Thessaloniki

This book shares the conclusions of a remarkable conference marking the centennial of Thessaloniki's incorporation into the Greek state in 1912. Like its Roman and Byzantine predecessors, Ottoman Salonica was the metropolis of a huge, multi-ethnic Balkan hinterland, a center of modernization/westernization, and the de facto capital of Sephardic Judaism. The powerful attraction it exerted on competing local nationalisms, including the Young Turks, gave it a paradigmatic role in the transition from imperial to national rule in southeastern Europe.

Twenty-three articles cover the multicultural physiognomy of a 'Levantine' city. They describe the mechanisms for cultivating national consciousness (including education, journalism, the arts, archaeology, and urban planning), the relationship between national identity, religious identity, and an evolving socialist labor movement, anti-Semitism, and the practical issues of governing and assimilating diverse non-Greek populations after Greece's military victory in 1912. Analysis of this transformation extends chronologically through the arrival of Greek refugees from Turkey and the Black Sea in 1923, the Holocaust, the Greek civil war, and the new waves of migration after 1990. These processes are analyzed on multiple levels, including civil administration, land use planning, and the treatment of Thessaloniki's historic monuments.

This work underscores the importance of cities and their local histories in shaping the key national narratives that drove development in southeastern Europe. Those lessons are highly relevant today, as Europe reacts to renewed migratory pressures and the rise of new nationalist movements, and draws lessons, valid or otherwise, from the nation-building experiments of the previous century.

Dimitris Keridis is Professor of International Relations at the Panteion University in Athens, Greece, and has been a member of the Greek Parliament since 2019. He has written widely on foreign policy, particularly on the Balkans and on modern Greek history.

John Brady Kiesling is an archaeologist and former U.S. diplomat, whose work includes *Greek Urban Warriors* (2014), *Diplomacy Lessons* (2007), the ToposText application, and various edited works on Greek history.

Routledge Studies in Modern European History

70 Strange Allies
Britain, France and the Dilemmas of Disarmament and Security, 1929–1933
Andrew Webster

71 1989 and the West
Western Europe since the End of the Cold War
Edited by Eleni Braat and Pepjin Corduwener

72 Margins for Manoeuvre in Cold War Europe
The Influence of Smaller Powers
Edited by Laurien Crump and Susanna Erlandsson

73 The European Illustrated Press and the Emergence of a Transnational Visual Culture of the News, 1842–1870
Thomas Smits

74 Interwar East Central Europe, 1918–1941
The failure of Democracy-building, the fate of Minorities
Edited by Sabrina P. Ramet

75 Free Trade and Social Welfare in Europe
Explorations in the Long 20th Century
Edited by Lucia Coppolaro and Lorenzo Mechi

76 Immigrants and Foreigners in Central and Eastern Europe during the Twentieth Century
Edited by Włodzimierz Borodziej and Joachim von Puttkamer

77 Europe between Migrations, Decolonization and Integration (1945–1992)
Edited by Giuliana Laschi, Valeria Deplano, Alessandro Pes

78 Steamship Nationalism
Ocean Liners and National Identity in Imperial Germany and Atlantic World
Mark A. Russell

For more information on this series, please visit www.routledge.com/history/series/SE0246

Thessaloniki
A City in Transition, 1912–2012

Edited by Dimitris Keridis and
John Brady Kiesling

LONDON AND NEW YORK

First published 2020 by Routledge

2 Park Square, Milton Park, Abingdon, Oxon OX14 4RN

605 Third Avenue, New York, NY 10017

Routledge is an imprint of the Taylor & Francis Group, an informa business

First issued in paperback 2021

Copyright © 2020 selection and editorial matter, Dimitris Keridis and John Brady Kiesling; individual chapters, the contributors

The right of the editors to be identified as the authors of the editorial material, and of the authors for their individual chapters, has been asserted in accordance with sections 77 and 78 of the Copyright, Designs and Patents Act 1988.

All rights reserved. No part of this book may be reprinted or reproduced or utilised in any form or by any electronic, mechanical, or other means, now known or hereafter invented, including photocopying and recording, or in any information storage or retrieval system, without permission in writing from the publishers.

Notice:
Product or corporate names may be trademarks or registered trademarks, and are used only for identification and explanation without intent to infringe.

Publisher's Note

The publisher has gone to great lengths to ensure the quality of this reprint but points out that some imperfections in the original copies may be apparent.

British Library Cataloguing-in-Publication Data
A catalogue record for this book is available from the British Library

Library of Congress Cataloging-in-Publication Data
Names: Keridis, Dimitris, editor. | Kiesling, John Brady, 1957- editor. | Thessaloniki, a city in transition, 1912-2012 (2012: Thessalonikē (Greece))
Title: Thessaloniki, a city in transition, 1912-2012 / Dimitris Keridis and John Brady Kiesling.
Description: Abingdon, Oxon ; New York : Routledge, [2020] | Series: Routledge studies in modern European history | Includes bibliographical references and index.
Identifiers: LCCN 2019053650 (print) | LCCN 2019053651 (ebook) | ISBN 9780367192822 (hardback) | ISBN 9780429201561 (ebook)
Subjects: LCSH: Thessalonikē (Greece)–History--20th century–Congresses. | Thessalonikē (Greece)–History–21st century–Congresses. | Thessalonikē (Greece)–Ethnic relations–Congresses.
Classification: LCC DF951.T45 T335 2020 (print) | LCC DF951.T45 (ebook) | DDC 949.5/65--dc23
LC record available at https://lccn.loc.gov/2019053650
LC ebook record available at https://lccn.loc.gov/2019053651

ISBN: 978-0-367-19282-2 (hbk)
ISBN: 978-1-03-217272-9 (pbk)
DOI: 10.4324/9780429201561

Typeset in Times
by Deanta Global Publishing Services, Chennai, India

Contents

List of figures	viii
List of tables	xi
List of contributors	xii

**Introduction: Continuities and discontinuities in the transition
from imperial to national order**   1
DIMITRIS KERIDIS

PART I
Searching for identity

1   Towards a history of Thessaloniki's future   15
MARK MAZOWER

2   Thessaloniki and the cities of the Enlightenment   26
PASCHALIS M. KITROMILIDES

3   Was Salonica a Levantine city?   35
PHILIP MANSEL

**4   The place of Thessaloniki in Greek national awareness: From
Greek independence to 1912 and beyond**   49
SPYRIDON G. PLOUMIDIS

5   Salonica through Bulgarian eyes   63
YURA KONSTANTINOVA

**6   The municipality of Salonica between old regime, Ottoman
reforms, and the transition from empire to nation state**   81
NORA LAFI

vi *Contents*

7 **Amateur and professional theatre in Ottoman Thessaloniki: Multicultural identity and its implications**   95
OLIVIA PALLIKARI

8 **A new look at an ancient city: Thessaloniki in Ottoman archaeology, 1832–1912**   105
EDHEM ELDEM

9 **Urban transformation and the revolution: Salonica and the Young Turks, 1908–1912**   126
SOTIRIS DIMITRIADIS

10 **Bulgarian newspapers in Thessaloniki, 1869–1913**   139
VLASIS VLASIDIS

PART II
A city in transition

11 **The boundaries of Hellenism: Language and loyalty among Salonican Jewry, 1917–1933**   154
DEVIN E. NAAR

12 **In the aftermath of the Balkan Wars: The incorporation of Thessaloniki into the Greek state**   169
ELPIDA K. VOGLI

13 **Refugee resettlement, 1922–1924: A watershed in the ethnic, social, and economic transformation of Thessaloniki**   183
CONSTANTINOS KATERINOPOULOS

14 **Integration through the past: Jewish scholars write history in inter-war Salonica**   193
EYAL GINIO

15 **Destruction and reconstruction of Thessaloniki's class structure, 1912–1940**   207
EVANGELOS HEKIMOGLOU

16 **From the call to prayer to the silences of the museum: Salonica's soundscapes in transition**   227
ELENI KALLIMOPOULOU, KOSTIS KORNETIS, AND PANAGIOTIS C. POULOS

Contents vii

PART III
Mapping the future of Thessaloniki

17 **The Muslims of Thessaloniki, 1912–2012: A discontinuous and uncomfortable presence**   243
KONSTANTINOS TSITSELIKIS

18 **Urban change and the persistence of memory in modern Thessaloniki**   260
ELENI BASTÉA AND VILMA HASTAOGLOU-MARTINIDIS

19 **French interests and Salonica's port, 1872–1912: Entrepreneurial and architectural innovation**   291
VILMA HASTAOGLOU-MARTINIDIS

20 **The post-war transformation of the Thessaloniki periphery: Urbanization and landscape**   310
CHARIS CHRISTODOULOU

21 **Land policy in Thessaloniki and the transition to a contemporary metropolitan area, 1922–1967**   333
ATHENA YIANNAKOU

22 **The care of monuments in modern Thessaloniki: Perceptions and practices**   352
KORNILIA TRAKOSOPOULOU-TZIMOU

23 **A past for every possible future: Concluding remarks**   375
BASIL C. GOUNARIS

Index   381

Figures

3.1	Photograph of women at the summer theatre beside the White Tower, 1908	43
3.2	Postcard, mounted officers of the Ottoman garrison of Thessaloniki parading by the White Tower, 1908	44
3.3	Postcard, Thessaloniki post office employees marching in support of the constitution, 1908	45
5.1	Teachers and students of the Bulgarian high school in 1888	69
5.2	The Bulgarian Men's High School in 1888–1889	71
5.3	The villa of Osman Bey at 36 Vasilissis Olgas Str., housing the Bulgarian Consulate in the early 20th c. (2014 photograph by the author)	72
8.1	Sarcophagus of Phaedra and Hippolytus, inv. 125	107
8.2	Copy of the inscription and shape of an altar found in the house of Ligor Bağlamalı	110
8.3	Certified copy of a funerary inscription from Vodena (Edessa) sent to the high school for preservation	111
8.4	Copy and translation of the inscription on a sarcophagus found in the Greek cemetery	112
8.5	Great ambo of Salonica (Hagios Georgios), inv. 1090	118
8.6	Ambo of Salonica in *verd antique* (Hagia Sophia), inv. 1627	119
18.1	Thessaloniki, Greece	264
18.2	Thessaloniki. Refugee houses in the Upper Town	266
18.3	Thessaloniki. Urban growth from 1930 to 1990	268
18.4	Thessaloniki. Street in the Upper town in 1900	269
18.5	Thessaloniki: the death of the neighborhood: From the original historic fabric, only the monuments survived	271
18.6	Thessaloniki. The landscape of Modernism: the International Fair Grounds, the Museums, and the lower part of the historic center	272
18.7	Thessaloniki. The creation of the modern seafront in the south-eastern shore	272
18.8	Thessaloniki. The Aristotelous civic axis in the 1980s	273

Figures ix

18.9	Thessaloniki. The enhancement of the old harbor with the surviving harbor market	273
19.1	Plan of the quay of Salonica, October 29, 1871, by Roch A. Vitalis	295
19.2	Louis Barret's draft project for Salonica's harbour, 1872	297
19.3	'Port de Salonique: Nouveau Project étudié par Monsieur Aslan' (1892)	300
19.4	The dockside transit sheds in 1904, postcard published by David M. Assael, Salonique	302
19.5	Alexandre Vallaury's design for the façade of Salonica's custom house, 1911	305
19.6	Plan of the harbour in 1914, showing the completion of the works	306
20.1	Diagram of the area of research in the perimeter of the Thessaloniki Urban Complex	312
20.2	Diagram of official urban plan limits for the years 1979 and 2000	313
20.3	The area of research imposed on Thessaloniki urban fabric of the 1930s	314
20.4	Aerial view of the eastern periphery of Thessaloniki in the early 1950s; Pylea, Toumpa, Votsi, Nea Krini in the foreground	315
20.5	Part of the north-western periphery in the late 1970s; densification of unstructured fabric of in-between areas of Kordelio, Evosmos, and Menemeni	318
20.6	Out-of-the-official-plan settlements (in black) in the Thessaloniki periphery of the late 1970s	320
20.7	Parts of the northern periphery in the 1980s; extensive fragmentation of suburban parcels in preparation for settlement in Efkarpia	322
20.8	Views of the western periphery in the 2000s; Roma organized settlement in Menemeni, 2004	325
20.9	Views of the northern periphery in the 2000s; Efxinoupolis, new Pontian neighborhood in Evosmos–Efkarpia, 2001	326
20.10	Views of the south-eastern periphery in the 2000s; images of new urbanity and peri-urban consumption, 2001	327
20.11	Views of the south-eastern periphery in the 2000s; mixture of primary and tertiary sector activities in the peri-urban area of Pylea, 2005	328
21.1	Refugee settlements in the province of Thessaloniki	335
21.2	Land allocated to refugees by the Refugee Rehabilitation Programmes, including land allocated to building co-operatives	337
21.3	The distribution of exchangeable landed property in Greater Thessaloniki in 1966	347
22.1	Thessaloniki. The quay in the early 20th century	353
22.2	Thessaloniki. New-style buildings in the Customs House district	354

x *Figures*

22.3	Thessaloniki 1916. The arch of Galerius	355
22.4	Thessaloniki: *Las Incantadas*, by Stuart and Revett 1794	355
22.5	Vitaliano Poselli, Government House	357
22.6	The church of Saint Sophia (Aya Sofia Mosque) after restoration	360
22.7	The 'liberation' of Agia Sophia from its surroundings, extract from the city plan, 1924	363
22.8	Hamza Bey Mosque. View of the atrium, before 1912	366
22.9	Karavan Serai. General view of the remains from the fire in 1917	366
22.10	Saatli Mosque. General view, 1916	367
22.11	Nikolaos Mitsakis Anotaton Parthenagogeio Thessalonikis: Thessaloniki Secondary Girl's School, Elevation 1933 ANA_14_37_05	369
22.12	Yako Modiano's villa, after restoration	370
22.13	The workshop of the School of Arts and Crafts Hamidié (*Islahhane or Midhat Pasha Polytechnic*) in Eleni Zographou Street	371

Tables

8.1	Objects from Thessaloniki in the Imperial Museum collections	113
10.1	Bulgarian-language newspapers and journals known to have been published in Thessaloniki	141
15.1	The re-planning and reconstructing process	210
15.2	The fate of some Rogos residents after the fire of 1917	212
15.3	The size of the old plots	213
15.4	The 'ancient' and the 'capitalist'	217
15.5	Population of Thessaloniki in 1904 and 1928	218
19.1	Harbour works: projects, engineers, contracting companies, and urban transformations	292
21.1	Land disposed under the jurisdiction of the EAP, the MSW, and building co-operatives for the URP	336
21.2	Distribution of the URP and per area of GT	336
21.3	Number of families settled by the URP in different periods	337
21.4	Distribution of settled families by the RRP per community	340
21.5	The Rural Rehabilitation Programme and the distribution of land per 'Farm'	341
21.6	The implementation of the RRP over time	343
21.7	Average size of farming land in the allocation areas	344
21.8	Land allocation to refugee building co-operatives	348

Contributors

Eleni Bastéa (†2020) was born and grew up in Thessaloniki, Greece. She held a BA in Art History from Bryn Mawr College, US, and an MA of Architecture and a PhD in Architectural History, both from the University of California at Berkeley, US. She taught at the University of New Mexico, US, where she was Regents' Professor of Architecture and Director of the International Studies Institute. Bastéa's books include *The Creation of Modern Athens: Planning the Myth* (Cambridge University Press 2000), also published in Greek (Libro 2008), *Memory and Architecture* (University of New Mexico Press 2004), and *Venice without Gondolas*, a poetry collection (Finishing Line Press 2013).

Charis Christodoulou is Assistant Professor at the School of Architecture, Aristotle University of Thessaloniki (AUTh), Greece. She holds a PhD in Planning from the Department of Urban and Regional Planning and Development, AUTh. She has worked as a professional architect-urban designer and a consultant to local authorities on urban strategies, and has written on housing issues and social exclusion, urban design and public space, urban planning and socio-spatial transformations.

Sotiris Dimitriadis is a historian of the late Ottoman Empire, with a special interest in urban and social history. He completed his PhD dissertation at the Department of History at SOAS-University of London, UK, and is currently Post-Doctoral Fellow at the Department of Balkan, Slavic and Oriental Studies of the University of Macedonia, Greece.

Edhem Eldem is Professor in the Department of History of Boğaziçi University, Turkey, and holds the International Chair of Turkish and Ottoman History at the Collège de France. His fields of interest include the Levant trade, funerary epigraphy, Istanbul, the Ottoman Bank, the history of archaeology, Ottoman first-person narratives, and Ottoman photography. Publications include: *French Trade in Istanbul in the Eighteenth Century* (1999); *The Ottoman City between East and West: Aleppo, Izmir and Istanbul* (1999, with D. Goffman and B. Masters); *Pride and Privilege: A History of Ottoman Orders, Medals and Decorations* (2004); *Consuming the Orient* (2007); *Scramble for the Past: A Story of Archaeology in the Ottoman Empire* (2011, with Zainab Bahrani and Zeynep Çelik); and *Camera Ottomana: Photography and Modernity in the Ottoman Empire* (2015, with Zeynep Çelik).

Eyal Ginio is Associate Professor in Middle Eastern and Islamic Studies at the Hebrew University of Jerusalem, Israel, and Director of the Ben-Zvi Institute for the Study of the Jewish Communities in the East. He holds a doctorate from the Hebrew University. He has published numerous articles on the social and cultural history of Salonica during the Ottoman period and following the transition to Greek rule and on the Balkan wars. He is currently preparing a study on the modernization of the Ottoman Sultanate after the 1908 revolution.

Basil C. Gounaris is Professor of Modern History in the Department of History and Archaeology at Aristotle University of Thessaloniki, Greece. He studied History at the Aristotle University (BA, MA) and holds a DPhil from St. Antony's College, Oxford, UK. He has edited and published numerous books and articles on Modern Greek, Balkan, and Mediterranean History. Two of his monographs won awards from the Academy of Athens.

Vilma Hastaoglou-Martinidis is Professor Emerita of Urban History and Design at the School of Architecture, Aristotle University of Thessaloniki, Greece. She holds a degree in Architecture and a PhD in Urban Planning from the School of Architecture, Aristotle University of Thessaloniki, and a Diploma in Urban Sociology from the École des hautes études en sciences sociales, Paris, France. Her research interests include planning history, urban modernization, and heritage preservation. She is the author of many books on urban history and planning in Greece and the Eastern Mediterranean. She is currently working on a book, *Harbor Building and the Modernization of the East Mediterranean Cities in the Late 19th Century*.

Evangelos Hekimoglou is Principle Curator of the Jewish Museum of Thessaloniki (former Director of the National Bank of Greece/Cultural Center for Northern Greece). He studied at the Aristotle University, Thessaloniki, Greece, and holds a PhD from the same university ('The historical and Spatial Nature of the Economic Surplus'). He has published more than a hundred articles and thirty books on the history of Thessaloniki and the economic history of the Ottoman and the Greek states.

Eleni Kallimopoulou is Assistant Professor in Ethnomusicology at the University of Macedonia, Greece. She received her PhD in Ethnomusicology from the School of Oriental and African Studies (SOAS), University of London, UK. She is author of the book *Paradosiaká: Music, Meaning and Identity in Modern Greece* (Ashgate 2009), and co-editor of *Introduction in Ethnomusicology* (Asini 2014). Her research interests center on Greece and the Mediterranean; musical performance and ethnography; public folklore and the politics of culture; nationalism, religion, and ritual; oral history; and auditory culture and urban space.

xiv *Contributors*

Konstantinos Katerinopoulos is a lawyer and economist based in Athens. He has studied and written on refugee resettlement issues in Greece.

Dimitris Keridis is Professor of International Relations at Panteion University of Athens, Greece. As of July 2019, he is an elected member of the Greek Parliament, representing Athens-North for center-right New Democracy. He directs the Olympia Summer Academy in Politics and International Studies (www.olympiasummeracademy.org) and the Navarino Network, a public policy think-tank based in Thessaloniki (www.navarinonetwork.org). He is a senior fellow at the Konstantinos G. Karamanlis Foundation. He has been a regular political commentator and host of a weekly TV show on foreign affairs. Past positions include senior consultant at the Greek Ministry of Foreign Affairs, the Constantine Karamanlis Associate Professor in Hellenic and European Studies at the Fletcher School, director of the Kokkalis Foundation in Athens, director of the Kokkalis Program on Southeast and East-Central Europe, and adjunct lecturer at the John F. Kennedy School of Government, Harvard University.

John Brady Kiesling is an archaeologist and former U.S. diplomat, whose work includes *Greek Urban Warriors* (2014), *Diplomacy Lessons* (2007), the ToposText application, and various edited works on Greek history.

Paschalis M. Kitromilides obtained a PhD Harvard University, USA, and is Professor Emeritus of Political Science at the University of Athens, Greece, and Director of the Center for Asia Minor Studies. From 2000 to 2011, he was Director of the Institute of Neohellenic Research at the National Hellenic Research Foundation. He has held visiting appointments at Cambridge and Oxford, the École des hautes études en sciences sociales, the European University Institute and the Harvard Center for Renaissance Studies, Villa I Tatti, Florence. His books in English include: *The Enlightenment as Social Criticism*; *Iosipos Moisiodax and Greek Culture in the Eighteenth Century*; *Enlightenment Nationalism Orthodoxy*; *An Orthodox Commonwealth*; *Symbolic Legacies and Cultural Encounters in Southeastern Europe*; *Enlightenment and Revolution. The Making of Modern Greece* (Harvard University Press 2013); and *Enlightenment and Religion in the Orthodox World* (Voltaire Foundation 2016).

Yura Konstantinova is Associate Professor in the Institute of Balkan Studies, Center of Thracology at the Bulgarian Academy of Sciences. She studied History and Greek philology at the Sofia University, Bulgaria, 'St. Kl. Ohridski' and holds a doctorate from the Institute of Balkan Studies, Bulgarian Academy of Sciences, on the topic 'The Balkan policy of Greece at the end of 19th and the early 20th century'. She has published numerous articles on Modern and Contemporary Balkan History, Greek-Bulgarian Relations, Political Propaganda, and is currently preparing a study about Bulgarian community in Thessaloniki in the end of nineteenth and the early twentieth centuries.

Kostis Kornetis is CONEX-Marie Sklodowska Curie Experienced Fellow at the Universidad Carlos III de Madrid, Spain. He did his BA in History and

Contributors xv

Political Science at Ludwig Maximilian University, Munich, Germany, and in War Studies and Modern Greek at King's College London, UK. He received his MA from University College London, UK, and PhD in History and Civilization from the European University Institute, Florence, Italy. From 2007 to 2015, he taught at the History Department at Brown University and the Center for European and Mediterranean Studies at New York University. His research focuses on the study of social movements, authoritarianism, and democratic transitions and the methodology of oral and sensory history. His book *Children of the Dictatorship. Student Resistance, Cultural Politics and the 'Long 1960s' in Greece* (Berghahn Books 2013) received the 2015 Edmund Keeley Book Award of the Modern Greek Studies Association.

Nora Lafi is Senior Research Fellow in Berlin at the Leibniz-Zentrum Moderner Orient. She also teaches at the Freie Universität Berlin, Germany, in the Department of Islamic Studies. She studied history and Arabic language at the University of Aix-en-Provence, France, and holds a PhD from this University. She has published numerous articles on the history of the cities of the Ottoman empire and is currently preparing a study on the civic sphere in an Ottoman urban context.

Philip Mansel is Fellow of the Royal Historical Society and the Institute of Historical Research, London. He studied History and French at Balliol College, Oxford, UK, and received his PhD from the University of London, UK, in 1978. His books include histories of Constantinople City of the World's Desire and Smyrna, Alexandria, and Beirut (*Levant: Splendour and Catastrophe on the Mediterranean*). He is one of the founders of the Society for Court Studies (www.courtstudies.org) and is a founding trustee of the Levantine Heritage Foundation (www.levantineheritage.com). In 2016, he published a short history of Aleppo. He is currently preparing a biography of Louis XIV.

Mark Mazower is Ira D. Wallach Professor of History at Columbia University, US. He studied classics and philosophy at Oxford, and international affairs at Johns Hopkins and he holds a doctorate in history from Oxford. His books range on topics from Salonica (*Thessaloniki City of Ghosts*) to international governance and he recently finished a family memoir, entitled *What You Did Not Tell* that has been published in Greek by Agra.

Devin E. Naar is Isaac Alhadeff Professor in Sephardic Studies and Associate Professor of Jewish Studies and History at the University of Washington in Seattle, US, where he directs the Sephardic Studies Program and is a member of the Hellenic Studies faculty. Naar received his PhD in History from Stanford University, US, in 2011 and was a Fulbright Scholar in Greece. His book, *Jewish Salonica: Between the Ottoman Empire and Modern Greece* (Stanford University Press 2016), won the 2016 National Jewish Book Award for Best Archival Research and the 2017 Keeley Prize for best book in Greek studies awarded by the Modern Greek Studies Association.

xvi *Contributors*

Olivia Pallikari is a PhD student at the faculty of Theater Studies—School of Philosophy at the National and Kapodistrian University of Athens, Greece. She studied at the Faculty of German Language and Literature at the University of Athens and did her MA at the Faculty of Theater Studies. She has worked as Lecturer of Semiotics at the same program and as Lecturer of Theater History in several acting schools. She has taken part in several conferences and has written articles about the history of theater in the Greek press.

Spyridon G. Ploumidis is Assistant Professor in Modern Greek History at the National and Kapodistrian University of Athens, Greece, in the Department of History and Archaeology. He studied History at the Ionian University, Corfu, and holds a PhD from the University of London, UK (his PhD thesis was on 'Ethnic symbiosis and friction between Greek Orthodox and Bulgarians in Plovdiv/Philippoupolis, 1878–1906'). He has published numerous books and articles on nationalism in Greece, Bulgaria, and the Balkans; agrarianism; corporatism; the Metaxas regime (1936–1941); the Asia Minor Question (1891–1922); and is currently preparing a study on the Greek Great Idea (1844–1912).

Panagiotis C. Poulos is Lecturer in the Arts of Islamic World at the Department of Turkish and Modern Asian Studies, National and Kapodistrian University of Athens, Greece. He studied ethnomusicology with a focus on the musical traditions of the Near and Middle East at the School of Oriental and African Studies at the University of London, UK, where he also completed his PhD dissertation on Ottoman classical music. His publications center on cultural history of late Ottoman and Turkish music and arts, and the history of everyday life in Ottoman cities. He is currently scientific coordinator (with E. Kolovos) of the research project 'Histories, Spaces and Heritages at the transition from the Ottoman Empire to the Greek state'.

Kornilia Trakosopoulou-Tzimou is former Director of the Ministry of Culture and Sports and Lecturer at the Democritus University of Thrace, Greece, in the Department of Architecture. She studied at Sapienza University of Rome (Faculty of Architecture). She pursued her postgraduate studies at the School of Specialization in Restoration of Monuments and Sites at the same university and later on at the University of London—Faculty of Science—Bartlett School of Architecture and Planning, UK. She holds a doctorate from the National Technical University of Athens (dissertation title: Ο Εκσυγχρονισμός της Βορειοελλαδικής Αρχιτεκτονικής και Πόλης στη διάρκεια του 19ου αιώνα και στις αρχές του 20ου). She has published numerous articles on Restoration of Monuments and History of Architecture. She is the author of the book: Η αρχιτεκτονική του Konrad J. J. von Vilas (1866–1929), στη Δράμα και την ευρύτερη περιοχή της, Δράμα 2002–2003.

Konstantinos Tsitselikis is Professor in Human Rights and International Organizations at the University of Macedonia, Greece. He has taught at the Universities of Thrace and Bilgi, Istanbul. He is author of several books, studies, and articles on human rights, focused on minority, refugee, and migrants'

Contributors   xvii

rights. He has worked for the Council of Europe (1992–1995), the OSCE, the UN, and the EU (1997–1999) in human rights and democratization field missions. Member of the Secretariat of the Research Center for Minority Groups (KEMO, www.kemo.gr) and chairman of the Hellenic League for Human Rights (www.hlhr.gr) (2011–2017).

Vlasis Vlasidis is Associate Professor at the University of Macedonia, Department for Balkan, Slavic and Oriental Studies, in Thessaloniki, Macedonia, Greece. He obtained his PhD in Contemporary History in 1997 from the Aristotle University of Thessaloniki, Greece. His most recent books are *Between Memory and Forgetfulness. Monuments and Cemeteries of the Macedonian Front*, Thessaloniki, 2016 and *The Memory of the Great War*, Thessaloniki, 2017.

Elpida Vogli is Assistant Professor of Modern Greek History at the Department of History and Ethnology, School of Classics and Humanities, at the Democritus University of Thrace, Greece. She holds a PhD from the Department of History at the Aristotle University of Thessaloniki (AUTh), Greece, and has taught Hellenic and European History at the Department of Journalism and Mass Media at AUTh and the Hellenic Open University. Her research interests include citizenship and national identity, the processes of nation- and state-building, political development, migration policies, and diaspora-homeland relations. She is the author of (all in Greek) *Works and the Days of Greek Families, 1750–1940* (Athens: ELIA 2005), *'Greek by Descent': National Identity and Citizenship in Modern Greece, 1821–1844* (Heraklion: Crete University Press 2007), *Metaxa, The Real Story: The Development of a Greek Family Industry* (Athens: Livanis 2010), and *What a Historian Should Know About His Science* (ebook: Kallipos 2015—https://repository.kallipos.gr/hand le/11419/3821).

Athena Yiannakou is Associate Professor in Urban Policy and Urban Development at the School of Spatial Planning and Development, Aristotle University of Thessaloniki, Greece. She studied Architecture at the Aristotle University Thessaloniki and Regional and Urban Planning at the London School of Economics, UK, and holds a PhD from the London School of Economics. She has worked as a professional planner and has published articles and books on the subjects of sustainable cities and urban planning, urban regeneration, strategic spatial planning, and spatial planning and climate change.

Introduction

Continuities and discontinuities in the transition from imperial to national order

Dimitris Keridis

The publication of *Thessaloniki: A City in Transition 1912–2012* fulfils a promise made by the Organizing Committee as the international conference of that name came to a close on October 21, 2012, in Thessaloniki. This four-day conference was the chief scholarly event marking the one-hundredth anniversary of the liberation of Thessaloniki from Ottoman rule in 1912. It featured dozens of presentations in Greek and English and a series of round table discussions on the past, present, and future of Thessaloniki, attended by hundreds of Thessaloniki residents and foreign visitors. The high quality of the papers submitted, the broad range of subject matter they covered, and their utility for the historiography of Thessaloniki, were an irresistible argument for publishing them, first in Greek and now at last in English for an international audience.

Our city was founded by Cassander, son-in-law of Alexander the Great, in honor of his half-sister Thessalonike. It counts a history of twenty-three centuries of unbroken urban continuity from Hellenistic times to the present. Often the second city of the empire but never the first, Thessaloniki was a magnet for heretics and radicals escaping the limitations imposed by the capital: Zealots of the late Byzantine period, the cabbalists of Sabbatai Zevi, the Young Turks, Federation socialists of Avraam Benaroya, and most recently the demoticists of modern Greece.

The Christian community of Thessaloniki, the second oldest in Europe after that of nearby Philippi, was founded by the Apostle Paul himself, who wrote two of his famous epistles to his Thessalonian brethren. From Thessaloniki came Cyril and Methodius, the evangelists of the Slavs, and here too preached the Hesychast Gregorios Palamas, a key shaper of Orthodox Christian tradition. Thessaloniki was the birthplace of Mustapha Kemal, founder of the modern Turkish Republic, and of many other key figures in the Young Turk and Kemalist movements. At the beginning of the twentieth century, Thessaloniki was at the center of the great upheavals that dismantled the Ottoman Empire and created modern southeast Europe.

The entry of the Greek army into Thessaloniki in October 1912 was a key event of the First Balkan War, shaping the modern history of Greece and the southern Balkans. With Thessaloniki and its Macedonian hinterland, Greece doubled its territory and resources, expanded its borders and its horizons, and hastened its

2 Dimitris Keridis

urban modernization. Greece was no longer an insignificant state at the tip of the Balkan peninsula; instead it claimed a leading role in the eastern Mediterranean.

The year 1912 represented a sharp break in the history of the city as well. The transition, however, was not completely abrupt. Thessaloniki retained its Turkish mayor for a decade after 1912. During World War I the city reached the high point of its doomed cosmopolitanism, when its Jewish, Christian, and Muslim residents found themselves living side by side with tens of thousands of Entente soldiers on the 'Balkan Front'.

The Asia Minor Catastrophe of 1922 followed, with the 1923 exchange of populations, and then the horrific extermination of almost all its numerous Jewish communities by the Nazis in 1943. These tragedies were followed by impressive successes, such as the assimilation of the refugees from Anatolia, industrialization and economic growth during the interwar years, and evolution as a modern metropolis and center of commerce and education. Thessaloniki developed as essentially the only urban counterweight to Athens and the hydrocephalous Greek state. The opening of the borders with Eastern Europe after 1989 and the arrival of economic migrants changed the face of the city once again.

The modern form of Thessaloniki results from three major developments: the urban planning interventions of late Ottoman reformers who aspired to free the city from its medieval past and turn it into a modern Mediterranean port; the great fire of 1917, which destroyed its historic center and allowed Ernest Hébrard to redesign it as a Greek city; and finally, the frequently anarchic construction boom of the first post-WWII decades and the attempts of Konstantinos Karamanlis to preserve and, if possible, reinforce its metropolitan character (new sea front, university campus, port, etc.).

The 1917 catastrophe left the Upper City and a handful of monuments in the Lower City as reminders of continuity with the Ottoman and Byzantine past, while the villas of the eastern 'extensions' symbolized the city's commercial prosperity at the end of the nineteenth century. Ambitious plans for reshaping the city center withstood the pressure of building contractors and property speculators in a few cases only, such as the monumental Aristotle square with the rectangular and diagonal street grid surrounding it. The display and conservation of surviving historic monuments reflected a nationalist agenda that emphasized the city's Roman-Byzantine rather than Ottoman heritage.

In short, Thessaloniki is a city with strong 'continuities' reflecting its long and glorious history, but equally strong 'discontinuities'. These continuities and discontinuities of a city in transition were the focus of the conference and are the chief thematic axis of the book you are reading.

At the beginning of the summer of 2011, new Thessaloniki mayor Giannis Boutaris invited a group of active Thessalonians, under the leadership of businessman Stavros Andreadis, to draw up a new plan for commemorating the centennial of the liberation of Thessaloniki. Ambitious early ideas had fallen victim to the economic crisis and various organizational weaknesses. Fortunately, the idea of a large, open international conference survived intact. Initial planning had focused on the city's Greekness but, as reconsidered, the conference would become

Introduction 3

the opportunity for a genuine international encounter that would highlight new approaches to the city's rich and diverse past and confirm Thessaloniki's place in international historical bibliography. The support of a dynamic mayor with a fresh concept of Thessaloniki was a strong guarantee for the success of the enterprise.

The conference became an exercise in self-knowledge for Thessaloniki through a convergence of modern historiographic currents with the related social sciences: social anthropology, economics, law, international relations, political science, archaeology, architecture, city planning, and the arts. We called on the help of distinguished Greek academics and of foreign scholars from neighboring or distant countries, including Bulgaria, Turkey, Israel, and the United States. The enthusiastic response proved that Thessaloniki still has power to inspire.

No other Greek city and very few in southeast Europe can boast so rich a historiography as modern Thessaloniki. Some studies have had global success, particularly the landmark *Salonica: City of ghosts* by Mark Mazower (2004), still widely available after fifteen years in print. Mazower's book has been translated into several languages and enjoyed great commercial success because its main subject, the transition from the imperial past to the nation-state present, remains a subject with global appeal, especially after the explosion of interest in nationalism and ethnic identities that followed the end of the Cold War in 1989.

Thessaloniki and its recent history constitute outstanding raw material for a narrative of that transition. The key drama centers on nationalism and liberalism as the two principal modernist ideologies. Old Thessaloniki, where different religions, languages, and ethnic groups coexisted under the autocratic rule of the Ottomans, with strict social stratification and guild organization of the economy its chief characteristic, was shaken by the infiltration of western capitalism, the progress of industrialization, and the arrival of new radical concepts of rights, including national rights.

At the end of the nineteenth and beginning of the twentieth centuries, Thessaloniki was at the center of developments aimed at creating a new, post-imperial order. This was a result both of history and geography. From its founding, it was a major port and important commercial crossroads. After the 1878 Congress of Berlin, it found itself, as capital of the Ottoman province of Macedonia, at the center of colliding efforts to preserve or obliterate Turkey's shrinking foothold in Europe.

The westernmost and most exposed large city of the Empire, Thessaloniki emerged as the headquarters of the Young Turk movement. It is no accident that the Young Turk leadership originated in the city and surrounding region, that the Young Turk revolution broke out in this specific city in July 1908, that the Young Turks drew from it the forces that crushed the counterrevolution that broke out in Istanbul in April 1909, and that it was here that Abdul Hamid was exiled, since only here could they be sure the deposed sultan would be hard put to find local allies.

In this context, it is worth repeating that Thessaloniki was the birthplace of Mustapha Kemal, the future Ataturk, founder of the modern Turkish Republic. Raised in a multi-ethnic and cosmopolitan imperial city gradually encircled by

4 Dimitris Keridis

the hostile nationalisms of the bordering Christian states, with an insecure hinterland ravaged by the struggles between Bulgarian Exarchists and Greek followers of the Patriarch, exposed him, from a young age, to modernist ideas of progress, science, and nationalism, Ataturk distilled the ideas but also the contradictions of Young Turk nationalism. Already in 1907 he was proposing the dissolution of the Ottoman Empire and the creation of a Turkish national state through an exchange of populations (Hanioğlu 2011, 37). The irony was that the applying of such a policy would turn Ataturk himself and most of the Muslims of Ottoman Macedonia into refugees. Ataturk would go on to build a Turkish state in Asia Minor, which until the end of World War I he had never visited and knew little about.

Ataturk's personal journey demonstrates the role of Thessaloniki and Ottoman Macedonia's place in the rise of the Young Turks and Turkish nationalism and the creation of Turkey amid the ruins of the collapsed Ottoman Empire. Şükrü Hanioğlu, the prominent Turkish historian of the late Ottoman period, called Thessaloniki the womb from which both the key ideas and the leading characters of post-Ottoman Turkey were bred, gestated, and hatched, with all this implies for the history of the broader Near and Middle East.[1]

However, Thessaloniki in the decades prior to 1912 was not solely or even chiefly Muslim. The dominant element, in population, wealth, and culture, was the Jewish community. That community could not remain isolated from developments, whether local or international. The crisis of the Ottoman Empire, suspense regarding its future, and the strong reservations felt by Thessaloniki Jews regarding the Christian nationalisms laying claim to the city, were linked to the rise of the Zionist movement and also the Labor movement across Europe.

Thus, even if for most of the community the solution to the 'Jewish problem' was assimilation, one part of it sought to imitate other European nationalisms through Zionism and the creation in Palestine of a Jewish national state along European lines. Finally, for a third group, the solution was the labor union movement and socialism, which promised to transcend nationalist differences and, by introducing a new, class-based differentiation, to soften the dividing lines of religion, language, and national conscience.

The result of this attempt in Thessaloniki was the creation of the Federation in 1909. The Federation was the forerunner of similar labor and socialist movements in the Balkans. In due course, after the liberation, it took part in founding both the General Confederation of Greek Workers (GSEE) and the Greek Communist Party (KKE). The gradual industrialization of Thessaloniki and its region, with the development of weaving and the fur industry to the west and tobacco processing to the east, and the existence of a sizeable Jewish proletariat little moved by the call of local nationalisms, was the raw material for the comparatively early development of unionism and socialism in the city. Thessaloniki would continue to take a leading role in labor struggles even after 1912, and the refugees, chiefly tobacco workers, would assume the inheritance of the Federation in the interwar period, culminating in their large mobilizations in 1936.

It would be a mistake, of course, to assume that the relationship between socialism and nationalism was purely hostile. The two would be compelled to

Introduction 5

interact and sometimes to form an alliance. This alliance assumes particular importance in the case of Macedonia, since from it would emerge a new nationalism, Slavo-Macedonian, in opposition to the traditional Bulgarian. Already in 1893, the Internal Macedonian Revolutionary Organization (IMRO/VMRO) was founded in Thessaloniki with the goal of 'Macedonia for the Macedonians'. The Organization would import new terrorist methods from Russia to the Balkans, blowing up buildings and murdering local personalities. A few years later, an analogous act in Sarajevo, Bosnia, would spark World War I.

If Thessaloniki's Muslims and Jews agonized over the survival of the Ottoman Empire, the city's Christians, particularly the Greek community, looked for that Empire's expulsion from its remaining European possessions or from the world stage. From the end of the nineteenth century and for more than half a century afterward, Thessaloniki was the apple of discord for Greek–Bulgarian conflict. There is an interesting paradox, however. Although Greeks could invoke the city's glorious Hellenistic and Byzantine past and the existence of a flourishing Hellenic community to support their nationalist claims, the truth is that Thessaloniki, as Paschalis Kitromilides states in his contribution to this volume, was largely absent from the Greek Enlightenment and from rising Greek nationalism.

In the end, Thessaloniki's future proved Greek. The mass arrival of refugee populations from the east—Greeks from Asia Minor, the Black Sea, Eastern Thrace, and Eastern Rumelia—contributed to this outcome. The 'Jerusalem of the Balkans' gave way to the 'refugee capital', as Thessaloniki's faithful literary icon Giorgos Ioannou characterized it.

To the dramas and traumas these upheavals provoked must be added the pan-European tragedy of the Holocaust during World War II. This tragedy sealed the 'Europeanness' of the city, since it bound its history to that of the other cities of Central and Eastern Europe, while at the same time it cut the city loose from that of the Middle East. If modernity is characterized by the rejection of the 'hybridity' of traditional societies and the crystallization of clear, mutually incompatible national identities, then the Nazis were the most extreme laborers in clearing away the city's pre-modernist cosmopolitan hybridity, otherwise known, as Philip Mansel describes it in this volume, as Levantinism.

Thessaloniki was a Levantine city *par excellence*, one that more than any of its Eastern Mediterranean peers such as Izmir, Beirut, or Alexandria, found itself at the vortex of history on the eve of 1912. It was also a city of revolutions, as Mansel says. Here converged a series of trends and movements that defined the twentieth century, including every shade of nationalism, socialism, and labor unionism, terrorism and antisemitism.

Above all, however, Thessaloniki remained a great city, with all this implies for its function and history. Empires came and went, but Thessaloniki continued to shine as the most important port city of the southern Balkans. Even the hydrocephalous Greek state, which concentrates 40% of Greece's population in its capital, could not pauperize it.

This fundamental urban continuity of Thessaloniki is another reason that makes its history so appealing. We live in an age of rapid urbanization. For the

6 Dimitris Keridis

first time, the majority of the world's population lives in cities. Cities are not simple population concentrations within a broader state whole. Today's era of globalization is characterized by increased interest in the local as well as the international, and not only in relations between states but also in the international networks linking nodal cities. Thessaloniki is such a nodal city for its Balkan region, with a strong trans-local and a growing transnational role. Moreover, cities such as Thessaloniki offer historical researchers a rich field for analysis of economic and social developments on the micro-level, going beyond the political history of the macro-level.

Focus on the city foreordains a series of challenges and reversals. The first victim of this focus is the 'national history' reproduced by power structures such as Greece's highly centralized educational system, the mass media, and the Orthodox Church. A simplified national historical narrative is undermined and the horizons of historical narrative expand, revealing paradoxes, nuances, juxtapositions, and interactions that official history would prefer to ignore. To the extent that we live in an age of 'revisionism', where old precepts and 'grand narratives' are challenged, the history of one city, especially a city such as Thessaloniki, as Mazower knows well, offers a marvelous context for applying this revisionism.

More or less in this way, Thessaloniki found itself at the epicenter of modern historiographic discussion, 'stealing the spotlight' of international attention from its southern rival, Athens. Thessaloniki was fortunate to attract a series of particularly inspired and gifted historians and researchers. The present volume is a representative but by no means exhaustive sample of their work. By rights, this book is dedicated to all of them.

Thessaloniki's complex contours are a poor fit with official Greek historiography's categories and divisions. To many, therefore, a conference and book dedicated to the city is a somewhat heretical undertaking. When the question was posed, whether the centennial would be a commemoration centered on Thessaloniki or on the overall Greek conquests in Macedonia, the answer was not self-evident. Putting the focus on Thessaloniki raised the issue of the permissibility of the word 'liberation', with all the reaction that issue would provoke.

The undertaking becomes more unorthodox when scholars from different academic disciplines and national origins take part. The aim was to 'cross-pollinate' using the different levels of analysis of each social science, from the micro-level of anthropology to the macro-level of political science, but also by involving differing, usually competing, national viewpoints. It is worth noting here that the success of the endeavor required a clear political decision by the sponsor of the enterprise, namely the Thessaloniki municipality under the leadership of Giannis Boutaris. Thessaloniki embraced the brave, honorable conviction that its past is a source of wealth for a dynamic, outward-looking, and innovative city.

The goal of this book, as of the conference, is certainly not to address the city's entire past. The subject was more narrowly defined as the 1912 events and their importance for the gradual incorporation of Thessaloniki into the Greek state, in relation to the immediately preceding period and the century that followed. Three basic axes were specified: first is the search for identity, not to specify some 'true'

Introduction 7

identity of the city but rather to understand the debates over that identity before and immediately after 1912. The second axis is the transition from an imperial to a national system and how that affects the city and its residents. The third axis, Thessaloniki's futures, aims to foster debate on what future the city deserves, as we lived, then and now, continuous cycles of unfulfilled dreams.

The questions that emerge from these three axes affect every city that survives through the centuries. For this reason, an attempt was made to emphasize comparative viewpoints as well. Judging from the response of the scholarly community, we are confident the lectures, papers, and discussions of this conference will contribute to reframing discussion of our city. A new dialogue with the past can illuminate the future we seek.

This collection of papers begins with the contribution of Mark Mazower, the best-known historian of Thessaloniki internationally. His contribution dissects how older scholars understood the future, in order to sketch out clearly the history of the ideas that influenced Thessaloniki's historic course, particularly in the critical period of the second half of the nineteenth century. The gradual inclusion of Thessaloniki in the global capitalist economy brought with it a teleological idea of History and the future together with the modernist idea of progress. The demolition of the medieval walls and the expansion of the port under an active governor, Sabri Pasha, during the 1870s, signaled a more active role for the state in shaping this future. Even more ambitious was Hébrard's planning after the 1912 liberation. The result was the physical separation of Thessaloniki between a traditional Upper City and a European Lower City, but also the new European neighborhoods, primarily toward the east. The physical transformation proceeded in parallel with the ideological, and the flourishing of modernist ideas such as nationalism, socialism, or ethno-tribalism, that aimed to shape the future. The post-Cold War period is characterized by greater suspicion of all such grand visions.

For Paschalis M. Kitromilides, the modern researcher *par excellence* on the transplantation of the Enlightenment into southeast Europe, Thessaloniki is a paradox. In western Macedonian cities such as Kozani, Kastoria, and Siatista, and northwards in Moschopoli, and even on monastic Mt. Athos, where the 'Athonian' Academy functioned, hotbeds of the Neohellenic Enlightenment developed, nothing similar happened in the Macedonian capital itself. The paradox intensifies because the city's commercial development did not lead to modernizing debates on education, as Enlightenment social theory dictates. Thessaloniki's absence from the geography of the Enlightenment cannot be blamed on a lack of education in the city, but on its demographic composition and a series of conjunctures. The dominance of the Jewish community in the city's life made the Jewish conduit the most important one for transmitting the spirit of the Enlightenment to the city. However, that conduit remained closed due to the reaction of the rabbinic leadership to the Sabbatai Zevi movement, which entailed serious losses for the community. The long-term results of this adventure were strict control over the spiritual life of the community and the exclusion of potential deviations from Talmudic tradition.

8   *Dimitris Keridis*

Philip Mansel offers an outstanding comparative study of Thessaloniki in relation to other port cities of the eastern Mediterranean such as Izmir, Alexandria, and Beirut. These cities shared common characteristics of geography, diplomacy, language, hybridism, trade, modernity, and vulnerability, and they comprised a common space, the Levant. For Mansel, Thessaloniki was a Levantine city *par excellence*, but also the first city of the east to be de-levantinized, with the entry of the Greek army in 1912. Levantinism concerned certain cities in a specific historical conjuncture, as the Ottoman Empire attempted to modernize and to negotiate its rescue with western modernism. The Levantine cities, such as Thessaloniki, were the intermediaries in this negotiation. As long as the negotiation continued, the Levantine cities amassed wealth, influence, autonomy from the state to which they belonged, but also the unquenchable hostility of nationalists who detested their cosmopolitanism. The collapse of the imperial east pulled down with it the Levantinism of these distinguished cities and they lost the autonomous role they had played until then.

Spyridon G. Ploumidis plunges into the archaeology of the Greek Macedonian movement, which emerged after the appearance of its rival Bulgarian movement in the 1860s. The 'Megali Idea' focused from the outset on incorporating Macedonia into the national core. The Greek national preoccupation concerned Macedonia as a geographic whole more than Thessaloniki in isolation, where the Jewish population was dominant. It intensified after the Ilinden uprising in the summer of 1903. The thwarting of Greece's 'Ionian Vision' in 1922 reconfirmed the importance of Macedonia for Greek nationalism. In the interwar period, interest in Macedonia developed on the geostrategic and, secondarily, economic level, since Macedonia offered Greece an important hinterland with rich productive resources.

From a different perspective, Yura Konstantinova describes Thessaloniki's place in Bulgarian nationalist thought before 1912. The history of 'Bulgarian' Thessaloniki is the history of the gradual emancipation of Macedonia's Slavophones from Greek cultural domination. In this evolutionary process, a key turning point was the recognition of the Bulgarian Exarchate by the Ottoman government in 1870. However, for a number of years thereafter, many wealthy Bulgarian merchants continued to see Greek education as a means of advancement and development, and to remain under the broad influence of Hellenism. The situation was complicated in 1878 with the foundation of the Bulgarian state, which would aspire to intervene in the region by funding Bulgarian education in Thessaloniki and, still more in 1893 with the creation of the IMRO and evolution of socialist and anarchist ideas to which the Bulgarian community of Thessaloniki proved susceptible. Ultimately Thessaloniki, where the Bulgarian population was at a significant disadvantage, became a problem for Bulgarian foreign policy which, immediately after the First Balkan War, was divided between the moderates, who recognized Greece's precedence in exchange for internationalizing the port, and the extremists, who finally prevailed, who considered possession of Thessaloniki and winning over its Jewish residents the precondition for full Bulgarian dominance in Macedonia.

Introduction 9

Nora Lafi supplements the analysis of the physical changes in Thessaloniki's urban environment during the second half of the nineteenth century by analyzing the institutional changes in municipal governance. Apart from the major changes in the hardware of the city, with the arrival of reformist governor Sabri Pasha in 1869, changes that included the demolition of the walls, expansion of the port, a rail connection first with Belgrade and then with Istanbul, construction of a tram line, and a series of large public buildings, Lafi presents the changes in the city's software, chiefly in the functioning of the municipal authority. Because of its geo-strategic importance, Thessaloniki was chosen by Ottoman Tanzimat authorities as one of the seven imperial cities in which to apply new, modern municipal institutions. However, Lafi emphasizes the continuities with the previous Ottoman regime, as it had been shaped over three centuries on the basis of ethnic coexistence. As she stresses, these were reforms based on an old system, rather than a break with that system.

Olivia Pallikari selected theater and its history in Turkish-ruled Thessaloniki to illustrate the gradual Europeanization of residents' entertainment but also the intensifying national rivalries expressed in the separate theatrical life of each of the communities that coexisted in Thessaloniki. The history of theater, a quintessentially urban pursuit, attests the city's increasing wealth, the gradual secularization of its morals, and the entry of Thessaloniki in the broader national and international cultural events of the age. Indeed, from 1850 until 1912, more than 150 performances of Greek and foreign plays took place, by amateur and professional companies, and the most important Greek professional theater companies and many foreign ones passed through.

Scientific interest in the past and archaeology are part of European modernism and are part of a teleological idea of historical time. On this basis, Edhem Eldem analyzes Ottoman interest in archaeology in Thessaloniki during the 1832–1912 period. Eldem sketches a charming history of Ottoman archaeology from its first disorganized steps to the improvement and systemization of its efforts and finally to the official calendars published by the Thessaloniki provincial administration, in which one section is devoted to the antiquities. Thessaloniki at the beginning of the twentieth century is recognized as a model city for modernization and westernization. However, unlike in other sectors such as education or industry, interest in archaeology began and ended in the imperial center, Istanbul. Thessaloniki was on the archaeological periphery, feeding the imperial collections in the capital with its finds. Finally, Ottoman Thessaloniki never acquired an archaeological museum, unlike other modernizing cities in the east, and this was remedied only in 1925 under Greek administration, using the New Mosque of the *Dönme* for the purpose.

Thessaloniki was not simply a city of revolutions, especially at the beginning of the twentieth century, but even further, it was the capital of the most important of them, the Young Turk revolution of 1908. Sotiris Dimitriadis addresses this key event to analyze the effect of the revolution on the city during the four years of 1908–1912. In 1908, the simmering discontent in the Ottoman army stationed in the city burst out in an uprising against the arbitrary government of

10   *Dimitris Keridis*

Sultan Abdul Hamid II. The Ottoman state's declaration of bankruptcy in 1897, the widening gulf between social classes, the instability in the wider region of Macedonia, and increasing tensions between Orthodox Greeks and Bulgarians, were some of the causes of the uprising. Mass gatherings, demonstrations, and public speeches were the chief characteristic of local life during the whole period of intense political activism that followed. However, the initial expectations for democratization of the Ottoman polity and safeguarding of workers' rights were disappointed, with an autocratic turn to one-party rule by the Committee of Union and Progress.

Thessaloniki was also in the vanguard in printing, once Don Yehuda Gedaliah established the first printing plant in southeast Europe at the beginning of the sixteenth century. Complementing Konstantinova's analysis, Vlasis Vlasidis studied the development of the city's newspapers, and particularly of a relatively neglected part, the Bulgarian newspapers. Already in the nineteenth century Thessaloniki had several Jewish, Greek, and Turkish papers. Indeed, the first Turkish/Ottoman newspaper, which was published in 1869 on the initiative of the local administration, in four languages, was entitled Selanik/Salonica/Thessaloniki/Solun! Until 1908, Thessaloniki's Bulgarian-language press lagged behind the others in number of imprints and in circulation. This changed in the four years prior to the Balkan wars, when the Young Turk revolution imposed pacification in Macedonia and returned the national rivalry to more political means. Study of Bulgarian newspapers and periodicals in Thessaloniki before 1912 reveals the quarrels within the Bulgarian-Exarchist community, but also the general hyper-politicization of the press in the service of nationalist aims.

Devin E. Naar opens the second section of the book by tackling a sensitive issue, the inclusion of Thessaloniki Jews in Greek national life in the 1917–1933 period. Naar offers a series of nuances to the standard account that sees Thessaloniki Jews as opposed to the city's being part of Greece. The Greek state handled the issue more sensitively and intelligently than is usually recognized. 'Hellenization' affected not only Thessaloniki Jews but also the Macedonian Slavophones and many Asia Minor refugees. This 'Hellenization' meant adopting a Greek national identity, one that for the whole first half of the twentieth century was still taking shape. Finally, at the beginning of the 1930s, knowledge of Greek had made important progress, particularly in the younger generations of Thessaloniki Jews, and the assimilation process was proceeding normally. Naar attributes the Campbell anti-Semitic Pogrom of 1931 to the success of the Venizelist assimilationist policy rather than to its failure.

Elpida K. Vogli studies the process of incorporating Thessaloniki into Greece after its seizure by the Greek army in 1912. The process of incorporating the 'New Lands' was complicated and time-consuming because of their size relative to the rest of the country, but also because of the internal conflicts provoked by the national schism that lasted the whole interwar period. As we know, the national completion of Greece was gradual, and the Greek state acquired the relevant experience early on, with the annexation of the Ionian Islands in 1864. Cosmopolitan Thessaloniki, however, had its own distinctive issues, expressed in its 'municipal

Introduction   11

question' and the intermittent dominance of anti-Venizelist candidates for city hall thanks to the Jewish vote.

The contribution of Constantinos Katerinopoulos concerns the installation of refugees after the Asia Minor Catastrophe of 1922, which radically changed the city's ethnic composition, residential patterns, economy, and political behavior. The first expansion outside the walls was launched by the visit of sultan Abdul Mecid in 1859, signaling the Ottoman government's renewed interest in reform. Major infrastructure works, an opening of the local economy to global trade, and rapid economic progress followed, prior to liberation. The arrival of the refugees gave a second, even stronger impetus to the city's development and transfiguration.

Eyal Ginio returns to the interwar Jewish community and to the effort to negotiate the new situation that emerged after 1912, especially on the part of its historians. Though part of the Jewish community decided to emigrate, the majority remained and, in time, became divided among Zionists, socialists, and moderates preaching assimilation. Jewish historians in the interwar period attempted to teach Greek history to their co-religionists, in order to ease their entry into Greece. In this effort they highlighted the long historical course of Greeks and Jews and their great contribution to shaping western civilization. One interesting element Ginio adds, with important ramifications in the current age, is the dominance and gradual decline of Judeo-Spanish, which had been the language of the Jewish community.

The Aristotelian University of Thessaloniki, the largest university foundation in Greece, recently announced creation of a Chair of Jewish Studies at the Philosophical School. This is in fact the refounding of a chair abolished by the Metaxas regime. The key point of interest is the language in which the Chair will teach: Judeo-Spanish, the language of the Thessaloniki Jews, or Hebrew, a language few spoke prior to the founding of modern Israel? In other words, is the target of this important educational initiative, with significant political implications, the city's Jewish community or today's Israel, with its wealthy potential investors.

The eminent Thessaloniki historian Evangelos Hekimoglou offers a breath of Marxism, focusing on class stratification and its reordering during the first decades after liberation. As has already been said, the history of Thessaloniki and, generally, all the formerly multi-ethnic cities of eastern Europe became fashionable after 1989 and the great international discussion of nationalism and ethnic identity triggered by the fall of Soviet communism and the dissolution of Yugoslavia. With the same ease that older generations of historians used to refer to 'social class' as the only analytical category worthy of their attention, younger historians refer to the 'nation', frequently excluding any other identity besides national/ethnic. In this way, however, Thessaloniki's history around 1912 is limited to a contest between its national-religious communities. Hekimoglou, on the contrary, presents not only a general economic history of the city from the end of the Ottoman period to World War II, with his analytical tool of the three-fold division of economic activity into archaic, colonial, and capitalist, but also the social stratification of the city as it was interwoven with its ethnographic composition.

12 *Dimitris Keridis*

Eleni Kallimopoulou, Kostis Kornetis, and Panagiotis C. Poulos offer an innovative piece on Thessaloniki's auditory landscape and how this changed after 1912, once the voices of the muezzin disappeared and the sound of cars and other modern technology increased. The value of the work lies in its reminder of the power of sound and hearing in shaping social, class, and national identities. Moreover, the mass arrival of refugees after 1922 did not necessarily imply homogenization and 'Hellenization' of the acoustic landscape, but strengthened its polymorphism, since many of the new arrivals brought with them their own customs and languages, such as Pontic and Turkish.

Mazower's work on Thessaloniki was criticized by various sides, including by Greek nationalists, since it challenged the national narrative of the city's uninterrupted Greekness from its founding to the present. The truth, however, is that if Mazower's history 'wronged' anyone, it was not the Greeks and other Christians nor, certainly, the Jews, but perhaps the city's Muslims, who were the masters for five centuries before 1912. These Muslims are perhaps those most left out of efforts to trace Thessaloniki's historical course during the twentieth century. The article by Konstantinos Tsitselikis makes an attempt to fill the gap. He reports on the Muslim presence in Thessaloniki after the 1912 change, which was especially painful for Muslims, many of whom emigrated. The Muslim population coexisted with the now-dominant Christian element for a decade, until the compulsory population exchange in 1923. Tsitselikis focuses on the legal devices used by the Greek state to incorporate but also to control the city's Muslim population.

Eleni Bastéa† and Vilma Hastaoglou-Martinidis have contributed an ambitious overview of the city's transformation. They juxtapose the changes in the built environment to key contemporary examples from the rich literary culture Thessaloniki inspired, to bring home how sweeping the changes were for the inner life of Thessaloniki residents, and how the anchors of personal and civic memory shifted over time.

It is said that Thessaloniki is first and foremost its port. However, Vilma Hastaoglou-Martinidis reminds us that until 1870 the city had no access to the sea, being shut in by its walls. Only then was decided, in addition to demolition of the sea walls, creation of a spacious waterfront that even today is one of the city's chief sights, and construction of a modern harbor. The 1869 opening of the Suez Canal preceded it, as did the development of port installations in other Eastern Mediterranean cities such as Izmir, Beirut, and Alexandria. This was the city's most important infrastructure project and, in conjunction with the rail links to Europe via Belgrade and to Istanbul, upgraded its geopolitical significance and economic potential. French companies undertook the construction and managed the port until 1930, thus even after liberation. It is impressive that the port of Thessaloniki and prospects for privatizing and improving it remain in the news even today.

Charis Christodoulou offers a gripping account of the post-war changes in Thessaloniki, by decade, from the standpoint of the urban periphery rather than the city center. This is an unusual but valuable look at the 'real' city, not the one on paper, which fills in the architectural and urbanistic course of Thessaloniki.

Introduction 13

Athena Yiannakou addresses the Greek state's housing policy in Thessaloniki from the interwar period through the construction explosion in the 1960s. Even though most of the urban expansion of the city, after the arrival of the refugees and the creation on the outskirts of new neighborhoods to shelter them, took place on land managed by the state, the policy it followed favored small property owners. Thessaloniki followed the rest of the country and avoided creating faceless, ghettoized dormitory suburbs around it.

Kornilia Trakosopoulou-Tzimou focuses with admirable care on the policy regarding protection of Thessaloniki's monuments from late Ottoman times until today. It is not particularly original to recognize that Thessaloniki is a city with a long, rich architectural heritage, certainly unique in Greece for the range of architectural currents meeting in it, eclecticism the most prevalent, but also neo-classicism, Ottoman baroque, and Italian influences that converge in the pre-1912 buildings of Greeks, Turks, and Jews, respectively. Many ideas and practices changed along the historical path she charts. Once walls were demolished, while today they are restored. The author adopts a critical stance toward the 'innovations' of Hébrard. It is worth noting, as was mentioned several times in other essays as well, that the Greek state was slow to recognize the cultural value of Islamic monuments, most of which were lost. A characteristic example is the mass destruction in 1926 of all the city's minarets except that of the Rotunda. Alexandros Papanastasiou protested in vain: 'I am sorry because many (Islamic) monuments were mutilated by demolishing the minarets ... history is not erased with the demolition of innocent monuments that beautified the city ... they are a national property, they are valuable, and they must be respected'.

The opening of the borders after the end of the Cold War and developments such as the expansion of the European Union in the Balkans, created an expectation that the city would take on a regional role as the most important nodal port in the area. Although these expectations, superficial and sometimes even imperialist in how they were cultivated, never became reality, Thessaloniki has been transformed today, thanks to immigration but also to the new economic networks that have developed, into a real Balkan city.

In closing, I want to express my gratitude to all those who worked for the successful realization of the Congress, but also to those who contributed to the present publication. Professor Vasilis Gounaris was crucial to this effort, and it is fitting that the final essay in this volume is his meditation on future histories of the city. Once the idea of a conference took hold, he played the leading role as president of the Scientific Committee. That committee also included historians Dimitris Lyvanios, Professor at the School of Journalism and Mass Media of the Aristotelian University of Thessaloniki; Konstantinos Svolopoulos, Emeritus Professor at the University of Athens and member of the Athens Academy; Giannis Stefanidis, Professor at the Law School of the Aristotelian University; and Mark Mazower, Professor of History at Columbia University in New York. Together they contributed their scholarly insights and were the guardians and guarantors of the whole endeavor from an academic perspective. For the publication, first in Greek and now in English, special thanks are due to researcher

14   *Dimitris Keridis*

Anastasia Lekka, and to Aspa Kyriaki who managed the Navarino Network in Thessaloniki until 2019.

Dimitris Keridis, M.P., Professor of International Relations, Panteion University, Greece, Founding Director of the Navarino Network, and Chair of the Organizing Committee of the International Conference 'Thessaloniki: A City in Transition, 1912–2012'.

Note

1   Indeed, the first chapter of Hanioğlu's 'spiritual biography' of Ataturk is entitled '*Fin-de-siècle* Salonica' (Hanioğlu 2011, 8–30).

References

Hanioğlu, Ş. M. Atatürk, *An Intellectual Biography*. Princeton: Princeton University Press (2011).
Mazower, M. *Salonica, City of Ghosts: Christians, Jews, and Muslims, 1430–1950*. London: HarperCollins (2004).

1 Towards a history of Thessaloniki's future

Mark Mazower

One hundred years ago, the future hung heavy over Thessaloniki. Although it was under the control of the Greek army, its legal status was provisional—a military occupation in which effective Greek control coexisted with the formalities of Ottoman sovereignty, and would coexist until its new legal status was definitively settled at the end of 1913 by the Treaty of London in favor of Greece. Greek authorities could not be at all sure that the diplomats of the Great Powers would come down in their favor. They found themselves in fierce competition with other would-be claimants for the city, a competition which manifested itself not only— and indeed not primarily militarily (as with Bulgaria)—nor through claims about the past or about historic rights but chiefly through rival claims about the city's future. For the city's new rulers, especially provisional governor Konstantinos Raktivan and his subordinates, laying claim to the future meant coming to grips as quickly as possible with the existing bureaucratic order of things and persuading the city's inhabitants that Greek rule was in their own interest.

Faced with early indications that prominent Jewish circles were going to call for the city's eventual internationalization, and with worrying signs that the Bulgarians were appealing for Jewish support for their own claim, the administration tried its own PR offensive. 'Members of the Chamber of Commerce', Raktivan's deputy for economic affairs, Georgios Kofinas, assured Athens confidentially at the start of 1913, expressed their pleasure 'with the administration's solicitude and their conviction in a rosy future' [*peri aisiou mellontos*] (Hekimoglou 1989, 28).

A very serious contender in this struggle over future scenarios for the city was the Habsburgs, who saw it as a means strategically of outflanking the Serbs and Russia. Austrian propaganda veered off into its own prognostics, stressing that:

> For Thessaloniki Austria means immediate communications between the North Sea and the Aegean. Instead of tardy, creaking trains ... we will have luxurious carriages that will ferry their international clientele at top speed. The India Post will make a great saving of time by following the route through Thessaloniki ... A German-Slav line, passing via Germany, Austria, Bosnia, Albania and Macedonia will shave between thirteen and eighteen hours off

16   *Mark Mazower*

the journey between Ostend and Port-Said. In this way, Thessaloniki will see days of great prosperity. All central Europe will use the port.

(Risal 1913, 358)

This the Greeks countered with visions of their own. Looking ahead in the summer of 1913, Kofinas argued for the creation of a Free Port under overall Greek management. This would not only help realize 'the economic dreams of Hellenism' but it would transform the city into a regional hub, linking the Balkans and the islands with the eastern shore of the Mediterranean, 'even Smyrna and Constantinople'. Here was a bid for a rival empire, with the new city at the heart of things—a commercial magnet but also a future industrial center for a new empire of Hellenism to counter the older fading rivals in Istanbul and Vienna.

The basic point is a simple one: we cannot tell the story of Thessaloniki, above all the history of its transformation into a major modern Greek city, unless we can also tell the history of the city's futures—those visions that have in modern times guided policy and sharpened conflicts and competition among those who sought to master it. 1912–1913 was the moment that revealed this future thinking more than any other; but it was not the end of this story and certainly not the start of it either.

But the history of the future? Is it not a contradiction in terms? Not at all. In fact, it is striking that recently more and more historians have been showing an interest in the way people have thought about the future over time. Some explore attitudes to the future as displayed in science fiction or utopian political philosophy; others are interested in the changing political economy of risk; or in changing attitudes to death. It is, I think, not at all surprising that, living as we do in an era subject to the tyranny of anxiety about the future—especially, but not only, in Greece right now—we should find it valuable, perhaps even consoling, to reflect on what the future has meant to previous generations. Because if one thing is clear, it is that the future has a history too: attitudes to it have changed very dramatically in the past and may do so again. And so what I propose to do briefly is to sketch out something of this story as it applies to Thessaloniki, to ask what futures have clustered around it and emerged from within its walls in the past, and how these futures changed around the time of the Balkan Wars and changed again in the century that has passed since then.

Let's begin by thinking about the tools at our disposal today to think about the future. We live in a world where financial institutions impute present value to assets of all kinds on the basis of projected future earnings, as compared with older theories of value based on past investments of labor or capital. To calculate those earnings, we rely on—or suffer from—a computerized system of extraordinary complexity, with instruments for estimating future values as precisely as possible. Never mind that much of this is mumbo-jumbo: it is our mumbo-jumbo—together with the credit ratings and the agencies that produce them, the forecasters, the risk assessment agencies and strategic planners, the derivatives contracts, and innumerable futures markets. And that is just the start. We are surrounded by automatic timekeepers, built into our computers, or on our wrists or

Towards a history of Thessaloniki's future 17

in our phones that fix us as data in a regularized flow between past and present. We have a political system in which political behavior is shaped by calculations of the needs of forthcoming elections. We have a consciousness of the world as an aggregate of natural resources, an ecological system of its own, whose future is directly affected by our own consumption patterns. And so on.

Nearly all of this is of recent vintage. Almost none of it can be traced back before the 19th century at the earliest (with a couple of exceptions I will return to). It is part of what the French historian, François Hertog, would call a new 'regime of historicity', a new way that is of ordering in our minds the relationship between past, present, and future (Hertog 2002). So, in order to understand the sheer oddity, in historical terms, of the way we now think about the future, we need to think ourselves back into a premodern world, to its economy and its patterns of thought. For of course, it is not as though the inhabitants, say, of medieval Thessaloniki never thought about the future at all. Surely, they did. Only they did so in such a very different way that we might scarcely recognize it as the same thing.

I would like to propose that roughly speaking, we can distinguish three epochs of future thinking, each quite distinct from one another, and view the city's history in their light. The earliest would be one in which the future was almost entirely out of men's hands. It offered no guide to action or morality, and was nothing like as important for either as the past. Instead it lay in the hands of God, or of fate. One could plan for the future, to a limited degree, but neither individuals nor states did so on anything like the scale we are accustomed to. There was no such thing as politics in this world, and nothing really resembling a modern economy either. Then came a rupture, a time, when in the words of Alexis de Tocqueville, 'the past no longer illuminated the future' and as a result 'the spirit marches amid shadows'. Catalyzed by the French Revolution—the very phrase *ancien régime* captures the new attitude to power—this rupture came some time in the early 19th century in western Europe, and later in the Ottoman lands, and marked the moment when teleological thinking—the idea that society was marching towards a given end, and that the present gained its meaning from the destination—triumphed across Europe, along with the emergence of capitalism, of liberalism, nationalism, and their closely conjoined intellectual companion, the professional study of history itself. Thessaloniki was shaped as much as any major city by this turn to the future, as we shall see in a little more detail below. And then there comes the third phase, towards the end of the 20th century, the phase in which we still live, in which confidence in the great schemes of future improvement, of progress, falters. For some, the future vanishes entirely as a horizon of action, or becomes simply a source of fear, anxiety, and risk reduction. For others, in a similar vein, it ushers in an epoch, our own, in which we are reduced to living in the present, incapable of taking seriously any projection of human aspirations or needs into the future. Let us turn now to Thessaloniki, and ask how the city's history might look under the sign of the future.[1]

How far back do we need to go? Perhaps to the Apostle Paul, who as you will remember passed through this city and got a rough reception for preaching faith in Christ. Things went better for him and his companions in Verroia but it is in Athens, challenged by some rather self-confident Epicurean and Stoic philosophers, that Paul defined the 'new teaching' most clearly. Standing in the Areopagus, as we learn from *Acts of the Apostles* (*Acts 17*), Paul stated uncompromisingly:

> The God who made the world and all things in it, since He is Lord of heaven and earth, does not dwell in temples made with hands; [25] nor is He served by human hands, as though He needed anything, since He Himself gives to all *people* life and breath and all things; [26] and He made from one *man* every nation of mankind to live on all the face of the earth, having determined *their* appointed times and the boundaries of their habitation, that they would seek God, if perhaps they might grope for Him and find Him, though He is not far from each one of us; for in Him we live and move and exist, as even some of your own poets have said, 'For we also are His children'. Being then the children of God, we ought not to think that the Divine Nature is like gold or silver or stone, an image formed by the art and thought of man. Therefore having overlooked the times of ignorance, God is now declaring to men that all *people* everywhere should repent, because He has fixed a day in which He will judge the world in righteousness through a Man whom He has appointed, having furnished proof to all men by raising Him from the dead.
>
> (Hertog 2012, 52–53)

Now by the time we come to the period with which we are concerned, Paul's gospel has become dominant. All the city's inhabitants, to the best of our knowledge, are monotheists, who govern their lives, and expect the city to be governed, in accordance with the word and laws of God as laid down by his messengers. The chief dispute is over who those messengers are and how their word is to be interpreted. These issues are of critical legal and political importance in a polity where the legitimacy of the rulers is bound up with the claim to divine approval—hence the radically disruptive potential of the Sabbataian movement in the 17th century, and the reason for its very careful handling by the Ottoman authorities.

How then do people think about the future in such a society? In the first place, they think about the City of Rome in the light of, and in anticipation of, the City of God (to put it in Augustinian terms) and their most important acts are conducted with an eye to the fate of their souls after death. The future exists as a day of judgement when heaven will submit the earthly world and earthly deeds to a reckoning. Life on this earth is preliminary to that, a brief entryway to eternity. Living in much closer proximity to death and the dead than we do today—cemeteries are scattered around the city, and private tombs may be found in very central locations—the future for them is not so much a guide to ethical practice as a destination that requires certain kinds of spiritual and economic preparations. Ethical guidance comes from holy books as interpreted by a class of spiritual advisers, and perhaps, for the few who are educated, from the instruction to be gleaned from the lives of great men. Preparing for the future means above all solicitude for the soul.

Towards a history of Thessaloniki's future 19

In an instructive article, Eyal Ginio used Ottoman wills to demonstrate the ways in which wealthy inhabitants of the city sought to secure rewards in the hereafter by endowing *waqfs* and mandating good deeds in their name—such as care for the poor or the reading out of passages from the *Qur'an*. One could not obviously control death; one could, however, aim to secure as favorable as possible an afterlife in this way. And of course, other strategies were there for this purpose—the pursuit of ethical purity through spiritual reclusion, for instance (Ginio 2001).

Society respected such choices and facilitated them. But they were essentially the choices of individuals. And the role for the state to demonstrate its own competence in matters of the future was thus limited. While the Ottoman dynasty might, like any other magnate family, pursue its own spiritual strategies for the afterlife, its solicitude for the future of its inhabitants in this world was strictly limited. The Ottoman state was surprisingly ambitious in tackling matters deemed necessary for its own survival—maintenance of a serious road and postal network for instance; raising taxes; levying troops; ensuring the Istanbul food supply. But in most of the areas of life where we are accustomed to the modern welfare state staking its claim, it was absent—no state-run school system, for instance, nor any system of health care. This is obvious: they did not exist anywhere before the middle of the 19th century at the earliest and there was nothing odd about the Ottoman case.

I think the first force to begin to transform attitudes to the future was capitalism. For decades in the late 18th century, European consuls railed against the refusal of Ottoman society—of all religions—to enter into the new consumer frenzy that was gripping Europe and upon which, historians now tell us, much of the industrial revolution was based. I cannot resist quoting from the remarks back home of one irritated consul from the city around 1800:

Always the same in his way of being, of living and of dressing, the pleasures and the wants of yesterday are to him the pleasures and wants of tomorrow. Rich or poor, he puts on every morning the same woollen cloth, and lays it aside only when he has worn it entirely out, in order to purchase another of the same quality, the same price and the same colour. He has drunk coffee in his childhood but he will drink it in his old age. He will not forsake old habits but he will not imbibe new ones. This stupid monotony in habits and tastes must set constant limits to the consumption of our commodities.[2]

In fact, despite the emergence of a class of 'Francos', closely linked to European trade, and with the city playing a significant role particularly in the development of the Greek wheat trade, so important for the future development of Greek society, overall Ottoman Selanik remained, well into the 19th century, as resistant as the rest of the empire to the new logic of capital. There were no banks in the city, merely private money-lenders, and no state borrowing and thus no public works. Money was, for the most part, tight, and much of the economy rested upon a barter basis. The export trade in particular was tightly controlled by the authorities, and this limited the capacity of the local society to afford foreign imports. A few notables

20   *Mark Mazower*

sported European watches by the end of the 18th century but their elite quality testified to the relatively closed circuit that comprised the Ottoman imperial economy.

With the Tanzimat this began to change. The Anglo-Turkish commercial convention of 1830 was a major turning point. But so was something else—closely connected with the spread of European capitalism—the emergence after the Napoleonic Wars of a new, culturally loaded conception of Europe itself. The idea of Europe as a civilization was part of the new future-thinking that was sweeping the continent. 'Europe' was not only the new Concert of Europe dedicated to keeping a conservative peace, nor the new rival radical Europes under discussion by free traders, nationalists, and communists at this time. It was also a cultural club open, on conditions, to other members, and presented as a recipe for future happiness: Europe was a policy prescription for modernity.

It was the desire to assert the Europeanness of the Empire that made Reshid Pasha so keen to advise Mehmed II to make reforms. It was the same desire that explained the overwhelming desire of Ottoman diplomats to achieve international recognition for the Empire as part of what contemporaries called 'the Public Law of Europe'. The desire to protect the empire in an increasingly harsh world was thus premised on a new view of what the state ought to do for the future welfare of its subjects.

Hence the new strategies—diplomatic and also economic—that we see pursued by Ottoman diplomats (and by Mehmet Ali and his successors in Egypt) in the middle of the 19th century: the first thinking about public works and urban transformation; the first recourse to European capital markets; the first debt crises. All of these left their mark on the city of Thessaloniki. Through them we first see the emergence of the idea that those in charge of the city, or those who love it, should imagine a future for the city itself.

The middle of the 19th century was a time of restless entrepreneurial energies, much of it directed towards land, whether urban or rural. The historian James Belich, in his recent study of the development of English-speaking settlement overseas, has identified the mid-19th century as the height of a global frenzy in land speculation, a frenzy that he sees as part and parcel of the spread of capitalism and of colonialism as well. Sometimes this frenzy correctly identifies opportunities for investment; as often, it gets them wrong, or just as bad, gets them right but the timing wrong. But what is common to them all is their orientation towards the future, a future of dynamic enterprises, bustling cities and entire new economies—think of Chicago, or Canberra, or San Francisco—made by human hands. Thus some 30 years after Reshid Pasha had first proposed public works investments to the Sultan, and 10 years after Abdul Mejid's visit to Thessaloniki, which had resulted in nothing but the usual charitable disbursements, a new *vali*, Sabri Pasha inaugurated the demolition of the sea walls and construction started on the new harbor that would eventually, after many fits and starts, allow the city to present a new, self-consciously European face to the world. It was, for the Ottoman Empire, an act of unprecedented financial daring and speculation, and profits were won and lost astonishingly rapidly in the early 1870s in the Salonica docks reclamation scheme.

Towards a history of Thessaloniki's future 21

Paradoxically but completely characteristically, the more the empire accumulated debt, the more this kind of thinking about the future proliferated. Take for instance an English pamphlet of 1875, which contains the following suggestion made by 'a Long Resident in Turkey', to resolve the empire's looming financial crisis:

A suggestion with regard to Turkey:

We think if a Financial Committee, could be formed in Turkey, composed of the Commissioners appointed by the Bondholders, and some other members representing the Turkish Government, with an agency in London, it would inspire confidence in all the friends of Turkey, and perhaps by this means the resources of Turkey might really be developed in a proper manner, and capital might again flow into the country, with some chance of opening up the various sources of wealth, now lying buried in one of the richest countries of the world, where Mines rich in Gold, Silver, and other Minerals, including vast deposits of Coal, situated near Mount Olympus, are only waiting to be properly worked in order to become a second El Dorado, and in the hands of really enterprising Englishmen, fortunes could soon be amassed, if only a proper understanding could be arrived at with the Turkish Government, and the present moment is the time to secure the necessary privileges for working capital in Turkey, with security and profit.

Vast tracts of land laying uncultivated in various parts of Turkey, for instance Macedonia, with the magnificent bay and port of Salonica, only a week's journey from London, can be purchased at a mere nominal price, and were it more generally known English gentlemen, young farmers seeking a home in the wilds of America, Canada, Australia, and other parts would adopt Turkey as their future home, instead of spending vast sums in the endeavour to find, what more often turns out to be a myth, an eligible farm in Missouri, Ohio, or some other out-of-the-way part.

There is an abundance of shooting in all parts of Turkey, fishing besides, and we have known more than one Sultan, one Duke, and one Ambassador to spend several days near the beautiful surroundings of Salonica, and Monastir, in order to enjoy the varied sports of shooting and hunting, in those enchanting districts renowned for their antiquities.[3]

For the rest of the century, and early into the new one, commentators on the city pontificated endlessly on the struggle that was being waged for its soul between a traditionalism exemplified by the Ano Poli and the Frankish modernity revealed below Egnatias Street and above all along the seafront—clubs, cinemas, banks, rectilinear street plans [permitted by the 1890 fire]. There were those who embraced the demolition of the city gates and the expansion west and eastwards, crowds who stood and cheered at the arrival of the first train from the north. And there were those whose Orientalism expressed itself in nostalgia for the city's vanishing ways. For some Westerners, such as the Frenchman Julien Viaud, better

22   *Mark Mazower*

known as Pierre Loti, Salonica represented the last of what he called the 'old Orient'. In his strange first novel, *Aziyade*, an early Orientalist bestseller based on his own experiences in the city in the summer of 1876, he incarnates in his passionate love affair with the Circassian girl of the title, a doomed meeting of West and East that could only be consummated, as he put it, 'outside time and place' and 'beyond all laws of nature' (Loti 2006, 276, 287).

An age so acutely self-conscious of history could not help but prognosticate. In Ottoman terms, the city in the final decade of the 19th century and the first of the 20th was the European face of the empire, an intellectual motor for change as well as a rising commercial entrepôt. Both evolutionists and revolutionaries were believers in political action for the sake of the future. The fascination of catching a glimpse of Abdul Hamid in captivity in the Villa Allatini—a kind of tourist attraction of 1909–1912 and a memory that crops up astonishingly often in later autobiographies—was that it offered the chance to see the past caged by the future. The Young Turks turned their backs on their elders, and projected the virtues of youth. But the Young Turks were riding the crest of a wave of new social forces, all demanding radical change. The burgeoning women's movement dreamed of uniting women of all classes towards a future that combined the education and freedoms of Western women with political activism and piety. The *Federacion* called for cooperation across national and linguistic dividing lines to advance the cause of workers' rights. Marx and Darwin were the joint deities of this new confidence in the future.

And of course, this confidence did not perish with the sudden ending of Ottoman rule. Far from it, no 19th-century ideology was more conscious of the burden of the future than nationalism. This had been evident nearly a century earlier as the Greeks won their independence further south. The Greeks had well understood the importance of appealing to their glorious past and saw its extraordinary appeal on hundreds of influential and classically trained philhellenes. But they soon came to grips with Europe's new obsession with the future too. No philosophical movement was more indifferent to history than Bentham and the utilitarians; yet Benthamites and even the master himself were quickly drawn to Greece as a possible laboratory to try out their new philosophical principles. Equally drawn to look ahead were the Saint-Simonians, and they were certainly more influential in the new Kingdom. The Bavarians were not much inclined to such flights of philosophical fancy—the real urge to the future was in Britain and France in these years—but note that when the new King George arrived in Athens, he defined his mission—'to make Greece ... a model Kingdom in the East'—once more in terms of a new future for the Orient. Everything, from administrative reform to ensuring that Greek was spoken at court, was justified in terms of 'our future', a future that was equated with 'the clear and unblemished Greek idea—in all parts of our life, in all stations of the nation's development' (Bastéa 2000, 34–35).

As we know from several outstanding recent scholarly works, urban planning was a key terrain in which this battle for the nation's future was to be waged. Pylos, Sparta, and above all Athens, were early examples of how the city itself might be used to gesture towards a better future. What the Ottomans had begun in Thessaloniki before the First World War, the new Greek authorities took much

Towards a history of Thessaloniki's future 23

further of course, following the fire of 1917. If anything, the future orientation of the Hébrard-Mawson plans for Thessaloniki was more accentuated than the Othonian-era plans for Athens had been. For the latter had labored under the burden of the past; in the shadow of the Acropolis even the future seemed neoclassical in inspiration. No such constraints held the masters of the plans of 1918–1919. Hébrard himself had been dreaming of a rationalist Universal City since before the First World War; Mawson came out of an Arts and Crafts tradition and was better known as a landscape gardener. Hébrard, the driving force, was sensitive to the city's Byzantine monuments, but they were scarcely allowed to impose themselves in the way that the Acropolis dominated all efforts to turn Athens into the capital of a modern state.

The future as something susceptible to human agency, to state planning—the rebuilding of Thessaloniki took this idea further than it had ever been taken in Greece before. But it also revealed its limitations. The discourse of planning—above all urban planning—is invariably followed by the sound of the planners lamenting what has happened to their plans. Plans are never realized in full, and not only in the former Soviet Union. Extraneous forces, unexpected events, impose and intrude. In the case of the city, one such event was, of course, the *catastrofi*; another was the civil war; a third would be the tyranny of the automobile. Unplanned shanty towns sprang up and took decades to clear away. Roads took on a life of their own, unimaginable to Hébrard or Mawson, whose designs generally feature a tram or two, or perhaps a horse-drawn cart. Individual human futures could not wait on the grand vistas of architects and ministers.

Moreover, planning for the future need not only take the form of rational functionalism. Other kinds of futures were also in the air in the mid-20th century. One was socialism, and nowhere in Greece was the socialist tradition more powerful especially in the 1930s than it was on the streets of the Macedonian capital. The 'days of 36' represented a continuation of that European struggle of ideological opposites—fascism and communism—already starting to play itself out in Spain. Another was racial, and it was again in Thessaloniki that the interwar era's only notable right-wing racial movement in Greece—EEE—made real headway for a time, hitting the headlines with the Campbell Pogrom of 1931. The German invasion and occupation once more threw the city's future into question; this uncertainty facilitated the genocide, which after all commended itself to some Greek nationalists on the grounds that it would finally usher in a future for the city without a significant Jewish presence. But it is also worth remembering that the Germans at least officially presented the genocide as a new future for the Jews themselves—the official story line was that they were going to settle in a new homeland in Poland—thus testifying—in the grimmest and most cynical way—to that epoch's ingrained tendency to always think ahead.

The question is how long and to what point ideas of progress, of collectively wrought social change, continued to shape the city. One would have to assume that, as elsewhere, the war did not mark any kind of break, that after the end of the civil war, reconstruction itself was conceptualized as a form of social and political planning. In Athens, a ministry, the then sub-ministry of Reconstruction, continued to be active into the 1950s, while a Ministry of Coordination existed until 1981. The complaint from Thessaloniki, of course, was always that the city was disadvantaged in the struggle for funds with Athens; on the other hand, the building of the main university campus and other major works testified to its continued importance as guardian of the northern frontier during the Cold War.

Historians of our attitudes towards the future are inclined to point to the 1970s as the era when attitudes to the future suddenly darkened, when the post-war social compact and the consensus in managed capitalism gave way to Reaganite individualism and the Thatcher revolution, when the future as an improved world of shared public goods was replaced by the future as a matter of individual self-interest, corporate forecasting, and private accumulation.

In Greece, the chronology was somewhat different. The fall of the junta and especially the emergence of PASOK meant that a future-oriented collective ethos remained powerful through the 1980s. Indeed, Thessaloniki's astonishingly rapid post-war growth—much faster even than that of Athens—meant that the city's population was overwhelmingly one with no memory of the city's past at all: the destruction of much of the city's remaining historical urban fabric even into the 1980s, when some kind of historic preservation movement first gathered support, reflected the newcomers' lack of sentimental attachment to its past. There was a past of course, an omnipresent one, an officially sanctioned one produced in the publications of such institutions as the Society for Macedonian Studies, and this was the city's past as bastion of Hellenism. With the end of the Cold War, and with the emergence of a new multi-ethnic population in the city, a workforce of Albanians, Georgians, Ukrainians, and others, this past began to be challenged. In retrospect, this was a key function of the 1994 designation of the city as Cultural Capital of Europe and the truly extraordinary outpouring of documents and photo albums that this generated. The city's past was suddenly open for debate again, and history seemed to come alive and to count. Of course, there was a sense in which this argument about history was also an argument about the future. But what strikes me now is how attenuated, how uncertain, the discourse about the city's future was, and has largely been since then. Thessaloniki, along with Greece as a whole, appears to have entered this third and final phase that I alluded to above, a phase in which we lose our faith to determine the shape of the future, and at best consider how we can immunize it or minimize its risks and dangers. The contrast with the confidence manifested by previous generations—of all ideological persuasions—is striking. Some may see this as a good thing and argue that exaggerated faith in big futures, in utopias, has been responsible for much suffering and harm. But I wonder whether this is entirely correct. For the future does not much occupy our political leaders any longer or indeed our intellectuals; but that is because, like so much else, it has been privatized and commodified. Do we really want to cede control of the future to the market too, like so much else? Is there not still a case to be made for a public debate about the kind of future we collectively desire for our city, our country, our continent?

Notes

1 Cited by Hertog 2012, 52–53.
2 Felix Beaujour, *A View of the Commerce of Greece* (Paris, 1800) cited in Mazower 2004, 117.
3 From 'A Plea for Turkey and a Proposal to the Bondholders', by A Long Resident in Turkey and Egypt (London, 1875).

References

Bastéa, E., *The Creation of Modern Athens: Planning the Myth*. Cambridge: Cambridge University Press (2000).
Ginio, E., 'Every soul shall taste death: Dealing with death and afterlife in eighteenth-century Salonica', *Studia Islamica* 92(93) (2001).
Hekimoglou, E., *Κοφινάς πρός Διομήδη: δοκίμια και τεκμήρια για την οικονομική ιστορία της Μακεδονίας* [Kofinas to Diomedes]. Thessaloniki: Athanasios Altintzis (1989).
Hertog, F., *Régimes de historicité: Présentisme et expériences du temps*. Paris: Le Seuil (2002).
Hertog, F., 'Faire du temps/faire avec le temps', In: Birnbaum, J. (ed.), *Ou est passé le temps?* Paris: Gallimard (2012).
Loti, P., *Journal intime 1868–1878, Tome I*, In: Quella-Villéger, A. and Vercier, B. (eds.), Paris: Les Indes savantes (2006).
Mazower, M., *Salonica, City of Ghosts: Christians, Muslims and Jews, 1430–1950*. London: HarperCollins (2004).
Risal, P. [Nehama, J.], *La ville convoitée (Salonique)*. Paris: Perrin (1913).

2 Thessaloniki and the cities of the Enlightenment

Paschalis M. Kitromilides

In what follows I wish to consider some questions arising from the absence of the Enlightenment movement in Thessaloniki.[1] From its founding and throughout the course of its over two-millennia-long history, the Macedonian capital, the justly called bride of the Thermaic Gulf, never ceased to be the great metropolis of the Balkan region, a sensitive receiver and relay station of reverberations through the Balkan and Mediterranean worlds. In modern times, the ethnic diversity of its population and its strategic position on the roads of commerce in Southeastern Europe conferred on the city of Thessaloniki both dynamism and an openness to social change. And yet the Enlightenment, the pre-eminent movement of ideological change, which brought Southeastern European society in direct contact with modernity, is absent from the history of Thessaloniki, or rather is deferred to late in the nineteenth century, by then a component of other cultural trends or ideological phenomena. But in terms of the classical Age of the Enlightenment, within the conventional time limits of the eighteenth and early nineteenth centuries, Thessaloniki is absent from the cultural map of such phenomena and processes in the Balkan region.

This is a somewhat paradoxical impression, especially in the context of the history of Macedonia, where we observe noteworthy manifestations of the Enlightenment in the broader periphery of Thessaloniki. To the northwest, in Western Macedonia, new schools teaching the curriculum of the Enlightenment appeared in Kastoria, Kozani, Siatista, and further to the north in Moschopolis; and closer to the metropolis, in its immediate southeastern periphery, on Mount Athos, where exactly at mid-century the Athonite Academy was run by two leading representatives of the Greek Enlightenment, Evgenios Voulgaris and Nikolaos Zerzoulis (Kitromilides 1992, 53–59; Dimaras 1982, 394–403; Psimmenos 1993, 285–291).

So then why not in Thessaloniki? I believe this is an interesting question, teeming with the potential of a critical discussion with the city's history. Yet, perplexingly, it has been posed neither by the historians of Thessaloniki, nor by us, the historians of the Enlightenment, who have focused on the various expressions of the Enlightenment throughout the Greek world, such as, for example, the Septinsular Enlightenment, the Enlightenment in the historic region of Aeolis and Ionia in Western Asia Minor, the Epirot Enlightenment pre-eminently in

Thessaloniki and the Enlightenment 27

continental Greece, etc. It is time, therefore, to ask this historiographic question, the search for answers to which may offer us viewpoints and perspectives that would highlight the dynamics of Thessaloniki's history, as well as the obstacles that occasionally hindered the dynamic flow of historical time.

A comparison of Thessaloniki and the cities of the Enlightenment in the Greek world might contribute to elucidating these questions. Let us summarize the geography of the Enlightenment in the Greek world within the greater environment of Southeastern Europe. The centers of the Enlightenment in this region of Europe included, to the north, the two princely academies of Bucharest and Jassy, which constituted the pre-eminent centers of Greek education throughout the century of the Phanariots, from 1711 to 1821. On the western front of the Greek world, centers of the Enlightenment appear in the Ionian Islands, and especially Corfu, Cephalonia, and Zakynthos. Because of the centuries-long Venetian occupation, the Ionian Islands were incorporated in Italian culture and formed a southern extension of the 'Adriatic Enlightenment' (Wolff 2001, 319–331).

On mainland Greece, the most important center of the Enlightenment was certainly Ioannina, an educational metropolis with direct affinities and relations to the Enlightenment centers in northwestern Macedonia, which we have already mentioned. Centers of Enlightenment that do not share the long prehistory of the movement in Ioannina appeared during the culmination of the period of cultural change in small towns in Thessaly, in the villages of Mount Pelion, in Tyrnavos, and Ambelakia. In regard to northern Greece, we have made reference to the Athonite Academy during the 1750s, while to the east, at the Thracian extremity of the European world, the Enlightenment was embraced by the Patriarchal School in Constantinople during the patriarchate of Seraphim II, between 1757–1761, and later, in the very early nineteenth century, at the Xirokrini School under Cyril VI (1813–1818). Finally, a dominant position in the geography of the Enlightenment during its apex in the Greek world is held by the triangle of the Eastern Aegean, comprising the schools of Kydonies, Smyrna, and Chios.

It is truly remarkable that Thessaloniki is absent from this geographical sketch. If we wish to assess the factors surrounding the appearance of the Enlightenment in the geographical regions mentioned above, we will observe certain significant differences making up the network of multiple causes that conferred dynamism and continuity on the movement through time. In the case of the principalities of Moldowallachia, the rise of the Enlightenment was linked to modernizing initiatives on the part of the Phanariot princes, initiatives that were due to Phanariot society's love of education, as well as to the will of their rulers to render their administration more efficient by producing cadres with modernized training. In Constantinople and the Athonite Academy, the Enlightenment was introduced on the initiative of the Church in order to improve the quality of the education received by its cadres. This observation is put forward to encourage alternative assessments of the relation between Orthodoxy and the Enlightenment, moving beyond the conventional view that presents this relation as a mere dialectical opposition (Kitromilides 2006, 187–209).

28   *Paschalis M. Kitromilides*

Finally, in other regions, in Epirus, Western Macedonia, Eastern Thrace, and the northeastern Aegean, the Enlightenment appeared and developed on the initiative of local communities and groups of merchants who saw in the scholars of the Enlightenment their natural allies in the struggle to bring about a new society. So why then should Thessaloniki be absent from the geography of the Enlightenment since, as the study of the city's history makes plain, during precisely the period under examination we can observe a significant growth in commerce and a reinforcement of the Greek element in its population? The historians of Thessaloniki, from Apostolos Vakalopoulos and Nikos Svoronos to Mark Mazower, underscore precisely this trajectory of the city's Greek community towards a pinnacle, violently interrupted but only temporarily and without being aborted, by the tragedy of May 1821 (Mazower 2004). So why then does Thessaloniki not witness the interplay between commerce, modern culture, and freedom pointed out as a historical regularity in the social theory of the Enlightenment from Montesquieu to Condorcet and Korais?

A dimension of the history in Thessaloniki, which constitutes a fundamental point of reference to which any answer to the question we have posed cannot help but be related, is the history of education. The Enlightenment did not bypass Thessaloniki because of a lack of local tradition in education within which new ideas could be received. Education in Thessaloniki was a continuous process throughout modern times. Perhaps this tradition of Greek letters in the Macedonian metropolis was not of the same breadth and importance as that expressed during the city's last Byzantine centuries, especially the fourteenth; however, the lamp of education was never extinguished, either in post-Byzantine Thessaloniki or in the early modern city. Thessaloniki was one of the cradles of those 'faint and thirsty lamps' of the education of the Greek nation, in the words of Constantinos Koumas (Koumas 1832, 534).

The older historians of the education of the Greek nation, to whose work the researchers of intellectual history always turn with a sense of gratitude and certain benefit, unequivocally testify to the continuous presence of Greek education in Thessaloniki. Both Manouil Gedeon and Tryphon Evangelidis tell us that as early as the end of the fifteenth century, a few decades after the fall of Thessaloniki in 1430, the city maintained a higher Greek school. Testimony of the first known name of a teacher of Greek letters, Ioannis Moschos, dates back to 1490. These testimonies increase regarding the sixteenth century, while for the seventeenth century Gedeon hypothesized: 'By the late seventeenth century, it was impossible that the Greeks of this populous and exceedingly wealthy city would not maintain a school of Greek letters, since Verria had one before 1690, and Kozani before 1680' (Gedeon 1941, 19). The information set forth by Gedeon himself and by Tryphon Evangelidis and other scholars since then has significantly increased our knowledge regarding this subject and confirms absolutely this hypothesis with respect to the seventeenth century (Evangelidis 1932, 111–118; Gedeon 1941, 1–24; Vakalopoulos 1983, 247–249; Karathanasis 1996a, 39–47; Papastathis 1999, 311–340).

The same applies to the eighteenth century, when the history of education in Thessaloniki records the first dramas concerning initiatives and possibilities of

Thessaloniki and the Enlightenment   29

intellectual change. Their failure to come to fruition explains the absence of the Enlightenment. Let us briefly recall what these dramas and possibilities entailed.

One drama was the clash in the early 1730s between Thessaloniki school principal Giannakos and the monk Pachomios, a student of Methodios Anthrakitis and an 'extreme vilifier of Aristotelian philosophy'. Pachomios obviously knew, from Anthrakitis's teachings, the philosophical ideas of Descartes and Malebranche, and his criticism of Aristotle no doubt involved fundamentally a criticism of Theophilos Korydalleus's neo-Aristotelianism. The dispute that resulted obviously originated in the 'envy between the two teachers', as Gedeon is quick to point out. But Pachomios's defeat and subsequent exile to Mount Athos precluded any possibilities that could be linked to his presence in the education of Thessaloniki. Thus, the 'early dawn of spiritual rebirth' to which Gedeon refers when he describes the incident did not lead Thessaloniki to a dawn of the Enlightenment (Gedeon 1930, 49–57). A supporter of traditional education, Giannakos remained dominant in the education of Thessaloniki, hindering any possibility of change or renewal (Tsoulkanakis 1975, 353–386).

In 1752, Giannakos encountered the young Iossipos Moisiodax, who came to Thessaloniki from Wallachia, motivated by an eager desire for education. But he was sorely disappointed, for in Giannakos he met 'a man who had exhausted his entire life in Aristotelianism' (Moisiodax 1780, 179). Soon Moisiodax left Thessaloniki for the Athonite Academy. Sometime later, in the 1760s, another Orthodox Balkan youth, Dositej Obradović, set out from Serbia and traveled the Greek world with the yearning for education. He mentions the Athonite Academy and Evgenios Voulgaris, of course; also Smyrna and Ierotheos Dendrinos; Corfu and Andreas Petritsopoulos; but he makes no mention of Thessaloniki. He too seems to have passed it by, disappointed. The great opportunity for the future of education of Thessaloniki appeared in the spring of 1759 when, following his disputes at the Athonite Academy, Evgenios Voulgaris left Mount Athos and took refuge in Thessaloniki, where he remained for some time. That was truly a great moment for Thessaloniki: to put its education in the hands of the dean of the scholars of the Greek nation, the originator of the Enlightenment in Greek culture. The Thessalonians, community leaders and the Church, did not do so, and the illustrious Evgenios accepted an invitation from Patriarch Seraphim II to serve in the Patriarchal School in Constantinople. That was the possibility that did not yield results, after the drama regarding Pachomios that had come before.

Education in Thessaloniki in 1758 was handed over to the Orthodox theologian Athanasios Parios (canonized in 1995) and his students. In 1778, Parios returned to Thessaloniki from Mesolonghi and was a school principal until 1786, at which point he left for the school of Chios. The presence of this opponent of the Enlightenment is enough to explain why Thessaloniki remained hermetically sealed to the Enlightenment and explains in particular why the Thessalonians remained indifferent to the services that Evgenios Voulgaris could have offered to their education, despite his prolonged sojourn in their city as a guest of Dimitrios Hoidas, the consul of the Venetian Republic, to whose protection he had resorted as a Venetian subject (Mertzios 1956, 417–420).

30   *Paschalis M. Kitromilides*

A typical indication of the baffling decline of education in Thessaloniki precisely at the peak of the Enlightenment arises from the comparison of the testimony of the geographical sources of that era. At mid-century, Grigorios Fatzeas (1760, 176) cites Thessaloniki as the seat of a higher school and as one of the centers of Greek education. On the contrary, in the late eighteenth century, in the much better informed and empirical survey of the Greek world carried out by the two authors of *Geographia Neoteriki* (Modern Geography), Daniel Philippides and Grigorios Konstantas, the following is written regarding Thessaloniki:

> Salonica, Thessaloniki is now the metropolis of Macedonia, a very old, famous, large, populous, beautiful and very commercial city, on the east side of the innermost part of the Thermaic Gulf, with a fine harbor, part of it on slopes, part on a plain. It was built by Kassandros, Philip's son-in-law, and was named after his wife, Thessaloniki; before that it was called Thermi, from where the Thermaic Gulf got its name, which is now known as the Gulf of Thessaloniki. The city is well known for the old monuments that still survive there, and indeed for its triumphal arches, of which one survives intact to this day. They say this city was sold by Andronikos Palaiologos to the Venetians in 1422, and it was taken from them by the Turks in 1431; but the French encyclopaedia includes the information that when the said Andronikos became emperor, Salonica was taken by William of Sicily, and from him it reverted back to Andronikos Palaiologos, and then shortly afterwards, the Sultan sent a general and subjugated it. The very holy fathers of the Tsaous Monastery colluded in the sack of the city in the way they were instructed in treachery by their teacher, the devil; when the Turks entered the city they put an administrator in charge so that their Holinesses wouldn't be harmed; later the Sultan rewarded them with a permanent tax exemption, with their share to be paid by those who wished to be masters of their freedom and their religion, and they would be rewarded by their teacher in their nether homeland, together with their schoolmate, Judas. It is inhabited by Romans [Greeks], Turks and a multitude of Jews, most of whom came here after they were driven out of Spain. It is honored by the throne of a Metropolitan, who has many bishops under him and lives in the castle like all the Romans, and performs the functions of religion somewhat more freely than in other parts. The Christians have churches, the Jews have synagogues. The city is also inhabited by Armenians. And there are also consuls of various nations.
>
> (Philippides and Konstantas 1988, 202–203)

We see that much is said about Thessaloniki, but not a word about schools or education, neither Greek nor Jewish. The impression created by the narrative in the *Geographia Neoteriki* is also confirmed by the explicit testimony of Athanasios Psalidas: 'it has a Greek school, but a neglected one' (Psalidas 1931, 56). The *Geographia*'s reference to Thessaloniki reminds us that during the period the authors describe, the Macedonian metropolis was primarily a Jewish city. We could, therefore, pose the question to what extent would it have been possible for

Thessaloniki and the Enlightenment   31

the Enlightenment to appear in Thessaloniki through Jewish channels. Could the *Haskalah*, the Jewish Enlightenment, have arrived in Thessaloniki through the contacts of the city's Jewish community with the communities of Central Europe, where, thanks to Moses Mendelssohn, this version of the Enlightenment had appeared within the Jewish tradition? (Sorkin 2008, 165–213). In his monumental history, Joseph Nehama, the historian of Thessaloniki's Jewry, offers ample evidence regarding the community's intellectual life between 1669–1816 to corroborate the view that not only did the *Haskalah* never arrive in Thessaloniki, but quite the opposite. For the Jews of the city, the Age of Enlightenment was a long period of, as he says, 'philological and philosophical drought' (Nehama 1978, 426). The reasons dated back to the reaction of the Rabbinical leadership to the movement of Shabetai Zvi and its consequences, which led to significant losses for the community due in part to the Islamization of a number of its members who had adopted the ideas of the pseudo-Messiah (Koutzakiotis 2011, 75–77, 98–99). The long-term results of this great ordeal were the enforcement of a stringent control on the community's intellectual life by the rabbis and the barring of any possible deviation from strict Talmudic tradition (Nehama 1978, 429–434). Maimonides's writings, especially *The Guide for the Perplexed*, which in the communities of Central Europe was the initial source of the *Haskalah*, were forbidden in Thessaloniki (Nehama 1978, 436). Thus, the Jewish channel remained closed to the Enlightenment.

Our reference to the Jewish community brings to mind the historical context in relation to which an answer to our question could be sought. This is obviously the multicultural and multi-ethnic character of Thessaloniki's population for the greater part of its modern history. If the question concerning the absence of the Enlightenment is approached through this prism, hypotheses could perhaps be formulated in order to produce an answer. The Enlightenment could find points of reception in the bosom of the Jewish community because this community, 'the multitude of Jews', as the *Geographia* refers to them, possessed demographic depth, and the large numbers inevitably contained a diversity within which groups could be found that would be open to the ideas of modernity. Joseph Nehama tells us of the appearance, towards the end of this period, of a group of Jewish doctors whose studies in the West and familiarity with the scientific spirit of modernity made them dynamic agents of the spirit of the Enlightenment (Nehama 1978, 475–477). The climate within the Jewish community began to change following the resettlement in Thessaloniki, from the mid-eighteenth century onwards, of Jews from Livorno, as for example Moses Allatini, who had studied medicine in Pisa. The forceful and strict enforcement of the conservative rabbinical spirit, nevertheless, cancelled this dynamic, or rather postponed its manifestation for several decades, after the middle of the nineteenth century.

The Greek Orthodox community, on the other hand, did not have an equal demographic depth. Its numbers were smaller and the community's diversity was more limited. It does not appear, therefore, that what had taken place in Ioannina and Smyrna—i.e., the diversification of interests and ideas within the community, which in turn provided a basis for the creation of a culture of modernity and

32   *Paschalis M. Kitromilides*

its educational institutions—could take place in Thessaloniki. As became evident from the failure of the monk Pachomios in the early eighteenth century, the Thessaloniki community, despite its frequent communal disputes, did not possess the dynamics of internal diversification, which could have provided the basis for the Enlightenment. But with the absence of this basis and the continually elusive dynamics of intellectual renewal, eventually education declined. Despite its prosperity and glory, the Macedonian metropolis remained outside the geography of the Enlightenment.

Certainly, much more could be said about our initial question, which proved more complex than it appeared at first. But I hope that the formulation of an array of possible hypotheses, which will provide a fuller answer, and the interconnection of these hypotheses with the history of education, with historical demography, and with the dynamics of social change put into motion by economic activity, have brought to the fore the historical variables that further research could pursue in greater detail, which in turn would outline a more satisfying answer. I also hope that all that has been said will have clearly shown the interest presented by the study of the Enlightenment, even as an absence or silence, for the understanding of the historical life of Thessaloniki. And perhaps the affirmation of this interest will contribute as much as possible to the incorporation of related concerns in the historiography of this great metropolis. These thoughts could be rounded up, therefore, with two concluding remarks: a methodological observation and a factual reminder.

On a methodological level, historical concern regarding the absence of the Enlightenment in Thessaloniki led us to identify the ethnic diversity of the city's history as the necessary framework within which the question should be examined. This observation stems from the indisputable importance of Thessaloniki's Jewish culture, highlighted long ago by Fernand Braudel, who pointed to the Jewish community's historical role as a conduit of cultural transfers (Braudel 1972, 760–761). It was through this channel that, among other things, printing arrived in Thessaloniki, long before it was introduced anywhere else in Southeastern Europe, and at the same time the city, as a pre-eminent haven for exiles, became the receiver of the ideas, attitudes, and lifestyles that also travel along the roads of exile. Hence, it was only natural to look for the arrival of the Enlightenment through these channels. For the reasons we explained, the *Haskalah* never arrived in Thessaloniki. This finding could become visible through the prism of a pluralist point of view on the city's historical past; a point of view which broadens the unilateralism which always results from the imposition of national exclusivity on historical reflection. The necessity of multilateralism and pluralism in the reading of sources and the reconstruction of the past constitutes the methodological observation I alluded to earlier.

Now, with respect to the factual reminder I also promised, attention could be drawn to the next stage in the history of Thessaloniki. Despite the absence of the Enlightenment, the city's society, both the cosmopolitan merchant community and the younger generations of Orthodox Greeks, did not remain distant or indifferent to the messages of the revolutionary age that began in 1789, messages

Thessaloniki and the Enlightenment 33

that intensified after the Serbian rebellion of 1804 (Karathanasis 1996b, 9–15). From various testimonies, we are informed that the revolutionary songs of Rhigas Velestinlis, the pre-eminent conductor of revolutionary ideas and of the longing for freedom among the Orthodox inhabitants of the Balkans, were being sung in Thessaloniki. The English traveler Henry Holland heard them in November 1812 and noted that these songs had been composed 'at the time when the French Revolution gave a passing impulse to the spirits of the Greeks' (Holland 1815, 322–323; Kitromilides 1980, 358–361). Not so transient an impulse, one might remark. Of course, Thessaloniki had to wait a long time, but the seed had fallen upon favorable soil and the tree of freedom finally blossomed and gave fruit exactly one hundred years after Henry Holland heard Rhigas's revolutionary songs on the shores of the Thermaic Gulf.

Note

1 I would like to thank Antonis Molho and Georgios Koutzakiotis for their observations and comments. This paper originally appeared in *(Mis) Understanding the Balkans. Essays in Honour of Raymond Detrez*, ed. by Michael de Dubbeleer und Stijn Vervaet, Gent: Academia Press, 2013. I am grateful to the editors and publisher for their permission to reprint.

References

Braudel, F., *The Mediterranean and the Mediterranean World in the Age of Philip II*, vol. II, New York: Harper & Row (1972).

Dimaras, K. Th., «Πνευματικός βίος» [Intellectual life]. In: M. V. Sakellariou, (ed.), *Μακεδονία. 4000 χρόνια ελληνικής ιστορίας* [Macedonia. 4000 Years of Greek History], Athens: Ekdotiki Athinon (1982), 394–403.

Evangelidis, T., *Η παιδεία επί Τουρκοκρατίας* [Education during the Turkish occupation], vol. I, Athens: A. P. Chalkiopoulou (1932).

Fatzeas, G., *Γραμματική γεωγραφική* [Geographical Grammar], vol. II, Venice: Antonio Zatta (1760).

Gedeon, M., «Λυκαυγές πνευματικής αναγεννήσεως παρ' ημίν: 1700–1731» [Early dawn of spiritual rebirth among us: 1700–1731], *Πρακτικά της Ακαδημίας Αθηνών 5* (1930) [Proceedings of the Academy of Athens], 5 (1930), 49–57.

Gedeon, M., «Θεσσαλονικέων παλαιαί κοινοτικαί διενέξεις» [Old communal disputes among Thessalonians], *Μακεδονικά 2* (1941–1952), 1–24.

Holland, H., *Travels in the Ionian Isles, Albania, Thessaly, Macedonia Etc. During the Years 1812 and 1813*, London: Longman, Hurst, Rees, Orme, and Brown (1815).

Karathanasis, A., *Θεσσαλονίκεια και Μακεδονικά* [Thessalonian and Macedonian Matters], Thessaloniki: Kyriakidis (1996a).

Karathanasis, A., *Θεσσαλονίκη και Μακεδονία 1800–1825. Μια εικοσιπενταετία εν μέσω θυέλλης* [Thessaloniki and Macedonia 1800–1825. Twenty-five years in the eye of the storm], Thessaloniki: Society for Balkan Studies (1996b).

Kitromilides, P. M., «Γνωσιολογικός εμπειρισμός και πολιτικός φιλελευθερισμός. Το ταξίδι του Henry Holland στην Ελλάδα (1812–1813)» [Cognitive empiricism and political liberalism. Henry Holland's Journey in Greece (1812–1813)], *Δελτίον της Ιστορικής και Εθνολογικής Εταιρείας της Ελλάδος*, XXIII (1980), 341–364.

34 Paschalis M. Kitromilides

Kitromilides, P. M., «Εστίες του Διαφωτισμού στη Μακεδονία» [Centers of the Enlightenment in Macedonia], *Νέα Εστία*, no. 1571 (Christmas 1992), 53–59.

Kitromilides, P. M., 'Orthodoxy and the West: Reformation to Enlightenment'. In: M. Angold, (ed.), *The Cambridge History of Christianity*, vol. *V, Eastern Christianity*, Cambridge: Cambridge University Press (2006), 187–209.

Koumas, C., *Ιστορίαι των ανθρωπίνων πράξεων* [Histories of Human Actions], vol. XII, Vienna: Anton v. Haykul (1832).

Koutzakiotis, G., *Αναμένοντας το τέλος του κόσμου τον 17ο αιώνα. Ο Εβραίος μεσσίας και ο μέγας διερμηνέας* [Awaiting the end of the world in the 17th century. The Jewish messiah and the great interpreter], Athens: National Research Foundation (2011).

Mazower, M., *Salonica City of Ghosts. Christians, Muslims and Jews, 1430–1950*, London: HarperCollins (2004).

Mertzios, K., «Περί Ευγενίου του Βουλγάρεως διατί εγκατέλειψε το 1759 την Αθωνιάδα Σχολήν» [On Evgenios Voulgaris, why he left the Athonite Academy in 1759], *Ηπειρω τική Εστία*, no. 5 (May 1956), 417–420.

Moisiodax, I., *Απολογία* [Apologia], Vienna: Ioannis Thomas Trattner (1780).

Nehama, J., *Histoire des Israélites de Salonique*, vols. VI–VII, Thessaloniki: Librairie Molho (1978).

Papastathis, Ch., *Θεσσαλονίκεια και Μακεδονικά ανάλεκτα* [Thessalonian and Macedonian Analects], Thessaloniki: University Studio Press (1999), 311–340.

Philippides, D. and Konstantas, G., *Γεωγραφία νεωτερική* [Modern Geography] (Koumarianou, A., Ed.), Athens: Ziti (1988)

Psalidas, A., «Η Τουρκία κατά τας αρχάς του ΙΘ´ αιώνος» [Turkey in the early 19th century]. In: G. Haritakis, (review article), *Ηπειρωτικά Χρονικά 6* (1931), 32–74.

Psimmenos, N. K., «Η φιλοσοφία των χρόνων της Τουρκοκρατίας (1453–1821)» [The philosophy of the years of the Turkish occupation (1453–1821)]. In: A. Paliouras, (ed.), *Μακεδονία, τομ. Β´: Αρχαιολογία—Πολιτισμός* [Macedonia, vol. II: Archaeology—Civilization], Athens: Elliniki Ethniki Grammi (1993), 285–291.

Sorkin, D., *The Religious Enlightenment: Protestants, Jews, and Catholics from London to Vienna*, Princeton: Princeton University Press (2008).

Tsoulkanakis, N. (Archimandrite Nafkratios), «Ιωάννης ο του Ιωάννου, διδάσκαλος της εν Θεσσαλονίκη σχολής» [Ioannis son of Ioannis, teacher at the school in Thessaloniki], *Κληρονομία 7* (1975), 353–386.

Vakalopoulos, A., *Ιστορία της Θεσσαλονίκης, 316 π.Χ.–1983* [History of Thessaloniki, 316 BC–1983], Thessaloniki: Stamoulis (1983).

Wolff, L., *Venice and the Slavs: The Discovery of Dalmatia in the Age of Enlightenment*, Stanford: Stanford University Press (2001).

3 Was Salonica a Levantine city?

Philip Mansel

The Levant means 'where the sun rises': the eastern Mediterranean. Levant is a geographical word, free from associations with race or religion. It is defined not by frontiers but by the sea. Levantine cities such as Smyrna, Alexandria, and Beirut shared the following characteristics: geography; diplomacy; language; hybridity; commerce; modernity; and finally, vulnerability. In the nineteenth century Salonica was one of those cities.

Diplomacy

The modern Levant was a product of diplomacy, not conquest. It flourished after 1535 partly as a result of one of the most successful alliances in history, between the Ottoman Empire and France, between the Caliph of the Muslims and the Most Christian King. It was based on international strategy, on their shared hostility to Spain and the House of Austria.

With the alliance came the capitulations: agreements between the Ottoman and foreign governments, which allowed foreigners to live and trade in the Ottoman Empire, for the most part under their own legal systems. (This is still a toxic issue today: most American soldiers were withdrawn from Iraq in 2011 not to please Iraqi or American opinion, but because the US government refuses to allow American soldiers to be subject to foreign, in this case Iraqi, law). As a result of the French-Ottoman alliance, French consuls—later joined by those of the Netherlands, England, and other countries—were appointed to most Levantine ports.[1]

These were the 'years of the consuls', to paraphrase the title of Ivo Andric's 1945 novel about nineteenth-century Bosnia, *The Days of the Consuls*. Janissaries guarded them from insult or attack. To show equality of status, they often refused to remove their hats in the presence of the local governor. The ports of the Levant became, at times, diarchies between foreign consuls and local officials. Many locals preferred the consuls' law courts, since they were often more convenient and less corrupt than their own. Consuls could be peace-makers. In 1694 and 1770, respectively, consuls in Smyrna persuaded the commanders of the Venetian and Russian navies not to attack the city, in order to prevent reprisals by Muslims against local Christians (Kontente 2005, 343; Anon. 1772, 107, 113).

36   *Philip Mansel*

Soon the French-Ottoman alliance acquired commercial and cultural momentum. Consuls acted both as servants of their own government and as local power-brokers and transmitters of technology and information. In a *danse macabre* of mutual manipulation that has lasted to this day, outside interference was at least matched by local desire for more of it. Consuls were equivalents of modern international organisations such as the World Bank, the IMF, or NATO: unpopular but effective. In nineteenth-century Alexandria, consuls protected criminals of their own nationality from Egyptian courts, but also helped introduce quarantine and fight cholera. Consuls also brought foreign post offices to the ports of the Levant.

The British consul-general played a vital role in the riots in Alexandria, which precipitated the British invasion in 1882. He was subsequently the senior British official in Egypt, which he helped to rule (Mansel 2010, 102–103). Consuls played a similar role in Beirut after the French invasion of 1860, helping to run the internationally guaranteed regime in Mount Lebanon, as they did in Crete after 1898. As the power of the Ottoman Empire declined, consuls could facilitate the transfer of Ottoman sovereignty and territory to foreign empires or local nation states.

Salonica after 1850 also had its 'years of the consuls'. They formed the aristocracy of the town, one of them recalled. A square was called Place des Consuls (Wratislaw 1924, 212). As in Smyrna, Alexandria, and Beirut, they were power-brokers. May 1876 was a time of rising tension in the city, owing to a Christian family's opposition to the desire of their daughter Itchko to convert to Islam to marry a Muslim called Hairullah. Her family appealed to the main non-Muslim source of authority—the consuls. The French consul-general and the German vice-consul, a local millionaire called Mr. Abbot, entered a mosque during Friday prayers, without protection. In front of the vali himself they were murdered.

In reprisal the great powers sent warships to train their guns on the city. On 16 May around fifty Muslims, many of whom had nothing to do with the murder, were hanged on the quay beside the White Tower, watched by officials, consuls, a vast crowd, and British sailors in full uniform. As had already happened during a similar public punishment after a brawl between a Frenchman and an Egyptian in Alexandria in 1863, Ottoman authorities were forced to advertise to the local population their humiliation by foreign powers (Sciacky 2000, 37–38; Risal 1913, 251–253; Vakalopoulos 1963, 116). The scene was watched by the French sailor Julien Viaud, who published his drawings of it in *Le monde illustré* (17 June 1876) and later, writing under the name Pierre Loti, described it in the opening pages of the novel which made him famous, *Aziyadé* (1879).

Consuls in Salonica were again crucial in 1912. In the first Balkan war, the Ottoman armies had been defeated by those of Serbia, Bulgaria, Greece, and Montenegro. To protect Salonica and its inhabitants, and ensure a peaceful transition from Ottoman to Greek rule, the municipal council and the foreign consuls seized the initiative: with the Ottoman governor, they decided that, while the Ottoman army would withdraw, the Ottoman police and gendarmes would remain in the city. On 7 November the consuls went to Greek army headquarters to negotiate the army's entry into the city. Negotiations were in French. To avoid what he called 'unnecessary bloodshed', Hasan Tahsin Pasha, the Ottoman commander,

Was Salonica a Levantine city?   37

agreed with the consuls not to defend Salonica; moreover, he knew the Greek army was stronger than his own (Leune 1914, 338–339, 344).

On 8 November Salonica was encircled by Greek and Bulgarian forces. Hasan Tahsin Pasha decided to surrender to the Greeks—in part to stop Bulgarians entering Solun, as they called the city some considered rightfully Bulgarian. The surrender took place 'in a relaxed and friendly manner'. On 9 November Greek forces reached the outskirts of Salonica. Ottoman forces handed over their rifles. 26,000 Ottoman soldiers marched into captivity (Erickson 2003, 223–225; Leune 1914, 363). On 10 November, led by Crown Prince Constantine, Greek troops entered the city. Greeks sang their national anthem, and trampled on the fezzes they had previously worn. Blue and white Greek flags covered the city. At a thanksgiving service the archbishop cried 'Hosannah to the glorious descendants of the fighters of Marathon and Salamis, to the valiant liberators of our beloved fatherland! … the golden rays of liberty must illuminate all the corners of the unredeemed nation'—in other words Constantinople, Smyrna, and beyond (Veinstein 1992, 250–253). Greek newspapers were printed in blue and white and ended articles with the cry 'To the city! To Constantinople!' (Leune 1914, 311, 316–317).

The foreign consuls had helped ensure a transfer of sovereignty in Salonica, from Turkey to Greece, far less lethal than that which would occur ten years later from Greece to Turkey in Smyrna, without their intervention.

Language

International languages for inter-community communication were another characteristic of the Levant. Before the triumph of English, the Levant used two international languages. First was *lingua franca*, the simplified Italian described by French travellers as

> généralement entendue par toutes les cotes du Levant, qui a cours par tout le Levant entre les gens de Marine de la Méditerranée et les Marchands qui vont négocier au Levant et qui se fait entendre de toutes les nations.
>
> (Dakhlia 2008, 81, 89, 100, 497)

A commercial rather than a literary language, *lingua franca* was rarely written down. It was spoken by slaves and sailors; by the Beys of Tunis and Tripoli; and by Byron, who learnt what he called 'Levant Italian' in Athens in 1810. The *Gentleman's Magazine* wrote in 1837 of an Englishman in the Levant: 'he has talked *lingua franca* till he has half forgotten English' (Mansel 2010, 14). *Lingua franca* was proof of the accessibility of the Levant to the outside world. It was not a cultural ghetto.

From 1840, thanks to the spread of schools and of steam and rail travel, French, then the world language from Buenos Aires to Saint Petersburg, became the second language of the Levant. The language of science, culture and diplomacy, it was spoken by pashas, viziers, and sultans; by Mustafa Kemal and by the poet from Smyrna, George Seferis; and as an official language of the municipalities of Alexandria and Beirut. Young Turk revolutionaries learnt French in Paris, which

38 Philip Mansel

they called a 'star brighter than my dreams'. 5,000 French words—such as *complot, metres, dansös*—entered the Turkish language, another form of integration with the outside world (Mansel 2010, 45–47).

Salonica shared these polyglot habits. Most inhabitants spoke some words of Spanish, known in the city as Ladino or *Judezmo*, the language of Salonica Jews, owing to their numerical and commercial predominance in the city (Veinstein 1992, 28–32; Risal 1913, 347). The Ottoman Sultan Abdulmecid spoke French to Salonica's Jewish and Levantine notables on his visit in 1859. Although many were nostalgic for the subtlety of Ladino, French became so popular in Salonica that all modern schools of whatever religion, even some German schools, taught it. A French-language newspaper called the *Journal de Salonique*, ('*publication bi-hebdomadaire, Politique, Commerciale et Littéraire'*) was founded in 1895; soon it had a circulation of about 1,000 (Veinstein 1992, 71, 211, 217; Molho 2005, 135).

Vidal Nahoum, father of the philosopher Edgar Morin, was born in Salonica in 1894. Through education in a French (*Alliance Israélite Universelle*) school, he became culturally French, even before becoming physically and legally so, after emigration to France in 1917. Like many other Frenchmen from Salonica, such as the Carasso and Modiano families, although he retained nostalgia for the Ottoman Empire and his native city, he did not feel '*dépaysé*' in France. His son wrote:

> *la France c'est pour lui la Poésie faite Nation ... Le prestige du francais est lié à celui de la patrie de la liberté, au mythe de Paris ... l'essor des idées laiques a favorisé la gallomanie laquelle amplifie en retour l'essor des idées laiques.*
>
> (Morin 1989, 28, 66, 88, 90, 356–357)

Hybridity

Hybridity and multiple identities were other characteristics of the Levant. The Lebanese-American historian William Haddad has written, 'the nation state is the prison of the mind'. The Levant was a jailbreak. The Ottoman Empire enforced few of the national restrictions and regulations of European governments. There were no ghettos. Travellers were attracted by the variety of races and costumes in these cities and the juxtaposition of mosques, churches, and synagogues, inconceivable in European cities before 1970 (Mansel 2010, 2, 4).

In Levantine cities no single group dominated demographically. In Smyrna and Beirut populations were roughly half Christian and half Muslim; in Alexandria approximately three-quarters Muslim and one-quarter Christian and Jewish (Mansel 2010, 55, 91, 96, 107). In Salonica in 1850 the population had been about 70,000; by 1906 it had risen to 110,438, of whom 47,017 were Jewish, 33,756 Greek, and 29,665 Muslim (of whom half may have been *dönme* of Jewish origin) (Veinstein 1992, 107).

Outside the home some men developed multiple identities: in the seventeenth century Sabbatai Zevi, the 'false Messiah' of Smyrna, founded his own religion, with Christian and Muslim as well as Jewish elements, and made many converts

Was Salonica a Levantine city? 39

in Salonica. His followers are still an important element in Izmir and Istanbul. There are three distinct groups: those who believe in Zevi and his eventual return to earth as the Messiah; those who remain officially Jewish, but secretly believe in Zevi; and the *Dönme*, those who converted to Islam but retained certain Jewish practices (Sciacky 2000, 90; Baer 2010, passim).

Mustafa Kemal, a Muslim born in Salonica in 1881, son of an official probably with Macedonian blood, after going to a traditional Koranic school, switched against his mother's advice to the Fevziye school, much frequented by *dönme*. Then he enrolled in a military school in order to join the army. Many attribute his zeal for reforms in part to his Salonica background, on the edge of the Ottoman Empire, exposed to other cultures. At military college in Constantinople, he was at first known as Selanikli Mustafa (Stavroulakis 1984, 3). I have been assured by elderly gentlemen in Istanbul that he knew, although he rarely used, Ladino.

In public, at places of work, or relaxation, from the *Cercle de Salonique* founded for wealthy businessmen in 1873 to the cafés, taverns, and '*musicos*' of the port, (and in the *Federacyon* labour union founded after 1908) the male population worked and played side by side. The official journal of the province of Salonica was in four languages: Ottoman, Greek, Bulgarian, and Judeo-Spanish. Some chose not only employees, but also wet-nurses and spouses, from other religions. Christians and Muslims visited each other's houses and made pilgrimages to the tombs of each other's holy men. Christians continued to pray in a section of the church of Saint Demetrios, although it had been turned into a mosque (Veinstein 1992, 105, 116; Levy 2000, 100n).

Daily coexistence did not, however, exclude eruptions of nationalism—as terrorist attacks in Macedonia, and the Balkan wars, would show. Hybridity affected public lives more than personal loyalties. Religious authorities generally restricted marriages to people within their own community and encouraged people to live near their place of worship. Postcards in Salonica used dress to emphasise national differences: they showed Greek peasant women bedecked in gold coins; Macedonians with thick leggings, white tunics, and embroidered aprons; Albanians in massive sheep-skin cloaks; Turks in suits and a fez. The inscription always mentioned the race of the person portrayed (Petropoulos 1980, 7, 22, 66–68). Jobs in the city were traditionally distributed by ethnicity. Grocers and waiters were Greek, yoghurt-sellers Albanian, clothes-sellers Jewish, tram conductors Turkish, shoeshine-boys gypsies (Veinstein 1992, 28–32; Risal 1913, 347). A French visitor called Ricciotto Canudo admired Salonica as 'a true crossroads of races … you think you find there the power of life itself, growling, boiling, a human whirlpool in the centre of an ocean of European, African and Asiatic activity' (Canudo 1992, 182).

Trade

Levantine cities were not romantic. They were trading cities, integrated into the economic systems of Europe and the Ottoman Empire. Many became boom cities, which experienced rapid rises in population. Principal hub of a vast network

40   *Philip Mansel*

of inland trade routes, Smyrna became the city where Asia came shopping for Europe, and Europe for Asia. From 5,000 in 1600, the population rose to around 100,000 in 1700 (Goffman 1990, 139).

Alexandria became a capitalist El Dorado, attracting a gold rush of Europeans and Syrians in the nineteenth century. In the cotton boom of the 1860s capital could double every two years. The population rose from 5,000 in 1800 to 100,000 in 1850 and 232,000 in 1882. It became the port linking the economies of Egypt and Europe, with the largest stock exchange outside Europe and North America (Mansel 2010, 56, 108).

Beirut in 1826 had been described as a republic of merchants, living according to its own law. Its rise was due not only to local merchants but also, like that of Smyrna and Alexandria, to the arrival of foreign merchants and consuls. By 1841 according to the American traveller A. A. Paton, it was 'a Levantine *scala*, a bastard, a mongrel'. Its population rose from 6,000 in 1800 to around 130,000 in 1900 (Mansel 2010, 151).

Salonica was also a trading city. Jews formed around half the population of the '*Madre de Israel*', as they called Salonica. Until 1923 most shops in the city closed on the Sabbath and on Jewish holidays (Veinstein 1992, 28–32; Risal 1913, 347).

Salonica also became a boom town after 1860. Entrepreneurs from the Allatini, de Botton, and Modiano families—often with links with the western Mediterranean port of Livorno—helped bring Salonica, in a few years, out of the Middle Ages into the nineteenth century. Brick, soap, and beer factories were opened. Dr. Moise Allatini, Salonica's great moderniser (whose family founded the famous Allatini flour mill), started the first French-language school in 1858. He offered help and medical care to all, whatever their religion. The city walls were demolished in 1866 and new boulevards created; French- or Austrian-style villas, such as the Villa Kapandji, appeared by the shores of the Aegean (Veinstein 1992, 34–35, 171–174; Desmet-Grégoire and Georgeon 1997, 83, 85).

One of the main commercial streets, as in Smyrna and Alexandria, was called Rue des Franques (Risal 1913, 143). The quay was constructed in the 1870s, at the same time as Smyrna's; streets were slowly paved, drains finally installed (Veinstein 1992, 107). Railway links to Vienna in 1888 and Istanbul in 1896 began to open up the hinterland. In 1888 the Banque de Salonique was founded with French and Austrian capital. European fashions began to replace traditional dress (Veinstein 1992, 187, 189; Levy 2000, 26–28).

Another characteristic of Levantine cities was their sense of separation from the hinterland. In an age when sea transport was more important than it is today, and usually quicker and safer than rail or road, regular boat services made it easier to travel from port to port than into the hinterland. Their role as ports facilitated Levantine cities' emergence as commercial and cultural centres. The corniche, where the boats docked, was the principal meeting place.

To many visitors Alexandria seemed part of Europe, Beirut the Paris of the Middle East, and Smyrna a different country from Constantinople, as Halid Ziya, author of *Kirk Yil*, remembered. Many of Salonica's inhabitants rarely left the city. The mountains of Macedonia were ravaged by *comitacis, cetniks,* and *cetes*—brigands who used nationalism (Greek, Albanian, Macedonian, Bulgarian, or Turkish) as an excuse for pillage and murder: trains were held up, villages burnt, 'traitors' shot (Bérard 1897, 151, 153, 162; Owen 1919, 19).

Modernity

Levantine cities also brought education and modernity. 'Smyrna illuminates like a beacon all the other provinces of the Ottoman Empire', wrote the Austrian consul-general Charles de Scherzer. It had the Ottoman Empire's first botanical collections, newspaper, American school, railway, electricity, cinema, and football club: Bournabat Football and Rugby Club, established by English merchants in 1894, fourteen years before the foundation of the legendary Galatasaray team in 1908 (Mansel 2010, 164–166). Alexandria had Egypt's first theatres (Arabic and Italian), feminist newspaper, and brewery, and in Cavafy the first publicly published homosexual poet since the ancient world (Mansel 2010, 144).

Smyrna, Beirut, and Alexandria attracted dynamic foreign schools, run by the *Mission Israélite Universelle*, Jesuits, the *Order of Notre Dame de Sion*, the *Frères des écoles chrétiennes*, or other organisations. Like the American University and Université Saint-Joseph in Beirut, they gave pupils the intellectual weapons, including language skills, with which to resist the cultural imperialism they represented. They were attended by Muslims and Jews as well as Christians (Mansel 2010, 135–136).

Salonica also spread education and modernity. As postcards at the 2012 exhibition at the Villa Kapandji showed, the city contained German, French, Italian, Jewish, Greek, and Serbian schools. Modern Turkey was born not in Anatolia or Istanbul, but in Salonica, birthplace of Mustafa Kemal (and of the great Communist poet Nazim Hikmet). Turks took advantage in Salonica of a measure of freedom unparalleled anywhere else in the empire, due to a combination of geography and demography. The liberal character of the least Muslim large city in the Empire (Muslims comprised at most 30% of the population), combined with the proximity of the largest army corps in the Ottoman empire, based eighty miles away in Monastir (now Bitola), made Salonica a more effective incubator and accelerator of political change than Constantinople or Smyrna. Some of the best schools in Istanbul today are continuations of schools founded in Salonica, that left, with staff, pupils, and charitable foundation, in 1912. The famous Istanbul newspaper *Cumhuriyet* is the successor of the Salonica newspaper *Rumeli*.[2] The publishers of the Salonica newspaper *Yeni Asır* ('New Century'), moved it to Izmir, where it is published to this day (Kontente 2005, 600).

More than other Levantine cities, Salonica became a city of revolutions. The Internal Macedonian Revolutionary Organisation (IMRO) was founded in 1893 in Salonica. Believing in 'Macedonia for the Macedonians' (though some wanted it to be part of greater Bulgaria, since the two nationalisms were at that time closely linked), it soon developed its own shadow law-courts, armed forces, and

42 *Philip Mansel*

taxes, like a state within a state (Veinstein 1992, 132, 135; Sciacky 2000, 72). Fanatically anti-Greek, it terrorised villages, most of which would have preferred to remain neutral. On 29 April 1903 in Salonica the office of the Ottoman Bank and the surrounding cafés, as well as a French boat in the harbour, were blown up by Bulgarians, led by a teacher called Delchev, who hoped to shake Macedonia out of its lethargy and force European intervention. In reprisal Bulgarians—recognisable by their dress—were killed in the street, until the governor Fehmi Pasha came to restore order in person, despite a bomb thrown at his carriage (Sciacky 2000, 81).

Another organisation of revolutionaries opposed to the Sultan, called the Committee of Union and Progress (CUP), was established in Salonica in 1904. Its nucleus was provided by two young officers, Enver and Cemal, and Talaat Bey, a telegraph employee. Like the IMRO, the CUP created a state within the state. The army was infiltrated. Like many others from Macedonia, members of the CUP had the ultra-nationalism of the frontier. Enver had a Christian Turk or Gagauz background, while Talaat was a Pomak, a Bulgarian Muslim. Cemal came from the island of Mytilene in the Aegean. Other early members of the CUP included Niyazi, of Albanian origin; Cavid, head of the Salonica school of arts and crafts, a *dönme*; and Dr Nazim, born in Salonica, who had studied in Paris. All were united in hatred of what Enver's uncle Halil called 'the imbecile rule of the palace'— which, moreover, failed to pay the troops on time (Kansu 2007, 89).

The presence of foreign consuls in Salonica assisted revolutions. The CUP communicated with political exiles in Paris, and smuggled in subversive men and books, using Greek consuls and foreign post offices as well as their own networks (Hacisalihoglu 2004, 168–169; Sciacky 2000, 120; Panayotopoulos 1980, 87–95). In Salonica they planned revolution in the cafés near the White Tower or at the Café Cristal (Desmet-Grégoire and Georgeon 1997, 88, 89). Salonica was a political and national time bomb.

On 3 July 1908, fearing an investigation by the Sultan's police, the CUP officers began a military coup in Monastir. As more soldiers joined, or refused to suppress the coup, the movement turned into a constitutional revolution. On 24 July the Sultan capitulated and announced that elections to the Ottoman parliament would be held in the autumn. In front of the Salonica konak, the Inspector-General of the Macedonian provinces Huseyin Hilmi Pasha read out the Sultan's decree. Three times he called for cheers for the Sultan; each time he was greeted by silence (Veinstein 1992, 236). On the main square, Enver Bey, the handsome young leader of the revolution, proclaimed: 'we are no longer Turks, Greeks or Bulgarians but brothers. Long live the fatherland!—the nation!—liberty!' Speeches, ovations, flag-waving processions—one led by a virgin dressed in white, to symbolise the purity of the Ottoman constitution—succeeded each other.

In the following days, the city appeared to be united. Bristling with cartridges, pistols, and daggers, brigands laid down their arms (or rather those too old to be useful) and proclaimed their love of Liberty, Fraternity, and Justice, from the balconies of the Olympos Palace Hotel and the *Cercle de Salonique*.

Their photographs were taken in Salonica studios, and sold as postcards of 'brigand bands' or 'bandit chiefs', titled 'Hassan Cavus', 'Livanos', or 'Paulos with his companion' (Sandalci 2000, 853–870). As in Constantinople, imams, priests, and rabbis embraced each other (Koker 2008, passim; Morin 1989, 59). The number of murders in Macedonia fell from 1,768 in 1907 to 291 in 1909 (Cumali 2007, 274).

The whole city seemed to be wearing cockades or 'liberty ribbons' in the white and red colours of the Young Turk revolution: white to show that Turkey must be pure, and red to show willingness to shed blood to make it so. Until 1912, the revolutionary ruling party, the Committee of Union and Progress, held its congresses and published its newspaper *Yeni felsefe* (new philosophy) in Salonica. Everything was discussed: the organisation of labour; women's rights (Figure 3.1); the settlement of Bosnian Muslims in Macedonia; and the reform of the Turkish language. In 1911, a group of Young Turk writers called *Genç Kalemler*—young pens—was formed there, including the Turkish nationalist Tekinalp (born Moise Cohen) (Figure 3.2).

Figure 3.1 Photograph of women at the summer theatre beside the White Tower, 1908. From the French periodical *L'Illustration*, 15 August 1908. Original caption: '*A Salonique. - Réunion de femmes turques et européennes écoutant une oratrice musulmane conférencier sur les droits de la femme, au théâtre d'été de la Tour Blanche. Deux clichés de Turquie qui n'eussent pas été possibles avant la révolution*'. (Macedonian Struggle Museum 61178, Giannis Megas Collection; used by permission of the Macedonian Struggle Foundation)

44 *Philip Mansel*

Figure 3.2 Postcard, mounted officers of the Ottoman garrison of Thessaloniki parading by the White Tower, 1908. (Macedonian Struggle Museum 57530, Papaioannou Collection; used by permission of the Macedonian Struggle Foundation)

The Young Turk revolution had international impact. Salonica was hailed as the holy city of the revolution, *'le berceau de la liberté ottomane'*. Olympos square was renamed Place de la Liberté; there were plans to rename Salonica itself 'the *kaaba* of Liberty'. Few Muslims considered that it might soon be lost to the empire (Veinstein 1992, 114, 238). The ancient family of Evrenoszade, which had helped conquer the Balkans for the Ottomans in the early fifteenth century, decided to restore its ancestors' tombs, in what is now Giannitsa, forty kilometres west of Salonica, in 1908, as if they would be there for another 500 years (Lowry 2008, 1–192).

On 13 April 1909 there was an attempt at counter-revolution in Constantinople by troops faithful to the Sultan and horrified by the Committee's alleged irreligion. In Constantinople many supported the Sultan. Salonica, however, remained true to the revolution. 30,000 demonstrators in Liberty Square promised to protect the constitution (Figure 3.3). The 'operation Army' under Shevket Pasha, Enver, and Mustafa Kemal, with volunteers from Albanian, Greek, and Bulgarian brigand bands, advanced by train to Constantinople. To win popular support they had to promise to protect the Sultan. Instead, on 23 April troops surrounded Yildiz Palace and deposed him. He was sent by train to exile in Salonica, where he lived under house arrest in the Villa Allatini. He was replaced by a younger, more liberal brother, who reigned as Mehmed V (Kansu 2000, 90, 118). When he visited Salonica in 1911, Mehmed V did not call on the brother he had deposed.

Figure 3.3 Postcard, Thessaloniki post office employees marching in support of the constitution, 1908. Original caption: '*Fêtes de la Constitution: Manifestation Populaire*'. On reverse, '*editeur: Albert J. Barzilai*' and note in French dated 1 January 1916. (Macedonian Struggle Museum 56668, Papaioannou Collection; used by permission of the Macedonian Struggle Foundation)

Vulnerability

Salonica also shared the vulnerability of other Levantine cities. A riot or a change of regime could change it overnight. After the entry of the Greek army in November 1912, Salonica was the first major city to be de-levantinised, before Smyrna or Alexandria. The Rotunda of Galerius, which had first been transformed from a Roman temple into a church, then after 1430 into a mosque, in 1912, like many other mosques, became a church again (Kiel 1990, 145). Shop and street

46 *Philip Mansel*

signs henceforth had to be in Greek. People talking French in the streets were sometimes assaulted for doing so—already in Constantinople since 1908 Greek diplomats had been trying to persuade local Greeks to leave French schools, stop speaking French, and hellenise their shop signs (Oztuncay 2008, 26–27).

The assassination of King George I in Salonica on 13 March 1913 led to 'reprisals' against Muslims and Jews, often by Greek policemen and soldiers. Many died. After the Bulgarian school was attacked and fighting broke out between Greek and Bulgarian soldiers on 1 June 1913, Bulgarians fled the city. Although Jews kept some privileges such as exemption from military service, and the right to keep accounts in Spanish, many regarded the Greek 'liberation' as more oppressive than Ottoman rule. Many left for France (Morin 1989, 90, 115, 120; Sciacky 2000, 157; Molho 2005, 46).

Identity was not immutable. Some Salonicans preferred to abandon their city, emigrate, and become American or French. An unknown number, whether Jewish, Muslim, *Dönme*, Slav, or Albanian, changed religion and language and became officially Greek and Orthodox (as, for self-protection, Czechs in Vienna became Austrian, Slavs in Trieste Italian, and the people of Strasbourg switched identity four times between France and Germany in 1871–1945).

Thousands of embittered Muslims had already fled terrorism in the countryside—descendants of Christian converts to Islam, as well as Turks. After 1912 Muslims left Salonica as well, including Mustafa Kemal's mother. They moved to Constantinople or Izmir. Perhaps as many as 150,000 Muslim refugees arrived in the Aydin vilayet alone in 1912–1914 (MacCarthy 1995, 141–142, 145, 156, 159, 261). Beginning with Mustafa Kemal himself, Balkan refugees, living proof of Turkey's European roots, would provide much of the driving force behind its modernisation (cf. Tesal 1997).

British and Austrian proposals for Salonica and the surrounding area to become an autonomous, neutral city or province, like Tangier or Mount Lebanon, protected by international guarantees and an internationally officered gendarmerie (as Macedonia had possessed since 1903) were supported mainly by Jews. Joseph Nehama, author of *Salonique, la ville convoitée* (1913), believed Salonica should be a new Venice, 'the threshold of central Europe', the great port between Germany and Suez. Few others, however, put their city before their nation (Risal 1913, 365; Molho 2005, 175–177, 190, 365).

Once the commercial dynamo of Turkey in Europe, after 1912 Salonica sank to being the second city of Greece, cut off from its former hinterland by the new frontiers of Albania, Serbia, and Bulgaria. The creation of nation states weakened the city's Levantine character, its trade, its hybridity, its multilingualism, and the power of the consuls.

Benefiting from its geographical distance from the capital, however, Salonica again played a role as revolutionary capital in 1916–1917. This revolution was led by Venizelos against King Constantine in Athens, as in 1908–1909 it had been led by the CUP against Abdulhamid in Constantinople. As a result, the city experienced a last international incarnation, as headquarters of the allied *Armée d'Orient*. Its streets filled with troops from Annam, India, Senegal, Serbia, and

Russia, as well as France and Britain (Mansel 2010, 201–203; cf. Scheikevitch 1922, passim). Levantine ports, being accessible to foreign navies, were easy to occupy, as Beirut (in 1860) and Alexandria (in 1882) had already discovered.

In conclusion Salonica in its Levantine heyday between 1850 and 1918 shows the political as well as the cultural and commercial independence of cities. Geography, demography, trade, and diplomacy can empower them to play an independent role, often against the orders of the state and its capital. Through the flight or transfer of its Muslims, and above all the destruction of its Jews by the German state in the Second World War, the history of Salonica also shows that, as one Salonican who emigrated to America, Leon Sciacky, wrote, 'civilisation was but a thin crust, a layer so tenuous that one dared not trust it' (Sciacky 2000, 16).

Notes

1 For a survey, see Mansel 2010, 6–15, 19.
2 I am grateful for this point to Professor Zafer Toprak.

References

Anon., *An Authentic Narrative of the Russian Expedition against the Turks by Sea and Land*, London: S. Hooper (1772).
Baer, M. D., *The Dönme: Jewish Converts, Muslim Revolutionaries, and Secular Turks*, Stanford: Stanford University Press (2010).
Bérard, V., *La Macédoine*, Paris: Calmann Lévy (1897).
Canudo, Ranuccio, *La France et la Grèce dans la grande guerre*, Thessaloniki: Institut d'études balkaniques (1992).
Cumali, N., *Macedoine 1900: nouvelles*, Paris: Actes Sud, (2007)
Dakhlia, J., *Lingua Franca: histoire, d'une langue métisse en Méditérranée*, Arles: Actes Sud (2008).
Desmet-Grégoire, H., F. Georgeon, *Cafés d'Orient revisités*, Paris: CNRS éditions (1997).
Erickson, E. J., *Defeat in Detail: The Ottoman Army in the Balkans 1912–1913*, Westport: Greenwood Publishing Group (2003).
Goffman, D., *Izmir and the Levantine World 1550–1650*, Seattle: University of Washington Press (1990).
Hacisalihoglu, M., 'The negotiations for the solution of the Macedonian question', *Turcica*, 36, (2004), 165–190.
Kansu, A., *Politics in Post-Revolutionary Turkey 1908–1913*, Leiden: Brill (2000).
Kansu, A., *The Revolution of 1908 in Turkey*, Leiden: Brill (2007).
Kiel, M., *Studies on the Ottoman Architecture of the Balkans*, Vol I, Aldershot: Variorum (1990).
Koker, O., *Souvenir of Liberty. Postcards and Medals from the Collection of Orlando Carlo Calumeno*, Istanbul: Birzamanlar Yayincilik (2008).
Kontente, L., *Smyrne et l'Occident, de l'Antiquité au XXIe siècle*, Paris: Montigny (2005).
Leune, J., *Une revanche, une étape*, Paris: M. Imhaus et R. Chapelot (1914).
Levy, S., *Salonique à la fin du XIXe siècle*, Istanbul: Isis Press (2000), 100n.
Loti, P., *Aziyadé*, Paris: Eds. Gallimard (1879).

48 *Philip Mansel*

Lowry, H., 'The Evrenos dynasty of Yenice Vardar', *Journal of Ottoman Studies*, XXXII, (2008), 1–192.

MacCarthy, J., *Death and Exile: The Ethnic Cleansing of Ottoman Muslims 1821–1922*, Princeton: Princeton University Press (1995).

Macedonian Struggle Museum, *Αρχείο Μουσείου Μακεδονικού Αγώνα* [Archive of the Museum of the Macedonian Struggle], Thessaloniki.

Mansel, P., *Levant: Splendour and Catastrophe on the Mediterranean*, London: John Murray (2010).

Molho, R., *Salonica and Istanbul: Social, Political and Cultural Aspects of Jewish Life*, Istanbul: Isis Press (2005).

Morin, E., *Vidal et les siens*, Paris: Seuil (1989).

Owen, H. C., *Salonica and After: The Sideshow that Ended the War*, London, New York: Hodder and Stoughton (1919).

Oztuncay, B., ed., *100th Anniversary of the Restoration of the Constitution*, Istanbul (2008).

Panayotopoulos, A. J., 'Early relations between the Greeks and the Young Turks', *Balkan Studies*, 21, (1980), 87–95.

Petropoulos, E., *Old Salonica*, trans., John Taylor, Athens: Kedros (1980).

Risal, P. [Nehama, J.], *La ville convoitée Salonique*, Paris: Perrin (1913).

Sandalci, M., *Max Fruchtermann Kartpostallari*, 3 vols, Istanbul: Koçbank (2000), III, 853–870.

Scheikevitch, A., *Hellas? ..., Hélas! Souvenirs de Salonique*, Paris: P. Catin (1922).

Sciacky, L., *Farewell to Ottoman Salonica*, Istanbul: Isis Press (2000).

Stavroulakis, N., *The Jews of Greece*, Athens: American Friends of the Jewish Museum of Greece (1984).

Tesal, R. D., *Selanik'ten Istanbul'a*, Istanbul: İletişim (1997).

Vakalopoulos, A. E., *A History of Thessaloniki*, Thessaloniki: Institute for Balkan Studies (1963).

Veinstein, G., ed., *Salonique 1850–1918. La ville des juifs et le réveil des Balkans*, Paris: Éds. Autrement (1992).

Wratislaw, A. C., *A Consul in the East*, Oxford: W. Blackwood (1924).

4 The place of Thessaloniki in Greek national awareness
From Greek independence to 1912 and beyond

Spyridon G. Ploumidis

The Balkan Wars in the context of the Macedonian question

The triumphal entry of the Greek army into Thessaloniki, the first key accomplishment of the Greek armed forces in the First Balkan War, was a milestone in modern Greek history. It was in Thessaloniki that the discourse about Greater Greece took a new impetus. Gennadius, the Metropolitan of Thessaloniki, in his address to King George I on 29 October 1912, stated: 'Lo! Here comes greater Greece, liberating and regaining one by one the enslaved Greek lands' (Molossos 1914, 1032).

Since the 1870s, Thessaloniki was considered the heart of the Hellenism of Macedonia (e.g. Merkouris 1876, 30). The city had great significance for Greek national awareness and self-understanding, not only because of the Greek Orthodox population of Ottoman Macedonia but also from a geographic, economic, and symbolic point of view. For instance, on 26 October 1912, Mayor of Athens Spyridon Merkouris, in an address to the Athenians, hailed 'the liberation of the homeland of the most Greek of all Greeks Alexander' [the Great] (*Embros*, 27 October 1912, 2). Along the same lines, the novelist Babis Anninos (1852–1934), in his chronicle of the First Balkan War, paralleled the liberation of Thessaloniki with the Greek national dream of recapturing Constantinople from the Ottomans:

> Next to the great dream that captured the mind of the enslaved Nation right after the fall of Constantinople and final loss of its freedom; next to this luminous dream that strengthened and consoled several generations [of Greeks], here stands Thessaloniki, which, along with the holy City on the Seven Hills, is one of the two pinnacles of Greek desires.
>
> (Anninos 1913, 13)

The London *Times* reporter W.H. Crawfurd Price commented in his account of the Balkan Wars:

> With the entry of King George of Greece on 11th November, another chapter was opened in the history of the Macedonian capital. It was an event

50 *Spyridon G. Ploumidis*

of vast political, historical and sentimental importance. But few of the onlookers remembered they were celebrating a victory over the Turks. The thoughts uppermost in their minds were that once again the Greeks were masters of Salonika, that a long exile had ended and that a dream had been realized.

(Crawfurd Price 1914, 139)

This 'dream' actually belonged to a wider issue that answered to the name Macedonia. Indeed, Macedonia was the epicenter of the two Balkan Wars, and had attracted the interest of European diplomats and politicians particularly since the Ilinden uprising in 1903.

The British journalist framed the two Balkan Wars in the context of 'the fascinating tale of Macedonian strife' (Crawfurd Price 1914, vi). Macedonia attracted the interest of European diplomats and politicians well before, though particularly after the Ilinden uprising of 1903. In 1898 the renowned French historian Édouard Driault (1864–1947) had placed the Macedonian Question within the broader context of the Eastern Question and of 'the history of the relations of Islamism with the Christian world'. He viewed the clashes in Macedonia between the Christian subjects of the Sultan and their Ottoman rulers as 'a crusade and struggle of the Cross against the Crescent'. And he envisaged that:

Macedonia will be of course—and already is—along with Armenia and Crete the land that will preoccupy European diplomacy in the future. In contrast to Thrace, which is almost completely Turkish, and Albania, which is fully Muslim, Macedonia on the contrary has only a few dozen thousand Ottomans. What is more, the points on the ethnographic map of this land that indicate the positions of the Turks are becoming more scarce and smaller every day, until they are completely obliterated. Such points are, for example, Yenice on the right bank of the Vardar river, Demir Hissar, and Drama, along the road that leads to Constantinople.

(Driault 1898, viii, ix, 280)

Driault made a useful analysis of Greek national interests in Ottoman-ruled Macedonia and the expectations linked to a possible annexation of Macedonia and Thessaloniki:

At first, the Greeks were the sole heirs apparent of the Ottoman patrimony in Macedonia, as well as the successors of the Ottoman Empire both in Europe and in Asia Minor. For they consider themselves as the legal inheritors of Philip [of Macedon] and the Byzantine emperors; exactly because of this, before 1860 all the enemies of the Turks were identified as Greeks. [...] the Greeks preserve until today the hope that they might again conquer Macedonia [...] In that case, Macedonia could become their granary. The farmers of Macedonia, by capacity of their prudence and wisdom, would be, in Greece's best interests, a counterweight to the light-mindedness of the

Thessaloniki in Greek national awareness 51

seaman of the Greek islands. This would be a collateral for the restitution of the Greek empire; and is the focal point of the Great Idea.

(Driault 1898, 280–281)

Greek 'Macedonism'

Greek expectations from the acquisition of Macedonia were indeed high (though partly eclipsed after 1915, when Asia Minor and its natural wealth entered the diplomatic agenda), and were an integral part of the Great Idea for a national unification of Hellenism. Certainly, Macedonia's inclusion in the Greek 'national' space' was commonplace in Greek imagery. The *Totius Graeciae Descriptio*, a map drawn by the Renaissance cartographer Nikolaos Sophianos (Rome 1540) and reprinted by a fellow Greek scholar Andreas Moustoxydis in 1843, included all of Ottoman Macedonia (along with the lands below the Danube) within its borders (Tolias 2010, 106–109). In their *Geographia Neoteriki* [Modern Geography], published in Vienna in 1791, the cartographers of the Greek Enlightenment, Daniel Philippides and Gregorios Konstantas, positioned Macedonia within 'mainland Greece' and 'European Greece' (Philippides and Konstantas 1988, 109). Finally, both ancient and early modern Macedonia were included in the Map of Greece of the revolutionary poet Rigas Feraios (Velestinlis) published secretly in Vienna in 1797 (Tolias 2010, 106, 110, 112). The same was the case with the 'ethnocratic' *Chart of the Greek Lands* produced by the Society for the Dissemination of Greek Letters (est. Athens 1869) in 1878 (Wilkinson 1951, 74–75; Tolias 2010, 113; Karavas 2003, 83, 89n).[1] Macedonia, both as a historic and a geographic entity, was presented as an integral part of modern Greek national identity (cf. Tolias 1998, 29). This coincides with the efforts in 1849–1859 by Konstantinos Paparrigopoulos, the founder of modern Greek historiography and of the concept of historical continuity of Greece from antiquity to the present, to reintroduce Alexander the Great and the royal house of ancient Macedonia in the discourse of Modern Greek scholarly education and national awareness (Dimaras 1986, 71–74, 207, 279; Gounaris 2007, 134).

What is surprising, given this trend, is the limited number of works on Thessaloniki in Greek literature of the eighteenth and the nineteenth centuries. The conservative and introverted character of Thessaloniki society has some bearing on this. Despite the efforts of Pachomios, a scholar who opened a school in Thessaloniki in the early eighteenth century, and its Levantine trading community, Thessaloniki never became a learning center of the Greek Enlightenment like Ioannina or Smyrna (Kitromilides 1985, 38–39). Philippides and Konstantas provide one of only a few Greek depictions of Thessaloniki and ethnic relations there:

Salonica, Thessaloniki, now the capital city of Macedonia, is a very old, renowned, sizeable, populous, most beautiful and very commercial city, situated on the eastern side of the head of the Thermaikos gulf, with a good port,

52 *Spyridon G. Ploumidis*

built partly on the slopes of a hill and partly on the plains. [...] Its inhabitants are Romaioi, Turks, and plentiful Jews, who came here after they were expelled from Spain. It is the metropolitan diocese of an [Orthodox] bishop, under whose jurisdiction there are many Episcopal sees. The metropolitan palace is inside the walls of the castle, as is actually the case with all the Romaioi. The bishop of Thessaloniki practices religion somewhat more liberally than in other places. The Christians have churches, whereas the Jews [have] synagogues. There are also Armenians residing in the town. And several foreign consuls.

(Philippides and Konstantas 1988, 202–203)[2]

Likewise, the suspicions that existed between the local Greek Orthodox community and the city's large Jewish population were not such as to arouse the concern of Greek commentators (cf. Mazower 2004, 165–167).

The seeming lack of interest by Greek intellectuals and officials came to a definitive end at the turn of the twentieth century. What prompted the new attention was the rise of the Bulgarian national movement in Macedonia beginning in the early 1860s, a challenge to the position of Hellenism in the area. Greek interest intensified after the Eastern Crisis of 1875–1878, which resulted in the establishment of a Bulgarian national state and almost, through the abortive Treaty of San Stefano, of a Great Bulgaria including Macedonia (minus Thessaloniki and Halkidiki) and Thrace. The Greek public had a new source of alarm in the terrorist attacks of the *Gemidji* [Boatmen], a group of Bulgarian anarchists in Thessaloniki in April 1903 and the Ilinden uprising that same summer (Gounaris 2007, 149, 151, 158, 162, 410). A leading role in arousing Greek public interest in Macedonia was played by Stefanos Dragoumis, an MP for Athens and former Foreign Minister, whose family originated from Macedonia. On 11 September 1903, in the aftermath of the Ilinden uprising, Dragoumis made a dramatic appeal in the Athens daily *Akropolis*:

And lo! Here appears again the specter of Greater Bulgaria, and actually it is even thicker today, with the addition of Thessaloniki and Halkidiki.
The numbers, the voice, the strength of Hellenism in Macedonia, are neutralized, strangled and suffocated. Macedonia is absorbed and devoured.
The continuity of Hellenism is severed. Its cohesion is dissolved. [...]
Guards, snap out of it!
Greeks wake up!

(Dragoumis 1906, 3)

Next, the self-sacrifice of Pavlos Melas (a Greek second lieutenant of *haute bourgeois* descent killed by Ottoman forces near Kastoria on 13/26 October 1904), thrilled the Greek public, and signaled the apogee of Greece's national involvement in Macedonia's affairs (Gounaris 1997, 108; Ploumidis 2012, passim).

By the outbreak of the Balkan Wars, the preoccupation of the Greek public with Macedonia had been established. Alexandros Mazarakis-Ainian (a future

Thessaloniki in Greek national awareness 53

Chief of the General Staff, who took part in the Macedonian Struggle of 1904–1908) noted in 1912:

> We all had heard, from a very young age, about Macedonia, yet the name of Macedonia was sounded particularly in the last few years. [...] we all thrilled to hear this name, which reminded us of so many misfortunes and sacrifices, as well as so many glorious and heroic acts.
>
> (Mazarakis-Ainian 1912, 9)

By this he particularly meant the feats of Alexander the Great and of the emperors of the Macedonian dynasty of Byzantium, and especially the 'armed defence of Hellenism' in 1904–1908.

We might call this intense irredentist interest and highly politicized rhetoric over Macedonia, which developed in 1903–1912 in response to emerging 'Bulgarianism' regarding the disputed region, as 'Macedonism'. Greek national 'Macedonism', however, was qualitatively different from its Bulgarian equivalent, which developed into a place obsession (*topophilia* as I have lately defined it), or the 'Slavo-macedonism' of Yugoslav Macedonians, which made the history and political issue of Macedonia central to their national identity (Gounaris 2010, 31, 38; Ploumidis 2011, 23–27, 419). Far from becoming an obsession, Greek claims on Ottoman Macedonia, as they were set forth in detail in 1919 by Major Vladimiros Colocotronis for the Paris Peace Conference, drew chiefly on the principle of nationalities, and relied on ethnographic statistics to assert that the boundaries of ancient Macedonia coincided roughly with those of Greater Greece of 1913 (Colocotronis 1989, 603–619; Wilkinson 1951, 2, 71, 75, 241).[3] In addition, the discourse of Greek 'Macedonism' entailed political, geographic, and economic facets this paper will discuss.

Alexandros Mazarakis-Ainian (reacting to the rumored expansionist agenda of Austria-Hungary and its drive toward Thessaloniki) neatly characterized Greek political-geographic calculations, referring to Macedonia as 'the Gordian knot of the Eastern Question':

> Macedonia, in itself and because of its geographical position, is destined to provide its future owner overall mastery of the Balkans and the Near East. Due to its vast population and its natural wealth, Macedonia is already in a position to provide to its possessor unchallenged supremacy over all its neighbouring countries in the Balkan peninsula. Yet, the greatest importance of Macedonia is found in its key geographical position. This is proven by the fact that, in addition to the neighbouring countries, which have a more or less close racial affiliation to its native population and so they naturally desire its annexation, Macedonia has also attracted the lust of Great Powers that do not any legal claim upon it either in terms of history or ethnography, but still hope that they will conquer it by the use of force against the small, mutually hostile Balkan countries, and thus find their desirable outlet to the Aegean Sea.

54   *Spyridon G. Ploumidis*

For Hellenism and Greece in particular, he saw Macedonia as an issue of life and death:

> possible conquest [of Macedonia] by somebody else, especially by the Bulgarians, would mean breaking the continuity of Hellenism and the loss of any hope of national unification, as well as the suffocation of the Greek state, which in this case would inevitably be cut off from the eastern [Greek] lands. Any Greek that underestimates these dangers should reflect for a moment on the power the annexation of Macedonia would provide to the Bulgarian state, and what disadvantage this would be for Greece's position. If for the Bulgarians the annexation of Macedonia is purely annexationist or at least the fulfillment of its requirement for an outlet to the Aegean, for us this is an issue of life and death of Hellenism. And by saying life we do not mean the anemic existence of a statelet [...] by this we mean the continuation of the great historic mission of our Nation, which can only be accomplished by means of our national unification.
>
> (Mazarakis-Ainian 1912, 210, 212)

This veteran of the Macedonian Struggle placed Macedonia at the apex of the Greek irredentist agenda, arguing that

> none of the enslaved Greek provinces runs the dangers that Macedonia does; and the annexation or the loss of any of these provinces will not have the same grave consequences for the rest of them and for the whole Nation as the loss of Macedonia would.

And he concludes that 'the fate and the future of the whole Nation will be defined by Macedonia and in Macedonia' (loc. cit., cf. Helmreich 1938, 170–178).

The dramatic analysis of Mazarakis-Ainian was not, by any means, isolated or eccentric. At the same time, on the eve of the Balkan Wars, a Greek-American, in his call to fellow Greeks to join the Greek army, identified Macedonia as the actual Promised Land of Hellenism:

> There are more than 300,000 Greek men in America. This great and glorious country, far from being harmed by us, can still exist and progress without us. Our America is Macedonia, which offers to us much bigger opportunities for prosperity than any other place, and the restitution of which demands from us much fewer efforts, sacrifices and dangers than those efforts that we made and are still making, than those sacrifices that we suffered and are still suffering, and than the dangers we ran and are still running in America. It is therefore not only in our best national interest but also in our individual, both practical and commercial, interest to rally round the agenda of the liberation of Macedonia and of all our unredeemed homelands. For only through the fulfillment of our national aspirations will we benefit ourselves and others, not just materially but also mentally.
>
> (Kastritsis 1912, 207–208)

Thessaloniki in Greek national awareness   55

Thus, by 1912 Macedonia had assumed the image of a mythical El Dorado that would bring prosperity, wealth, and geopolitical supremacy to Greece. The roots of this perception can be traced back to 1880, when a confidential report on the economic prospects of Macedonia by Athanasios Eftaxias (1849–1931), a young Greek economist (and future Minister of Finance and National Economy), was published privately and circulated in establishment circles of Athens. Eftaxias traveled to Macedonia in the spring of 1877, on the eve of the Russo-Turkish War, on an official commission. In his report, Eftaxias identifies Macedonia as the land 'wherein the future of Hellenism lies':

> The land that can arguably be considered as the centre and the core of the present-day European Turkey, because of its large size and its fertile soil as well as because of the many and rich mines underground, and thanks to its excellent geographic position, which in the near future, upon the completion of the railway line that will connect Thessaloniki to Vienna, will be of great importance for global trade; the land with greatest value and importance, I say, for all these reasons is definitely Macedonia.

The Greek economist placed particular emphasis on the prospects of agriculture, industry, and trade:

> Agriculture is one of the main foundations of [Macedonia's] present and future prosperity. [...] For a long time past, Macedonia was renowned as one of the major granaries of the world; and still today it is competitive, in the large cereal markets, with the greatest wheat-producing countries in Europe. If transport were developed further and its interaction with the outside world was strengthened, the records of its trade and industry would seriously improve, and the prospects of its agriculture would become much greater and more splendid than they are already now.
>
> (Eftaxias 1880, iv–vi, 13–14)

Eftaxias implied that the natural resources of Macedonia would boost the economic growth of Greece. However, the main concerns in his report were political not economic, namely the acquisition of land in Macedonia in order to enhance Greek national aspirations. To this end, he suggested the purchase of Ottoman rural estates (*çifliks*) by Greek capitalists as the best means for the Hellenization of Macedonia, since 'two thirds of the land in Macedonia, especially the most fertile grounds, today are *çifliks* that belong to Muslim landlords', while 'the tillers of these estates are, in their majority, Bulgarians', who are 'almost serfs' (Eftaxias 1880, 13–14; cf. Chatziiosif 1993, 146; Gounaris 2007, 173; Karavas 2010, 43–47, 99–120).

Much more anguished and existential were the questions put to the Greek public in 1886 in a report on the economy and geography of Macedonia by Ioannis Kalostypis (1851–1918), an Athens-based publicist and publisher of the *Sfaira*

56 *Spyridon G. Ploumidis*

newspaper. This was in 1886, in the wake of the unilateral annexation of Eastern Rumelia to the Bulgarian Principate:

> Macedonia is the heart of Hellenism. Macedonia is in danger. Without Macedonia, Greece, either small or greater, cannot exist. [...] Truly, Macedonia is the bastion of Greek self-existence and the guarantee for its great future. [... Macedonia is] the queen of the Greek provinces.
>
> (Kalostypis 1886, 8)

Kalostypis stressed 'the political importance of sizeable and most beautiful Macedonia', and argued that without Macedonia Greece would remain 'an embryonic nation', its existence would be problematic, and the Great Idea would remain a mere dream. He also emphasized 'the significance of Macedonia for the safety and the grandeur of Greece', and lamented the 'ignorance' of the Greek public and 'governing circles' about Macedonia and its potential. He exhorted his compatriots to defend Macedonia and the Greeks who lived there against 'the threat of "Panslavism"', since 'the Bulgarians are attempting to seduce a great part of Macedonia's population, by making every sacrifice, and using every trick and threat that this takes to be accomplished'. He referred extensively to 'the fabulous wealth' and 'immeasurable economic capacity' of Macedonia, especially in the agricultural sector and the mining industry:

> The produce of Macedonia is famous for its diversity, abundance and in many cases superior quality. Its main products are cereals; wines; rice grains; cotton; olive oil; silk; excellent legumes; top-rated fruits; tobacco; saffron; animals of various species; timber suitable for ship and house-building; unprocessed and tanned hides; cheeses; butter; animal fibers; coal; and precious metals such as gold, silver, copper and iron, still unexploited, like most of the resources of this glorious land.

Kalostypis commented that 'such a country, which is so rich in natural resources, obviously has the potential for industrial development'. And he reasoned that, exactly because of all this, the Greeks would 'struggle to the very end to secure this great and most productive country for Hellenism'. Not least because of Macedonia's geopolitical value, and its 'key role' in the Eastern Question:

> From a geographic point of view, Macedonia is even more valuable for Greek security and the future of Greece than it is vital from an economic viewpoint. For Macedonia is the great bastion of Thessaly and Greece itself; the buttress and shelter of Epirus; and the impregnable, from both the North and the East, citadel of Hellenism. Through Halkidiki, which in terms of its shape reminds us of Poseidon's trident, Macedonia supplements Greek supremacy in the Aegean. And through the varied and wooded Rhodope

Thessaloniki in Greek national awareness 57

mountain, it secures the land connection with the Greek populations of Thrace. [...] Macedonia is the key to the Eastern Question. The master of Macedonia is the moral hegemon of the whole Near East. Greece, therefore, must always have its eyes set upon Macedonia. And every national concern must be directed there.

(Kalostypis 1886, 8–11, 14–17, 23, 70, 96; cf. Gounaris 2007, 184)

Eftaxias' and Kalostypis' strategic analyzes on Macedonia and its connection with Greece were the most well-structured and explicit on the subject; they were certainly not the only ones. Several others with the same message appeared in Athens before 1912 (Gounaris 2010, 33).

Geopolitical analyzes of Macedonia in the inter-war period

Greek 'Macedonism' continued unabated after the conclusion of Greece's national wars and during the process of national unification in 1923. Greek analyzes on Macedonia (and Thessaloniki) continued to be published in the inter-war period, placing special emphasis on political geography, geopolitics, and economics. The first in a series of such works was a *History of Hellenism*, 'centered and based on Macedonia', which was published in 1923 by Kleanthes Nikolaides, a professor of Linguistics at the University of Vienna. Nikolaides highlighted the central position of Macedonia in Great Power politics, drawing particular attention to the contention between Russia and Austria-Hungary in the area, and arguing that Macedonia was the real culprit for the outbreak of the Balkan Wars as well as the First World War. Understandably, the main concern of Nikolaides was the close association of Macedonia with Hellenism 'from ancient times to the present' (i.e. before 1914):

History proves that Macedonia lay at the root of the Greek Nation's unification into a genuinely single State. It was not until Macedonia [under Philip II and Alexander the Great] came to exercise its hegemony over Greece that Greece acquired a solid natural base. It was not until then that the entire Greek Nation found its mother earth, wherein it could safely plant its roots and flourish.

(Nikolaides 1923, xi–xii)

In other words, Macedonia was always the geopolitical axis of Greek national unity and existence:

Most importantly, Macedonia is the backbone of mainland Greece. It is what, in modern political discourse, we normally call '*hinterland*'. Thessaly will develop only when the land route from Athens to Monastir meets the standards of modern times. Any closer cultural and economic ties either between Greece and Albania or between Greece and Thrace (up to Adrianople and the Black Sea) can only be achieved through Macedonia. On the other hand, if

58 *Spyridon G. Ploumidis*

Macedonia is ever lost for the Greek Nation, Thessaly would be condemned to eternal stagnation; Albania would be detached from any influence that Greece exercises on it; the Hellenism of Thrace would be lost forever for Motherland Greece; and Epirus itself would prove a mixed blessing for Greece. On the other hand, if Macedonia remains in Greek hands, all the western, northern and eastern Greek lands will be firmly secured to our nation, and their economic contribution to Free Greece will highly raise the economic prosperity and development of the Greek Nation. [...] this backbone [i.e. Macedonia] can definitely secure a great future for Greece and make our country strong and viable, and able to retain those limbs [i.e. the Greek lands] that are scattered through Europe, Asia Minor, and the Mediterranean.

(Nikolaides 1923, xiii)

Nikolaides' analysis is germane to the course of Greek political thinking in the inter-war period. The issue of Greece's viability, in geopolitical and geo-economic terms, was high on the agenda of politicians, intellectuals, and journalists (Chatziiosif 1986, 330–368; Ploumidis 2011, 361–390).

On the matter of Macedonia, most influential was the analysis of Konstantinos Sfyris, a German-trained professor of geopolitics and economics in the Athens School of Economics and Business Studies. In 1930–1931, he argued that 'the shores of the Aegean are the dynamic natural outlet of both the Balkan and the Central European hinterland to the broad international routes of the Eastern Mediterranean'. Subsequently, he opined that Greece 'is a Mediterranean country and a Balkan country because of its Balkan trunk, as well as an Aegean country with an outlet to Central Europe'. He identified Thessaloniki as a '*Standort*', 'a natural junction of international trade':

First, Thessaloniki has the natural local advantage of serving the exigencies of its Macedono-Albanian hinterland. Secondly, Thessaloniki is destined, thanks to its geographical position as an international intersection of international land and sea routes of transport, to be the natural outlet, in terms of international transport, to the Eastern Mediterranean not just of the Balkan hinterland, strictly speaking, but also of the vast and diverse Central European hinterland up to the line of segregation of the sectors of the two Northern European maritime *Standorts* of Hamburg and Danzig. [...] In its capacity as a junction of international transport, Thessaloniki can, and indeed is destined to, flourish commensurately with its valuable position.

(Sfyris 1930, 256–257)

Rather surprisingly, Sfyris came to the conclusion that, if Greece wanted to become a viable 'economic, politico-territorial and ethno-racial unit', it would be in its best interest to promote its neighbours' access to the Aegean:

It is in Greece's interest to facilitate by any means the Slavic outlet into the Aegean, firstly and mostly because Slavism generally does not have

Thessaloniki in Greek national awareness 59

anywhere its individual outlet [i.e. to the sea] for the development of its dynamism freely, i.e. free from any constrictive or steadfast political sub-servience. At the same time, it is also in Greece's interests to serve by any means the free development of the shores of the Aegean as a Central European outlet, and therefore not to disrupt the unity and development of Central Europe.

(Sfyris 1930, 262)

Sfyris, whose arguments had a great impact at the time, explained that the 'prime interests' of Greece derived from the country's need 'to procure its grain from places that offer the most favorable conditions and the biggest opportunities for Greek exports, and serve in the best manner Greece's multiple economic inter-ests' (by this he alluded to Bulgaria and Yugoslavia, two Slavic countries, major producers and exporters of grain whose relations with Greece were tense). He did not make clear whether his suggestion for 'a Slavic outlet into the Aegean' would entail territorial concessions from Greece to its northern neighbors in its Macedonian or Thracian provinces (Sfyris 1931, 300–301, 347; Ploumidis 2011, 95–99).

Epilogue

Notwithstanding all challenges, post-1912 Macedonia and Thessaloniki seem to have met the great expectations of Greek publicists and political analysts. For example, in 1931 the journalist Antonios Chamoudopoulos and the Liberal MP for Thessaloniki Michael Mavrogordatos (who in 1925–1932 also served as the Venizelos government's commissioner in the Free Zone of Thessaloniki), in a joint economic study, identified Macedonia as 'one of the most productive parts of the Greek State', adding that:

It is not an exaggeration to claim that Macedonia is the most productive and the richest Greek province [...] In the new age that is looming after the Asia Minor Catastrophe, Macedonia is destined to play the main role. [...] Greek Macedonia took the lead in the accomplished and the ongoing campaign for the economic regeneration of Greece.

The two authors placed particular emphasis on the monetary value of tobacco (Greece's main export commodity in the inter-war years) produced in Macedonia. After 1912, 'by the liberation of Macedonia', Greece's economy virtually became a 'tobaccoist' economy, and its production of Oriental tobacco increased dra-matically in volume (from 8,744,838 *okas* in 1912 to 21,505,977 *okas* in 1914) (Mavrogordatos and Chamoudopoulos 1931, 5, 67).

Still, for all its advantages, Macedonia was not by any means the only 'unre-deemed' land to be the object of grandiose economic aspirations. At the turn of the century, Asia Minor also attracted the serious attention of scholars and publicists. Most of these were of Asia Minor extraction; they exalted the natural resources of

60   Spyridon G. Ploumidis

their homeland out of local pride and prejudice. One example is the Athens-based doctor Dimitrios Giassas, who wrote in 1898:

> There no other land in this world so populous and so fertile as Asia Minor. First, the plains of Kotiaion [Kütahya], Ikonion [Konya] and Ankara produce prime and plentiful grains, bountiful fruits, etc. [...] Secondly, the meadow of Meander [Büyük Menderes], this earthly paradise, flowery, graceful and joyful with its temperate climate, produces everything that is lacking in any other part. The scent from the lemon and the orange trees fills the air on the slopes of the Mediterranean coastline and around Smyrna. [...] The people who live on this charming and lush place, which is endowed with such beauties and virtues and blessed so lavishly by nature, are renowned for being industrious and caring for the embellishment and the maintenance of this verdant plain. [...] Asia Minor conceals also many mineralogical treasures. All of its mountains have plenty and various mines, few of which are in operation at present.
>
> (Giassas 1898, 3)

Between 1915 to 1922 this 'Ionian vision' (as Michael Llewellyn Smith phrased it) overtook Macedonia as the most popular topic for nationalist dreams (Smith 1998, xv–xx; Ploumidis 2016, 79–83, 156–157, 209–218). The Asia Minor Catastrophe, however, caused a rapid reversal. Greek national interest shifted back from the East to the North. As Greece responded to Bulgarian revisionist and Yugoslav pretensions in the Balkans, Greek 'Macedonism' revived and flourished for the rest of the inter-war period and beyond (Hatzivassiliou 2006, 6).

Notes

1 This map relied heavily on the *Tableau ethnocratique des Pays du Sud-Est de l'Europe* of the renowned German cartographer Heinrich Kiepert.
2 According to these humanist travelers and geographers, 'modern Greeks are usually miscalled *Romaioi*' (Philippides and Konstantas 1988, 120).
3 Colocotronis maintained that the Greek/Patriarchist population of (pre-1913) Ottoman Macedonia was double that of the Bulgarian/Exarchist, and also that the connection between the Slavic-speakers of Macedonia with the Bulgarians was 'artificially constructed by Bulgarian propagandist activity'.

References

Anninos, B., *1912: Νίκαι κατά βαρβάρων* [Victories against Barbarians], Athens: n.e. (1913).
Chatziiosif, Ch., 'Απόψεις γύρω από τη βιωσιμότητα της Ελλάδας και τον ρόλο της βιομη χανίας' [Views on the viability of Greece and the role of industry]. In: Kremmydas, V., Maltezou, Ch., Panagiotakis, N.M.(eds.), *Αφιέρωμα στον Νίκο Σβορώνο* [Dedication to Nikos Svoronos], vol. II, Rethymno: Panepistimiakes Ekdoseis Kritis (1986), 330–368.
Chatziiosif, Ch., 'Η εξωστρέφεια της ελληνικής οικονομίας στις αρχές του 20ού αιώνα και οι συνέπειές της στην εξωτερική πολιτική' [The extroversion of the Greek economy in

Thessaloniki in Greek national awareness 61

the early twentieth century and its consequences on foreign policy]. In: *Η Ελλάδα των Βαλκανικών Πολέμων 1910–1914* [Greece of the Balkan Wars, 1910–1914], Athens: ELIA (1993).

Colocotronis, V., *La Macédoine et l'Hellénisme. Étude historique et ethnologique*, Paris: Berger-Levrault 1919, Reprinted by Etaireia Makedonikon Spoudon, Thessaloniki (1989).

Crawfurd Price, W. H., *The Balkan Cockpit: The Political and Military Story of the Balkan Wars in Macedonia*, London: T. Werner Laurie (1914).

Dimaras, K. Th., *Κωνσταντίνος Παπαρρηγόπουλος, η εποχή του—η ζωή του—το έργο του*, [Konstantinos Paparrigopoulos: His Times—His Life—His Work], Athens: Morfotiko Idryma Ethnikis Trapezis (1986).

Dragoumis, S. N., [as *'Gnasios Makednos'*], *Μακεδονική κρίσις 1903–1904* [Macedonian Crisis, 1903–1904], Athens: n.e. (1906).

Driault, É., *La question d'Orient depuis ses origines jusq'à nos jours*, Paris: Félix Alcan (1898).

Embros Daily Newspaper, Athens: D. Kalapothakis (1896–1969).

Giassas, D., *Περί Μικράς Ασίας προς χρήσιν παντός εν τη περικλεεί ταύτη χώρα κατοικούντος* [About Asia Minor for the Use of All the Inhabitants of This Glorious Land], Athens: n.e. (1898).

Gounaris, B. C., 'Social gatherings and Macedonian lobbying: Symbols of irredentism and living legends in early twentieth-century Athens'. In: Carabott, Philip (ed.), *Greek Society in the Making, 1863–1913*, Aldershot: Ashgate Variorum (1997).

Gounaris, B. K., *Τα Βαλκάνια των Ελλήνων: Από τον Διαφωτισμό έως τον Α΄ Παγκόσμιο Πόλεμο* [The Balkans of the Greeks: From the Enlightenment to the First World War], Thessaloniki: Epikentro (2007).

Gounaris, B. K., *Το Μακεδονικό Ζήτημα από τον 19ο έως τον 21ο αιώνα: ιστοριογραφικές προσεγγίσεις* [The Macedonian Question from the Nineteenth to the Twenty-First Century: Historiographical Approaches], Athens: Alexandria (2010).

Hatzivassiliou, E., *Greece and the Cold War: Frontline State, 1952–1967*, London and New York: Routledge (2006).

Helmreich, E. C., *The Diplomacy of the Balkan Wars 1912–1913*, Cambridge, MA: Harvard University Press (1938).

Kalostypis, I. N., *Μακεδονία ήτοι μελέτη οικονομολογική, γεωγραφική, ιστορική και εθνολογική της Μακεδονίας* [Macedonia: An Economic, Geographic, Historical and Ethnological Study of Macedonia], Athens: n.e. (1886).

Karavas, S., *'Μακάριοι οι κατέχοντες την γην': Γαιοκτητικοί σχεδιασμοί προς απαλλοτρίωση συνειδήσεων στη Μακεδονία 1880–1909* ['Blessed Are Those Who Own the Land': Land-Purchasing Plans for the Expropriation of Consciousnesses in Macedonia, 1880–1909], Athens: Vivliorama (2010).

Karavas, S., 'Οι εθνογραφικές περιπέτειες του "ελληνισμού" (1876–1878)' [The ethnographic vicissitudes of 'Hellenism'], *Ta Historika* 38 (June 2003), 23–74.

Kastritsis, G. P., *Η. Μεγάλη Ιδέα* [The Great Idea], New York: O Kosmos (1912).

Kitromilides, P. M., *Ιώσηπος Μοισιόδαξ: Οι συντεταγμένες της βαλκανικής σκέψης τον 18ο αιώνα* [Iosepos Moisiodax: the coordinates of Balkan thought in the 18th century], Athens: Morfotiko Idryma Ethnikis Trapezis (1985).

Mavrogordatos, M. I. and Chamoudopoulos, A. Ch., *Η Μακεδονία: μελέτη δημογραφική και οικονομική* [Macedonia: A Demographic and Economic Study], Thessaloniki: n.e. (1931).

Mazarakis-Ainian, A. ['Almaz'], *Αι ιστορικαί περιπέτειαι της Μακεδονίας από των αρχαιο τάτων χρόνων μέχρι σήμερον (και ιδία τα από του 1903–1908 γεγονότα)* [The Historical

62   Spyridon G. Ploumidis

Vicissitudes of Macedonia from Ancient Times to the Present, especially the events of 1903–1908], Athens: Kratos (1912).

Mazower, M., *Salonica: City of Ghosts. Christians, Muslims and Jews 1430–1950*, London: HarperCollins (2004).

Merkouris, S., *Λόγοι εκφωνηθέντες κατά τα εγκαίνια του εν Θεσσαλονίκη διδασκαλείου* [Speeches delivered upon the opening of the Thessaloniki Teachers' Training College], Thessaloniki: Hermes (1876).

Molossos, S., *Ιστορία του Βαλκανοτουρκικού πολέμου* [History of the Balkano-Turkish War], Athens: n.e. (1914).

Nikolaides, K., *Ιστορία του ελληνισμού με κέντρον και βάσιν την Μακεδονίαν από των παναρχαίων χρόνων μέχρι της σήμερον* [History of Hellenism, Centred and Based on Macedonia, From the Most Ancient Times to the Present], Athens: n.e. (1923).

Papalouka Eftaxias, A., *Το έργον του ελληνισμού εν Μακεδονία* [The Work of Hellenism in Macedonia], Athens: n.e. (1880).

Philippides, D. and Konstantas, G., *Γεωγραφία Νεωτερική* [Modern Geography], Koumarianou, A. (ed.), Athens: Hermès (1988).

Ploumidis, S. G., 'Συνέχειες και ασυνέχειες του ελληνικού εθνικισμού: Από την ήττα του 1897 στη μακεδονική εξόρμηση' [Continuities and discontinuities of Greek nationalism: From the defeat of 1897 to the campaign for Macedonia], *Clio* 6, Thessaloniki (2012), 149–178.

Ploumidis, S. G., *Έδαφος και μνήμη στα Βαλκάνια: Ο 'γεωργικός εθνικισμός' στην Ελλάδα και στη Βουλγαρία (1927–46)* [Land and Memory in the Balkans: 'Agrarian Nationalism' in Greece and Bulgaria], Athens: Patakis (2011).

Ploumidis, S. G., *Τα μυστήρια της Αιγηΐδος: Το Μικρασιατικό Ζήτημα στην ελληνική πολιτική (1891–1922)* [The Mysteries of the Aegeid: the Asia Minor Question in Greek Politics, 1891–1922], Athens: Hestia (2016).

Sfyris, K. D., 'Γεωοικονομία και οικονομία. Μεθοδολογική έρευνα' [Geoeconomics and economics: A methodological analysis], *Archeion Oikonomikon kai Koinonikon Erevnon* 10/3(July—September 1930), 215–265.

Sfyris, K. D., 'Υπό ποίας προϋποθέσεις η Ελλάς είναι βιώσιμος' [Under which conditions Greece is viable], *Archeion Oikonomikon kai Koinonikon Erevnon* 11/3 (July—September 1931), 289–354.

Smith, M. L., *Ionian Vision: Greece in Asia Minor, 1919–1922*, London: Hurst, (1998).

Tolias, G., *Challenged Territories: Cartographers of Greece and the Levant during the Ottoman Era*, Istanbul: Isis Press (2010).

Tolias, G., '"της ευρυχώρου Ελλάδος": η "Χάρτα" του Ρήγα και τα όρια του "ελληνισμού" ['Of spacious Greece': Rigas' map and the boundaries of 'Hellenism']', *Ta Historika* 28–29 (June–December 1998), 3–30.

Wilkinson, H. R., *Maps and Politics: A Review of the Ethnographic Cartography of Macedonia*, Liverpool: Liverpool University Press (1951).

5 Salonica through Bulgarian eyes

Yura Konstantinova

Early in the 20th century, Bulgaria tried and failed to achieve its national goal through warfare. Bulgarian society paid a heavy price during the two Balkan Wars and the First World War. After the humiliation of defeat, Bulgarians swung between revanchism and pacifism. In 1938, a Bulgarian lawyer and public figure, Todor Krainichanets from Veles, intervened in the political debate of the era with a booklet on the importance of Thessaloniki, in which he strongly opposed the increasing militarist sentiment at that time.[1]

> Nature has destined for Salonica to become a unifying link, the pillar around which the surrounding countries are to be built with flourishing economy and glamorous culture ... Enough of fighting and discord for this beautiful city of Salonica! Let's stop dividing it among each other! And let us create for it, with the efforts of every one of us, such conditions that it may serve us as a place of mutual understanding, of collective cooperation ... and will grow to the point of actually becoming what God himself has allotted to it—to be the center and capital of the Balkans! ... I really hope that through everyone's efforts, those who sincerely and soberly wish brighter days to their homelands, will create from Salonica, instead of an 'apple of discord', the 'Balkan Hamburg'.
>
> (Krainichanets 1938, 40)

Indeed, the beautiful city of Thessaloniki should be 'a place of mutual understanding and collective cooperation' for the Balkan peoples. In its long history, however, the city has often become an arena of confrontation not only for the neighboring peoples but also for Arabs, Crusaders, and the Great Powers. An exceptional geographical position on the Thermaikos Gulf destined it for economic dominance in the region and naturally attracted the covetous eyes of populous nations and the powerful states. Bulgarian writer Aleko Konstantinov satirically described the importance of the city in his classic work 'Various people, different ideals':

> If only I could get you—the Customs of Salonica, I do not need much; just two years, leave me for just two years as customs manager or appraiser, come and have a talk with me then ... Salonica is crowded with Jews: There are

64 *Yura Konstantinova*

maybe fifty or sixty thousand of them, who knows, but all of them are traders: you can milk it as much as you want, and still enough will remain—it's not like our indigence in Sofia ... The Salonica customs! California, God damn it!

(Flag newspaper, 05.02.1897)

It is clear, however, that this dream of profiting from the Thessaloniki Customs does not exhaust the topic of the city's place in Bulgarian cultural and historic memory. I will try to show the Bulgarian view of Thessaloniki in historical perspective, focussing on the period from the end of the 19th century and the early 20th century, when the Bulgarian presence in the city was most noticeable. Based mainly on Bulgarian sources, I will seek an explanation for the romantic aura around Thessaloniki that Bulgarians created between the two world wars. My goal is to explore the reasons which led to the emotional perception of Thessaloniki as a Bulgarian city. This idea, not based on any serious scientific arguments, was propagated even by respected Bulgarian scientists such as the medievalist Ivan Snegarov, who proclaimed Thessaloniki the 'Bulgarian Bethlehem', the 'oldest Bulgarian sanctuary' that illuminated the Bulgarian fatherland (Snegarov 1937, preface).

The assertion of Thessaloniki as part of Bulgaria cannot seriously be justified because Thessaloniki was never part of medieval Bulgaria. Moreover, the city was remote from the strategic priorities of Bulgarian rulers and was their target only sporadically during the Middle Ages. As a good professional, Ivan Snegarov understood the groundlessness of the historical arguments by which he attempted to justify his claim that Thessaloniki since ancient times had been 'a Bulgarian sanctuary'. His justification was based instead on the theory that the city was bonded spiritually to the Slavic population of its hinterland. The creators of the Cyrillic alphabet, Cyril and Methodius, had a key role in this theory. They are traditionally associated by Bulgarians with the literature and spirituality of the Bulgarian nation. Through them Macedonia is bound with Bulgarian culture (Kaychev 2006, 101). In the 19th century, however, they were recognized as creators of the Slavic Bulgarian nationality and their work was directly related to the modern era. This led to the claim that Thessaloniki was the 'first hearth' and 'cradle' of the Bulgarian Revival.

The first mention of a Bulgarian population in Thessaloniki was in a travelogue of Evliya Çelebi in 1668. In *Geography of Neofit Bozveli and Emmanuil Vaskidovich*, printed in 1835 and in the *General Geography in Brief for the Whole World* of Konstantin Fotinov, there was no claim that the city was Bulgarian. Nor were such claims made in Bulgarian folk songs from the Ottoman period (Dinchev 1993, 109). In the 19th century, with the rapid growth of the population of Thessaloniki, there was an increase in the number of people of Bulgarian ethnic origin, as residents of the neighboring villages and urban centers flocked there in search of livelihood (Moskov 1974, 25, 61; Mazower 2004, 264). Despite this, one could hardly speak of Bulgarians in Thessaloniki before the middle of the 19th century, because the settlers quickly learned Greek and integrated with

Salonica through Bulgarian eyes 65

the Greek community in the city. This process of voluntary Hellenization was typical for the largest commercial centers in the European *vilayets* of the Ottoman Empire, where the dominance of the Greek-speaking commercial, artisan, and intellectual elite was undeniable.

However, the situation began to change with the arrival in Thessaloniki of Bulgarian artisans, mainly builders, tailors, milkmen, and coppersmiths, from smaller urban centers of Western Macedonia: Debar, Veles, Kukush, Krushevo, Prilep, Resen, and Ohrid (Yaranov 1934, 225). Representatives of the Bulgarian tailors' and masons' guilds formally established the Bulgarian community of Thessaloniki at a meeting in 1868 (Snegarov 1937, 56). This, however, was not the first manifestation of the Bulgarian spirit in the city. Between 1838 and 1843, a Bulgarian printing house functioned in Thessaloniki, founded by Theodosiy of Sinai (Antov 1934, 308; Papastathis 1968, 252). In 1866, Konstantin Darzhilovich provided his home, located in the parish of St. Athanasios Church in Thessaloniki, for the creation of the first Bulgarian school in the city. His daughter Slavka Dinkova, the sister of Georgi Konstantinov-Dinkata, was a teacher in this school, where 30 boys and girls studied (Snegarov 1937, 46–55).

Immediately after the establishment of the Bulgarian community, an elementary school opened in the city. At that time, it was decided that the local newspaper *Selanik* would be issued in four languages: Ottoman Turkish, Greek, Ladino, and Bulgarian. According to contemporary memoirs, initially the Bulgarian language was supported by the then governor Akif Pasha. A change in Turkish policy came with the arrival of the new governor Sabri Pasha in 1869, who agreed to eliminate Bulgarian from the newspaper and to expel Bulgarian teacher Stoyan Bozhkov from the elementary school (Salgandzhiev 1906, 33).

The establishment of a Bulgarian community in Thessaloniki was an indication of the emergence of Bulgarian national consciousness among part of the population, but this was not a turning point for the Bulgarian element in the city. In the coming years, the community remained weak and shaken by constant strife between the representatives of different towns (Veles, Kukush, Ohrid, etc.), while the school interrupted its activities several times. Voluntary Hellenization among Bulgarians remained strong and found its outward expression through clothing. Men wore trousers reaching to the knees, and short waistcoats, and used to throw over their shoulders a cloth (*choha-fermene/salmatarka*) with a red lining. Women also wore traditional Greek outfits in which, according to memoirs of the time, they looked like 'overdressed dolls' (Salgandzhiev 1906, 21).

The foundation of the Bulgarian Exarchate in 1870, which led to the official recognition of Bulgarian nationality by the Ottoman Empire, had a considerable impact on the development of the Bulgarian cause in Thessaloniki. The schism imposed by the Ecumenical Patriarchate alienated the most prominent representatives of the Bulgarian community in the city. This was the case with the Hadzhilazarou family, which had come to Thessaloniki from Vodena (Edessa) and was of Bulgarian ethnic origin. It owned large plots of land, developed successful commercial and banking activity, and was among the most respected and influential Christian families in the city. Three members of the Hadzhilazarou

66   *Yura Konstantinova*

family were among the founders of the Bulgarian community in Thessaloniki, while Yanis Hadzhilazarou even promised Methodiy Kusevich money for the construction of the Bulgarian church in the city (Snegarov 1937, 56, 84). During this period, Yanis Hadzhilazarou and his two sons Periclis and Nikolaos were Russian nationals, and their sister married the doctor of the Russian Embassy in Constantinople, V. Karakanovski.[2] The wedding ceremony, which took place in Thessaloniki in November 1872, made a 'painful' impression on the Greek community because the mass was celebrated by both an Orthodox priest of the Patriarchate and the 'schismatic' Archimandrite Ilarion of the Zographou Monastery (Stamatopoulos 1998, 90–91). It was clear that the Hadzhilazarou family for some time oscillated between the Patriarchate and the Exarchate, but it eventually made its choice in favor of the Patriarchate. There was no doubt that one of the reasons for this was the desire to maintain its position in the 'good society' of Thessaloniki (Anastasiadou 2008, 495–497).

The decision of this important family certainly deterred representatives of smaller commercial and artisan families from supporting the Exarchate and the Bulgarian idea. Indicative of their concerns was a report in the newspaper *Makedonia*, that raised the question: 'if the Bulgarian idea was something good, why didn't the Hadzhilazarev brothers, as pure Bulgarians and so intelligent ... involve themselves in this cause?' (Snegarov 1937, 95). Several decades later, at the beginning of the 20th century, Stefan Salgandzhiev wrote in his memoirs that although Yanis Hadzhilazarou from Vodena, Konstantin Gerasimov from Ohrid, and the Papa Dimitrovi brothers from Bitola still demonstrated their Bulgarian nationality, their children 'did not want to hear even a word about it' (Salgandzhiev 1906, 19). The example of the son of Yanis Hadzhilazarou, Periclis, who married an American and became the honorary U.S. consul in Thessaloniki, suggests the correctness of his observation. P. Hadzhilazarou was over the course of many years among the most prominent and wealthy members of the Greek community. In the years of armed struggle for Macedonia (1903–1908), he and the whole Hadzhilazarou family stood fully on the Greek side and proposed, as the only effective way to strengthen the Greek position, replacement of the Bulgarian population by Greeks (Karavas 2010, 135–143).

The traditional dominance of Orthodox Greeks among traders, their close ties with the political and economic elite, and their good economic position, were among the reasons Bulgarians in Thessaloniki remained under the influence of Hellenism until the early 1880s. This reality is reflected in a letter of Bulgarian Exarch Joseph to the Ministry of Foreign Affairs of the Principality of Bulgaria at the end of 1882. According to him, although Bulgarians predominated in the southern parts of Macedonia, the major and even the minor centers of the *Vilayet* of Salonika were 'entirely under the influence of the Greeks and the Grecomans', and in Thessaloniki one could count only about 200 Bulgarian families (Georgiev and Trifonov 1994, 29–33).

In parallel, however, although with some delay compared to other areas, a new commercial and entrepreneurial class developed in Thessaloniki comprised of Bulgarians originating from the urban centers of Western Macedonia.

Some representatives of this class in Thessaloniki were the families of Vesov (from Veles), Zlatarev (Kukush), Kondov (Prilep), Shavkulov (Prilep), and Hadzhimishev (Veles), who imported textiles from England and France and exported leather, tobacco, wheat, and other agricultural and animal products (*Peace* newspaper, 03.07.1937). These families gradually entered into economic competition with the Greeks and supported the Bulgarian national idea. A typical example of this category was the Bulgarian trading family of Hadzhimishev, which supported the Exarchate and later sponsored the activity of the Internal Macedonian and Adrianople Revolutionary Organization (IMARO). For this reason, in 1905, members of the Greek armed organization in Thessaloniki beat Pancho Hadzhimishev,[3] and a few years later in 1908, killed his father Todor, the then interpreter of the Russian consulate in Thessaloniki (Hadzidis and Mihailidis 2010, 131–132). As a consequence of this, the family was forced to flee to Bulgaria.

For the Bulgarians in Thessaloniki, the turning point came with the establishment of the Bulgarian state and, to a greater extent, with the decision of the Bulgarian Exarchate to open a Bulgarian high school in Thessaloniki. The undisputed geographic position of the city as 'the capital of Macedonia', its economic importance as the largest commercial port in the European *vilayets* of the Ottoman Empire, connected by road and railway networks to the other urban centers, and its administrative functions as the center of the *vilayet*, were appreciated by the activists of the Exarchate, who aimed at making the high school accessible to all students from Macedonia (Georgiev and Trifonov 1994, 34). It was also important that in the city there were representatives of the Great Powers, on whom Bulgarians could rely to protect them from the authorities (as happened in 1882 and in 1883) and to whom they wanted to show that Macedonia was inhabited by Bulgarians with a desire for education (Shapkarev 1984, 312–313).

The idea of founding a school in Thessaloniki itself belonged to a well-known activist of the Bulgarian national revival in Macedonia, Kuzman Shapkarev, supported by Naum Sprostranov, the interpreter at the Russian Consulate in Thessaloniki (Shapkarev 1984, 296–297). Originally the Exarchate opposed the idea with the argument that Bulgarian educational activity in Thessaloniki was not going well. Indeed, during the school year 1880, in the Bulgarian schools in the city there were only 60 boys and 40 girls (Snegarov 1937, 180). According to most supporters of the Exarchate, it would have been better to found a school in Bitola or Prilep. Only in the winter of 1880 did Shapkarev succeed in persuading the Exarchate to found the Bulgarian high school for the Ottoman Empire in Thessaloniki. His main argument was the city's geographic and administrative importance. The idea to make the new high school in Thessaloniki a 'stumbling block for the Greek *Megali Idea* in Macedonia' was fully in the spirit of the struggle for the formation of a Bulgarian nation, which emerged in the struggle against the Greek one (Shapkarev 1984, 305).

In the summer of 1881, the teachers of the high school began to visit the countryside and invite students. Prospective students from all over Macedonia flocked to Thessaloniki, dressed in their traditional costumes and speaking the

68   *Yura Konstantinova*

dialects typical of their home towns and villages. At the same time the *Sveto Blagoveshtenie* (Holy Annunciation) Girls' High School was founded. Most students in the two Bulgarian high schools did not come from Thessaloniki, which immediately raised the need to provide boarding houses in which they would live. This problem was solved, thanks to the Bulgarian merchant and benefactor Evlogi Georgiev, who in 1894, following the mediation of Ivan Ev. Geshov, granted the sum of 50,000 Levs for the purchase of a building for the Girls' High School and of a building to serve as the boarding house for the Girls' High School. With a donation from the Bulgarian tradesman Georgi Shopov, a Bulgarian central elementary school, St. Kliment Ohridski, acquired in 1898 its own building on 64 Ag. Sofia Str. (Geshov 1994, 109–112).

With its excellent education in humanities and science, its well-arranged rooms, and even a meteorological station, the Sts. Cyril and Methodius Boys' High School of Thessaloniki became the pride of the Bulgarian educational system. During the 33 years of its existence, it educated a total of 6,259 students, who represented various Bulgarian communities of the European *vilayets* of the Ottoman Empire.[4] Among the graduates, students from the *Vilayet* of Salonica predominated (172), followed by those from the *Vilayet* of Kosovo (143), and the *Vilayet* of Monastir/Bitola (142), but children from the *Vilayet* of Adrianople (15), and even from Bulgaria (26), completed their secondary education at the high school as well. The situation was similar in the girls' high school: 222 students from the *Vilayet* of Salonica, 195 from the *Vilayet* of Monastir, 169 from the *Vilayet* of Kosovo, 38 from the *Vilayet* of Adrianople, and 7 from Bulgaria graduated from the high school (Kandilarov 1930, 104–107, 177–178). After completing their training, the graduates of the Bulgarian high schools in Thessaloniki returned to their homelands and spread the ideas they had absorbed in Thessaloniki. They were appointed as teachers by the Exarchate which, following up on the idea of K. Shapkarev, even prior to 1879 sought to send to Macedonia Bulgarian teachers with family ties to this area (Shapkarev 1984, 298). Their natural desire to return to their homelands was encouraged by the fact that they were Ottoman subjects, a requirement for their appointment (Figure 5.1).

The divergent ideas professed by the teachers at the high school were the best evidence of the absence of a unified plan for action in Macedonia, either by the Bulgarian state or by the Exarchate. This was confirmed by the first principal of the school Bozhil Raynov, who noted that they had not received any instructions from anywhere, and private initiative had complete freedom. The goal of the high school was 'to enlighten the Bulgarian element, in order to take a worthy place among other nations' (Raynov 1934, 120–121). Many teachers and students of it, however, believed that the methods of the Exarchate were inadequate or inappropriate for that purpose. Some of them (e.g. Damyan Gruev) were concerned about the actions of the Serbs, who attracted Bulgarian students by granting scholarships to study in Belgrade, where the Serbian language was imposed on them. Others (Gyorche Petrov) believed that they could overthrow the Sultan by bombs. All those dissatisfied by the Exarchate, however, were united by the idea that education alone was insufficient and the creation of revolutionary committees in the

Figure 5.1 Teachers and students of the Bulgarian high school in 1888. (Photographer not listed, public domain. Image from the Archives of the Macedonian Scientific Institute in Sofia, used by permission)

vilayets of Salonica and Monastir was necessary, modelled after the activities of Bulgarian revolutionary organizations before the Liberation (Petrov and Bilyarski 1995, 19–20).

The revolutionary ferment at the Boys' High School was a fact since the mid-1880s, when, for the first time, students were expelled from the school for involvement in revolutionary organizations. Despite that, revolutionary activity continued, and in 1893 it was in the Bulgarian high school of Thessaloniki that the IMARO was established, which gradually brought together the other revolutionary societies. The IMARO's founders had a direct connection with the Boys' High School—either they had studied there or had worked in it (Pandev 1983, 96). Among the sponsors of the organization in this period were Thessaloniki merchants—the Hadzhimishev brothers, the Shavkulov brothers, Peter Sarafov, and others (Bilyarski 1989, 63–64).

The emergence of the IMARO was a result of growing Bulgarian national self-awareness and the overall ideological climate in the region. Only three years after the IMARO, in 1896, a division of the Young Turks' Committee of Union

70 Yura Konstantinova

and Progress was founded in Thessaloniki; in 1908 it overthrew the power of the Sultan. In the early years of the 20th century, Thessaloniki was also the center of Greek armed struggle for Macedonia and the scene of bloody clashes between the various nationalities. This allows us to define the city as a center of the 'national idea' in European Turkey. Simultaneously, anarchist and socialist ideas also found fertile soil in Thessaloniki; the Bulgarian presence in their dissemination was also important.

Suffice it to recall briefly the activity of the so-called 'Gemidzhii' ('Boatmen'), who in April 1903 carried out a series of bomb attacks against various sites in Thessaloniki, the most famous of which was the buildings of the 'Ottoman Bank' and the French ship 'Guadalquivir' (Shatev 1983; Megas 1994). These young people were strongly influenced by anarchist ideas and did not follow the advice of the IMARO, although for some period of time they had received money from the organization. The result of the bombings was disastrous for Bulgarians in Thessaloniki. According to information from Bulgarian commercial agent Atanas Shopov, the authorities killed more than a hundred people and arrested more than three hundred. These included all principals and teachers in the Bulgarian schools, four priests, 25 members of Bulgarian commercial families, 52 wealthy entrepreneurs, and many members of the artisan guilds. Most of these people had no connection with the 'Gemidzhii' or the IMARO. Some of them had even moved to Thessaloniki in order to be closer to the authorities and guarantee a safer and more comfortable life for their families. The arrests of prominent Bulgarians in the smaller towns and villages of Macedonia continued for a month after the attacks. More than 400 of them remained in the prisons of Thessaloniki for months.[5]

The presence of Bulgarian socialists in Thessaloniki was also visible. The Socialist Society appeared in the Bulgarian Boys' High School during the school year 1907/08 (Pandev 1983, 103). After the victory of the Young Turks, the socialist movement grew stronger. Among its members the following activists stood out by their ideas and deeds: Pavel Deliradev, Vasil Glavinov, Dimo Hadzhidimov, and a Jewish socialist from Vidin, Avraam Benaroya (Apostolidis et al. 1989, 39–44; Parvanov 1991, 55–70). It should be noted, however, that the Bulgarian anarchist and socialist groups in the city were most often directly or indirectly related to the IMARO, whose members were heavily influenced by the national idea. For this reason, a clear distinction between the representatives of these currents and the IMARO is difficult, and at times impossible.

The development of the Bulgarian educational institutions in Thessaloniki, together with the presence of a strong revolutionary organization, encouraged Bulgarians in the city to declare their national consciousness openly. Thus, in the first decade of the 20th century, the head of the secret Greek terrorist organization in Thessaloniki, At. Souliotis-Nikolaidis, counted 8,000 Bulgarians in the town (Souliotis-Nikolaidis 1959, 27). According to Bulgarian statistics, shortly before the Balkan Wars their number already reached about 10,000, slightly more than 8% of the population of the city (Ishirkov 1934, 12). In the first official counting of the city's population, performed by the Greek authorities in April 1913, 6,263 people declared themselves as Bulgarians.[6] In the beginning, Bulgarian families lived together with the Greeks in the neighborhood around today's Egnatia Boulevard, between the streets now called Ethniki Amina and Venizelou, i.e. mainly in the parishes of the St. Athanasios and St. Nicholas Churches (Anastasiadou 2008, 531). In the central part of the city, about 100 meters south of Egnatia Blvd., the first Bulgarian church, dedicated to Sts. Cyril and Methodius was built in today's Kapetan Patriki Str. in 1873.

In 1882, the Sts Cyril and Methodius Boys' High School acquired its own building at the St. Athanasios neighborhood. It was auctioned by its owner, Ms Mariola Vangalli. To the west the school bordered on Ag. Sofia Str., to the south on 125 Aristotelou Str. (today Olimpou Str.), to the north on Turkish houses and to the east on Evripidou Str.[7] The location of the building was assessed by the Bulgarian teachers as excellent: situated on high ground, in good sanitary condition, and quiet. It was a two-story building, with a high-ceiling basement but the rooms were dark, which rendered them inadequate for schooling purposes, the more so that they were highly insufficient for the large number of individuals willing to study at the high school (Figure 5.2).

The building of the Bulgarian community was exactly across the street. It was directly connected through a yard with the Bulgarian Primary School and the Bulgarian Girls' High School. From 1898, the Bulgarian commercial agency was housed in the same neighborhood, at the house of Dimosten Angelaki at 6 Hamidiye Blvd., modern Ethnikis Amynas. Later, in 1905, the Bulgarian government bought the villa of Osman Bey (now 36 Vasilissis Olgas Str.) to house the Bulgarian Consulate (Konstantinova 2015, 229–241) (Figure 5.3). The seat of the IMARO, the Boshnak Han, in which all meetings of the leaders of the organization

Figure 5.2 The Bulgarian Men's High School in 1888–1889. (Photographer 'G. David, Paris'; public domain: WikiCommons with date 1891)

Figure 5.3 The villa of Osman Bey at 36 Vasilissis Olgas Str., housing the Bulgarian Consulate in the early 20th c. (2014 photograph by the author)

took place, was near the Vardar Gate. As one of its visitors noted, 'if Thessaloniki is the capital of revolutionary Macedonia, the Boshnak Han is the palace where the leaders of the revolutionary ideology lived'. During the Balkan Wars, the offices of the Bulgarian National Bank and of the Bulgarian Posts were housed in Egnatia Blvd., in the building of the Grand Hotel, known as the Bulgarian Hotel.

In the eastern part of the city, by the castle wall, where the Greek Evangelistria Cemetery was located, Milosh Kalfa and Lazo Kalfa, Bulgarian carpenters from Debar, purchased a plot of land and donated it for a Bulgarian cemetery.[8] In 1900, a small stone chapel called St. Paul, one of the four Bulgarian churches in the city, was built there. It exists even today, transformed into a warehouse. North of the cemetery, the Bulgarian Military Hospital was housed in the Turkish hospital during the First Balkan War. In 1886, the Bulgarians in the city obtained permission from the authorities, and made a second cemetery near the Vardar Gate neighborhood (Megas 1994, 220–221). This was the biggest Bulgarian neighborhood in the city, known among the Bulgarians as the Kukush neighborhood because of the numerous settlers from Kukush who lived in it. The Bulgarian St. Dimitar Church was also located in this district. In its yard was a primary school. Later, during the school year 1905/1906, in the same neighborhood a second Bulgarian primary school opened. Just behind the old port, the Bulgarian High School of Commerce opened its doors in the first decade of the 20th century (Alexiev 1934, 378–394). The offices of the Bulgarian merchants and the two Bulgarian bookstores, with

Salonica through Bulgarian eyes 73

the printing houses of K. Samardzhiev and I. Hadzhinikolov, were located in the same area.[9]

The Bulgarian Catholic High School was housed north of Kukush Mahalla, in the Zeytinlik district (now Kolokotronis Str. in Stavroupoli). From the start of the Greek-Bulgarian church dispute, some Bulgarians in Thessaloniki and its surroundings adopted Catholicism in order to be emancipated from the Ecumenical Patriarchate. They chose mainly French Catholic orders, and specifically the Lazarist Order, whose curriculum did not include the Greek language. In addition to the Lazarists, some Bulgarians joined the Order of St. Jean Baptiste de la Salle, and the sisters of St. Vincent de Paul, who also offered boys' and girls' primary and secondary schools after the French model (Vanchev 1982, 98). The Bulgarian Catholic School in Thessaloniki was founded by the Lazarist Order in 1858. Several years later (1864), it moved to the Zeytinlik district, where in 1886 the building of the high school was completed. It had two departments: a general one, where the children were trained using the curriculum of the Bulgarian Boys' High School, and an artisanal one, which taught sewing, shoemaking, carpentry, cooking, and gardening. For several years, the training was conducted only in Bulgarian, using Bulgarian textbooks. Later, gradually, the French language was introduced, and Bulgarian was limited to one hour per day. The diplomas of the students of the Catholic High School were signed by the teachers, the principals, and Consul of France (Stamatov 1934, 318–326; Tapkova-Zaimova, Zaimova 2011, 420–431). In the vicinity of the high school, between 1860 and 1867, a Catholic cemetery was founded. Next to it, a war cemetery was later created for the Allied soldiers who died during the First World War. Bulgarian prisoners of war from this period were also buried in this cemetery.

Bulgarians, primarily those working in the factories of the Allatini brothers, also lived in the eastern part of the city in the neighborhoods of Pirgi and Transvaal. There were two Bulgarian primary schools there. One of them was founded in 1895–1896 close to the Greek Holy Trinity Church on 39 Andoraki Str., and the other one was the Bulgarian-American Agricultural School, founded by American Protestant missionaries. In 1908, with the voluntary contributions of Bulgarians from these two neighborhoods the construction of the St. George Church began. It remained unconsecrated before the Balkan Wars (Alexiev 1934, 389). This is today's church of St. John Chrysostom, at 55 Perdika Str.

Even in the period of greatest prosperity of the Bulgarian element in Thessaloniki, it was always outnumbered by the Jews, Muslims, and Greeks. The Bulgarian population, however, was predominant in the hinterland, and it was on this superiority that Bulgarian territorial claims relied during the Balkan Wars. 'For the Bulgarian people'—the Consul General of Bulgaria in the city, Atanas Shopov, wrote—'the localities of: Kostur, Lerin, Kaylyar, Voden and Yenice-Vardar, which are populated by a pure Bulgarian and relatively developed population, are of much greater value and importance than the city of Thessaloniki itself.' Shopov insisted that by its behavior during the years of the Macedonian Struggle, this population proved that it was Bulgarian and feared Greek vengeance if it should end up within the boundaries of the Kingdom of Greece (Shopov 1995,

74 *Yura Konstantinova*

221–222). The Bulgarian ambassador in Athens, Pancho Hadzhimishev, who had grown up in Thessaloniki and had studied at the Bulgarian Boys' High School in Thessaloniki, did not succumb to sentimentality, and was ready to accept a political solution to the question. He believed that it is better for Bulgaria to give up Thessaloniki in order to obtain Southwest Macedonia and avoid the creation of 'an irreconcilable enemy' in Greece.

In the early 20th century, Bulgaria claimed Thessaloniki not because it considered it a Bulgarian city, but because it was the capital of Macedonia, which was a major part of the Bulgarian national programme. The most emotional expression of this idea is offered by the representatives of the IMARO, who called Thessaloniki 'Macedonia's doors, or more correctly, its heart' (Gotsev 1981, 99). For them, 'Macedonia without Thessaloniki was like a corpse without a head', and the city was likened to the 'lungs of the living Macedonian body, through which it feels alive and active' (Krainichanets 1938, 39).

It should be noted, however, that Thessaloniki was not a primary target of Bulgarian political propaganda leading up to the Balkan Wars. This role was played initially by Istanbul and Edirne, and afterwards by Silistra. The focus of the Bulgarian press on these three cities reflected Bulgarian objectives during the Balkan Wars (Konstantinova 2011, 79–116). Thessaloniki was a lesser priority until the Bulgarian-Greek disputes that eventually led to the Second Balkan War. In Bulgaria, there were two views on the possible future of Thessaloniki. Most extreme and emotional were the Bulgarian politicians from Macedonia. For example, the Bulgarian ambassador in Rome, Dimitar Rizov, whose family came from Bitola, pleaded with Prime Minister Ivan Ev. Geshov not to make any compromise for the city, and if necessary, to fight for it with Greece. 'I charge you before the Bulgarian God', he wrote, 'do not make any compromise with this, even if you must leave power' (Markov 1989, 173). Although not for emotional reasons, Ferdinand also insisted that Thessaloniki should become Bulgarian.

The issue of Thessaloniki stood between the leaders of the two parties in the coalition government that ruled Bulgaria. Prime Minister Ivan Ev. Geshov believed that it was important to maintain good relations with Greece and to prevent its union with the Serbs, even if it would mean giving up Thessaloniki. The President of the National Assembly, St. Danev, opposed any compromise. He was against arbitration concerning the city because he believed that the countries of the Entente would support Greece on this issue (Markov 1989, 205).

In Bulgarian arguments concerning the city, the desire to extract real economic and political benefits was closely intertwined with emotions. Bulgarian politicians usually focused on the close economic links of Thessaloniki with its surroundings and the fact that the city would decline without it. The connection of the city with urban centers in the interior was the main argument of Bulgarian diplomats soliciting the accession of Thessaloniki to Bulgaria. In support of this argument, they pointed out the passage of the major road arteries to Thessaloniki through Bulgarian territory.[10] Public figures and politicians insisted that if Thessaloniki remained Greek it would lose two-thirds of its importance, because Bulgaria

Salonica through Bulgarian eyes 75

would be forced to make another port on the Aegean Sea, which would assume the trade with the provinces of Sofia and Kyustendil, while the city would have to satisfy itself with the markets of Thessaly and Epirus, and that would inevitably lead to its diminution (Lisichkov 1913, 26–27). This was also the opinion of Greek economists, according to whom if Greece received only the lands it had occupied until December 1912, the value of imports of goods through Thessaloniki would be reduced by 70%. They also assessed that the loss of the plain of Serres would leave cotton cultivation to Bulgaria and would deprive the industry of Thessaloniki of this raw material. These rational economic considerations were at the heart of Greece's willingness to discuss the transformation of Thessaloniki into a free-trade zone and offer concessions to Serbia and Bulgaria for trade via the city (Gounaris 1990, 138–140).

The moderate wing of Bulgarian foreign policy, represented by Shopov, was inclined to support the idea of Thessaloniki and the Halkidiki peninsula as a separate entity, a '*porto franco*', administered jointly by the Balkan states (Shopov 1995, 214–215). But the extreme elements in Bulgarian politics prevailed, declaring that if Thessaloniki remained in Greek hands it would be 'a daily casus belli, a smouldering ember ready to flare up at any moment' between Greeks and Bulgarians (*People's rights* newspaper, 02.05.1913).

Another argument that Bulgarian diplomats raised in support of the idea that Thessaloniki should remain within the boundaries of the Bulgarian state, was the purported desire of the majority of the population of the city. They therefore proposed to solve the question by plebiscite (Markov 1989, 216). This view was derived mostly from the belief that, for religious reasons and economic considerations, the Jews of Thessaloniki would prefer to see the city in Bulgarian hands. Clashes between Jews and Greeks in the city were not uncommon in previous years (Anastasiadou 2008, 560–561), while in Bulgaria at that time the Jews enjoyed full civil rights and liberties. Greek diplomats also noted the fear felt by the Jewish population, provoked by Greek Orthodox fanatics, and they were afraid that if Thessaloniki remained Greek, all Jews would leave it.[11] This fear was heightened by the raising of Bulgarian flags on Jewish houses when the Allied forces entered the city (Markov 1989, 93).

In order to strengthen the pro-Bulgarian sentiments of the Jewish community, as early as November 1912 Shopov proposed to the government to enter into an agreement with the Jewish Rabbinate of Sofia to establish contacts with some Jewish families in Thessaloniki. The idea was to send an influential person from the Jewish community of Sofia, who together with Jews from Thessaloniki would draw up a plan on how to work for the inclusion of the city within the boundaries of the Bulgarian state. Independently from the Consul, the Chief Rabbi of Sofia arrived at a similar idea and propagated it during his travel in Europe. Shopov, however, insisted that Thessalonian Jews should take the lead in the implementation of the conceived plan, and proposed to act through Mr. Salem, an experienced lawyer of Thessaloniki and a 'great authority' in the city, who had served for many years as a free legal advisor of the Bulgarian General Consulate, as well as to send Mr. Cohen, who would act among the Jewish community in the city.

76   *Yura Konstantinova*

It was the Consul's idea again to send all the Jewish officers of the Bulgarian Army to Thessaloniki in order to work for the Bulgarian cause and to strengthen pro-Bulgarian feelings among the Jewish population (Shopov 1995, 217–219). Naturally this did not remain unnoticed by Greek authorities; through the immediate intervention of foreign minister L. Koromilas and personally of Prime Minister Eleftherios Venizelos, Greek soldiers of Jewish origin were also sent to Thessaloniki to try to balance the Bulgarian influence.[12]

It was chiefly during the interwar period that the romantic aura developed and Thessaloniki began to be perceived by the public as Bulgarian. This image of Thessaloniki was created mostly by Bulgarians who left their homelands in Macedonia and found refuge within the Bulgarian state. The life path of many of them was connected with the Bulgarian schools of Thessaloniki; others had been taught by graduates of these schools, and a third group had been members of the IMARO. For them, their families, and friends, Thessaloniki remained the capital of Macedonia, the city of their youth, their dreams, and longings. For Bulgarians of Macedonia, Thessaloniki was a beacon illuminating their path, and its loss was experienced as a deep emotional trauma.

Bulgarian emotions concerning Thessaloniki were best described in the classic novel by Dimitar Dimov, *Tobacco*. For Kostov, the main protagonist in the book, who had studied in Thessaloniki, the most vivid memory was the one of the 'strange excitement' the Macedonian revolutionaries awakened in his soul when they planted their bombs. There follows the euphoria of speechifying in the 1908 revolution for socialism, equality, and justice. Last but not least is his memory of love, embodied in the well-educated and beautiful Greek girl he then wanted to marry. D. Dimov describes these memories as 'wonderful and bittersweet' (Dimov 1967, 233).

Notes

1 This paper was supported by the Bulgarian Ministry of Education and Science under the Cultural Heritage, National Memory and Social Development National Research Program.

2 Dr. Vasil Karakanovski (1804–1905) was born in Lovech, studied medicine in Russia, and was a close friend of Count Ignatiev. In 1878, he was a member of the Bulgarian Constituent Assembly, and later was a member of the delegation that brought Prince Battenberg to Bulgaria.

3 Historical and diplomatic archives of the Ministry of Foreign Affairs, Greece [ΙΔΑΥΕ 1905, В. α.α.κ, φάκελος 90, υποφάκελος 4, L. Koromilas report from Thessaloniki to the Ministry of Foreign Affairs in Athens, No. 250 of 11.08.1905].

4 TsDA, fond 334k, inv. 1, a.u. 13, fol. 1-34 [ЦДА, фонд 334к, оп. 1, а.е. 13, л. 1-34]. See the list of graduates from the school in Kandilarov, 1930.

5 Bilyarski, www.sitebulgarizaedno.com/index.php?option=com_content&view=article &id=414:2012–05–03–08–02–41&catid=29:2010–04–24–09–14–13&Itemid=61

6 Historical Archives of Macedonia, Greece, [Ιστορικό Αρχείο Μακεδονίας, ΓΔΜ, φάκελος 27β, 1].

7 TsDA, fond 719k, inv. 14, a.u. 408 [ЦДА фонд 719к, оп. 14, а.е. 408].

8 Salgandzhiev does not mention the year in which the first Bulgarian cemetery was created, but from his memoirs it can be concluded that this happened before he left

Salonica through Bulgarian eyes   77

Thessaloniki for Serres in 1871. According to Greek sources, the cemetery was established in 1882, although Bulgarians had started burying their dead there since the end of the 18th century. Probably the plot for a separate Bulgarian cemetery was purchased in the beginning of the 1870s, while the official permission for its opening was given in the 1890s, since the first permission for an Orthodox cemetery in the city was given only in 1875. See: Salgandzhiev 1906, 21, Megas 1994, 219–220.

9 The first Bulgarian bookshop in Thessaloniki was opened in 1873 by Dragan Manchov from Batak, and existed until 1876 when it was closed since it distributed free school books, and as a result suffered losses. Six years later the bookshop of Kone Samardzhiev opened. For more details see: Ilieva 2000, 373–387.

10 TsDA, fond 176k, inv. 2, a.u. 1195, fol. 253 [ЦДА, фонд 176к, оп. 2, а.е. 1195, л. 253].

11 Historical and diplomatic archives of the Ministry of Foreign Affairs, Greece [ΙΔΑΥΕ 1913, φάκελος 22, υποφάκελος 4, P. Panas to L. Koromilas No. 834 of 03.04.1913].

12 Historical and diplomatic archives of the Ministry of Foreign Affairs, Greece [ΙΔΑΥΕ 1913, φάκελος 22, υποφάκελος 4, L. Koromilas to the Ministry of War No. 5594 of 23.02.1913].

References

Archives

Central State Archive, Bulgaria (TsDA)
Historical and diplomatic archives of the Ministry of Foreign Affairs, Greece (ΙΔΑΥΕ)
Historical Archives of Macedonia, Greece, [Ιστορικό Αρχείο Μακεδονίας]

Newspapers

Flag [*Знаме*], Sofia: People's Party 1897, 05.02.
Peace [*Мир*], Sofia: People's Party 1937, 03.07.
People's rights [*Народни права*], Sofia: Liberal Party 1913, 02.05

Books and periodicals

Alexiev, V. [Васил Алексиев], Бележки върху българските просветни учреждения в Солун [Notes on the Bulgarian educational institutions in Thessaloniki notes on the Bulgarian educational institutions in Thessaloniki]. In: Сборник Солун. *Издание на възпитателите и възпитаниците от солунските български гимназии* [Corpus Thessaloniki. Issue of teachers and students in the Bulgarian high schools in Thessaloniki], Sofia: Hudoznik, (1934).

Anastasiadou, M. [Μερόπη Αναστασιάδου], *Θεσσαλονίκη 1830–1912. Μια μητρόπολη της εποχή των Οθωμανικών μεταρρυθμίσεων* [Thessaloniki 1830–1912. A Metropolis of the Era of Ottoman Reforms], Athens: Estia (2008).

Antov, H. [Христо Антов], Първата българска печатница в Солун [The first Bulgarian printhouse in Thessaloniki]. In: Сборник Солун. *Издание на възпитателите и възпитаниците от солунските български гимназии* [Corpus Thessaloniki. Issue of teachers and students in the Bulgarian high schools in Thessaloniki], Sofia: Hudoznik (1934).

Apostolidis, A., Dankas, A., and Papadopoulos, K. [Άκης Αποστολίδης, Αλέκος Δάγκας, Κώστας Παπαδόπουλος], *Η σοσιαλιστική οργάνωση 'Φεντερασιόν' Θεσσαλονίκης,*

78 Yura Konstantinova

1909–1918. Ζητήματα γύρω από την δράση της [The socialist organization 'Fédéracion' of Thessaloniki, 1909–1918. Issues surrounding its action], Athens: Sinhroni Epohi, (1989).

Bilyarski, Ts. [Цочо Билярски], *Ползите и вредите от солунските атентати* [The benefits and the damages of the Thessaloniki attacks]. www.sitebulgarizaedn o.com/index.php?option=com_content&view=article&id=414:2012–05–03–08–02–41&catid=29:2010–04–24–09–14–13&Itemid=61.

Bilyarski, Ts. (ed.) [Цочо Билярски, съст.], *Др Христо Татарчев—спомени, документи, материали* [Dr. Hristo Tatarchev – memoirs, documents, materials], Sofia: Nauka I Izkustvp (1989).

Dimov, D. [Димитър Димов], *Тютюн* [Tobacco]. In: *Събрани съчинения* [Collected works], vol. 4, Sofia: Bulgarski Pisatel (1967).

Dinchev, K. [Костадин Динчев], *Юнаци, още комити. Легенди и предания* [Heroes, even rebels. Legends and stories], Sofia: Orbel (1993).

Georgiev, V. and Trifonov, St. [Величко Георгиев, Стайко Трифонов], *Българите в Македония и Тракия 1879–1912. In: Нови документи. Екзарх Български Йосиф I. Писма и доклади* [The Bulgarians in Macedonia and Thrace 1879–1912. New documents. Exarch Bulgarian Joseph I. Letters and reports], Sofia: Club 90 (1994).

Geshov, I. [Иван Гешов], *Лична кореспонденция* [Personal correspondence], (Съст.) Радослав Попов, Василка Танкова [Ed. Radoslav Popov, Basilka Tankova], Sofia: BAN (1994).

Gotsev, D. [Димитър Гоцев], *Национално-освободителната борба в Македония 1912–1915* [National Liberation struggle in Macedonia 1912–1915], Sofia: BAN (1981).

Gounaris, B. [Βασίλης Γούναρης], Η οικονομική ζωή στη Μακεδονία πριν από τη υπογραφή της Συνθήκης του Βουκουρεστίου [The economic life in Macedonia before the signing of the Treaty of Bucharest]. In: Gounaris, V. (ed.), *Η Συνθήκη του Βουκουρεστίου και η Ελλάδα. Συμπόσιο 75 χρόνια από την απελευθέρωση της Μακεδονίας, Θεσσαλονίκη, 16–18 Νοεμβρίου 1988* [The treaty of Bucharest and Greece. Symposium 75 years from the liberation of Macedonia. Thessaloniki 16–18 November 1988], Thessaloniki: Institute for Balkan Studies (1990).

Hadzidis, A. and Mihailidis, Y. [Άγγελος Χατζίδης, Ιάκωβος Μιχαηλίδης], «Μαύρη ζωή την έκαναν κι αυτοί»: Θύτες και θύματα στην ελληνική Μακεδονία (1901–1912) ['They made life black': Victimizers and victims in Greek Macedonia (1901–1912)]. In: Gounaris, V., Stefanidis, I., Kalyvas, S. (eds), *Ανορθόδοξοί πόλεμοι: Μακεδονία, Εμφύλιος, Κύπρος* [Un-Orthodox wars: Macedonia, Civil War, Cyprus], Thessaloniki: Patakis, (2010).

Ilieva, A. [Ана Илиева], *Първата българска книжарница в Солун* [The first Bulgarian bookshop in Thessaloniki]. In: *Θεσσαλονίκη και Φιλιππούπολη σε παράλληλους δρόμους. Ιστορία, τέχνη, κοινωνία 18ος–20ός αιώνας* [Thessaloniki and Plovdiv on parallel roads. History, art, society 18th–20th century], Thessaloniki: Northern Greece Entrepreneurs Cultural Society (2000).

Ishirkov, A. [Атастас Иширков], 'Град Солун. Географски чертици' [City Thessaloniki. Geographical markers]. In: Сборник Солун. *Издание на възпитателите и възпитаниците от солунските български гимназии* [Corpus Thessaloniki. Issue of teachers and students in the Bulgarian high schools in Thessaloniki], Sofia: Hudoznik (1934).

Kandilarov, G. [Георги Кандиларов], *Българските гимназии и основни училища в Солун* [Bulgarian high schools and primary schools in Thessaloniki], Sofia: P. Glushkov (1930).

Salonica through Bulgarian eyes 79

Karavas, S. [Σπύρος Καράβας], 'Μακάριοι οι κατέχοντες την γην.' Γαιοκτητικοί σχεδιασμοί προς απαλλοτρίωση συνειδήσεων στη Μακεδονία (1880–1909) ['Blessed are the possessors of the earth.' Master planning to expropriate consciences in Macedonia (1880–1909)], Athens: Vivliorama (2010).

Kaychev, N. [Наум Кайчев], Македонийо, възжелана. Армията, училището и градежът на нацията в Сърбия и България (1878–1912) [Macedonian, wished. The army, the school and the structure of the Nation in Serbia and Bulgaria (1878–1912)], Sofia: Paradigma (2006).

Konstantinova, Y. Political Propaganda in Bulgaria during the Balkan Wars, Etudes balkaniques 2–3 (2011), 79–116.

Konstantinova, Y. The un/believable story of a Salonica building, Etudes Balkaniques 1 (2015), 229–241.

Krainichanets T. [Тодор Крайничанец], Солун като икономически и културно-просветен център на Македония [Thessaloniki as the economic, cultural and educational center of Macedonia], Sofia (1938).

Lisichkov, I. [Иван Лисичков], Как и защо се предаде Солун? (Според сведенията на чуждите военни кореспонденти и рапорта на ген. Тодоров) [How and why is Thessaloniki delivered? (According to reports by foreign military correspondents and the report of Gen. Todorov], Shumen (1913).

Markov, G. [Георги Марков], България в Балканския съюз срещу Османската империя 1912–1913 [Bulgaria in the Balkan Union against the Ottoman Empire 1912–1913], Sofia: Nauka I Izkustvo (1989).

Mazower, M., Salonica, City of Ghosts: Christians, Muslims and Jews, 1430–1950, London: HarperCollins (2004)

Megas, Y. [Γιάννης Μέγας], «Βαρκάριδες» της Θεσσαλονίκης. Η αναρχική βουλγαρική ομάδα και οι βομβιστικές ενεργές του 1903 ['Barkarides' of Thessaloniki. The Anarchist Bulgarian group and the bombing attacks in 1903], Thessaloniki: Trohalia (1994).

Moskof, K. [Κωστής Μόσκωφ], Θεσσαλονίκη 1700–1912. Τομή της μεταπρατικής πόλης [Thessaloniki 1700–1912. Cross section of a retail city], Athens: Stohastis (1974).

Pandev, K. [Константин Пандев], Солунската гимназия и националноосвободителното движение в Македония и Одринско [The Thessaloniki High School and the national liberation movement in Macedonia and the Adrianopol Region]. In: Светилник [Candlestick], съст. Йордан Ванчев [ed. Iordan Vanchev], Sofia: Narodno obrazovanie (1983).

Papastathis, Ch. [Χαράλαμπος Παπαστάθης], 'Τα πρώτα ελληνικά τυπογραφεία της Θεσσαλονίκης' [The first Greek printing houses in Thessaloniki], Μακεδονικά 8 (1968), 239–256.

Parvanov, G. [Георги Първанов], Димо Хаджидимов и националноосвободителното движение (края на XIX век–1912 г.) [Dimo Hadzhidimov and the national liberation movement (late 19th–1912)], Исторически Преглед [Historical Review XLVII (1991), 55–70.

Petrov, T. and Bilyarski, Ts. (eds.) [Тодор Петров, Цочо Билярски, съст.], ВМОРО през погледа на своите основатели. Спомени на Д. Груев, Х. Татарчев, И. Хаджиниколов, А. Димитров, П. Попарсов [IMARO through the eyes of its founders. Memoires of D. Gruev, H. Tatarchev, I. Hadjinikolov, A. Dimitrov, P. Poparsov], Sofia, (1995).

Raynov, B. [Божил Райнов], Две години в Солун [Two years in Thessaloniki]. In: [Sbornik Solun] Сборник Солун. Издание на възпитателите и възпитаниците от

80   Yura Konstantinova

солунските български гимназии [Corpus Thessaloniki. Issue of teachers and students in the Bulgarian high schools in Thessaloniki], Sofia: Hudoznik (1934).

Salgandzhiev, S. [Стефан Салгънджиев], *Лични дела и спомени по възраждането на солунските и серски българи или 12-годишна жестока и неравна борба с гръцката пропаганда* [Personal affairs and memoirs of the revival of the Bulgarians in Thessaloniki and Serres or 12 years of cruel and unequal fight against Greek propaganda]. Plovdiv: Trud (1906).

Shapkarev, K. [Кузман Шапкарев], *За възраждането на българщината в Македония. Неиздадени записки и писма* [About the Bulgarian revival in Macedonia. Unpublished notes and letters], Sofia: Balgarski pisatel (1984)

Shatev, P. [Павел Шатев], *В Македония под робство. Солунското съзаклятие (1903), подготовка и изпълнение* [In Macedonia under slavery. The Thessaloniki Conspiracy (1903), preparation and execution], Sofia: Patriotičen Front (1983).

Shopov, A. [Атанас Шопов], *Дневник, дипломатически рапорти и писма* [Diary, diplomatic reports and letters], Sofia (1995).

Snegarov I. [Иван Снегаров], *Солун в българската духовна култура: историче ски очерк и документи* [Thessaloniki in Bulgarian spiritual culture: History and documents], Sofia: Pridvorna Pečatnica (1937).

Souliotis-Nikolaidis, A. [Αθανάσιος Σουλιώτης – Νικολαΐδης], *Ο Μακεδονικός αγών. Η «Οργάνωση Θεσσαλονίκης» 1906–1908. Απομνημονεύματα* [The Macedonian struggle. The 'Organization of Thessaloniki' 1906–1908. Memoirs], Thessaloniki (1959).

Stamatopoulos, D. [Δημήτριος Σταματόπουλος], *Εθνικοί ανταγωνισμοί και κοινοτική ανασυγκρότηση: η ενδοκοινοτική σύγκρουση στη Θεσσαλονίκη (1872–1874) και η σύνταξη του πρώτου κοινοτικού κανονισμού»* [National competitions and community reconstruction: the intra-communal conflict in Thessaloniki (1872–1874) and the drafting of the first Community Regulation]. *Βαλκανικά Σύμμεικτα* , Vol. 10 (1998), 49–96.

Stamatov, I. [Йероним Стамов], 'Зейтинлъка в Солун' [Zeytinlik in Thessaloniki]. In: *[Sbornik Solun] Сборник Солун. Издание на възпитателите и възпитаниците от солунските български гимназии* [Corpus Thessaloniki. Issue of teachers and students in the Bulgarian high schools in Thessaloniki], Sofia: Hudoznik (1934).

Tapkova-Zaimova, V. and Zaimova, R. [Василка Тъпкова-Заимова, Рая Заимова], Историята на една учителска фамилия в Македония [The history of a teacher's family in Macedonia]. In: Grebenarov, A. (ed), *Гласовете ви чувам. Личностите на гимназията и България. Доклади и съобщения от национална научна конфе ренция Благоевград, 29–30 април 2010 г.* [I hear your voices. The persons of the high school and Bulgaria. Reports and Communications from the National Scientific Conference Blagoevgrad, 29–30 April 2010], Blagoevgrad (2011).

Vanchev I. [Йордан Ванчев], *Новобългарската просвета в Македония през Възраждането до Сгодина* [Bulgarian Education in Macedonia from the Renaissance until 1878], Sofia: Nauka I Izkustvo (1982).

Yaranov, A. [Атанас Яранов], Солун като стопанско средище [Thessaloniki as an economic center]. In: *Sbornik Solun Сборник Солун. Издание на възпитателите и възпитаниците от солунските български гимназии* [Corpus Thessaloniki. Issue of teachers and students in the Bulgarian high schools in Thessaloniki], Sofia: Hudoznik (1934).

6 The municipality of Salonica between old regime, Ottoman reforms, and the transition from empire to nation state

Nora Lafi

Introduction

The history of Thessaloniki-Salonica-Selânîk is now well-documented. Many aspects of urban life during the last decades of the Ottoman Empire and during the transition to Greek sovereignty have been explored; the image we have of the history of the city is now much more nuanced than it was a few decades ago. Its historiography, however, remains splintered among different disciplines without a common sphere of questions and scholarly dialogue: the history of Thessaloniki's Jews, general history of the Ottoman Empire (e.g. Hall 2002), national struggles in the region, and local history of the city's integration into the Greek kingdom. These fields have evolved during recent decades, but not necessarily converged. It is partly an issue of competences, with historians working on different periods using archival and other resources of different nature and languages. But it is also a question linked to the sociological *milieu* of historians, with a diversity of points of view. The historiography of Thessaloniki remains highly ideological, with different traditions corresponding to different interpretations of history. Even if the era of national historiographies is now largely over, or at least the object of critical re-examination, history writing about and on Thessaloniki is far from being the object of consensus. Divergent views on the Ottoman period, for example, continue to characterize the city's narratives.

The context, however, is favorable for a fresh discussion: on the one side, Greek nationalist narratives are now much more nuanced, and on the other side, studies on cosmopolitan Salonica and the Ottoman reforms of the last third of the 19th century have changed our vision of the late Ottoman period. In this article, I try, by studying urban governance and municipal institutions, to propose a new reading of the municipality under its late Ottoman form and to propose alternative interpretations to the still widely accepted opposition between empire and nation state. The main argument is that from the 16th century if not before, up until the 19th century, Thessaloniki's 'old-regime' form of urban government was more complex than often described, and this system was reformed during the second half of the 19th century, when the municipality became an instrument for promoting an Ottoman modernity. I argue that this Ottoman municipal modernity was consistent and coherent, in spite of its limits, and that a re-evaluation

82 *Nora Lafi*

of this feature is necessary for a correct interpretation of the passage to Greek sovereignty.

Cosmopolitan Salonica and Ottoman governance: an 'ancien régime' municipal system

Thessaloniki was characterized since antiquity by the diversity of its population and numerous changes in its composition. This diversity was not simply a juxtaposition of communities under a more or less external imperial element. In light of recent progress in Ottoman urban history, specifically in the field of local governance, it is possible to propose alternative interpretations based upon a new reading of the relationship between cities and the central power in Istanbul (Lafi 2011a; Barkey 2008). This in turn becomes an invitation to re-examine the nature of the Ottoman Empire itself (Lafi 2011, 73–82).

Salonica under Ottoman rule was the object of the progressive construction of a bureaucratic and ideological apparatus that can be called the Ottoman urban *ancien régime*. Its diversity was not only a demographic datum but also the object of political construction through the participation of different collective bodies in a general urban system of governance. "Minorities" were granted a certain access to the civic sphere, in spite of limitations pertaining to the very nature of this old regime.

The Ottoman municipal reforms of the years 1850–1890 cannot be read accurately without a re-reading of the previous system. Modernity was introduced as the reform of an existing order facing new challenges, not as the importation into a local vacuum of solutions inspired from abroad. This has been illustrated for numerous Ottoman cities, from Beirut to Tunis, Edirne to Baghdad, and Aleppo to Jerusalem. Salonica, with its local specificities, followed a similar path.

Salonica had in old-regime times a key particularity as one of the very few cities in the Empire with a Jewish "majority" or dominant "minority" (Mazower 2006); Jews had been present in the city since Antiquity. The Romaniote presence during the Byzantine Empire was consistent. Notwithstanding inferences made from the 1478 Ottoman census, which does not mention Jews, it is quite obvious that there were Jews in the city during the first Ottoman period, even before the massive Jewish immigration from Spain (Ben-Naeh 2008, 503). When that happened, the Jewish population of Salonica, like that of Tunis, Algiers, and Tripoli, grew rapidly, bringing new cultural patterns into the city, for example the influence of medieval Arabic governance of diversity as experienced in al-Andalus. The new Jewish immigrants also brought in new commercial networks and professional skills, of which the local guild took great profit.

Among the Jews of Salonica, there were both Sephardim and populations of Eastern European origin (see Benbassa 2002; Levy 1992; Smuelevitz 1984; Olson 1979, 75–88; Franco 1897). This Jewish element was part of the construction of the old-regime Ottoman balance in the governance of diversity: immigration was favored and Jewish communities were seen by imperial authorities as elements promoting loyalty to the Empire (Inalcik 2002). This has long been interpreted as

Salonica: old regime, reforms, transition   83

an anti-Greek move: bringing new population into a recently conquered city was an element of the Ottoman strategy of urban control and domination. But it was also something more complex, pertaining to imperial equilibriums at the scale of both the Empire and the city: between forced migrations and implicit invitations to migrate, many cities of the Empire in old-regime times were subject to population changes. Such changes must not be interpreted in the light of similar events in the early 20th century, when ethnic homogenization was a response to new ideologies.

In the 16th century, about half of Salonica's population was Jewish. Each Jewish community had its own council (*cemaat*) (Kolçak 2005, 133). Each Christian community was also granted the right to have communal institutions. The old-regime Ottoman urban system integrated such communal institutions into urban governance, delegating to them a number of competences.

Communal institutions and the Empire were much more entangled than what has long been thought. The organization of the Jewish communities has been extensively studied, its articulation with the Ottoman imperial sphere less so. In the Empire, communities were granted a certain degree of autonomy, and many urban issues were dealt with at this scale. Communal governance was in no way only religious: it was an element of an old-regime municipal system, along with other elements such as neighborhoods and guilds. Communities were also part of the collective body of the city, and the articulation between this collective body and confessional institutions and assemblies is at the heart of the Ottoman urban form of cosmopolitanism: a system of governance that did not organize equality, a notion extraneous to old-regime political thought, but managed diversity and integrated it into the imperial sphere. Notables from all communities took part in the city council: Muslims in their own name as heads of notable families, Jews and Christians as heads of their relative *cemaat*, in the collective name of their relative communities.

This Ottoman old-regime form of political municipal cosmopolitanism is to be seen in the archives, when for example notables from diverse confessions signed a petition together (BOA, Shikayet, ADVN). The city was in no way a juxtaposition of communities held together only by an imperial governor and a military caste of Janissaries extraneous to urban society, but was also a collective body with a rich civic life, the relevance of which was not only at the level of confessional communities. Guilds, which could be multi-confessional, also had a crucial importance in urban governance.

Reading old-regime Salonica under this perspective allows one to set aside culturalist visions of the city, and to interpret its imperial identity in a different way. It was indeed more a negotiated balance between local notables and the center than just the presence in the city of extraneous elements representing the Empire. Streets and quarters had their urban institutions, and there was above them a general urban assembly of notables, which was the interlocutor of the imperial governor. The imperial and local dimensions were intimately entangled, and local notables, mostly merchants, were part of imperial networks. Their activities spanned the scale of the whole Empire. The main specificities of this

84   *Nora Lafi*

Salonica form of Ottoman old-regime cosmopolitanism were linked to the diversity within each community (Jewish and Christian, but also Muslim) and to the fact that confessions and ethnic origins did not necessarily match: the identity map was much more complex than the simplistic picture imposed by 19th- and 20th-century nationalisms.

Identity had nuances. Salonica's specificity was also linked to the fact that Muslims were not a "majority". The articulation between communal institutions and civic institutions at the scale of the city was reformed different times, for example after the creation of the Talmud Torah Hagadol, in 1520, which headed all Jewish communities. In the 17th century, different reforms of the Ottoman old-regime organization were also promoted, resulting each time in a renegotiation of local features with urban notables. The question of Sabbatai Zevi's followers also added to the complexity of the situation. The conversion to Islam in 1686 of many Thessaloniki notables following this episode has to be interpreted in the framework of the relationship between local governance and imperial structures. Many converted in order to escape Jewish communal justice (Gion 1998, 185–209). The *Dönme* community that resulted from this conversion also has to be interpreted in the framework of old-regime relationships between the Empire and communal organizations (Baer 2010). The balance between communities constituted a kind of imperial Ottoman *Pax Urbana* and even embodied the very nature of this empire. This equilibrium was challenged, however, at the turn of the 19th century, with important consequences for municipal institutions.

The 1826 revolt of the Janissaries, which resulted in months and even years of unrest in the city, should be analyzed in this context of intertwined scales of conflict at the imperial level and local rivalries (Üstün 2002, 103). The episode must be viewed in the context of the revolts of this kind that various cities of the Empire experienced. In Thessaloniki, 1826 can be seen as the beginning of the end of the old-regime balance of urban faction and communities in relationship to an imperial framework that included, among other things, special prerogatives for groups like the Janissaries. Local historiographies tend to analyze such events mainly in the light of local factors. But there seems to be a relative convergence between such events at the scale of the Empire which might reveal a moment of change in the very organization and logic of it and in the relationship between local elites (and their bodies of urban governance) and the Empire. The Empire and the city were linked not by a dichotomy but instead by complex mutual entanglements.

During the first half of the 19th century, various migration waves and the first manifestations of modern forms of nationalism began to challenge the traditional balance between communities. There is of course the context created by Greek independence. But Salonica also became during these decades a nest for diverse forms of nationalism as a challenge to the Ottoman *Pax Urbana* and the old-regime municipal system. Geopolitical issues had consequences for urban life, down to the scale of the neighborhood, street, and even family. Every wave of migration, e.g. of Roma, was also a challenge to the communal balance and to their representation within old-regime forms of municipal institutions (Ginio 2004, 117). Salonica, moreover, was to be for the next decades a city situated in a region of

Salonica: old regime, reforms, transition 85

wars and battles, with here again entanglements of scales between locality and Balkan geopolitics and with the direct impact of war on the city with the arrival of numerous refugees from the Balkans (Şimşir 1968). Ottoman municipal reforms have to be analyzed in this context, just as those in Tripoli of Libya or in Tunis have to be analyzed in the context of French colonial occupation of Algeria: geopolitics had a strong impact on urban politics and on the very organization of the Empire. In cities of the Empire, the municipal reforms were an imperial response to new threats to local equilibriums and indeed to the Ottoman character of the cities, and first took the form of a negotiation with local notables for the passage of their old-regime municipal prerogatives into a new institutional framework.

The municipality of Salonica in the era of the Ottoman reforms

This local process has to be interpreted in the context of what happened at the scale of the whole Empire (Lafi 2005). If Salonica was one of the seven test cities for the implementation of the municipal reforms, with cities like Tunis, Jerusalem, or Damascus, it is precisely because the stakes there were high for the Empire. It was not necessarily because the local population was thought to be, by nature, more prone to understanding modernity than that of other cities, as has long been asserted about the municipal experiment in the Pera neighborhood of Istanbul, but rather because Salonica was one of the most important cities in the Empire and potentially the object of anti-Ottoman intrigues.

The era of municipal reforms in Salonica is generally interpreted according to a top-down logic, with the Empire sending modernist governors to the city in order to enact a modernization programme whose inspiration is seen as foreign. Modernization is often described as a movement of westernization, or Europeanization. Though foreign inspiration and imported expertise were important, interpretations of this era need to be nuanced. The reform programme was made of both institutional reforms and public works. If historiography now acknowledges the reality and consistence of the Ottoman urban modernization effort in Salonica between 1850 and 1910, the local urban dimension of it is often neglected, as well as aspects pertaining to the definition of a new form of Ottoman imperiality in the city.

The question of Ottoman modernity in Salonica deserves to be inserted into a wider framework of interpretation. The symbol of the opening of this period is the 1858 visit of the Sultan Abdülmecid. At the end of that year, a decree created a new municipal institution, with a mayor and a municipal council (BOA, A.}MKT. MHHM 430 20 1285 N 04 [19.12.1868]). Historiography has also underlined the role of Sabri Pasha, starting in 1869.

The installation of the reformed municipality happened in this context of special imperial attention, but does not imply a uniquely top-down process. Local notables were part of the negotiation during all phases, with episodes of conflict and negotiation. The Ottoman imperial pact with local elites, e.g. Jewish notables, was renewed (Cooperman 1991). The birth of the Ottoman reformed municipality is often interpreted in the context of a certain underestimation of

86 *Nora Lafi*

what existed before. Meropi Anastassiadou, for example, states that before the reforms, 'there was no municipal body, nor any will of global governance of urban affairs. Administration was atomized and its only aim was to ensure peace, combat injustices, and provide for the regular collection of taxes' (Anastassiadou 1997, 137).

This is a paradox: ensuring civic peace, social justice, and fiscal efficiency is already a huge achievement for something which is not even an administration. And appreciations have to be revised about it. Reforms, indeed, were reforms, and not the creation of something new in an institutional vacuum. The reforms, in Salonica and other Ottoman cities, were implemented in the context of the existence of a strong old-regime urban administration. The authority of local notables was reinforced, just like their control over the urban territory through neighborhood institutions. The communal organizations of the various confessional communities remained important (Rodrigue and Abrevaya Stein 2012). The council of the notables and elders was formalized in a new way, that of a municipal council, on the same social and functional basis. The 1869 creation of the modern municipality, a few weeks after the 1868 decree, is only the consecration of two decades of reforms and the result of a long negotiation with local notables (Ergin 1995). It was not the importation into an empty shell of a foreign inspiration. As for the modernization programme, a new reading of the relationship between mayor and governors is necessary. Of course, the new municipality had to struggle from the very beginning for its financial independence, and archives in Istanbul show that most correspondence between the mayor and the ministry was about the insufficient budget allocated to the institution and about the limits on its capacity to collect taxes.[1] But the municipality, beyond this matter of fact, was the expression of a dynamic civic life, the nature of which had been deeply modernized. The 1877 imperial law on municipalities also provided partial answers to the early limitations.[2] The situation in 1880 or 1890 should not be analyzed only in terms of the tensions at the turn of the 20th century.

A modernization programme, generally interpreted as directed by governors, transformed the city space, with for example the destruction of the city walls during the 1870s (municipal engineer Wernieski's plans of the walled city date back to this period), with the construction in 1870 of the promenade on the seafront of the avenue Sabri Pasha (today Venizelou) and of Midhat Pasha Street (Agiou Dimitriou).[3] The 1871 railroad station and the 1875 Municipal Hospital are also symbols of this great programme of public works, just like the modernization of the harbor during the 1880s and the opening at the end of this decade of the first tramway line.

There is a necessity today to interpret this considerable effort of modernization, comparable to what happened in Beirut, in the context of the reform of local governance, and not only as external imperial impulses being applied to the city with recourse to foreign expertise. The central archives of the Ottoman Empire in Istanbul, where numerous documents about the municipality of Salonica are kept, show that the functioning of this institution was, between the 1870s and the Balkan Wars, that of a modern municipality.[4]

Salonica: old regime, reforms, transition 87

The career of engineer Wernieski (also known as Vrenski in Ottoman documents) is an invitation to revise views on this process. Wernieski supervised the preparation of a map of the city by the municipal technical services (BOA, Y..MTV.2972 1305 R 09 [3.1.1888]). These technical services launched a process of modern town planning, in which municipal engineers, in connection with landowners and investors, were very active.[5] During the last decades of Ottoman rule, this trend was reinforced, the municipal services facilitating investment in new neighborhoods by investors often belonging to the Christian and Jewish communities (Yerolympos 1988, 141–166).

This observation applies more generally to the role of foreign technical expertise and investment. Salonica, just like all major Ottoman cities, benefited from the work of the best engineers on the European and Mediterranean market, a fact which is not a sign of submission to an external order but rather of insertion into dynamic networks. The concession system chosen for the implementation of the modernization programme of numerous public services has to be interpreted according to a similar logic. It was accompanied by the growth of the municipal technical apparatus. The position of municipal engineer in Salonica was very attractive on the international market of expertise.

In the case of water, for example, the 1888 concession to a Belgian firm and to the investor Nemli-Zade Effendi Chamdi, under the name of *Compagnie Ottomane des Eaux de Thessalonique*, was a sign of the close relationship between local interest, municipal civic conscience, European capitalism, and imperial logic. The work of the engineer Campion is to be read in this context. Public fountains were built in all major streets of the city, just like in all Ottoman cities, and were a sign of the civic and social dimension of the modernization programme. They were also a sign of the imperial pact with local elites. Municipal engineers in Salonica were very active, and were also inserted into the Ottoman network of municipal connections, with other cities of the Empire.

A new interpretation of this period is emerging: it was not necessarily a westernization, but a true Ottoman modernization. Many new neighborhoods were built, and the age of Ottoman reforms was a period of strong urban dynamism for the city. Entrepreneurs, often belonging to the Christian and Jewish parts of the population, benefited from the new political and regulatory context (old limitations on land ownership by Christians and Jews outside the walls or former walls were lifted) to launch ambitious urban projects. Alexandra Yerolympos illustrated how the municipal technical services were key in planning the extension of the city outside of its traditional limits, with a plan from 1879 and with the municipal acceptance of the 1889 planning initiative by the former municipal engineer Achille Campanakis (Yerolympos 2005, 113–142). The planning of a neighborhood of social housing for the Jewish community after the 1890 fire was made in close collaboration with the planning services of the municipality. The public/municipal, communal, and the private spheres were linked. The common point was that they were all controlled by the same *milieu* of notables.

The achievements of mayor Ahmed Hamdi Bey (1893–1895 and 1901–1907), a rich *Dönme* merchant and landowner, also have to be reinterpreted: he was a

88   *Nora Lafi*

typical figure of Ottoman modernity, with strong roots in the old-regime past of the city. Both Young Turks and Greeks later diminished his importance, but the fact is that the *fin de siècle* Ottoman municipality was an efficient instrument in the hands of local notables working in the framework of a highly imperial ideology of reinvention of the imperial pact with local elites. Not only governors acted for modernization; local society was highly involved, while the central government was not inactive.[6]

Architecture is also a symbol of this complexity of the late Ottoman period. The embodiment of architectural modernity in Salonica was a Sicilian architect sent by the Ottoman government. This was a typical Ottoman practice, that happened in dozens of other Ottoman cities. In the same way, Greek architects were active in many cities of the Empire (Colonas 2005, 155). Once in Thessaloniki, Vitaliano Poselli also worked with and for local elites. He was born in the region of Catania and studied architecture in Rome. Invited to Istanbul by the Catholic Church for the restoration of the Santo Stefano Church, he then entered the service of the Ottoman government and was sent to Salonica in 1886 to build a school. He remained to construct many public buildings, including the Ottoman governorate building (Konak) in 1891. But he also built churches, synagogues, and mosques, a sign of his acceptance by local notables of the various communities and a sign as well that the Ottoman modernity he embodied reflected shared values.

The work of architect Xenophon Paionidis follows the same logic: whether working on a charitable endowment by a rich Greek merchant, for the construction of the orphanage under Ottoman municipal auspices, or building what is now known as Villa Mordoch, he was acting in a typically Ottoman way seen in dozens of other Ottoman cities.

The main question in this reinterpretation is thus not on the nature of modernization, but on the nature of the reformed municipal institutions. The Ottoman municipality had four decades of functional existence, and was able to renew the pact between local elites and the Empire. But it failed on different levels: it was never granted enough financial resources to achieve a sufficient level of intervention except in the large-scale works conducted in conjunction with the governor. (Note, however, that such works should not be read simply as top-down intervention; local notables were partners, not only as landowners, but also as members of the municipal council.) And it was not able to invent a system of representation of the diverse identities present in the city that could really replace the old regime with modernity. In other words, it proved an efficient solution for renewing an alliance between the urban sphere and the Porte, but not for finding a modern form of urban cosmopolitan governance.

This failure to reinvent Ottoman cosmopolitanism for a new era, in the context of growing nationalist activities of different natures, poses the question of the relationship between the modern municipal idea and the governance of diversity, a question which affects not only the Ottoman municipality, but also the Greek one of the post-1912 period.[7] During the Ottoman era of reforms, the municipality as the urban body of representation of urban diversity was always challenged for its incapacity to both be as flexible as the old form it replaced, and be based on a

Salonica: old regime, reforms, transition 89

new idea of urban citizenship. It was a half-measure in that sense, and this was its limit. Bulgarian, Greek, Turk, and also, in a more marginal way, Zionist nationalists (Dakin 1966; Benbassa 1990, 127–140), were providing a new ideological framework, and relation to the world, which was not easily reducible to municipal coexistence. The last period of Ottoman rule in Thessaloniki was also marked by strong conflicts between Greeks and Bulgarians, for example riots following the 1908 assassination of Greek consul Askitis (Michailidis 2008, 169–180; Vermeulen 1984, 225–246).

The Ottoman reforms were an attempt in the direction of the invention of a modern form of cosmopolitanism, but not complete enough to ensure civic harmony, nor strong enough to counter the winds of nationalism. The difficulty of the Empire to gather consensus on the imperial idea illustrates the limits of the process of Ottoman modernity (Ginio 2005, 156–177). But it does not cancel the fact that the reforms were partly successful. The growth of a working class also challenged the old-regime relationship between notables and the population, and the modern municipality did not really address this mutation (Quataert 2002, 194–211). On the other hand, in many other cities and countries, the invention of municipal democracy took time, and was often made at the cost of an ethnic homogenization.

Questions on the passage to municipal governance after the annexation to Greece

Many issues regarding the transition to a Greek municipality are common to those for the Ottoman one. It is not only a question of institutional continuity, but also of common features in the face of common challenges. The institutional change was not huge: municipal law in Greece had a lot in common with that of the Empire: it was designed in a similar cultural context of reform of the same old-regime system and was implemented in a negotiation process involving notables from often similar sociological *milieux*. The challenges the Ottoman municipality had to face remain the same for the Greek one: the governance of diversity, the relationship between a city with a "minority" in "majority" and the center, the financing of modernization, the role of notables, the institutional pact between a local elite of landowners and merchants and the central government.

Many aspects of continuity need to be emphasized, from the confirmation of the private-sector concession system for public services to the operational framework of the technical services. The same holds for the operation of municipal social services. As for the question of the governance of diversity within the Greek municipal system between 1912 and World War I, the impression is one of limitations in embodying a modern form of urban cosmopolitanism. Concerns were already expressed among the Jews during the first weeks and months of Greek rule and negotiations with Jewish notables proved difficult (Molho 1993, 253–264).

The idea of internationalization of the city left its legacy. During the first months of Greek rule, despite assurances given by the Greek government on the

90   *Nora Lafi*

representation of non-Greek communities, the situation remained tense (Molho 1992, 127–140). Internationalization plans raised the question of having a Jewish mayor (Gelber 1955, 105–120). The guarantees for continuity of communal life and political rights for Jews were unclear regarding the implementation of equal civic representation at the municipal level (Molho 1988, 391–403; Fleming 2010, 271). Venizelos used the influence of Greek Jews to reassure the local Jewish community.

How diversity was managed under Greek rule, during the short period in which the Greeks were still a "minority", is crucial to our understanding of the fate of the idea of cosmopolitanism in this city in transition between empire and nation state.[8] The 1912–1917 period is fascinating, as we have the situation of a nation state with one of its most populous cities inhabited by a "majority" that is not the "majority" in the rest of the country.

The fact that urban planning became a central government competence was in this context a first challenge to the municipal sphere and of course to the competences of non-Greek notables.[9] The career and achievements of Osman Sait Ibrahim Chaki have to be looked at in this light. He was mayor from 1912 to 1916 and then from 1920 to 1922, but the decisions on the reconstruction after the 1917 fire, and the fire itself, happened under mayor Konstantinos Angelakis.

Everything changed indeed in 1917, when the city and its 135,000 inhabitants experienced the Great Fire, an event the interpretation of which has to be made in this framework of communal tension. The Jewish quarters were most affected and the balance of communities in the city was permanently altered (Vasilikou 1999). The fire marked the beginning of a massive Jewish emigration to the U.S.A., to Palestine, and to Paris. It also marked a big change in the functioning of the municipality, more, perhaps, than that of 1912. Very important is the recourse to expertise external not only the municipality, but also to the municipal sphere for the planning of reconstruction.

Ernest Hébrard (1875–1933) arrived in Salonica as an archaeologist working for the French troops stationed in Thessaloniki during World War I. He was one of the ideologists of the project of (re)hellenization of the city. The recourse to this expert has nothing to do with what had happened many times between 1850 and 1917: calling a foreign expert for a specific municipal project. The ideological dimension of the project of (re)hellenization of the city, against its Jewish, Turkish, and Slavic urban components, was inherent in the very choice of the expert (Yerolympos 1993, 233–257). The image of a European city as conceived by Hébrard was an ideological challenge to urban cosmopolitanism, but also to municipal practices of planning as formalized during the late Ottoman period. Hébrard worked in Thessaloniki with Aristotelis Zachos (1871–1939), not a local engineer or architect working in the municipality since Ottoman times, but a Greek from Macedonia, exiled to Germany, who returned to Greece (not Salonica or Macedonia) in 1905.

Zachos came to Thessaloniki in 1913. He drew up the master plan, by appointment of the Greek central government, not the municipality. Then, between 1915 and 1917, Zachos was head of the planning department of the Athens municipality. He returned to Thessaloniki after the Great Fire. After 1920, Hébrard was sent to Indochina, where he became the official planner of Hanoi for the French colonial administration. Again he implemented the planning of a city corresponding to a precise ideological project.

The population exchanges of 1921–1922 (20,000 Thessaloniki Muslims expelled to Turkey, 160,000 Greeks refugees installed in Thessaloniki) must be read in the context of a challenge to the very concept of management of diversity, for which the municipality had been the instrument (Kontogiorgi 2006; Loizos 1999, 237–263; Sundhausen 2010). Mayor Osman Sait Ibrahim Chaki was himself expelled. The arrival of the Greeks from what had become Turkey changed the city in the same proportions the arrival of Jews from Spain had centuries earlier. It posed the same kind of questions on the role of institutions of urban governance as had the previous municipal transition: Thessaloniki became a city with a Greek "majority". Jews became a minority in a system in which the articulation between communal institutions and municipal representation was unclear (Vasilikou 1999). The programme of hellenization that followed is to be interpreted in relation to the link between planning and ideological visions (Hastaouglou-Martinidis 1997, 493–507; Mangana 1995).

Conclusion: new research perspectives on cities in transition

The municipal history of Thessaloniki invites us to reflect on urban transitions at different levels. It illustrates the importance of knowledge of the pre-reform situation for understanding the reforms undertaken; it also illustrates the fact that what is at stake in the reform of municipal governance is intertwined with the stakes in the relationship between local society, central government, and the world in general. When analyzing urban transitions, historians tend to exaggerate the degree of novelty of the reformed situation. The example of Thessaloniki invites us to a reappraisal of the consistence of the Ottoman urban old regime, without which no adequate interpretation of the reforms of the Tanzimat era is possible. Only with a reappraisal of the achievements of this era can we understand the stakes and processes of passage to Greek sovereignty. As for municipal history, what the Thessaloniki case illustrates is the importance of the old-regime heritage, the limits of political modernity for the conceptualization and practice of the governance of diversity, and the tragic end of a cosmopolitanism, which was abolished before being given the chance of inventing its own modern form.

Notes

1 For example: BOA, A.}MKT MHM 47665 1291 B 17 (29.08.1874). In this file, a request by mayor Faik Bey for more budget in order to pay municipal employees is to be found.
2 BOA, MAD. d1065. Maliyeden Müdevver Deftere. The case of Salonica was treated together with those of cities such as Aleppo, Tripoli, or Beirut. See also: BOA, I..MVL.204 6222 1867 CA 24 (28.3.1881).
3 On the programme of public works: BOA, I.MVL.00522 23467 1281 b 26 (1.12.1864).

92   Nora Lafi

4 For example, about mayor Ibrahim Bey: BOA, BEO 85 6351 1310 Ra 18 (9.10.1892). The file BEO 90 6449 1310 Ra 27 (18.10.1892) provides the correspondence between the municipality and the ministry in Istanbul.
5 About these early steps in modern planning: BOA, A{AMKT.16633 1265 S 1 (29.12.1848).
6 Hannsen 2005 illustrates similar dynamics in Beirut.
7 For a reflection on urban cosmopolitanism in the age of nationalisms, see for example Davies and Moorehouse 2003; Fuhrmann and Kechriotis 2009, 71–78; Vasilikou 2001, 155–172; Cesarini 2001, 1–11.
8 For a reflection on the notion of cosmopolitanism in Salonica: Benveniste 2002, 8.
9 On the relationship between the national ideal and urban planning in Greece see Hastaoglou-Martinidis 1995, 99–123.

References

Anastassiadou, M., *Salonique, Une ville ottomane à l'âge des réformes*, Leiden: Brill (1997).

BOA = Ottoman State Archives.

Baer, M., *The Dönme: Jewish Converts, Muslim Revolutionaries and Secular Turks*, Stanford: Stanford University Press (2010).

Barkey, K., *Empire of Difference: The Ottomans in Comparative Perspective*, Cambridge: CUP (2008).

Ben-Naeh, Y., *Jews in the Realm of the Sultans. Ottoman Jewish Society in the 17th c.*, Tübingen, Mohr Siebeck (2008).

Benbassa, E., *Histoire des Juifs sépharades, de Tolède à Salonique*, Paris, Seuil (2002).

Benbassa, E., 'Zionism in the Ottoman Empire at the end of the 19th and the beginning of the 20th century'. *Studies in Zionism* (1990), 11–12, 127–140.

Benveniste, A., 'Salonique, ville cosmopolite au tournant du XIXe siècle'. *Cahiers de l'Urmis* 8 (2002), online at https://journals.openedition.org/urmis/18 [accessed 20191230].

Cesarini, D., 'Port Jews: Concepts, cases and questions'. *Jewish Culture and History* (2001), 4–2(2), 1–11.

Cooperman, E., *Turco-Jewish Relations in the Ottoman City of Salonica (1889–1912): Two Communities in Support of the Ottoman Empire*, PhD dissertation, New York University, New York (1991).

Dakin, D., *The Greek Struggle in Macedonia (1897–1913)*, Thessaloniki, Museum of the Macedonian Struggle; Institute for Balkan Studies (1966).

Davies, N., Moorehouse, R., *Microcosm: Portrait of a Central European City*, London, Pimlico (2003).

Ergin, O. N., Mecelle-I Umûr-i Belediyye, 8 vol., Istanbul, Istanbul Büyüksehir Belediyesi (1995) (1st edition 1914–1922).

Fleming, K., *Greece, A Jewish History*, Princeton, Princeton University Press (2010).

Franco, M., *Essai sur l'histoire des Israélites de l'empire Ottoman depuis les origines jusqu'à nos jours*, Paris, Durlacher (1897).

Fuhrmann, M., Kechriotis, V., 'The late-Ottoman port-cities and their inhabitants: Subjectivity, urbanity and conflicting orders'. *Mediterranean Historical Review* (2009), 24–2(2), 71–78.

Gelber, N. M., 'An attempt to internationalize Salonika (1912)–1913'. *Jewish Social Studies* (1955), 17–2, 105–120.

Salonica: old regime, reforms, transition 93

Ginio, E., 'Mobilizing the Ottoman nation during the Balkan Wars (1912–1913): Awakening from the Ottoman dream'. *War in History* (2005), 12–12, 156–177.

Ginio, E., 'Neither Muslims nor Zimmis: The gypsies (Roma) in the Ottoman State'. *Romani Studies* (2004), 14–2(2), 117–144.

Ginio, E., 'The Administration of Criminal Justice in Ottoman Salânik (Salonica) during the 18th c'. *Turcica* (1998), 30, 185–209.

Hall, R., *The Balkan Wars (1912–1913): A Prelude to the First World War*, London, Routledge (2002).

Hanssen, J., *Fin de Siècle Beirut: The Making of an Ottoman Provincial Capital*, Oxford: Oxford University Press (2005).

Hastaoglou-Martinidis, V., 'A Mediterranean City in Transition: Thessaloniki between the two World Wars'. *Facta Universitatis* (1997), 1–4, 493–507.

Hastaoglou-Martinidis, V., 'City form and national identity: Urban designs in 19th c. Greece'. *Journal of Modern Greek Studies* (1995), 13–11, 99–123.

Inalcik, H., 'Foundations of Ottoman-Jewish cooperation'. In: Levy, A., (ed.), *Jew, Turks, Ottomans, A Shared History*, Syracuse, NUP (2002).

Kolçak, O., *Osmanlilarda Bir Küçük Sanayi Örneği: Selanik Çuha Dokumaciliği (1500–1650)*, History Dpt Licence Thesis, Istanbul University (2005).

Colonas, V., *Greek Architects in the Ottoman Empire (19th–20th c.)*, Athens: Olkos (2005).

Kontogiorgi, E., *Population Exchange in Greek Macedonia: The Rural Settlement of Refugees (1922–1930)*, London, Clarendon (2006).

Lafi, N. (ed.), *Municipalités méditerranéennes: Les réformes urbaines ottomanes au miroir d'une histoire comparée*, Berlin: Klaus Schwarz (2005).

Lafi, N., *Esprit civique et organisation citadine dans l'Empire ottoman, Thèse d'habilitation à diriger des recherches*, Habilitation: Aix-Marseille I University (2011a) [published Leiden : Brill (2019)].

Lafi, N., 'Petitions and accommodating urban change in the Ottoman Empire'. In: Özervarlı, Özdalga (Elisabeth) (Sait) Tansuğ (Feryal) (eds.), *Istanbul as Seen from a Distance. Centre and Provinces in the Ottoman Empire*, Istanbul, Swedish Research Institute (2011b), 73–82.

Levy, A., *The Sephardim in the Ottoman Empire*, Princeton, Darwin Press (1992).

Loizos, P., 'Ottoman half-lives: Long term perspectives on particular forced migrations'. *Journal of Refugee Studies* (1999), 12–13, 237–263.

Mangana, V., *Westernization and Hellenicity: Form and Meaning in Thessaloniki (1850–1940)*, Ann Arbor, University of Michigan (1995).

Mazower, M., *Salonica City of Ghosts, Christians, Muslims and Jews (1430–1950)*, London, Vintage (2006)

Michailidis, I., 'From Christians to members of an ethnic community: Creating borders in the city of Thessaloniki (1800–1912)'. In: Klusakova, L. and Teulières, L. (eds.), *Frontiers and Identities: Cities in Regions and Nations*, Pisa, Plus (2008), 169–180.

Molho, R., 'Popular antisemitism and State policy in Salonika during the city's annexation to Greece'. *Jewish Social Studies* (1993), 50(3–4), 253–264.

Molho, R., 'Salonique après 1912: Les propagandes étrangères et la communauté juive'. *Revue Historique* (1992), 1(1), 127–140.

Molho, R., 'The Jewish Community of Salonika and its incorporation into the Greek State (1912–1919)'. *Middle-Eastern Studies* (1988), 24(4), 391–403.

Olson, R. W., 'Jews in the Ottoman Empire in light of new documents'. *Jewish Social Studies* (1979), 41(1), 75–88.

94 Nora Lafi

Quataert, D., 'The industrial working class of Salonica (1850–1912)'. In: Levy, A., (ed.) *Jews, Turks, Ottomans: A Shared History*, Syracuse (NY), Syracuse UP (2002), 194–211.

Rodrigue, A., Abrevaya Stein, S. (eds.), *A Jewish Voice from Ottoman Salonica: The Ladino Memoir of Sa'adi Besalel a-Levi (1820–1903)*, Stanford: Stanford University Press (2012).

Shmuelevitz, A., *The Jews of the Ottoman Empire in the Late 15th and the 16th c.*, Leiden, Brill (1984).

Şimşir, B. (ed.), *Rumeli'den Türk Göçleri*, 2 vol., Ankara, Türk Kültürünü Araştirma Enstitüsü (1968) (1970).

Sundhaussen, H., *Forced Ethnic Migration, European History Online*, Mainz: IEG (n.d.).

Üstün, K., *Rethinking Vaka-I-Hayriye: Elimination of the Janissaries on the Path to Modernization*, Master Thesis, Bilkent University Ankara (2002).

Vasilikou, M., 'Greeks and Jews in Salonika and Odessa: Inter-ethnic relations in cosmopolitan port cities'. *Jewish Culture and History* (2001), 4–2(2), 155–172.

Vasilikou, M., *Politics of the Jewish Community of Salonica in the Inter-Wars Years: Party Ideologies and Party Competition*, PhD Dissertation, University College London (1999).

Vermeulen (H.), 'Greek cultural dominance among the Orthodox population of Macedonia during the last period of Ottoman rule'. In: Block, A. and Driessen, H. (eds.), *Cultural Dominance in the Mediterranean Area*, Nijmegen: Katholieke Universiteit (1984), 225–246.

Yerolympos, A., 'A New City for a new state. City planning and the formation of national identity in the Balkans (1820s–1920s)'. *Planning Perspectives* (1993), 8–3(3), 233–257.

Yerolympos, A., 'Formes spatiales d'expansion urbaine et le rôle des communautés non-musulmanes à l'époque des réformes: Etudes de cas dans les villes des provinces européennes de l'Empire ottoman (1839–1912)'. *Revue du monde musulman et de la méditerranée*, 107–110 (2005), 113–142.

Yerolympos, A., 'Thessaloniki (Salonica) before and after 1917: 20th c. Planning versus 20th c. Urban Evolution'. *Planning Perspectives*, 3 (1988), 141–166.

7 Amateur and professional theatre in Ottoman Thessaloniki

Multicultural identity and its implications

Olivia Pallikari

In the year 1809 the Scottish novelist John Galt visited Thessaloniki, a brief halt on his route to Constantinople, Plovdiv, and Sofia (Grigoriou and Hekimoglou 2008, 106). In the book he published a few years later, we find a reference to entertainments the inhabitants of the city of Thessaloniki enjoyed:

> It being the Ramazan, during which the Turks abstain all day from every kind of refreshments, converting the day into night, there were several nocturnal amusements. Among others, we heard of a comedy to be performed by puppets and made arrangements with acquaintance to see the exhibition. It was rude and most indecent, equal in every respect to the rites and mysteries with which the ancients worshipped Priapus.
>
> (Galt 1812, 230)

Unfortunately, we could find no further information about this performance. Still, Galt's description is perhaps the earliest evidence available for theatre in Thessaloniki during the modern era. During the 19th century and first years of the 20th Thessaloniki developed. Theatre developed as well, reflecting the ethnic and linguistic diversity of a city comprised not only of Turks, Jews, and Greeks, the three main components, but also Serbs, Vlachs, Armenians, French, Italians, Austrians, and Roma. In addition to Turkish, Judaeo-Spanish, and Greek, Italian, French, Russian, Latin, Arabic, and Bulgarian played a role in the commercial and cultural life of Thessaloniki (see Anastassiadou 1997; Moskof 1978; Gorgeon 1994; Georgiadou 1994; Lory 1994; Ter Minassian 1994; Anastassiadou 1994; Enepekidis 1998; Risal 1997; Vafopoulos 1985; Kouzinopoulos 1997; Hasiotis 1985; Mazower 2004).

During the last quarter of the 19th century, the Ottoman administration made an effort to beautify Thessaloniki in accordance with western models. This coincided with modernising reforms that including the expansion of education of all nationalities. Education and a growing spirit of freedom helped the development of theatre and led, as in Istanbul, to the appearance of the first professional theatre companies (Vasilakou 1996).

Prior to 1875, when the first Greek newspaper was introduced, evidence about theatre life in Thessaloniki is sporadic. Theodoros Chatzipantazis tells us that in

96 *Olivia Pallikari*

the winter of 1858–1859 a young theatre company—its name, origin, and composition unknown—visited Thessaloniki. This group returned in 1860, perhaps because of its success in the previous year. Hadjipantazis suggests on the basis of its repertoire of comedies and light opera that the theatre company was a group of semi-professional actors from the Ionian Islands (Hadjipantazis 2002, 487). The company gave some 40 performances in Thessaloniki, where it stayed for the whole spring, and probably continued its performances in Manastir for one more year (*Journal de Constantinople* 28 December 1859; *Athina* 20 January 1860; *Filopatris* 23 January 1860). The Greek newspaper *Faros tis Makedonias*, however, would report (17 September 1883) that 'Vasilis Andronopoulos, who first performed Greek plays in Thessaloniki 23 years ago, is arriving at the city', i.e. in 1860.

The first identifiable theatre company to visit Thessaloniki, that of Demosthenes Alexiades, arrived at the beginning of March 1870 (Hadjipantazis 2002, 730). Alexiades came from Smyrna through Syros, where he often performed. This was probably one of his first managerial attempts; he founded *Elliniko Dramatiko Thiaso* (Greek Drama Company), his permanent company, only in 1876 (Exarchos 1995, 24). The company consisted of Pipina Vonasera—with whom Alexiades had collaborated at the beginning of his artistic career on several tours, even outside the borders of the Ottoman Empire—Antonios Tasoglou, Nikolaos Kyriakos, and Perikles Aravantinos (Hadjipantazis 2002, 730). All were known actors and actresses of their time.

The company gave seven performances: French musicals such as Théodore D' Aubigny's *The Two Sergeants*, Victor Hugo's *Hernani*, and *Lucrezia Borgia* and a modern Greek tragedy, *Merope* by Dimitrios Vernardakis (Hadjipantazis 2002, 730). The emphasis on musical theatre, especially French or Italian, illustrates the influence of European culture on the renaissance of Greek society. Light opera was accessible to an ethnologically and linguistically diverse audience. The performance of a modern Greek tragedy, however, was an expression of national identity at a time when Greeks dreamed of a free and independent Greece. The ancient past was one more argument for the national demands.

Alexiades' company was performing for an audience not yet used to going to the theatre. He tried to gauge its preferences by using his experience from other cities he had visited and by choosing plays he knew had great success. It should be noted however, that Alexiades' performance in Thessaloniki was not very profitable for the company, because the weather conditions were bad and few attended (Hadjipantazis 2002, 727).

Ten years after his first appearance, Alexiades visited the city again in 1880, this time wiser regarding audience's preferences. He kept Vernadakis' *Merope* from his previous visit. He added French drama, Narcisse Fournier's *Jocelin the coastguard* (*Ermis* 21 March 1880) and Molière's *Bourgeois Gentilhomme* (*Ermis* 11 April 1880). His new repertoire also included Shakespeare's *Othello* (*Ermis* 11 April 1880). His practice, like that of other companies of the time, was to fill theatre seats by presenting both a drama and a one-act comedy. On the same evening the audience could hear Theodoros Orfanidis' dramatic poem *I Chios*

Theatre in Ottoman Thessaloniki 97

Douli [Chios the Slave] and then the comedy *Kideia kai Choros* [Funeral and Dance] by Cameroni (*Ermis* 15 April 1880); or *Othello* followed by *To Kokkino panteloni* [The Red Trousers] (*Ermis* 11 April 1880); or *The Two Sergeants* and then *Ta Vasana tou Vasilaki* [The Torments of Vasilakis] (*Ermis* 11 April 1880). Alexiades also combined prose with music, presenting *Le diable*, a French drama by Lambert Thiboust and Alfred Delacour, and the Verdi opera *Un Ballo in Maschera* (*Ermis* 8 April 1880). Opera and musical theatre in general gave the audience a better chance to approach theatre, by overcoming the barriers of language. This was necessary in the case of Thessaloniki if someone wanted to show his work to an audience of more than one nationality.

By 1912 many of the most important Greek professional theatre companies had visited the city, some among them more than once. Apart from the company of Alexiades, which visited Thessaloniki four times, the list includes the company of Vasiliades and Halkiopoulou, of Spyropoulos-Vekiarelli, the *Euripides* company of Ioannis and Aikaterini Vasiliades, the *Sophocles* company, *Aristophanes* company, and *Menandros* company of Dionysios Tavoularis. Other theatre companies that also visited and performed in the city were those of Evangelia Paraskevopoulou, Ioannis Ralis, Emmanouil Lorandos, the Konstantinidis pair, and the Greek Drama Company of Athens, which presented the Dimitrakopoulos pair. Furthermore, the audience of Thessaloniki also saw the company of Marika Kotopouli and had the chance to enjoy the melodrama companies of Lavragas and Papaioannou.[1]

As we have seen, Greek professional theatre groups generally favoured French and Italian over Greek playwrights. The Greek plays that reached Thessaloniki tended to be the most famous ones, such as the successful 1865 verse tragedy *Maria Doxapatri* by Dimitris Vernardakis, which was performed in 1874 by the theatre group of Spyropoulos-Neri-Vekiarelli (Hadjipantazis 2002, 730). The poet Christoforos Samartzides from Lefkada was present at the performance of his play *Armatoloi kai Kleptai*, also performed in Thessaloniki in 1874 (Hadjipantazis 2002, 903). The *katharevousa* poet Spyridon Vasileiades became known to the Greek audience of Thessaloniki with his plays *Kallergai, Skylla*, and *Galateia* performed there for the first time in 1883 (*Faros tis Makedonias* 11 May 1883). The audience of the city knew the works of Theodoros Orfanides through his play *I Chios Douli*. Dimosthenes Misitzis, with his *Fiakas*, and Vyzantios with *Vavylonia*, introduced typical Greek comedies. Michalis Arniotakis, actor and playwright, presented his play *Koinonikai Taxeis* and Marinos Koutouvalis his play *Daphne*, played for the first time from the *Sophokles* theatre group (*Ermis* 11 November 1880). These were probably the most important Greek playwrights to reach the Thessaloniki public.

Vasilis Andronopoulos, who arrived at the city in 1894, after extended wandering through the territories of the Ottoman Empire, was a special case for Thessaloniki. He tried to put on theatre with local Greek participation, and also broke with the pattern of presenting only smooth popular pieces aimed at amusing the audience. Andronopoulos chose a Greek and foreign repertoire that would appeal to the patriotic feelings of his audience. He presented plays of Ioannis

98   Olivia Pallikari

Zambelios with themes from the Greek Revolution as well as foreign plays with messages against tyranny. He also used theatre not only as a means for entertainment but also as a way to enlighten and to awaken the national conscience of his audience (Kounenakis 1997).

In February 1912, not long before Thessaloniki's liberation, the Lagadas company visited Thessaloniki to present various well-known operettas, including *Ein Walzertraum* by Oscar Straus (*Makedonia* 10 January 1912), Franz Lehar's *Der Graf von Luxemburg*, and Hervé's *Mam'zelle Nitouche*. Operetta was an international medium directed to a multicultural audience. On the evening of 9 February, amid heightened tensions among the different nationalities of Thessaloniki, five officers went to the Union Park a few hours before the beginning of the benefit performance for the *Omonoia* [Concord] Association. They found the advertising poster at the gate of the park and tore off the part written in Turkish (*Makedonia* 10 February 1912).

In March of 1912, seven months before the liberation of the city, Marika Kotopouli also gave a series of performances in Thessaloniki. The plays she chose to present were of a kind 'unsuitable for young ladies'. One play, however, *Israel* by Henri Bernstein, showed both Kotopouli's artistic side and also her intent to attract people from the Jewish community of the city. The newspaper *Makedonia*, where the announcement of this performance can be found, anticipated that many Jews would watch the performance. Indeed they did, and the performance was a great success (*Makedonia* 10 February 1912).

Theatre companies devoted their performances to charitable causes on many occasions. Several times a performance was given to support an asylum, an association, or even an individual.[2] Charitable performances were also given to benefit actors. It was not always important to which nationality the beneficiary belonged. A charitable performance by the *Aristophanes* theatre company for the Ottoman orphanage is typical of this practice (*Ermis* 12 August 1875).

A big problem, which often provoked conflicts among the artists, was the absence of theatre buildings. This meant it was impossible for two or more theatre companies to give performances in the city at the same time. This problem was solved in a peaceful manner, once, in the summer of 1875. The city simultaneously hosted two productions, of *Euripides* and *Aristophanes*, and for that reason constructed two open theatres. These theatres were built on the newly constructed waterfront and can be included in the efforts of the Ottoman authorities to modernise the city and reform imperial institutions (Hadjipantazis 2002, 730). But in 1880, conflict between the theatre company of Alexiades and an Italian melodrama company broke out. The Italian company, which was already in Thessaloniki, gave performances in the only theatre of the city. The two companies were unable to come to an agreement about alternate use of the theatre, so Alexiades' company gave its performances in a club (*Leschi syntechnion*), which was rearranged for this purpose (*Ermis* 21 March 1880). This problem became less acute after 1880, when theatre buildings began to be built. Theatre began to be regarded not only as pleasant and uplifting, but also as a profitable business worthy of capital investment. The Apollon theatre was built, for

Theatre in Ottoman Thessaloniki 99

example, by Stefanos Ioannou, whose prior business was a coffee house (*Ermis* 1 July 1880).

This was an eventful period. Theatre could provoke an upsurge of patriotic emotion, which could lead, in turn, to sharp reactions from the Ottoman administration. Thessaloniki authorities suspended the licenses of all theatre companies indiscriminately after the patriotic excitement roused by the performance of Zambelios's play *Christina* by the *Euripides* theatre company (Hadjipantazis 2002, 1017). Andronopoulos was forced in 1896 to take great precautions to be able to present his patriotic plays to the audience of Thessaloniki.

Despite this, performances were often given in the presence of, or even in honour of, some Turkish official, possibly in order to ensure his support. The presence of the officials in the theatre also served to demonstrate the reforming spirit of the Ottoman Empire. Thus, for example, we are informed that governor-general Abedin Pasha honoured with his presence the performance of *Othello* by Demosthenes Alexiades in 1880. During this period, moreover, European theatre began to penetrate into Turkish society, along with the other changes and reforms that were ongoing in the empire (*Ermis* 12 April 1880).

The city's newspapers played an important role in promoting Greek professional theatre companies and in creating the audience to support theatre in general. From the first issue of the *Ermis* newspaper, and more regularly and systematically as time progressed, we see news regarding the arrival of various theatre companies. The newspapers took care to announce upcoming performances and encourage spectators to watch the shows of each theatre company. They commented, mostly favourably, on the staging of each play. They praised the acting skills of each group, expressing objections when necessary, and in this way shaped popular taste for the theatre.

The Thessaloniki press saw theatre—at least that presented by the Greek professional companies—less as entertainment than as a source of education and spiritual uplift for the Greek audience. Newspapers saw support for Greek theatre as a national duty, since they regarded it as a tool for the development of a national conscience and the cultivation of a national spirit. For those reasons, newspapers saw in theatre a moral benefit for its audience.

On the other hand, newspapers recognized that the audience knew little about theatre. They tried in their articles to inculcate appropriate theatre behaviour as well as to cultivate a better appreciation of dramatic arts. Negative comments regarding the inappropriate, often 'loud', behaviour of the audience during a performance were not uncommon, and there were frequent efforts to encourage readers to attend those performances where the audience was lacking.

The Thessaloniki newspapers commented not only on the value of the plays presented, but also on the translations. It is important to say here that these translations were done for the specific performance, often by one of the actors. The press often asked theatre companies to choose and present Greek plays that could make a positive contribution to national affairs. The comments on the plays referred to the language, to the quality of the plot, and, in general, to the talent of the playwright. Furthermore, the newspapers also evaluated the talent of the actors and actresses of

100   *Olivia Pallikari*

each show. The basic acting criteria, for almost all the newspapers of the city, were naturalness, realism in the performance of a role, and beautiful declamation.

More Greek theatre was a universal demand of the Greek press of Thessaloniki, though each newspaper and each editor interpreted Greek theatre in a different way. One definition was companies and theatres where only Greek performances would be given. Another was merely the presence of Greek plays in the repertory, while another was more contact of the Greek audience with Greek plays, whether in theatres or through their publication in the newspapers.

European theatre companies were frequent visitors to Thessaloniki as this period progressed. The first testimony of such a visit is in 1870, when the press reported that a nameless group presented plays in Italian. Unfortunately, we don't have more information about this company or others which also visited Thessaloniki in the same period (*Konstantinoupolis* 17 February 1870). Western Europeans had established themselves in Thessaloniki from the 17th century. This 'Frankish' community was not large, but it was certainly influential in the 19th century, powerful not only economically but also culturally, as the source of most innovations. For example, it was through the European schools that education was promoted; through foreign music teachers' western music; through the charitable associations the spirit of the Enlightenment. The European melodrama theatre companies that visited the city, primarily Italian and French, didn't choose Thessaloniki for its small community of Europeans. They chose the city in order to present their plays in front of an expanding range of spectators. In this multilingual city, it was only inevitable that music would become a means of communication with a large number of spectators.

During Christmas of 1874, the Italian musical theatre company *Labruna* came to Thessaloniki for the first time, with soprano Angela Rossi, as its leading actress. It presented several performances in the French theatre, beginning with Verdi's *Ernani*. Although the opera was a great success, the company split apart (Tomanas 1994, 21). It was followed by other known companies, such as that led by Eugenio Castagna, which started its performances with the tragic operetta *Ruy Blas* (*Ermis* 18 November 1880), the company of *Salvini*, which gave a series of performances (*Faros tis Makedonias* 29 September 1881), and Italian soprano Adelina Calzoletti, who sang *Traviata*, *Trovatore*, *Condessa d'Amalfi*, *Rigoletto*, *Ruy Blas*, and others (*Faros tis Makedonias* 20 February 1881).

More interesting for 19th-century Thessaloniki theatre history is the presence of professional Armenian-Turkish theatre companies. In Constantinople of the 19th century, in addition to traditional forms of Turkish theatre, one could also find European theatre. French and Italian companies frequently performed in Pera, while in Constantinople one could find less distinguished groups but also a few major names in theatre. There were also local stages presenting European plays in translation but also original Ottoman plays. Between 1870 and 1880 plays written in Turkish were presented in the 'Ottoman Theatre, the first big repertory theatre in Constantinople. Almost all the actors were Armenians, as the Ottoman Turks involved in theatre were very few. Armenians and Levantines were the first to give the Ottoman Empire a western theatre' (Faroqhi 2003; And 1979; Martinevich 1933).

Theatre in Ottoman Thessaloniki 101

In 1884 the Armenian-Turkish theatre company of *Venlian* visited Thessaloniki. The press, particularly the Athens press, had made very flattering comments about this company. Thanks to its reputation, the press and public were awaiting its arrival with great anticipation. The theatre company started its performances with the 1874 French comic opera *Girofle Girofla*, watched by a large crowd. The next play was *Leplepitzis Hor Hor agas*, an Armenian-Turkish operetta, which was a hit in Athens when first performed. The success in Thessaloniki was also great; 500 men were left outside the theatre, because they couldn't find a seat. The music of the play was not particularly French, and in many parts of the drama a strong oriental influence was present (*Faros tis Makedonias* 28 January 1884). The same company demonstrated its dramatic versatility with a performance of Molière's *L'Avare* (*Faros tis Makedonias* 26 January 1884). Four years later, in 1888, another Turkish theatre company, this one unnamed, presented with great success the comic opera *La Fille de Madame Angot* (*Faros tis Makedonias* 1 January 1888).

An interesting aspect of the theatre in Thessaloniki was the development of amateur theatre, particularly in the city's Jewish community. Jewish theatre reached the city in 1880, after Constantinople and Smyrna. It combined Judaeo-Spanish and European culture. As rabbis gradually lost their hold and a western, reformist, and modernising spirit started being established, Judaeo-Spanish plays were performed for the first time. The audience was primarily people influenced by European culture through education in western schools. Jewish theatre performances took place mainly in the context of charitable organisations to support their work financially, focused on school groups and Jewish holidays. The influence of French culture was strong, thanks to the penetration, expansion, and impact of the *Alliance Israélite Universelle*.

After the establishment of local theatre in Thessaloniki, the number of plays translated and adapted grew quickly. Jewish theatre shifted from Bible episodes to focus more on social life. Thessaloniki's Jewish theatre became a model for other Jewish communities in Turkey as well as Greece. The plays were short productions on specific themes, and often there was no formal script (Romero 1979; Romero 1983).

The first known amateur theatre activities of the Jewish community took place in 1873 and 1884 in the *Cercle des Intimes* with the play *Saul* by Vittorio Alfieri, adapted to Judaeo-Spanish by local poet Yosef Errera. He also directed the theatre productions of the *Cercle*. Influenced by French and Italian writers, Errera wrote biblical plays in Judaeo-Spanish and directed a group of amateur actors (Kerem). We can also find intense theatre activity at schools, by teachers and by students. Moshe Ottolenghi from Livorno, director of the *Talmud Torah* school, translated two Italian plays into Judaeo-Spanish. They were performed by his students in 1885 and 1887 (Kerem).

Judaeo-Spanish was not the only language for drama in the Jewish community. Especially during school performances, dialogues and monologues were given in Italian, French, and even in Turkish (Romero 1983, 52–54). The shows consisted of short pieces, songs, and recitation of poems, and even the most distinguished members of the Jewish community used to take part. A typical example

102   *Olivia Pallikari*

is the performance of Girolamo Ocoferi's play *Ideales Contrastados* in the Italian Philological Circle, where amateurs from the best families of the city appeared. The performance was a great success (Romero 1983, 53–54). By 1912 the Jewish community had given more than 40 performances.

The Greek community was responsible for a creditable number of amateur productions as well. The philanthropic clubs and educational societies founded after 1850 also identified theatre as a means of generating resources for educational activities, for supporting vulnerable social groups, and for promoting Greek national ideas on the eve of the city's liberation. Characteristic examples were the benefit performance of Hugo's play *Hernani* in front of a large audience of both genders by 'dutiful and artistic' young people to support the *Filekpaideutikos Syllogos Thessalonikis* (Society for the promotion of education) (*Ermis* 6 May 1880); and the performance, over the Christmas holidays of 1881 by a group of high school students to raise money for their physics laboratory (*Faros tis Makedonias* 16 December 1881). These amateur performances presented French comedies but also patriotic plays such as the *Katsantonis* of Antonios Antoniades (*Faros tis Makedonias* 9 January 1891), and the *Galateia* of Vasileiades, in which young members of Greek society took part (*Faros tis Makedonias* 22 May 1912).

From 1850 until 1912, amateur and professional theatre groups in Thessaloniki put on more than 150 performances of Greek and foreign plays. These performances covered the needs of almost all the communities of the city. The most important Greek and foreign theatre companies came through the city. Tragedies, comedies, melodramas, French, Italian, even Turkish operettas were presented, including the most famous or important plays of that time. Theatre was entertainment and a tool for the formation of national consciousness. It was amusement but also a reflection of the influence of European civilisation. It was a part of the social life of the upper class of Thessaloniki, but also a way to show the new, contemporary face of a city that among other things also loved and supported theatre.

Notes

1 This list is derived from systematic research in all Greek newspapers of Salonica at this time: *Ermis, Faros tis Makedonias, Alitheia, Nea Alitheia, Makedonia, Pammakedoniki, Fos.*
2 According to an announcement in the newspaper *Konstantinoupolis* of Constantinople, on February 1870 a theatre company, name and play unspecified, gave a performance to benefit the Greek hospital of the city.

References

Newspapers

Alitheia newspaper,editor I. Kouskouras, Thessaloniki, 1903–1909
Athina newspaper, Athens, 1832–1864
Ermis newspaper, editor S. Garpolas, Thessaloniki, 1875–1881
Faros tis Makedonias newspaper, editor S. Garpolas, Thessaloniki, 1881–1895

Filopatris newspaper, Athens, 1855–1862
Fos newspaper, editor Demosthenis Rizos, Thessaloniki 1914–1922
Journal de Constantinople newspaper, Istanbul, 1839–1845
Konstantinoupolis, newspaper, editor Dem. Nikolaidis, Istanbul 1867–1880
Makedonia newspaper, editor K. Vellidis, Thessaloniki, 1911–1923
Nea Alitheia newspaper, editor Athanasios Kouskouras, Thessaloniki, 1909–1971
Pammakedoniki newspaper, editor K. Vellidis, Thessaloniki, 1912

Books and articles

Anastassiadou, M., *Salonique 1830–1912, Une ville ottoman a l' age des Reformes*, Leiden: Brill (1997).
Anastassiadou, M., 'Οι Δυτικοί της περιοχής' [The westerners of the region]. In: Veinstein, G. (ed.), *Θεσσαλονίκη 1850–1918: Η 'πόλη των Εβραίων' και η αφύπνιση των Βαλκανίων* [Thessaloniki 1850–1918: The 'city of the Jews' and the awakening of the Balkans], Athens: Ekati (1994).
And, M., *Karagoz Turkish Shadow Theatre*, Istanbul: Dost (1979).
Enepekidis, P., *Η Θεσσαλονίκη στα χρόνια 1875–1912* [Thessaloniki in the Years 1875–1912], Thessaloniki: Adelfon Kyriakidi (1998).
Exarhos, T., *Έλληνες ηθοποιοί - Αναζητώντας τις ρίζες* [Greek actors - seeking the roots], Athens: Dodoni (1995).
Faroqhi, S., *Kultur und Alltag im Osmanischen Reich: Vom Mittelalter bis zumAnfang des 20, Jahrhunderts*, Munchen: C.H. Beck Verlag (2 Auflage 2003).
Galt, J., *Voyages and travels in the years 1809, 1810 and 1811: Containing statistical, commercial, and miscellaneous observations on Gibraltar, Sardinia, Sicily, Malta and Turkey*, London: Printed for T. Cadell and W. Davies (1812).
Georgeon, F., 'Η «Σελανικ» των Μουσουλμανων και των Ντονμεδων' [Selanik of the Muslims and Donmes]. In: Veinstein, G. (ed.), *Θεσσαλονίκη 1850–1918: Η 'πόλη των Εβραίων' και η αφύπνιση των Βαλκανίων* [Thessaloniki 1850–1918: The 'city of the Jews' and the awakening of the Balkans], Athens: Ekati (1994).
Georgiadou, K., 'Οι Έλληνες της Θεσσαλονίκης' [The Greeks of Thessaloniki]. In: Veinstein, G. (ed.), *Θεσσαλονίκη 1850–1918: Η 'πόλη των Εβραίων' και η αφύπνιση των Βαλκανίων* [Thessaloniki 1850–1918: The 'city of the Jews' and the awakening of the Balkans], Athens: Ekati (1994).
Grigoriou, A. H. and Hekimoglou, E., *Η Θεσσαλονίκη των περιηγητών 1430–1930*, [Salonica of the travelers 1430–1930], Thessaloniki: Etaireia Makedonikon Spoudon-Militos (2008).
Hadjipantazis, Th., *Από του Νείλου μέχρι του Δουνάβεως: το χρονικό της ανάπτυξης του ελληνικού επαγγελματικού θεάτρου, στο ευρύτερο πλαίσιο της Ανατολικής Μεσογείου, από την ίδρυση του ανεξάρτητου κράτους ώς την Μικρασιατική καταστροφή vol A2* [From the Nile to the Danube: The chronicle of the development of Greek professional theatre in the wider context of the eastern Mediterranean, from the founding of the independent Greek state to the Asia Minor catastrophe], Irakleio: Panepistimiakes Ekdosis Kritis (2002).
Hasiotis, I. K., *Η Θεσσαλονίκη της Τουρκοκρατίας* [Thessaloniki under Turkish rule], Nea Estia: Afieroma sti Thessaloniki, Athens: Vivliopoleion tis Estias (1985).
Kerem, Y., 'The Greek-Jewish theater in Judeo-Spanish, ca. 1880–1940' www. sephardicstudies.org/greek-t.html (consulted July 2019).
Kounenakis, P., 'Αφιέρωμα: Θεσσαλονίκη: πρωτοπόρες θεατρικές αναζητήσεις'. In: *Kathimerini* (Athens newspaper) weekly supplement *Epta Imeres* (21 September 1997).

104 Olivia Pallikari

Kouzinopoulos, S., *Το μεγάλο άλμα – Η απελευθέρωση της Θεσσαλονίκης* [The great leap: The Liberation of Thessaloniki], Athens: Kastaniotis (1997).

Lory, B., 'Σολούν, Σλάβικη πόλη'. In: Veinstein, G. (ed.), *Θεσσαλονίκη 1850–1918: Η 'πόλη των Εβραίων και η αφύπνιση των Βαλκανίων* [Thessaloniki 1850–1918: The 'city of the Jews' and the awakening of the Balkans], Athens: Ekati (1994).

Martinevich, N., *The Turkish Theatre*, New York: Theatre Arts INC (1933).

Mazower, M., *Salonica, City of Ghosts: Christians, Muslims and Jews, 1430–1950*, London: HarperCollins (2004).

Moskof, K., *Θεσσαλονίκη: 1700–1912, τομή της μεταπρατικής πόλης* [Thessaloniki 1700–1912: Profile of a retail city], Athens: Stochastes (1978).

Rizal, P. [Nehama, J.] *Thessaloniki I peripothiti poli* [La Ville Convoitée], Thessaloniki: Nisides (1997).

Romero, E., *El mundo teatral de los Sefardies orientales*, Madrid: C.S.I.C (1979).

Romero, E., *Repertorio de noticias sobre el mundo teatral de los Sefardies orientales*, Madrid: C.S.I.C (1983).

Ter Minassian, A., 'Μια μικρή Αρμενική κοινότητα' [A small Armenian community]. In: Veinstein, G. (ed.), *Θεσσαλονίκη 1850–1918: Η 'πόλη των Εβραίων' και η αφύπνιση των Βαλκανίων* [Thessaloniki 1850–1918: The 'city of the Jews' and the awakening of the Balkans], Athens: Ekati (1994).

Tomanas, K., *Το θέατρο στην παλιά Θεσσαλονίκη 1872–1944* [The theatre in old Thessaloniki 1872–1944], Thessaloniki: Nisides (1994).

Vafopoulos, G., 'Το παραμύθι της Θεσσαλονίκης' [The fairytale of Thessaloniki]. In: *Nea Estia periodical, Afieroma sti Thessaloniki*, Athens: Vivliopoleion tis Estias Nea Estia (1985).

Vasilakou, Ch. S., *Το ελληνικό Θέατρο στην Κωνσταντινούπολη το 19ο αιώνα* [The Greek theatre in Konstantinoupoli in the 19th century], Athens: Neos Kyklos Konstantinoupoliton (1996).

8 A new look at an ancient city
Thessaloniki in Ottoman archaeology, 1832–1912

Edhem Eldem

Introduction: modernity and magic

If any Ottoman city best exemplifies the nineteenth-century drive of the Ottoman elite and, later, of the middle classes, to modernize and westernize, it may well be Salonica/Selanik/Thessaloniki. Historians have pointed to a number of areas where Thessaloniki seemed to play the role of pioneer or prototype of Ottoman modernity (Anastassiadou 1997; Mazower 2004; Özdemir 2003). Urban development is the best-studied aspect of this transformative process, whereby Thessaloniki created its own modernity while at the same time benefiting from external motors of change, from Europe but also from the center of the empire (Yerolympos 1996). Trade, industry, and education have also been studied, more or less thoroughly, as a complex three-way interaction between Europe, Istanbul, and Salonica (Alkan 2003). For a certain section of the Turkish political spectrum, Salonica, Atatürk's birthplace, became a sort of mythical symbol or shrine of modernity, almost to the point of changing the age-old expression into '*ex Thessalonica lux*'.

One aspect of modernization that does not seem to have been studied from this perspective is archaeology. Unlike Thessaloniki's other modernizations, this one was managed almost exclusively from the center, and the roles played in it are not the ones generally assigned to the major actors of the cultural struggles of the nineteenth century. There is some irony in the idea of Ottomans conducting archaeological research and acquiring antiquities that belonged to a Greek, Roman, or Byzantine past, in a city that, while not actually Greek, was inhabited by a sizeable Greek population and formed part of a geographical and cultural space that fell under the rubric of Greece.

As I will try to show, Thessaloniki was an early, prime target of the Ottomans' newly discovered interest in antiquities. From the 1850s on, Thessaloniki was incorporated into the archaeological 'periphery' of the Ottoman center. As a result, it was somewhat systematically exploited to feed the rapidly growing collections of the Imperial Museum in Constantinople. Its rapid compliance with one of the most sophisticated requirements of modernity came at the cost of fulfilling the desires of a demanding capital.[1]

Thessaloniki's archaeological history begins with a mixture of respect for timeless objects, traditions passed on through the generations, and an element

106   *Edhem Eldem*

of magic. I begin with a report by the *naib* of Salonica, the assistant to the *kadı* or judge of the city. On 12 April 1832, the said *naib*, Şiranizade Abdullah Şakir Efendi, reported to Istanbul that the city and its entire region had suffered a terrible drought.[2] Prayers and lamentations had had no effect, until the octogenarian el-Hac Mustafa Efendi, originally from Anatolia but a resident of Salonica for almost fifty years, had a dream, in which he saw the Sultan, Mahmud II, who told him that 'there are some stones inside the holy mosque of Hagia Sophia, which is an ancient temple',[3] and decreed that prayers be said and that they be placed in water. As soon as Mustafa Efendi recounted his marvelous dream, they all rushed to the mosque, found the stones—the document does not say how—recited in their direction a Koranic verse that had proven efficient in provoking rain, placed them in water according to the Sultan's commandment and suddenly the rain started to fall, not to be interrupted for four days and three nights.

The document had been written and submitted as an expression of gratitude to the Sultan, who, by guiding his pious subject, Mustafa Efendi, had saved the city and the entire region from drought and famine. Yet the power that had unleashed the merciful rain was not really his. Three elements had had to come together to create a miracle: the Koran, of course, although previous failures showed that it was not sufficient alone; the Sultan, who knew how to make things work; and, finally, the stones of Hagia Sophia, that 'ancient temple', which had brought into the equation the powerful contribution of a sanctity that went back to time immemorial. There was nothing really exceptional about this event, and there is little doubt that such practices were not uncommon; what seems to have been rather striking was that it was documented in such detail and with such care as to end up not only in the state archives, but also in the official gazette (*Takvim-i Vekayi*, 1832),[4] thus providing a precious insight into one of the many ways in which early modern and preindustrial societies approached the notion of antiquity.

The first finds

It would not take very long before ancient objects would start to acquire a new meaning no longer embedded in magical and mythical narratives. Exactly twenty years later, in October 1852, the first documented Ottoman archaeological acquisition in Thessaloniki took place. In a letter dated 31 October, a certain Tahir Efendi, representing Salonica's governor, Yusuf Sıddık Mehmed Pasha (d. 1859), informed the Porte that his master had 'added to other antiquities one antique trough' (*tekne taşı*)[5] and had it shipped to the Arsenal in Istanbul on a ship of the Admiralty laden with timber.[6] The Grand Admiral, Mahmud Pasha (d. 1857), requested instructions as to what he should do with the stone, now described as a coffer (*sandık taşı*).[7] Following consultation with the palace and the issuance of an imperial decree, it was decided that the governor's stone should be placed in the museum.[8]

The documents do not describe the object, but the label trough or coffer indicates that this was a sarcophagus, probably without its lid. This information dovetails with the much-discussed hypothesis that the famous sarcophagus of Phaedra

A new look at an ancient city 107

and Hippolytus (Figure 8.1) may have come from Thessaloniki. Ever since Otto Frick had spotted it in the courtyard of Hagia Eirene in the mid-1850s (Frick 1857, col. 33), archaeologists had pondered the rumor of a Thessaloniki origin, without fully accepting it for lack of concrete evidence (Dumont 1868, 247; Goold 1871, 28; Reinach 1882, 18–19; Joubin 1898, 31–34; Mendel 1912–1914, I.98). The only evidence for this provenance had been a remark to this effect by the German consul in Izmir, Spiegelthal;[9] quite a number of objects in the early collection, however, were wrongly attributed to Thessaloniki (Schmidt 1881, 134; Mendel 1912–1914, I.xviii–xix). The match between this information and the official reports in the Ottoman state archives gives us grounds to assert, more than 150 years later, that the sarcophagus of Phaedra and Hippolytus was indeed a Thessaloniki acquisition.

It is too early to call this practice archaeology. When the Ottomans transformed part of the church of Hagia Eirene, until then an arsenal, into a 'museum' in 1846, what they had really done amounted to little more than hoarding unidentified and unclassified antiques in an improvised warehouse. The source of inspiration behind this project was obvious: the major excavations undertaken by the Europeans in the 1840s had inspired them to do the same as part of the ongoing project of westernization. Fellows in Xanthos, Newton in Bodrum/Halicarnassus, Botta in Khorsabad, and Layard in Nineveh had been carrying off huge chunks of the monuments they had unearthed in Anatolia and Mesopotamia; the Ottomans had decided they would simply do the same and store their own finds in this warehouse of a museum within the palace grounds. Yet, as they had no archaeologists—or adventurers, to be accurate—they had to resort to the bureaucratic and

Figure 8.1 Sarcophagus of Phaedra and Hippolytus, inv. 125. (Photograph courtesy of the Istanbul Archaeological Museums)

108   Edhem Eldem

military chain of command to obtain antiquities from what they thought would be the most promising provinces. From Iraq to Tripolitania, from Palestine to Salonica, governors and administrators were instructed to dig, find, and ship anything that might fall within the category of antiquities (BOA, C. MF. 5/221 *ca.* August, 1846). In that sense, Yusuf Sıddık Mehmed Pasha was simply following orders, shipping an undetermined number of 'old stones' to the capital.

Setting up a system

It would take another twenty years for this erratic pattern to develop into a real system. By the early 1870s, the museum was slowly acquiring an institutional character: the first bylaw on antiquities was passed in 1869 and the museum was entrusted in 1872 to Philipp Anton Dethier, its first director with a scientific background and a plan for the future. In 1870, at least two objects were sent to the Imperial Museum by the then governor of the province, Sabri Pasha. One of these was the famous funerary relief of a young warrior, wrongly attributed to Pella by Salomon Reinach (Mendel 1912–1914, I.132–135), and the funerary relief representing a couple, wrongly identified as Asklepios and Hygieia (Mendel 1912–1914, I.239–242). In 1872, it appears from a note by Tony Terenzio, then director or rather caretaker of the Imperial Museum, that Sabri Pasha had sent to Istanbul a copper vase and a dram of gold leaves found in a quarry exploited by a certain Ahmed Agha in the village of Akbekâr (Terenzio 1871–1872a, 66). In October, the museum received a statue depicting a naked man leaning on a tree laced with vine, a woman's head in the form of a mask, the fragment of a male head, two consoles ending in female heads (Terenzio 1871–1872b, 2, 5, 17).[10]

The quest for antiquities in Salonica really took off thanks to a local entrepreneurial figure, Giovannaki Efendi, who rapidly became a self-appointed provider of antiquities for the museum, a sort of tout (Mendel 1912–1914, I.xix). Documents in the archives attest to several massive shipments of objects, eleven in 1873,[11] eighteen in 1874,[12] destined to enrich the collection in Istanbul. For his services, Giovannaki expected compensation for his expenses together with a 'finder's fee'. In 1873, in return for services rendered, he was awarded the Mecidî order;[13] in 1874, when he had retrieved fourteen objects, mostly funerary stelae, he was awarded the handsome sum of 30 liras (£27);[14] finally, in 1880 he was promoted to third rank in the Ottoman bureaucratic hierarchy,[15] although there were some hesitations as to where he really stood: in one document, the word *memur* (civil servant) had been replaced by *muhbir* (informant) next to his name.[16]

Interestingly, Giovannaki's understandable zeal was the indirect cause for a rise in consciousness and professionalism among Ottoman officials. Once they found themselves under the obligation to pay 30 liras for a dozen objects, they came to realize that perhaps not everything Giovannaki found was of the utmost importance. It was therefore decided that henceforth objects would first be examined and their photographs sent to Istanbul to see if they were worth the acquisition. If not, the document added, they would have to be properly preserved by the local authorities; a measure that started immediately to be applied to a number of

A new look at an ancient city 109

objects.[17] That same year, on his way back from Athens, where he had defended Ottoman claims against Schliemann over Trojan finds, the museum's director, Dethier, visited Salonica with the purpose of examining the existing antiquities and the sites where they had been found.[18] In a very modest way, Salonica had thus been officially integrated into a formal archaeological service.

Towards a local collection

By the mid-1880s, it seems that the system was already working properly. Some major pieces, such as the Dionysiac sarcophagus (Mendel 1912–1914, I.119) and that of the Putti[19] were officially sent by the governor of the province, at that time, Abdullah Galib Pasha. More ordinary finds were systematically examined and investigated locally, and the information sent to Istanbul. As the museum's archives are not entirely open to research, we can only speculate on what kinds and numbers of objects were thus processed. Nevertheless, a few examples that have transited through the bureaucracy provide an insight into such specific cases, where the local authorities were summoned to the site of a find and then conducted an investigation. Assisted by the governor's dragoman, who would conduct a cursory inspection of inscriptions, the province's director for Education and/or the chief engineer would examine the finds, sometimes providing transcriptions and drawings (Figures 8.2, 8.3, and 8.4). As to the location where the objects were stored, the choice had fallen, as in many other Ottoman cities, on the local high school, the *Mekteb-i İdadi*. This may have started earlier, in 1887, when the school was first established, but it is clearly documented only from 1308/1892 on, corresponding to the date when the school was moved to the newly established Hamidiye Boulevard, today's Ethnikis Aminis.

Typical of this type of operation was, for example, the preservation of an ancient sarcophagus found in the city's Greek cemetery, which had been converted into a fountain.[20] Even more telling was the 1902 episode concerning the discovery of five funerary stelae in the city's Jewish cemetery. The investigation had been carried out by a team consisting of the accountant and the interpreter of the Education directorate, accompanied by an official appointed by the Rabbinate. Following a rough description of the size and volume of these stelae, the report noted that they all bore a few lines in Greek; but that they were too worn by time to be read, and that some had been erased on purpose. Only one could be read, with great difficulty. It had been erected in the memory of a man called Hector, and had two hands engraved on its side. Interestingly, the report noted that

> one of the stones had been reused as a tombstone 249 years earlier by the Jews for a member of their community and had been inscribed with a few words in Hebrew in memory of the Jew who had thus been buried.

'Our humble observations consist of this', concluded the report, 'and it therefore appears that these stones have no historic value today, and that they were brought in from various places by Jews in order to be used as tombstones'.[21]

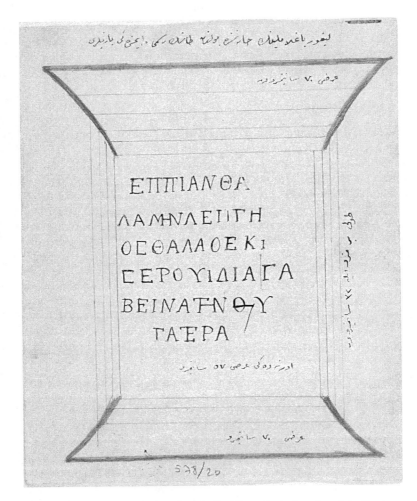

Figure 8.2 Copy of the inscription and shape of an altar found in the house of Ligor Bağlamalı. BOA, MF. MKT. 578/20, 18 Haziran 1317 (1 Temmuz 1901). (Turkish State Archives)

By and large, then, most of the archaeological finds from the 1890s on were preserved in Thessaloniki, instead of being systematically shipped to Istanbul as previously.[22] The phenomenon is confirmed to a large extent by the examination of the Imperial Museum's final catalogue, established by Gustave Mendel and dated from 1912–1914. The number of objects from Thessaloniki entering the collections drops drastically after that date. In fact, it is practically limited to only two pieces, both major, the ambos of Hagios Georgios and Hagia Sophia (Mendel 1912–1914, II.393–408) (See Table 8.1).

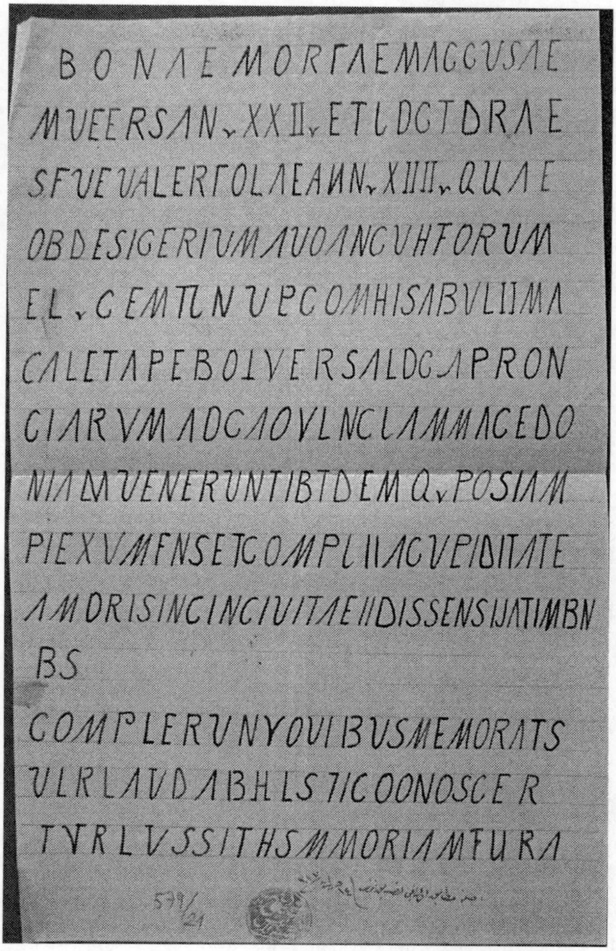

B O N A E M O R T A E M A C C V S A E
M V E E R S A N . X X II . E T L D C T D R A E
S F V E V A L E R T O L A E A A N . X III . Q U A E
O B D E S I C E R I V M A V O A N C V H F O R V M
E L . C E M T L N V P C O M H I S A B V L II M A
C A L E T A P E B O I V E R S A L D C A P R O N
C I A R V M A D C A O V L N C L A M M A C E D O
N I A M V E N E R V N T I B T D E M Q . P O S I A M
P I E X V M F N S E T C O M P L II A C V P I D I T A T E
A M O R I S I N C I N C I V I T A E II D I S S E N S I J A T I M B N
B S
C O M P L E R V N Y O V I B V S M E M O R A T S
V L R L A V D A B H L S T I C O O N O S C E R
T V R L V S S I T H S M M O R I A M T U R A
57 9/21

Figure 8.3 Certified copy of a funerary inscription from Vodena (Edessa) sent to the high school for preservation. BOA, MF. MKT. 579/21, 14 Haziran 1317 (27 June, 1901). (Turkish State Archives)

Mosques, churches, or monuments?

This brings us back to the very beginning of this study, to the episode concerning the sanctity and magical powers attributed to the mosque of Hagia Sophia. Indeed, while most of the archaeological concerns of the Imperial Museum focused on Greek and Roman remains, the Byzantine monuments of the city were only rarely referred to. One reason was that the major monuments of the Byzantine period were churches, which in many cases had been converted into mosques. Gradually, however, the developing Ottoman antiquarian gaze would start to differentiate

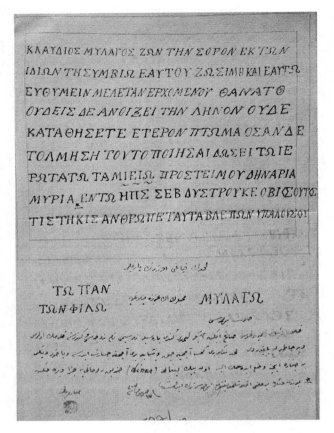

Figure 8.4 Copy and translation of the inscription on a sarcophagus found in the Greek cemetery. BOA, MF. MKT. 577/53, 14 Haziran 1317 (27 June, 1901). The translation is signed and sealed by a certain 'Jan' (probably Jean for Yanni), translator for the office of Education. (Turkish State Archives)

between the present use of these buildings and their original nature. Rather telling in this respect is the way in which the perception of the famed Hagia Sophia evolved in time, as illustrated by the documents concerning its frequent restorations after recurrent fires and overall deterioration. One needs only to compare the way in which such repairs were justified in 1875[23] and 1883.[24] In both cases, the argument was that it was 'not appropriate to leave it in such a state of disrepair'. Yet in 1875, the building itself was described as a 'holy mosque friends and foes had set their eyes on'; in 1883, however, it had become 'the second example after the holy mosque of Hagia Sophia in Istanbul, and a building of great antiquity'. This new perception of churches as monuments is illustrated, some ten years later, in 1892, by the mobilization of the local authorities upon

Table 8.1 Objects from Thessaloniki in the Imperial Museum collections

Date	Sender/Provider	References	Description
1853	Yusuf Sıddık P.	Goold 66; Reinach 121; Mendel 21 (125)	Sarcophagus of Phaedra and Hippolytus
1870	Sabri Pasha	Goold 127; Mendel 91 (109)	Funerary relief of 'Asklepios and Hygieia'
1870	Sabri Pasha?	Goold inv. 138	Two reliefs with figures
1870	Sabri Pasha?	Goold inv. 142	Four marble reliefs
1870	Sabri Pasha	Goold 128; Reinach 120; Mendel 39 (85)	Funerary stela of a young warrior
1872	Sabri Pasha?	Terenzio inv. statues 46; Reinach 28	Statue of Dionysos leaning against a tree
1872	Sabri Pasha	Terenzio corr. 66	Copper vase and gold leaves
1872	Sabri Pasha?	Terenzio inv. têtes 40	Mask in the form of a woman's head
1872	Sabri Pasha?	Terenzio inv. têtes 41	Man's head
1872	Giovannaki	Terenzio inv. reliefs 112; Mendel 953 (234)	Funerary relief
1872	Giovannaki	Terenzio inv. reliefs 111; Mendel 1047 (75)	Funerary stela of Gamos
1872	Giovannaki	Terenzio inv. varia 1,2	Two consoles decorated with female heads
1873?		Mendel 828 (81)	Statuette of a child
1873?		Mendel 322 (82)	Statuette of a sleeping nymph
1873?		Reinach 129; Mendel 1163 (203)	Fragment of a sarcophagus decorated with garlands
1873?		Reinach 208; Mendel 971 (222)	Funerary banquet
1873?		Reinach 202; Mendel 989 (188)	Funerary banquet
1873?		Reinach 211; Mendel 992 (227)	Funerary banquet
1873?		Reinach 200 bis; Mendel 978 (201)	Funerary banquet
1873?		Reinach 217	Funerary banquet
1873?		Reinach 235; Mendel 968 (272)	Funerary stela of Proklos
1873	Giovannaki	Reinach 122; Mendel 492 (31)	Great relief of the 'Thracian rider' type
1873	Giovannaki	Mendel 827 (84)	Statuette of a child
1873	Giovannaki	Mendel 905 (95)	Funerary stela
1873	Giovannaki	Mendel 1076 (118)	Funerary stela of Agatheanis
1873	Giovannaki	Mendel 961 (174)	Funerary stela of Ailios Ioulianos' family
1873	Giovannaki	Mendel 960 (195)	Funerary stela
1873	Giovannaki	Mendel 861 (209)	Votive stela dedicated to Tyche
1873	Giovannaki	Reinach 237; Mendel 1049 (258)	Funerary stela of Dizalas and his family

(*Continued*)

Table 8.1 Continued

Date	Sender/Provider	References	Description
1873	Giovannaki	Mendel 853 (264)	Votive stela dedicated to Apollo and Artemis
1874	Giovannaki	Mendel 865 (117)	Votive stela dedicated to the Dioscuri
1874	Giovannaki	Reinach 529; Mendel 1039 (196)	Funerary stela of Mestrios and Philla
1874	Giovannaki	Reinach 280; Mendel 914 (260)	Funerary stela
1874	Giovannaki	Mendel 920 (267)	Funerary stela of Stolos
1874	Giovannaki	Mendel 967 (271)	Dedicatory inscription
1874	Giovannaki	Mendel 921 (478)	Funerary stela of Heraklides and Heraklios
1874	Giovannaki	Mendel 909 (483)	Funerary stela of Manta, Paramonos, and Torko
1874	Giovannaki	Mendel 934 (2238)	Funerary stela of Lysanias
1880	Giovannaki	Mendel 1037 (226)	Funerary stela
1878	Giovannaki?	Dethier inv. 84	Funerary stela of Titus Flavius Demetrius
1878	Giovannaki?	Dethier inv. 85; Mendel 966 (240)	Funerary stela of Gaios Kousonios Krispos
1878	Giovannaki?	Dethier inv. 86	Funerary stela of Demetrius
1878?	Giovannaki?	Dethier inv. 87	Right fragment of a funerary stela
1878?	Giovannaki?	Dethier inv. 88	Funerary stela with five figures and inscription
1878?	Giovannaki?	Dethier inv. 89–90	Two fragments of a funerary stela
1878?	Giovannaki?	Dethier inv. 91; Reinach 143; Mendel 935 (216)	Funerary stela of Tyranna (from Veria)
1878?	Giovannaki?	Dethier inv. 92	Funerary stela fragment in the form of a small sarcophagus
1878?	Giovannaki?	Dethier inv. 93	Funerary stela with two busts and no inscription
1878?	Giovannaki?	Dethier inv. 94	Funerary stela with three heads and no inscription
1878?	Giovannaki?	Dethier inv. 95	Funerary stela with man pouring liquid and woman offering cup
1878?	Giovannaki?	Dethier inv. 96; Mendel 788 (2246)	Dedicatory inscription
1878?	Giovannaki?	Dethier inv. 97; Mendel 913 (2206)	Funerary stela
1878?	Giovannaki?	Dethier inv. 98; Mendel 918 (2208)	Funerary stela
1878?	Giovannaki?	Dethier inv. 99; Mendel 916 (213)	Funerary stela of Baios Nikomakhos and his family
1880	Giovannaki	Mendel 1041 (252)	Funerary stela of Thrason and his family

A new look at an ancient city 115

Table 8.1 Continued

Date	Sender/Provider	References	Description
1880	Giovannaki	Mendel 1064 (253)	Funerary stela of the gladiator Nikephoros
1885		Mendel 32 (366)	Dionysiac sarcophagus
1887	Abdullah Galib P.	Mendel 23 (511)	Sarcophagus decorated with putti
1887	Abdullah Galib P.	Mendel 144 (1230)	Archivolt
1893		Mendel 1034 (668)	Funerary stela of Agathon
1895		Mendel 939 (723)	Funerary stela of Hippostratos and Ammia
1897		Mendel 321 (774)	Child asleep and standing
1899	Rıza Pasha	Mendel 1018 (1004)	Funerary banquet
1899	Rıza Pasha?	Mendel 1048 (1006)	Funerary stela of Demetrios and Maxima
1899	Rıza Pasha	Mendel 945 (1007)	Funerary stela of Leontis
1900		Mendel 952 (1103)	Large bust of a man
1900		Mendel 643 (1090)	Great ambo of Salonica
1905		Mendel 644 (1627)	Ambo of Salonica in ancient green

Sources used: Goold, 1870; Goold, 1871; Terenzio, 1871-1872a; Terenzio, 1871-1872b; Dethier, 1873-1881; Reinach, 1882; Mendel, 1912–1914.

a report that an underground church had been discovered inside the property of a Jewish subject, and that it was about to be destroyed.[25] I have not been able to find out which church this might have been; nor have I managed to check whether this report may have been triggered by anti-Semite feelings among some Greek Orthodox residents of the neighborhood. After all, such sentiments may well have been involved, all the more so since most of these monuments had a complex and multi-layered history, which made it possible for individuals to perceive them in very different and ambiguous ways according to their own identity. I would put under that category the very interesting complaint placed in 1907 by a certain Lambros Christidi concerning the protection of Hagia Sophia:

> Although your servant is a resident of the neighborhood of Aya Tanaş (Hagios Athanassios), considering that Jewish children in the neighborhood of the holy mosque of Hagia Sophia are throwing stones at a place of daily worship and at antiquities, I request and beg that this information be forwarded to the appropriate authority in order to ensure the protection of the said holy mosque.[26]

Was Lambros Christidi really concerned with the welfare and protection of a mosque? Probably not, and the chances are that he saw in this building the embodiment of a Christian and/or Byzantine past under Jewish threat. Nevertheless, he knew exactly how to appeal to Ottoman sensitivity by combining the traditional and modern definitions of the site as both a mosque and an ancient monument.

Telling stories

Perhaps one of the most telling indicators of the Ottomans' new gaze on the city and its monuments, and more particularly on its mosques, was the inclusion of a section devoted to antiquities (*asar-ı atika*) in the official almanacs (*salname*) published by the provincial administration. This publication started in 1287/1870; from the outset, surprisingly, antiquities were mentioned among the resources and characteristics of the city. The second edition (1871) had a three-page section devoted to this topic. First among the antiquities came the mosque of Hortacî, the famous Rotunda. The almanac provided rather dubious information about the building's origins, claiming that it had been built some 3,000 years earlier by the idolaters (*put perest*) as a fire temple (*ateşgede*) honoring a *Kabir* (Cabeiri) god by the name of *İfestos* (Hephaistos) before it was converted into a church by the Greeks. It was noted that in its courtyard stood a three-stepped ambo carved out of a single block of marble, from which Saint Paul was said to have preached. The second building so treated was the mosque of Eski Cuma (the Acheiropoietos church), described again as a former temple of the idolaters, dedicated to the goddess Venus, and then converted into a church by the Greeks. Of course, the description of these two monuments as antiquities did not exclude a rather detailed account of the way in which they were both converted into mosques, the first after a certain Hortacî Süleyman, and the second by the Ottoman warriors who conquered the city. In that sense, the only 'pure' antiquity of the city that was listed was the Arch of Galerius, wrongly identified as a triumphal arch erected in 312 AD by the population of the city to honor Constantine the Great on his way to occupy Rome, which he had wrested away from Maxentius and Maximian in 312. One interesting feature of this text was that it lamented the state of dereliction in which this monument now stood (*Salname* 1871, 124–126).

This narrative was repeated almost verbatim in several of the following editions (e.g. *Salname* 1873, 117–118) before it evolved, probably in the 1880s, into a new version which was integrated into a broader description of the city, including its history. The section specifically devoted to antiquities disappeared; however, the treatment of the monuments and their history was much more sophisticated. Interestingly, in this second phase of the official narrative, it was the mosque of Ayasofya (Hagia Sophia) that provided a starting point for the discussion. Its description started with the observation that this former church had been *purchased* from Christian priests by İbrahim Pasha—a way of suggesting a peaceful transition—but then immediately shifted to the artistic and historic importance of the building. It was described as filled with sculptures, and particularly with an 'ambo made of a single block of green porphyry decorated with beautiful flowers and motifs', thought to weigh 5–6 tons, which qualified as a 'truly rare antiquity'. The Rotunda followed, with a description that had obviously been cut and pasted from the previous edition, including the three-stepped ambo; and so did the mosque of Eski Cuma, described in exactly the same terms as in the earlier version. A novelty was the inclusion of a fourth church, Hagios Dimitrios, known to the Ottomans as Kasımiye Mosque. The saint was buried there, the almanac

A new look at an ancient city 117

noted, and not only would Christians visit his tomb every year on 26 October, but the mosque also enjoyed great fame among Europeans. The text then reverted to its previous version, describing the Arch of Galerius in exactly the same terms,[27] but adding that another triumphal arch could be found within Vardar Gate, one that had been erected in gratitude for the protection granted to the city against neighboring tribes by the Roman emperor Octavian (*Salname* 1886, 124–127).

After a brief interruption in or around 1890 (*Selanik Vilayeti Salnamesi* 1890, 74–84),[28] the format changed once again, reverting to the original idea of having a separate section devoted to antiquities. The new text returned to the initial order, starting with the Rotunda and then moving on to Hagia Sophia, Hagios Dimitrios, and Acheiropoietos, before finishing with the Arch of Galerius. The descriptions were still similar to those of the preceding version, but there were also some significant changes. In the case of the Rotunda, which was again presented with its remarkable ambo, the Cabeiri had disappeared but Hephaestus remained, his name transformed into an unlikely İfemenos;[29] the building was 'dated' from 1000 BC; and its conversion into a church now explicitly mentioned the name of Hagios Georgios. Hagia Sophia came next, with the usual description of its green ambo, but with the additional mention of its 'dome decorated with beautiful mosaics'; however, the text lamented, the church had fallen prey to the flames during the great fire of 1306/1890. Kasımiye Mosque (Hagios Dimitrios) received exactly the same treatment as previously. As to Eski Cuma (Acheiropoietos), one could now discover that it had once been named after Hagia Paraskevi; the claim that it had been the first mosque to be used by the city's conquerors was further reinforced by recounting the tradition that the preachers delivering the Friday homily (*hutbe*) did so with a sword in hand: 'For this reason, this holy mosque has gained particular importance in Ottoman history'. Once again, the Arch of Galerius, still linked to a victorious Constantine the Great, now also described as 'the founder of Istanbul (*sic*)' came last; as a novelty, its decorative program was highly praised, while the names of Maxentius and Maximian simply disappeared from the narrative. The last sentence of the new version, also a novelty, was strangely dismissive: 'While there are other antiquities in Salonica, they are not important enough to deserve to be noted or remembered' (*Salname* 1895, 179–181; *Salname* 1900, 286–289).

Discovering Byzantium

The last editions remained pretty much faithful to the text as it had settled just before the turn of the century. There was, however, one striking addition that concerned both Hagios Georgios and Hagia Sophia. The ambos, repeatedly described as exceptional pieces, were now explicitly mentioned as having been removed and taken to the Imperial Museum in Constantinople (*Salname* 1904, 268–70; *Salname* 1906, 211–4; *Salname* 1907, 526–528). This was a drastic step in a totally new direction, that of treating Byzantine remains with the interest until then reserved for Greek and Roman antiquities. The first ambo to go had been that of Hagios Georgios, half of which was preserved in the church of Saint Panteleimon (İshakiye Mosque). This major piece of Christian church sculpture, with its remarkable figures, entered the Imperial Museum in 1900, under inventory number 1090 (Mendel 1912–1914, II.393–405) (Figure 8.5).

The conflict that arose around the acquisition of this piece may help explain the broader context of the museum's new interests. In a letter to Osman Hamdi Bey, director of the Imperial Museum in Istanbul, the German archaeologist Theodor Wiegand bitterly complained that despite the fact that the 'great ambo of Salonica' had been on the list of objects promised to Kaiser Wilhelm in October 1898, Halil Edhem Bey, Osman Hamdi's brother, had declared that the ambo could not be moved from the two mosques where it stood, which had prompted him to ask for that of Hagios Menas as a replacement. Nevertheless, Wiegand had been dismayed at the sight of the said ambo standing in the halls of the Istanbul museum, and this had triggered his irate letter to Hamdi Bey.[30] Wilhelm had developed the idea of setting up a major collection of early Christian and Byzantine antiquities at the Kaiser-Friedrichs Museum in Berlin, and had sent out a 'shopping list' to his ally in Istanbul, Abdülhamid II, with the Salonica ambo third on his list.[31] Evidently, following the German example, the Ottomans had started to pay more attention to Byzantine remains, and the ambo of Hagios Georgios had been the cause of a tug-of-war between the two museums.

Four years later, in the summer of 1904, the same fate awaited the ambo of Hagia Sophia. The argument for its removal was that the building had been much damaged by fire and its 'decorated marble pulpit was an antique worthy of display'[32] (Figure 8.6). Every removal was a step in the direction of the recognition of churches—independently of their being used as mosques—as ancient buildings worth protecting and preserving.

Figure 8.5 Great ambo of Salonica (Hagios Georgios), inv. 1090. (Photograph courtesy of the Istanbul Archaeological Museums)

Figure 8.6 Ambo of Salonica in *verd antique* (Hagia Sophia), inv. 1627. (Photograph courtesy of the Istanbul Archaeological Museums)

This redefinition of sacred buildings went hand in hand with the rapid development of tourism during the same period and the consequent 'museification', as it were, of these structures. A telling example of this is the conflict that opposed two brothers, Mehmed Fehmi and Hasan, over the right to reap the benefits to be obtained from Christian visitors to Hagios Dimitrios, known as Kasımiye Mosque since 1493. In 1906, Mehmed Fehmi Efendi, as muezzin and caretaker of the said mosque, explained to the General Inspectorate of Rumelia that he and his brother Hasan, also muezzin and caretaker of the same mosque, had always shared the gifts and tips left by Christian and European visitors to whom they showed the mosque and 'an ancient grave belonging to the Christians and located inside the mosque', taking turns in performing this duty. His brother, however, had gotten greedy, and had maneuvered to force him into retirement, thus seizing all the attractive profits from visitors.[33] Trivial as it may sound, this family feud was a good indicator of how the effects of tourism could contribute to a form of secularization of Muslim sacred space.

The restoration of Hagia Sophia, undertaken in 1906, was another clear indication of this gradual change. The projected cost was set at a total of 570,000 piasters, the equivalent of almost £5,200. More importantly the project specified that the building should be restored 'without bringing any change to its original state'. To what extent this clause was truly respected is open to question, if one considers that 'the inner floor consisting of old gravestones and most of them being broken, it would be redone with marble flagstones over cement' and that only Allatini bricks would be used in restoring the walls.[34] Nevertheless, the fact that the Imperial Museum dispatched its architect, Edhem Bey, Osman Hamdi's son, to supervise the whole operation does indicate a concern for a restoration in conformity with the historic importance of the building.[35] That same year, when the governor of the city, Ali Daniş Bey, asked for the Friday mosque (probably Eski

120   *Edhem Eldem*

Cuma) to be restored, he invoked the fact that 'many foreigners visit this mosque and its state of dereliction is a disgraceful sight in the eyes of friends and foes'.[36]

The final stage: change and continuity

Following the collection of objects for the Imperial Museum, the restoration of historic churches, and the constitution of a local collection housed in the city's high school, the logical step would have been to open a local museum, the Salonica branch of the Imperial Museum. There were important precedents: Konya had acquired a museum in 1902 and Bursa in 1904; in that sense one could even claim that Salonica was lagging behind. As we learn from a piece of news in the local *Alitheia* newspaper cited in Vassilis Kolonas' dissertation, a first project in this direction seems to have sprung in the city's mayor Adil Bey's mind by August 1908. The White Tower would be turned into a museum, with 'heavy' antiquities on the first floor and ethnographic material on the second (Kolonas 1992, 55). It seems, however, that the project was dropped for some time, probably due to the shaky political situation in the months that followed the Young Turk Revolution, not to mention the chronic financial difficulties of the Empire. It was only in 1911 that the project seems to have been taken up again, this time at the initiative of the Imperial Museum.[37] Salonica had already been on the agenda of the Museum's new director, Halil Edhem. He had first intervened in late January in reaction to reports that the city walls were being torn down. This, he noted, was against the clauses of the bylaw on antiquities and should be prevented at all cost, for fear that it might create a dangerous precedent.[38] There was some irony in the fact that Salonica owed in great part its modernity and development to the demolition of its walls some forty years earlier, and that now modernity required that the remaining fortifications be spared and preserved. The danger was imminent and real, and it also concerned other cities of the Empire, including Istanbul itself. The museum was therefore seriously fighting back against an ongoing movement of urbanization that threatened the preservation of the historic fabric of urban centers.[39]

That same year, at the end of the month of June, Halil Edhem asked permission to set on a weeklong mission to Salonica. His objective was 'to investigate the location that had been prepared for the projected museum branch'.[40] It was clear that this time a serious project was underway, and that Salonica could soon add a museum to the long list of modernizing achievements. However, that particular project never saw the light of day, as the Ottomans lost the city to the Greeks before they could set up a proper museum. In an article published in 1913 in the *Bulletin de correspondance hellénique*, French archaeologists Charles Avezou and Charles Picard noted that the Ottoman administration had left some 150 ancient pieces in the basement, attic, and classrooms of the city high school which, following the fall of the city to Greek troops, had been transferred to the custody of the Greek authorities (Avezou and Picard 1913, 84). Interestingly, the transfer of power does not seem to have had the expected 'liberating' effect on the antiquities of Thessaloniki. The occupation of the city and its region by British and French forces from 1915 to 1918 led to a rather systematic archaeological

A new look at an ancient city 121

campaign throughout Thessaloniki and its hinterland. The result was the constitution of a museum, first housed in the White Tower, and then built on the grounds of the general headquarters, located in the Papapheion orphanage, where it would open its doors in May, 1918. However, this positive step towards the constitution of a local collection ended with an unexpected spoliation, as the commander-in-chief of the British forces obtained that the newly found antiquities be 'very generously ... given by the Greek Government to the British nation', as a result of which this 'free gift by Greece' was packed and sent to the British Museum (Mazower 2004, 317; Gardner and Casson 1918, 10–12, 27–28, 43).

With respect to the remaining collections, which had been taken from the Ottomans, it seems that the Greek administration showed no greater hurry than its predecessors in setting up a formal museum. Indeed, if one is to consult the website of the Archaeological Museum of Thessaloniki, it appears that the existing collection was kept in the Ottoman high school and that additional antiquities were stored in the Residency building. It was not until November 1925 that the much-dreamed museum was finally opened, inside the New Mosque (Yeni Cami) of the *dönme* community. An intriguing detail concerns the fact that the *minbar* of this particular mosque—its ambo, if it had been a church—was removed soon after, in 1926, and stored in Hagia Sophia (A. M. Thessaloniki; Sabanopoulou 2008). Would it be over-reading to suggest that this action may have been in some measure revenge for the removal of the Hagios Georgios and Hagia Sophia ambos some twenty-five years earlier?

Notes

1 I must express my most heartfelt thanks to a number of colleagues who have greatly helped me in this endeavor, particularly with respect to my deep ignorance of purely archaeological matters. Zeynep Kızıltan, director of the Archaeological Museums of Istanbul, and her deputy, Tuğçe Akbaytogan, have provided me with excellent photographs of the Thessaloniki ambos in their collection. I have benefited from the precious and expert help of Pantelis Nigdelis, from the Department of History and Archaeology of the Aristotle University of Thessaloniki, with respect to the identification of a number of objects described in Ottoman archival documents. Panagiotis C. Poulos, from the Department of Turkish and Modern Asian Studies of the University of Athens, has shared with me invaluable information concerning later developments, and has drawn my attention to the relevance of *salnames* (official almanacs) in this matter. Finally, I am grateful to Murat Şiviloğlu, from Trinity College Dublin, for drawing my attention to the fact that the 1832 report by the *naib* of Salonica appeared that same year in the Ottoman official gazette.
2 BOA, HAT 651/31803, 11 Zilkade 1247 (12 April, 1832).
3 '*Selanik derununda kâin kadim mabed olan Ayasofya cami-i şerifinde mevcud bir takım taşlar vardır*' (loc. cit.).
4 One wonders how the document could have been published in *Takvim-i Vekayi* nine days *before* the date it bears. However, I do not see any point in trying to solve a mystery that is irrelevant to the issue at hand.
5 '[…] *sair antikalar zeyline vaz ü ilave [olunan] bir aded antika tekne taşı*'.
6 BOA, İ. DH. 263/16351, 17 Muharrem 1269 (31 October, 1852).
7 BOA, İ. DH. 263/16351, 21 Muharrem 1269 (4 November, 1852).

122 *Edhem Eldem*

8 BOA, İ. DH. 263/16351, 4 Rebiyülevvel 1269 (16 December, 1852).

9 'Zunächst kann jetzt der Fundort, welcher damals nicht ermittelt werden konnte, augegeben werden. Es ist einer Mittheilung des General-Consul Spiegelthal zu Smyrna zu Folge die Umgegend von Salonichi' (Frick 1858 col. 131).

10 The detail of these objects is as follows: p. 2, n° 46: 'Belle statue sans tête nue appuyée sur un tronc d'arbre qui est orné de pampre et raisins en marbre. Bacchus. Provenant de Salonique 12 oct. 1872'; p. 5, n° 40, '[tête] de femme masque en marbre de Salonique 12 oct. 72.'; n° 41, '[tête] d'homme fragm. la face [?], très gâté[e] en marbre de Salonique 12 oct. 72;' p. 17, n° 1–2, 'Deux consoles finissant en têtes de femmes de l'un il n'y a que la tête de femme en marbre de Salonique 12 oct. 72.' The female head may be Mendel 636 (49), 'Tête de Méduse' (Mendel 1912, 383–384).

11 BOA, İ. DH. 667/46451, 19 Rebiyülevvel 1290 (17 May, 1873).

12 BOA, MF. MKT. 18/66, 4 Rebiyülevvel 1291 (21 April, 1874).

13 BOA, İ. DH. 667/46451, 19 Rebiyülevvel 1290 (17 May, 1873).

14 BOA, MF. MKT. 18/66, 4 Rebiyülevvel 1291 (21 April, 1874).

15 BOA, İ. DH. 808/65326, 27 Receb 1297 (5 July, 1880).

16 BOA, MF. MKT. 30/136, 24 Cemaziyülahir 1292 (27 July, 1875).

17 BOA, MF. MKT. 18/66, 4 Rebiyülevvel 1291 (21 April, 1874).

18 BOA, MF. MKT. 18/116, 8 Cemaziyülevvel 1291 (22 June, 1874).

19 BOA, MF. MKT. 93/92, 3 Receb 1304 (28 March, 1887); (Mendel 1912, 105–107).

20 BOA, MF. MKT. 577/53, 14 Haziran 1317 (27 June, 1901). It appears that this particular sarcophagus was first discovered in June, 1895, in the vicinity of Telli Kapı, when a path was being built between the Orthodox and Protestant burial grounds in the Northeast of the city. It was first published by J. H. Mordtmann (1896, 7–8; Edson 1972, n° 557, 179–180).

21 MF. MKT. 640/39, 28 Mayıs 1318 (10 June, 1902).

22 A typical example is the altar bearing a Latin inscription discovered in June 1901 near Kasımiye Mosque (Agios Dimitrios), for which the Imperial Museum issued the following verdict: 'Considering that this inscribed stone is not a piece of great importance, it has been deemed unnecessary to have it brought to the Imperial Museum, and it should remain in place'. According to the Ottoman document, this monument, inscribed in 'ancient Greek' (*'kadim Yunanice'*), was examined by a certain Dimitriadis Efendi, assistant road engineer of the province, but could not be removed, as it was found on the property of the late Bağlamalı Ligor, former dragoman of the Austrian consulate, whose family was also of Austrian nationality (BOA, MF. MKT. 578/20, 18 Haziran 1317 (1 Temmuz 1901); BOA, MF. MKT. 578/20, 29 Ağustos 1317 (11 Eylül 1901). This piece seems to have been first spotted by Vidal de La Blache (Husson, 1869, 63). Interestingly, however, this author locates it in the house of a certain Mpithos, probably to be read as Bitzo, dragoman of the British consulate, as suggested by Edson, who also notes that the object is lost today (Edson 1972, n° 217, 91).

23 İ. DH. 699/48912, 1 Safer 1292 (9 March, 1875).

24 BOA, İ. ŞD. 64–3741, 2 Receb 1300 (9 May, 1883).

25 BOA, MF. MKT. 145/118, 28 Zilhicce 1309 (24 July, 1892); BOA, MF. MKT. 147/52, 15 Muharrem 1310 (8 August, 1892).

26 '*Acizleri Aya Tanaş mahallesi sakinlerinden isem de Aya Sofya Cami-i şerifi orada bulunan Yahudi çocukları her gün ibadet olan bir yere ve antikalara taş atmakda bulunduklarından lutfen ve merhameten mezkûr cami-i şerif muhafaza edilmesi zımnında keyfiyetin lazım gelen mahalle emr ü havale buyurulmasını niyaz ve istirham eylerim*' (BOA, TFR. İ.SKT. 136/13517, 6 Kânun-ı Evvel 1323 (19 December, 1907).

27 An interesting detail reveals how the text was copied from one edition to another. In the early lithographed editions (e.g. 1871), the name of Maxentius was phonetically transcribed from the French 'Maxence' in the form of 'Maksent'; when it reappeared in the later editions (e.g. 1886), the emperor's name was spelled 'Hafsent', the result of an unfamiliar name and confusion between similar letters.

A new look at an ancient city   123

28 Like the previous editions, the 10th edition had a lengthy historical narrative, but no section devoted to antiquities as such (*Salname* 1890, 74–84). I have not been able to access the 11th (1310/1892) and 12th (1311/1894) editions, but it is clear that the section on antiquities was restored at least in the 13th edition (1312/1895).
29 Again, this is the result of a clumsy reading of the earlier version.
30 Draft of a letter from Theodor Wiegand to Osman Hamdi Bey, Arnavutköy, 16 May, 1900. (Deutsches Archäologisches Institut, Berlin, Zentrale Archiv (DAI), Wiegand 4, Briefe H–J)
31 The Ottoman archives list nine pieces that were to be ceded to the Kaiser: seven column capitals from Istanbul, one 'stone' from Alaçam, on the Black Sea coast, and one other 'stone' from Thessaloniki, evidently the coveted ambo (BOA, MF. MKT. 479/41, 4 Receb 1317 (8 November, 1899); İ. MF. 5/91, 15 Şaban 1317 (19 December, 1899); BEO 1431/107262, 20 Şaban 1317 (24 December, 1899); Y. PRK. ASK. 163/11, 22 Temmuz 1316 (4 August, 1900).
32 BOA, DH. MKT. 865/84, 10 Mayıs 1320 (23 May, 1904).
33 BOA, TFR. İ. ŞKT. 87/8614, 14 Rebiyülevvel 1324 (7 May, 1906).
34 BOA, TFR. İ. SL. 106/10501, 20 Rebiyülevvel 1324 (14 May, 1906).
35 Osman Hamdi Bey to Alexander Conze, 9 June, 1908 (DAI, Conze 2 Briefe an Conze A–Z).
36 TFR. İ. SL. 197/19609, 15 Eylül 1324 (28 September, 1908).
37 BOA, MF. MKT. 1173/16, 20 Haziran 1327 (3 July, 1911).
38 BOA, MF. MKT. 1165/84, 16 and 20 Kânun-ı Sani 1326 (29 January and 2 February, 1911).
39 BOA, DH. İD. 86/12, 2 Safer 1329 (2 February, 1911); 19 Şaban 1329 (15 August, 1911); 22 Şaban 1329 (18 August, 1911).
40 BOA, MF. MKT. 1173/16, 20 Haziran 1327 (3 July, 1911).

References

Alkan, M. Ö., *İmparatorluk'tan Cumhuriyet'e Selanik'ten İstanbul'a Terakki Vakfı ve Terakki Okulları 1877–2000*, Istanbul: Terakki Vakfı (2003).

Anastassiadou, M., *Salonique, 1830–1912: une ville ottomane à l'âge des réformes*, Leiden: Brill (1997).

Avezou, C. and C. Picard, 'Inscriptions de Macédoine et de Thrace', *Bulletin de Correspondance Hellénique*, 37 (1913), 84–154.

BOA = Prime Ministry, Ottoman State Archives, Istanbul.

Dethier, Ph.-A., 'Inventory', Istanbul Archaeological Museums Archives (IAMA) (1873–1881).

Dumont, A., 'Le musée Sainte-Irène à Constantinople', *Revue Archéologique*, XVIII (1868), 237–263.

Edson, C., (ed.), *Inscriptiones Graecae Epiri, Macedoniae, Thraciae, Scythiae, Pars II, Inscriptiones Macedoniae, Fasciculus I, Inscriptiones Thessalonicae et vicinae*, Berlin: G. de Gruyter (1972).

Frick, O., 'Phädra und Hippolyt, Ariadne auf Naxos (Sarkophagrelief zu Constantinopel)', *Denkmäler und Forschungen, Archäologische Zeitung*, XV, N° 100–102 (April–June 1857) col. 33.

Frick, O., 'Zum Hippolytus-Sarkophag in Constantinopel', *Denkmäler und Forschungen, Archäologische Zeitung*, XVI, N° 109–110 (January–February 1858) col. 131.

Gardner, E. A. and Stanley Casson, 'Macedonia. II. Antiquities Found in the British Zone, 1915-1919', *Annual of the British School at Athens*, 23 (1918/19), 10–43.

124   Edhem Eldem

Goold, E., *Catalogue explicatif, historique et scientifique d'un certain nombre d'objets contenus dans le Musée impérial de Constantinople*, Constantinople: A. Zellich (1871).

Husson, H., 'Nouvelles archéologiques et correspondance', *Revue Archéologique*, XX, 60–72 (June–December 1869).

Joubin, A., *Musée impérial ottoman. Monuments funéraires. Catalogue sommaire*, 2e édition, Constantinople: Musée impérial (1898).

Kolonas, V., Η εκτός των τειχών επέκταση της Θεσσαλονίκης: Εικονογραφία της συνοικίας Χαμηδιέ 1885–1912 [The 'Extra Muros' Extension of Thessaloniki. Iconography of The Hamidiye Area 1885–1912], PhD thesis, Aristotle University, Thessaloniki (1992).

Mazower, M., *Salonica, City of Ghosts: Christians, Muslims and Jews, 1430–1950*, London: HarperCollins (2004).

Mendel, G., *Catalogue des sculptures grecques, romaines et byzantines*, vol. I, Constantinople: Musées impériaux (1912–1914).

Mordtmann, J. H., 'Inschriften aus Makedonien', In: *Mittheilungen des deutschen archäologischen Institutes in Athen*, vol. XXI (1896), 97–101.

Özdemir, B., *Ottoman Reforms and Social Life: Reflections from Salonica, 1830–1850*, Istanbul: Isis Press (2003).

Reinach, S., *Catalogue du Musée impérial d'antiquités*, Constantinople: Ministère de l'Instruction publique, Musée impérial (1882).

Sabanopoulou, L., 'Yeni Cami (aka Old Archaeological Museum)', In: Brouskari, E. (ed.), *Ottoman Architecture in Greece*, Athens: Ministry of Culture, Directorate of Byzantine and Post-Byzantine Antiquities (2008), 226–229.

Salname-i Selanik, 2nd edition, Thessaloniki: Hamidiye Mekteb-i Sanayi Matbaası (1288/1871).

Salname-i Selanik, 3rd edition, Thessaloniki: Hamidiye Mekteb-i Sanayi Matbaası (1290/1873).

Schmidt, J., 'Aus Constantinopel und Kleinasien', *Mittheilungen des deutschen archäologischen Institutes in Athen*, VI (1881).

Selanik Vilayeti Salnamesi, 9th edition, Thessaloniki: Hamidiye Mekteb-i Sanayi Matbaası (1303/1886).

Selanik Vilayeti Salnamesi, 10th edition, Thessaloniki: Hamidiye Mekteb-i Sanayi Matbaası (1307/1890).

Selanik Vilayeti Salnamesi, 13th edition, Thessaloniki: Hamidiye Mekteb-i Sanayi Matbaası (1312/1895).

Selanik Vilayeti Salnamesi, 16th edition, Thessaloniki: Hamidiye Mekteb-i Sanayi Matbaası (1318/1900).

Selanik Vilayeti Salnamesi, 18th edition, Thessaloniki: Hamidiye Mekteb-i Sanayi Matbaası (1322/1904).

Selanik Vilayeti Salnamesi, 19th edition, Thessaloniki: Hamidiye Mekteb-i Sanayi Matbaası (1324/1906).

Selanik Vilayeti Salnamesi, 20th edition, Thessaloniki: Hamidiye Mekteb-i Sanayi Matbaası (1325/1907).

Takvim-i Vekayi, 24, p. 2 (2 Zilkade 1247/3 April, 1832).

Terenzio, T., 'Correspondence Book', Istanbul Archaeological Museum Archives (IAMA) (1871–1872a).

Terenzio, T., 'Inventory', Istanbul Archaeological Museum Archives (IAMA) (1871–1872b).

'The Story of the Archaeological Museum of Thessaloniki', www.amth.gr/en/story-arch aeological-museum-thessaloniki (accessed July 2019).

Yerolympos, A., *Urban Transformations in the Balkans (1820–1920), Aspects of Balkan Town Planning and the Remaking of Thessaloniki*, Thessaloniki: University Studio Press (1996).

9 Urban transformation and the revolution

Salonica and the Young Turks, 1908–1912

Sotiris Dimitriadis

In the summer of 1908, the discontent that had been simmering for years among the Ottoman military stationed in Salonica and other garrisons in Macedonia erupted in full rebellion against the autocratic government of Sultan Abdulhamid II. The opposition to the sultan's regime, officially united under the rubric 'Committee of Ottoman Union and Progress', but collectively known in the foreign press as the 'Young Turks', had been content in years past to operate from exile in Europe and Egypt. By that time, however, they had actively recruited new members among the bureaucracy and the army. In June 1908, officers affiliated to the Committee began abandoning their posts to form insurgent bands in the countryside. After the local military authorities proved unwilling or unable to move against them, opposition supporters in Salonica decided to move openly. The morning of July 23, 1908 leaflets were distributed calling on the people of Salonica to demonstrate for the restoration of constitutional rule, which had been introduced in 1876, but suspended the year after by the sultan. The streets were soon filled with large crowds; speeches on the virtue of Ottoman brotherhood, liberty, and the rule of law were delivered by the mayor, the president of the Commercial Court, and other notables.

With similar demonstrations springing up throughout the Ottoman Balkans and local authorities coming out in support of the opposition, the sultan capitulated. The following day, Hilmi Paşa, the Inspector General of Ottoman Macedonia, read from the steps of the *konak*, the local Government House, to a crowd of about 15000 people a telegram he had received from the palace, promising the restoration of the constitution and elections for a new Chamber of Deputies. In the words of Harry Lamb, the British consul:

> The rest of the day was given up to demonstrations of popular rejoicing, of which I doubt if the like has ever been seen in Turkey. The whole town was dressed in flags, processions paraded the streets, speeches were delivered in every public place, and the populace, half intoxicated with a sense of unwonted freedom, applauded uproariously on every possible occasion.[1]

The unexpected success of the 'Revolution' of 1908 had a far-reaching impact on future developments. Salonica found itself at the centre of events; as the birthplace

Urban transformation and the revolution   127

of the movement, as well as the seat of the Committee of Union and Progress and a bastion of constitutionalist support, the city became known as the 'Capital of Revolution'. The pre-existing local elites, which had controlled the political and economic life of the city and had contributed to its rise as a major urban centre in the Eastern Mediterranean, were now confronted with a new reality: new forms of political mobilisation and participation, emerging challenges from subaltern political groups, and a growing rift between state and non-state elites. By offering an account of the history of Salonica between 1908 and 1912, this paper will attempt to follow the emergence of the city as a model late Ottoman port and how that model unravelled under the historical processes released by the Revolution of 1908.

The rise of an Ottoman port city: Salonica 1870–1908

Salonica, the major port of the Ottoman Balkans, was radically transformed during the last third of the 19th century. As was the case with other, comparable port cities in the Eastern Mediterranean, the city experienced population growth, an increase in economic activity, and growing Western influence on social and cultural life. These effects can be traced to two long processes which defined the last century of the empire's history: One was the consolidation and expansion of the authority of the central state. The period of *Tanzimat* that followed the edicts of 1839 and 1856 attempted to reinvent the Ottoman state and reorganise its military along lines that combined European administrative and legal models with pre-existing practices. After the traumatic war with Russia in 1877–1878, Sultan Abdulhamid II would oversee his own brand of reformist projects, with the palace keen on maintaining much closer control over developments throughout the empire.[2]

Another factor was the on-going integration of the Ottoman economy into a world system dominated by the industrial powers of Western Europe. The need for diplomatic support against Russia and the costs of administrative and military reorganisation led to the opening up of the empire to foreign imports. Access to the financial institutions of Western Europe was secured during the Crimean War (1853–1856), and the empire quickly accrued increasing levels of public debt. However, the expectations for economic growth fuelled by free trade proved unrealistic and the Ottoman state had to declare insolvency in 1875 (Clay 2002). A settlement with debtors was reached only in 1881, with the founding of the Ottoman Public Debt Administration. This compromise allowed for the penetration of European financial capital into a significant part of the Ottoman economy; conversely the Ottoman state benefitted from renewed access to international loans, stabilisation of its currency, and reorganisation of its tax collecting agencies (Kasaba 1999, 77–88).

In port cities such as Salonica, these two processes converged. For the reforming state, these cities functioned as the administrative centres for larger areas; from the European perspective, they would be staging points for the expansion of economic activity into their hinterland. As the port cities eclipsed the cities of the interior in importance, wealth, and population, two groups emerged as the main

128 *Sotiris Dimitriadis*

agents of—and beneficiaries from—this process: an increased number of officials and civil servants, operating within an expanding institutional framework; and the emerging commercial elites, profiting from the increasing importance of international trade in the Ottoman port cities. While such traders had initially functioned as middlemen between producers in the hinterland and European traders, they were soon competing with the latter on equal terms for the trade with Europe (Findley 1980; Tabak 2009).

Both groups were very conscious of the fact that they were a product of the Ottoman reform process. They were united in their acceptance of a modernising discourse, even if they were uncomfortable with an uncritical adoption of European ideas and habits (Mardin 1974; Exertzoglou 2003). During the Hamidian period, Ottoman intellectuals, Muslim and non-Muslim alike, attempted to fashion ties between the modernisation of the empire and what each respective group perceived as 'traditional' (Deringil 1991). All the same, in a 19th-century context the requirements for being 'modern' were largely imposed from outside. Elites in places such as Salonica soon became very sensitive to the perception the Europeans had of their cities (Skopetea 1992).

The adoption of a modernising discourse by both the Ottoman state and by non-state elites had a direct impact on the urban fabric of the major urban centres of the empire. During the first half of the 19th century, a specific set of criteria developed in Western Europe concerning town planning, architecture, sanitation, safety, and public order, as well as services provided to the citizens. Recognising the importance of such a transformation, from the 1840s onwards the Ottoman state drafted a series of laws regulating town planning and the construction of buildings (Çelik 1986).

Most interventions in urban space were carried out by local administrative authorities: the province, or *vilayet*, and the municipalities. Set up as an attempt to improve the quality and extent of state functions in the Ottoman provinces, and at the same time to secure the co-operation of local notables, both institutions were open to the representation of local elite groups, while retaining ultimate control by the centre (Davison 1968; Hanssen 2003). The Hamidian system guaranteed a restricted public space and the opinions of the 'civil society' of the empire's cities were expressed through the press; while the state and its representatives were out of bounds, journalists were allowed to comment critically on the dealings of municipal authorities (Yerolympos 1997).

Beyond the ideological importance of reordering the cityscape, the process entailed concrete material gains for those involved in the process. In 1869 Sabri Paşa, the newly appointed *vali* of Thessaloniki, began the demolition of the coastal walls of the city. The rubble resulting from the demolition would be used to reclaim land from the sea and construct a quay; the plots were auctioned off (Yerolympos 1996, 62–67). When the Eastern walls of the city were demolished about ten years later, the fields of Kalamaria attracted large numbers of affluent locals who built their mansions there (Yerolymbos 1992, 63–67). The impoverished centre of the city remained in stark contrast to the newly developed areas until 1890 (Mazower 2004, 189–193). When a fire devastated a large expanse, the

Urban transformation and the revolution 129

municipality intervened, forbidding all reconstruction until a new town plan had been drafted for the area.[3] The centre was redesigned according to a grid pattern, and the new plots filled with large buildings designed in the Eclecticist and classicist architectural style. The original inhabitants of the burnt areas were forced to relocate in settlements on the outskirts (Dimitriadis 1983, 73–76, 162–170).

The concessions issued by the Ottoman state for large-scale infrastructure projects from the 1880s onwards promised the inhabitants of Salonica modern services and amenities, and at the same time offered good returns to local investors. The main actor in the concession trade in Salonica was Nemlizade Hamdi Bey, member of a notable *Dönme* family and an accomplished businessman with strong ties to Belgian economic interests. Hamdi Bey acquired the concessions for the construction of a local tram line, the supply of the city with water, and the enlargement of the Axios River so as to make it navigable. He then sold these concessions to Belgian companies, maintaining the role of a mediator between the new owners and the Ottoman authorities. In 1893 he was appointed mayor, exemplifying the convergence between public and private interests (Anastassiadou 1997, 160 ff.).

While the different elites of Ottoman Salonica maintained their mutual understanding, increasing instability in the surrounding countryside fuelled tensions inside the city, as well. Building on local traditions of brigandage and the dissatisfaction of a mainly landless peasantry now exposed to market relations, the region soon became the site of armed confrontation between bands equipped and supplied from the neighbouring states (Gounaris 1995; Hanioğlu 2008, 106–107). The Ottoman state was unable to curb the steady decline of public order. Its troops were often left without pay or supplies and their undisciplined and often brutal behaviour only fuelled the cycle of violence.[4] Salonica itself was not unaffected: In May 1903, a group of Bulgarian anarchists executed a series of bombing attacks on government and business targets, spreading chaos and prompting a violent reaction by the authorities.[5] In the following years, the streets and cafes of the city would witness a series of assassinations, which could only be attributed to the growing tensions between the Greek Orthodox and the Bulgarian element.

The growing instability in Macedonia, the failure of the Ottoman state to impose order, and the prospect of intervention by the Great Powers contributed to the disillusionment of the Ottoman officers stationed in the region with the Hamidian regime and their alignment with the opposition. During the winter and spring of 1908, the secret police attempted to neutralise the clandestine opposition groups within the troops (Hanioğlu 2001, 232 ff.). Faced with the prospect of arrest or demotion, a number of junior officers took a leap of faith and escaped to the countryside, launching the chain of events which would eventually lead to the 1908 revolution and the restoration of constitutional rule in the empire.

The aftermath of the revolution: July 1908–March 1909

The 1908 revolution created a vastly different reality for Ottoman society. The changes were especially pronounced in Salonica, one of the initial centres of the movement and the seat of the Committee of Union and Progress. The city now

130   *Sotiris Dimitriadis*

attracted visitors from the empire and abroad, eager to visit the capital of the revo-lution.[6] The element of public participation, first seen on and immediately after July 23, was a novelty that would irrevocably change the way politics was conducted on the local and the imperial level: whether one was a member of the municipal coun-cil or a candidate for parliament, a career once advanced by serving on a school board, attending services in the synagogue or church, and joining the gentlemen's club now had to be legitimised from the balcony and the street. Informed by a rapidly multiplying number of local papers, the people of the city remained mobi-lised even after the initial euphoria subsided; mass gatherings, demonstrations, and public speeches remained a feature of local life throughout this period.

Political activism spread to all classes of the population. Industrial and commer-cial workers across the empire decided to put their newly acquired rights to the test and formed associations and unions. Salonica was the city with the highest concen-tration of industrial workers, and they were soon protesting against long work hours, lack of pension rights, and salaries that remained stagnant in the face of rising living costs. On August 31, the workers at the tobacco manufacturing plan refused to go to their shifts, starting a wave of strikes that paralysed the local economy for about a month. Virtually all strikes ended with some compensation for the workers, who succeeded in negotiating pay raises that ranged between 20% and 45%.[7]

The strike wave of September 1908, which had spread around the empire, put the Committee in a delicate situation. On one hand, the striking workers embodied the same spirit of public participation that was evident during the constitutional revolution, and their appeals to the spirit of that revolution were frequent and constant. Committee members or public functionaries regarded as affiliated to the group, such as mayor Osman Adil Bey, played a crucial role in the negotiations between the strikers and their employers, to the point that a significant portion of the public thought the Committee itself was behind the strikes. On the other hand, it was of utmost importance to the Young Turk movement that the transition to constitutional rule be an orderly and controlled process—preferably controlled by the Young Turks themselves. The strikes had to be curtailed, and legislation was drafted at Istanbul to this goal.

The ambivalent position of the Committee was indicative of a concept of society formed in close connection to *fin-de-siècle* French positivism: that of a mechanical whole constituted by different parts. That whole would be operated by a national party, playing the role of the moderator between the state, established elites, and the 'Ottoman nation'. The participation of the latter was crucial: Given all the problems faced by the new regime, the utilisation of public participation and mass politics was a means for the Committee to reinvent itself, and from a secret organisation of junior officers and disgruntled exiles turn into a hegemonic political force with a structure reaching throughout the empire. Groups such as workers, the youth, and women had to be encouraged into greater public par-ticipation, under the guidance of the Committee and its affiliated organisations (Karakaya-Stump 2003).

Conversely, the new conditions challenged the control of established elites over the local politics. The Ottoman constitution guaranteed their individual

Urban transformation and the revolution   131

rights against the state; but these had been previously maintained as communal rights, common material interests, and networks of patronage and patrimony, all now under question. The administrative order was disrupted, and scores of officials were replaced, some removed in disgrace and others promoted in recognition of their constitutionalist sympathies (FO 195/2328, Lamb to Lowther, 6/2/1909). Local administrative structures continued to function, but their authority was challenged by the mere existence and operation of the committee in the city. Though the committee initially made moves at reconciliation with the local notables, the response of the commercial classes and the communal leaders oscillated between enthusiasm among the Jews and *Dönme*, who welcomed the modernist and Ottomanist discourse, and suspicion from the Muslim *ulema* and the Greek Orthodox church and community, who feared for their established privileges (Cooperman 1996; Veremis 1990, 17–22; Baer 2007, 157–158).

The elections for the restored Ottoman parliament, which were to be held throughout the autumn, were expected to shed some light on the intentions of the Committee and its relations with the city's elites. The elections were to be held under a complicated two-stage electoral system, with the franchise restricted to adult, male holders of property and with deputies elected from a joint list at the level of the *sancak*. The *sancak* of Salonica was to elect six deputies, with another five for the rest of the *vilayet*. The Committee succeeded in entering into an agreement with the Jewish and the Greek communities of the city, as well as with the pro-Bulgarian Constitutional Clubs, to jointly support six candidates: two Muslims, two Greeks, one Bulgarian and one Jew.[8]

Despite these arrangements, the election campaign proved quite tumultuous. On October 5, Bulgaria unilaterally declared itself independent; the next day, Austria-Hungary, also unilaterally, formally annexed Bosnia and Herzegovina, which had been under its military control since 1878. Both developments had important repercussions in the diplomatic field. On the local level, the Committee organised the public reaction against Bulgaria and Austria-Hungary to further its influence and secure its electoral success. On October 10, thousands of people congregated on the open ground in front of the Third Army headquarters (FO 195/2298, Lamb to Lowther, 22/9/1908 and 11/10/1908). The following day, the dockworkers refused to handle the cargo of an incoming Austrian steamer; despite the protests filed by the consular corps and the intervention of the Chief Rabbi and the *vali*, the boycott remained strong until it was called off the next spring (FO 195/2298, Lamb to Lowther, 23/11/1908).

Despite the tense atmosphere, the elections themselves were peaceful, if not entirely fair: The Bulgarian and Greek communities claimed that extensive fraud took place, in order to return a majority of Muslim second degree electors. Nonetheless, the Committee honoured the electoral pact it had signed, and the Muslim electors of the second degree voted *en bloc* for the non-Muslim candidates. The Committee swept the elections in the *vilayet*, returning all eleven designated candidates. The six new deputies for the *sancak* of Salonica were, for the Committee, Rahmi Bey, Emmanuel Carasso, and Mehmet Cavid Bey; Dimitar Vlahof, a socialist schoolteacher; and the Greeks G. Artas and G. Honaios.[9]

132   *Sotiris Dimitriadis*

The elections to the Ottoman parliament were expected to be a first step towards the normalisation of political life of the empire, under a parliamentary and constitutional regime. These expectations remained unfulfilled. Instability remained, as the Committee, still officially seated at Salonica, the Palace, the bureaucracy, and the parliamentary opposition fought for political power. Outmanoeuvred by the Committee, its opponents were drawn closer into an unlikely alliance of liberals, ethnic nationalists, and supporters of absolute rule by the sultan. On April 13, 1909, things in the capital came to a head, as troops from the Istanbul garrison, along with students from the religious schools and crowds of people, stormed the parliament and forced the appointment of a new government, which would be more in accordance with religious law.[10]

News of the movement in Istanbul was met with anger in Salonica. Mahmud Şevket Paşa, head of the Third Army, agreed to mobilise the troops to advance towards Istanbul. Crowds were again on the streets, denouncing the threat to the constitution and volunteering to go to the capital and defend the new order once and for all. By April 23, the army had taken control of Istanbul with minimal fighting; four days later the deposition of Abdulhamid and his replacement by his brother Mehmet Reşad was publicly announced (FO 195/2328, Lamb to Lowther, 21/4/1909).

At the news of Abdulhamid's deposition, Salonica was illuminated, and the following day was declared a public holiday (FO 195/2328, Lamb to Lowther 27/4/1909). The city became a rehabilitation centre of sorts, as those arrested as complicit in the events of April 13 were imprisoned there and the soldiers who had taken part in the mutiny were also brought to Salonica, before being gradually decommissioned. Abdulhamid himself arrived at Salonica by a special train on the night of April 28. His train stopped at the military station, in the outskirts of the city, to avoid the crowds that had gathered in front of the passenger station. The sultan boarded a carriage and was driven through the less frequented streets of the city accompanied by mounted gendarmes, until he reached his destination, the Villa Allatini.[11]

Capital of the revolution

The failure of the movement of April 1909 gave a great boost to the influence of the Committee. The appointment of Mahmud Şevket Paşa to the post of Minister of War symbolised the bond between the army and the Committee. Faced with the growing intransigence of the Committee and without recourse to the palace or the bureaucracy, the opposition splintered and became ineffective. Inside Salonica itself, the control of the Committee seemed absolute. The population was supportive, the civil and military authorities affiliated to it and the press was sympathetic. In the short period between July 1908 and April 1909, the city had become known as the 'capital of the revolution', a bastion of support for the constitution, the parliament, and the Committee, and the only place safe enough to keep the former sultan imprisoned.

Urban transformation and the revolution   133

The stranglehold of the Committee over imperial and local politics, however, gradually bred discontent. Constant pressure from abroad made the Committee less inclined to accommodate the demands of ethnic and religious minorities. A number of intellectuals active at Salonica had become advocates of Turkic nationalism. This caused alarm to the non-Muslim communities. The Muslim *ulema* were becoming increasingly suspicion of the attitude of the Committee in regard to religion and its place in Ottoman society. There were merchants who feared that measures such as the boycott would endanger their commercial interests, and workers who were unsatisfied with the gains of the September strike wave and thought that independent action was the only way to defend and extend them. Support for or opposition to the Committee cut across ethnic, religious, and class groups, which led to a greater fragmentation of local society (Boura 1999).

The 1908 revolution greatly expanded the space available for public expression, by initiating elections and mass politics and abolishing the restrictive legal framework. It had also politicised the spaces that existed already: the broad, straight streets became sites for rallies, which ended up in the open spaces of the city; coffeehouses were booked for political meetings; otherwise, the speaker could address the crowds from the balcony of a hotel; streetlamps and telegraph posts were placarded with pamphlets and posters; and the theaters, which once only played comic operas or tragedies, now had their share of satires and patriotic plays. Since 1908 the Committee had frequently employed these spaces to expand its influence in the city. Now it found itself challenged in the same spaces, with the same means it had used before. Aware that an attack on the freedom of expression would undermine the legacy of 1908 and its own legitimacy, the Committee had no other choice but to combine some restrictive measures with enhancing its own presence in the public spaces of the city (Seckin 2007).

Challenging the order imposed locally by the Committee, workers returned to the streets and celebrated May Day for the first time in the city. On June 19, a crowd of thousands gathered in Olympos Square, known as the Square of Liberty ever since the revolution of 1908 was proclaimed there, to protest against the introduction of anti-strike and anti-union legislation and for the defence of workers' rights. One of the speakers, a Bulgarian Jew called Avraam Benaroya, had gathered around him a growing group of workers, who assembled regularly and debated workers' rights, progressive politics, and socialist theory. By the summer of that year, the group had been reorganised as the *Fédération Socialiste Ouvrière*. Its publication, *The Worker's Journal*, appeared in August in four editions: Judeo-Spanish, Bulgarian, Ottoman Turkish, and Greek.[12]

From its emergence, the nascent labour and socialist movement in Salonica was entangled with the national question. Some of the unions in the city were organised on a communal basis and others on the corporation level. The *Fédération*, conversely, developed into a staunchly Ottomanist organisation. The socialist transformation of the Ottoman Empire it envisaged would alleviate ethnic tensions and promote a federal, decentralised structure of government. In practice, socialist internationalism had difficulties in expanding beyond the Jewish and, to

134 *Sotiris Dimitriadis*

a lesser extent, Bulgarian workers, and the *Fédération*'s newspaper soon had to suspend its Ottoman and Greek editions (Quataert 1995).

From the summer of 1909 onwards, the city remained embroiled in agitation over Crete and the alleged violation of Ottoman sovereignty over the island. In the spring, a public meeting of protest was followed by a call for a boycott against Greek shipping as well as all commercial establishments owned by Greek subjects.[13] Kerim Ağa, head of the guild of porters and lightermen, was established at the Customs House and was given the responsibility to provide Ottoman Greek businessmen with certificates of Ottoman citizenship in return for a small charge, the proceeds of which were supposed to compensate his men for the losses incurred. The collection of that fee soon escalated into acts of violence against shops whose owners refused to pay. The effects were felt not only by Greek subjects and Ottoman Greeks, but also by Jewish merchants and foreign protégés.[14]

The tense climate persisted until the spring, when it was announced that the sultan would be visiting the city. The visit, which had been originally intended for Abdulhamid and postponed in the chaos of the events of April 1909, was set first for March 31, then for June 7. The preparations for the sultan's visit constituted the last large-scale intervention in the cityscape of Ottoman Salonica: The streets on which the sultan would pass (the quay, the *Hamidiye* Boulevard, and Midhat Paşa Street, where the *konak* was situated) were re-paved and widened. The walls that surrounded the White Tower were demolished and the public gardens enlarged to incorporate the structure. The restoration of the Ayasofya mosque, where the sultan would attend Friday prayers, was accelerated. The religious communities and the political and cultural clubs were encouraged to participate in the festivities and to prepare large archways with celebratory slogans, which would be placed around the sites the sultan would visit. Thousands of visitors started arriving days before, and all accommodation in the city was booked.[15]

The sultan arrived at Salonica on board the warship *Hayreddin Barbarossa* on the evening of June 7. He disembarked at the harbour the next morning and was driven around the city in a carriage to the applause of thousands of spectators, until he reached the *konak*, where he received various delegations. In the evening, the clubs of the city organised a parade of torchbearers, which was accompanied by a luminous fountain, courtesy of M. Cuypers, the Belgian consul and head of the city's Water Company. The following day, the sultan went to Ayasofya to pray, then proceeded to the gardens of *Beş Çinar* where he attended an exposition of local manufactures. The sultan sent his first secretary to the Villa Allatini, to ask after his brother's health, but direct communication between the two men was denied. After the sultan visited the Third Army headquarters and inspected the officers on the morning of the third day, he departed by train for Kosovo.

The sultan's visit was perhaps the last manifestation of the Ottoman city. In the following months, war and an increasingly restrictive state would lead first to the segmentation of local society, then to its eventual neutralisation.

Urban transformation and the revolution 135

The unravelling of Ottoman Salonica, 1911–1912

The summer of 1911 was marked by the escalation of the crisis between Italy and the empire over Tripoli. When war was formally declared in September, the Committee organised counter-measures against the local Italian presence.[16] Italian trade was boycotted and commercial and financial establishments owned by Italian subjects were closed (FO 195/2382, Morgan to Lowther, 3/10/1911). Since a significant part of the Jewish upper class of the city had Italian protection, these measures, along with the gradual flight of those targeted in this way, exacerbated an already critical financial situation.[17]

As the weakness of the Ottoman military damaged the prestige of the government, opposition groups formed the Liberal Entente, hoping to effectively challenge the Committee. The municipal elections that took place in February 1912 were regarded as a first round between the Committee and the opposition, in anticipation of the parliamentary elections, which were to take place in that spring. In the event, the Committee suffered a humiliation, as none of its candidates were re-elected.[18] By this point, however, the relative power and autonomy of the municipality had diminished and the victory of the opposition proved to be hollow. The Committee had taken control of the provincial bureaucracy and its leading members all held managerial positions in the *vilayet* (FO 195/2359, Lamb to Lowther, 16/12/1910). By appointing weak individuals without administrative experience at the post of *vali*, they could ensure their control of provincial administration from their secondary posts (FO 295/21, Lamb to Lowther, 31/1/1912).

That control proved crucial during the parliamentary elections that took place in the spring of 1912, appropriately remembered as the 'big stick elections'. As the date for the selection of the first degree electors approached, the opposition press reported numerous cases of fraud, disruption of political rallies, intimidation, and violence on the part of the authorities (FO 295/21, Lamb to Lowther, 30/3/1912). Unfazed by such allegations, the *vali*, Hüseyin Kâzim Paşa, publicly endorsed the Committee and the candidacy of Rahmi Bey, who was running again along with Cavid Bey and Carasso (FO 295/21, Lamb to Lowther, 30/3/1912). The final results of the elections seemed largely unrepresentative of public opinion: Only nine of 86 second degree electors recorded their votes for the opposition in the *kaza* of Salonica, only one in the *kaza* of Vodena, none in the *kazas* of Kasandra and Yenice, i.e. in those areas of the *vilayet* which it was expected to perform well.[19] The Committee elected all six candidates on its ticket; these included, apart from the three mentioned, Halil Bey, J. Nikolov, and K. Kotsanos (*Nea Alitheia* 870, 3/4/1912). Honaios and Vlahov were not returned, while Artas ran successfully in Istanbul with the support of the Committee (Boura 1999, 203–205; *Nea Alitheia* 872, 5/4/1912).

The elections of 1912 had a depressing effect on political activity in the city. They proved, if anything, the extent of the control the Committee exercised over the state apparatus, and its willingness to use it to further its political aims, and, conversely, the weakness of local civil society in maintaining its influence vis-à-vis the state. The ideals of constitutionalism and Ottoman brotherhood, which

136 *Sotiris Dimitriadis*

seemed triumphant after July 1908, now were unsalvageable and perhaps irrelevant. With the war with Italy showing no signs of abating, and tensions rising with the neighbouring Balkan States, local society withdrew from public life and held its breath, as the city passed into a state of emergency. By November of that year, the Balkan Wars would break out and the city would be occupied by Greek troops.

Notes

1 Public Records Office, Foreign Office archives [from now on FO] 195/2298, Lamb to Barclay, 23/7/1908 and 24/7/1908. See also Megas 2003, 115 ff.
2 For the 'fine-tuning' of Ottoman society and administration by the Hamidian regime, see Selim Derngil's work, especially Derngil 1998.
3 *Faros tis Makedonias*, August 25 [old style] 1890; FO 78/4287, Blunt to White, September 5, 1890.
4 Akhund 2009, 451–452; FO 295/16, Du Vallon to embassy, 22/9/1904 and 25/9/1904.
5 Megas 1994; FO 195/2156, Billioti to O'Conor, 2/5/1903.
6 According to the British Consul, more than 30,000 visited the city in August 1908! FO 195/2328, Lamb to Lowther, 6/2/1909.
7 Mentzel 1994, 112–115; FO 195/2298, Lamb to Lowther, 9/9/1908 and 24/9/1908.
8 Megas, *Η Επανάσταση των Νεότουρκων*, 331–346; FO 195/2298, Lamb to Lowther, 22/9/1908.
9 FO 195/2298, Lamb to Lowther, 22/9/1908; 9/11/1908 and 15/11/1908.
10 Hanioğlu 2008, 151–154; FO 195/2328, Lamb to Lowther, 17/4/1909; 18/4/1909 and 19/4/1909.
11 FO 195/2328, Lamb to Lowther, 57, 29/4/1909; Mazower 2004, 277–278.
12 Mazower 2004, 286–287; FO 195/2329, Lamb to Lowther 21/6/1909.
13 FO 195/2357, Lamb to Lowther, 15/5/1910; FO 195/2358, Lamb to Lowther, 10/6/1910.
14 FO 195/2358, Lamb to Lowther, 18/6/1910; 28/6/1910 and 29/6/1910. For the importance of Greek banking for the commerce of the Aegean port cities, see Frangakis-Syrett 2009.
15 Theoharidou 1989, 179–180; FO 195/2381, Lamb to Lowther, 11/6/1911; Cohen 2008, 217 ff.
16 FO 195/2382, Morgan to Lowther, 28/6/1911; interestingly, the largest demonstration against the war was not that of the Committee, but the one organised by the *Fédération*. Mazower 2004, 289.
17 FO 195/2382, Lamb to Lowther, 2/12/1911; Meron, 2005.
18 *Nea Alitheia* 12/2/1912; FO 295/21, Lamb to Lowther, 26/2/1912 and 9/3/1912.
19 The authorities refused to allow Honaios and Vlahov, who were contesting the elections on the Liberal ticket, to visit Vodena (*Nea Alitheia* 25/2/1912). The electors of second degree in Kassandra, which was the last *kaza* to send its votes, claimed that when they arrived at the seat of the district, in order to cast their votes, the authorities pressured them to vote for the Committee candidates (*Nea Alitheia* 6/4/1912).

References

Akhund, N., 'Muslim representation in the Three Ottoman Vilayets of Macedonia: Administration and military power (1878–1908)', *Journal of Muslim Minority Affairs* 29 (2009), 451–452.
Anastassiadou, M., *Salonique, 1830–1912: une ville ottomane à l'âge des réformes*, Leiden: Brill (1997).

Baer, M., 'Globalization, cosmopolitanism and the Dönme in Ottoman Salonica and Turkish Istanbul', *Journal of World History* 18.11 (2007), 157–158.

Boura, C., 'The Greek millet in Turkish politics: Greeks in the Ottoman Parliament', In: Issawi, C. and Gondicas, D. (eds.), *Ottoman Greeks in the Age of Nationalism: Politics, Economy and Society in the Nineteenth Century*, Princeton, NJ: Darwin Press (1999), 193–206.

Çelik, Z., *The Remaking of Istanbul: Portrait of an Ottoman City in the Nineteenth Century*, Seattle, WA/London: University of Washington Press (1986).

Clay, C., *Gold for the Sultan: Western Bankers and Ottoman Finance 1856–1881: A Contribution to Ottoman and to International Financial History*, London: I.B. Tauris (2002).

Cohen, J. P., *Fashioning Imperial Citizens: Sephardi Jews and the Ottoman state, 1856–1912*. PhD dissertation, Stanford University, Stanford, CA (2008).

Cooperman, E., 'The Young Turk revolution of 1908 and the Jewish community of Salonica', In: Altabe, D. F., Atay, Erhan and Katz, I. J. (eds.), *Studies on Turkish-Jewish History*, New York: Sepher-Hermon Press for the American Society of Sephardic Studies (1996), 168–180.

Davison, R., 'The advent of the principle of representation in the government of the Ottoman Empire', In: Polk, W. R. and Chambers, R. L. (eds.), *Beginnings of Modernization in the Middle East: The Nineteenth Century*, Chicago, IL/London: University of Chicago Press (1968), 93–108.

Deringil, S., 'Legitimacy structures in the Ottoman state: The Reign of Abdülhamid II (1876–1909)', *International Journal of Middle East Studies*, 23 (1991), 345–359.

Deringil, S., *The Well-Protected Domains: Ideology and the Legitimation of Power in the Ottoman Empire, 1876–1909*, London: I. B. Tauris (1998).

Dimitriadis, V., *Η Τοπογραφία της Θεσσαλονίκης κατά την Εποχή της Τουρκοκρατίας, 1430–1912* [A Topography of Thessaloniki under the Turks, 1430–1912], Thessaloniki: Etairia Makedonikon Spoudon (1983).

Exertzoglou, H., 'The cultural uses of consumption: Negotiating class, gender, and nation in the Ottoman urban centers during the 19th century', *International Journal of Middle East Studies*, 35 (2003), 77–101.

Faros tis Makedonias [Φάρος της Μακεδονίας], Thessaloniki daily newspaper, 1874–1912.

Findley, C. V., *Bureaucratic Reform in the Ottoman Empire: The Sublime Porte, 1789–1922*, Princeton, NJ: Princeton University Press (1980).

Frangakis-Syrett, E., 'Banking in Izmir in the early twentieth century', *Mediterranean Historical Review* 24:2 (December 2009), 115–132.

Gounaris, B. C., 'Social cleavages and national "awakening" in Ottoman Macedonia', *East European Quarterly*, 29 (1995), 418–424.

Hanioğlu, M. Ş., *A Brief History of the Ottoman Empire*, Princeton, NJ/Oxford: Princeton University Press (2008).

Hanioğlu, M. Ş., *Preparation for a Revolution: The Young Turks, 1902–1908*, Oxford: Oxford University Press (2001).

Hanssen, J., *Fin de Siecle Beirut: the making of an Ottoman provincial capital*, Oxford: Clarendon Press (2003).

Karakaya-Stump, A., 'Debating progress in a "serious newspaper for Muslim women": The periodical *Kadın* in post-revolutionary Salonica, 1908–1909', *British Journal of Middle Eastern Studies*, 30.2 (2003), 155–181.

Kasaba, R., 'Economic foundations of civil society: Greeks in the trade of Western Anatolia, 1840–1876', In: Issawi, C. and Gondicas, D. (eds.), *Ottoman Greeks in the Age of*

138 *Sotiris Dimitriadis*

Nationalism: Politics, Economy and Society in the Nineteenth Century, Princeton, NJ: Darwin Press (1999), 77–88.

Mardin, Ş., 'Super westernisation in urban life in the Ottoman Empire in the last quarter of the nineteenth century', In: Benedict, P., Tümertekin, E. and Mansur, F. (eds.), *Turkey: Geographic and Social Perspectives*, Leiden: Brill (1974), 403–446.

Mazower, M., *Salonica: City of Ghosts, Christians, Muslims and Jews, 1430–1950*, London: HarperCollins (2004).

Megas, Y., *Η Επανάσταση των Νεότουρκων στη Θεσσαλονίκη* [The Young Turk Revolution in Thessaloniki], Thessaloniki: University Studio Press (2003).

Megas, Y., *Οι «Βαρκάρηδες» της Θεσσαλονίκης: Η Βουλγαρική αναρχική ομάδα και οι βο μβιστικές ενέργειες του 1903* [The 'Boatmen' of Thessaloniki: The Bulgarian Anarchist Group and the Bombing Action of 1903], Thessaloniki: Trohalia (1994).

Mentzel, P. C., *Nationalism and the labor movement in the Ottoman Empire, 1872–1914*. PhD dissertation, University of Washington, Seattle, WA(1994).

Meron, O. C., 'Sub-ethnicity and elites: Italian-Jewish professional and entrepreneurs in Salonica, (1881–1912)', *Zakhor: Revista di storia degli Ebrei d'Italia* 8 (2005), 177–220.

Nea Alitheia[Νέα Αλήθεια] Thessaloniki daily newspaper, 1909–1971.

Quataert, D., 'The workers of Salonica, 1850–1908', In: Quataert, D. and Zürcher, E. J. (eds.), *Workers and the Working Class in the Ottoman Empire and the Turkish Republic, 1839–1950*, London: Tauris Academic Studies (1995), 59–74.

Seckin, B., *Staging the Revolution: The Theatre of the Revolution in the Ottoman Empire, 1908–1909*. Unpublished MA thesis, Boğazici University (2007).

Skopetea, E., *Η Δύση της Ανατολής: Εικόνες από το Τέλος της Οθωμανικής Αυτοκρατορίας* [The West of the East: Images from the End of the Ottoman Empire], Athens: Gnosi (1992).

Tabak, F., 'Imperial rivalry and port-cities: A view from above', *Mediterranean Historical Review*, 24.2 (2009), 79–94.

Theoharidou, K., *The Architecture of Hagia Sophia, from Its Erection up to the Turkish Conquest*, Oxford: BAR International Series 399 (1989).

Veremis, T., 'From the national state to the stateless nation, 1821–1910', In: Veremis, T. and Blinkhorn, M. (eds.), *Modern Greece: Nationalisms and nationality*, Athens: ELIAMEP (1990), 17–22.

Yerolympos, A., 'Conscience citadine et intérêt municipal à Salonique a le fin du XIX siècle', In: Dumont, P. and Georgeon, F. (eds.), *Vivre dans l'empire Ottoman: Sociabilites et relations intercommunautaires (XVIIe–XXe siècles)*, Paris: L'Harmattan (1997), 123–144.

Yerolympos, A., 'Urbanisme et Modernisation en Grece du Nord a l'Epoque des Tanzimat (de 1839 a la Fin du XXe s.)', In: Dumont, P. and Georgeon, F. (eds.), *Villes Ottomanes a la Fin de l'Empire*, Paris: l'Harmattan (1992), 63–67.

Yerolympos, A., *Urban Transformations in the Balkans (1820–1920): Aspects of Balkan Town Planning and the Remaking of Thessaloniki*, Thessaloniki: University Studio Press (1996).

10 Bulgarian newspapers in Thessaloniki, 1869–1913

Vlasis Vlasidis

Introduction

The importance of the Thessaloniki press as a key resource for the history of the city and its society was not fully appreciated until the end of the 1970s. The archives of most Thessaloniki newspapers did not survive the vicissitudes of time. In the 1990s, however, the surviving archives began to be valued by the community and became the subject of research. A pioneer in this was the redoubtable Manolis Kandylakis from the University of Thessaloniki (Kandylakis 1984, 12; 1993, 99–108), followed by other researchers. Their first emphasis was on systematic study of the Greek press, followed by research on Jewish newspapers and those of the labor union movement. The Turkish-language press has also received a share of scholarly attention. For the Bulgarian-language newspapers published in pre-1912 Thessaloniki, however, there are few published studies: that of Stojan Simeonov (1934, 227–259); Dimitar Ivantsev's bibliographical references for the creation of a newspaper archive at the National Library of Sofia (1962, 1966); Boro Mogrob and Tome Gruevski, who followed Ivantsev but rebaptized the press Macedonian (1993); and Kandylakis's *Newspapers of Thessaloniki* (1998, 2000).

The first printing houses appeared in Thessaloniki centuries before the first newspapers were published. The first Jewish printing house, the oldest in the Balkan peninsula, was founded in 1515 by Don Yehuda Gedaliah with a press brought from the printing house of Eliezer Toledano in Lisbon (Papastathis 1968, 239; Toledano 2000, 3). In 1727, the first Turkish printing house was set up (Papastathis 1968, 239). The first Bulgarian printing house in Thessaloniki was founded in 1838 by Hadzi Theodosij Sinajtski, and it operated until 1841 or 1843, when it was destroyed by fire for the second time (Antov 1934, 308, 311; Snegarov 1937, 28; Papastathis 1968, 251; Hekimoglou 2017, 157). The first Greek printing house was founded by Miltiadis Garbolas in 1850. It operated for only a year (Papastathis 1968, 240–241).

Thessaloniki's first journal was *El Lunar* (the lunar month), which appeared in 1864, published by Rabbi Judah Nehama (1826–1899). This short-lived journal carried translations of articles from Jewish newspapers from central Europe and also articles by Nehama and his assistants (Frezis 1999, 95; Kerem 1999, 69). *Salonica (Selanik)* followed in February 1869. It was the official newspaper of

140   *Vlasis Vlasidis*

the Vilayet and appeared in four languages including Judeo-Spanish; a page was compiled by Rabbi Jacob Uziel. The first daily newspaper containing news stories in Judeo-Spanish, *La Epoca*, was launched on 20 October 1875 by Saadi Halevi Ashkenazi (Frezis 1999, 96–97; Kerem 1999, 70). The same year Saadi and his sons Betsalel, Daout effendi, and Samuel published a French newspaper, *Journal de Salonique* (Kerem 1999, 70). By 1923–1924, more than fifty Jewish newspapers had been published in total (Frezis 1999, 96–97).[1]

The first Turkish, or rather, Ottoman newspaper was the four-language *Selanik/Salonica/Thessaloniki/Solun*, begun in 1869 at the initiative of the Ottoman administration to inform local people about its activities (Fotopoulou 1995, 15; Kandylakis 1999, 415–417). The first private Turkish newspaper was *Roumeli*, published by Mustapha Bey in 1872. A year later it was renamed *Zaman* (Fotopoulou 1995, 15). This newspaper was short-lived, but *Asir*, which first came out in 1895, was published in Thessaloniki until 1924 and is still published in Izmir. In total, 73 Turkish-language newspapers existed, 13 before 1908, 49 between 1908 and 1912, and nine from 1912–1924 (Fotopoulou 1995, 15).

The first Greek-language newspaper was the official *Thessaloniki (Selanik)* (Kandylakis 1999, 37). The Greek community got its own newspaper on 13 May 1875, *Ermis*, published by Sophocles Garbolas. This was a bi-weekly newspaper with a combative attitude to many issues in the news. *Alitheia* (Truth) followed, and then dozens of others. One of them, Vellidis' *Makedonia*, is still in circulation today (Christianopoulos 1992, 8–12; Kandylakis 1999, 51).

Bulgarian newspapers and journals

Table 10.1 lists the Bulgarian-language newspapers and journals, many of them ephemeral, known to have been published in Thessaloniki. It excludes reprints or translations of journals from other countries.

Apart from the official *Solun (Selanik)*, at least 26 Bulgarian newspapers and periodicals were published between 1891 and 1913. At first glance this seems a substantial number relative to the size of the Bulgarian Exarchist community in Thessaloniki and its environs.[2] For the period before the end of the 19th century, however, the output is very limited: three literary journals, and four hand-written newspapers.[3]

The first documented Bulgarian journal, *Knizhiitsi za prachit*, published extracts from Bulgarian and world literature, linguistics, and science. This journal was evidently directed not at the general population of Macedonia, but at an educated population with an interest in the Bulgarian national idea (Simeonov 1934, 231). The first edition of the journal *Godishen otchet na meteorologitseska stantsia* was published by the Bulgarian High School in Thessaloniki, edited by Ivan Diakovich. It published texts on atmospheric measurements, the weather, and so on, and had no particular political agenda beyond that of the school authorities. It remained in circulation for a number of years (Ivantsev 1962, 215).

The four newspapers were written out by students at the Thessaloniki Bulgarian High School under the guidance of some of their teachers. There are no

Table 10.1 Bulgarian-language newspapers and journals known to have been published in Thessaloniki

Publication	Years	Description
Solun (Selanik)	1869	Bulletin of the Ottoman administration
Knizhiitsi za prachit	1889–1895	Literary journal
Godishen otchet na metereologitseska stantsia	1895–1911	Journal
Vastanik	1894	Hand-written political newspaper
Borba	1898	Hand-written political newspaper
Veriga	1899	Hand-written student political newspaper
Snop	1899	Hand-written student political newspaper
Konstitutsionna Zarya	22 August 1908–3 January 1909	Political newspaper
Edinstvo	27 September 1908–5 January 1909	Political newspaper
Nachalo	25 October 1908–25 July 1912	Weekly political and social review
Kulturno Edinstvo	1 October 1908–1 March 1909	Social and literary journal and review
Narodna Volya	17 January 1909–5 June 1910	Political and social newspaper
Otechestvo	21 February–19 December 1909	Political and social newspaper
Rabotnicheski Vestnik	14 August–15 October 1909	Weekly newspaper
Uchitelsko Saznanie	2 September–12 October 1909	Journal for teachers
Rodina	19 February–2 July 1910	Informative and political newspaper
Istina	26 February–6 April 1912	Informative and political newspaper
Uchitelski Glas	15 June 1910–20 September 1912	Journal for teachers
Pravo	18 September 1910–7 May 1913	Daily political and social newspaper
Rabotnik	1911–1912	Weekly workers newspaper
Rabotnicheska Iskra	1 January 1909–20 May 1911	Workers socialist newspaper
Iskra	1 December 1911–September 1912	Political, social, and literary journal
Svetlina	8 February–24 May 1912	Political pro-Turkish newspaper
Belomoretch	2–7 November 1912	Political and social newspaper
Bulgarin	5 November–1 December 1912	Political and social newspaper
Nova Bulgaria	1–5 December 1912	Political and social newspaper

142   *Vlasis Vlasidis*

surviving copies to be found either in Greece or Bulgaria. Our information about them is thus indirect and concerns the aspiring political figures who published them rather than their content. These were presumably not school newspapers, but rather political tracts concerned with national awaking and the revolutionary ideas of the newly formed Internal Macedonian Revolutionary Organization (IMRO). In any event, it is hard to imagine Dame Gruev's or Ivan Garvanov's newspapers not promoting revolutionary ideas in Macedonia during this decade of political ferment (Simeonov 1934, 238; Mokrob and Gruevski 1993, 44).

In the next period, from 1900 to the rise of the Young Turks, there was almost no Bulgarian-language publishing activity. During these years of ethnic conflict between Exarchists and the Patriarchists, only one journal continued publication, *Godishen otchet na meterologitseska stantsia*, and no newspapers. In other cities of Macedonia, the situation was the same. In this period around the Ilinden uprising, Bulgarian nationalists relied on 'propaganda of the deed' directed both against the Greeks and against their own communities: supporters of annexation by Bulgaria and supporters of IMRO sometimes sneered at one another and sometimes fought with weapons. The fact that other ethnic communities continued their publishing activities during this period, and not only in Thessaloniki, suggests that this view is not far from the truth.

This situation changed drastically with the rise of the Young Turks, the cessation of clashes between the armed bands, and the declaration of elections for the Ottoman parliament. Between 1908 and 1912, 11 Bulgarian social and political newspapers were published as well as six literary and educational periodicals. All of these promoted political views and took part in the political competition for representation in the Ottoman parliament.

The Young Turk revolution and the promise of elections found the ethnic communities in Macedonia divided, particularly the Bulgarians. In the November/ December 1908 elections for the 275 seats in the Ottoman parliament, Exarchists split into two main groups within IMRO, which in the first decade of the 20th century played a more important political role than the Exarchate. The right wing played a key role in the founding of the Bulgarian Constitutional Clubs, which took part in the elections with the slogan of a self-governing Macedonia containing all the ethnic communities (Parvanova 1994, 68; Parvanov 1991, 23–49). The left wing of IMRO, with the collaboration of the socialists, started the People's Federative Party (Bulgarian Section) aiming for local and regional self-government and the creation of separate units on the basis of ethnic boundaries and economic conditions, and the creation of an Eastern federation (Parvanova 1994, 69; Parvanov 1989, 32–42).

In 1909, the Union of Bulgarian Constitutional Clubs developed into the Progressive Constitutional Party. The People's Federative Party took the word Bulgarian out of its name and essentially broke up in 1910. Dimitar Vlahov, who had been elected with the Federative Party, joined the Ottoman Socialist Party, and other members preferred to create the Workers' Social Democratic Party (Parvanova 2001, 53, 55; Despot 2012, 27). There were some attempts to create other political groups.

Bulgarian newspapers in Thessaloniki 143

The Bulgarian parties were in disarray at the time of the elections of 1912. The right wing created a Central Election Committee, whose main demand was respect for constitutional freedom, self-government, cultural autonomy, and solutions to the agricultural issue (Parvanova 2001, 66). Most people supported the Central Election Committee, even Vlahov (*Iskra*, 1 February 1912).

Newspapers sprang up. Supporters of the Union of Bulgarian Constitutional Clubs promoted: *Otechestvo* (21 February–19 December 1909); *Rodina* (19 February–2 July 1910); *Pravo* (18 September 1910–7 May 1913); *Istina* (26 February–6 April 1912). Their periodicals were: *Uchitelsko Saznanie* (21 September–12 October 1909); and *Iskra* (1 December 1911–11 September 1912).

Supporters of autonomy and the transformation of the Ottoman Empire to a federative state published the following newspapers: *Konstitutsionna Zarya* (22 August 1908–3 January 1909); *Edinstvo* (27 September 1908–5 January 1909); *Narodna Volya* (17 January 1909–5 June 1910); *Rabotnicheski Vestnik* (14 August–15 October 1909); *Rabotnicheska Iskra* (1 January 1909–20 May 1911); *Rabotnik* (1911–2 July 1912). Their periodicals were: *Nachalo* (25 October 1908–25 July 1912); *Kulturno Edinstvo* (1 October 1908–1 March 1909); and *Uchitelski Glas* (15 June 1910–20 September 1912).

All these newspapers were closely linked to Bulgarian political parties. *Otechestvo* was the chief mouthpiece of the Union of the Bulgarian Constitutional Clubs (Ivantsev 1966, 114). Its aim was to be the main source of information and influence for supporters of the Exarchate in Thessaloniki. It had lots of news from the Ottoman Empire but also from other countries.[4] It also published news items from all over Macedonia, including Greek activities.[5] It played an important role in political developments by criticizing the Exarchate[6] and the educational system of the Bulgarian schools.[7] It was also concerned with non-local problems such as the Cretan Issue.[8]

Rodina was a weekly paper that started on 19 February 1910. It supported the traditional Bulgarian stance on the national question. Its contents were similar to *Otechestvo*, especially on the issue of news from Macedonia and the Macedonian Question. According to Ivantsev (1962, 114) it stopped publishing in July 1910, making room for *Pravo*. According to other sources it continued to circulate until December 1910, the 87th edition (Gros and Caglar 1985, 148).

The daily *Pravo* replaced *Otechestvo* in September 1910. This was a regular newspaper with news from the Ottoman Empire and from other countries. It had an unusual feature, a column called '*Proizshestvija*' or 'Incidents' giving a detailed account of the activities of the rebels and criminal bands of every nationality in Epirus, Macedonia, and Thrace. In the edition of 22 April 1912, four armed incidents are reported, giving the names of the rebel groups. A second column called '*Posledni Tsas*', refers to last-minute news from news agencies and by telegraph (*Pravo*, 22 April 1912, 3). The editor's personality and influence on the Exarchist community meant that the newspaper took the initiative at the end of 1911 to promote the election of its representatives to the Ottoman parliament and to heal the divisions and drift in the community; these issues were also addressed in the *Vesti* newspaper of Constantinople and the review *Iskra*

144   *Vlasis Vlasidis*

(Parvanova 2001, 56). According to Kandylakis, it stayed in circulation until 10 May 1913 (Kandylakis 2000, 608).

The review *Iskra* was a social-political and literary journal. It took on the issue of large agricultural estates in Macedonia and Thrace (Razboynikov 1911, 8–12) and that of the Exarchate as the national Bulgarian Church (Montsev 1911, 19–22); it dealt with issues of historical awareness, such as the story of the Milandinov brothers (Bazhdarov 1912, 1–5), and it had permanent columns with news about the internal affairs of the Ottoman Empire and news from other countries. *Iskra* from February 1912, under pressure of Young Turks policies directed against the Christian minorities, published an article arguing that, since no ethnic group in the Ottoman Empire constituted an absolute majority, the Empire belonged to all of them. Thus, the efforts of the Young Turks against the ethnic communities were against the interests of the country (*Iskra*, 1 February 1912, 13–19).

The journal *Uchitelsko Saznanie* was the mouthpiece of the Association of Bulgarian Teachers in the Ottoman Empire. Its material was compiled in Thessaloniki and printed in Sofia.[9] It was concerned with the constitution of the Association and its first conference,[10] and with Bulgarian national education in the Ottoman Empire, which should resist the Phanariots and Phanariotism.[11] It also had articles about the teaching profession in other countries.[12]

The newspaper *Istina* was first published by Sreben Poppetrov in the pre-election period of 1912. The main purpose of the paper was to promote his personal point of view. Ideologically he was compatible with the Bulgarian Election Committee, which promoted the idea of a unity slate,[13] but opposed the initiatives of *Pravo* editor Naumov, and his paper was really in opposition to *Pravo*.[14] Discontent and a desire to disentangle himself caused Poppetrov to waver and approach the other side, that of Turkophile Bulgarians promoted by Danev.[15]

This other side also displayed great publishing activity. The first newspaper to be published immediately after the Young Turks revolution was *Konstitutsionna Zarya*, the mouthpiece of the left wing of IMRO, the followers of Yane Sandanski. The purpose of the paper was to support the autonomy of Macedonia inside the Ottoman Empire,[16] and to promote IMRO's programme for the upcoming elections, although ideologically it showed support for the Unity and Progress Party.[17] At first, however, since there was no other Bulgarian newspaper, it covered the political activities of the Bulgarian clubs in the Ottoman Empire and the proceedings of their conference,[18] although it firmly supported separate organizations for the Bulgarians.[19] Its texts were long, sometimes published in instalments.[20] Naturally it covered the activities of IMRO, which until recently had been illegal.[21]

The *Edinstvo* newspaper was similar to *Konstitutsionna Zarjia*, since its main contributor was another IMRO leader, Hristo Chernopeev. The newspaper's goal was action against the Exarchate and the followers of the Union of Constitutional Clubs and in favor of federalism as it had begun to develop in 1908. Sometimes *Edinstvo* and *Konstitutsionna Zarjia* printed the same texts.[22] According to another source, however, the newspaper reflected the ideas of Bulgarian social democrats, or at least of Vasil Glavinov's group (Haupt 1975, 25).

Bulgarian newspapers in Thessaloniki   145

Narodna Volya first appeared on 17 November 1909 in place of *Edinstvo* and *Konstitutsionna Zarja*, which stopped publication for that reason.[23] This newspaper was concerned with the politics of the new National Federal Party,[24] the work of the Ottoman parliament,[25] and the new government.[26] It carried news from the interior of the Ottoman Empire, mainly from Macedonia, but very little about the politics of the Great Powers and the Balkan states. It wanted to show in this way that the new party was completely independent of all types of influences. The newspaper chose agricultural reform as a key issue to promote.[27]

Rabotnicheski Vestnik was a different matter: it belonged to Abraham Benaroya's socialist organization *Federation*, which embraced or collaborated with Bulgarians who had abandoned the National Federal Party or were followers of socialism but not of the Federation. The newspaper was first issued in August 1909. At first it was published in four Balkan languages (and in French) but afterwards only in Bulgarian and Judeo-Spanish. The editor of the Bulgarian edition was Angel Tomov. Even though the newspaper could not survive financially and stopped being publishing in the spring of 1910, it managed to publish nine issues. It was a labor newspaper, basically internationalist in its principles (Benaroya 1975, 53).

At the same time, at the end of 1910 and the beginning of 1911, the newspaper *Rabotnicheska Iskra* began to be published in Thessaloniki. It started in Bitola (Manastir) as the newspaper of Vasil Glavinov, a follower of the veteran Bulgarian socialist Dimitar Blagoev. In Thessaloniki, five issues were printed. The newspaper embraced the ideas of Marx on class struggle and favored union of all the workers in the Ottoman Empire, and opposed the leftist Federalists such as Sandanski and Chernopeev (Ivantsev 1966, 208).

Rabotnik was the third worker's weekly newspaper. Published in 1911, it was the organ of the Workers Socialist Democratic Party, promoting socialist ideology throughout the Ottoman Empire. Nineteen editions were published in all. It was very close to Federalists Yane Sandanski and Hristo Chernopeev.[28] From another source we are told that the newspaper *Rabotnik* was also published in December 1908, but with no further information (Mokrob and Gruevski 1993, 97).

Nachalo was a political, social, and literary journal, printed in Sofia for the Bulgarians of Macedonia. The editor was the socialist Nikola Harlakov. It welcomed political articles and reprinted articles from other European periodicals and by politicians from the broader Left.[29] It differed from other publications in being more the journalistic outlet for the views of a particular political group and less as a source of information on internal developments in the Ottoman Empire (Haupt 1975, 25).

Uchitelski Glas was the mouthpiece of the Union of Bulgarian teachers in the Ottoman Empire, a different organization from the association that published *Uchitelsko Saznanie*. Its main contributors were from the Bulgarian High School of Thessaloniki, but it hosted articles by teachers in the various Bulgarian schools of Macedonia.[30] It often expressed its opposition on chronic problems as well as current events.[31] It was opposed to the Exarchate,[32] especially on the issue of the underfunding of schools[33] and its relationship to the Bulgarian nation.[34] Frequently it carried articles on labor union issues,[35] as well as on meetings of the Union itself.[36]

146 *Vlasis Vlasidis*

Kulturno Edinstvo was a journal on society and literature. It was published by the *Edinstvo* newspaper and the editor was Anton Strasimirov. The content was not purely literary: it printed articles such as 'Proskynesis in Kilkis'[37] and 'Pro-Turkish Bulgarians',[38] about the agricultural issue in Macedonia and more specialized subjects such as the Prilep landowners.[39] It covered social issues such as emigration to America[40] and local folklore, for example on the village of Tsapari in Monastir.[41] Politically it favored cooperation of all the Balkan peoples, but it always referred to the Slav population of Macedonia as Bulgarians rather than Macedonians.[42]

During the election campaign of 1912, a new group appeared, led by Pancho Dorev. This group was not particularly well organized and had little impact. It advocated Bulgarian-Turkish cooperation, preserving the integrity of the empire, and supporting the Ottoman constitution. To promote these ideas, it published *Svetlina*.[43] This newspaper took a stand against national rivalries in the Ottoman Empire, against the policies of IMRO,[44] and against *Pravo*,[45] while it favored good relations with the Greeks,[46] and tried to ensure the support of the Exarchate.[47] It claimed to be ideologically very close to the Patriotic Committee of the Stambolovists.[48]

In general, the explosion of publishing activity between the rise of the Young Turks movement and the elections of 1912 was a direct result of the new right of the various political groups to compete for representation. These newspapers and journals were published not to promote rivalry with other ethnic groups, especially the Greeks, but to gain influence within their community. Their existence made obvious both the bitter antagonism within IMRO but also the strong influence it had attained in the Exarchist community, even after the split. According to the newspapers themselves, this influence was considerably stronger than the Exarchate's or any other institutions of the Bulgarian state. The dispute was so strong that it extended to the trade union publications.

The result of this rivalry was to drive other news off their pages, apart from that coming from foreign news agencies. Political and social news from urban areas of Macedonia was completely missing. There were hardly any letters from readers. Advertisements were few, though this could be because of the negative economic consequences of ethnic rivalries and disputes. In every case, communication was top-down, from the editors and journalists to the readers, and indifference prevailed regarding the idea of a two-way relationship. Perhaps for that reason, the life span of each paper was brief. Once the political goal was accomplished, i.e., the election, they ceased to publish.

The daily *Pravo* was the exception, since apart from its goal of steering the representation of the Bulgarian communities, it also aimed to cover its readers' need for information with news from both inside and outside the Ottoman Empire. For that reason, it stayed in print, with interruptions, until the beginning of the second Balkan War.

The fourth period was very brief but full of publishing activity. It covered the time from the first Balkan War until the eve of the second Balkan War, the first few days of December 1912. *Pravo* continued to circulate, and three other newspapers managed to publish a few issues before Greek authorities shut them down.

Bulgarin was launched on 5 November 1912 as a replacement for *Pravo*, which was temporarily barred from publication the previous day since it had continued to promulgate anti-Greek propaganda despite a warning from Greek censorship authorities. In particular, *Pravo* editor Nikola Naumov had characterized the Bulgarian army in Thessaloniki not as guests of the Greek authorities but as co-rulers.[49]

Bulgarin opened its first issue with a leading article 'To our liberators' (*Na nashite osvoboditeli*),[50] the Bulgarian army in other words, ignoring the Greek army that had officially occupied the city.[51] This paper strongly supported Bulgarian national aspirations. It devoted most of its space to the victories of the Bulgarian army, with bulletins from the front and articles on the opinion of the Great Powers on the war and on the Macedonian and Eastern Questions more generally.[52] *Bulgarin* took for granted that the solution to the Eastern Question must be the forcible break-up of the Ottoman Empire in Europe.[53] It considered as Bulgarian territory all the areas covered by the 1903 Mürzsteg Agreement (the vilayets of Thessaloniki, Manastir, and Kosovo), or where IMRO was active. Greece should be content with annexing Crete, the Aegean islands, Thessaly, and Epirus.[54]

From 20 November, the newspaper started to publish articles that would greatly anger the Greek authorities.[55] It continued over the next few days to urge that the Greek army should turn to Epirus, Crete, and the Aegean and leave the 'Bulgarian areas' to the Bulgarians.[56] The Bulgarian Army came to Thessaloniki 'not as a guest, but as a liberator'.[57] The contributors to the newspaper clearly anticipated the probable response of the authorities.[58] Still they continued with more aggressive articles like that of 27 November 1912, which expressed the view that since Thessaloniki was the capital of Macedonia and Macedonia was Bulgarian, it should be annexed to Bulgaria. According to the newspaper, the fact that there were twice as many Greeks as Bulgarians was not important, since the Turks and the Jews were even more numerous.[59] For economic reasons as well, Macedonia should be annexed to Bulgaria.[60] The Greek newspapers of Thessaloniki, *Nea Alitheia* and *Makedonia*, raised a strong outcry against *Bulgarin*, and the Greek authorities finally stopped its publication on 1 December 1912.[61]

Bulgarin was immediately succeeded by *Nova Bulgaria*. This newspaper had an even shorter life, since the Greeks forced it to stop on 5 December 1912 (Ivantsev 1966, 66; Simeonov 1934, 258; Kandylakis 2000, 618). There is not much information on this newspaper. One issue of this paper is in a private Greek collection, but it remains inaccessible to researchers.

Another Bulgarian daily, *Belomoretch*, started on 1 November 1912. The newspaper's intentions became obvious right away. It welcomed the Bulgarian army, which had liberated them from the tyranny of the Turks,[62] and expressed the idea that the Bulgarian army came to free Macedonia, the land of the Bulgarian tsars Simeon and Krum.[63] Most of the contents was battle news and the war in general.[64] The third issue carried articles on the activities of the Bulgarian rebel groups of the IMRO under the leadership of Todor Alexandrov, mainly in the Thessaloniki and Kilkis districts.[65]

The first few days, the newspaper was not openly against the Greek authorities. It reported the arrival of King George in Thessaloniki, the establishment of

148   *Vlasis Vlasidis*

the Greek administration,[66] and the creation of a secure feeling because of the arrival of the policemen from Crete.[67] The Greek authorities, however, quickly imposed censorship, which the newspaper deeply resented.[68] Soon the newspaper expressed its worry, complaining that the Bulgarian army of 300,000 men fought the Turks on a large front at Adrianople while the Greeks and Serbs easily conquered the territory of Macedonia.[69]

Belomoretch was much more restrained towards the Greek authorities than *Bulgarin*, more informative, and less political. Still, the rivalry over control of Thessaloniki prompted the Greek authorities to shut down *Belomoretch* after six issues, on 7 November. According to some sources, it was sold to other publishers who continued to publish it in French from December 1912, but this could not be confirmed (Simeonov 1934, 256. Kandylakis 2000, 617). The only Bulgarian newspaper that remained intermittently in circulation, until it was shut down on 7 May 1913 shortly before Greece and Serbia fought Bulgaria in the second Balkan War, was *Pravo*.

Where were newspapers printed?

At the beginning of the 20th century, Bulgarian newspapers and journals were printed at four printing houses. The best Bulgarian printing press was that of Samardzhiev and Karavelev, and most newspapers and periodicals were printed there (Snegarov 1937, 170),[70] including *Bulgarin, Nova Bulgaria, Rodina, Svetlina, Otechestvo, Konstitutsionna Zarya* from its thirteenth edition, some editions of *Uchitelski Glas*, the journal *Iskra*, the *Knizhiitsi za prachit*, and the *Meditsinska Beseda* (Ivantsev 1962, 116, 379; 1966, 66, 114, 236–237; 266; Simeonov 1934, 258; *Knizhiitsi za prachit*, no. 6.1, 6.4).

The newspapers *Istina, Edinstvo*, and *Konstitutsionna Zarya*, and the journal *Uchitelski Glas* were printed at the Italian-owned printing house Aquarone (Ivantsev 1962, 273, 382, 408; 1966, 456).[71] Depending on the circumstances, they sometimes used K. Tentsov's printing house, where *Rabotnik* in 1909 was printed and later *Belomoretch* (Ivantsev 1962, 382; 1966, 83, 207).[72] At least in the beginning, the journal *Knizhiitsi za prachit* was printed at the Mouratori printing house (Ivantsev 1962, 400). Finally the journal *Uchitelsko Saznanie* was printed at the Sfeta Petka printing house, and the *Nachalo* at the Union printing house, both in Sofia.[73] *Pravo*, a daily, could not use the same printing house as the other newspapers, but was printed at Yordan Jarchev's printing house.[74] At least one edition, however, was printed in K. Pentsov's printing house in Kolomvou Street, and *Narodna Volya* was printed there too (Ivantsev 1966, 20).[75]

Conclusions

The publishing of Bulgarian newspapers and periodicals is directly linked to the rise of the Exarchist community in Thessaloniki, in particular the teachers and pupils of the Bulgarian High School and a group of people with influence in this community. At first, these publications tried to promote ethnic self-awareness,

Bulgarian newspapers in Thessaloniki 149

but afterwards they supported the political pursuits of those that published them. In practice, the most important factor in publishing was the needs of the different factions of IMRO. With one or two exceptions, editors were indifferent to the need for information faced by imperial citizens in Thessaloniki.

The number of newspapers published, especially by the Federalists, was out of proportion to their voting strength. Otherwise, that strength would have been manifest in the Ottoman parliament, and not only with the election of Vlahov, and publishing would have continued even after the entry of the Bulgarian army into Thessaloniki. This did not happen, both because Greek and Bulgarian authorities had opposing opinions and also because personal disputes and choices seriously weakened their operational ability. The brief presence of Bulgarian newspapers in Thessaloniki in 1912 marks the end of an age of co-existence of national communities in a broader state entity, and the dawn of a national state, which would impose homogenization. Newspapers and education would serve this policy, not the promotion of distinctive ethnic or cultural identities.

Notes

1 Rena Molho's study of the Jewish press cites only 42 newspapers published in Thessaloniki between 1865–1941 (Molho 2005, 107–113).
2 According to Vasil Kanchov, the inspector of Bulgarian schools in Macedonia, in 1900 there were 16,000 Greeks, 10,000 Bulgarians, and 28,000 Turks in a Thessaloniki population totalling 118,000 (Kanchov 1970, 440). According to the census made by Hilmi Pasha and published in Athens, in 1905 there were 30,000 Greeks, 1,000 Bulgarians, and 20,000 Muslims in a population of 135,000 (Chalkiopoulos 1910, 1).
3 An earlier Bulgarian periodical is mentioned by one source. There are no copies of this journal in any archive or library in Bulgaria, which is why its existence is in doubt. T. Krajnitsanech wrote that it appeared in Thessaloniki in 1882 in one edition only, and that its purpose was to defend Bulgarian claims on Macedonia (Krajnitsanech 1941).
4 E.g., 'Okolo sabitijata v Tsarigrad', *Otechestvo*, 10 April 1909, p. 1; 'Otomanskite bjuzhet', *Otechestvo*, 17 July 1909, 1.
5 'Gartsi razboinitsi v Drama', *Otechestvo*, 10 October 1909, 3.
6 'Mjastoto na Eksarhiata', *Otechestvo*, 7 June 1909, 1.
7 'Nuzhdata ot reformi v nasheto delo', *Otechestvo*, 4 July 1909, 1.
8 'Kritskijat vapros', *Otechestvo*, 8 July 1909, 1.
9 'Otriva se podpiska za I godishina na v. Uchitelsko Saznanje', *Uchitelsko Saznanie*, 21 November 1909, 1.
10 'Utsreditelnija kongres na Balgarskija Uchitelski Sajuz v Otomanskata darzhava', *Uchitelsko Saznanie*, 21 September 1909, 2.
11 'Trudovite uslovija na balgarskija naroden utsitel v Otomanskata darzhava', *Uchitelsko Saznanie*, 28 September 1909, 2.
12 'Profesionalnoto dvizhenie v stranstvo', *Uchitelsko Saznanie*, 28 September 1909, 3; 'Uchitelsko dvizhenie v Italija', *Uchitelsko Saznanie*, 12 October 1909, 3.
13 'Tsijala naroda s naroda, i za naroda', *Istina*, 28 February 1912, 1.
14 'Tselijat narod e s nas', *Istina*, 8 March 1912, 1. See also Mokrob, *op. cit.*, p. 57.
15 A much more typical example is the article '*Eksarhia I izborite*', *Istina*, 20 March 1912, 2 which is the same as the article with the same name in *Svetlina*, of 15 February 1912.
16 'Programme de l' Organisation Revolutionnaire Macedono-Adrianolitaine', *Konstitutsionna Zarya*, 22 August 1908, 2; 'Konstitutsionnite klubove i organizatsija', *Konstitutsionna Zarya*, 1 September 1908, 2.

150 *Vlasis Vlasidis*

17 'Pravilnik za izbori', *Konstitutsionna Zarya*, 22 August 1908, 3; 'Partijata obedinenije i napred', *Konstitutsionna Zarya*, 19 September 1908, 1; 'Mlada Turtsija i nobite sabitija', *Konstitutsionna Zarya*, 18 October 1909, 1.

18 'Konstitutsionnite klubove i organizatsija', *Konstitutsionna Zarya*, 1 September 1908, 2–3; 'Utsreditelen kongres na B.K.Klubove', *Konstitutsionna Zarya*, 14 September 1908, 3; 'Deklaratsija na Sajuza na B.K.Klubove na Otomanskata Imperija', *Konstitutsionna Zarya*, 29 September 1908, 3; 'Kongres na B.K.Klubove', *Konstitutsionna Zarya*, 3 October 1908, 2.

19 'Organiziraneto na utsilishte', *Konstitutsionna Zarya*, 15 November 1908, 2.

20 'Harakternoto v Turskata Revolutsija', *Konstitutsionna Zarya*, 27 August 1908, 2.

21 'Do okolniskite komiteti', *Konstitutsionna Zarya*, 27 August 1908, 2; 'Miting v Poroi', *Konstitutsionna Zarya*, 5 September 1908, 4.

22 Ivantsev 1966, 273; 'Konstitutsionnite klubove i organizatsija', *Edinstvo*, 27 September 1908, 2.

23 *Narodna Volya*, 17 January 1909, 1.

24 'Partien zhivot', *Narodna Volya*, 7 February 1909, 2–3.

25 'Iz parlamenta', *Narodna Volya*, 7 February 1909, 2.

26 'Ministerska kriza', *Narodna Volya*, 7 February 1909, 1.

27 'Nuzhda li e navremena petitsijata po agrarnija vpros', *Narodna Volya*, 28 February 1909, 1; 'Petitsija ot seljanite tsifligari v Makedonija', *Narodna Volya*, 7 March 1909, 1; 'Agrarija Vapros', *Narodna Volya*, 27 June 1909, 1.

28 Ivantsev 1966, 207. According to Benaroya, this was a Constantinople newspaper which came out in Greek, Jewish, and Turkish but not in Bulgarian. This information is doubtful however since the Worker's Socialist Democratic Party was against Benaroya's Federation (Benaroya 1975, 60–61).

29 Jaurès 1909, 3; Sh. Segnodos, 'Mirit i Istotsna vpros', *Nachalo*, April 1909, 3–5; Kr. Rakovski, 'Istotsnijat vpros I silite', *Nachalo*, January 1909, 241–245.

30 'Na oproverszhenijata', *Uchitelski Glas*, 10 October 1911, 3.

31 'Iskanjat ot Veritas otgovor', *Uchitelski Glas*, 20 October 1911, 4.

32 'Klikata v Eksarhijata v borba s sajuza', *Uchitelski Glas*, 26 August 1910, 2.

33 'Eksarhija posobie I selskite Utsiteli', *Uchitelski Glas*, 10 October 1911, 2.

34 'Eksarhijata I naroda', *Uchitelski Glas*, 10 October 1911, 3.

35 'Kak mozhe da zajakne utsiteskijat sajuz', *Uchitelski Glas*, 20 October 1911, 3.

36 'Nashata konferentsija', *Uchitelski Glas*, 10 October 1911, 9; 'Tsetvjrtijat izvinreden kongres na Otomanskite balgarski utsiteli', *Uchitelski Glas*, 20 January 1912, 1–3; 'Petijat kongres na Otomanskite balgarski utsiteli', *Uchitelski Glas*, 11 August 1912, 1.

37 Anton Strasimirov, 'Na poklonie v Kukuc', *Kulturno Edinstvo*, 15 October 1908, 3–4.

38 'Motivi na turskofilstvo i balgarite', *Kulturno Edinstvo*, 15 October 1908, 1–2.

39 'T. km agrarnija vapros v Makedonija', *Kulturno Edinstvo*, 15 October 1908, 19–20; Asia, 'Tsifligarstvoto v Prilepsko', *Kulturno Edinstvo*, 15 December 1908, 30–34.

40 Gortse Petrov, 'Emigrantskoto dvizhenie za Amerika v Makedonija', *Kulturno Edinstvo*, 15 January 1909, 3–6.

41 N. Vasilev, 'Selo Tsapari', *Kulturno Edinstvo*, 15 January 1909, 26–27.

42 'Polititseska perspektiva', *Kulturno Edinstvo*, 1 December 1908, 1–2.

43 Parvanova, 'Organizational', 66, *Svetlina*, 15 February 1912, 1–5.

44 'Deputatski mesta I fondove', *Svetlina*, 8 January 1912, 2.

45 'Na v.Pravo I s', *Svetlina*, 8 February 1912, 3.

46 'Parvite opiti za savmestno deistvie na balgarite s gartsite I itiliftsiite po izborite', *Svetlina*, 15 February 1912, 1; 'Gartsko-balgarskoto sporazumenije za praktika', *Svetlina*, 15 February 1912, 2.

47 'Eksarhijata I izborite', *Svetlina*, 15 February 1912, 1.

48 'Protokolite na stambolskata patriotarska komisija po prestojastite parlamenti izori', *Svetlina*, 8 February 1912, 1.

49 Kandylakis, *op. cit.*, vol. 2, pp. 606–607.

Bulgarian newspapers in Thessaloniki 151

50 'Na Nashite osvobooditeli', *Bulgarin*, 5 November 1912, 1.
51 For the way in which the Bulgarian press looked at the Serbian and Greek successes in the first Balkan War, the occupation of Thessaloniki in particular, see Vlasidis 2004, 38–44.
52 'Balkanskata voina I velikite sili', *Bulgarin*, 5 November 1912, 1; 'Istotsnijat vapros v minaloto I sega', *Bulgarin*, 8 November 1912, 1; 'Italia I balkanskata problema', *Bulgarin*, 10 November 1912, 1; 'Velikite sili I Balkanskata problema', *Bulgarin*, 11 November 1912, 1; 'Avstrija I voinata', *Bulgarin*, 16 November 1912, 1; 'Istotsna kriza I Frantsija', *Bulgarin*, 27 November 1912, 1.
53 'Nasheto gledishte po balkanskija vapros', *Bulgarin*, 9 November 1912, 1.
54 ibid.
55 'Kakvo govorijat faktite za privzimaneto na Solun', *Bulgarin*, 20 November 1912, 1; 'Prietite ot grtskata voiska turtski uslovija na Solun', *Bulgarin*, 20 November 1912, 1–2.
56 'Balkaskija vapros I makedonskite Balgari', *Bulgarin*, 21 November 1912, 1; 'Okupiranite ot sajuznitsite balgarski zemi', *Bulgarin*, 22 November 1912, 1.
57 'Prevzimaneto na Solun', *Bulgarin*, 23 November 1912, 1.
58 'Tsenzurata na gartsija voenen shtab', *Bulgarin*, 22 November 1912, 2.
59 'Bzhdashteto na Solun', *Bulgarin*, 27 November 1912, 1.
60 'Bzhdashteto na Solun', *Bulgarin*, 28 November 1912, 1.
61 'Nashite gartski oponenti', *Bulgarin*, 30 November 1912, 1; 'Koi s grobarite na balkan-skija sajuz', *Bulgarin*, 1 December 1912, 1.
62 'Dobre dosli', *Belomoretch*, 2 November 1912, 1.
63 'Nii doidohme', *Belomoretch*, 3 November 1912, 1.
64 'Voennite deistvija', 'Kavala e zaet', *Belomoretch*, 3 November 1912, 2.
65 'Tsetite', *Belomoretch*, 4 November 1912, 1–2.
66 'Upravlenijeto na G. Solyn', *Belomoretch*, 2 November 1912, 2.
67 'Sigurnosta v Solun', *Belomoretch*, 2 November 1912, 2. 113 'Opasnosta', *Belomoretch*, 7 November 1912, 1.
68 'Tsensurata', *Belomoretch*, 4 November 1912, 1.
69 'Opasnosta', *Belomoretch*, 7 November 1912, 1.
70 This printing house depended on the bookshop belonging to Kone Samardzhiev and D. Mantsov, which operated from 27 August 1883 (Snegarov 1937, 170).
71 Aquarone burned in the great fire of 1917 (Virvilakis 1981, 7).
72 I could discover no other information about the Tentsov printing house.
73 Ivantsev 1966, 42, 458; *Uchitelsko Saznanie*, 21 September 1909, 4.
74 Ivantsev 1966, 168. The Jarchev Bulgarian printing house is mentioned by Antov 1934, 313 and Megas 1994, 225.
75 *Pravo*, 22 April 1912, 1. There is no other information about the Pentsov printing house.

References

Antov, H., 'Parvata petsatnitsa v Solun' [The first Bulgarian printhouse in Thessaloniki]. In *Sbornik Solun*, (eds.), *Izdanie na vazpitatelitie I vazpitanitsitie ot Solunskitie Balgarski Gimnazii*, Sofija: Hudozhnik, (1934).
Bazhdarov, G., 'Bratija D. i K. Miladonovi', *Iskra*, 1 December 1912, 1–5.
Benaroya, A., *Η πρώτη σταδιοδρομία του ελληνικού προλεταριάτου* [The first stage of the Greek proletariat], Athens: Olkos (1975).
Chalkiopoulos, A., *Η Μακεδονία : εθνολογική στατιστική των βιλαετίων Θεσσαλονίκης και Μοναστηρίου* [Macedonia: Ethnological statistics of the vilayets of Thessaloniki and Monastir], Athens: Nomiki (1910).

152 Vlasis Vlasidis

Christianopoulos, D., *Οι ελληνικές εφημερίδες της Θεσσαλονίκης επί τουρκοκρατίας, 1869–1912* [Greek newspapers in Thessaloniki during Turkish rule 1869–1912], Thessaloniki: Diagonios (1992).

Despot, I., *The Balkan Wars in the Eyes of the Warring Parties: Perceptions and Interpretations*, Bloomington: iUniverse (2012).

Fotopoulou, A., 'Τουρκικές εφημερίδες. Εκδόσεις που κυκλοφόρησαν από την εμφάνιση της "Selanik" από το 1869 έως το 1924' [Turkish newspapers: Publications that circulation from the appearance of 'Selanik' in 1869 until 1924], *Kathimerini, Epta imeres*, 26 February 1995, 15.

Frezis, R., *Ο εβραϊκός τύπος στην Ελλάδα*, Volos: Jewish Community of Volos (1999).

Gros, G. and Caglar, I., *La presse française de Turquie de 1795 à nos jours: Histoire et Catalogue*, Istanbul: Edition Isis (1985).

Haupt, G., 'Εισαγωγή στην ιστορία της Federacion' [Introduction to the history of the *Federacion*], In Benaroya, A., (ed.), *Η πρώτη σταδιοδρομία του ελληνικού προλεταριάτου* [The first stage of the Greek proletariat], Athens: Olkos (1975).

Hekimoglou, E., 'Η σχέση των εκπαιδευτηρίων της Ελληνικής Ορθοδόξου Κοινότητος Θεσσαλονίκης με τον ναό του Αγίου Μηνά. Επανεξέταση των πηγών' [The relationship of the educational institutions of the Greek Orthodox Community of Thessaloniki with the church of Agios Minas], In Dalakoura, K., Deligianni-Koumitzi, V., Tzikas, Ch., Foukas, V. A. (eds.), *Θέματα Ιστορίας της Ελληνικής Εκπαίδευσης και Φύλου (19ος και 20ός αιώνας)* [Issues of the history of Greek education and tribe], Thessaloniki: Kyriakidis (2017), 142–163.

Ivantsev, D. P. (ed.), *Balgarski perioditsen petsat 1844–1944. Anotiran bibliografski ukazatel*, vol. 1, vol. 2., Sofija: Nauka I Izkustvo (1962, 1966).

Jaurès, J., 'Balkanskata problema', *Natsalo*, April 1909.

Kanchov, V. Izbrani Proizvedenia [Selected Works], т.1, Sofia: Nauka I Izkustvo (1970), 7–27.

Kandylakis, M., 'Άγνωστη η ιστορία και οι εφημερίδες της Θεσσαλονίκης' [Unknown the history and newspapers of Thessaloniki], *Ellinikos Vorras*, 16 December 1984, 12.

Kandylakis, M., 'Ο Τύπος της Θεσσαλονίκης ως μη προσιτή πηγή της ιστορίας' [The Thessaloniki press as inaccessible historical source], In Sambanopoulos, V., (ed.), *Η νεότερη ιστορία της Θεσσαλονίκης και ο Τύπος* [The modern history of Thessaloniki and the Press], Thessaloniki: University Studio Press (1993), 99–108.

Kandylakis, M., *Εφημεριδογραφία της Θεσσαλονίκης* [Newspaper-writing of Thessaloniki], Vol. 1, Turkish rule, Thessaloniki: University Studio Press (1999).

Kandylakis, M., *Εφημεριδογραφία της Θεσσαλονίκης* [Newspaper-writing of Thessaloniki], Vol. 2, 1912–1923, Thessaloniki: University Studio Press (2000).

Kerem, Y., 'The Europeanisation of the Sephardic Community of Salonika', In Stillman, Y. K. and Stillman, N. A., (eds.), *From Iberia to Diaspora: Studies in Sephardic History and Culture*, Leiden: Brill (1999), 58–74.

Krajnitsanech, T., 'Balgarskijat petsat v Makedonija', *Dnevnik*, 17 May 1941.

Megas, Y., *Οι «Βαρκάρηδες» της Θεσσαλονίκης: Η Βουλγαρική αναρχική ομάδα και οι βομβιστικές ενέργειες του 1903* [The 'boatmen' of Thessaloniki: The Bulgarian anarchist group and the bombing action of 1903], Thessaloniki: Trohalia (1994).

Mokrob, B. and Gruevski, T., *Pregled na Makedonskiot petsat (1885–1992)*, Skopje: Studentski Sbor (1993).

Molho, R., 'Ο εβραϊκός τύπος στην Ελλάδα' [The Jewish Press in Greece], In Droulia, L., (ed.), *Ο ελληνικός τύπος 1784 έως σήμερα. Ιστορικές και θεωρητικές προσεγγίσεις* [The

Bulgarian newspapers in Thessaloniki 153

Greek press, 1784 until today: Historical and theoretical approaches], Athens: National Research Foundation (2005), 107–113.

Montsev, B., 'Balgarskata eksarhija- natsionalna tsirkva', *Iskra*, 1 December 1911, 19–22.

Papastathis, Ch., 'Τα πρώτα ελληνικά τυπογραφεία της Θεσσαλονίκης' [The first Greek printing houses of Thessaloniki], *Makedonika* 8 (1968), 231–256.

Parvanov, G., 'Narodno-federativnata partija v natsionalnoosvoboditelnoto dvizhenie', *Vekove*, 18.3 (1989), 32–42.

Parvanov, G., 'Polititseskata deinost na Sajuza na balgarskite konstitutsionni klubove', *Makedonski Pregled* 14.4 (1991), 23–49.

Parvanova, Z., 'Political programmes of the national liberation movements in European Turkey following the coup of the young turks (1908–1909)', *Etudes Balkaniques*, 30.1 (1994), 51–78.

Parvanova, Z., 'Programme and organizational transformations of National Movement in European Turkey (1910–1912). Part One. Legal political organizations', *Etudes Balkaniques*, 37.4 (2001), 53–55.

Razbojnikov, A., 'Tsifligarstvoto v Makedonija I Odrinsko', *Iskra*, 1 December 1911, 8–12.

Simeonov, S., 'Balgarski perioditsen petsat na Makedonija', In Sbornik Solun, (ed.), *Izdanie na vazpitatelitie I vazpitanitsitie ot Solunskitie Balgarski Gimnazii*, Sofija: Hudozhnik (1934), 227–259.

Snegarov, I., *Solun v bulgarskata duhovna kultura. Istoričeski očerk i dokumenti* [Thessaloniki in Bulgarian spiritual culture: History and documents], Sofia: Pridvorna Pečatnica (1937).

Toledano, Y. T., 'The history of the Toledano families', *Sharsheret Hadorot*, 15/1 (2000), 3–7 (online at http://members.tripod.com/~Yacov_Tal/sub-pages/history-english.html viewed July 2019).

Virvilakis, Y., 'Εντυπωσιακή η τυπογραφική τέχνη της Θεσσαλονίκης' [Impressive typographic craft in Thessaloniki], *Ellinikos Vorras*, 17 July 1981, 7.

Vlasidis, V., 'Η απελευθέρωση της Φλώρινας μέσα από το βουλγαρικό Τύπο της εποχής' [The liberation of Florina through the Bulgarian press of the period], In Photiadis, K., (ed.), *Πρακτικά του συνεδρίου 'Φλώρινα 1912–2002, Ιστορία και Πολιτισμός* [Conference proceedings, Florina 1912–2002: History and culture], Florina: Kessopoulos (2004), 38–44.

11 The boundaries of Hellenism

Language and loyalty among Salonican Jewry, 1917–1933[1]

Devin E. Naar

For Jews in Salonica, caught in the crossfire of nationalist antagonisms amidst the Balkan Wars, the future was uncertain. The well-known banker, writer, and director of the local *Alliance Israélite Universelle*, Joseph Nehama, captured the fraught tenor at the time of the arrival of the Greek army in October of 1912:

> The Greeks have covered all the walls of their homes with banners in the Greek colors, blue and white. … And here is the problem with which we [the Jews of Salonica], are wrestling: should we join in the general rejoicing? Common Jews, with surprising unity, have refrained from cheers and applause. They have maintained a most dignified and proper attitude. Certainly they have shown no hostility, but neither have they shown satisfaction. … What will be the new conditions created for our fellow Jews …?
>
> (Rodrigue 2003, 236–238)

Scholars agree that Jews in Salonica responded to the incorporation of the city into the Greek nation-state in 1912 with the kind of ambivalence and uncertainty described by Nehama (Molho 2001; Pierron 1996; Fleming 2008). Would Salonican Jews be able to preserve their preeminent role in the city? Would they be able to adapt to the new context of modern Greek society? Could they retain their Jewish identity and also somehow become 'Greek'? Would 'Greekness' be defined according to citizenship, political allegiance, language and culture, religion, ethnic origin and race, or some combination thereof?

Scholars have largely assumed that in Salonica, throughout the interwar years, 'Greeks' and 'Jews' remained two discrete, even antagonistic, categories fixed along ethnic lines.[2] According to this view, the Jews of Salonica suffered from cultural, economic, and demographic decline under the nationalizing Greek government, especially under Venizelos, who was intent on transforming Ottoman Selanik/Jewish Saloniko into Greek Thessaloniki. In this context, scholars have characterized the Jews as 'under siege' (Kallis 2006), 'doomed' (Bowman 2009, 10), or 'unwanted compatriots' (Margaritis 2005), at least in part because they were perceived as resisting Hellenization and never really became 'Greek' prior to the Second World War. A provocative study argues that Salonica's Jews established a 'nascent but inchoate' Greek-Jewish identity in the 1930s, under Metaxas,

The boundaries of Hellenism   155

but only came to identify themselves and be identified by others as fully 'Greek' once they left Greece—either in Auschwitz, Israel, or New York (Fleming 2007).

I would like to reconsider this narrative by emphasizing that the very nature of national identity in Greece was in the making throughout the first half of the 20th century. The 'Hellenization' of Northern Greece was a protracted process that targeted not only Salonica's Jews, but also Slav speakers, as well as Orthodox Christian refugees arriving from Asia Minor and beyond—many of whom spoke Turkish as their primary language—as well as a variety of other culturally diverse populations. The city's autochthonous Orthodox Christians, who constituted the *Rum millet* of the Ottoman Empire, had to be recast as the standard bearers of the consolidating Greek nation (Michailidis 2008). In this context, the state did not unequivocally impose a policy of Hellenization; rather the cultural transformation of the various populations resulted from negotiation with, and re-education initiated by, the state. Greece's Jews, including those in Salonica, played an active role in this process and, in so doing, also shaped the boundaries of the Hellenic collectivity and the very meaning of being 'Greek' (Mackridge and Yannakakis 1997; Gazi 2005). For this reason, during the 1920s, the Director of the Salonica Press Bureau observed, 'The question of education is the most important issue concerning the Jews' (Constantopoulou and Veremis 1999, 122). The schools became the laboratory in which to test and contest the possibilities and processes of transforming the children of the last generation of Ottoman Jews into the first generation of Greek Jews, proficient in the Greek language and loyal Greek citizens.

Instead of focusing on Greek government policy regarding interwar Jewish education (Vasilikou 1999; Lagos 2005; Anastassiadis 2010), or exclusively on Jewish resistance to Hellenization, I would like to provide a fresh perspective derived from a previously unexplored source, the surviving archives of the Jewish Community of Salonica. During the German occupation, the Nazis confiscated the archives of the Jewish community. Miraculously, extensive fragments of these archives survive in New York, Jerusalem, Moscow, and in Thessaloniki at the Jewish Museum (Naar, 2014). The archives include extensive documentation on the Superior Commission for Jewish Instruction, a council that functioned under the auspices of the Jewish Community of Salonica. The vast majority of these archives, including the minutes of the Commission for Jewish Instruction from 1917 to 1934, were penned in Judeo-Spanish, in the traditional handwritten Hebrew script known as *soletreo*. Few scholars have consulted these archives, in part, because this script can be extremely difficult to read. It is this set of materials, supplemented by the local press as well as other sources in English, Greek, Hebrew, and French, on which the present paper is based.

The precursor to the transformation in Jewish education in Salonica during the interwar years, as documented in the archives, can be traced to the 19th century. During this period, the Ottoman Empire introduced a series of reforms, the *Tanzimat*, which sought, at least in theory, to transform its various subject populations into Ottoman citizens, regardless of ethno-religious affiliation. While working toward the implementation of these equalizing legal reforms, the Ottoman

156   *Devin E. Naar*

state did not enforce a uniform culture on its new citizenry. Instead, by solidifying the formal structure of each ethno-religious community (*millet*), the Ottoman state permitted Christians and Jews to retain a certain degree of communal autonomy, including in the realm of education and language instruction (Rodrigue 1995). In this context, the emergent vision of Ottomanism as a supranational ideology ostensibly demanded little cultural allegiance from each ethno-religious community, but rather political allegiance alone. According to this model, in its ideal form, one could be shaped into a good and loyal Ottoman by supporting the continued integrity of the empire, even without necessarily knowing Turkish (Cohen 2014).

The Paris-based *Alliance Israélite Universelle* filled the void in Jewish education and language instruction left by the Ottoman state's hands-off approach. Motivated by a 'civilizing mission', the leaders of the *Alliance* sought to uplift their fellow Jews in the Orient. During the last quarter of the 19th century, established a network of Jewish schools throughout the Ottoman Empire, Salonica included, in order to accomplish this goal. Through its program of modern education, the *Alliance* introduced the study of secular subjects, vocational skills, and the French language to a traditional curriculum focused on religious education (Rodrigue 1990). The Jewish communal schools and a number of newly established private schools, such as Alcheh, Gattegno, and Pinto, soon followed suit (Daccarett 2008). The resulting acquisition of French by a significant swath of the Jewish population, especially the upwardly mobile, did not, however, cause alarm from the perspective of the Ottoman state. Rather, added to Judeo-Spanish as the mother tongue, French was unproblematically folded into Jewish bourgeois identity in Salonica without impeding claims to being true and loyal Ottomans (Stein 2004).

The situation changed once Salonica came under Greek control, although not immediately. The Greek government promulgated Law 2456, 'Concerning Jewish Communities', in 1920. Law 2456 stipulated that the Jewish communities throughout the country, including in Salonica, preserved aspects of their autonomy in continuity with Ottoman practice: the right to collect certain taxes from its members, maintain its own rabbinical court, philanthropic institutions, and civil registry (Constantopoulou and Veremis 1999, 103–110). However, Law 2456 introduced a major departure from Ottoman practice in the realm of education and language. While the law permitted the Jewish Community, as a legal corporate entity, to retain its own communal schools, it dictated—for the first time—much of the school curriculum and especially the language of instruction, specifically Greek, which was to be taught 'adequately'. The law continued:

> Apart from the teaching of Greek as a language, the teaching of history, geography, and science is to be conducted in Greek. The staff to teach the Greek classes will be appointed in the same manner as the staff of Greek state schools. All the other lessons in the curriculum drawn up by each community may be taught in whichever language the community may wish.
>
> (Constantopoulou and Veremis 1999, 103–110)

The boundaries of Hellenism   157

I would like to trace the ways in which the Greek state and the Jewish community negotiated Jewish educational practices and policies in the wake of Law 2456, and assess the impact of these processes on Jewish language acquisition and political loyalty. First, I will highlight the practical difficulties that the Commission for Jewish Instruction encountered in implementing the new educational policies, including Greek language instruction. Second, I will highlight unrecognized successes in rebuilding the Jewish educational system in the Greek mold and integrating Jewish students into the Greek state school system. Finally, I will offer some suggestions as to how the transformation of Jewish education may have impacted Jewish-Christian dynamics in Salonica, especially among the youth.

First, in terms of practical obstacles to Jewish education, the massive fire of 1917 was a major roadblock. The fire devastated the entire city and left 70,000 residents homeless, including 50,000 Jews. The fire also destroyed most of the Jewish communal institutions, including eight schools. The case of the main Jewish school, the *Talmud Torah*, is instructive. Over a year after the fire, the *Talmud Torah* offered classes for only 300 of its previous 1,000 students; most of the other 700 students did not receive any formal education during this period.[3] Furthermore, in conformity with the Greek government's policy regarding the reconstruction of the city following the fire of 1917, the National Bank of Greece outbid the Jewish Community for the plot of land on which the half-burnt *Talmud Torah* was located. When the building was demolished, some students were relocated to the 151 District, where the Cazes school was founded.[4] Others were transferred to a nearby *matza* factory. Due to the terrible odor emitted from the adjacent tobacco processing plant, however, students were relocated yet again.[5] Finally, by 1928, the new *Talmud Torah* was operational, along with seven other Jewish communal schools and over a dozen private Jewish schools.[6]

The lack of stable and hygienic settings was not the only reason that Greek language instruction in Jewish schools seemed to develop slowly. The inability of the government to provide the necessary Greek language instructors for Jewish schools, despite a legal requirement to do so, was a perennial problem. In the fall of 1922, for example, when the Greek teachers did not arrive at the beginning of the school year, the 14 weekly hours intended for Greek instruction were instead dedicated to the study of Hebrew liturgy.[7] The Commission for Jewish Instruction appealed to the Inspector General of Public Education again in 1928, 1930, 1931, 1932, and 1933, at one point renouncing all responsibility for poor results in Greek language instruction that may stem from the absence of qualified teachers, and demanded that a 'radical solution' be implemented immediately.[8]

Despite challenges in rebuilding the Jewish school system in Salonica after the fire of 1917, and various impediments to instruction of the Greek language, the Commission for Jewish Instruction made considerable strides in educating the first generation of 'Greek Jews' and achieving a certain degree of rapprochement. For most of the 1920s and early 1930s, Prime Minister Venizelos hoped that the legal status of Jews in Greece as a 'religious' (rather than 'national') minority would compel them to readjust, and would encourage Salonican Jews to follow the example of their *Romaniote* co-religionists in Old Greece, who spoke Greek

158   *Devin E. Naar*

fluently, gave their children Greek names, and expressed their Judaism exclusively as religious difference (Rivlin 1998, 18). Venizelos offered an ostensibly liberal promise that if Jews adjusted their cultural and political orientation, they would become Greeks and be accepted as such. The Inspector of the Commission of Jewish Instruction, Jacques Kohn, molded Jewish communal educational policies in line with Venizelos' demands that Jews adopt the Greek language and a Greek consciousness. Kohn even succeeded in introducing Jewish students to Greek state schools for the first time.

Known in Greek government circles for his 'pro-assimilation views' (Constantopoulou and Veremis 1999, 113), Kohn was instrumental in founding the B'nai B'rith Lodge, an organization whose ideology dovetailed with that of the *Alliance Israélite* and shaped the trajectory of Jewish education in interwar Salonica. Part of a Jewish fraternal order founded in New York in 1843, the B'nai B'rith Lodge in Salonica outlined its goals for 'Social Education' in 1925: to strengthen relations between Jews and Christians—or in B'nai B'rith's language, 'Christian Hellenes' and 'Jewish Hellenes'.[9] According to this discursive shift, Jews and Greek Christians were to be understood as two kinds of 'Hellenes'. It was with this spirit of rapprochement that B'nai B'rith established the first Greek language Jewish newspaper in Salonica, *La Tribune Juive de Grèce/Evraïkon Vima tis Ellados*, which sought to promote the good of the Jews of Greece for the good of Hellenism.[10]

Motivated by the same spirit, B'nai B'rith also mobilized the Alumni of the *Alliance Israélite Universelle* and even the New Zionist Club and the Theodor Herzl Club to encourage the Jewish Community to work for the benefit of all of the city's residents, including through the distribution by the Jewish Community of clothing to Greek-Christian refugee children.[11] This kind of goodwill was recognized in the public sphere at the same time that tensions mounted. The American consul in Salonica, for example, reported that a group of 650 Christian refugees inaugurated a new 'anti-Semitic movement' on the grounds that the city's Jews were disloyal to the country due to their anti-Venizelist vote in a recent election.[12] Yet simultaneously, *To Fos* celebrated the foundation of the 'Greek-Jewish League' at the Chamber of Commerce, which expressed gratitude to the Jews for their goodwill toward the refugees. A certain Dr. Papazoglou even went so far as to proclaim: 'The Jews are our brothers. They have lived in this city for more than 2,000 years. Salonica is as much theirs as it is ours'.[13]

Animated by the promise of Jewish-Christian rapprochement and the program of B'nai B'rith, Kohn utilized the Jewish communal schools as a vehicle to promote Jewish integration in the educational institutions of Greece. A key B'nai B'rith initiative that Kohn funneled into the Jewish communal schools encouraged graduates to attend Greek state high schools through the establishment of a scholarship program. In 1925, the first five Jewish students entered Greek state schools.[14] Through Kohn's intervention, B'nai B'rith received financial support for the scholarship program from the Jewish Communal Council.[15] This signified that the Jewish Community officially approved of and encouraged sending Jewish students to Greek schools. Given the fact that the Commission for Jewish Instruction

The boundaries of Hellenism 159

discouraged Jewish students from attending foreign schools, especially the Lycée Française,[16] the decision to support attendance at Greek schools reinforced the desire of the Jewish Community to partake in the Greek national project.

The gradual integration of Jews into Greek state schools formed part of a set of policies voluntarily initiated by the Commission of Jewish Instruction to accommodate the new realities of the Greek state, and emerged without any pressure from the government. Already in 1921, the Commission had decided that the language of instruction for arithmetic, left to the discretion of the Jewish Community according to Law 2456, would be in Greek.[17] The same year, the Commission also decided that all teachers would be paid not according to the Western (Gregorian) calendar, but rather the Greek (Julian) one.[18] In 1930, in celebration of the 100th anniversary of Greek independence, Kohn instructed the Jewish and Christian teachers to spend an entire day teaching students in every Jewish communal school about the history of the Greek War of Independence, recalling the 'great and beautiful accomplishments of the Greek heroes', and inspiring in them 'sentiments of patriotism'.[19]

Despite tentative beginnings, at a well-publicized conference given in 1927 at the B'nai B'rith Lodge, Kohn had already boasted of the successes of the Jewish communal schools. Forty-six Jewish students attended Greek high schools, of whom 41 were graduates of the Jewish communal schools. The following year the first graduates of Jewish schools would enroll in the recently established University of Thessaloniki, evidence that Jewish youth were successfully learning the language of the country.[20]

Kohn indicated that the question of languages was indeed key to the educational enterprise. It was a juggling act that sought to satisfy the government with regard to Greek; the Zionists with regard to Hebrew; and parents, who saw French as key to their children's future success (Constantopoulou and Veremis 1999, 119; Ginio 2002). Rather than reduce instruction of Greek, Judeo-Spanish was virtually removed from the curriculum. Kohn announced that the dedication of two-thirds of classroom hours to Greek could not but satisfy even the 'most intransigent of our assimilationists'.[21] He further proclaimed that 'the day is not far when there will not be any [Jewish] youth who will not have assimilated the Greek language to the point of speaking it like someone of the Greek race'.[22]

Improved knowledge of the Greek language, combined with scholarships offered by B'nai B'rith, increased the number of Jewish students at Greek state high schools—especially those from poor families. *El Puevlo* congratulated the Jewish students as well as the Jewish communal schools for this accomplishment. However, *El Puevlo* noted that integration also produced a kind of social isolation. Jewish students initially attended the same school, the First Gymnasium of Salonica. They often studied together after school in Judeo-Spanish. Most importantly, the Jewish students remained apart because most of their classmates were Christians from well-to-do families, and their being poor stood out more than their being Jewish.[23] This also explains why the Commission of Jewish Instruction periodically distributed at no cost appropriate clothing to the poor Jewish students at the state gymnasia.[24]

160   *Devin E. Naar*

Local Jewish private schools, following the trend, also made the teaching of the Greek language a priority. When the national census was undertaken in 1928, for example, the Pinto school provided 30 Jewish students to serve as interpreters in the Vardar district, home to many impoverished Jews who, especially women, typically spoke only Judeo-Spanish. The Greek census takers, so impressed by the knowledge of Greek among the Jewish students, wrote a flattering letter to the Greek press, quickly reproduced in *El Puevlo*, which congratulated the Pinto school for advancing Greek education and thereby decreasing the divide between Jewish and Christian youth in Salonica.[25] What is striking here is how 'impressed' the Greek Christians were with the progress that Jewish youth had made in learning Greek, as if they had not expected it at all.

Scholars have often focused on editorials in the influential *Makedonia* newspaper decrying what its editor conceived to be Jewish antipathy toward the Greek language—and by extension, the Greek nation as a whole. Yet, as we see, *Makedonia* did not represent the totality of public opinion expressed in the Greek press. Other Greek newspapers were indeed more sympathetic. In 1928, *To Fos* defended Salonica's Jews, proclaiming that they did not disparage the Greek language; rather, they studied it and continued to perfect their knowledge of it. *To Fos* further explained that relatively few Jews attended Greek schools not because Jewish youth did not know Greek, but rather because Greek schools did not make accommodations for Jewish religious instruction or the Hebrew language. If these aspects of Jewish difference were respected and developed within the context of Greek schooling, *To Fos* surmised that more Jewish students would attend state schools for the betterment of both communities.[26]

It is striking that, only a few years later, the state adopted the plan advanced by *To Fos* and established five special state schools for Jewish students.[27] The creation of these schools constituted a major revolution in educational practice: never before had the state intervened so extensively in Jewish education nor had it sought to accommodate Jewish difference in state schools. These government schools for Jewish students, which began operating in the autumn of 1930, followed the state curriculum and even enrolled a number of Christian students.[28] Unlike existing state schools, the new schools dedicated specific class periods to Jewish religion and Hebrew language instruction for Jewish pupils. To accommodate these additional classes, the Inspector of Public Instruction requested that the Commission for Jewish Instruction provide the necessary teachers.[29] Some, such as the well-known teacher and historian, Michael Molho, refused.[30] Ironically, the Commission ultimately had to import 'foreign' Hebrew teachers from Palestine to meet the demands of their own schools as well as those of the Greek state.[31]

The consequences of the transformation in the nature of Jewish education in Salonica as a result of the creation of these new state schools cannot be emphasized enough. By the early 1930s, 2,271 Jewish students—that is, more than one quarter of Jewish students in Salonica—were attending some kind of Greek state school: 1,440 began attending the five Greek state schools designed specifically for Jewish pupils;[32] 831 attended 15 general Greek state schools,[33] nearly 100 of whom at any given time had scholarships from B'nai B'rith.[34] These numbers are

The boundaries of Hellenism   161

staggering in comparison with the initial five Jewish students sent to Greek gymnasia barely five years before.[35] Notably, the government implicitly accepted the Zionist (and religious) claim that Hebrew, rather than Judeo-Spanish, constituted the Jewish language and thus ought to be taught in the government schools. Most importantly, through this decision, the state accepted the proposition that instruction in a language other than Greek, although not to the exclusion of Greek, could be possible without compromising one's loyalty to the Greek polity.

In addition to the increased Jewish attendance at state elementary and high schools, the University of Thessaloniki also emerged as a key forum for the public expression of anticipated Christian-Jewish cooperation, and tested the limits to which linguistic difference would be accommodated. The first four Jewish students enrolled at the University in 1928. The following year, in 1929, as a result of negotiations initiated by the Jewish members of parliament, the University established a new and unprecedented chair in Hebrew language and literature.[36] The Hebraic scholar and Corfu native Lazarus Belleli assumed the position. Fluent in Greek, Belleli had attended the University of Athens and represented Greece at a congress of Orientalist scholars in Rome (Papastathis 1983, 6–8; Phoukas 2009b, 350; 2009a, 93–100, 193–195). *El Puevlo* hailed the inauguration of the chair as a 'beautiful manifestation of Greek-Jewish rapprochement'.[37]

The University rector, Kondos, also lauded the new position. He proclaimed that the aim of the chair was to 'work toward reciprocal appreciation between Greeks and Jews in order to enhance their relations ... for the common good and the greatest benefit of the shared homeland'.[38] Belleli reiterated this stance, assuring his audience that the Jews of Salonica already fulfilled all of their obligations toward their homeland and that with deepened knowledge of the Greek language, their 'profound love' for Greece would only expand. While both *El Puevlo* and *La Verdad* complained about the low attendance at Belleli's initial courses and public lectures,[39] his position at the University constituted an important symbolic expression of the developing category of 'Hellenic Judaism'. The discourse of Hellenic Judaism sought to emphasize long-standing Hellenic-Jewish symbiosis since the era of Apostle Paul, and to recast Salonican Jewish identity in a Greek mold. It should also be mentioned that in 1929 at the same time that the Hebrew Studies chair was being created, the University also approached the Jewish Community demanding that a quadrant of the Jewish cemetery be ceded for the expansion of the University[40]—a task ultimately initiated under Metaxas and completed during the Nazi occupation (Hesse and Laqueur 2005).

Remarkably, while the state educational institutions in Salonica, both the University and the public schools, accepted the introduction of the Hebrew language into the curriculum, they avoided Judeo-Spanish completely. The matter does not appear to have been raised for the state elementary and high schools. At the University, however, the prospect of creating a chair of Spanish Language and Literature emerged in 1930. The Spanish Embassy in Athens requested the creation of the chair, at the expense of the Spanish government, in order to 'satisfy the needs of the seventy thousand Spanish-speaking Sephardim in the city' (Philippis 2010, 199–201). Since a chair in Hellenic Studies had been in operation at the

162 *Devin E. Naar*

University of Barcelona since 1928, the establishment of a chair of Spanish in Thessaloniki, the Spanish Embassy argued, would be a welcomed act of diplomatic reciprocity. While neither the Greek Ministry of Education nor the Ministry of Foreign Affairs objected, the University itself responded that the creation of such a chair 'will perniciously counter the work of Hellenizing the Jewish element of the city' (Philippis 2010, 199–201).

The Spanish chair thus never materialized. A language with the backing of a foreign state, Spanish (or, more accurately, Judeo-Spanish) was also actively used by the Jews of Thessaloniki, and therefore could be construed as a threat to the Greek nationalizing project. In contrast, Hebrew, perceived by the Greek state as a language of religious difference, with no state to back it, and which very few Jews in Salonica actually spoke, seems to have been less of a challenge to the state program of Hellenization. The processes in Greece found a parallel in the new Republic of Turkey, where the project of 'Turkification' sought to diminish the use of the Judeo-Spanish 'jargon' among Jews, but did not oppose attempts to revive Hebrew, a 'dead language'.[41]

The Jewish Community negotiated with the state to incorporate additional hours of Hebrew into the educational system. In 1928, for example, when the government ordered that the number of weekly hours dedicated to Greek language instruction be increased from 14 to 20 in the Jewish communal elementary schools, the Commission of Jewish Instruction successfully negotiated with the Inspector of Public Instruction and reached a comprise of 17 or 18 hours of Greek (depending on the grade level), with the other hours dedicated to Hebrew.[42] Greek nonetheless became the dominant language, one that dictated the parameters of education—Jewish or otherwise—in interwar Salonica and became a prime measure of the boundaries of Hellenism.

Scholars have generally characterized the interwar period, after the Asia Minor catastrophe, as one in which the boundaries of Hellenism contracted. According to this interpretation, the 19th-century vision of Hellenism, as advanced by historians such as Constantinos Paparrigopoulos, had been more flexible, animated by the promise that populations such as Albanians, Vlachs, and Slavs within the borders of Greece could be Hellenized in terms of their cultural orientation. With the demise of the irredentist vision of Greek nationalism, the *Megali Idea* (Great Idea), the perceived need to defend the territorial integrity of the Greek state and guard against possible internal threats—communists, Slavs, Albanians—increased. The possibilities of absorbing minorities into the Hellenic collectivity therefore were severely curtailed (Koliopoulos and Veremis 2010, 98–100). The case of the Jews of Salonica, however, requires the process of Hellenization to be reconsidered. A window of accommodation that offered the possibility and promise that Jews could also become Greeks, while continuing to develop certain aspects of their cultural difference, such as the Hebrew language, increased after the Asia Minor catastrophe, and remained open until the early 1930s.

In fact, the unparalleled, rapid increase in the number of Jewish students proficient in the Greek language, those attending state schools—including the first

The boundaries of Hellenism   163

few at the University—and the number of Jewish teachers employed by the state, including one at the University, marked a new high point in Jewish integration into Greek society and educational structures. This apogee of Jewish integration emerged just as the economic crisis hit and, while never previously recognized, corresponded to a new high point in anti-Jewish violence. The so-called Campbell riots in the summer of 1931—the first major anti-Jewish violence in 20th-century Thessaloniki—is usually explained as the result of emergent ethnic Greek nationalism stirred up by the anti-Jewish rhetoric of the editor of *Makedonia*, who decried what he claimed to be Jews' disloyalty, their refusal to align their interests with Greece, and their obstinacy in the face of demands to learn the Greek language and to assimilate (Kallis 2006; Vasilikou 1993).

The preliminary research presented here, based on a new set of sources, raises several questions: could the anti-Jewish violence of 1931 have been triggered not by Jews' apparent refusal to assimilate or be loyal, but perhaps by the opposite, the unexpected and rather successful acquisition of the Greek language and sense of identification with Greece among of a section of the Jewish population, especially the youth but including the lower classes? May we understand the violence of 1931 as a backlash against a sense that certain social, linguistic, and political boundaries between 'Jews' and 'Greeks', seemingly well entrenched and scrupulously maintained since the Ottoman era, were now beginning to break down?[43]

Certain segments within the Jewish population successfully navigated the transition from the Ottoman Empire to the Greek nation-state, accepting and fulfilling Venizelos' demand that they learn Greek, identify with Greece and the Greek people. On the ground in Salonica, did a segment of Greek-Christian society come to reject Venizelos' ostensible liberal promise to accept Salonica's Jews as part of Greece, precisely as Salonica's Jewish youth began to meet the challenge? When an anti-Venizelist politician described the Jews of Salonica as 'more Greek' than the Christian refugees from Asia Minor, many of whom did not arrive speaking Greek (Mazower 2004, 416), could he have been presenting a reasonable portrait of the situation? Could a realization that Jews had become, or could become, just as 'Greek' or even more Greek, in terms of language and loyalty, than Christians, have provoked a sense of resentment that sparked some of the anti-Jewish sentiment and violence that transpired in the early 1930s?

The key role of youth must be emphasized. It is well-known that disaffected Greek-Christian youth, especially those from refugee families, some of whom very likely had Jewish classmates, supplied a considerable portion of the membership of *Tria Epsilon*, the ultra-nationalist organization that perpetrated the Campbell riots. In the months after the Campbell riots, Christian youth also instigated a series of desecrations of the Jewish cemetery—*El Puevlo* debated whether this was antisemitism or child's play.[44] Furthermore, the *Panfititikis Enosis* (Student Union) of the University of Thessaloniki, also a youth organization, passed out fliers that called for an anti-Jewish boycott and helped precipitate the riots.[45] Notably, the Maccabi sports club, a meeting place for Jewish youth, was the first target of attack.

164   *Devin E. Naar*

In fact, Maccabi was not only a meeting place for Jewish youth (Zaikos 2010). Normally understood as a Zionist organization, and accused of promoting Bulgarian irredentism as a pretext for the attack, Maccabi was, in many ways, a Greek-Jewish youth organization. As early as 1927, *El Puevlo* had celebrated the Maccabi club as a center of 'Hellenic-Jewish fraternization'. An article reported that on a Saturday in May, 45 Greek-Christian scouts arrived in Salonica from the suburb of Langadas specifically to spend the weekend with the Maccabi. The master of each scout troop, it was reported, made enthusiastic speeches emphasizing Greek-Jewish camaraderie, and their shared goal of creating strong and moral youth. The scouts played 'mixed games'—Jews and Greek Christians together.[46] The fact that their meeting transpired on Saturday, the Jewish Sabbath, suggests that the Jewish scouts were not observing Jewish tradition, and were thus even more similar to their Christian 'brothers'. Furthermore, the Maccabi patriotically participated in the annual parades with the other Greek scout troops on 25 March in celebration of 'Hellenic independence'.[47] Certain segments of Jewish youth in interwar Thessaloniki were becoming—if they had not already become—Greek Jews.

By reference especially to the archives of the Jewish community of Salonica, as well as the local press, I have emphasized the challenges the Jewish Community, as represented by the Commission for Jewish Instruction, faced in educating the first generation of Jewish youth born in Greek Thessaloniki, but also the seemingly successful, albeit fleeting, rapprochement that was achieved. For Jewish youth who passed through the Jewish communal schools, Greek state schools, or participated in clubs such as the Maccabi, allegiances to Jewish sentiments and Hellenic sentiments were by no means mutually exclusive. Much like French culture had been folded into Jewish identity since the late Ottoman period, now Greek culture also became part of Jewish identity. The difference was that Jews who acquired Greek culture also had Greek citizenship and developed a Greek political identity and sense of loyalty to Greece. This kind of political orientation had never developed among Ottoman Jews vis-à-vis France. Yet, the recasting of Jewish identity in a Greek mold by no means signified the abandonment of affinities to the Jewish collectivity. The extent to which Thessaloniki's now demographically preponderant Christian population, many of whom undergoing a process of Hellenization themselves, was willing to accept a configuration of identity that accommodated both Jewish and Greek sentiments of belonging requires further study.

A long-time journalist and Member of Greek Parliament, Mentesh Bensanchi, insisted, in numerous articles published in *El Puevlo*, that there was no contradiction between being Greek and being Jewish. This was because he envisioned the Hellenic polity 'as truly liberal'—a country that, if true to the ancient liberal Hellenic spirit, would recognize and respect cultural and communal differences. In this version of Hellenism, Jews and Christians constituted two types of Hellenes. Such an idealized vision of Hellenism was in some ways a repackaged Ottomanism of a previous generation, according to which each 'community' could retain its own cultural distinctiveness while still playing an integral

The boundaries of Hellenism 165

and loyal role within the politics and society of the country. Or maybe this flexible vision of Hellenism echoed that of the 19th-century era of the *Megali Idea*. Or perhaps it was a model for a new kind of pluralistic society. Was it in vain that, referring to mother Greece and her Christian and Jewish citizens, Bensanchi asked: *una madre no puede amar a muchos ijos?* 'Cannot a mother love her many children?'[48]

Notes

1 This article is based on research now published as Devin E. Naar, *Jewish Salonica: Between the Ottoman Empire and Modern Greece*, Stanford: Stanford University Press (2016). The scholarship on Jews in Salonica, and specifically on the question of Jewish education, continues to develop. A future paper will engage with the historiographic discussion my work prompted.

2 Mazower (2004) chapter 21, 'Greeks and Jews', suggests the mutually exclusive nature of the two categories.

3 'Prochesos verbales dela komision superiora de instruksion', 10 October 1918, 47, Central Archives for the History of the Jewish People in Jerusalem [CAHJP], Gr/Sa 8. This notebook contains the minutes of the Commission from 1917 until 1921. The Ben Zvi Institute in Jerusalem holds the subsequent minutes from 1922 to 1934, cited below, in the Amariglio Collection, 1719: v. 1, 1922–1927; v. 2 1927–1928; v. 3: 1929–1930; v. 4: 1931–1932; v. 5: 1932–1934. All of the minutes are handwritten in Judeo-Spanish in the Sephardic Hebrew cursive, *soletreo*.

4 *Ibid.*, 15/28 February 1922, 162; 22 February 1922, 167; 3/16 March 1922, 169; 26 April 1922, 176.

5 *Ibid.*, 11 November 1924, 54; 2 February 1925, 68.

6 See statistics compiled in December 1928, Jewish Museum of Thessaloniki [JMTh], file 138.

7 'Prochesos verbales', 23 August 1922, 195.

8 *Ibid.*, 17 April 1928, 64; 9 December 1930, 195; 31 December 1931, 40; 8 January 1932, 42; 7 November 1933, 150.

9 'Oeuvre d'education sociale: Fondation B'nai B'rith' (15 March 1925), Archive of the *Alliance Israélite Universelle* (Paris), Grèce IIC 54.2; cf. B'nai B'rith to the Communal Council, 6 July 1925, CAHJP Gr/Sa 343.

10 'To programma mas', *Evraïkon Vēma tēs Ellados*, 8 April 1925, 1.

11 B'nai B'rith to the Jewish Communal Council, 8 September 1924, CAHJP Gr/Sa 343.

12 Sidney O'Donoghue to the Secretary of State, 'The Anti-Semitic Movement in Saloniki', 19 December 1923, National Archives and Records Administration (Washington, D.C.), RG84, volume 113, document 840.1/3217.

13 'La liga grega djudia', *El Puevlo*, 25 December 1923, 3.

14 'Prochesos Verbales', 5 August 1924, 46; 19 August 1924, 48.

15 B'nai B'rith to the Jewish Communal Council, 9 November 1925, CAHJP Gr/Sa 343.

16 'Prochesos Verbales', 9 October 1921, 144.

17 *Ibid.*, 2 January 1921, 127–128; 20 September 1921, 143.

18 *Ibid.*, 15 February 1921, 116.

19 Kohn to the directors of the Jewish communal schools, 22 October 1930, JMTh, file 147.

20 *Las Eskolas Komunalas de Saloniko—Loke eyos son loke eyos deven ser. Konferensia echa por s. J. Kon, inspecktor de las eskolas komunales. En la lodja Bene Berith, el Shabat 5 Marso 1927* (Salonica: Brudo 1927), 19.

21 *Las Eskolas Komunalas*, 18.

22 *Ibid.*, 20.

166 *Devin E. Naar*

23 'Los djidios en las eskolas gregas', *El Puevlo*, 19 July 1931, 1.
24 'Prochesos Verbales', 7 April 1927, 4.
25 'La lingua grega en la eskola Pinto', *El Puevlo*, 18 May 1928, 1.
26 'Gregos i djidios. Una ermoza letra de un djornalista', *El Puevlo*, 24 January 1928, 1.
27 'Prochesos Verbales', 16 October 1930, 185.
28 *Ibid.*, 3 November 1931, 23.
29 *Ibid.*, 23 October 1930, 186–187.
30 *Ibid.*, 4 November 1930, 189.
31 *Ibid.*, 16 December 1930, 197; 9 February 1932, 52.
32 *Ibid.*, 21 January 1932, 46–47.
33 Statistics of Jewish students attending Greek schools [early 1930s], CAHJP, Gr/Sa 273.
34 B'nai B'rith to the Jewish Community of Salonica, 15 May 1939, YIVO Institute for Jewish Research in New York, RG–207, file 87.
35 Michael Molho provided the following statistics concerning Jewish school attendance on the eve of the war: 934 in four government schools for Jewish pupils; 839 in Greek gymnasia; and 1,584 in government primary schools. According to Molho's figures, 3,357 of 7,690 school-age Jews—over 40 percent—attended Greek state schools. To this number, he added 50 Jewish students who had attended the University of Thessaloniki (Molho 1948, 23).
36 The position was originally supposed to be in Jewish history, but was changed. 'Salonica University Will Have Jewish History Chair', *Jewish Telegraphic Agency*, 10 November 1927; 'Jew to teach Hebrew at Salonica University', *Jewish Telegraphic Agency*, 4 January 1929.
37 'El diskurso de inogurasion del Profesor Belleli', *El Puevlo*, 14 February 1929.
38 *Ibid.*
39 'Los kursos de Me. Belleli', *El Puevlo*, 11 April 1929.
40 'La ekspropriasion del simiteryo', *El Puevlo*, 12 November 1929, 2.
41 'Turkish Paper Attacks Jews for Using Judeo-Spanish Language', *Jewish Telegraphic Agency*, 12 December 1924.
42 'Prochesos Verbales', 18 September 1928, 81; 30 October 1928, 89.
43 Cf. medieval precedents in Nirenberg 1996.
44 'Las profanasiones al simiteryo. Se trate de sakrelidjio o de echas de kriaturas? *El Puevlo*, 4 February 1932; 'Las profanasiones al simiteryo djidio', *El Puevlo*, 7 June 1932, 1.
45 *Le Progès*, 24 June 1931, 1.
46 'Fraternizasion eleno-djudia', *El Puevlo*, 24 May 1927, 4.
47 'Efimerides de los Drorim-Makabi', *El Makabeo* (1925/1926): 59.
48 M. Bensanchi, 'Sentimientos relijiozo i nasional. Se puede ser djidio i eleno? Balansa para pezar los sentimientos!' *El Puevlo*, 1 October 1928, 1.

References

Abrevaya Stein, S., 'The Permeable Boundaries of Ottoman Jewry', In: Migdal, J. S., (ed.), *Boundaries and Belonging: States and Societies in the Struggle to Shape Identities and Local Practices*, London: Cambridge University Press (2004): 49–70.

Anastassiadis, A., 'À quoi servent les langues aux enfants? Elèves juifs et apprentissage des langues dans les écoles de Thessalonique durant les années 1922–1932', In: Bocquet, J. (ed.), *L'enseignement français en Méditerranée: les missionnaires et l'Alliance israélite universelle*, Rennes: P.U. de Rennes (2010): 239–262.

Bowman, S., *The Agony of Greek Jews, 1940–1945*, Stanford, CA: Stanford University Press (2009).

The boundaries of Hellenism 167

Cohen, J. P., *Ottoman Brothers: Sephardi Jews and Imperial Citizenship in the Modern Era*, New York: Oxford University Press (2014).

Constantopoulou, P. and Veremis, T. (eds.), *Documents on the History of the Greek Jews: Records from the Historical Archives of the Ministry of Foreign Affairs*, Athens: Kastaniotis Editions (1999).

Daccarett, P., *Jewish Social Services in Late Ottoman Salonica (1850–1912)*, PhD Dissertation, Waltham: Brandeis University (2008).

Fleming, K. E., 'The stereotyped "Greek Jew" from Auschwitz-Birkenau to Israeli popular culture', *Journal of Modern Greek Studies* 25 (2007): 17–40.

Fleming, K. E., *Greece: A Jewish History*, Princeton, NJ: Princeton University Press (2008).

Gazi, E., 'Constructing the national majority and ethnic/religious minorities in Greece', In: Eriksonas, L. and Müller, L. (eds.), *Statehood Beyond Ethnicity: Minor States in Northern and Eastern Europe, 1600–2000*, Brussels: Peter Lang (2005): 303–317.

Ginio, E., '"Learning the beautiful language of Homer": Judeo-Spanish speaking Jews and the Greek language and culture between the Wars', *Jewish History* 16 (2002): 235–262.

Hesse, C. and Laqueur, T., 'Orata kai Aorata Sōmata. Ē Exaleiphē tou Evraïkou Nekrotapheiou apo tē Zōē tēs Synkronēs Thessalonikēs', In: Mihailidou, M. and Halika, A. (eds.), *Ē Paragōgē tou Koinōnikou Sōmatos*, Athens: Katapi/Dini (2005): 31–56.

Kallis, A. A., 'The Jewish community of Salonica under siege: The antisemitic violence of the summer of 1931', *Holocaust and Genocide Studies* 20.1 (Spring 2006): 34–56.

Koliopoulos, J. and Veremis, T., *Modern Greece: A History since 1821*, Malden, MA: Wiley-Blackwell (2010).

Lagos, K., 'The Hellenization of Sephardic Jews in Thessaloniki in the interwar period, 1917–1941', In: Aradas, M. and Pappas, N. C. J. (eds.), *Themes in European History: Essays from the 2nd International Conference on European History*, Athens: ATINER (2005): 401–406.

Mackridge, P. and Yannakakis, E. (eds.), *Ourselves and Others: The Development of a Greek Macedonian Cultural Identity Since 1912*, Oxford: Berg (1997).

Margaritis, G., *Ανεπιθύμητοι συμπατριώτες. Στοιχεία για την καταστροφή των μειονοτήτων της Ελλάδας. Εβραίοι, Τσάμηδες* [Unwanted compatriots: Evidence regarding the destruction of the minorities of Greece: Jews and Chams], Athens: Bibliorama (2005).

Mazower, M., *Salonica, City of Ghosts: Christians, Muslims and Jews, 1430–1950*, London: HarperCollins (2004).

Michailidis, I., 'From Christians to members of an Ethnic Community: Creating borders in the City of Thessaloniki (1800–1912)', In: Klusáková, L. and Teulières, L. (eds.), *Frontiers and Identities: Cities in Regions and Nations*, Pisa: Plus-Pisa University Press (2008): 169–180.

Molho, M., *Memoriam: Hommage aux Victimes Juives des Nazis en Grèce*, Thessaloniki: Communauté Israélite de Thessalonique (1948).

Molho, R., *Οι Εβραίοι της Θεσσαλονίκης 1856–1919. Μια ιδιαίτερη κοινότητα* [The Jews of Thessaloniki 1856–1919: A special community]. Athens: Patakis Editions, [2001] (2014).

Naar, D., 'Removing the "Shroud of Forgetfulness": The dispersal and recovery of the libraries and archives of the Jewish Communities of Greece', In: Ginio, E. (ed.), *Ha-Yehudim be-Yavan* [The Jews of Greece], Jerusalem: Ben Zvi Institute (2014).

Nirenberg, D., *Communities of Violence: Persecution of Minorities in the Middle Ages*, Princeton, NJ: Princeton University Press (1996).

168   *Devin E. Naar*

Papastathis, Ch., 'Ο Λάζαρος Βελέλης ως καθηγητής του Πανεπιστημίου Θεσσαλονίκης' [Lazaros Velelis as professor at the University of Thessaloniki], *Chronika* 61 (September 1983): 6–8.

Philippis, D., *Προφασισμός, εκφασισμός, ψευδοφασισμός, Ελλάδα, Ιταλία και Ισπανία στον Μεσοπόλεμο* [Pre-fascism, fascisticization, pseudo-fascism: Greece, Italy and Spain in the interwar period], Thessaloniki: University Studio Press (2010): 199–201.

Phoukas, V., *Η Φιλοσοφική Σχολή του Πανεπιστημίου Θεσσαλονίκης* [The Philosophical School of the University of Thessaloniki], PhD Dissertation, University of Thessaloniki (2009a): 93–100, 193–195.

Phoukas, V., 'Οι ιστορικές σπουδές στη Φιλοσοφική Σχολή Θεσσαλονίκης κατά την περίοδο του μεσοπολέμου' [Historical studies in the Philosophical School of Thessaloniki in the interwar period], In: *30th Panelliniko Istoriko Synedrio, 29–31 Maiou 2009, Praktika*, Thessaloniki: Greek Historical Society (2009b): 337–358.

Pierron, B., *Juifs et Chrétiens de la Grèce Moderne: Histoire des relations intercommunautaires de 1821 à 1945*, Paris: Editions L'Harmattan (1996).

'*Prochesos verbales dela komision superiora de instruksion'* [Minutes of the superior commission on education], Central Archives for the History of the Jewish People in Jerusalem [CAHJP], Gr/Sa 8. Minutes of the Commission from 1917 until 1921. The Ben Zvi Institute in Jerusalem holds the subsequent minutes from 1922 to 1934, in the Amariglio Collection, 1719: v. 1, (1922–1927).

Rivlin, B. (ed.), Pinkas HaKehillot. *Encyclopaedia of Jewish Communities from their Foundation till after the Holocaust: Greece*, Jerusalem: Yad Vashem (1998).

Rodrigue, A., *French Jews, Turkish Jews: The Alliance Israélite Universelle and the Politics of Jewish Schooling in Turkey, 1860–1925*, Bloomington, IN: Indiana University Press (1990).

Rodrigue, A., 'From millet to minority: Turkish Jewry', In: Birnbaum, P. and Katznelson, I. (eds.) *Paths of Emancipation: Jews, States, and Citizenship*, Princeton, NJ: Princeton University Press (1995).

Rodrigue, A., *Jews and Muslims: Images of Sephardi and Eastern Jewries in Modern Times*, Seattle: University of Washington (2003).

Vasilikou, M., *The Anti-Semitic Riots in Thessaloniki (June 1931) and the Greek Press: A Case-Study of 'Scapegoating' Theory*, Masters Thesis, London: King's College London (1993).

Vasilikou, M., 'Εκπαίδευση των Εβραίων της Θεσσαλονίκης στο Μεσοπόλεμο' [Education of Thessaloniki Jews in the interwar period], In: Stefanopoulou, M. (ed.), *Ο Ελληνικός Εβραισμός* [Greek Jewry], Thessaloniki: Etaireia Spoudon Neoellinikou Politismou kai Genikis Paideias (1999): 129–147.

Zaikos, N., *Γυμναστικός Σύλλογος Μακαμπή Θεσσαλονίκης: Έλληνες Εβραίοι αθλητές και αθλήτριες* [Gymnastic club Maccabi of Thessaloniki: Greek-Jewish athletes], Thessaloniki: Municipality of Thessaloniki (2010).

12 In the aftermath of the Balkan Wars

The incorporation of Thessaloniki into the Greek state

Elpida K. Vogli

States engaged in occupation of foreign lands during armed conflicts are forced to deal with two complicated issues. The first is the establishment of effective administration over the territory under control for the period until a peace treaty is signed. The second emerges during the negotiations for the signing of a peace treaty and pertains to the incorporation of new territory into the state's administrative and juridical system. These two issues are distinct but complementary, insofar as military occupation—which does not equate to sovereignty—is indispensable for the annexation of foreign territories. Furthermore, the process of incorporation of new provinces, which commences at the time a peace treaty recognizes their transfer from one state to the other, is complex, time-consuming, and complicated by the successor state's desire to safeguard its sovereignty and ethnic homogeneity.

Taking the above considerations into account, this article explores the incorporation of Thessaloniki over a period of almost two decades after its occupation by the Greek armed forces in October 1912. Greece lends itself to such a case study partly through its long experience as a successor state. The cession of the Ionian Islands by Britain in 1864 inaugurated Greek territorial unification. In 1881, Greece, again without fighting a war, gained its first Ottoman lands (in Epirus and Thessaly), while in the Greek-Ottoman War of 1897 it saw a few of its provinces temporarily occupied by hostile forces (for Greek unification policy, see Karipsiadis 2000; Sfika-Theodosiou 1989; Dakin 1972; Divani 2000). There is no doubt, however, that its military success in the course of the Balkan Wars brought to the fore the significant role of territory in the development of nationalist thought. Territory, construed either as the specific space to which its native residents are attached through their history, memory, and myths, or as the concrete area of a nation-state's legitimate power that binds its co-national residents together, remains the primary and overriding factor in defining group and individual identities (Penrose 2002). During the annexation of the provinces occupied by the Greek army in 1912–1913, a first set of difficulties arose related to the large geographical space they covered, only slightly smaller than the old Greek territory into which they were going to be absorbed. More complications resulted from the fact that this territory was ethnically heterogeneous.

170   *Elpida K. Vogli*

In addition to highlighting the complexity of the incorporation process after the Balkan Wars, this article explores the motivations behind the policy Greek authorities followed for 'Hellenizing' the 'New Lands' and specifically their largest city, Thessaloniki, whose strategic location made its annexation an important goal for both Greece and Bulgaria. Thessaloniki was known for its cosmopolitan society as well as for its image as the 'place where Ottoman and European values and aspirations met'. Its occupation by the Greek army was greeted with enthusiasm throughout Old Greece. However, the national and religious heterogeneity of its population was one of the major problems the politicians of Old Greece had to cope with in organizing its Greek administration. Mark Mazower points out the disdain some of the first Greek visitors to the city expressed for its multicultural character. He also makes clear, though, that neither its history nor its ousted former rulers were the source of Greek anxiety. From the outset, it was the Bulgarians who posed the most serious threats to the Greek military regime (Mazower 2004, 256, 275–278). All of the above reasons render the incorporation of Thessaloniki into the Greek state an ideal case study.

This process can be divided into two phases. The main feature of the first was the attribution of Greek citizenship to those inhabitants who would remain in the city, and the establishment of their civil rights. The creation of a Greek citizenry was combined with the voluntary or forced emigration of many of its non-Greek residents, while the city was acquiring an administrative and legal framework, similar to the system of Old Greece. From this perspective, the ultimate purpose in this first transitional phase of Thessaloniki's incorporation was the spread of Old Greece's political and nationalist control.

It is also important to point out that 'civic equality and political representation are distinct elements of modern citizenship, with ideological and institutional roots in different sociohistorical contexts' (Brubaker 1996, 40). Thus, studying the 'Hellenization' of Thessaloniki allows us to control for the different meaning ascribed to the civil and political rights during the annexation of new lands in a sovereign state. We may assume that the municipal elections, conducted in Thessaloniki for the first time in 1925, were the starting point of its second incorporation phase in the Greek state. Nevertheless, we must keep in mind that the main feature of the election campaign in the city, which had already welcomed hundreds of thousands of co-national refugees from Asia Minor and the Soviet Union, reflected the attitudes the principal Greek political forces had adopted towards the New Lands and its population.

From the occupation to the Hellenization of Thessaloniki

Once Greek forces were in possession of Thessaloniki, many eminent legal experts of Athens volunteered to enlighten their compatriots about the constraints and the necessities that the procedure of territorial annexation imposed. An example of their contribution to this public debate was Pantelis Tsitseklis' dissertation on the development of the international law of land occupation since ancient

In the aftermath of the Balkan Wars   171

times, published in instalments over a full month in Athens daily *Skrip* from mid-November 1912.[1] Before the end of this month, the diplomatic incident resulting from the Greek military landing on the island of Sazan (*Sason* in Greek), gave rise to a proliferation of pertinent disquisitions, many of which became also accessible to the general public through the Athenian press. This small island where the Adriatic and Ionian Seas met was ceded to Greece with the rest of the Ionian Islands in 1864, but was never annexed since it was not placed under the authority of the Greek army before November 1912. The incident encouraged legal experts to emphasis the latent complexities and hidden dangers of the territorial annexation procedure. Embracing the opportunity, George Filaretos, a 64-year-old distinguished jurist and well-known liberal politician, concluded that the Greek government should pay close attention to the 'lessons of [national] experience' while planning its policy.[2] His conclusion reflected the assumption that the Great Idea provided both the state and the nation with a program of territorial enlargement as well as 'a certain perspective on politics and civic identity' (Stouraiti and Kazamias 2010, 11–34).

However, Filaretos' purpose was to point out not only the national consequences of a state's failure to fulfil international requirements but also the effects the intervention of neutral foreign Powers might have on the political outcome. Italy and Austria-Hungary had declared at once their dissatisfaction against the landing of Greek forces on the island of Sazan. Neither Filaretos and the other Greek jurists nor the Greek politicians of the time could have predicted what surprises the intervention of the Great Powers in the peace conference would have in store for them as far as the fate of Thessaloniki and their other possessions were concerned. Besides, it was the first time Greece had gained control over foreign territories as a result of its involvement in war. Far more worrying, though, was the fact that Greece was fighting as a member of a fragile Balkan alliance, which was formed gradually after its major competitors on the 'Macedonian question' had agreed to set aside the issues that divided them. The treaties Greece had signed with each of them strengthen the impression that their reconciliation was temporary. In other words, the most threatening feature of the Balkan League was the lack of a generally accepted demarcation line between its members' national claims.

'Disputed zones' presaging conflicts existed in most of the bilateral treaties the Balkan states had signed between them. The first problem that separated the victorious allies arose between Greece and Bulgaria and centered on the city of Thessaloniki. From the outset, it was not the ousted Turkish government but the Bulgarians who put in jeopardy the regime the Greeks established in accordance with the regulations embodied in the Hague Convention of 1907.

Despite their inter-alliance problems, all of the Balkan allies were obliged to demonstrate their compliance with international law. The government of Eleftherios Venizelos took advantage of article 42 of the 1907 Hague Regulations, which provided that an area was considered occupied once it had been placed under the occupier's authority. Without delay, Venizelos put in force Greek Law

172   *Elpida K. Vogli*

4069, which was adopted a day after the Greek declaration of war in order to establish an administration system 'for the regions under siege'.[3] As a result, Thessaloniki was subsumed in a transitional administrative 'environment' that could be considered similar to Old Greece's insofar as it was controlled by the Greek forces but which was obliged to respect Ottoman laws in accordance with article 43 of the Hague Regulations.[4] In other words, differences in taxation, customs, and criminal law put a clear dividing line between the Greek provinces and those under occupation. In the first weeks after the establishment of the Greek administration, a visitor of the city might have been astonished to see Ottoman officers still patrolling its streets alongside their Greek counterparts. In fact, the Greeks chose to cooperate with the Turks in order 'to ensure public order and civil life', having in mind not only their 'duty', as it was defined in the Hague Regulations, but also the need to confront their Bulgarian competitors, whose soldiers, still in the city, constituted 'a daily challenge' to the legitimacy of the Greek occupation regime (Mazower 2004, 278–279).

Although the signature of a peace treaty that would determine their fate had not been signed, Konstantinos Raktivan, Minister of Justice in the Athenian government and its representative in the occupied lands after his appointment as 'Civilian Governor-General of Macedonia',[5] was already preparing to inaugurate the 'Hellenization' process of the occupied lands. His preparatory work was in accordance with article 43 of the Hague Regulations, which did not absolutely prohibit changes in the economic and legal system left by the ousted government. Raktivan took advantage of the vagueness of the above article. He represented himself as 'respecting' existing laws, while at the same time enacting new ones. He made unambiguously clear that he would put forward any changes he thought necessary to safeguard the civil rights and welfare of the 'conquered peoples' (Benvenisti 1993, 3–31). In fact, he had prepared the ground for changes from the beginning. In the first proclamation he addressed to the local population a few hours after his arrival in Thessaloniki, he committed himself to introducing a system of effective administration, 'worthy of a civilized State', that would prevent racial or religious discrimination and inequality.[6] The early signs of his policy are discernible in his resolution to keep the Ottoman Mayor of Thessaloniki, Osman Sait Chaki, in his position. Implicit in this resolution was his intent to pave the way for the separation between the military and the civilian powers of the occupation authority. Law 4134, which was enacted in February 1913 but had retroactive effect for the whole period since the Greek declaration of war, enshrined this separation of powers[7] and simultaneously initiated the economic and judicial unification of the occupied lands with Old Greece. A few days later the establishment of the 'Central Financial Service of the Occupied Lands' on the basis of the structure of the Greek Ministry of Economics, into which it was to be incorporated, could be considered as evidence that the unification project had already begun.[8]

Meanwhile, both the Governor of the occupied lands and the officers involved in their administration admitted that there were two major problems to be solved. The first one was closely connected with their ignorance of local conditions. The most urgent task Raktivan assigned to his administrative and financial commissioners in the region, immediately after their appointment, was the preparation of a detailed 'agricultural, industrial and generally economic and financial study of Macedonia'. Their report, which was to be completed by 20 February 1913, should also include detailed demographic and ethnological data. According to the requirements put forth by Raktivan, this report was expected to be equivalent to a census conducted by the state statistical service. In other words, it should include information on agricultural practices in the new regions; what was commercially produced at what price range; employment figures; wages; the buying power of the local populace; the number of livestock; modes of transportation; natural resources such as rivers, lakes, and mineral resources; as well as information on the types of property possessed by the populace and the nationalities living in the new regions.[9] Not surprisingly, such a detailed report was not completed in a few weeks. This failure did not discourage Raktivan from entrusting the preparation of a second detailed report to his close friend, leading jurist Konstantinos Polychroniades. This time a thorough study, consisting of concrete proposals for the organization of the administration of the occupied regions, was completed within a few months, but it did not offer the guidance Raktivan hoped for (Polychroniades 1913). It could be assumed, though, that Raktivan's vain attempts to be acquainted in a few months with such a broad and unknown area was a sign of his recognition of the impossibility of managing 'from the center' all the economic, legislative, and political affairs involving its residents. It could be also assumed that Raktivan wished to assimilate both Greek and non-Greek groups into a Greek identity before the signing of a peace treaty. Such a goal, of course, was not only ambitious but also unfeasible; and Raktivan was aware of its impossibility. Indeed, the existence of several minorities was the second major problem he had to handle.[10]

The significant reforms Raktivan sought revealed his determination to expand Greek sovereignty over the occupied region even before the signing of a peace treaty. On the other hand, his effort to present the reforms he promoted as beneficial to the interests of the indigenous communities under occupation was designed to ingratiate his administration with the local population; their expressed preference for Greek sovereignty was expected to provide incontrovertible evidence for the Greek character of the region. In conjunction with this effort, Raktivan presented the 'Hellenization' process as equivalent to the modernization or 'Europeanization' of the region. In symbolic terms, modernization equated to the replacement of an outmoded Ottoman system with a Greek one developed in conformity with European models. Examples of Greek intentions to identify their nationalizing policy with modernization include the establishment of a committee responsible for the examination of taxpayers' complaints[11] and later on the reform of the healthcare system. The first could be compared to the inauguration of a liberal financial reformation that would prevent the violation of individual rights. The latter, designed in accordance with the rules in force in Greece and

174   *Elpida K. Vogli*

other European states of the time, was to protect public health. In particular, it prohibited doctors, dentists, and pharmacists who did not hold a university degree or diploma, from the exercise of medical professions within the borders of the occupied lands.[12]

This remained, however, an uncompleted reform. Though it probably helped Raktivan collect information about health services in the region, in practice it created more problems than it solved. Greek administrators lacked the jurisdiction to take measures for the re-education of locals practicing medical professions without a university degree. Strangely, they did not even discuss how to address the problems that would arise from the lack of qualified doctors.

A reform that met with greater success, although it proved equally complicated, was the expansion of the Greek judicial system to the occupied lands. From the outset, this was a high priority on the Greek political agenda, since it was expected to determine the future of the occupied territory at the peace conference. Not quite forty days after Raktivan had assumed his duties, the Greek military courts transferred their jurisdiction to municipal courts (*eirinodikeia*) and courts of first instance (*protodikeia*), which were established throughout the occupied regions, and to a court of appeal (*efeteio*) established in Thessaloniki.[13] The organization of the new courts was based on the legal principles and structures of the Greek judicial system. These courts were authorized to try all crimes committed in the region after its occupation by Greek forces according to the rules of Greek legal procedure. Raktivan explained that this change of the existing system did not deviate from the rules of international law. The reason was that the military courts were not sufficient to adjudicate the huge number of outstanding cases that had not been brought in court yet as well as those which were added daily. Many Muslims, Jews, and Greeks placed in custody by the Ottoman authorities were still awaiting trial, although a number of them had already remained in custody longer than allowed by Greek law.[14]

The staffing of the police and the recruiting of a sufficient number of bailiffs required time and funds that were not available; still, the creation of the structures necessary for the judicial and legislative unification of the occupied lands with Old Greece had already begun. This was confirmed by the measures taken to house the new courts and court archives as well as the commencement of translating court files into the Greek language. The first such translator was hired in December 1912 to serve the municipal courts and the Court of Appeal of Thessaloniki.[15] Until early 1914, he was the sole translator for the Greek courts.

Certainly, it was not the rules of international law that prevented the recruitment of translators or the organization of translation agencies in the Greek occupied lands.[16] Recruitment of translation agencies, court personnel, administrative officers, and police forces proved one of the most severe problems the Greek authorities had to deal with. From the outset, the transferring of employees from Old Greece provided a convenient solution, since they knew Greek law and how the Greek system worked. Their most important asset was their assumed loyalty to the Greek state. In any case, article 3 of the 1911 constitution, which limited employment in the public service to Greek citizens, would bar the appointment of residents of the occupied regions. The retroactive law 4134 'on the administration of the occupied lands' provided the staffing of state services with employees transferred from Southern Greece, but also allowed the General Governor of Macedonia to keep in their positions employees of the predecessor state on condition that they would 'make a declaration under oath about their conscientious fulfilment of their duties under the new Government'.[17]

The Greek government and General Administration of Macedonia had no need to clarify whether the decision to transfer employees from the south was dictated by security reasons and national interest, or was aimed at gratifying the expectations of citizens of Old Greece. Raktivan chose to focus on lawyers and notaries who had worked in Northern Greece prior to October 1912. He contended that many of them appeared to be inferior to their colleagues in Old Greece and Crete since they had no degree but only a permit 'awarded to them in a totally peculiar way' by the Ottoman state.[18]

Transfers of employees from Old Greece were not necessarily published in the *Government Gazette*. They were often, however, the subject of political articles in the Athenian newspapers. The press, sensitive to national issues, took on an active role in the inevitable 'reformation' of Greek nationalism. The answer given by a columnist of the Thessaloniki afternoon newspaper *Nea Aletheia* showed the bitterness felt by city residents at their treatment by the citizens of Old Greece: 'The day the citizens of Thessaloniki welcomed Raktivan in his new position, and also welcomed the policemen from Crete and the public servants transferred from South Greece, was the day the second conquest of the city started', he commented. The first was that completed by the Greek army. The second, however, the columnist explained, was being achieved day by day by the people of Old Greece, together with a 'whole legion' of Athenian journalists eager to convey images of an 'unknown' Thessaloniki to the public of the capital.[19]

On the other hand, the unprecedented experience of extending Greek domination to provinces without a homogeneous Greek population brought to public debate a number of unspoken worries regarding the Great Idea, as well as the fear Greek society felt regarding the new parts of Greek territory. Under the circumstances, the 'mission' of the nation was to extend the indisputably 'superior' political culture of Old Greece to the new provinces. The editor of *Hestia* newspaper put the question openly: 'How shall we teach our new fellow citizens gentle morals and lawfulness?' His answer was quite revealing: 'By proving ourselves to be a gentle, liberal, willing and beneficent State, but also a State of unyielding status and even with a ... fist', which would not trust the new societies so much as to cede 'local rights' to them. This was his assessment of the situation, even if this Greek policy appeared 'colonial', as liberal newspapers of the capital claimed.[20]

The split in public opinion as well as that of the politicians, was proved by the conversations that took part in the Greek parliament regarding the 'rights' of the New Lands. Pressure was applied to Venizelos, who agreed to conduct local

176   *Elpida K. Vogli*

elections only in Old Greece, because it was only a month after the signing of the peace treaty that endorsed the Greek domination over these lands.

According to Venizelos's interpretation, the 'Hellenization' of Thessaloniki had been achieved, since the residents of the city, like the residents of the other new lands, gained Greek citizenship automatically with the ratification of the Treaty of Athens. Alternatively, they had the right to choose between the citizenship of the predecessor or the successor state within three years. The 'naturalization' of the new provinces and their population extended smoothly within the diaspora as well. Members of the indigenous population who lived abroad also gained access to Greek civil rights as long as they followed the relevant procedures within six months from the ratification of the treaty. On the other hand, those who rejected the offer of Greek citizenship were obliged to leave the Greek territory within three years. It was expected that by the second half of the 1920s there would be at least partial homogeneity of the population, since it was almost certain that at least one significant minority, the Turks, would leave.[21]

In the first days of 1914, an amendment was made to article 23 of the 1856 Civil Code, which defined that those who opted for foreign citizenship would be deprived of their rights as Greek citizens. The aim of this amendment was to discourage residents of the New Lands from choosing the citizenship of another state in order to avoid military service or other duties while continuing to live in Greek territory.[22] In the following months, residents of the New Lands who wanted to be appointed as translators or participate in exams to work as lawyers and notaries[23] had to declare that they would keep Greek citizenship and give up the right of choice offered by the peace treaty.[24]

The intent to create a homogeneous Northern Greek society—at least as far as the civil identity of its members was concerned—was based on the *de facto* extension of Greek sovereignty to their birthplaces. In December 1914, after stormy debate, a law was passed regarding the final administrative division and administration of the New Lands.[25] A number of juridical reforms undertaken by the Ministry of Justice seemed to change the legislative and administrative environment of the state, to the extent necessary to absorb the local communities of the New Lands. However, this appeared to be part of the reforms promoted by Venizelos and the Liberals in accordance with their program, thus combining internal reform and territorial expansion.

After 1915, the modernization of the New Lands ended and their right to local government was almost forgotten. The abolition of the General Administration of Macedonia in March 1915 could be received as the closing act in the unification of Thessaloniki and the New Lands with Old Greece, insofar as it reinforced the administrative unity of Greek territory (Dimakopoulos 1993, 222).

In May 1915, the citizens of the New Lands exercised their electoral rights for the first time, taking part in the parliamentary elections of the Greek state. However, the problems that a few months earlier had led the Greek government to the decision not to conduct municipal elections in the New Lands had not yet been overcome. Participation in the parliamentary election of 1915 was connected with the need to ensure the unity of Greek territory and was an unavoidable

In the aftermath of the Balkan Wars 177

development. Symbolically, though, it seemed to stress the integration of the hitherto unredeemed Greeks into the Greek state which, according to the Venizelist position, was on the verge of entering the European War on the side of the Entente in order not only to complete 'its irredentist mission' but also to ensure its gains of the Balkan Wars (Mavrogordatos 1983, 26–28, 283). During the National Schism (*Ethnikos Dichasmos*), which 'split state and nation into two "political worlds"', this internal competition was transferred to the New Lands. After the settlement of the refugees, which rendered Greece the most homogeneous state of the Balkans (Mavrogordatos 1983, 226), there was no point in continuing or completing the integration of the New Lands which had been already ceased.

Making Thessaloniki a Greek city

The residents of Thessaloniki headed to the polls to elect their mayor for the first time in 1925. Both politicians and citizens focused their attention more on the election's outcome rather than on the importance the beginning of the local political life had for the city. Both in the October elections, the results of which were overturned by dictator Pangalos, and in the December repeat elections, the lawyer Minas Patrikios, a refugee born in eastern Thrace, was elected mayor with the support of the Labour Center of Thessaloniki, the Left party, and the refugees. Patrikios served as mayor until 1929. He performed his duties during only half his tenure, being suspended for several months and under continuous investigation for financial and other 'scandals' he was allegedly involved in. This meant there was no effective municipal administration organized until the late 1920s. In the interim, municipal issues were managed by the council, which made the impression of political instability even clearer. This issue also prevented the Municipality from contracting loans that would allow the public works to move forward that were absolutely necessary for Thessaloniki to reach the level of cities elsewhere in Greece and become at last, as its residents expected, a 'European' city (Vogli 2006, 48–52).

The administrative problems of the Municipality of Thessaloniki, the so-called 'municipal issue', hindered the development of the city and was not resolved by the parliamentary or municipal elections of 1928–1929. The issue was a direct repercussion of the National Schism, which had rendered Thessaloniki its theater even from its early beginning in October 1912—when Venizelos passed over the Commander in chief and heir to the throne and named a minister of his government as the Governor of the city and the wider occupied area (Mavrogordatos 1993, 228). It is worth noting that in 1928 Venizelos went to Thessaloniki to launch his campaign and announce his political program, which was essentially a national reform program after the long period of political instability that followed the Asia Minor Disaster. In 1929, however, Thessaloniki again elected an anti-Venizelist mayor, the candidate of the People's Party, Nikolaos Manos. A year later, Thessaloniki became the single Greek city to face the dismissal of a second elected mayor: Mayor Manos was dismissed, like Patrikios, on allegations of illegal management of municipal finances.

178   *Elpida K. Vogli*

In the December 1930 special municipal elections, held exceptionally due to Manos' dismissal, the Venizelist candidate, Charisios Vamvakas, won a clear victory. It might be assumed that the citizens of Thessaloniki, regardless of their adherence to a political party, had concluded it would benefit their city to vote for the governing party's candidate. Unsurprisingly, the Liberal Party played the leading role during the campaign for Thessaloniki's municipal elections in 1930. Two weeks before the election, Prime Minister Venizelos visited Thessaloniki on the occasion of the opening of the Chamber of Trade and Industry building and the foundation of two school complexes in the center of the city, as well as a new orphanage in the refugee settlement of Kalamaria.[26]

The outcome of the election can be considered positive for the city for several reasons. First of all, it ensured a stable municipal administration for two years. Until then, none of its mayors were given the opportunity to deal with the reorganization of municipal services. The first appointed mayors, Osman Sait Chaki (1912–1916) and Konstantinos Aggelakis (1916–1920), governed the city under extraordinary circumstances, since Greece was either on the verge of civil war or participating in war or diplomatic negotiations. After Venizelos' defeat in the November 1920 elections, Osman Sait Chaki was reappointed Mayor of Thessaloniki. During his term of office, he had to handle the repercussions of World War I. Petros Syndikas, who was appointed Mayor of Thessaloniki in December 1922 (and remained in office until his death at the beginning of 1925), had to deal with a wide range of problems resulting from the Asia Minor Disaster and the settlement of hundreds of thousands of refugees in the city. As it has already been mentioned above, Mayors Patrikios and Manos were subjected to terms of probation even before being dismissed.

In contrast, Vamvakas obtained a loan of 200,000 English pounds from the Mortgage Bank, without being obliged to seek state guarantees or searching for any additional guarantee at the expense of the municipal revenues. For the first time, thus, construction works were carried out to improve the city's infrastructure. Due to the hiring of hundreds of workers on these public projects, another benefit of this loan was the lessening of the unemployment rate.[27] Vamvakas would claim that more that 70 million drachmas were spent during his tenure on public works projects. In response to an article of an anti-Venizelist newspaper of the city, he boasted that 'more projects were carried out in the city than ever before since Thessaloniki was liberated'.[28]

However, after an anti-Venizelist government came in power in November 1932, action was taken to form a new committee to audit municipal finances. In July 1933, Vamvakas was temporarily suspended from office, and that autumn he became the third elected mayor of Thessaloniki to be dismissed. All of them were accused of financial mismanagement: specifically, for using money from the municipal treasury to pay municipality expenses before they had legally received the payment mandate. In practice, they had followed the traditional methods used before 1912. Such methods, however, were illegal according to Greek law. For example, in the financial year 1932–1933, the Municipality of Thessaloniki spent more than 10,000,000 drachmas instead of the approved 7,000,000 drachmas to run the municipal soup kitchens. The rest of the amount was covered through fundraising. There was, however, a deficit of about 600,000 drachmas, which was covered out of a municipal loan destined for public works. Since neither the Municipal council nor the Ministry of Internal Affairs had given approval for such use, the Mayor's decision was declared illegal (Vogli 2006, 48–52). Vamvakas was dismissed in October 1933.

In lieu of conclusion

It may be easy to identify when the process of integration of a province into a dominant state begins. In the case of Thessaloniki, this process started a few hours after its occupation by the Greek army, in the cabinet meeting convoked by Venizelos to appoint his delegate, 'the General Governor of Macedonia'. It is not equally easy to define when this process is completed. The question raised in this article is how a state defines the integration process after having achieved international recognition of its sovereignty. Did successive Greek governments necessarily retain the completion of the new provinces' integration among their priorities once Greek sovereignty was established, and under what conditions did they attempt to achieve the 'homogenization' of old and new provinces.

The extension of legislation and the judicial system to the new provinces is one of the state's duties connected with international recognition of their annexation. A necessity for the completion of the new provinces' integration is organization of their local administration to the standards of the old provinces and cities of the state they are annexed to. Another is the construction of public works to extend to the new provinces the civil, sanitation, and other infrastructures of the old provinces.

The case of Thessaloniki also suggests that a successor state may have to solve a wide range of problems before planning its policy. Some of these problems may be closely connected with the national ideology it had cultivated in favor of its expansionist or irredentist claims. Other problems may be associated with the expectations expressed by its 'old' or new local societies. However, as was proved in the case of Thessaloniki, the most important problems ensued from the conflicts between the two 'political worlds'—Venizelists and anti-Venizelists—into which the Greek state was split at least since 1915–1916. Both camps claimed a leading role in the local politics of the New Lands. As a consequence, the Schism crystallized 'as a developing conflict between Old Greece and the New Lands' (Mavrogordatos 1983, 284).

Under these conditions, we can assume that a second phase of Thessaloniki's integration into the Greek state started in the mid-1920s, when the first municipal elections took place in the New Lands. Its outset and especially its end cannot be defined accurately. In any case, after the First World War little reference is made to Thessaloniki's need for integration. By way of conclusion, we could quote the opinion expressed by Venizelos: 'We conquered Macedonia with our army in 1912, we conquered it nationally in 1922, with the settlement of our refugee brothers after that tragedy'. 'Nationally we are already secure', he added, 'at least

180 *Elpida K. Vogli*

for the reason that the delegates of all the Great or the lesser Powers have recognized its absolute Greekness'. In Venizelos' opinion, the only thing still pending was the financial integration of Thessaloniki and the other New Lands; this was the goal he included in his party's political program before winning his sweeping victory in the 1928 elections.

Notes

1 Pantelis Tsitseklis was an eminent lawyer of Athens and, at a later time, Minister of Justice. The first instalment of his dissertation was published on 11 November and the last one on 10 December 1912. See the corresponding sheets of the Athenian daily *Skrip.*
2 George Filaretos (1848–1929) exposed the above arguments in one of his articles in the monthly Greek law journal *Gazette of Greek and French Jurisprudence* which was re-published as a leaflet under the title *The Military Occupation in the Law of War: The Administrative, Legal and Taxation System in Macedonia, Epirus and the island under their occupation by the Greek Military and Naval Forces in 1912*, Athens: (November) 1912, p. 30 [in Greek].
3 Law 4069/6.12.1912, *Greek Government Gazette*, no. 317/6.10.1912. The dates mentioned here are according to the Julian calendar used in Greece until 1923.
4 For the development of the law of occupation (usually referred to as 'belligerent occupation') until 1912, see Benvenisti 1993, 3–31; Filaretos 1912, 17–18, 22, 24–25; Dimakopoulos 1993, 205–206.
5 It is worth noting that almost all the Athenian newspapers approved of his appointment. See, for example, *Hestia*, 26.10.1912 and *Akropolis*, 27.10.1912.
6 For his first Circular addressed to the residents of the occupied lands (31.12.1912), Raktivan 1913, 97–98.
7 See the Law 4134/28.2.1913 'on the administration of the military occupied lands', in the *Greek Government Gazette*, no. 41/2.3.1913. For a detailed description of the law, see Dimakopoulos 1993, 214–217.
8 Circular no. 5915/26.3.1913 (Raktivan 1913, 197–204).
9 See Raktivan's Instructions, no. 1065/22.1.1913 (Raktivan 1913, 121–126).
10 After the recognition of the Greek sovereignty over the occupied lands, Raktivan conducted a census in the 'New Lands'. For the 1913 census, see Mazower 2004, 284–285.
11 Circular no. 5941/17.3.1913 (Raktivan 1913, 206–220). See also Kofinas 1914.
12 Mandate no. 1049/14.12.1912 (Raktivan 1913, 36–37).
13 See Raktivan's Mandate no. 300/14.11.1912 as well as his Circular no. 293/11.12.1912 (Raktivan 1913, 5–7, 12).
14 See further information on this issue in *Bulletin of Justice Review* 3.1 (January–March 1913), p. 53 [in Greek].
15 Circular no. 1121/1.12.1912 (Raktivan 1913, 13–14).
16 Law 148/26.12.1913 provided for the establishment of the first translation agency. See *Greek Government Gazette*, no. 25/1.2.1914.
17 See the articles 3 and 4 of the Law 4134, *ibid.*
18 See Raktivan's report (6.11.1913) in the *Bulletin of Justice Review*, 3.2–4 (April–December 1913), Athens 1915, p. 268–272 [in Greek].
19 *Nea Aletheia*, 31.10.1912.
20 See, for instance, *Hestia*, 1.11.1913, *Athena*, 18.12.1913, and *Makedonia*, 5–9.11.1913.
21 See article 4 of Law 4213, which ratified the peace treaty of 1/14 November 1913 between Greece and Turkey, in the *Greek Government Gazette*, no. 229/14.11.1913.

In the aftermath of the Balkan Wars 181

22 Law 120/31.12.1913, *Greek Government Gazette*, no. 1/2.1.1914.
23 Royal Decree, 28.2.1914, *Greek Government Gazette*, no. 54/6.3.1914.
24 Royal Decree, 22.2.1914, *Greek Government Gazette*, no. 89/11.4.1914.
25 Law 524/24.12.1914 in *Greek Government Gazette*, no. 404/31.12.1914.
26 *Makedonika Nea*, 1.12.1930.
27 Vamvakas' letter to the Prime Minister, 15.11.1932, The Hellenic Literary and Historical Archive, Archive of Vamvakas, folder 4.2.
28 *Ibid.*, folder 4.1.

References

Benvenisti, E., *The International Law of Occupation*, Princeton/Oxford: Princeton University Press (1993).

Brubaker, R., *Citizenship and Nationhood in France and Germany*, London: Harvard University Press (1996).

Dakin, D., *The Unification of Greece, 1770–1923*, London: Ernest Benn Limited (1972).

Dimakopoulos, G. D., 'Η διοικητική οργάνωσις των καταληφθέντων εδαφών (1912– 1914)' ['The administration of the occupied lands (1912–1914)'], In: *Η Ελλάδα των Βαλκανικών Πολέμων 1910–1914* [Greece during the Balkan Wars, 1910–1914], Athens: Hellenic Literary and Historical Archive (1993), 203–226.

Divani, L., *Η εδαφική ολοκλήρωση της Ελλάδας 1830–1947* [The territorial integration of Greece (1830–1947)], Athens: Kastaniotis (2000).

Filaretos, G.N., *Κατάληψις πολεμική κατά τους νόμους του πολέμου*. [The Military Occupation according to the law of war, Athens: Law School Printing House (1912)

Karipsiadis, G., *Η Ελλάδα ως διάδοχο κράτος. Θέματα διαδοχής κρατών κατά την ίδρυση του Ελληνικού κράτους και την ένωση των Επτανήσων* [Greece as successor state: Issues of state succession during the foundation of the Greek state and the union with the Ionian Islands], Athens/Komotini: Sakkoulas (2000).

Kofinas, G. N., *Τα οικονομικά της Μακεδονίας* [The economics of Macedonia], Athens: National Printing House (1914).

Mavrogordatos, G. Th., *Stillborn Republic. Social Coalitions and Party Strategies in Greece, 1922–1936*, Berkeley: University of California Press (1983).

Mavrogordatos, G. Th., 'Τα σπέρματα του διχασμού' [The seeds of the schism], In: *Η Ελλάδα των Βαλκανικών Πολέμων 1910–1914* [Greece during the Balkan Wars, 1910– 1914], Athens: Hellenic Literary and Historical Archive (1993).

Mazower, M., *Salonica: City of Ghosts, Christians, Muslims and Jews, 1430–1950*, New York: Alfred A. Knopf, Borzoi Books (2004).

Penrose, J., 'Nations, states and homelands: Territory and territoriality in nationalist thought', *Nations and Nationalism* 8.3 (2002), 277–297.

Polychroniades, K. D., *Μελέτη περί της διοικήσεως των ανακτηθεισών χωρών της Μακεδον ίας* [A study on the administration of the regained Macedonian lands], Athens: National Printing House (1913).

Raktivan, K. D., *Οργανικαί διατάξεις, εγκύκλιοι και οδηγίαι του επι της δικαιοσύνης υπουργού ως αντιπρόσωπος της ελλ. κυβερνήσεως εν ταις υπο του ελληνικού στρατού καταληφθήσαις μακεδονικαίς χώραις* [Instrumental provisions, circulars and Instructions put forth by the Minister of Justice], Thessaloniki (1913).

Sfika-Theodosiou, A., Η προσάρτηση της Θεσσαλίας. Η πρώτη φάση στην ενσωμάτωση μιας ελληνικής επαρχίας στο Ελληνικό Κράτος (1881–1885) [The Annexation of Thessaly: The first phase of incorporating a Greek province into the Greek State], PhD thesis, Thessaloniki: Aristotle University of Thessaloniki (1989).

182 *Elpida K. Vogli*

Stouraiti, A. and Kazamias, A. 'The imaginary topographies of the Megali Idea: National territory as Utopia', In: Diamandouros, P. N., Dragonas, T. and Keyder, Ç. (eds.), *Spatial Conceptions of the Nation. Modernizing Geographies in Greece and Turkey*, London: I. B. Tauris (2010), 11–34.

Vogli, E. K., 'Το "δημοτικόν ζήτημα" και η πολιτική στη Θεσσαλονίκη του μεσοπολέ μου (1919–1933)' [The 'Municipal Issue' of Thessaloniki (1919–1933)], In: *Θεσμοί και τοπική αυτοδιοίκηση στη Θεσσαλονίκη, διαχρονικά*, (Πρακτικά του διεθνούς επιστημονικού συνεδρίου) [Institutions and Local Government in Thessaloniki in the Course of Time, Proceedings of the International Conference, Thessaloniki, 24–25 November 2005], Thessaloniki: Municipality of Thessaloniki and Thessaloniki Historical Center (2006), 48–52.

13 Refugee resettlement, 1922–1924

A watershed in the ethnic, social, and economic transformation of Thessaloniki

Constantinos Katerinopoulos

Beginning late in 1912, Thessaloniki began to receive refugees from Macedonia, Thrace, and Asia Minor. A second wave of refugees followed after the Treaty of Bucharest in the summer of 1913. The flow of refugees kept going throughout the decade. These changes substantially increased the Greek population in Thessaloniki. The movement of refugees was compulsory to a certain extent, driven by the policy of the respective states to seek ethnic homogeneity in the areas they controlled (Mazower 2000, 116 ff.). However, the decisive shift was the arrival of a flood of refugees after the Asia Minor Catastrophe, and the formal population exchange of 1923, which forced the departure of Thessaloniki's Muslim residents.

After the fall of Smyrna in September 1922, thousands of refugees arrived by ships on a daily basis from Smyrna and other areas of Asia Minor. On September 16 alone, 15,000 refugees arrived aboard six ships. The Minister of Social Welfare, Doxiadis, said while visiting the city in mid-October 1922 that 'Thessaloniki's superhuman effort does not compare to any other action of any other Greek city' (Karatzoglou 2012). This statement depicts strongly the overall effort put by the city's inhabitants (Greeks, Jewish, and Muslims) to mitigate the dire circumstances of the refugees by all means possible, such as fundraising and donations of clothing and food. According to a statement released by the League of Nations, Thessaloniki, with a population of 174,000 on November 9 1922, had admitted 100,000 refugees. Thessaloniki was also the transit point for another 270,000 refugees destined for other areas of Macedonia.

In the population census of 1913, which gives an image of the city at the time of liberation, Thessaloniki's population outstripped that of Athens. Of 157,889 total inhabitants, Greeks were 39,956 (25%), Muslims 45,867 (28.8%), Jews 61,439 (39%), Bulgarians 6,263 (4%), and miscellaneous 4,364 (2.7%). In March 1916, without significant change in the overall population, now 165,704, the Greeks were 68,205 (41%), Muslims 30,000 (18%), Jews 61,400 (37%), Bulgarians 1,800 (1%), and miscellaneous 4,300 (2.6%) (Hastaoglou 1999, 317). There was a major increase in the number of Greeks and a significant decrease of Muslims and Bulgarians.

During World War I, English and French troops had been deployed in Thessaloniki since 1915. In September 1916, Venizelos's Government of National

184   *Constantinos Katerinopoulos*

Defense settled in Thessaloniki where it would remain until June 1917. Its presence had a great impact on and enhanced the democratic character of political life of the city before the decisive influence of the refugee wave in 1922.

The settlement of refugees after 1922

The census of 1928 shows a total Thessaloniki population of 251,254, of whom 48,000 were Jewish and almost all the rest were Greek, approximately 200,000. The critical parameter in this change was the resettlement of 117,000 refugees in combination with the compulsory departure of almost 250,000 Muslims who had remained until that time. The refugees of the previous decade had either integrated into the urban environment or moved to other areas, and the changes that they effected on the ethnic composition, although essential, were not of the scale caused by the settlement of refugees after the Asia Minor Catastrophe and the exchange of populations.

Of the refugee families in 1922, a percentage of 10% had property exceeding the amount of 2,000 pounds, 36% had a property of 500–2,000 pounds, and 54% less than 500 pounds. The richest 10% preferred not to live in the refugee resettlement projects: 70% of this 10% lived in the centre, 20% in the Towers, and only 10% lived in the projects (Hekimoglou 1996, 374–375). Of the 117,000 total, 40,000 stayed temporarily in exchangeable Turkish properties, while approximately 70,000 people were added to the homeless of the 1917 fire, primarily poor Jews forced into the settlement projects around the city. In this manner, the city's ethnological character changed decisively and its population was almost completely homogenised.

The city became Hellenised, losing its multinational character. The decrease of the Jewish population, the only significant non-Greek community, completely changed its ethnological nature. Greeks, from 40,000 out of a total of 157,000 people in 1913, were now 200,000 of a total of 251,254 people in 1928. Thus the city of 1928 was completely different from the one that had been liberated just 16 years before (Mazower 2004, 395–438).

Urban transformation

Refugees, except those living temporarily in exchangeable properties until construction was complete, were settled in temporary quarters made from sheet metal or in the army camps left behind by the allies. The refugees' living conditions were marginal, and a large number actually died. Their final settlement was in housing built by the Welfare and Refugee Settlement Commission (EAP), within the scope of the big residential project, or through parallel self-housing programs, managed by special-purpose organisations and refugee cooperatives rather than by the competent Ministry of Transport. The settlements were built on the city's periphery, in locations that had been selected for resettlement of victims of the 1917 fire, or in camps that were extended into the entire area around them. Some of the settlements were entirely new. This program lasted

Refugee resettlement 1922–1924 185

for a decade until 1932. The total number of refugee residences erected was 9,084, in 48 settlements forming an arc that embraced the city externally at its western, central, and eastern sides, having a total population of 114,750 inhabitants in 1932 (Hastaoglou 1999, 335).

In this way, the refugee residences extended outside the city, within the scope of a policy that kept the refugees separated from the local population, which led also to an ethnological, social, and class segregation. The few refugees that kept their financial strength for a brief time, purchased houses or lands at the areas of the exchangeable properties or the areas that had been destroyed by the fire. At this time, the city had expanded and reached six times the size of its original core, with gradual and constant expansions of the city plan which were completed in 1929.

In 1913, approximately 73% of the population lived inside the city walls, while in 1928 more than 50% lived outside the city walls, mostly refugees and poor Jewish people affected by the fire. The refugees were almost half the population of the city and the majority of the Greeks. In their vast majority, refugees were cheap labour. They were settled outside the city walls to avoid disturbing the social balance in the city centre and create socially homogeneous subdivisions.

This specific formulation of the refugee settlements and their position in terms of the city centre and amongst the settlements themselves defined to a significant extent the future development and spatial separation of activities in the city. In essence, the city's future layout was predetermined by the nature of the residential rehabilitation of the refugees, whereas all the infrastructure works such as streets, water supply and sewage, electricity network were adjusted and developed on the basis of this rehabilitation.

This specific spatial arrangement of the settlements at the city's periphery, a long distance from its centre, at a time when transportation was far from easy or available, in combination with bad road conditions, as streets were packed dirt that the rain turned into mud, intensified social and class segregation.

Regardless of the urban layout, the residences that had been built by EAP and the Welfare were small-footprint single-family residences, two-storey, joined together to form quadruplex units. They were standardised, mass-produced houses, with austere lines, but using various styles. They were built under pressure, to meet a huge need for housing during the first years, and with limited resources. Those people who managed to build their own houses, using their own resources, assisted by small cooperatives and lending, clearly acquired more comfortable and spacious quarters, with 'Saranta Ekklisies' the most characteristic of such developments.

This refugee resettlement transformed the social geography of the city and created a new city at the perimeter of the old one, which would take years to integrate functionally into a single city. This integration was achieved by urbanisation and massive housing, mainly after the establishment of the General Building Construction Code (GOK) of 1973. After the 1985 GOK, which provided for even more intense building construction, the vast majority of the 9,000 refugee houses of Thessaloniki were demolished.

186 *Constantinos Katerinopoulos*

The government had no program for preserving even some parts of these settlements and did not take any measures to protect them. As a result of this policy, almost all the refugee settlements of Thessaloniki lost their original urban and historic character by massive building constructions. This violent change of the old refugee settlements contributed strongly to loss of collective memory of the old refugee Thessaloniki, as association of memory with space is the tool to preserve it for the generations to come. Archives, depictions, and books can only record it and address mainly people who have a specific interest in it. The refugee rehabilitation in Thessaloniki was the biggest governmental housing program in the world, for its time, and developed parallel to rebuilding the centre of the city after the 1917 fire, which was the first important European urban design program in the beginning of the 20th century.

Economic transformation

This gigantic building activity supported the city's economic life at a time when it had lost its Balkan hinterland, its Black Sea and Asia Minor connections, and its critical role in transit commerce, while at the same time it had not yet connected productively and commercially to the rest of Greece. Overall, of course, this building activity was combined with the development of the construction materials industry, to an extent that it fully substituted for imports. This particular sector of industry was based primarily on non-specialised refugee laborers. Sixty-five percent of Asia Minor refugees declared themselves to be merchants, manufacturers, or craftsmen, and 35% unspecialised, therefore as laborers. These declarations defined the character of employment that refugees were looking for.

Refugees contributed to the increase in birth rate and demographic growth. Overall in the country, births reached 30.7 per thousand in 1930, while births outstripped deaths by 16.5 per thousand in 1926. This figure, which remained stable until 1934, contrasted to only 4.3 per thousand in 1924. This was Greece's highest birth rate (Lampsidis 1992, 165–176).

The presence of refugees maintained consumption and demand in general at relatively high levels, and became the basis for the development of agricultural productive activities in the city, as well as for economic and commercial revitalisation after a period of wars and destructions. The building construction activity enhanced all the other related professions and increased the number of people employed in this sector. Farm production saw a marked increase due to the arrival of refugees who settled at rural areas, mostly in Macedonia. Wheat cultivation increased by approximately 70%, corn by 45%, while there was a significant increase in planting intended for animal fodder, not previously practised. The agricultural rehabilitation of refugees, which was implemented by expropriations of large country estates ('*tsiflikia*') and exchangeable properties, gave a big boost to agricultural production as it created a large basis of free small landowners, who changed both the nature of the agricultural class and the map of agricultural production in Macedonia. In all the places where the refugees settled, cultivations multiplied and diversified.

Refugee resettlement 1922–1924 187

After 1924, cotton culture and viniculture began to grow in Macedonia, along with tobacco cultivation. Moreover, large-scale land reclamation works were done, and refugees were given fertile lands. In the prefecture of Thessaloniki alone, these lands covered an area of 1,303,500 *stremmata* (1 *stremma* = 1,000 square metres). Agricultural production is connected to the food industry: flour mills, spinning, and weaving plants, and the carpet industry flourished in inter-war Thessaloniki.

Refugees were seeking employment and a large part of them provided cheap labour that gave Thessaloniki's industrial development a significant boost, particularly those living in the western settlements. The country's total industrial production multiplied in value six times between 1921 and 1929. However, Thessaloniki, despite the establishment of the International Exhibition in 1926, remained significantly isolated from the economic, business, and decision centre, Athens. During the first years of its operation, no Athenian businesses took part in the Exhibition.

Business activity

Of the business families in the beginning of the century, few managed to continue to play the same role in the inter-war period. There had been a significant change in their composition and origin, but refugees' participation to this was not especially big. According to an estimate based on research about families participating in businesses, those of refugee origin were less than 30%. Moreover, the refugees who became involved in business life were those who had been businessmen back home. As refugees were more than those needed for salaried work, and as they were very creative people, they managed to establish small businesses of their own and professional units. Both the government and EAP, and the National Bank too, offered loans to assist this effort. EAP's job was to rehabilitate the refugees in productive activities. Besides, refugees were not proletariats by definition as they owned land and houses due to the housing rehabilitation program. Most of them had similar business activities back home, within the scope of the Ottoman empire, as commerce was mostly in the hands of populations with Greek origin in Asia Minor, along with the Armenians and Jews.

According to the official newspaper of the League of Nations of July 1927, refugees should settle in a location where they would be able to exercise their previous profession or some other profession, without which securing a residence in the city would be useless (Leontidou 1999, 351). EAP's belief was that the large majority of refugees who lived in the city were engaged in the field of commerce and other forms of self-employment as they did back home. By virtue of Law 3142/1924, a financial subsidy, guaranteed by the state, was established for refugees of Greek origin, organised in groups and in small-scale industrial and manufacturing co-operatives.

The National Bank offered loans both to cooperatives and individuals. EAP gave subsidies for the replacement of tools used by craftsmen or to small cooperative production units which had to find their own materials and, of course, the markets in which they would sell their merchandise or to seek employment

188   *Constantinos Katerinopoulos*

in the construction field, as many groups of craftsmen were working in this field (construction workers, marble technicians, carpenters). The carpet manufacturing and other related small-scale manufacturing businesses operated in the same manner. As a result of this, during the first decade of the inter-war period, unemployment rates were relatively low and negative consequences arising from the abundant human resources that were available, which otherwise would remain unemployed, were avoided. Refugee merchants, according to Adamantios Pepelasis, managed to overtake their Jewish rivals in terms of commercial activity in Thessaloniki, as they had significantly profited from the credits offered by banks and the low inflation rate of that period (Mazower 1991). This activity gave rise to many large enterprises after the war, which played an important role in the city's economic life.

Refugees and the city's working class

The arrival of refugees during the period of 1922–1924 had an initial negative impact on the city's labour class and trade unions, due to the fact that up until then the role of the trade unions was to control the labour process, the prices of products such as bread, and of course the salaries. This was effected by regulating the hiring and lay-off conditions, which were rights prohibited to employers without the approval of the competent trade union. Unionism in Thessaloniki before the Minor Asia Disaster had great achievements and was more controlling and powerful than in the rest of the country, as recorded by Benaroya (1975).

The arrival of refugees and the offer of cheap labour overturned these conditions. There was competition between local and refugee laborers, who had their own unions. Every year after 1924, 14 new unions were established in Thessaloniki, however not all of them were actually active.

Moreover, the arrival of refugees caused an important overturn in the products market. All the production fields were affected as demand increased and production had to keep up with the demand. The need for bread grew so big that the employment protocols could not be observed for those working in the bread industry; however, other old sectors were affected too, such as the tobacco industry, railroad workers, and workers employed in shoe manufacture, who went on many strikes during the 1920s. Strikes were also recorded after 1931, primarily in new sectors that were created such as the printing industry, rail track workers, civil servants, textile industry, while strike rates decreased in the more traditional sectors. After the law 4229/1929, known as 'Sui generis', became effective, there was a slowdown both in the establishment of unions and in their unionism and strike presence, which changed again after 1934 when the economic crisis grew. This led to the strengthening of the labour movement and the Communist Party, which, after the elections of January 1936, became a regulating force in the parliament. The exacerbation of the labour and union fight led to the events of May 1936 in Thessaloniki, which although started from the tobacco workers striker, soon took over all other fields and led Metaxas's government initially to repression and then to bloodshed, leading finally to the dictatorship of August 4, in view of the new strike that had been announced for the August 5 1936. After 1929, strikes no longer turned against employers for the control of the employment process, which was now infeasible after the massive entry of refugees in the employment market, but rather against the government's policy in order to secure workers against the consequences of unemployment and the economic crisis.

Refugee associations

Since the very beginning, refugees had organised into cooperatives and trade unions. This applied to various aspects of their social life both in terms of the production activity and those relevant to the rehabilitation, as provided for by the relevant laws. Refugees had a tradition in union organisation back home where they had established educational, sports, and professional unions and associations.

More than 250 refugee trade unions and associations were established in Thessaloniki between the years 1923 to 1936. Amongst them were sports and cultural associations which played a decisive role in the preservation of the cohesion, traditions, and commonly shared elements that kept the refugees together, on the basis of their place of origin per settlement. Settlements were formed on the basis of the refugees' place of origin and were named after these places of origin. However, large athletic associations such as PAOK, were not limited to one settlement but were very popular among all the refugees of the city. A very characteristic fact of the wide influence that refugees had over Thessaloniki is that PAOK continues to be, up to the present day, the principal sports ambassador of Thessaloniki, as opposed to AEK which did not manage to have such a decisive presence in Athens's athletic life.

The purpose of the associations was, through various events, to preserve the cultural features that united the refugees by maintaining a mechanism for the preservation of collective memory, which was very important as it offered refugees a particular bond that differentiated them from the locals.

The refugees influenced cultural life as examples of behaviour and through their traditions, but not through formal governmental speech, from which they were almost excluded. Especially in Thessaloniki, however, they had a strong influence on popular culture and tradition, to the extent that Giorgos Ioannou, an important figure of the intellectual community during the 20th century, called his city 'the capital of refugees' (Ioannou 1984). Refugees remained the majority of the Greek population until the second post-war decade, when a wave of internal migration became the decisive factor in the city's population composition.

Inter-war political and electoral attitudes among refugees

The electoral behaviour and political attitude of the refugees were shaped decisively by the tragedy of the Asia Minor Catastrophe. Pro-royal political parties abstained from the elections of December 1923. In Thessaloniki, the joint Liberal-Democratic slate included 15 local candidates and 15 refugee candidates, which

190 *Constantinos Katerinopoulos*

clearly shows the political and electoral significance of the refugees but also their distinctive identity.

The presence of refugees was a catalytic factor in changing the city's political representation. The elections of November 7 1926 were critical, as they were won by the Liberals, whose percentage in Thessaloniki was well above their average nationwide. The (conservative) Popular Party had a percentage 16% lower than its national average. Lacking analytical data, a rough estimation is that the sum of the conservative parties in the areas inhabited by refugees (Popular Party and Freethinkers) did not exceed 10%.

When the 1928 elections were held, housing rehabilitation had been completed to a significant degree, and the refugees were 47.8 % of the city's total population. The Liberal Party won a percentage of 85–90% in the areas inhabited by refugees, as opposed to a percentage of 50–60% in the areas inhabited by locals. It is worth mentioning that the Popular Party support did not exceed 5% in refugee districts.

However, things begin to change in the elections of 1932. The Greek-Turkish Friendship Treaty put an end to refugee hopes of returning to their lost homelands; at the same time, the government's refusal to take responsibility for repayment of debts to EAP alienated refugees enrolled in the agricultural rehabilitation program; the breach with the Liberal Party became evident for all refugees (Mazower 1991). As a result of this, the Radical Party (Kondylis) gained significant ground amongst the refugees in Thessaloniki, as it was against the Greek-Turkish treaty. The Communist Party (KKE) as represented by the United Front also gained ground in the elections. The Kalamaria settlement, consisting almost exclusively of refugees, is an eloquent example of the changes. In 1928, the Liberals won 92% of the votes, the Popular Party won 3.6% of the votes, and the United Front won 3.5% of the votes. In the same settlement in the 1932 elections, the Liberals won 35% of the votes, the (conservative) Popular Party 8.7% of the votes, the United Front 17.8% of the votes, the Radical party (Kondylis) 24.4% of the votes, and Progressive Party (Kafantaris) 3.9% of the votes.

Correspondingly, in Agia Sofia, an area of Thessaloniki almost exclusively inhabited by locals, in the 1928 elections the Liberals won 62.3% of the votes, and the Popular Party 33%. However, in 1932, the Liberals won 39.1% of the votes, the Popular Party 34.1% of the votes, the United Front 6.5% and Radical Party (Kondylis) 9%. It is clear that the different electoral attitude of the refugees as opposed to the locals is determined by their particular problems, in comparison to the problems that would determine a political choice based only on ideological foundations or current issues of political conflict. The refugees who voted for Kondylis in 1932 or other parties did not return to the Liberals, and after 1932 the refugee settlements ceased to be fortresses of the Liberals, while the Communist Party (KKE) made a strong showing through the United Front (Dodos 2010, 161–178).

The political clout of the refugees became more important after the Second World War, as the annihilation of the Jewish population of Thessaloniki by the Nazis essentially turned the refugees into the majority of the city's inhabitants, given that from 1922 to 1944 they had preserved their 'endogamy' to a significant

Refugee resettlement 1922–1924 191

degree. During the first two decades after the war, the refugees' political positioning was, in general terms, in favour of Plastiras, and afterward, generally of the centrist parties. EDA, the legal left party, however, kept some influence.

In the 1970s, the expansion of migration flows to urban areas, which in the beginning also included refugees from rural Macedonia, hence internal migration to Thessaloniki, together with the mixing of populations and gradual improvement of living conditions, slowly and gradually caused the specific characteristics of the refugees to fade, especially once the second refugee generation gave way to the third, while the fourth generation is not an unmixed refugee generation, with refugee 'endogamy' no longer a consideration.

Mixing of populations, and the full integration of old refugee neighbourhoods into a unified urban complex, resulted in a decrease in differentiation of the political and social reference points of the refugees. This development is the result of the full integration of the third refugee generation, which had not experienced the deprivations and strong struggle to survive of the first and second generations. Nor had the first generation's memories and narratives regarding their lost homelands defined their childhood.

Instead of a conclusion

The refugees left their mark on the city. They contributed decisively to Greece's ethnic integration and were a key factor in the important changes in social and political life during the inter-war period. Thessaloniki's current image remains largely the result of refugee resettlement. Let me conclude by citing Giorgos Ioannou, who wrote when the city's transformation was beginning, and with it the disappearance of the differences between refugees and non-refugees:

A few decades ago one could not call the inhabitants of this city Thessalonians, unless by convention. At that time, Thessalonians meant only the local Greeks, those who had inhabited it since antiquity. But these people were few in comparison to the refugees. [...] During the last decades, a fair number have moved to Athens with this or that excuse. However, no Athenian of the arts of letters, despite all the hymns about Thessaloniki's charms and the nobility of its people, has come to settle here. So what is going on?

(Ioannou 1984; Anastasiadis 2010, 68–71)

References

Anastasiadis, G., 'Ο Γιώργος Ιωάννου και η πρωτεύουσα των προσφύγων' ['George Ioannou and the capital city of refugees'], *Θεσσαλονικέων πόλις* [City of the Thessalonians], 09, (2010), 68–71.

Benaroya, A., *Η πρώτη σταδιοδρομία του ελληνικού προλεταριάτου* [The first stage of the Greek proletariat], Athens: Olkos (1975).

Dodos, D., 'Οι πρόσφυγες στις εκλογές: από τον Βενιζέλο στον Κονδύλη' ['The Refugees in the elections: From Venizelos to Kondylis'], In: Ioannidou, E. (ed.) *Η μεταμόρφω*

192   Constantinos Katerinopoulos

ση της Θεσσαλονίκης: Η εγκατάσταση των προσφύγων στην πόλη (1920–1940) [The transformation of Thessaloniki: The settlement of refugees in the city (1920–1940)], Thessaloniki: Epikentro (2010), 161–178.

Hastaoglou, V., 'Η προσφυγική εγκατάσταση και ο βίαιος μετασχηματισμός του αστικού χώρου στη Θεσσαλονίκη, 1922–1930' ['The settlement of refugees and the violent transformation of urban space in Thessaloniki, 1922–1930, conference proceedings'], In: Ο ξερριζωμός και η άλλη πατρίδα: Οι προσφυγουπόλεις στην Ελλάδα [The uprooting and the other homeland: Refugee towns in Greece], Athens: Moraitis School (1999).

Hekimoglou, E., Θεσσαλονίκη: Τουρκοκρατία και μεσοπόλεμος [Thessaloniki. Turkish rule and inter-war period], Thessaloniki: University Studio Press (1996).

Ioannou, G., Η πρωτεύουσα των προσφύγων [The capital of the refugees], Athens: Kedros (1984).

Karatzoglou, G., 'From the steaming ruins of Smyrna to the ashes of the Thessaloniki', Θεσσαλονικέων πόλις [City of the Thessalonians], 16, (2012), 4–21.

Lampsidis, G., The Refugees of 1922, Thessaloniki: Kyriakidi Publications (1992).

Leontidou, L., 'Η άτυπη οικονομία ως απόρροια της προσφυγικής αποκατάστασης' ['The informal economy as after-effect of refugee resettlement'], In: Conference Proceedings, Ο ξερριζωμός και η άλλη πατρίδα: Οι προσφυγουπόλεις στην Ελλάδα [The uprooting and the other homeland: Refugee towns in Greece], Athens: Moraitis School (1999), 341–368.

Mazower, M., Greece and the Inter-War Economic Crisis, Oxford: Oxford University Press (1991).

Mazower, M., The Balkans; A Short History, New York: Modern Library (2000).

Mazower, M., Salonica: City of Ghosts, Christians, Muslims and Jews, 1430–1950, London: HarperCollins (2004).

14 Integration through the past
Jewish scholars write history in inter-war Salonica[1]

Eyal Ginio

This chapter examines the different ways in which Jewish intellectuals narrated Greek history in inter-war Thessaloniki. My main argument is that history served them in their efforts to promote Jewish integration into Greek society and the national community. This desired integration was not an easy mission to accomplish. Under the terms of the Treaty of Bucharest (10 August, 1913) that ended the Balkan Wars, Thessaloniki and its hinterland became part of Greece. Consequently, almost 80,000 Jews, clearly the largest community in the city, found themselves perplexed in the face of political and economic marginalization and under pressure to assimilate into Greek society, about which they knew little. Some of them opted to emigrate—mostly to France, but also to Palestine, South and North America, Istanbul, and even Spain. A second wave of emigration followed in the early 1930s after the infamous Campbell pogrom (1931). This time, most departures were for Mandatory Palestine.

However, the majority of Jews chose to stay in their natal city and to adapt themselves to the new and uncertain political reality. How did the Jewish community and individuals respond to these new circumstances? The thriving local Jewish press reveals a community in confusion and internal conflict. The notion of modernization and its ramifications was certainly not new to the community. Yet, when the Greek army entered Thessaloniki, the local Jewish community was ill-equipped to cope with the new situation.[2] For one thing, Greek had never before been counted among the suggested languages that might serve the future generation of what was perceived as 'modernized Jews': During the late Ottoman period French and, to a lesser extent, other western languages, seemed to offer the right path for modernization and emancipation. Ottoman Turkish, as the state's language, had some supporters as well among local Jewish intellectuals. However, Greek language and modern Greek culture drew only little interest among them prior to the Balkan Wars.[3] Shim'on Burla, a local Jewish journalist, described the community: 'We were ignorant of Greek customs, of Greek culture, of the Greeks' race, of its past, its history, its language, its national ideal, its hope, its hatreds'.[4] Indeed, Katherine Fleming rightly claims that 'until 1912 there was very little indeed about them [Salonican Jews] that could be considered Greek, in any sense of the term' (Fleming 2008, 51). The absorption of Greek culture had to occur virtually from scratch and required plenty of time and effort.

194   *Eyal Ginio*

The Jews understood that adaptation meant the acquisition of a new cultural identity that could dovetail with their newly required Greek citizenship. Already during the late Ottoman period, the Jewish community searched for a cultural transformation that would enable it to survive in the changing world. However, following Thessaloniki's incorporation into the Greek nation-state, this need became more urgent and specific. The Greek authorities and Greek society demanded from the Salonican Jews a swift and radical change of identity and culture. The Jews' Ottoman and Sephardi heritages were deemed Oriental by their Christian co-citizens and, therefore, alien to the Greek spirit of the nation. Language was the key issue. Fragiski Abatzopoulou, who discusses literary stereotypes of the Jew in inter-war Thessaloniki, remarks that for the local Greek press of Thessaloniki, led by the infamous anti-Jewish daily *Makedonia*, the ubiquitous, damning accusation against the local Judeo-Spanish (Ladino) speaking community was their alleged reluctance to learn Greek. Other common stereotypes accused the local Jew of being a religious fanatic, a coward, and a complainer (Abatzopoulou 1997, 222).

While the surrounding Christian society admonished Salonican Jews for being indifferent or even hostile to the national ideals, the local Jewish press, even though representing different ideologies and agendas, almost unanimously reiterated the Jews' readiness to become part of the Greek nation, with all its cultural demands. Acquaintance with the national language was the main requirement demanded from the local Jews, but knowledge of Greece's history was deemed essential to the acquirement of the 'Greek spirit' in general. It should be noted that following the inclusion of Thessaloniki in Greece, the state established national cultural institutes to promote the cultural integration of both the refugees from Asia Minor and Eastern Thrace who settled in Thessaloniki and the other 'new lands' annexed by Greece and the non-Greek-speaking native Orthodox Christian communities of these lands. However, most of the Greek literary activity in the inter-war period that aimed to integrate the new lands did so by emphasizing their continuing Greek character, thus excluding native Jews (and other non-Orthodox Christians), who were often regarded as foreign remnants of Ottoman rule (Mackridge 1997, 175–186).

How did the Salonican Jews respond to the above-mentioned challenges? Of course, we cannot describe the Jewish community of Thessaloniki as speaking in one voice. On the contrary, the community was engulfed in bitter debates concerning its identity and agenda. Most of these debates were conducted during the 1920s and 1930s in Judeo-Spanish, still their prevailing language. There were basically three competing views, represented by the Zionists, the socialists, and the assimilators, or 'moderates' as they preferred to call themselves, who championed cultural assimilation. Each group had its own agenda and program for the future of Jews in Thessaloniki. Yet, the prevailing assumption shared by all of them was that Jews would always live in Thessaloniki. The major debate was whether they should be considered a national minority or merely a religious minority within the Greek state.

All political factions inside the Jewish community concurred that Salonican Jews must learn Greek and be acquainted with Greek culture. Even the Zionists

Integration through the past   195

who advocated the study of Hebrew in the communal schools eventually accepted that Jewish children should study Greek, 'the country's language' (*lingua del payíz*), as well. Mastering Greek, they understood, was a condition for finding a decent job, for claiming citizens' rights, for being able to fulfil one's obligations towards the state, for example serving in the army (Ginio 2002a, 243–244). Consequently, one of the major changes that dominated the Jews' cultural agenda in inter-war Thessaloniki was the attempt to define and adopt a new cultural identity that could transform Salonican Sephardi Jews into Greek Jews, a new concept whose exact ingredients and definitions were still ambiguous and under debate.

Shaping of a historicist discourse: ancient Greece and ancient Israel

The most efficient channel of acculturation opened to Salonican Jews was the communal and the general educational systems catering for the new generation of children born after Thessaloniki's incorporation into Greece. In this case, we can speak of a clear communal strategy that aimed to make the children Greek.[5] For the important group of adults educated during Ottoman times, however, the options for acculturation were probably more diversified, but less organized. The study of history, I would like to claim, offered one important channel of educating the adults on their newly assumed Greek identity.

Much was dependent on individual initiatives. Some adults joined Greek evening courses that were offered in Jewish clubs. Another option was to become acquainted with Greek civilization through the translation of Greek works into Judeo-Spanish.[6] Some translations were of historical novels, such as *El kapitán Leonidas Babanis*[7] ('Captain Leonidas Babanis'). This novel recounted the adventures of legendary bandits in the mountainous areas of Macedonia. John Koliopoulos claims that during the 1920s, when bandits were no more than 'outlaws, survivors of an era that had come to an end', tales of their adventures and exploits became a source for popular literature that viewed them with nostalgia for a bygone world (Koliopoulos 1999, 58).

Other translations from Greek narrated quasi-historical love affairs and adventures, such as *Los Amores del Rey Aleksandro* [The Love Affairs of King Alexander], which offered a melodramatic narrative of the brief life of King Alexander (1893–1920). Published after the overthrow of the monarchy and the restoration of the Republic, the book recounted the numerous love affairs of the former king, especially with Aspasia Manos (1896–1972), a commoner who later became the king's wife, while putting these stories in some historical context. The translator emphasized that the book was based on 'documents taken from the Greek Royal court' in an attempt to provide the book with some credibility.[8] The translation to Judeo-Spanish indicates the attractiveness of this popular literature to a Jewish audience. While we can assume that its scandalous character was the main trigger for its translation, this kind of book nevertheless introduced scenes from Greek politics to Judeo-Spanish readers in Thessaloniki.

196   *Eyal Ginio*

Even Zionist activities could be regarded as a proper venue for promoting identification with Greek heritage. For example, the celebrations held to commemorate the opening of the Hebrew University in Jerusalem, a clearly Zionist project, also represented an opportunity to observe the common roles of Jewish and Greek ancient civilizations. On 1 April 1925, when the Hebrew University opened its doors on Mount Scopus, its inauguration was celebrated in many parts of the Jewish Diaspora (Kolat 1997, 3–74). In Jewish Thessaloniki, meetings were held at the various local clubs, a short film of the opening ceremonies was screened at a local cinema, enthusiastic speeches were given to cheering audiences, and the first pages of most Jewish journals were devoted to the occasion. A special issue published by the Judeo-Spanish journal *El Progreso* [Progress] in Xanthi (Western Thrace), where no more than 600 Jews lived at the time, indicates the significance of this event even in small Jewish communities in Greece.[9]

This interest should not come as a surprise. The opening of the Hebrew University was one of the first occasions on which the whole Zionist enterprise in Palestine was presented in depth to local Jewish audiences worldwide. This was true also for the Jewish community of Thessaloniki. For many Jews of this city, we can assume, taking part in the ceremonies was an opportunity to demonstrate their attachment to the Zionist project and to publicly display their Jewish ethnic identity. Zionism, it should be noted, gained much popularity and legitimacy among Salonican Jews following the city's incorporation into the Greek kingdom. Marginalized by Greek nationalism, many Jews perceived Zionism as an ideology that could assist Jews in shaping a national identity that could safeguard their position in 'new' Thessaloniki. In fact, Jewish nationalism became a major way for Salonican Jews to resolve the problem of not quite belonging to general society. For many local Jews, however, Zionism meant securing a future in Thessaloniki rather than fulfilling political ambitions in Palestine or creating a movement of mass emigration towards that land, at least until the early 1930s.[10]

However, this is only part of the story. I would like to argue that these festive events in Thessaloniki had more general significance for relations between Christians and Jews living in the city. By following the speeches given in these gatherings and their treatment in the local Jewish press, we can discern another discourse that was present during these celebrations—one that highlights the historical contribution and cultural mission of Jews and Greeks. While each had its own civilization and could claim its particular contribution to Western civilization, they shared a common, even complementary, historical role in developing and shaping that civilization. Though different in any cultural aspect, this common role could connect Greeks and Jews. At the central ceremony, both the communities' leaders and eminent members of the local Greek community and regional administration took part. The central speech was read by the local Zionist leader Moïse Uzilyo in fluent Greek, a choice highlighted by the local Jewish press. In his speech, Uzilyo elaborated on the significance of the Hebrew University to the Jewish world in general; however, he did not fail to mention the participation of the University of Athens in the celebrations. This marked for him the common past and likewise the potential common destiny of Jews and Greeks—both

Integration through the past   197

peoples boasted ancient civilizations that flourished in the East and both were meant to play a major and civilizing role in the region again after long years of silence and submission (Ginio 2002b).

This remark reveals an awareness of Greek history—both ancient and modern. The popular historiography written in Judeo-Spanish during the inter-war period in Thessaloniki sheds light on an important conduit of acculturation. Not only was the classical heritage of Greece presented in detail, but also the history of Byzantine and Modern Greece since its independence. It is true that Jewish intellectuals' interest in non-Jewish history was certainly not new among Sephardi Jews, who represented the vast majority of the Salonican Jewish community. Esther Benbassa and Aron Rodrigue claim that an 'infatuation with history', clearly shown in the publication of popular history books and the translation of some major historical works into Judeo-Spanish, demonstrate the growing openness of Sephardi Jewry to the outside world during the late Ottoman period (Benbassa and Rodrigue 2000, 110). Yet, the choice of which history to study and teach was not fixed or frozen. It reflected the changing political and cultural circumstances and, therefore, it merits out attention

In addition to general history, local Jewish scholars began to write the history of their own communities. Take for example the work of the pioneer educator and historian Abraham Danon (1857–1925), born in Edirne. In December 1900–January 1901, he published a series of articles on the Jews of Thessaloniki in *La Epoca*. This weekly was published in Judeo-Spanish by Saadi Bezalel Halevy (1820–1903) in Thessaloniki. These articles, Halevy proclaimed, would be the beginning of a series exploring the origins of 'the Jewish communities of the Orient'. This, in turn, would serve as the basis for a full history of Judaism in this part of the world.[11]

Such an ambitious project reveals the framework of locality as understood by scholars at the beginning of the twentieth century: scholars such as Abraham Danon envisioned the 'Orient' as the relevant space in which the history of the Sephardi Jews should be written. However, the shift from the Ottoman Empire to the Greek kingdom required also a gradual change in the definition of that space. Scholars Joseph Nehama, Merkado Yosef Kovo, and Michael Molho are representative of the small group of historians of Sephardi Jewry active during the late Ottoman era and in inter-war Thessaloniki. While Kovo died in 1940, Molho and Nehama survived the war and continued to write and publish after the Holocaust, mostly devoting their writing to commemorating a community that lost most of its members during WWII. They were all, according to Benbassa and Rodrigue (2000, 109), champions of modernity and guardians of a past that was no more. Like Salomon Rozanes in Bulgaria[12] and Avram Galanté in Turkey,[13] these Salonican scholars wrote the history of their community and described it in the framework of the Ottoman Sephardi world. Yet, they also wrote history in the framework of their own locality.

In fact, while their main mission was certainly to describe the Jewish history of their communities, it is clear that classical, Byzantine, and modern Greek history had an appeal for them during the inter-war period. These Jewish intellectuals

198 *Eyal Ginio*

took pain to demonstrate that ancient Greek achievements embodied the core and base of Western civilization. Absorbing Greek civilization was presented not only as coming to terms with the state's culture but also as discovering the roots of the enlightened West, with which Jewish intellectuals were hitherto acquainted mostly through French schools, institutions, and literature. But that was not all: studying Greek history and emphasizing a common past and similar historical role was meant to draw Greeks and Jews nearer to each other. Furthermore, indicating the Jews' role in Greece's recent history was a strategy for claiming a common present and future.

One important aspect of the popular history books published by Sephardi authors all over the former Ottoman-Sephardi cultural area was the choice of language. Interestingly, none of these books were published in the state language—Bulgarian, Turkish, or Greek. The mega-works of the history of Sephardi communities, including Nehama's book on the Jews of Thessaloniki (see below), were written in French (Galanté and Nehama) or Hebrew (Rozanes). We can assume that the choice reflected the prestige French enjoyed as a universal language and Hebrew as a national language. This choice also mirrored the authors' attempts to reach wider audiences. In contrast, the popular history books published in Thessaloniki appeared in Judeo-Spanish, thus revealing their authors' wish to reach local Salonican Jews and to serve their urgent need to learn more about their new state.

Unlike the more famous and academic history books written by these authors, their popular books on Greek history and politics were written in simple language without academic footnotes or original documents. The books followed their original format as popular lectures or press reports. Here again, the motive of reaching larger audiences in the local community may explain this choice.[14]

The presentation of Classical and Byzantine history

How could history serve mutual understanding and respect between Jews and Christians in Greece? The book by Joseph Nehama (1880–1971) is an illustrative example. Nehama, who served as a headmaster of an Alliance school in Thessaloniki, was a prolific author who advocated assimilation during the interwar period (Rozen 2005b, 298). He is known primarily for his multi-volume study of the Jews of Thessaloniki (Nehama 1935–1978). Nehama also lectured about Greek history to local Jewish audience. His book—*Bizansyo i Sivilizasyón Bizantina* [Byzantium and Byzantine Civilization][15]—appeared in Thessaloniki in 1938 at the initiative of the Zionist daily *Aksyón* [Action],[16] one of the last Judeo-Spanish journals to appear in Thessaloniki. The journal's initiative to publish the lectures in the form of books demonstrates the significance of the local press in disseminating historical knowledge. The book was the outcome of a conference organized in February 1937 by B'nai-B'rith, an international Jewish social and cultural organization that had a branch in Thessaloniki.

In this book, Nehama outlines Byzantine history and culture from the origins of the Byzantine Empire, through its different dynasties, cultural achievements,

Integration through the past 199

internal organization and military defeats, to its diplomacy, and its final surrender to the Ottoman Empire. The glory of Constantinople and the continuity between classical Greece, Byzantium, and modern Greece are emphasized: 'This Empire was one of the most powerful in the world. It provided significant services for all humanity. If it had not existed, all humans today would be merely barbarians. Without the Byzantine Empire, civilization could not exist'. Nehama further claims that 'Humanity owes much to Byzantium. Byzantium is Greek, the Byzantines are the Greeks of the medieval period' (Nehama 1938, 4–5). Furthermore, since the modern Greek state is the 'natural outcome' of Byzantium with its Hellenic and Orthodox heritages, 'our country' can boast 'thirty-five centuries of continuous civilization' (Nehama 1938, 47).

While Byzantium and its history and culture (but not the Byzantine Jews!) stand at the center of the book, Nehama also shows how both Jews and Greeks created civilizations on the shores of the Mediterranean that later influenced the whole world. For him, the Hebrews contributed moral ideas through monotheism, the ideas of a just God, before whom all people are equal and who gave the world a religion of love, harmony, and solidarity. The Greeks gave the world philosophy, science, and the arts. The Jews, Greeks, and Romans together created the basis of a universal civilization. Later European and Near Eastern civilizations, Nehama maintained, benefitted from Byzantine achievements. Furthermore, the Ottomans ('the Turks' for Nehama) owed everything to Byzantine as they shaped their administration, politics, etiquette, and ceremonies of power on Byzantine models; without this Byzantine heritage they would have remained ignorant barbarians (*una masa de bárbaros*) (Nehama 1938, 46–47).

Both ancient Greece and Palestine, as political entities, succumbed to Roman might: 'Greece and Palestine, thus, disappeared from the world map' and thus entered a long period of subjection. However, he claims, the Greeks and the Jews did not disappear as cultural entities; on the contrary, they were able to take advantage of their advanced cultures to influence the Romans who had defeated them in battle. Through Christianity, the daughter of Judaism, the Jews were able to gain the souls of the Romans, while the Greeks became the patrons of the Romans' spirit thanks to their literature, philosophy, and art (Nehama 1938, 7). Nowadays, both ideals survive as eternal flames from the distant past: the first one, representing justice, was lit on Mount Sinai and kept burning on the Temple Mount in Jerusalem; the other one, representing reason and science, was set alight on the Acropolis in Athens. Both of them continue to illuminate the world. Their universal messages will forever exist (Nehama 1938, 47–48).

Nehama's lecture was one in a series of five given at the B'nai-B'rith club. Four of them were dedicated to 'our beautiful country, Greece' and the fifth focused on the history of the Prophets and the ancient Hebrews. Merkado Yosef Kovo (1870–1940) gave a lecture about Classical Greece at the same venue, in which he went into detail about its remarkable cultural and scientific achievements. His lecture appeared later as a book under the title *Kólpo de ojo sóvre la Antiguedád Gréga* [A Glance at Greek Antiquity].[17] Kovo was born in Serres in 1870. He graduated from the Ottoman high school there and mastered Turkish and French

200   *Eyal Ginio*

in addition to his mother tongue, Judeo-Spanish. He moved to Thessaloniki and became a teacher of French and of Jewish history in various communal schools. Later on, he studied Greek as well—a knowledge that enabled him to teach various courses at institutions of higher education in the city.

The introduction to his lecture offers an insight into the purpose of this lecture series. Kovo explains the need to give popular lectures about Greek history because of the overwhelming ignorance of those Jews above the age of forty, who grew up in the Ottoman educational system, which did not cover Greek history. For him, learning about past Greek achievements was a way to understand the origins of civilization, as well as to love their Greek homeland and freedom. This need, he claims, was behind his decision to accept the challenge to present his lecture in a popular mode and not as a scientific lecture (*ovra de vulgarizasyón i no ovra de sensia*).[18]

As these two examples indicate, ancient and medieval history served Jewish intellectuals in presenting modern Greece, the state in which Thessaloniki Jews became citizens, as the cradle of Western civilization and therefore worthy of their allegiance. In addition, remote history offered a common role for Jews and Greeks on the basis of their contributions to the shaping of culture around the Mediterranean. It seems that this perception of a common Jewish-Greek distant past was quite easy to absorb. However, more recent history presented much more challenging issues regarding the relations between Greeks and Jews. Several authors tried to cope with this challenge as well.

The late Ottoman period: justifying Jewish loyalties

In 1937, the name of Ioannis Metaxas, the prime minister of Greece since 1936, was inscribed in the Golden Book of the Jewish National Fund on the initiative of Zionist activists in Greece. On this occasion, Metaxas conveyed a greeting in support of the Zionist Movement. Among the guests of honor were several Zionist and communal leaders of the Jewish community of Greece. One of them, Rabbi Tzevi Koretz, the incumbent chief rabbi of Thessaloniki,[19] expressed the gratitude of the Jewish community and referred to the inspiration the Greek Revolution gave to many Jews in Greece and elsewhere. He claimed that the 'heroic example of the Greek nation' influenced the Jews who were seeking to create 'a refuge for the persecuted Jews in their ancient Promised Land'.[20] By referring to the 'persecuted Jews' as the target audience of Zionism, Koretz intentionally excluded Greek Jews from the Zionist project. In this manner, he could reconcile his strong conviction regarding the Greek identity of the Jews living in Greece with his proclaimed support for Zionism.

Metaxas' message was published as a booklet by one of the Jewish journals of Thessaloniki. The publishers attached to the speech a short introduction in which parts of the speech were translated into Judeo-Spanish. The introduction highlighted the similarities between the Greek national movement and the Zionist movement. This comparison underscores one use of modern Greek history by Jewish leaders in inter-war Greece. Indeed, the modern history of Greece could

Integration through the past 201

offer inspiration for Jewish organizations, such as the Zionist movement. It could also raise various delicate questions.

Thus, as an illustrative example, one history book in Judeo-Spanish dealt with the more recent past, the Balkan Wars (1912–1913). It was published in 1931 under the symbolic title *La Liberasión de Saloniko* [The Liberation of Thessaloniki].[21] Its anonymous author retraced the political and military developments that surrounded the capture of the city by the Greek army. This discussion served as a framework for exploring Jewish-Greek relations in Thessaloniki. The author's aim was explicitly stated at the end of the book: to heal the wounds of the recent past and to restore mutual confidence between the two communities. His thesis is clear: Jews and Greeks always lived in Thessaloniki in harmony and mutual confidence under the Turks. However, very recent events, starting with the Young Turk Revolution of 1908, hampered these good relations and caused unprecedented and lingering antagonism between the two communities (*dos elementos*). His book is shaped around both apologetics and attempts to refute what he perceived as false allegations often voiced by the Greek side against Salonican Jews.

Thus, for example, the Jewish community's reluctance to demonstrate its joy at the entry of the Greek army is explained by the long benevolence of the Ottoman authorities towards the Jews during their lengthy dominion over Thessaloniki;[22] the allegations of Jewish enmity towards the Greeks and their attempts to deter the city's annexation to Greece are fully laid on the table and then contested. The author concludes with the wish that once all mutual allegations are laid bare and explained or refuted, Jewish-Greek relations will improve and return to their former good course. For him, the more distant past is a clear indication of the potential future—Jews and Greeks always lived together in harmony and they can do so again.[23]

For those Jewish authors and publicists who championed the hellenization of the Jews, a major challenge was the integration of Jews into Greek politics. In this case as well, ignorance of Greek could perpetuate the marginalization of Jews in national politics. To solve this lack of knowledge among local Jews, other popular books in Judeo-Spanish attempted to acquaint readers with the political events unfolding around them.

Contemporary history: Jews as integral players in Greek politics

Several books were published in Judeo-Spanish describing the Greek political system, its main players, and their relation to the Jews. The bitter conflict between Venizelists and Royalists that marred Greek political life was also the centerpiece of these books. Their authors depicted incidents in a popular fashion that included extracts from the Greek press and also apparently invented dialogs and scenarios. The books interpreted the internal political situation for readers who probably did not have full access to the Greek language; still, they were not written from the point of view of a foreign bystander. The authors instead inserted Jewish attitudes and positions into the political maelstrom. They emphasized that Greek Jews were

202   *Eyal Ginio*

an integral part of Greek politics; for the authors, local Jews were not only victims of the Venizelists' criticism, verbal attacks, and discriminatory legislation, but they were also the supporters of a major and legitimate political trend inside Greek society.

La matansa de los 6, or the Execution of the Six, can serve as an illustrative example.[24] The title derives from one of the major events in inter-war Greece, the execution of five members of the Royalist Government and the commander of the Greek forces in Asia Minor, convicted of high treason for their responsibility for the Greek defeat in Anatolia.[25] Published more than a decade after the executions took place, it also dealt with the events that led to the trials: the political schism in Greece during WWI (*la divizyón*; known in Greek as the *ethnikós dihasmós*), the deposition of King Constantine I (September 1922), the Asia Minor Catastrophe, the Venizelist revolution of 1923, and the subsequent restoration of the republic.

Another example is a book entitled 'Twelve Days that Tormented Greece' (*Dodje dias ke estemperearon la Grecha*).[26] The book describes the attempt of Venizelist officers and civilians (who benefitted from Venizelos' active and public support) to stage a military coup during the first days of March 1935 against the incumbent government of Panagis Tsaldaris, a moderate conservative and opponent of the Venizelists, in an attempt to avert an impending return of the monarchy.[27] Published only three weeks after the events, the book is described as the only authorized report on the abortive coup. It strives to explain the Jews' negative attitude towards the military uprising and to project the Jews as playing an integral and legitimate role in Greek politics as active supporters of the anti-Venizelists and the governing royalist party against the insurgents.[28] Interestingly enough, the author used the Greek term *andartes* to label the insurgents.

Conclusions

The story of Salonican Jewry during the inter-war period can be told from different angles. I discussed the process of acculturation of local Jews into Greek culture through the use of history. While this was only a small part of the community's attempt to absorb Greek culture and language, it nevertheless sheds light on several aspects: the wish of Jewish scholars to acquaint local Jews with Greek history—both ancient and modern—as a way to better integrate them into Greek society, to make Greek history relevant to Greek Jews, and to insert the local Jews into Greek history since ancient times.

Three decades of Greek sovereignty in northern Greece indeed transformed the Jewish community of Thessaloniki. Most local Jews chose to stay in their native city, and they understood and accepted the need to absorb the state's language and culture. Popular history books were part of a deliberate effort by local Jews to incorporate Jews into Greek society. Their first, overt mission was to acquaint Judeo-Spanish speakers with the history of their new homeland and to make them proud of it. The focus of these quasi-academic lectures was the Classical and Byzantine past, which assigned to Greece a prominent place

Integration through the past 203

in Western civilization. Another aim was to draw Greeks and Jews closer to each other through their claimed roles in history. Both peoples, according to the authors, contributed enormously to world civilization by providing it with its most fundamental perceptions and ideals. Both peoples were subjected to foreign political domination that ended with a national renaissance, and both were destined to enjoy a glorious future thanks to their civilizing mission in the East. The publishing of popular books on contemporary Greek politics aimed to explain this subject for the Jewish audience and to render it more intelligible, while emphasizing the role of Jews as legitimate and equal players in Greek politics.

This literature, published in Judeo-Spanish, thrived thanks to the existence of a large audience who wanted to learn more about the surrounding society and saw history as a channel through which they could achieve membership in Greek society. The study of history allowed Jewish scholars to work through their ambivalence about being Greek citizens. Claiming a common cultural mission for both Jews and Greeks in the past and indicating partnership in Greek politics could reconcile the Jews' particular identity with their new citizenship. The use of Judeo-Spanish as the language of publication reflected its continuing importance as the main language of communication among adults. However, this role was clearly perceived as temporary. The decline of the Judeo-Spanish press in the 1930s, and the decision of some of the journals (including Zionist journals) to publish some pages in Greek in order to reach the young Jewish generation, prove that Judeo-Spanish was gradually losing ground. It seems that Zionists and assimilators, though bitter rivals and for different reasons, both would come to terms with this outcome.

The gradual decrease in the use of Judeo-Spanish in publishing during the 1930s indicates the gradual assimilation of Jews into Greek culture. Katherine Fleming claims, however, that during the inter-war period, Thessaloniki Sephardim were undergoing a painful, forced, and only partially successful process of Hellenization (Fleming 2008, 209–210). For the vast majority of Salonican Jews, World War II brought these attempts to integrate into Greek society to a sudden and deadly end. The surviving Judeo-Spanish books on Greek history, published in inter-war Salonica, are one significant witness of this attempt at cultural assimilation.

Notes

1 An earlier version of this article was published as a section in Ginio 2002.
2 The literature on the absorption of Salonican Jews into the Greek state has increased significantly in the last decade or so. For some of the main studies, see Bowman 2002, 64–80; Mazower 2004, chapter 21; Rozen 2005b, chapters 8–9; Rozen 2005a, 111–166; Molho 2005; Fleming 2008; Ginio 2014; Naar 2016; Devin E. Naar, *Jewish Salonica between the Ottoman Empire and Modern Greece* (Stanford: Stanford University Press, 2016).
3 On the language question among Sephardi Jews in the late Ottoman period and their different linguistic choices, see Bunis 1996, 226–239.
4 Shim'on Burla, 'Los Djudiós de Saloniko i La Grecha', *El Puevlo*, 13 March 1925.
5 On Jewish education in inter-war Greece, see Molho 2014.

204 Eyal Ginio

6 On translations from Greek to Judeo-Spanish in inter-war Salonica, see Ginio 2002, 247–250; Cohen 2008, 161–166.
7 *El kapitán Leonidas Babanis. Pajinas de la vida del 'Rey de las Montanyas'* (Salonico [Thessaloniki]: Aksyón, 1930).
8 *Los Amores del Rey Aleksandro: Eskritos sovre baza de dokumentos de la korte reala grega*, trans. from Greek by Yosef Angel (Salonico: La verdad, 1925).
9 *El Progresso* (Xanthi), 8 April 1925. On this journal, see Rivlin 2002, 504.
10 On the rise of Zionism following Salonica's annexation to Greece and its role in inter-war Salonica, see Molho 1988, 391–403. For the beginning of Zionism in Ottoman Salonica, see Benbassa 1990, 127–140; Rodrigue 1995, 254–255.
11 Abraham Danon, 'Los Djudiós de Saloniko atrás 400 anyos', *La Epoca*, November 1900–January 1901.
12 Rozanes 1907–1945; in Hebrew. However, his book on the Jews of his natal city Rusçuk/Ruse was published in Judeo-Spanish (Rozanes 1914). On this book, see Keren 2005, 136–138; in Hebrew.
13 Galante 1985. In 1937, the journal *El Mesajero* published a booklet written by Avraham Galanté on Don Yosef Nasi, one of the major historical personalities of Ottoman Jewry. The publication of this booklet in Judeo-Spanish in Salonica, and the publication of several other books that dealt with Ottoman and Ottoman Jewish history, indicate the continuing interest in these topics as well (Galanté 1937).
14 It should be mentioned here that many of these books survive thanks to the donation of a large private library owned by Yehuda Haim Aharon Ha-Cohen Prahia. Prahia was a wealthy tobacco merchant from Xanthi, a Zionist leader and an amateur author who survived the Holocaust. He donated his library and archives to the Ben-Zvi Institute in Jerusalem, where those books are kept today.
15 Nehama 1938. Unlike previous Jewish publications which mentioned Salonico or Salonique, the traditional names of Salonica in Judeo-Spanish, as the place of publication, Nehama's book uses the name of Thessaloniki as used by Greeks. Apparently, this change is the outcome of legislation sanctioned under the Metaxas regime (1936–1941). However, it may also indicate an attempt to adapt the state's terminology for the city.
16 The journalists Eliyahu Biazi, Eli Franses, Yosef Angel, and Alberto Molho published *Aksyón* in 1929–1940. On this Zionist daily, see Hadar 2014.
17 Kovo, M. K., *Kólpo de ojo sóvre la Antiguedád Gréga* (Salonico: Aksyón, 5697 [1937/8].
18 Ibid., 4–5.
19 On the contested tenure of Rabbi Koretz as the chief rabbi of Salonica (1933–1943), see Rozen 2005a, 111–166.
20 *Una Deklarasión del Primo Ministro s. Ioannis Metaxas en favor de los Djidiós i del Sionismo* (Thessaloniki, no publisher, [1937]). Greek title: *Δήλωσις της Α.Ε. του Προέδρου της Εθνικής Κυβερνήσεως Κ. Ι. Μεταξά Υπέρ των Ισραηλιτών και του Σιωνισμού*. See also Rozen 2005a, 136.
21 *La Liberasión de Saloniko* (Salonico: Aksyón, 1937).
22 Ibid., 17–18.
23 Ibid., 63.
24 *La matansa de los 6* (Salonico: Aksyón, 5693 [1933/4]).
25 On this contested trial, see Koliopoulos and Veremis 2002, 129.
26 *Dodje dias ke estemperearon la Grecha: El úniko rakonto otorizado* (Salonico: Prensa, 1935).
27 On the failed pro-Venizelist coup of 1935 and its significance to Greek politics and the establishment of the Metaxas Dictatorship, see Veremis 1997, 99–133.
28 See, for example, the discussion of the Jews' attitude towards the insurgents and its causes: *Dodje dias*, 275; 282–283.

References

Abatzopoulou, F., 'The Image of the Jew in the Literature of Salonica', In: Mackridge, P. and Yannakakis, E. (eds.), *Ourselves and Others: The Development of a Greek Macedonian Cultural Identity since 1912*, Oxford: Berg (1997).

Benbassa, E., 'Zionism in the Ottoman Empire at the End of the 19th and the Beginning of the 20th Century', *Studies in Zionism*, 11:2 (1990), 127–140.

Benbassa, E. and Rodrigue, A., *Sephardi Jewry: A History of the Judeo-Spanish Community, 14th–20th Centuries*, Berkeley: University of California (2000).

Bowman, S., 'Jews', In: Clogg, R. (ed.), *Minorities in Greece: Aspects of a Plural Society*, London: Hurst (2002), 64–80.

Bunis, D. M., 'Modernization and the Language Question Among Judezmo-Speaking Sephardim of the Ottoman Empire', In: Goldberg, H. E. (ed.), *Sephardi and Middle Eastern Jewries: History and Culture in the Modern Era*, Bloomington: Indiana University Press (1996), 226–239.

Cohen, D., 'Traduksiones del Grego al Djudeo-Espaniol, publikadas en Salonika', In: Molho, R. (ed.), *Judeo Espagnol: Social and Cultural Life in Salonika through Judeo-Spanish Texts*, Thessaloniki: Fondation Ets Ahaim (2008), 161–166.

Fleming, K. E., *Greece: A Jewish History*, Princeton, NJ: Princeton University Press (2008).

Galante [sic], A., *Histoire des Juifs de Turquie*, 9 vols. [reprint], Istanbul: Isis (1985).

Galanté, A., *Don Yosef Nasi: Duke de Naxos según nuevas dokumentos*, Salonica: El Mesajero (1937).

Ginio, E., (ed.), *Greece: Jewish Communities in the East in the Nineteenth and Twentieth Centuries*, Jerusalem: Ben Zvi Institute (2014) [in Hebrew].

Ginio, E., '"Learning the Beautiful Language of Homer": Judeo-Spanish Speaking Jews and the Greek Language and Culture between the Wars', *Jewish History*, 16 (2002a), 235–262.

Ginio, E., 'The Inauguration of the Hebrew University and Its Impact on the Jewish Press of Istanbul and Salonica', In: Harvet, W. Z., Hasan-Rokem, G., Saadoun, H. and Shiloah, A. (eds.), *Zion and Zionism among Sephardi and Oriental Jews*, Jerusalem: Misgav Yerushalayim (2002b), 261–274.

Hadar, G., 'The Jewish Press', In: Ginio, E., (ed.), *Greece: Jewish Communities in the East in the Nineteenth and Twentieth Centuries*, Jerusalem: Ben Zvi Institute, (2014), 201–218 [in Hebrew].

Keren, Z., *The Jewish Community of Rusçuk: From the Periphery of the Ottoman Empire to Capital of the Tuna Vilayet-i 1788–1878*, Jerusalem: Ben Zvi Institute (2005), 136–138 [in Hebrew].

Kolat, I., 'The Idea of the Hebrew University in the Jewish National Movement', In: Katz, S. and Heyd, M. (eds.), *The History of the Hebrew University of Jerusalem: Origins and Beginnings*, Jerusalem: Magness Press (1997), 3–74 [in Hebrew].

Koliopoulos, J., 'Brigandage and Insurgency in the Greek Domains of the Ottoman Empire, 1853–1908', In: Gondicas, D. and Issawi, C. (eds.), *Ottoman Greeks in the Age of Nationalism*, Princeton, NJ: Darwin Press (1999).

Koliopoulos, J. and Veremis, T., *Greece: The Modern Sequel from 1831 to Present*, London: Hurst (2002).

Mackridge, P., 'Cultivating New Lands: The Consolidation of Territorial Gains in Greek Macedonia Through Literature, 1912–1940', In: Mackridge, P. and Yannakakis, E. (eds.), *Ourselves and Others: The Development of a Greek Macedonian Cultural Identity since 1912*, Oxford: Berg (1997), 175–186.

206   Eyal Ginio

Mazower, M., *Salonica: City of Ghosts, Christians, Muslims and Jews, 1430–1950*, London: HarperCollins (2004).

Molho, R., 'Education in the Jewish Communities of Salonica and Greece in the Twentieth Century', In: Ginio, E., (ed.), *Greece: Jewish Communities in the East in the Nineteenth and Twentieth Centuries*, Jerusalem: Ben Zvi Institute (2014), 163–178, [in Hebrew].

Molho, R., *Salonica and Istanbul: Social, Political and Cultural Aspects of Jewish Life*, Istanbul: Isis (2005).

Molho, R., 'The Jewish Community of Salonika and its Incorporation into the Greek State 1912–19', *Middle Eastern Studies*, 24 (1988), 391–403.

Naar, Devin E., *Jewish Salonica between the Ottoman Empire and Modern Greece*, Stanford: Stanford University Press (2016).

Nehama, J., *Bizansyo i Sivilizasyón Bizantina*, Thessaloniki: Aksyón (1938).

Nehama, J., *Histoire des Israélites de Salonique*, 7 vols, Thessaloniki: The Jewish Community of Thessaloniki (1935–1978).

Rivlin, B., 'Incipient Hebrew Culture in Early 20th-Century Thrace', In: Harvet, W. Z., Hasan-Rokem, G., Saadoun, H. and Shiloah, A. (eds.), *Zion and Zionism among Sephardi and Oriental Jews*, Jerusalem: Misgav Yerushalayim (2002).

Rodrigue, A., 'From Millet to Minority: Turkish Jewry', In: Birnbaum, P. and Katznelson, I. (eds.), *Paths of Emancipation: Jews, States, and Citizenship*, Princeton, NJ: Princeton University Press (1995).

Rozanes, S., *History of the Jews of Turkey and of the Middle East*, Tel Aviv/Sofia: Devir, Rav Kook Institute, Husijstin (1907–1945) [in Hebrew].

Rozanes, S. *Istoría de la komunidad Israelita de Rusçuk*, Rusçuk [Ruse]: Yaakov Abraham Levy Publications (1914).

Rozen, M., 'Jews and Greeks Remember Their Past: The Political Career of Tzevi Korets (1933–43)', *Jewish Social Studies*, 12:1 (2005a), 111–166.

Rozen, M., *The Last Ottoman Century and Beyond*, Tel Aviv: Tel Aviv University Press (2005b).

Veremis, T., *The Military in Greek Politics: From Independence to Democracy*, Montreal: Black Rose Books (1997).

15 Destruction and reconstruction of Thessaloniki's class structure, 1912–1940

Evangelos Hekimoglou

The history of Thessaloniki is often considered as a narrative of facts concerning a major Ottoman and later Greek city (a narrative usually focusing on the religious classification of the population).[1] Although a number of academic papers and studies concerning the economic aspects of the city's history have been published during the last 20 years (Gounaris 1993; Dagkas 1998; Roupa and Hekimoglou 2004; Hekimoglou 2004; Meron 2012), not even one paper, to my knowledge, discussed the changes that occurred in the class structure[2] of Thessaloniki during the period of its incorporation into the Greek state.[3] This may be attributed to the fact that religious differentiation is a convenient, albeit ineffective, substitute for social analysis whenever the latter has difficulty in giving answers to social questions.[4]

Economic underdevelopment

If one compares late 18th-century data on Macedonian production to that for the early 20th century, one will easily trace a pattern of relative stagnation. Cotton production was reduced to one third; tobacco production increased by one third; raw wool production seems to remain unchanged; silk production reduced to one-tenth of its former size (extrapolating from Beaujour 1800, 41–62, 72–89, 99, 361–364; Kofinas 1914, 3–14, 167, 174–175, 219–221, 276).

The only exception to this pattern is cereal production, which increased by 300 per cent (Beaujour 1800; Kofinas 1914).[5] On the other hand, the population increased by 26 per cent in the same period.[6] Given the increase in the urban population by the early 20th century, in combination with the decrease of the agrarian population,[7] there is no doubt that the increase in cereal production was achieved by a number of cultivators not significantly higher than that of the late 18th century. Taking also in consideration the degree of technological underdevelopment,[8] we may conclude that the increase in cereal production occurred as a result either of intensification of labour or local reduced consumption.

In contrast to the relative stagnation in production, the aggregated value of imports and exports in 1910 was several times greater than that of the late 18th century. The volume of trade increased more rapidly than the volume of production, while the volume of imports increased faster than the volume of exports (Gounaris 1993, 210).

208 Evangelos Hekimoglou

The cumulative increases in the trade deficit point out that the local economy became more dependent upon the Western European economy, especially for food and raw materials. Moreover, direct European investment occurred in banking, urban infrastructure, and transportation (e.g. port construction, tramways, railways, etc.). These direct investments enhanced the dependency, because the main infrastructure of the city belonged to European entities.

In the early 20th century, Thessaloniki, as the main urban centre and the basic port of the Macedonian region, manifests the typical characteristics of a so-called 'gateway economy'. It was a relatively developed urban centre that facilitated the diffusion of European merchandise in the Macedonian interior and the export of food and raw materials to Europe.

Three different social contexts

It is crucial for our analysis to distinguish specific historical-social contexts[9] that corresponded to different modes of production.[10] First was the 'ancient' context, which embraced all the obsolete[11] characteristics of the Ottoman economy. The land was not fully a commodity; it could not be sold in the meaning of Greco-Roman Law. Only long-term leasing was possible, with ownership always retained by the Ottoman State. In fact, 'proprietors' were only possessors under conditions. Cultivators were paid in products, not in money.[12] The transportation of crops to the market was very difficult and expensive because of the lack of infrastructure. No fertilisers, even natural ones, were used. Cultivators were dependent upon local money-lenders and millers for credit, on onerous terms (Palamiotes 1914, 79–80; Gounaris 1993, 16–24). Political power remained in the hands of local Ottoman bureaucrats and was exercised in a fully arbitrary way.[13]

Second was a 'quasi-colonial'[14] context, which included the influx of Western capital,[15] the massive importation of Western merchandise (Christodoulou 1936, 60–122; Gounaris 1993, 206–233), and the indirect political control some European countries exercised on Macedonia through diplomatic pressure on the Ottoman state and inter-state conventions (Dakin 1993, 86–91, 112–116, 155–161, 320–359).

Third, there was a 'capitalist' context, including typical—although delayed—capital accumulation, which occurred in the textile and food industries, in banking, and commerce (Kofinas 1914, 207–240; Christodoulou 1936, 123–149; Roupa and Hekimoglou 2004, 12–68).

Class structure in Thessaloniki in the early 20th century

This social and economic milieu favoured certain social groups, such as the possessors of the agrarian land, local money-lenders, capitalists (in industry, commerce, and banking) and bureaucrats.[16] The increase in imports resulted in the formation of a group of smaller entrepreneurs, who served as mediators between importers and potential consumers in the hinterland and sometimes as money-lenders to the peasants. Although they should not be considered as a part of the capitalists proper, these lesser entrepreneurs played a major political role in the communal processes because of their large number (Hekimoglou 2015).

Thessaloniki's class structure, 1912–1940   209

A question is raised about the possible correspondence between the above-mentioned social groups on the one hand and the typical social classes of the capitalist mode of production on the other. There is no correspondence between the capitalist mode of production and ancient elements, such as Ottoman bureaucrats[17] and possessors of agricultural land.[18] In fact, these groups were contradictory to the capitalist mode of production, because they absorbed much of the economic surplus; besides, they stood as obstacles to the further commercialisation of the economy. Some other groups, i.e. the mediators and the money-lenders, might be considered as by-products of a transitional historical process in the Ottoman society, which has not yet been explored. The obvious lack of correspondence between the existing social groups and the theoretical forms constitutes an open question for Marxist-inspired theories. Another question is raised about the prosperous importers and exporters, who were obviously organised on a capitalist basis, usually being part of a multi-national entrepreneurial network.[19] In spite of their clearly capitalist looking, these merchants were the spinal column of the 'quasi-colonial' context, in close link with ancient elements, such as the landowners and the local money-lenders.

Changes in ownership relations after 1912

This class structure suffered many changes after the incorporation of Macedonia into the Greek State. In the period of 1912–1925, large farms were gradually confiscated by the state in favour of landless cultivators (Nakos 1990, 153–173; Hekimoglou 2009, 105–130). Before the official confiscation, the rights of old possessors (including the communities) and proprietors (including *waqfs*) had been left unprotected against claims by cultivators.

Besides, after the changes in the frontiers between the Balkan states, local industry's bonds with the Ottoman market were cut; local industrial products were left unprotected, in favour of Southern Greek industries (Gounaris 1990, 127–141). Another impact of the frontier changes with Serbia and Bulgaria was a massive capital loss for some hundreds of Thessalonian companies, which had credited their customers in the interior with huge sums; not a penny was paid back (Gelber 1955, 105–120; Hekimoglou 1989, 33–35).

In other words, the 'Gate' closed; commerce and industry were reduced. Important business families such as the Modianos (Hekimoglou 1991) and Allatinis (Roupa and Hekimoglou 2004, 372; Kavala et al. 2012) fled from Thessaloniki to European cities. Ottoman bureaucrats were deported. The Greek state immediately replaced Ottoman personnel with Greeks in every public agency.

The fire of 1917 and especially the re-planning of the city after the fire (Yerolympos 1995) were also important factors for the changes in the class structure, because they destroyed the urban middle class and created massive pauperisation.

There was a rich production of laws and decrees in the years 1917–1925 concerning the redistribution of the urban land and the reconstruction of the city

Table 15.1 The re-planning and reconstructing process

DATE	EVENT
1917, August 5–8	The fire.
1917, September 4	Law 823 prohibited 'temporarily' the reconstruction of the burned buildings. A committee was assigned to produce a new city plan for Thessaloniki.
1917, October 11	A Royal Decree permitted the reparation of the burnt buildings which belonged to the Jewish Community, to be used 'temporarily' for the housing of the homeless fire-stricken Jewish families.
1918, January 1	Law 1122 ordered: (a) 'the delimitation and the verification of the legal form of all the real estates in the limits of the city plan of Thessaloniki', (b) the estimation of the value of each plot. The Law concerned 4,100 plots.
1918, May 9	Law 1394 abolished land ownership in the private zone, with the elegant phrase: 'The real estate of the burnt zone comprise a land group with the goals of implementing a new city plan and distributing in justice all the future benefits concerning the value of real estate, which will derive from the implementation of the new plan'.
1919, January 15	Law 1660 modified some details of Law 1122.
1919, February 19	Law 1745 modified Law 1394, in an effort to cope with the many problems which rose in the meantime.
1919, March 7	Law 1719 authorised the expenses for developing the new city plan.
1919, May 7	A Legislative Order issued on that date modified Laws 1394 and 1745.
1919, June 8	All the Laws, Orders, and Decrees concerning the implementation of a new city plan were codified in a single text, which was given the legal form of a Royal Decree.
1919, September 6	A Legislative Order issued on that date modified Law 1394.
1919, October 22	A Royal Decree issued on that date permitted the National Bank of Greece to give loans pledging the legal papers (ktimatographa), which confirmed the value of the old plots.
1920, February 4	Law 1946 validated the Decrees issued in 1919, which had modified Laws 1394 and 1745.
1920, March 14	Minister Papanastassiou advised the National Bank of Greece to buy two plots for its own use and to pay not with cash, but with ktimatographa of small value, which it would buy from the old owners to 'facilitate them'.
1920, March 14	A Royal Decree issued on that date modified Law 1394 once more.
1920, March 28	The National Bank of Greece announced it was ready to give loans secured by ktimatographa. The maximum of the loan would not surpass 50% of the plot's estimated value.
1921, June 7	Law 2633 determined how the plots of the new city plan would be disposed.
1921, July 21	The Lower Civil Court of Thessaloniki authorised the official estimation of the value of 332 old plots in the area between Aghias Sophias, Egnatia, Venizelou, and Philippou Street. The Rogos neighbourhood is included in this area.

Thessaloniki's class structure, 1912–1940 211

Table 15.1 Continued

DATE	EVENT
1921, December 7	The public sale of the new plots (Section A) begun.
1921, December 30	*Makedonia* newspaper claimed that 'trusted interests' of persons who never had real estate in Section A (the central one) 'intruded in the place of the silly auction' and having bought all the ktimatographa of this Section, 'grabbed the large plots'. The Government had approved ktimatographa of the other Sections to be excluded from the auction.
1922, March 3	The decision of the Lower Civil Court of Thessaloniki mentioned above is formally published in the Appendix of the Official Government Gazette. It took eight months for the publication.
1922, March 7	The public sale of the new plots (Section E) begun but interrupted. Unsold plots were put into a new auction in June 1924.
1922, June 28	The public sale of the new plots (Section D) begun.
1923, February 8	The public sale of the new plots (Section B) begun.
1923, September 23	A Legislative Order issued on that date modified Law 2633.
1924, June 25	The public sale of the new plots (Section C) begun.

(see Table 15.1). In their combination, these laws violated the traditional land property rights of the residents, the religious communities, and *waqfs* in the burned area, resulting in a compulsory redistribution of the urban land.

A clear example is the Jewish population of the Rogos neighbourhood. Only one-tenth of the residents reclaimed their property.[20] The residents of one sample city block (No. 202, selected at random) were forced by hunger to sell their claims in the burnt area to third parties (see Table 15.2). The older family members died, and the younger male members emigrated. Perhaps the same happened in every other Jewish neighbourhood.

Even if the affected families were prosperous, the new city plan made it very difficult for them to repurchase their property. Half of the old plots had an area less than 150 square meters, and one third were less than 100 m². Besides, each plot was owned by more than one family. Therefore, it was impossible for the majority of middle-class families to buy even the cheapest new plots, which had an average area of 250 m², even if the price of land had remained unchanged in the competition that emerged during the auctions. Table 15.3 is based on a sample of 1,562 deeds out of 4,100 (the full list is in Mantopoulou-Panaghiotopoulou and Hekimoglou 2004).

The exchange of populations between Turkey and Greece was another catalyst of social change, because it resulted in the complete loss of rights of the old possessors of the urban and agrarian land; besides, it eliminated ownership without usufruct, i.e. the rights of the *waqfs* to urban and agrarian land; it eliminated the massive Muslim middle class; it established numerous class segments of small, heavily indebted, Christian landowners in the rural areas and poor proprietors of urban land in the cities, as the result of the urban planning decisions of the

212   *Evangelos Hekimoglou*

Table 15.2 The fate of some Rogos residents after the fire of 1917

Plot Number	Possessing Family	Area m²	What happened to the Ktimatographon
202/1	Saltiel Saltiel	137	Sold
202/2	Djoya Pessah	60	Sold
202/3	Corridor	8	
202/4	Yuda, Aharon, Samuel Arditti	200	Sold
202/5	Florentin (a book-binder) and Esformes (a smith)	191	Sold
202/6	Mallah Yuda Kohen	117	No data
202/7	Yako Almosnino	132	In the hands of the mortgage holder
202/8	Muson Jakob Kapon (a musician), Yako Menahem Algava	76	Sold
202/9	Myrjam Salomon Beraha, wife of Simon Molho	135	No data
202/10	Jakob Muson Saltiel (a tailor)	139	In the hands of the mortgage holder
202/11	Panaghia Chalkeon Church [Kazandjilar Djami during the Ottoman period]	520	
202/12	Isac Mordohai Azaria (a musician)	97	Sold
202/13	Sarah Levy, Saltiel Amiras	604	Sold

Source: Cadastral Documents (see endnote 35).

Refugee Settlement Committee and the Greek State. In sum, the old ruling classes almost disappeared, the old middle class was destroyed, and new poor social strata were formed.

The new social powers

Businessmen from Southern Greece and the Ottoman territories and Greek bureaucrats established themselves in Thessaloniki and replaced the older dominant classes (see above). Of course some of the old industrialists and merchants kept their position. But no more than ten out of the 60 richest Thessalonians of a list compiled by the Orient Bank in 1906 continued to live in Thessaloniki in the 1920s (Roupa and Hekimoglou 2004, 8–10). New middle classes and a stratum of paupers made their appearance in the new slums around the city.

The formation of a massive social category of small farm owners in Macedonia and Thrace, who came out from the homeless refugees, was to the benefit of the Greek bureaucrats, for two reasons: (a) the number of the families who paid the agrarian taxes (the main fiscal tax in Greece) increased; (b) the bureaucrats kept control on every subject in regard to the establishment of the refugees and consequently on the formation of the new middle classes for a long time.[21]

Table 15.3 The size of the old plots (out of a specimen of 1,562 cases)

Area m^2	Frequency	Cumulative Frequency	Cumulative Percentage Frequency
0–25	103		
26–50	118	221	14%
50–75	133	354	23%
75–100	166	520	33%
100–125	152	672	43%
125–150	136	808	52%
150–175	102	910	58%
175–200	85	995	64%
200–225	71	1066	68%
225–250	60	1126	72%
250–275	52	1178	75%
275–300	31	1209	77%
300–325	40	1249	80%
325–350	46	1295	83%
350–375	30	1325	85%
375–400	23	1348	86%
400–425	23	1371	88%
425–450	20	1391	89%
450–475	13	1404	90%
475–500	14	1418	91%
500–525	7	1425	91%
525–550	11	1436	92%
550–600	18	1454	93%
600–625	7	1461	94%
625–650	5	1466	94%
650–675	7	1473	94%
675–700	7	1480	95%
700–725	11	1491	95%
725–750	3	1494	96%
750–775	2	1496	96%
775–800	4	1500	96%
800–825	4	1504	96%
825–850	2	1506	96%
850–875	1	1507	96%
875–900	3	1510	97%
900–925	1	1511	97%
925–950	3	1514	97%
950–975	2	1516	97%
975–1000	2	1518	97%
1000–1025	2	1520	97%
1025–1050	2	1522	97%
1050–1075	1	1523	98%
1075–1100	2	1525	98%
1100+	37	1562	100%

Source: Cadastral Documents.

214 *Evangelos Hekimoglou*

Comparing the schemes before 1911 and after 1925

With respect to the pattern of our analysis, the changes in the period of 1911–1925 included the destruction of Thessaloniki's ancient context, the near destruction of the quasi-colonial context, and the strengthening of the capitalist context. However, the involvement of the Greek bureaucracy was not a favourable condition for further capitalist development. Another weakness of the new social scheme was that the indigenous middle class was destroyed, due to the new city plan of Thessaloniki.

The strengthening of the capitalist context might be seen in the profile of 146 share-holding companies, which were founded in Thessaloniki during the interwar period.[22] Only 21 out of the 146 companies were owned by 'native' families, in the sense that they used to live in Thessaloniki in the 19th century. Seven out of these 21 families were Christian, one was Muslim (Christianised), and the remaining 13 were Jewish. That means that capital accumulation was linked with the establishment of newcomers rather than with the 'natural' development of the 'native' capital. Indeed, more than half of the factories' owners came from the Macedonian interior and 30 per cent from Asia Minor, Thrace, and Eastern Rumelia (Hekimoglou 2010, 127–136).

The same pattern arises with respect to the middle class. The pauperisation of the indigenous small owners and shopkeepers, who lost their fortunes in the re-planning process of the 1920s, in combination with the establishment of thousands of merchants from the interior or the Ottoman territories, changed dramatically the composition of the local middle class.[23]

The new adventures of the middle class

Middle class is an empirical term, which involves 'intermediate strata' and 'obliterates lines of demarcation' of the capitalist mode of production (Marx 2007, vol. 3, ch. 52).[24] Although this term is used to facilitate the cognitive approach to the social reality, usually it helps to confuse it. In fact, the term 'middle class' means anything that does not include: (a) the traditional (blue-collar) waged labour in the secondary sector, and (b) the owners of the means of mass production.[25] The classic form[26] of the middle class consists of crafts and trades, i.e. self-employed artisans and small-scale merchants who rarely use waged labour and usually work by themselves. Their common economic characteristic is that

> They confront me as sellers of commodities, not as sellers of labour … they are producers of commodities. But their production does not fall under the capitalist mode of production … The means of production become capital only in so far as they have become separated from labourer and confront labour as an independent power' (…) 'It is therefore only through his ownership of these [the means of production] that he takes possession of his own surplus-labour, and thus bears to himself as wage-labourer the relation of being his own capitalist.
>
> (Marx 1969, 1328)

Thessaloniki's class structure, 1912–1940 215

Artisans possess means of production (i.e. tools and instruments, even a workshop), but these are not capital, because they have not been separated from their labour. In that sense, and in order to be consistent with the terms of our analysis, crafts and trades of interwar Salonika should be classified in the 'ancient context'.

In fact, the market value of artisans' 'means of production' varied significantly. In many cases their value was so small, that it would be easily absorbed by an accidental fall in orders or by a credit difficulty. Following that, the handicraftsman would fall into a condition of unemployment and eventually would be transformed into a wage-labourer. So, the lines between arts and crafts, and between unemployment and waged labour were (and remain) very thin.

The officials of the League of Nations, who came to Greece in 1926 to report on the condition of the refugees, found themselves puzzled amidst these lines. They faced a difficulty, which is clearly illustrated in their report in the chapter about refugee employment (Société des Nations 1926, 182–183). The compiler of the report traced 12 industrialist refugees, 300 merchants, 2,700 craftsmen and tradesmen, and 13,000 workers in Thessaloniki, and admitted that '*Il est évident que les chiffres concernant Salonique sont incomplets, 16,000 individus, vivant de leur travail sur un total de 170,000 habitants, c'est-à dire de 42,000 familles*' (p. 182). In conclusion, the compiler presumed the existence of another 13,000 unregistered workers, who lacked specialisation in work, besides 10,000 jobless chiefs of families (p. 182). The compiler based his hypothesis on the conclusions of a similar investigation concerning Attica, where a significant difference in the refugees' settlements in Athens was traced and illustrated in a classification between '*de tous les habitants exerçant une profession dans les mêmes quartiers*' and the '*individus sans profession définie, homes de peine, manoeuvres, etc*' (p. 181).[27]

The refugees from Asia Minor, Thrace, etc., who were settled in Thessaloniki, originated from social contexts similar to the three already mentioned local contexts. Their majority (trades and crafts) came from an 'ancient' social context; a few were linked with the quasi-colonial context and a small number with the capitalist context. Of course, as a Greek statesman remarked, 'all the merchants of Smyrna in particular and the Asia Minor in general retained their identity as merchants. The industrialists did not change their occupation. The artisans remained artisans' (Kalevras 1930, 9). But how did all of these people retain their bourgeois or petit bourgeois way of thinking and at the same time they were traced as unregistered or unoccupied or in the best case, as labour workers? There is a difference of time to be considered. The League of Nations official wrote his report in 1926; Kalevras wrote his pamphlet in 1930. What has happened in the meantime? 50,000 refugees' families, established in Thessaloniki, were poorly compensated for the loss of their property in Turkey (Christodoulou 1936, 316). For a moment, they had cash at their disposal and they rushed to enter the market.

In 1926, the members of the Chamber of Commerce were less than 1,500 and the members of the Chamber of Professions and Artisans hardly exceeded 8,000. According to Kalevras (1930, 9), in the period 1926–1929, 21,300 new members (27,844 entries less 6,550 exits) were registered in the two chambers, mainly in the second one. Besides the spending of the refugees' compensation,

216   Evangelos Hekimoglou

another autonomous increase in local spending occurred, due to the rebuilding of Thessaloniki.[28] But the period of prosperity was short. Very soon, the market of the city was over-stuffed due to the excess of craftsmen and tradesmen. The number of trades and crafts became excessive even before the Great Depression, let alone after the Depression hit Thessaloniki and the demand for goods collapsed (Robbins 2007).

During the crisis, seven out of ten small shops, five out of ten butcher shops, eight out of ten groceries, and six out of ten restaurants closed in Thessaloniki.[29] It was not only the newcomers that lost their 'means of production'. Two out of every three shops that had opened before 1922 went bankrupt during the Depression; the same happened with half of those that had opened up in the period 1922–1924. The Association of Salonika Merchants retained only half of its members in comparison with 1926, i.e. before the large increase in the number of tradesmen (Roupa and Hekimoglou 2004, 40).

In conclusion, a sudden boom of the middle class occurred in the period 1926–1929 and a new destruction of the middle class (the second one after the fire) took place in the succeeding period 1930–1935.

Wage workers and the traditional middle class

The unpredictable and volatile situation of the middle class stabilised in the mid-1930s (Roupa and Hekimoglou 2004, 42). Making use of the detailed information collected by Dagkas (1993), I re-classified into three groups a large number of occupations, which were registered in the contemporary statistics. The first group consists of waged workers; the second group of traditional crafts and trades; the third group of the remaining occupations and professions, civil servants, the unemployed, and those who did not declare their profession or had no formal employment. My hypothesis is the following: Presuming that waged labour is a result of the development of the capitalist mode of production, the increase in the number of the waged workers may be taken as a strong indication of the strengthening of the 'capitalist' context. On the contrary, the increase in traditional crafts and trades is conceived to be an indication of the strengthening of the 'ancient' context.

According to the data presented in Table 15.4, in 1936, 22,300 wage workers resided in Salonika, in comparison with 18,500 craftsmen and tradesmen (leaving 25,300 for the 'rest' category). The percentage of waged workers to active population increased steadily from 28 per cent in 1915 to 34 per cent in 1936, despite the extended unemployment caused by the great recession. On the other hand, the craftsmen and tradesmen percentage increased from 24 per cent in 1915 to 28 per cent in 1936, an increase that would have been much larger without the recession which caused the above-mentioned decrease of the number of shops and workshops.

In conclusion, although the 'ancient' context remained strong, a clear superiority of the 'capitalist' context is traced in the interwar period. It is important that this superiority is traceable both before and after the Great Recession, which hit the traditional middle-class strata harder than any other.

Thessaloniki's class structure, 1912–1940 217

Table 15.4 The 'ancient' and the 'capitalist'

Wage Workers			
Survey of the year	1915	1926	1936
Wage workers in the secondary sector	4.124	7.125	11.176
Wage workers in the tertiary sector (civil servants excluded)	5.889	6.604	11.107
Wage workers in total	10.013	13.729	22.283
Active population (farmers and gardeners excluded)	35.68	44.984	66.104
Wage workers as a percentage of the active population	28%	31%	34%
Traditional crafts and trades			
Survey of the year	1915	1926	1936
Traditional crafts in the secondary sector	2.945	5.801	8.158
Traditional trades in the tertiary sector	5.566	7.573	10.310
Traditional crafts and trades in total	8.511	13.374	18.468
Active population (farmers and gardeners excluded)	35.68	44.894	66.104
Traditional crafts and trades as a percentage of the active population	24%	30%	28%
Wage workers and traditional crafts and trades as a percentage of the active population	52%	61%	62%

Source of the data: Dagkas 1998, 394–395; (according to my calculations).

Replacement or reconstruction?

We have to stress that the already mentioned changes in respect to the bourgeois and petit bourgeois strata were not just a replacement of persons or a change in quantity. They were structural changes in the context through which these social strata functioned. From this point of view, interwar Thessaloniki was not a linear descendant of the Ottoman Selanik, but another, very different city.

The symptoms of this dramatic change are often confused with the process of 'Hellenisation'[30] of Thessaloniki, in the meaning of a series of deliberate political actions taken by the Greek state with the goal of changing the character of the city.[31] This interpretation is an offspring of misunderstanding the class reconstruction in the Macedonian geographical area; besides, it overestimates the ability of the Greek bureaucracy to pursue effective interventionist policies in complex social matters. Once more, the 'Hellenisation' concept overestimates the political factor in contrast to the social and economic factors. Last, but not least, the changes which took place in the 1920s as a result of the exchange of the populations and the mass migration of Thessalonians (Dagkas 1998, 157–165), were stronger than any bureaucratic intention, if they were any. In 1904 there was one Orthodox Greek for three Jews and two Muslims. In 1928 there were three Orthodox Greeks for one Jew, and almost no Muslims (see Table 15.5).

218   *Evangelos Hekimoglou*

Table 15.5 Population of Thessaloniki in 1904 and 1928

Group	1904*	1928	Difference
Jews	47,322	55,290	7,968
Muslims	32,703	1,182	−31,521
Orthodox Greeks	15,012	180,052	165,040
Total	95,037	236,524	141,487

*Note: For reasons of comparability, some 4,000 'Exarchists' registered in 1904 survey accounts, are omitted. Most of the Bulgarian population was exchanged soon after 1919.
(Şaşmaz 1994, App.; Dagkas 1998, 164)

The same remarks are valid with respect to the overstressing of religious differentiation in the interwar period. In fact, although a number of Jewish capitalists and lesser entrepreneurs survived in Thessaloniki, anything 'Jewish' was considered to be a reflection of the past, i.e. of the abolished 'contexts'. On the contrary, anything 'Greek' and 'Christian' represented the new class structure, i.e. the combination of the capitalist context and the dominant Greek bureaucracy. The anti-Semitism,[32] as it was expressed in everyday life in interwar Thessaloniki, even or especially among the Venizelist lower middle class against the Jewish proletariat and pauper families, was an ideological weapon of the newcomers against the indigenous population. Anti-Semitism was not legitimised on the ideological ground of racial differences, but as an expression of the rights the Greek conqueror asserted over the conquered, i.e. the rights of the victorious newcomers against the defeated indigenous 'tribes'.

The indigenous 'tribes' were not useful for the new capitalist context. Invoking the alleged refusal of the Jews to 'be adopted' into the Greek state, the fascist organisation EEE (National Union Hellas)[33] and its mentors, i.e. the Press Office of the General Administration of Northern Greece[34] and the *Makedonia* newspaper, expressed their belief that the Jews of Thessaloniki were a useless remnant of the past, which blocked the potential progress of the city.

In 1931, a group of at least 200 people, most armed, marched from Kalamaria to the Jewish 'Campbell' neighbourhood in the middle of the night. Their goal was to kill and rape, not simply to terrorise. It is not a coincidence that the EEE did not attack the houses of prosperous Jewish families but instead a poor neighbourhood.[35] They acted against people

> condemned to live in a black misery, residing in unhealthy huts, fed only with black bread and water, who wither from day to day; beings who do not deserve this name, joyless, living without sun, shadowed even in the best of their moments with the concern of tomorrow.
>
> (*El Puevlo*, 9 December 1932)

But those who burnt the Campbell neighbourhood, in June 1931, were workers, car drivers, and coffee-makers, destined to share that same misery (*Makedonia*, 3 April 1932, 1).

Thessaloniki's class structure, 1912–1940 219

It is true that 'Jewish entrepreneurs functioned as minority group entrepreneurs, recruiting Jewish workers and utilising Jewish information networks' (Meron 2012, 94). But we must not press this point too hard. The Christian entrepreneurial 'majority' was not a homogenous group; specifically, they were split in local groups linked by common origin and intermarriage (e.g. migrants from Kozani with others from Kozani) (Roupa and Hekimoglou 2004). Besides, even before 1912 non-Jewish businessmen had difficulties getting loans from Jewish bankers, for reasons related to the security of the loan: credit habits, access to information about the prosperity of the debtor, etc. (Hekimoglou 1999, 35–37). On the other hand, we have to evaluate properly the fact that Jewish firms suffered waves of anti-Jewish boycotts (Meron 2012, 108) motivated by nationalist sentiments, primitive and hostile to capitalist development. The official policy regarding Jewish businessmen, as expressed by the anti-Semitic director of the Press Office of the General Administration of Macedonia, was that the Greek State wanted them to stay in Thessaloniki to employ their co-religionists; if they emigrated, already high unemployment would increase and available capital would diminish.[36]

Conclusion

The interwar history of Thessaloniki may include narrations about labour strikes, anti-Semitic activities, the reconstruction of the city, and the economic progress or even full reestablishment of the refugees. But interwar history is not only a narrative nor a series of facts; it is a history of the destruction and reconstruction of social classes. This process was rather violent, not always bloodless, and completed in less than 25 years.

Notes

1 Apostolos Vakalopopulos (1909–2000) was the first who attempted to write a 'history of Thessaloniki', based on poor sources, as early as in 1947; his second and better documented attempt occurred in 1983 (Vakalopoulos 1993, English translation of the 1983 edition). Since 1983, more than 10,000 titles affiliated with the history of Thessaloniki have been published. Kostis Moskof's work (Moskof 1978) was a serious step, in the sense that he linked the historic narrative with a certain social structure. Being seriously ill since 1970, he examined unpublished archival material, took notes, and published some parts of it. Although valuable, his work was not disciplined and found no successors, with the exception of Dagkas 1998.

2 See the modern discussion about the Marxist notion of 'social class' and the relevant bibliography in Milios 2000, 283–302. By the term 'class' I mean a social group of a specific society, defined by its function in the processes of the production, extraction, and distribution of the economic surplus of the society (see f. 9). This notion is different from the typical Marxist notion of class, which is based on the notion of the mode of production.

3 Dagkas (1998) collected and studied a huge quantity of sources. He focused on the description of the economic activities, taking the social context as granted, i.e. as a typical capitalist context. The same remark might be made with regard to his voluminous subsequent work (Dagkas 2003, 25–37), which includes 12 pages under the title 'Les Balkans et le développement du capitalisme'. There he reports the number of factories

220 *Evangelos Hekimoglou*

in the Ottoman Empire and the problems which the Young Turks faced every time they attempted to determine their social identity. In another section of the same book under the title 'La concentration et la centralisation des capitaux dans l'industrie du tabac' (pp. 366–389), Dagkas refers to the competition between the European and the American tobacco companies. Despite his detailed documentation, his conclusions do not exceed the limits of a linear interpretation of capitalist development. He ignores the crucial combination between different modes of production, seeing only capitalism and nothing else. Although he presented an impressive quantitative analysis and he found significant geographical differences in the type of participation in the labour unions, he insisted seeing social classes only in the context of capitalism. Despite his elaborate analysis, the same remarks apply for Dagkas 2008.

4 This observation applies in particular to Mazower's *Salonica, City of Ghosts* (Mazower 2004). This study gained in popularity mainly because it is a narrative of facts and fictions, with three heroes, those named on the cover of the book. The term 'class' is not mentioned in that book; a couple of pages are dedicated to the '*Federation*', just to stress the religious differentiation inside the local labour class. About the credibility of his documentation in respect with the conversions to Islam, see Hekimoglou 2006, 134–139.

5 According to Gounaris 1993, 16, cereal production was already important in the middle of the 19th century.

6 Beaujour 1800, 10, estimated the population density at 375 persons per square league, i.e. 23 persons per square kilometre. According to the survey of 1906 the population in the *vilayets* of Thessaloniki and Manastir was estimated at 1,848,000 persons. The area of these *vilayets* was 63,000 square kilometres, so the density of the population was 29 persons per square kilometre. This is the safest way to estimate the increase in general population for the period 1800–1900, because there is not any trustworthy and comparable data for such a long period.

7 This trend is clearly seen in the survey of the population of Thessaloniki, according to which one out of four residents was a newcomer who moved to the city from the hinterland. For the analytical survey see Şaşmaz 1994, 349–377.

8 To my knowledge, the best description of the underdevelopment in the agrarian sector is included in an unpublished report, which was compiled by Austrian experts in 1913; National Bank of Greece Historical Archive [hereafter NBGHA], Alexandros Diomidis archive, owned by N. S. Pantelakis (1907–1950), Code A13, ff. D/70, D/71, D/85 and D/86.

9 The term 'social context' refers to the specific social conditions under which the economic surplus is extracted. For the notion of 'economic surplus' see Stanfield 1973; Szlajfer 1979; Hekimoglou 1987; Theodoropoulos 1993; Danielson 1994.

10 The term 'mode of production' is used in the Marxist meaning, i.e. as a theoretical scheme which explains the extraction of the economic surplus under different historical conditions; see Hekimoglou 1987, 12–68. According the neo-Marxist trend, a social formation comprises modes of production (Wright 1976, 3–42; Wright 1985; Marshall 1988, 141–154). Existing social groups do not always correspond with the classes of a mode of production. The later are ideal types, useful for the understanding of existing social formations, while existing social groups lack conceptual and operational perfection, as well as stability.

11 The term 'obsolete' is used as opposed to the term 'capitalist'. 'Obsolete' includes the 'whole series of inherited evils (...) arising from the passive survival of antiquated modes of production, with their inevitable train of social and political anachronisms' (Marx 2007, 13).

12 This mode of distribution was obsolete even according to the medieval standards. For a short description of the local relations of production, see Dakin 1993, 23–24; Gounaris 1993, 18.

Thessaloniki's class structure, 1912–1940 221

13 The political power of the Ottoman bureaucracy became stronger when the Young Turk Revolution occurred, and the Sultan accepted their demands. Dakin (1993, 24) notes that 'it was not so much the presence of official Turkish rule in Macedonian villages as the total lack of rule that made for abuses. The Turks had no tradition of ruling in the generally accepted sense of the term. True, they maintained a bureaucracy in the towns, but the main officials had not much work to do'. This is a stereotyped approach that underestimates the power of the Ottoman bureaucracy. Gounaris (1993, 13) stresses 'the continuation of the Ottoman rule in the Balkans for almost 35 years (1878–1912), while it was evident that the Empire could no longer safeguard these possessions'. This is a pragmatic approach, because it rejects the notion of Turkish 'incompetence' and associates 'the continuation of the Ottoman rule' with certain conditions.

14 The colonial mode of production is regarded as a variant of the capitalist mode. 'In the colonial mode of production we have a mode which might best be defined as deformed: Extended reproduction has been imposed from the outside, leading to a relative openness in trade with the metropolitan centre but a closed or "disarticulated" internal economy. Commodity production is also generalized but again imposed from outside …' (Harrison 1990, 123).

15 Western capital was invested in banking, railways, port construction, electricity power, and tramways. In the sphere of production, foreign investments occurred only in mining. The quasi-colonial context included also the monopoly on tobacco (controlled by English and French capital) and the Ottoman Public Debt Administration, an agency that via the Ottoman Bank collected a large portion of the local taxes and tariffs.

16 The so-called Young Turk Revolution was a political process concerning the differentiated interests in the interior of bureaucracy, not a 'bourgeois' revolution. The whole process had disastrous results for the Ottoman economy in the period 1908–1913.

17 This social group was only accidentally synonymous to the bureaucracy of the capitalist mode of production. For a bibliography on the Marxist approach to bureaucracy see Goldman and Van Houten 1977, 108–125.

18 There is no historical analogy between this group and the transformation of the feudal ownership into a capitalist type (complete ownership of the land). Milios (2000, 296) thinks that this transformation was a typical example for a new class, which originated through transition processes as the feudal mode of production was being dissolved, although the class of landowners did not constitute a component element of the capitalist mode of production.

19 A very good example is the Allatini-Morpourgo-Fernandez family. For the relevant bibliography and an extensive family tree, see Gregoriou 2008, 137–200; Hekimoglou 2012.

20 For a list of the old owners see in the Annex of the Government Gazette no. 63, March 29, 1922; for a list of the new owners, see *Efimeris ton Valkanion*, 12 June 1922.

21 Political life in interwar Greece comprised successive parliamentary elections, coups d'etat, and authoritarian governments, the later expressing army and civil servants' factions. With the exception of a few statesmen loyal to parliamentarism, there was no clear divide between the parliamentarians and the authoritarians. Parliament and authoritarian governments were two different forms of the same phenomenon, which originated from the army officers' 'pronunciamento' in Athens, in 1909. The economic and social basis of this process was the increasing role of the state in everyday life, especially since WW I. For a clear analysis see Koliopoulos 1996. The Marxist approach of Psyroukis (1974) retains its value as well.

22 All these companies were family owned. Although the legal share-holding scheme was only a trick used by family companies to evade income taxes, a minimum limit of capital was required for the establishment of a shareholding company. Consequently, the shareholding company legal form is an indication for the accumulation of capital.

222　*Evangelos Hekimoglou*

23 For a significant sample of middle-class businessmen see Hekimoglou 2004. Note that fewer than 10% of the merchants registered in the Commerce of Chambers records had a Jewish name.

24 I approach middle class as an existing social group, which originates from older social forms. The theory that the middle class is constructed in reference to a 'form' of production, which is not identified with the capitalist mode of production, puts in question the notion of the mode of production, without solving the problem where the middle class comes from.

25 Although in modern sociological terms this approach to the concept of the middle class is obviously incomplete, because it does not include social factors (i.e. education and income) besides the occupational ones, I adopt it for the purposes of the present paper, which is focused in the economic aspect of class structure and restructure.

26 The modern form includes the 'new middle strata', i.e. salaried professionals, civil servants, etc. A long and open discussion has developed in the milieu of the Greek Marxist historiography whether these strata are just a modern social output of the old middle classes, or rather a product of the development of the capitalist mode of production. The practical output of this discussion is the following question: Is modern middle class an 'obsolete' remnant (which 'obliterates lines of demarcation') or a 'capitalist' product? I deliberately kept this aspect out of the present paper; see Hekimoglou 1987 for the milieu of the whole discussion.

27 The report traced a location pattern, based on the vocational specialisation. The more specialized the refugees were, the closer to the centre of Athens their settlement was. Perhaps, a measure to evaluate the refugees who applied for urban settlement was their specialisation in work.

28 Kalevras 1930, 13. The majority of the proprietors of the new plots were not Salonikans, so the money used for the rebuilding came from elsewhere.

29 In trade fluctuation the tradesman or the artisan or even the peasant producer are not literary unemployed; 'but they suffer an "automatic" reduction of money-income, leading to the wiping out of middle-classes resources'; Robbins 2007, 187.

30 The term 'hellenisation' had been used since the 18th century in respect to the Hellenistic period to describe 'the diffusion of the Greek language, and the military organisation, discipline and administration of the Macedon'. On the other hand, 'Hellenism, properly so called—the aggregate of habits, sentiments, energies, and intelligence, manifested by the Greeks during their epoch of autonomy—never passed into Asia' (Grote 1856, 362–364). The term was also used to describe the creation of national consciousness among the Orthodox Christians of the Ottoman Empire through the use of Greek language during the 19th century: 'Hellenization [...] [made] language the distinguishing mark of an ethnic group and implicitly gave language and ethnicity a higher political priority than religion' (Karpat 2002, 637).

31 Fleming maintained that 'hellenisation' was the product of the conflict between Jews and refugees: '... Asia Minor Greeks were more hostile toward Jews than their Salonikan Christian counterparts—who after all, unlike Asia Minor Greeks, had cohabitated with large numbers of Jews for centuries' (Fleming 2008, 84). The same author seems to believe that 'hellenisation' was the product of legislation, which was introduced with the target of reducing the influence of the Jewish population.

32 The new (interwar) Thessaloniki anti-Semitism was different in quality from the old (pre-1912) one. The old anti-Semitism referred to the behaviour of a Christian minority against a Jewish majority. In social terms, the old anti-Semitism referred to the behaviour of craftsmen and tradesmen, guided by newcomer professionals, against old and prosperous Jewish bourgeois families with European roots and branches, families with strong economic foundations, who led the Jewish population majority. On the contrary, interwar anti-Semitism referred to the relations between pauperised Jews and pauperised Christian newcomers. If the old anti-Semitism had to do with the distribution of

Thessaloniki's class structure, 1912–1940   223

a developing economy, the new one referred to survival in a shrinking economy with fewer and fewer opportunities, the best of which was migration.

33 For fascist groups in interwar Thessaloniki see Tsironis (2003), 31–40.

34 Senator Isaac Siacky to the Prime Minister of Greece, November 29, 1932; a petition for the discharge of the Director of the Press Office, named Minardos, by the General Administration of Northern Greece. Minardos is characterised as 'the instigator and animator of every anti-Jewish action in Thessaloniki'; Gennadeios Library; Philippos Dragoumis archive; f. 38.2. It is very interesting that Minardos kept his important position for more than 15 years.

35 For a rich but not always accurate description of the events in Campbell, see the *Rizospastis* newspaper, issues 30 June 1931 to 8 July 1931.

36 Minardos to Dragoumis, Confidential memorandum dated 13 December 1932, Gennadeios Library; Philippos Dragoumis archive; f. 38.2.

References

Beaujour, L.-A. F., *A view of the Commerce of Greece: Formed after an Annual Average, from 1787 to 1797*, translated from the French by Thomas Hartwell Horne, London: James Wallis (1800).

Christodoulou, G., *Η Θεσσαλονίκη κατά την τελευταίαν εκατονταετίαν* [Thessaloniki During the Last Century], Thessaloniki: Enosis (1936).

Dagkas, A., *Συμβολή στην έρευνα για την οικονομική και κοινωνική εξέλιξη της Θεσσαλονίκης: Οικονομική δομή και κοινωνικός καταμερισμός της εργασίας. 1912–1940* [Contribution to the Research of the Economic and Social Development of Thessaloniki: Economic Structure and Social Distribution of Labour, 1912–1940], Thessaloniki: Professional Chamber of Thessaloniki (1998).

Dagkas, A., *Recherches sur l'histoire sociale de la Grèce du Nord: Le mouvement des ouvriers du tabac 1918–1928*, Editions de l'Association de Recherchers Interdisciplinaires Pierre Belon, No 6, Paris: De Boccard (2003), 779–795.

Dagkas, A., *Le mouvement social dans le Sud-est européen pendant le XXe siècle: questions de classe, questions de culture*, Thessaloniki: Epicentre (2008).

Dakin, D., *The Greek Struggle in Macedonia 1897–1913*, Thessaloniki: Institute for Balkan Studies (1993).

Danielson, A., *The Economic Surplus: Theory, Measurement, Applications*, Praeger: New York (1994).

Efimeris ton Valkanion, liberal daily newspaper, Thessaloniki: N. Kastrinos (1918–1950).

Fleming, K. E., *Greece: A Jewish History*, Princeton, NJ: Princeton University Press (2008).

Gelber, N. M., 'An Attempt to Internationalize Salonika, 1912–1913', *Jewish Social Studies*, 17 (1955), 105–120.

Goldman, P. and Van Houten, D. R., 'Managerial Strategies and the Worker: A Marxist Analysis of Bureaucracy', *The Sociological Quarterly*, 18.1 (Winter 1977), 108–125.

Gounaris, B., 'Η οικονομική ζωή στη Μακεδονία πριν από την υπογραφή της Συνθήκης του Βουκουρεστίου' ['Economic life in Macedonia before the Treaty of Bucharest'], In: *Πρακτικά του Συμποσίου: Η Συνθήκη του Βουκουρεστίου και η Ελλάδα* [Proceedings of the symposium: The Treaty of Bucurest and Greece], Thessaloniki: Institute for Balkan Studies (1990), 127–141.

Gounaris, B., *Steam over Macedonia: Socio-economic Change and the Railway Factor*, New York: Boulder (1993).

224 *Evangelos Hekimoglou*

Gregoriou, A., 'Η Θεσσαλονίκη των Allatini 1776–1911' [Allatini's Thessaloniki (1776–1911)], *Thessaloniki. Series of the Historical Centre of Thessaloniki*, 7 (2008), 137–200.

Grote, G., *History of Greece*, vol. XII, London: John Murray (1856).

Harrison, D., *The Sociology of Modernization and Development*, London: Routledge (1990).

Hekimoglou, E., *Η ιστορικότητα και η χωρητικότητα του πλεονάσματος: Χώρος και μηχανισμοί απόσπασης του πλεονάσματος στην Ελλάδα, 1800–1870* [The Historical and Spatial Character of the Economic Surplus: Space and Mechanisms for Surplus Extraction in Greece, 1800–1870], PhD Thesis, Aristotle University of Thessaloniki, Department of Economics (1987). http://thesis.ekt.gr/0554, retrieved July 2019.

Hekimoglou, E., *Κοφινάς προς Διομήδη: δοκίμια και τεκμήρια για την οικονομική ιστορία της Μακεδονίας* [Kofinas to Diomedes], Thessaloniki: n.e. (1989).

Hekimoglou, E., *Υπόθεση Μοδιάνο: τραπεζικό κράχ στη Θεσσαλονίκη το 1911* [The Modiano Affair: A Banking Crash in Thessaloniki in 1911], Thessaloniki: Altintzi (1991).

Hekimoglou, E., '*Hazakah*: Land Market Practices in Ottoman Thessaloniki', *Justice* 33 (Spring 1999), 35–37.

Hekimoglou, E., *Λεξικό επιχειρηματιών της μεσοπολεμικής Θεσσαλονίκης* [A Dictionary of Businessmen in interwar Thessaloniki], Thessaloniki: Businessmen Cultural Society for Northern Greece (2004).

Hekimoglou, E., 'Τα "φαντάσματα" των γιών του Αμπντουλλάχ : εξισλαμισμοί στη Θεσσαλονίκη κατά τον 15ο αιώνα' ['The "Ghosts" of the Sons of Abdullah: Conversions to Islam in Thessaloniki during 15th Century'], *Θεσσαλονικέων πόλις* [City of the Thessalonians], 19 (2006), 134–139.

Hekimoglou, E., 'The Greek Community of Thessaloniki and the Challenge of the Young Turks, 1908–1912', In: Stamatopoulos, D. (ed.), *Balkan Nationalism(s) and the Ottoman Empire*, Vol. III, Istanbul: ISIS Press (2015), 7–32.

Hekimoglou, E., 'Η αγροτική μεταρρύθμιση της τριανδρίας (1916–1917)' ['The Agrarian Reform of the Triumvirate (1916–1917)']. In Eleutherotypia editors, *Εθνικός διχασμός 1916–1917*, Athens: Eleftherotypia (2009), 105–130.

Hekimoglou, E., 'Επαγγελματικές πτυχές της εγκατάστασης των προσφύγων στη Θεσσαλονίκη του Μεσοπολέμου' ['Occupational Aspects of the Refugees' Establishment in Thessaloniki'], In: Ioannidou, H. (ed.), *Η μεταμόρφωση της Θεσσαλονίκης: Η εγκατάσταση των προσφύγων στην πόλη (1920–1940)* [The Transformation of Thessaloniki. The Refuges' Establishment], Thessaloniki: Epikentro (2010), 127–136.

Hekimoglou, E., *The 'Immortal Allatini': Ancestors and Relatives of Noémie Allatini-Bloch (1860–1928)*, Thessaloniki: Jewish Museum of Thessaloniki (2012).

Kalevras, A., *Αστυφιλία, Παρασιτισμός Και Μικροαστική Εγκατάστασις* [Rush to towns, Parasitism, and the Petit Bourgeois Establishment], Thessaloniki: Efimeris ton Valkanion (1930), 9.

Karpat, K., *Studies on Ottoman Social and Political History: Selected Articles and Essays*, Leiden: Brill (2002).

Kavala, M., Hekimoglou, E. and Kaplidjoglou, E., 'From the Global to a Local: The Transition of "Fratelli Allatini" from a Multi-national Enterprise Based in Ottoman Selânik to a Local Company of Greek Salonica (1906–1926)', *Paper Presented to the XVI Annual Conference of the European Business History Association*, Paris (August 30th–September 1st 2012).

Kofinas, G. N., *Τα οικονομικά της Μακεδονίας* [The Economics of Macedonia], Athens: National Printing House (1914).

Thessaloniki's class structure, 1912–1940   225

Koliopoulos, I., *Η δικτατορία του Μεταξά και ο πόλεμος του '40* [The Metaxas Dictatorship and the War of 1940], Thessaloniki: Paratiritis (1996).

Mantopoulou-Panaghiotopoulou, Th. and Hekimoglou, E., *Η Οθωμανική περίοδος: Κτηματολογικές πηγές, Θεσσαλονίκη τέλη 19ου αρχές 20ού αιώνα* [Cadastral Documents as Sources: Thessaloniki, late 19th–early 20th century], volume 2b in the series History of Entrepreneurship in Thessaloniki, vols. 1–4, Thessaloniki: Businessmen's Cultural Society for Northern Greece (2004).

Marshall, G., 'Classes in Britain: Marxist and Official', *European Sociological Review*, 4.2 (1988), 141–154.

Marx, K., *Theories of Surplus Value*, Moscow: Progress Publishers (1969).

Marx, K., *Capital*, New York: Cosimo (2007).

Mazower, M., *Salonica, City of Ghosts: Christians, Muslims and Jews, 1430–1950*, London: HarperCollins (2004).

Meron, O. C., *Jewish Entrepreneurship in Salonica, 1912–1940: An Ethnic Economy in Transition*, Eastbourne: Sussex Academic Press (2012).

Milios, J., 'Social Classes in Classical and Marxist Political Economy', *American Journal of Economics and Sociology*, 59.2 (2000), 283–302.

Moskof, K., *Θεσσαλονίκη: 1700–1912, τομή της μεταπρατικής πόλης* [Thessaloniki: Profile of a Retail City], Athens: Stochastes (1978).

Nakos, G., 'Δικαιικοί "μεταβολισμοί" της ιδιοκτησίας στις Νέες Χώρες μετά την ένταξή τους στην ελληνική επικράτεια' ['Changes in the law of Ownership in the New Lands, After their Incorporation in the Greek State'], *Πρακτικά του Συμποσίου: Η Συνθήκη του Βουκουρεστίου και η Ελλάδα* [Proceedings of the symposium: The Treaty of Bucharest and Greece], Thessaloniki: Institute for Balkan Studies (1990), 153–173.

Palamiotes, G., 'Γεωργία και κτηνοτροφία εν τη περιφερεία (καζα) Θεσσαλονίκης' ['Farming and Stock Farming in the Kaza of Thessaloniki'], *Deltion Vasilikes Georgikes Hetaireias*, 3 (1914), 79–80.

Psyroukis, N., *Ο Φασισμός και η Δικτατορία της 4 Αυγούστου* [Fascism and the Dictatorship of 4th August], Athens: Epikairotita (1974).

Robbins, L., *The Great Depression*, Auburn: The Ludwig von Mises Institute (2007) (first published 1934).

Roupa, E. and Hekimoglou, E., *Η επιχειρηματικότητα στην περίοδο 1900–1940 : Μεγάλες επιχειρήσεις και ... και επιχειρηματικές οικογένειες* [Entrepreneurship in the period 1900–1940: Large companies and businessmen families], Thessaloniki: Businessmen's Cultural Society for Northern Greece (2004).

Şaşmaz, M., 'Analysis of the Population Table of the Census of Salonica of 1903–4', *Osmanlı Tarihi Araştırma ve Uygulama Merkezi Dergisi OTAM*, 5 (1994), 349–377.

Société des Nations, *L'établissement des Réfugies en Grèce*, Geneva: League of Nations (1926).

Stanfield, J. R., *The Economic Surplus and Neo-Marxism*, London: Lexington Books (1973).

Szlajfer, H., *Economic Surplus and Surplus-value: An Attempt at Comparison*, Dar es Salaam: University of Dar es Salaam (1979).

Theodoropoulos, S., *Το Κοινωνικό Πλεονασμα. Η παραγωγή του και διάθεση. Η Περίπτωση της Ελληνικής οικονομίας και του κλάδου των μεταφορων* [The Social Surplus: Production and Consumption: the Case of the Greek Economy and the Transportation Sector] Thesis, P., University of Piraeus, Department of Shipping (1993) http://thesis.ekt.gr/2453.

Tsironis, Th., 'Επίδοξοι εθνοσωτήρες στη Θεσσαλονίκη (1925–1934)' [Would-be Nation-Saviours in Thessaloniki (1925–1934)], *Thessalonikeon Polis*, 10 (April 2003), 31–40.

226　*Evangelos Hekimoglou*

Vakalopoulos, A. E., *Ιστορία της Θεσσαλονίκης* [History of Thessaloniki], Thessaloniki: Institute for Balkan Studies (1993).

Wright, E. O., 'Class Boundaries in Advanced Capitalist Societies', *New Left Review,* 98 (1976), 3–42.

Wright, E. O., *Classes*, London: New Left Books (1985).

Yerolympos, A., *The Replanning of Thessaloniki after the Fire of 1917*, Thessaloniki: University Studio Press (1995) (second edition).

16 From the call to prayer to the silences of the museum

Salonica's soundscapes in transition

Eleni Kallimopoulou, Kostis Kornetis, and Panagiotis C. Poulos

A modern city's soundscapes[1] constitute part of its functionality as a locus of collective memory (Boyer 1996).[2] They provide access to overlapping acoustic communities that construct and experience them, and to which they are meaningful and intelligible (Schafer 1993). The various 'soundmarks'[3] of these communities (ranging from religious sound practices, such as church bells and calls to prayer, to the sounds of craftsmen and music-making) shape individual and collective identities (ethnic, gendered, religious, professional) and help community members make sense of urban culture overall (Garrioch 2003, 5–25). Salonica qualifies beyond doubt as such a modern city, having undergone over the 20th century— especially its first half—a rapid transformation of its soundscapes that both reflect and articulate the changes in its social and material fabric.[4]

Though the collapse of the Ottoman Empire and the transition to nation-states has been the subject of extensive historical research, a sensory or sound approach to this history has not been adequately explored. The current article aims to highlight aspects of this transition that reside outside literary, visual, and conceptual representations, in the sphere of the senses, and in particular of sound. More specifically, the purpose of this article is to trace those soundmarks, using a specific case study: that of Yeni Cami (1902),[5] the mosque associated with the *Dönme* community of late Ottoman Salonica, through its subsequent use as part of the web of structures for refugee aid and relief (1922–1925), and then as the first Archaeological Museum of Salonica (1925–1962).[6] Our focus is on the sound history of the building until 1940, when the museum was temporarily closed due to WWII. The changes that occurred in the soundscape of the building and its wider neighborhood, and the changes in the meanings of sounds for each specific auditory community, allow us to understand the transformed urban environment in the context of the emergence of the city's new identity, as well as the way in which the city's residents experienced this transformation. This case study points to the value of cultural listening as a tool for understanding social transformations from different subjective hearing-points. We propose this as a methodological model for approaching the history of sound in analogous transitions. Finally, a wider aim of our article is to promote a deeper understanding of the modern history of the city of Salonica and to approach the 'structure of feeling' of life in periods of transition, in Raymond Williams's famous term (2001).

228   E. Kallimopoulou, K. Kornetis, and P. C. Poulos

Call to prayer, languages, and tram horns: the soundscape of Hamidiye, 1902–1922

All accounts of late Ottoman Salonica, in particular its travelogues, mention the number of languages to be heard in the streets of the city. Few if any, however, discuss these languages in relation to the other sounds produced by social activities, as components of a soundscape that makes sense in particular ways to the people producing it. For the *Dönme* community of Salonica attached to the *Hamidiye Camii* (official name of the *Yeni Cami*, or 'new mosque'), language had always been a significant marker to distinguish between the private and public sphere, the two being historically identified with the use of Judeo-Spanish (Ladino) or Hebrew, and Ottoman Turkish and Arabic. In this respect, the *Dönme*s, unlike other communities of the city, who were bound to certain language barriers, could move freely between speech communities. For example, even if they did not publicly identify with the Ladino speech community, they recognized it as a 'sacred language'; at the same time, they identified with the 'Muslim' speech community in the use of Arabic language in the context of the mosque, and of Ottoman Turkish in their daily transactions and their newspapers. Therefore, in the case of the *Dönme*s, the notion of 'locality' differs significantly from that in all other speech communities of the city (Baer 2010, 17–18).[7]

The history of the *Dönme* community in the *Hamidiye* district is parallel to that of the *extra muros* expansion of the city to the east, following the demolition of the north-eastern walls in 1889, and to the need for settling of those affected by the fire of 1890, who were mainly Jews. In contrast to the traditional settlement pattern of the community at the borders between the Muslim and the Jewish communities, and to the internal community divisions that were reflected in the choice of specific neighborhoods within the city, the *Dönme*s of *Hamidiye* participated in a process of modern urban transformation which was dictated by social rather than strictly ethno-religious criteria (Anastassiadou 1997, 173–179, 182–187). In this process, it is mainly the wealthier members of the community, those playing an active role in the entrepreneurial life of the city, who chose to move to *Hamidiye* (Baer 2010, 50). This social group had greatly contributed to the educational life of the community, and the city in general, through the founding of schools, such as the *Terakki Mektebi*. This was a 'progressive school', as its title proclaimed, founded in 1879, with a particular emphasis on finance and commerce in its curriculum.

By 1907, the *Terakki Mektebi* had, in addition to its original premises in the city, new branches in the *Hamidiye* district (Baer 2010, 34, 50). The Yearbook of the Province of Salonica (*Selânik Vilâyeti Salnâmesi*) (1906, 263–263) lists the subjects taught at the *Yadikâr Terakki Mektebi*. In addition to Ottoman Turkish, one finds courses in Arabic and Farsi as well as French and German. For the sound historian, this is an example of a source that rather than being 'read' is being 'listened to'. The sounds of German and French, as well as of Farsi, complement in density the polyglot soundscape of the community; in addition to the use of Ladino and Ottoman Turkish, a further distinction is added by the use of French, which stands as a marker of social distinction within the community and in relation to the wider social stratification of late Ottoman Salonica (Dumon 2004, 225–244). Similarly, a wide variety of languages—including Greek, Albanian, and Bulgarian—was heard in their households due to the presence of wet-nurses, nannies, and daily helpers (e.g., Yalman 1957, 10). All this resulted in a marked hybridity.

This very vocal character of the soundscape of the *Dönmes* of *Hamidiye* should be conceived as part of the broader public soundscape. The loud sounds of the tram that regularly crossed the *Sahilhaneler* and the mosque's call to prayer that sounded five times a day implemented a certain periodicity in the everyday life of the inhabitants of the area. Yet, in *Hamidiye*, a socially and ethno-religiously diverse district, this periodicity—or better repetition, since the local press of the time is full of complaints regarding tram delays—did not mean the same to everyone. For certain inhabitants, the sound of the tram signified the very modern process of the urban expansion of the city, while for others it was simply noise, a 'sound out of place'.[8] After all, the notion of noise is culturally defined. The tram sound was conceptualized as noise due, firstly, to the antimodernizing discourse of religious elites and, secondly, to the discourse of travelers, mainly European, who were nostalgic for a serene, idyllic past (Mazower 2002).

Equally, the sound of the call to prayer structured the life of certain inhabitants, while being for others pure noise but also a powerful reminder of Muslim domination—for the Jews—and Ottoman rule—for the Greeks. For European residents who were followers of the orientalist trope vis-à-vis the city, it was a reminder of the presence of the Orient, just like the cypresses and the minarets, which shaped the skyline of the city visually. While the minaret and the tram are conceived as city landmarks, they are also soundmarks carrying specific, conflicting meanings for those who heard them. Modernity (and by consequence tradition) became the site of an acoustic struggle.

The soundscape of the Yeni Cami neighborhood was not stable, however, but ephemeral and fluid. The changes derived both from specific transformations to the anthropogeography of the neighborhood and from the wider processes of industrialization and technological progress. In 1906, for example, trams approaching the area were accompanied by people warning passers-by with horns in order to forestall accidents. An article in the *Journal de Salonique* evokes the soundscape surrounding such practices:

> The employees of the Tramway Company placed in charge of walking with their horn in front of the tram, cleaning the horse dung and clearing pedestrians out of the way, found it more relaxing to stand *on* the vehicle next to the coachman and to deafen the passengers with their obnoxious shouts and the sounds of the horns. Thus, despite the noise, passers-by don't have enough time to move aside and, consequently, too many accidents keep happening.
>
> (*Journal de Salonique*, 23 June 1906, cited in
> Τάμαριξ 1997: 6–7)

230   *E. Kallimopoulou, K. Kornetis, and P. C. Poulos*

In 1907, one year after the article in the *Journal de Salonique*, the tram ceased being drawn by horses and became electric (Anastassiadou 1997, 136).

In 1912, following the annexation of the city to the Greek Kingdom, the demography of the area changed as a significant number of Muslims left the city, followed by an increase of the Greek population in the district (Kolonas 1992, 59–65). The call to prayer addressed a shrinking community, while for the emerging dominant community the sound of the *ezan* sounded more and more incongruous, and in some cases irritating.[9] The sound was out of place in the soundscape, associated more and more with cultural difference. Although a good number of mosques were destroyed in the catastrophic fire of 1917[10] (Mazower 2004; Molho 2001, 120–133), by 1922–23 the minarets and their fate had become a favorite topic in the local press, particularly the leading Venizelist—and fiercely nationalistic—newspaper *Makedonia*. A number of articles argued for the non-necessity of minarets in Thessaloniki, their poor architectural and aesthetic value, and the 'barbaric' symbolisms they carried. One is a war chronicle from 1921, narrating a Greek soldier's traumatic experience of listening to the *ezan* in Sivri Hisar (Eski Şehir province) during the Asia Minor campaign:

> Suddenly, a voice cuts through the infinite silence like a knife. A loud and sharp voice. Yet, full of secretive harmony and grievance. It is a voice that comes from above and descends from the Sky. Lai-lalai-lalahi [...]. The city echoes with the cries of these hysteric barkers who, the more they climb up the stairs of the minaret towards the sky, the more they fall and squirm in a mire of an anti-humanitarian civilization.
>
> (*Makedonia*, 9 March 1923)

The publishing of this 'soldier's note' in the press of Salonica in 1923, almost a year after the war was over, signified that, to certain Greek sections of the local society, the call to prayer had started to sound very differently. Of course, this does not mean that reactions had not been reported in the past. As early as the times of the Young Turks, the anti-Muslim trope had started to appear, with regular reactions against the *Dönme*. However, whereas the careful minority politics of Eleftherios Venizelos had kept this tendency in check, the violent shift in the political (and geopolitical) landscape after the end of World War I rendered this tendency dominant. This dramatic reconfiguration of the semiotics of prayer meant that cultural difference was now seen as cultural dissonance, and therefore could not be tolerated and respected anymore. Nikolaos Fardis, an ultra-nationalist journalist, wrote in a similar tone:

> Who can tell me why that disgusting Hamza mosque remains on the key corner of Venizelos and Egnatia streets? Architectural value? None! Historical value? Less than none! [...] As soon as we can we must tear down the Hamza mosque.
>
> (Mazower 2004, 352)

To the Greek soldier and a section of the readership of the *Makedonia* newspaper, just like to journalists such as Fardis, the *ezan* signified neither time for prayer nor

Salonica's soundscapes in transition 231

a daily timer. Instead it meant that time had come for this already declining aural practice to be silenced once and for all.

A noisy coexistence: the refugee soundscape, 1922–1925

By the fall of 1922, the Greco-Turkish War had resulted in a massive influx of refugees from Asia Minor.[11] An estimated 1.1–1.5 million people flooded the Greek Kingdom, transforming dramatically the country's urban and rural social fabric (Katsapis 2011; Hirschon 2003; Pentzopoulos 2002; Clogg 2002). As a large number of refugees were placed strategically in Macedonia (Mazower 2004), the once predominant Jewish community—40% of the city's population in 1912—was decisively outnumbered by the Greek Orthodox community (Fleming 2010, 86).[12]

Those who arrived at the port of Salonica, with the aid of the various relief organizations or on their own initiative, found temporary shelter wherever they could, including in churches, synagogues, and mosques. This practice, common also after the Second Balkan War, caused considerable friction between the religious communities and the Greek authorities. Many families ended up sharing a single space, often for months or even years. Some village and neighborhood communities or families arrived together and were sheltered together; others were separated and found themselves scattered across Greece. Among the refugees, local dialects of Greek, Pontic Greek, and Turkish prevailed.

The soundscape of the Yeni Cami neighborhood was thus transformed:[13] first by the absence of the voice of the *muezzin* (the minaret itself would be demolished a few years later); second by a speech community in which Greek would eventually prevail. The surrounding area hosted a web of private and public facilities for refugee relief that also left their sonic imprint on the soundscape. In 1923, a wooden booth was erected at the square of Yeni Cami for the distribution of bread by the American Red Cross (*Makedonia*, 5 March 1923). During the same year, Yeni Cami was one of the points where the state census was conducted, of the refugee families who arrived after 1914. Through announcements posted in the daily press, the Chief of the Relief Service invited all 'heads of family, men or, in the absence of men, women' to present themselves with their refugee documents in hand to the census offices (*Makedonia*, 6 April 1923). The bread distribution outlet of Yeni Cami was used also by the state Relief Service for the distribution of a subsidy to refugee heads of family, and for the distribution of bedding to those in greatest need. Women who had come to register for the census or receive the relief distribution if they qualified as heads of family were the protagonists of an incident that unfolded at the Yeni Cami in August 1924.[14] The women's committee that had rallied a few days earlier in support of the return of prisoners and non-combatants still detained in Turkey, invited all those with relatives held hostage in Turkey to join the cause by sending letters to the Yeni Cami (*Makedonia*, 9 August 1924).

In the interior of the mosques and similar structures used as shelters for the refugees, the soundscape bore the signs of forced coexistence. In 1922, sound became central in defining the multiple spatialities of such buildings. What is more, the borders between private and public were blurred and rendered fluid. As numerous oral testimonies of refugees indicate, families hung pieces of cloth and rugs, or piled up sacks to partition the interiors of public buildings in order to achieve a degree of privacy and isolation. Yet the visual compartmentalization of space achieved by such improvised techniques with the help of material objects was far from soundproof. One interview is quite telling:

> We had difficulties in the tents. We used sacks to separate ourselves from each other, and from there what they said we too could hear. Sometimes they were decent people and they didn't talk and we didn't talk. Sometimes we quarrelled, we made [...] We had no isolation. In the tents one could hear everything.[15]

Here, sound tells a different story from sight: although spatial separation was achieved visually, the sounds and smells circulated rather freely and defined a different, porous condition of living together. Anthropologist David Howes has aptly noted the plurality of sensory regimes that can be generated from the interaction of the senses:

> The senses are not always in agreement with each other. At times, conflicting messages are conveyed by different sensory channels, and certain domains of sensory expression and experience are suppressed in favour of others.
>
> (Howes 2003, xxii)

This observation brings to the fore the recent theoretical discussion on 'intersensorality' (Smith 2007) or 'multisensorality' especially in the fields of sensory history and anthropology of the senses.[16] The critique to ocularcentrism (or visual bias) as a defining feature of modernity, came together with the realization that the pre-modernist era assigned an important role to vision, while touch, sound, smell, and taste continued to be significant bearers of meaning (Denney 2011, 601–616). Thus, we need to address how the senses work together in particular times and places rather than conduct separate analyses of each sense in isolation (Cockayne 2007). The plural ways in which sound and smell travel through space, bringing with them some of the most personal aspects of daily life, cancel out, in some sense, the distinction between 'private' and 'public'. In particular, the separation between visual and aural/olfactory sensory experience, perceptible via historical attention to the full range of the sensorium, displays the specific 'in between' regime—between individual and common, private and public—under which the refugees lived during their temporary residence in public buildings.

A silent 'Kaiadas' for antiquities: the Archaeological Museum, 1925–1940

Nineteen twenty-five was a crucial year for the monument and its soundscape. In that year, following a long-standing demand by archaeologists Giorgos Oikonomou and Efstratios Pelekidis, the decision was made to turn the Yeni Cami

Salonica's soundscapes in transition   233

into the city's first archaeological museum (Vokotopoulou 1986). After the rejection of a number of public buildings—the Rotunda included (Vokotopoulou 1986, 6)—Yeni Cami was selected, partly due to the fact that it was not affected by the great fire that had devastated the city center in 1917, partly due to the fact that it was a relatively novel space, and partly due to the eclectic characteristics in its architecture that rendered it supposedly more 'European' in nature. The building was assigned by the General Office of Exchange to the Ephorate of Antiquities of Salonica (Vokotopoulou 1986).

Despite all this rationale behind it, the decision to use this space as an archaeological museum is paradoxical. Archaeological museums function as the 'temples of the nation', to use archaeologist Yannis Hamilakis's apt description. In this case, however, the space used for this purpose was itself a temple, with all the historical, cultural, and semantic baggage attached. Hamilakis has pointed out the religious undertones in preserving antiquities in Greece as part of a wider sacralization of the past (Hamilakis 2007, 46–48), which makes the use of a former religious building towards that end in the case of Yeni Cami even more striking. It was a sure way to 'hellenize' the monument by re-writing its basic function and therefore 'cleansing' it from its past connotations, just like in the cases of other Ottoman buildings that changed function, such as the *Dioikitirio* [administrative building], the *Stratigeio* [military headquarters], and the *Teloneio* [customs].

Following on that argument, one might argue that even though the choice of Yeni Cami to shelter Greek antiquities was an act of secularization within the context of the modernizing task of the Greek state, the original worship place was preserved while the 'religious community changed'. The fact that Manolis Andronikos, the foremost Greek archaeologist of the second half of the 20th century, a figure Hamilakis calls a 'shaman' since he blurred the boundaries between archaeology and the supernatural, worked in this museum, adds to the validity of this argument (Hamilakis 2007, 162–167). At the same time, one cannot but think that the decision to house the Pedagogical Academy or '*Didaskaleion*' in the mansion of Mehmed Hayri Pasha, Ottoman commander of the Third Army Corps, a man with *Dönme* leanings (Theologou 2008), which happened to be across the street, was part of a wider project of 'hellenization' by giving this particular quarter a central cultural function. The fact that the city center remained destroyed and relatively dead throughout the interwar period rendered the 'hellenization' of the most bourgeois and Europeanized quarter almost imperative.

The 1926 refurbishment of Yeni Cami constituted a signpost in its history. In the context of the transition from a formerly religious building to a museum and with the interlude of diverse soundscape of the refugee shelter, the refurbishment acted as a rite of passage from one usage to the next. As in a large variety of rituals, this one included sound and silencing in a ceremonial catharsis that would render this monument compatible with the hegemonic national narrative, to paraphrase Yannis Hamilakis's comment on the Acropolis (Hamilakis 2007, 87–93). The detailed record of the conversion of the Yeni Cami into the first archaeological museum of Salonica described among other work the removal of

234   *E. Kallimopoulou, K. Kornetis, and P. C. Poulos*

the pulpit, the *minbar*, from where the preacher (*vâiz*) of the mosque performed his sermons and its transfer to Hagia Sofia, one of the city's most important Orthodox churches.[17] The significance of this document for sketching the sound history of this particular building is far greater than the epilogue to the story of Islamic prayer practice in the city: it narrates the story of the major demographic shift that had taken place in the first quarter of the 20th century in the city and consequently in this specific neighborhood, following a series of major political events. In other words, it tells the story of the major shift in the religious sound-scape of the city.

In order to make sense, the document of the extraction of the *minbar* needs to be cross-read with other documents, legal ones in particular. One is the *Convention of Athens*, signed by Greece and the Ottoman Empire in 1913, defining the legal status of the Muslim community of Macedonia after the latter's integration into the Greek Kingdom the previous year (*Gazette*, 14 November 1913, nr. 229). This document describes the right of the Muslim community to public exercise of its religious duties, as well as to appoint its religious leaders, including the positions of *mufti* and *imam*. This legal document testifies to the survival of the sound-life of the *minbar* after 1913. Yet, in the same document, this privilege was regulated by a subsequent article (protocol no. 3, article 1) that stated that the Ottoman state lost any right over mosques that were originally Orthodox churches. In Thessaloniki this applied to the major mosques of the historical center that, right after the integration of the city to the Greek Kingdom, were turned back into churches. Therefore, this legal document implemented the marginalization of Islamic ritual in the public space and consequently in the religious public soundscape of the city. Hence, the sound practices associated with the *minbar* were also marginalized.

Of particular importance for understanding the context of the minbar's removal are Law 2345 of 1920 (*Gazette*, 3 July 1920, nr. 148) on the administration of the property of the Muslim communities of the Greek state, and the Treaty of Lausanne that ended the Greco-Turkish war and stipulated the population exchange between the two countries' Christian and Muslim communities.[18] This put an end to the centuries-long presence of Muslims in Salonica and consequently to their imprint on the public religious soundscape of the city.[19] A cross-reading of administrative and legal documents facilitates understanding of how a specific sound practice, which was politically regulated and implemented, left its trace on archived documents and written texts.

As sound historians, we felt challenged by the task of exploring that space in the full picture inhabited by those who did not necessarily have a voice in legal documents. This challenge relates to how the members of the Muslim and/ or *Dönme* community of Salonica experienced this massive shift in their auditory world. This question takes more than legal documents in order to be answered. It takes for example the analysis of inscriptions. The function of inscriptions, which derives from their transitional life-stories, extends far beyond their monumental status. This issue has been discussed in detail by Yannis Hamilakis with reference to the establishment of archaeology in modern Greece.[20]

Salonica's soundscapes in transition 235

Among the preserved epigraphic elements of the Yeni Cami that can direct us is an inscription on one of the two fountains in the mosque courtyard. The three-line inscription reads:

> We made every living thing from water (*Qur'an* 21:30)
> Salonica Telegraph and Post ex-director
> El-Haj Agâh Beg from Serres, his charitable gift

> (Dimitriadis 1983, 335)

The centrality of water, underscored in this inscription, is hard to overlook. Two foreign visitors to Thessaloniki in 1921 noted the sound of the water in the fountain in their description of mosques:

> The ablution fountain, capacious and imposing, trickles with a refreshing sound and the wide open door shows the way to an interior which by its shade and cooler atmosphere affords a pleasing contrast to the glare and dust of the street.

> (Goff and Fawcett 1921, 195–196)

To these two Englishmen the sound of the water alluded to a specific sensation, expressed by the term 'refreshing'. This sensation carried on into their overall impression of the place. This particular inscription (in its rather short history) partook in another ritual; that of the conversion of the mosque into a museum. Among the works listed in the refurbishment of 1926 was also 'the destruction of the two fountains'.[21]

One could safely argue that the ritual destruction of the fountains equaled the 'hiding' or 'deleting' of an archive (Papailias 2005, 17), or more precisely its 'silencing' or its decontextualization (Hamilakis 2007). Despite all this, the inscription was preserved—presumably on the premises of the museum—as a monumental plaque, a relic of the Ottoman history of the building. Yet, even in its new displaced position 'within the archive', the inscription was subjected to all the 'nontextual' or 'antitextual' acts that followed its deposition in the archive, as it was examined, photographed, transcribed, published, and disseminated, to mention but a few of its subsequent treatments and afterlives (Papailias 2005, 17).

The transformation of this site in terms of aural practice and collective memory was not only the result of legal and administrative acts on an elite level. The neighborhood was transformed by the sweeping demographic changes brought about by the arrival of the refugees. The gradual exodus of a significant number of its Jewish population towards France, Italy, and Switzerland during the 1920s intensified this transformation (Mazower 2004; Pierron 1996). Consequently, the Yeni Cami could hardly hold the same signifiers anymore. As Mark Mazower aptly put it: 'by 1930, only a small proportion of Salonica's inhabitants could remember the city as it had existed in the days of [Sultan] Abdul Hamid' (2004, 331)—and this applies to the inhabitants of the quarter surrounding our monument.[22]

236   *E. Kallimopoulou, K. Kornetis, and P. C. Poulos*

Equally noteworthy, however, is the fact that despite the grandiose plans by local authorities to appropriate the ancient past of the city and region, the archaeological museum in Yeni Cami functioned more as a warehouse than anything else.[23] It was a dispirited space with hardly any visitors or exhibits until the 1950s, even though an entrance ticket was introduced in 1931 (Vokotopoulou 1986, 10). The condition of this ghost museum was so dire that a local newspaper castigated it as a highly unsuitable space to host the antiquities:

> No, this is not a Museum, this is a Kaiadas (pit of destruction), since so many treasures remain imprisoned and unknown, far from the light and the public, rotting, lost, destroyed. It is a disgrace, since the responsible officials hide these treasures just like the *Kizlar Agas* hid their harems, they squirrel them away like misers hoard their gold.
>
> (Vokotopoulou 1986, 10)

In this respect not only did the museum effectively camouflage and therefore silence the space's former functions but it was gradually transformed from a multi-sonorous milieu to a silent dead space—a 'Kaiadas'—despite its purpose of guarding part of the nation's 'symbolic capital' (Hamilakis and Yalouri 1999).

In the 1940s, another level was added to the above-mentioned process of silencing that prevailed in the building's history. The head of the Ephorate of Antiquities of Thessaloniki, Nikolaos Kotzias, with Charalambos Makaronas and other archaeologists, was placed in charge of the task of securing the antiquities against possible damage or loss due to the outbreak of WWII. The majority of the antiquities was buried in the city, to see the light of day again only in 1951 and finally in 1953, when a large exhibition took place in the building under the direction of Makaronas and Andronikos (Vokotopoulou 1986, 12–17).

While the shift in use of the Yeni Cami from refugee aid and relief to Archaeological Museum silenced a significant part of the recent social and cultural history of the building and the surrounding area, it also inaugurated a new sensory phase: namely, that produced by the new 'inhabitants' of the building. This new phase is interwoven with the life stories of the members of the Archaeological Ephorate and their paperwork, the archaeologists and technicians who moved around and catalogued the antiquities, the guards, and all those who occupied for longer or shorter periods the additional premises in the courtyard. The new soundscape produced by this complex network of people is to be studied in relation to the institutional principles and ideology of the museum, as these were conceived and spelled out at the time. Such an approach has a lot to offer the documentation and understanding of the sensory history of the antiquities hosted in the building and consequently of the history of archaeology and its relation to local and national politics in modern Greece in general. Ten years after the first exhibition, in 1962, a new Archaeological Museum was inaugurated in the city center—symbolically on the 50th anniversary of the city's 'liberation'—providing more space and less silence to a larger public, including a narrative regarding the past that was much more linear, more

Salonica's soundscapes in transition 237

homogenous, and less fragmented than that of the Yeni Cami and its various afterlives.

This article tried to underline the importance of sound and of aural perception in the articulation of social, class, and ethnic identities as well as in processes of modernization and secularization. In the words of ethnomusicologist Veit Erlmann:

> Hearing Culture suggests that it is possible to conceptualize new ways of knowing a culture and of gaining a deepened understanding of how the members of a society know each other. It is not only by accumulating a body of interrelated texts, signifiers, and symbols that we get a sense of the relationships and tensions making up a society. The ways in which people relate to each other through the sense of hearing also provide important insights into a wide range of issues confronting societies around the world as they grapple with the massive changes wrought by modernization, technologization, and globalization.
>
> (Erlmann 2004, 3)

We have tried to challenge the hegemonic narrative regarding the transition from empire to nation-state in Greece, demonstrating through the focus on soundscapes that multilingualism and cultural diversity not only survived but were often intensified, despite the official discourse regarding homogenization after 1922. The arrival of the refugees to the city did not necessarily denote its 'Hellenization' in terms of the linguistic landscape, since they brought with them Turkish, Pontic, and various local dialects. Instead of the 'Hellenization' of the soundscape, therefore, the result was a new form of 'multiculturalism', at least in as far as senses were concerned. Furthermore, parallel to our attempt to demonstrate through the historicization of the experience of sound the disjuncture that secularization and modernization brought about, we also tried to stress the importance of intersensorality—pointing to the crucial role of the relation between the senses in arriving to an alternative narration to the one of the image or the printed word. In terms of the studies of sound, this article asserts the usefulness of an intersensory or multisensory approach in historical and cultural inquiry, promoting the use of a different, so far understudied, theoretical tool for the study of the past.

Notes

1 This article is based on research carried out in the context of the research project entitled *Learning Culture through City Soundscapes*, which was funded by the John S. Latsis Public Benefit Foundation (http://sound-cities.turkmas.uoa.gr/). We are grateful to Spyros Tsipidis for his valuable contribution throughout the entire duration of this project, and to Paris Papamichos-Chronakis and Olga Touloumi for their valuable feedback and very thoughtful comments on a previous version of the manuscript. Thanks also goes to Alexandra Karadimou-Yerolympou for her important bibliographical suggestions. The sole responsibility for the content, nevertheless, lies with its authors.

2 The term 'soundscape' was originally coined by Canadian composer Murray Schafer ([1977] 1993) to describe 'the sonic environment', or the total experienced acoustic environment including all noises, and musical, natural, and technological sounds. The concept was subsequently taken up as an analytical tool by scholars from a range of disciplines with an interest in the study of culture, to denote 'an auditory or aural landscape', which 'like a landscape, is simultaneously a physical environment and a way of perceiving that environment; it is both a world and a culture constructed to make sense of that world' (Thompson 2002, 1). In this respect, this article focuses on sound and sound perception as a culturally constructed experience, placing emphasis on the ways that people listen to and understand sounds.

3 The term is analogue to 'landmarks' and refers to the sound of a community which has such properties as make it particularly recognizable by the members of that community (Schafer 1993, 10).

4 For a general history of the city, see Mazower 2004 and Hasiotis 1997. For the history of Salonica in the Ottoman period, see Moskof 1974, Dimitriadis 1983, and, especially for the later period, Anastassiadou 2008, 173–179 and Thémopoulou 2005, 343–348. For the social and urban transformation of the city during the first half of the 20th century, see Karadimou-Yerolympou 1995.

5 The Yeni Cami, an extraordinary monument of late-Ottoman architectural eclecticism, was built in 1902 by the Italian architect Vitaliano Poselli (1838–1918). For the history and architecture of the building, see Kolonas and Papamathaiaki 1980; Kolonas 2014, 176–179; Sabanopoulou 2008, 226–228. Also see Poselli 2002.

6 The Yeni Cami was built to cover the religious needs of the Ma'min community (Judeo-Spanish-speaking Muslim converts) of Salonica, known also as Donmedes (Tr. dönme; convert). See Poulos 2017; Mazower 2004, 75–79; Georgeon 1994, 117–130. For a recent articulate study on the history of the Dönme, see Baer 2010, as well as Papamichos-Chronakis 2011.

7 The language issue of the Dönme community remains disputed and requires further research. For the purposes of the present analysis it is worth considering the following information. According to Nikos Stavroulakis, the Yakobi branch were in general only Ottoman-Turkish speaking, while the Karakash might have retained Judezmo or some form of it at home. Also by the 19th century there was no interaction between Jews and Dönme and therefore less opportunity to keep Judezmo alive. However, Stavroulakis points out that in the context of business it may well be that the men used Judezmo. We are indebted to Paris Papamichos-Chronakis for sharing with us this piece of information.

8 A phrase coined by the cultural historian Peter Bailey, from a description by anthropologist Mary Douglas of dirt as 'matter out of place'; Weiner 2013, 4.

9 In greater depth regarding the function of mosques, their personnel, and their sound presence in the city's public space during this transitional period, see Kallimopoulou and Poulos 2015, 241–270.

10 List of Muslim community buildings destroyed by the Great Fire of 1917, Office of the Mufti of Thessaloniki, 24/12/1918. ΓΑΚ-IAM, GRGSA-IAM_ADM001.01.F000028

11 For the changes effected by the exchange of populations to Salonica's soundscape and the ways in which it was perceived, as well as the uses of the religious buildings, such as churches and mosques, for the temporary housing of refugees, and the political dimensions of these uses in the transformation of the city's physiognomy, see Kallimopoulou and Poulos 2015.

12 Despite its gradual weakening in this period, the Jewish community continued to maintain a strong presence in the public space. In the context of this article, it was not possible to examine this central dimension of the auditory history of the city. For the Jewish community of Salonica at the end of the Ottoman period, see Veinstein 1994; Molho 2014; Naar 2016.

Salonica's soundscapes in transition 239

13 Part of the following material appears in Kallimopoulou and Poulos 2015, 261–264.
14 For a discussion of the gendered auditory and sensorial dimensions of the refugee housing, see Kallimopoulou 2016, 151–168.
15 Oral testimony of Georgios Zografos; *Historical Archive of Refugee Hellenism of the Municipality of Kalamaria*, Oral Testimonies Archive. Thessaloniki, 20 September 1994. Interviewer Eleni Ioannidou. In our research at the Oral Testimonies Archive, we located a number of testimonies of people who found temporary shelter in tents and public buildings, though not specifically in Yeni Cami. Even so, such testimonies possibly reflect similar experiences of people who had to share indoor, undivided space.
16 For a more in-depth examination of the temporary refugee housing through the prism of intersensorality and the role that memory carries out in the sensory experience, see Kallimopoulou 2016.
17 Ministry of Transport, Public Works Directorate, Budget for the restoration of the Yeni Cami mosque [Προϋπολογισμός της Απαιτουμένης Δαπάνης δια την Επισκευήν του Τεμένους Γενί Τζαμί χρησιμοποιημένου ως Μουσείου] 1926, Yeni Cami File, 1926, Archive of the 16th Ephorate of Antiquities, Thessaloniki. Regarding the removal of the *minbar* and its transfer to Hagia Sophia see also document nr. 906 from the Ephorate of Antiquities of Macedonia to the Director of the Refugee Bank, 25 June 1926, in Mortgage Service Archive—Ministry of Finance, file 4154.
18 For a thorough overview of the relation and status of the Muslim communities of Greece and the state, see Tsitselikis 2012.
19 The gradual exodus of the city's Muslim population had already started after 1912–1913, with the Balkan Wars; Mazower 2004.
20 Hamilakis points to the central role of the materiality of inscriptions in the process of the sacralization of the classical past in modern Greece. In this process, inscriptions come at the center of a ritual by archaeologists and members of the national intelligentsia, invoking the multi-sensory and synaesthetic dimension of material culture (Hamilakis 2007, 9).
21 Ministry of Transport, Public Works Directorate, Budget for the restoration of the Yeni Cami mosque [Προϋπολογισμός της Απαιτουμένης Δαπάνης δια την Επισκευήν του Τεμένους Γενί Τζαμί χρησιμοποιημένου ως Μουσείου] 1926, Yeni Cami File, 1926, Archive of the 16th Ephorate of Antiquities, Thessaloniki.
22 This does not imply, however, an entire eradication of the past since important survivals remained. The sheer fact that the monument retained both names in everyday parlance, namely is referred to interchangeably as Yeni Cami and Old Archaeological Museum to the present day, demonstrates that survival of the Ottoman past had penetrated the everyday linguistic practices and the experience of the city.
23 For the archaeological projects of the new rulers of the city also see Davis 2000.

References

Anastassiadou, M., *Salonique 1830–1912: Une ville ottomane à l'âge des Réformes*, Leiden: E. J. Brill (2008).
Baer, M. D., *The Dönme: Jewish Converts, Muslim Revolutionaries, and Secular Turks*, Stanford, CA: Stanford University Press (2010).
Boyer, C., *City of Collective Memory. Its Historical Imagery and Architectural Entertainments*, Cambridge, MA: MIT (1996).
Clogg, R., *A Concise History of Greece*, Cambridge: Cambridge University Press, [1992] (2002).
Cockayne, E., *Hubbub: Filth, Noise and Stench in England, 1600–1770*, New Haven, CT/London: Yale University Press (2007).

240   *E. Kallimopoulou, K. Kornetis, and P. C. Poulos*

Davis, J. L., 'Warriors for the Fatherland: National Consciousness and Archaeology in Barbarian Epirus and Verdant Ionia, 1912–22', *Journal of Mediterranean Archaeology*, 13.1 (2000), 76–98.

Denney, P., 'Looking Back, Groping Forward: Rethinking Sensory History', *Review Essay, Rethinking History*, 15.4 (2011), 601–616.

Dimitriadis, V., *Η Τοπογραφία της Θεσσαλονίκης κατά την Εποχή της Τουρκοκρατίας, 1430– 1912* [The Topography of Thessaloniki Under the Turks, 1430–1912], Thessaloniki: Etairia Makedonikon Spoudon (1983).

Dumont, P., 'Τα γαλλικά πάνω απ'όλα', In: Veinstein, G. (ed.), *Θεσσαλονίκη, 1850–1918: Η 'πόλη των Εβραίων' και η αφύπνιση των Βαλκανίων*, Athens: Ekati (2004), 225–244 [= 'Le Français d'Abord'. In: Veinstein, G. (ed.), *Salonique, 1850–1918: La "ville des Juifs" et le reveil des Balkans*, Paris: Editions Autrement (1992)]

Erlmann, V., 'But What of the Ethnographic Ear? Anthropology, Sound, and the Senses', In: Erlmann, V. (ed.), *Hearing Cultures. Essays on Sound, Listening, and Modernity*, Oxford/New York: Berg (2004), 1–20.

Fleming, K. E., *Greece: A Jewish History*, Princeton, NJ: Princeton University Press (2008).

Garrioch, D., 'Sounds of the City: The Soundscape of Early Modern European Towns', *Urban History*, 30.1 (2003), 5–25.

Gazette of the Kingdom of Greece, Athens: National Printing Office.

Georgeon, F., 'Η 'Σελανίκ' των μουσουλμάνων και των ντονμέδων' [Salonique musulmane et deunmè], In: Veinstein, G. (ed.), *Θεσσαλονίκη 1850–1918. Η 'πόλη των Εβραίων' και η αφύπνιση των Βαλκανίων [Salonique, 1850-1918: La ville des Juifs et le réveil des Balkans]* (Kalamantis, G. tr.), Athens: Ekati [1992] (1994), 117–130.

Goff, A. and Fawcett, H. A., *Macedonia. A Plea for the Primitive*, London: John Lane and Bodley Head (1921).

Hamilakis, Y. and Yalouri, E., 'Sacralising the Past. Cults of Archaeology in Modern Greece', *Archaeological Dialogues*, 6.2 (1999), 115–135.

Hamilakis, Y., *The Nation and its Ruins: Antiquity, Archaeology, and National Imagination in Greece*, Oxford: Oxford University Press (2007).

Hasiotis, I. (ed.), *Τοις Αγαθοίς Βασιλεύουσα Θεσσαλονίκη: ιστορία και πολιτισμός* [Salonica, Capital of the Good: history and culture]. Thessaloniki: Paratiritis (1997).

Hirschon, R., (ed.) *Crossing the Aegean. An Appraisal of the 1923 Compulsory Population Exchange between Greece and Turkey*. New York/Oxford: Berghahn Books (2003).

Howes, D., *Sensual Relations: Engaging the Senses in Culture and Social Theory*, Ann Arbor, MI: University of Michigan Press (2003).

Journal de Salonique twice-weekly French-language newspaper, Thessaloniki (1895–1910).

Kallimopoulou, E. and Poulos, P. C., 'Ανταλλάξιμα κτήρια, σιωπηλές κληρονομιές: Η προσωρινή εγκατάσταση των Μικρασιατών προσφύγων και τα ισλαμικά τεμένη της Θεσσαλονίκης' , *Bulletin of the Center for Asia Minor Studies*, 19 (2015), 241–270.

Kallimopoulou, E. '"Ακούω-βλέπω-σιωπώ": Αισθητηριακή ιστορία και προφορικές μαρτυρίες στη Θεσσαλονίκη των προσφύγων' [Listen, Watch, Keep Quiet: Sensory history and oral testimony in refugee Thessaloniki], In: van Boeschoten, R. et al. (eds.), *Η μνήμη αφηγείται την πόλη ... Προφορική ιστορία αι η μνήμη του αστικού χώρου*, Athens: Plethron (2016), 151–168.

Karadimou-Yerolympou, A., *Η ανοικοδόμηση της Θεσσαλονίκης μετά την πυρκαγιά του 1917* [The Reconstruction of Thessaloniki after the Fire of 1917], Thessaloniki: University Studio Press (1995).

Katsapis, K., 'Το προσφυγικό ζήτημα' ['The refugee issue'], In: Liakos, A. (ed.), *Το 1922 και οι πρόσφυγες. Μια νέα ματιά* [1922 and the Refugees: A New Look], Athens: Nefeli (2011), 125–170.

Kolonas, V. S. and Papamathaiaki, L. G., *Ο αρχιτέκτονας Vitaliano Poselli* [Vitaliano Poselli, the architect], Thessaloniki: Paratiritis (1980).

Kolonas, V., *Η Θεσσαλονίκη εκτός των τειχών. Εικονογραφία της συνοικίας των εξοχών 1885–1912* [Thessaloniki Outside the Walls: Iconography of a Suburban Neighbourhood 1885–1912], PhD dissertation, Aristotelian University of Thessaloniki (1992), reprinted Thessaloniki: University Studio Press (2014).

Makedonia daily newspaper, Thessaloniki A Vellidis (1911–).

Mazower, M., 'Travellers and the Oriental City, c. 1840–1920', *Transactions of the Royal Historical Society*, Sixth Series, 12 (December 2002), 59–111.

Mazower, M., *Salonica: City of Ghosts, Christians, Muslims and Jews, 1430–1950*, London: HarperCollins (2004).

Molho, R., *Οι Εβραίοι της Θεσσαλονίκης 1856–1919. Μια ιδιαίτερη κοινότητα* [The Jews of Thessaloniki 1856–1919], Athens: Patakis [2001] (2014).

Moskof, K., *Θεσσαλονίκη: τομή της μεταπρατικής πόλης* [Salonica: Turning point of the comprador city]. Athens: Stohastis (1974).

Naar, D., *Jewish Salonica: Between the Ottoman Empire and Modern Greece*. Stanford: Stanford University Press (2016).

Papailias, P., *Genres of Recollection. Archival Poetics and Modern Greece*, New York: Palgrave Macmillan (2005).

Papamichos-Chronakis, P., *Οι έλληνες, εβραίοι, μουσουλμάνοι και ντονμέ έμποροι της Θεσσαλονίκης, 1882–1919. Ταξικοί και εθνοτικοί μετασχηματισμοί σε τροχιά εξελληνισμού* [Greeks, Jews, Muslims and Donme merchants of Thessaloniki, 1882–1919], Unpublished doctoral dissertation, Rethymno: University of Crete (2011).

Pentzopoulos, D., *The Balkan Exchange of Minorities and its Impact on Greece*, London: Hurst & Company, [1962] (2002).

Pierron, B., *Juifs et Chrétiens de la Grèce Moderne: Histoire des relations intercommunautaires de 1821 à 1945*, Paris: Editions L'Harmattan (1996).

Poselli, Z., *Ο Vitaliano Poselli της Θεσσαλονίκης. Η ζωή και το έργο του μεγάλου αρχι τέκτονα μέσα από το χειρόγραφο της εγγονής του* [Vitaliano Poselli of Thessaloniki: The life and work of the great architect through the manuscript of his grand-daughter], Thessaloniki: University Studio Press (2002).

Poulos, Panagiotis C., Challenging soundscapes: voicing the *müezzins* and *kayyıms* of late Ottoman Salonica's mosques, Unpublished paper, presented in the International Conference of Ottoman Social and Economic History, University of Sofia, St. Kliment Ohridski, 24–28 July 2017, Sofia, Bulgaria.

Qur'an: A New Translation, (tr. Muhammad Abdel-Haleem) Oxford: Oxford University Press (2004).

Sabanopoulou, L., 'Yeni Cami (aka Old Archaeological Museum)', In: Brouskari, E. (ed.), *Ottoman Architecture in Greece*, Athens: Ministry of Culture, Directorate of Byzantine and Post-Byzantine Antiquities (2008), 226–229.

Salname (Selânik Vilâyeti Salnâmesi) [Salonica vilayet almanac], Selânik: Hamidiye Mekteb-i Sanayi Matbaası (1324/1906).

Schafer, M. R., *The Soundscape. Our Sonic Environment and the Tuning of the World*, Rochester, VT: Destiny Books (1993).

Smith, M. M., *Sensing the Past: Seeing, Hearing, Smelling, Tasting, and Touching in History*, Berkeley, CA: University of California Press (2007).

242 *E. Kallimopoulou, K. Kornetis, and P. C. Poulos*

Thémopoulou, É.,'Les élites urbaines a l'époque du Tanzimat: Le Cas de Saloniques', In: Anastasopoulos, A. (ed.), *Provincial Elites in the Ottoman Empire*, Rethymno: Crete University Press (2005), 343–348.

Theologou, K., *Χώρος και Μνήμη: Θεσσαλονίκη 15ος-20ός αι.: Από τις παραδοσιακές κοινότητες στην αστική νεοτερικότητα [Space and memory: Thessaloniki 15th-20th c.: from traditional communities to urban modernity]*, Thessaloniki, University Studio Press (2008).

Thompson, E., *The Soundscape of Modernity: Architectural Acoustics and the Culture of Listening in America, 1900–1933*, Cambridge, MA/London: MIT (2002).

Tsitselikis, K., *Old and New Islam in Greece. From Historical Minorities to Immigrant Newcomers*, Leiden: Brill (2012).

Veinstein, G. (ed.), *Θεσσαλονίκη 1850–1918. Η 'πόλη των Εβραίων' και η αφύπνιση των Βαλκανίων [Salonique, 1850-1918: La ville des Juifs et le réveil des Balkans]* (trans. Giorgos Kalamantis), Athens: Ekati [1992] (1994).

Vokotopoulou, I., 'Τα πρώτα 50 χρόνια της εφορείας κλασσικών αρχαιοτήτων Θεσσαλονίκης' [The first 50 years of the Eforeia of Classical Antiquities, Thessaloniki], In: *Proceedings of the Conference Η Θεσσαλονίκη μετά το 1912*, (1–3 November 1985), Thessaloniki: Municipality of Thessaloniki (1986), 1–65.

Weiner, I., *Religion Out Loud: Religious Sound, Public Space, and American Pluralism*, New York: NYU Press (2013).

Williams, R., *The Long Revolution*, 1961. Reprint, London: Broadview Press (2001).

Yalman, A. E., *Turkey in My Time*, Norman, OK: Oklahoma University Press (1957).

17 The Muslims of Thessaloniki, 1912–2012

A discontinuous and uncomfortable presence

Konstantinos Tsitselikis

Introduction

The transition from Ottoman to Greek rule put the Muslims of northern Greece in a difficult position. This essay describes the institutional position of the Muslim community of Thessaloniki during the first years of Greek administration before the 1923 exchange of Greek and Turkish populations.[1] It then takes up the re-emergence of a Muslim community after a decades-long interruption, due to migration from the Middle East since the 1980s but especially after 2000, with the arrival of immigrants and refugees from Asia and Africa. This new Islamic presence appears under completely different circumstances than those that fostered Ottoman Islam in Thessaloniki. The Muslims of Thessaloniki left their homes as refugees in 1924. The new Muslim inhabitants of the city, almost a century later, are refugees as well, victims of poverty and war in their own countries.

Starting from the legal framework imposed by Islam, this essay examines the constitutional, social, financial, and ideological relations between majority and minority as they evolved during the transition from Ottoman to Greek administration. It attempts to shed light on a Muslim Thessaloniki that has been obscured due to its connection with the national 'other'. It also sets out to sketch the future of the city that seems once again to have been enriched—through gradual, steady migration—with a subtle Islamic element.

The present article derives from a larger study that examines the legal position of Muslim communities in Greece from the founding of the Greek state up to the present (Tsitselikis 2012). The sources, which patiently await the researchers who will exploit them in depth, are to be found in the archives of the Governorate General of Macedonia, the Eleftherios Venizelos archives, the archives of the Ministry of Foreign Affairs, various regional General State Archives, and particularly in the archives of the *Vakif* Administration in Ankara, which are almost unexplored but very promising.

It is no accident that the Muslim community of Thessaloniki under Greek administration (before and after the population exchange) has rarely been discussed (Mazower 2004; Hekimoglou 1996; Glavinas 2013; Dagkas 1998; Kandylakis 1998). The minimal scientific engagement with Muslim Thessaloniki probably reflects a hegemonic ideological selection of research topics, which

244 *Konstantinos Tsitselikis*

ultimately restricts the scientific community. It is particularly interesting to perceive Thessaloniki through its past and to project it to its present and future while focusing on the city's Muslim character: how this character remains invisible, how it imposes the use of certain terms, how it forms certain identities and blends together, how it harbours false nostalgia through a pathology of memory of simultaneous shared and multiple realities.[2]

Muslims in the Greek state

To understand what happened in 1912, when the relationship of sovereignty between the administration and the Muslim population was suddenly reversed, one must take into account the previous experience in Old Greece. Apart from the surviving Muslim community of Evia, the modern Greek state's first contact with a sizeable Muslim population occurred in 1881 with the annexation of Thessaly. Almost 40,000 Muslims acquired Greek citizenship, under a special legal status that would now be considered one of minority protection: the muftis, religious but also community leaders, retained the right to resolve civil right disputes; *waqf*—communal foundations and their properties—were retained; and the Turkish language continued to be taught in community schools, while a Greek teacher was added (in accordance with the Greek-Ottoman Convention of Constantinople in 1881).

This administrative autonomy model was extended to the Muslims of the New Lands when they were annexed to Greece. A Greek-Ottoman convention signed in Athens in 1913 gave these new Greek citizens a three-year window in which to opt for Ottoman citizenship, and a special protection regime similar to that for Thessalian Muslims. The protections offered Muslims in Greece, like those implemented in Bulgaria, Serbia, and Rumania, were a guarantee of stability aimed at minimising the Ottoman presence in the Balkans, but established a Muslim minority numbering millions. The minority was a potential playing card in the competition between the expanded Greek state and the aspirations of Turkish nationalism as expressed in the policies of the Young Turk governments. Though fragmented in different language groups and various, often heterodox, sects and religious orders (e.g., Sunni/Shia, Bektashi, Halveti, Mevlevi), this community was also the target of Muslim ecumenism under the supervision of the Sheik-ul-Islam in Istanbul.

The issue of 'Greek Islam' was not something that unexpectedly fell from the sky. Already in 1906, Greek politician Eleftherios Venizelos announced before the Cretan Parliament:

> the Greek Kingdom cannot be enlarged if the enlarged Greece does not incorporate elements belonging to foreign nations and religions. The foreign population belonging to another religion, that will possibly be incorporated within the boundaries of the enlarged Greece, is going to be Muslim. The Greece we are hoping for and are anticipating is bound to become one day a Muslim power just like Russia and England.[3]

The Muslims of Thessaloniki, 1912–2012   245

Therefore, Venizelos added, the Muslims of Greece should be the link between Greece and the Muslims of other countries if the latter are going to be detached from the Ottoman Empire. In this respect, Greece should secure the trust of the Balkan Muslims by granting them political privileges (*Gazette of the Cretan State*, 25 November 1906; Tsitselikis and Christopoulos 2008, 163).

1913 and the New Lands—Thessaloniki, the centre of Greek Islam

Transfer of sovereignty

Upon arrival, a primary concern of the Greek administration in Thessaloniki was to protect the life and the property of its Muslim inhabitants. A standard declaration to that effect was issued by all the new administrators in the New Lands, chiefly in the cities with a Muslim community. Though one can safely assume the city's 'liberation' was regarded as such only for by Christian and Greek-speaking or Greek-sympathising minority, a striking sign of retaining the old against the hegemonic new was the decision to retain the Muslim mayor of Thessaloniki, like those of Ioannina and Kailar (Ptolemaida) during the transfer of sovereignty. Osman Bey remained in office until 1916. He was reappointed mayor from November 1920 until September 1922.

Especially for the Muslim community the sovereignty change marked a period of occupation and reversal. Despite the assurances given, the presence of the Greek army in Macedonia and the establishment of the Greek administration in Thessaloniki were not welcomed enthusiastically by the Muslim (or Jewish or Bulgarian) population. Many started leaving for Ottoman territory or elsewhere. The vengeful behaviour of locals and the blind animosity of soldiers and police officers exacerbated this emigration,[4] despite Venizelos's repeated personal assurances regarding the safety of the Muslim population. The prime minister did not hesitate to approach the leaders of the Muslim communities personally when problems arose.[5]

Most of the complaints lodged against Greek authorities, principally the army and the police, regarded discriminatory treatment and mistreatment, but also the impunity with which Christian neighbours took violent revenge for whatever ills they had suffered at the hands of the Ottoman administration. In 1914 the arrival of the Greek refugees from Asia Minor[6] created acute problems, as private homes or community buildings were requisitioned for the needs of the refugees and the army. Reports record Muslim community complaints about the requisitioning of community buildings, mostly schools but also places of worship.[7] Moreover, Greek refugees engaged in frequent acts of blind revenge against local Muslims.[8] A large migration flow of Muslims ensued, not only from Thessaloniki but from all Macedonia and even Serbia and Bulgaria, using Thessaloniki as the transit point.[9] One should not forget the fire of 1917 as another factor contributing to emigration, as thousands of Muslims were among those made homeless.[10]

246 Konstantinos Tsitselikis

As complaints about acts of violence and threats accumulated, mostly concerning seizures of property by the army, the chances of finding effective protection diminished, especially for those who had not yet expressed their wish to acquire Greek citizenship. Thus, Muslims were *de facto* encouraged to leave their homes.

One goal of Greek policy, however, was to avert mass emigration from Thessaloniki and the New Lands in order not to undermine the position of Greece during its negotiations with the Great Powers. Thus, halting emigration was characterised as a matter of 'national interest', with a further goal of 'averting economic disaster in the region'.[11]

The community

According to the 1912–1913 population census, Muslim residents of Thessaloniki amounted to 45,867 in a total population of 157,889,[12] making them the second largest community group after the Jews. By 1917 the population of the community had fallen to approximately 30,000. The majority were Turkish-speaking Sunnis.

Thessaloniki was considered the Muslim capital for the wider region as it had the largest population and the most important economic and intellectual elite. The imams and the notables of every neighbourhood elected the members of the Community Council of Thessaloniki, all of whom were men. This council was the largest in Greece, numbering 24 members. Its committees administered communal property and schools, organised philanthropic activities to support the poor, managed the orphanage, etc. This model of communal organisation was in effect the pre-existing one, retained for Muslims (and Jews) but abolished for the Greek Orthodox community. The status of non-Christians was a counterpart to the Ottoman *millet* system, with many modernising elements, of course, and harmonisation of the legal system directed toward the concept of the citizen. The composition of the Muslim community council had to be ratified by the Greek administration, but it is not known to what extent the latter in fact intervened, except in the case of appointing a new Mufti and dismissing his predecessor, in the context of a broader political issue of that period (see below).

Naturally, after 1912 Muslims lost their administrative positions and other prerogatives they enjoyed at a local level but they kept their position in social and economic life, especially as merchants, landowners, lawyers, or other kind of professionals and participated actively in the economic life of the city.[13] Muslims also participated in the formation of trade unions and, of course, in the renowned 'Federation'. Muslim workers and employees participated in trade associations such as the League of Lemon Juice Makers (*Syndesmos Lemonatzidon*), the president of which was Muslim, the Butchers' Guild (*Synthehnia Kreopolon*) or the Agrarian Union (*Georgiki Enosis*). Two unions were solely for Muslims—the League of Grocers (*Syndesmos Pantopolon*, 1920) and the Association of Halva-Makers (*Syllogos Halvadopoion*, 1921).[14] It seems that in these sectors a broader intercommunal understanding existed, prompted by mutual interest, but this did not breach the dividing lines between the *millets*.

As already mentioned, the Greek administration rushed to maintain the basic structures of community autonomy. Act 4134 (ΔΡΛΔ΄) of 1913 and later Act 147/1914 regulated the application of Islamic law (Sharia) in family and inheritance disputes between Muslims by the mufti, who now acquired judicial competence (instead of the Kadi).

However, there were still many unsolved issues for the Muslims of Thessaloniki as for all Muslims in the New Lands: granting permanent citizenship after the three-year opt-out period; military service (compulsory, reduced, or exempt); return of seized property; shortfalls in assistance to homeless and impoverished victims of the Balkan Wars and the fire of 1917; delays in reopening community schools; prisoners of war who were now Greek citizens; and, in particular, uniform application of the new legal status governing Muslim communities.[15] Soon the need to solve these issues would disappear with the expulsion of the Muslim population, the outcome of the Greek disaster in Asia Minor and the ethnic cleansing decisions ratified by the Greek-Turkish population exchange convention signed in Lausanne on 30 January 1923.

The Mufti Office of Thessaloniki

As a prominent personality with great authority, the mufti played a crucial role in community issues as he acquired additional duties in the new Greek environment. In Thessaloniki the mufti was responsible for the Muslims of the city but also of the surrounding areas, the few Muslims in Halkidiki but also the many Muslims in Kilkis and Langadas and he was hierarchical head of the muftis of Macedonia. He chaired the religious court, the 24-member Council of the Community of the city, and the ten-member Council of Managers of the *waqf*. He was also responsible for the management of the schools and orphanage and, of course, for the operation of almost 50 mosques. There were over 15 *tekkes*, which apparently kept their administrative autonomy, each under the hierarchy of its order. However, the Sunni mufti probably had influence over issues concerning the relations between these heterodox orders and the Greek government.

By Decree of the provisional government of Thessaloniki (1449/1917, FEK special series 1917), the mufti of Thessaloniki was recognised as a 'first class' public servant and therefore received the highest salary among all the muftis on Greek territory. Hafuz Ahmet Efendi served as mufti and president of the Muslim Community of Thessaloniki from 1912 until 1922. But the political changes brought on by the Greek defeat in Asia Minor resulted in his removal from office (along with many other muftis) in December 1922 (*Makedonia*, 28 December 1922). He was replaced by Mehmet Houlousi, the former mufti of Adrianoupolis (Edirne) (*Makedonia*, 8 June 1924). Suleyman Sirri was the last mufti of Thessaloniki who finalised the pending affairs of the population exchange, closed the Mufti Office and left the city together with the last refugees in 1924 (*Makedonia*, 6 January 1925). It is perhaps worth mentioning that the legal advisor of the Mufti Office was Gavriil Filippidis, a Greek lawyer.[16]

248 *Konstantinos Tsitselikis*

Schools

As already mentioned, Muslim schools were communal under a special legal status. The community paid the salaries of the teachers and school maintenance costs which were funded from *waqf* incomes (see below). From 1919 the Greek language was introduced by law in Muslim community schools, as requested by the Community of Thessaloniki to the Governorate General of Macedonia.[17]

Six primary schools were in operation in the city, and one secondary school, the city school (the building now houses the Faculty of Philosophy of the Aristotle University of Thessaloniki), and 19 more schools in the region.[18] The 'Mithat Pasha' orphanage deserves special mention, as does the secular middle-school 'Terakki', which was a landmark (then but even today) for Muslims descended from Jews (*Ma'amin or Dönme*). This school was transferred to Istanbul before 1920.[19] These schools evolved in accordance with the educational ideas formed during the Tanzimat era but also after the Young Turk revolution, mostly concerning the educational role of the state in standardising secular education for all. Likewise, some schools implemented policies that stemmed from religious centres of power attempting to maintain the religious schools as the bastion of a religiously based Islamic society. The Muslim community of Thessaloniki, with strong influences from secular circles, had already developed schools of civil character and was promoting the use and standardisation of the Turkish language in schools.[20] This, however, did not mean that the Mufti's office had lost its supervisory role in educational affairs.

The *Vakif (waqf)*

The Management Committee of the *Vakif (waqf*, religious foundations) was a crucial administrative instrument of the community of Thessaloniki, as it was one of the richest in Greece. Under the supervision or chairmanship of the mufti, the Committee managed community property, deciding on its maintenance, the collection of revenues and the payment of expenses. Above all, it decided how to allocate annual revenues in accordance with the charitable aims of each institution (*waqf*) and for the benefit of the community as a whole. When these *waqf* were being incorporated in the Greek legal system, the applicable Ottoman law was retained in the intermediary role played by the community between members of the community and the Greek state. The *waqfs*, therefore, financed educational institutions, and the maintenance of mosques and *tekkes*, as well as every other charitable activity or institution belonging to the community (annual fundraiser for the poor, orphanage, nursing home, cemetery).

In practice, in the decade before the population exchange, *waqf* properties were not sufficiently protected and were often requisitioned—as already mentioned—for the needs of the Greek army or refugees, or else expropriated in order to expand or redefine the city's public spaces (Glarnetatzis 2012).

The standardisation of the law relating to religious foundations that resulted from Law 2345/1920 and the validation of the ownership status of charitable

The Muslims of Thessaloniki, 1912–2012   249

institutions and their property in favour of the Muslim communities did not, ultimately, have a significant effect. Three years later, the exchange of populations would entail the abolition of the Muslim communities and the nationalisation of community properties. However, during those three years the Community strengthened its administrative authority over *waqf* properties at the expense of their trustees (*muteveli*), while school properties[21] were put under the direct administrative oversight of special committees supervised by the mufti of Thessaloniki. However, family *waqfs* and those connected with the *tekkes* kept their relative autonomy from central community administration. In any case, even allowing for the unsettled situation, many problems remained unsolved, especially regarding community buildings seized by the Greek administration.[22]

Publications

During the decade from 1912 until the population exchange, Thessaloniki ranked first in newspaper circulation among the Muslim communities in Greece. Ten daily and two weekly newspapers were in circulation, notably: *Imdat* (Help), *Yeni Asır* (New Century), *Silah* (Weapon), *Hakikat* (Truth), *Balkanlar* (The Balkans), and *Havadis* (News) reflecting the different ideological tendencies of that time. Kemaledin Bey, initially a member of Parliament for Drama and then of Thessaloniki, was one of the most important publishers in the city, while Ali Sami Bey, an active anti-Kemalist and collaborator with the exiled Sultan Abdul Hamid, was exempted from the population exchange and remained in the city where he became a well-known photographer who even worked on Mount Athos. In 1915, Ali Sami Bey published a newspaper in French, *Le droit*, which in 1924 reappeared in Greek as *To dikaion*, with a pro-Greek attitude but also reliable analysis of the Greek political scene (Konortas 1985; Kandylakis 1998).

Political attitude and representation

During the decade between 1913 and 1923, the Muslims of Thessaloniki played an important role in the new, unstable political scene. In 1915, during the May and December elections but also in the elections of 1920, the Muslims of Thessaloniki had the right to vote as long as they had already opted for the Greek citizenship. So, the representatives of the Muslim community were incorporated within the national parliament in the midst of tensions dividing Greece. They tried to support the interests of the community rather than play a central role in the Greek political scene. However, because of the extreme rivalry between supporters and opponents of Venizelos, their attitude played an important role for the party they were advocating.

The Muslim elite of the city, merchants, landowners but also community officials exercised strong influence over the local Muslim population and could influence community votes on a large scale. Therefore, political parties sought their co-operation in an era characterised both by the major changes of the transition from the Ottoman to the Greek administration and by the rivalry between

250 *Konstantinos Tsitselikis*

supporters and opponents of Venizelos, the National Schism (Mavrogordatos 2015). Anti-Venizelos feelings rose because Muslim-owned estates were expropriated and promises for equal rights were not kept. Nor can we overlook the exceptional conditions created by military conflict, in World War I and the Greek expedition to Asia Minor. Influence campaigns were waged in northern Greece by the Greek authorities as well as by foreign agents, the Ottomans and the French, aimed at Muslim notables.

Seven Muslim deputies were elected in Thessaloniki in the elections of May 1915, and six in the December elections, all of whom were supporters of the pro-monarchy political party (Glavinas 2013, 602–603).[23] In 1920, they also voted against Venizelos, in opposition to the Greek campaign in Anatolia but also as a sign of discontent over the massive land expropriations affecting Muslims. In the crucial elections of 1920, the attempt of the Venizelos' Liberal Party (*Fileleutheroi*) to attract Muslim votes failed once again, while a significant part of Muslim workers voted for the socialist party SEKE. The majority of Muslims voted in favour of ending the war in Anatolia, which had put them in a difficult position. This time, four Muslims from Thessaloniki were elected as deputies with the anti-Venizelist party (*Laiko komma*). Public perceptions of the Muslim community improved, though only temporarily. It is noteworthy that during this period travel bans on Muslims were lifted and cannon fire for *iftar* (during the fasting of Ramadan) was resumed on a grand scale (Mazower 2004, 341). Two years later, the traumatic defeat of the Greek army in Asia Minor triggered anti-Muslim feelings in Greece, weakening the political power of Muslim officials: the Muslim mayor of the city was, for example, ousted from office and put in prison together with the mufti of Thessaloniki. The 'Revolution' of 1922 decreed that separate electoral groups would be established for Muslims and Jews. This measure, in force for a decade, was never implemented on the Muslims of Thessaloniki because of the population exchange.

After the population exchange

The population exchange was imposed in response to the disastrous Greek military expedition in Asia Minor (or the successful Turkish War of Independence). The Muslims of Greece were compelled to leave their homes and settle in the newly founded Turkish Republic, creating space for the larger number of displaced Greeks, who arrived in a wretched state from Asia Minor. The organisational structures of the Muslim community of Thessaloniki were dissolved in March 1924, when the last Muslims departed. Soon after, minarets and mosques were demolished,[24] while those remaining either changed their original use (see Yeni Cami) or were left to the ravages of time (e.g., Hamza Bey Mosque) without maintenance until the 1990s, when gradual renovation and maintenance of the Ottoman buildings began (Alatza Imaret, Yahudi Hamam, Bezesteni, etc.) thanks to European funding.[25]

Although many details are known about the departure of the mufti of Thessaloniki and his attempt to facilitate practical matters concerning his fellow

The Muslims of Thessaloniki, 1912–2012   251

citizens to be exchanged, it is generally not known that the Mufti Office of Thessaloniki was not legally abolished but was instead bequeathed to a group of Muslim Greek citizens who were exempted from the exchange: Muslims of Albanian origin and Circassians (*Çerkez*), many of whom already lived in Greece but had mostly come as fugitives to Greece after the collapse of the Asia Minor front, either because they collaborated with the Greek army or were anti-Kemalist dissidents. It is estimated that these Circassians totalled 9,000 throughout Greece.[26] The multiethnic Muslim community of northern Greece included other foreign Muslims exempted from the population exchange.

There is little evidence for this period regarding the Muslims who attempted to avoid being uprooted. In a Police Directorate document of January 1925, the Muslims who remained in Thessaloniki were listed: Serbian and Albanian citizens, 78 in total; 12 exchangeables who extended their stay; and seven of 'unknown citizenship'. Among them were confectioners, landowners, rentiers, and tobacco merchants, but also a cinema owner (Hekimoglou 1996, 381). It is worth mentioning the case of the Haciosman brothers, who acquired Albanian citizenship and remained in Thessaloniki. Their extensive properties in Halkidiki and elsewhere were expropriated by the Greek state without indemnification, leading the family to migrate to Turkey at the beginning of the 1950s.[27] Another case concerns Muslims working in a Dutch and Belgian tobacco factory who, as it seems, in the end did not succeed in staying for long.[28] According to a report of 1937, there were 47 anti-Kemalist Circassians residing in Thessaloniki.[29]

Under these population exchange conditions, Suleyman Osman Sirri, the exchangeable mufti of Thessaloniki, was replaced by Hatzi Ahmet. The new Mufti Office was founded in 1923 (according to the inscription on its seal, on a letter to the Mufti Office of Komotini).[30] It is not known whether the remaining Muslims of Thessaloniki had their own organisational structures based on ethnicity. In January 1928, two Mufti Offices were officially recognised by the Presidential Decree, one in Thessaloniki and one in Langada. It is not known why and for how long the latter operated. The Mufti Office of Thessaloniki was recognised as the 'Mufti Office of the Circassians'.[31] It is possible that in the context of the Greek-Turkish rapprochement of 1930 some Circassians were expelled, but it is not known to what extent. The first Circassian mufti, Hatzi Ahmet, was succeeded by Husein Housni Karaoglou who, in September 1938[32] was replaced by Moustafa Namouk Muan Zade, who appears to have been elected by the Muslim community. A retired colonel in the Greek army, he was appointed temporarily by the authorities as mufti (by a Royal Decree of 18.8.1938). From 1923 (and possibly for various periods until 1938), the secretary of the Mufti office and religious judge was Mahmud Tzellaledin (Tzezayrli). He was of Arab origin from Algiers, and a French citizen, the friend and secretary of the first mufti of the Circassians. However, as the archives reveal, the new mufti and the secretary of the Mufti Office were not in good terms.[33] When the mufti died in December 1943, a crisis over his succession broke out.

Mahmud Tzellaledin was an ambiguous personality with controversial activities as a mufti. He was sued for misuse of his religious authority by Ibrahim

252 *Konstantinos Tsitselikis*

Memis, who was acting as imam, and reciprocated with allegations made to the Greek governing authorities during the German occupation.[34] The latter was actually supported by the Bishop of Thessaloniki, Gennadios. During the next troubled months Nedim Almahsit Muan Zade (presumably the son of the deceased mufti) was allegedly the acting mufti while the secretary was again Mahmud Tzellaledin. In August 1948, Muan Zade was charged with forgery. It seems that the Mufti Office of the Circassians was operational, although divided, and the legitimacy of the mufti was doubted until the beginning of 1950. The office operated in one of the old mosques of Thessaloniki, the fate of which is unknown. According to the General Directorate of Aliens there was one mosque in operation in Thessaloniki as late as in 1952.[35]

This is the fragmentary information at our disposal about the Mufti Office of Thessaloniki operating for the Circassians but also for other Muslims that were not exchanged until the 1950s, when every trace of Muslim presence vanished.

Many small Albanian-speaking Muslim communities in Macedonia, mostly in Thessaloniki, were exempted extra-contractually from the population exchange as 'of Albanian origin' after long negotiations within the Mixed Commission overseeing the transfer.[36] Some Muslims, mostly wealthy merchants and landowners acquired foreign citizenship (Albanian, Serbian, Italian, Spanish, Turkish, or French) in order to be exempted. Before the Second World War, there were circa 500 Turkish citizens in Macedonia, the majority of whom resided in Thessaloniki (Gavrilidis 1931, 97; Hekimoglou 1996, 381).

Thessaloniki's New Islam

Due to its geographical position and status as a member state of the European Union, Greece attracted a large number of immigrants and political refugees from Muslim countries during the 1980s. Athens was the primary destination, but Thessaloniki hosted hundreds of Muslim students from Arab countries, drawn to its universities, but also political refugees from Turkey and elsewhere. During the 1990s, when the global geopolitical map changed dramatically, Thessaloniki received a large number of immigrants from Albania but also from the former USSR. The Muslim religiosity expressed by Albanian immigrants and Turkish or Kurdish refugees was weak to non-existent. Consequently, it would be wrong to consider this group part of Thessaloniki's New Islam. The Muslims for whom faith was a visible daily practice came to Thessaloniki after 2001, with the migration wave created by wars and instability in the Middle East and Africa and ecological disaster in Bangladesh and Pakistan. Although the majority of those people moved towards Athens, a large number settled in Thessaloniki in a more or less stable way. This New Islam in Thessaloniki is more a rolling phenomenon, with a population in constant flux. Gradually, many Muslims started living in the city permanently, notwithstanding the Greek economic crisis that started in 2009.

In any case, a near-total absence of Muslims in Thessaloniki has gradually ended. Since 1985, but mostly after 2001, a fluid Muslim community has arisen, fragmented in ethnic groups. During the same period, a stable community has

The Muslims of Thessaloniki, 1912–2012   253

been formed by Muslims from Western Thrace—Greek citizens, primarily Roma—who now reside permanently in Thessaloniki. Some of them express a clear Muslim identity (Tsitselikis 2012, 239–240). The Syrian refugee crisis in 2015–2016 brought a new Muslim population to Thessaloniki. By June 2015, many members of the various Muslim communities fled Greece with the refugee flow towards Northern Europe. Other refugees, mostly from Syria, Afghanistan, and Iraq, were settled in camps in the outskirts of Thessaloniki (or even at the port), with an uncertain perspective to be relocated to another European country.

Muslim immigrants and refugees face common issues with everyone else found in a similar position according to the current legal status. Their objective is to seek legal status and the documentation that will grant them access to legitimate work and residence in the country. Access to health services, family reunification, right to education and residence, and personal safety, are key issues that concern the whole immigrant population and particularly Thessaloniki's Muslims.

Muslims face special problems when seeking a place of worship, an issue connected with the overall negative attitude of the Greek political system toward the establishment of mosques. Discussion has focused on the long-delayed construction of a mosque in Athens after various initiatives,[37] stillborn due to the massive resistance they encountered from nationalist political forces. However, in Thessaloniki as elsewhere, the issue of Muslim places of worship remains unsolved. There is, instead, unstated agreement between the communities and the authorities, whereby the latter tolerate the operation of informal places of worship in apartments, basements, or garages.

Already since 1980, the basement of the Faculty of Theology was informally conceded for the needs of Muslim Arab students. In the late 2000s the Greek-Arab Association (*Ellinoaravikos Syllogos*) was founded. A prayer house functions in its offices during the major Islamic holidays. Four more similar places have been operating since 2012, for the Pakistani, Bangladeshi, and African Muslim immigrant communities on an irregular basis and according to their needs.[38] In 2011, at the request of the Bangladeshi community, the municipality of Thessaloniki in cooperation with the TIF (Thessaloniki International Fair) provided a place for prayer within the fairgrounds on a one-time basis. A proposal that the New Mosque (Yeni Cami), now used for art exhibits, should be made available for the religious needs of Thessaloniki Muslims, has not been implemented.

The lack of a Muslim cemetery also concerns the members of the Muslim communities of Thessaloniki as everywhere outside Thrace and the Dodecanese. The burial of the dead is a major psychological and financial burden, since the deceased must be transported quickly to a Muslim cemetery in Thrace or else repatriated to the home country, if any, at great expense. The municipal authorities of Thessaloniki had not taken, as of the date this was written, any initiatives concerning the founding of a Muslim cemetery. The issue encounters ideological resistance similar to that against establishing mosques.

The targeting of Muslims by far-right groups of neo-Nazi character has become a significant problem in recent years. The rapid rise of votes in favour of the ultra-right party *Chrysi Avgi* during the 2012 elections, along with rising Islamophobia,

254 *Konstantinos Tsitselikis*

can be linked to the financial crisis but also to the prevailing negative image of Islam in public opinion. Since 2010, threats and violence against Muslims and their places of worship have been recorded all over Greece. However, in Thessaloniki, reports do not indicate racist incidents specifically targeting Muslims. The lack of such incidents does not prove the non-existence of a climate of Islamophobia associated with the xenophobia and racism typical of segments of Greek society and expressed by a significant part of the society in public political discourse of a particular ideological coloration. In 2015, the current of Islamophobic discourse was encouraged by the local bishop Anthimos and by far-right extremists reacting to the presence of Muslim refugees in Thessaloniki by alleging a threat of islamisation of Greek society (Sakellariou 2015).

Conclusions

In October 1912, Thessaloniki's Muslim character was a key component of a complex status quo. When incorporated into the Greek state, a large Muslim community was the living continuity of the old regime. The situation of the community was inevitably connected in a particularly fatal way to Greek-Ottoman relations and the military confrontation that led to the Greek defeat in Asia Minor. In addition, it was shaped by internal political confrontations such as the National Schism and by events of local character such as the fire of 1917.

As Muslims and Turks, community members were identified with the main ideological 'other' and its negative connotations. This determined the fate of its monuments when the community vanished after the population exchange. The destruction in 1926 of the city's minarets and other places of worship (with very few exceptions), signified the beginning of the process of erasing Muslim Thessaloniki from collective memory. The presence of a few hundred Muslims until the 1950s, and very few thereafter, could not prevent the Muslim community from being erased from Thessaloniki's map of the past. The extermination of the vast majority of the Jewish community in 1944 created a linguistically and ethnically homogenised Greek Thessaloniki that conveniently renounced its multicultural past through an interleaving of collective memory to construct a past selectively according to the political expediency of the present.

However, with the arrival of immigrants and refugees since 1985 and, in particular, after 2000, a New Islam has reversed the flow to enrich the ethnic, religious, and linguistic diversity of the city, albeit in small amounts proportionally. Thus, a century of Greek Thessaloniki, as far as the Muslim presence is concerned, can be depicted for the most part as empty, with a visible Muslim population only at the beginning and in the recent present. There are many asymmetries between these two periods, but some issues are common. First, regarding the relation of Muslims to the Greek state, i.e., their legal status. Secondly, that Islam is viewed in a negative light by the majority of the public opinion and the political establishment. Last but perhaps most important, the reappearance of Muslim communities in the human geography of Thessaloniki raises the political issue of otherness: respect for diversity has to do not only with whatever ideological rigidity exists

The Muslims of Thessaloniki, 1912–2012 255

regarding the acceptance of other faiths and ethnicities, but ultimately with the core of the city's democratic collective memory: respect for pluralism is an inherent and constitutive element of democracy.

In brief, the incorporation of Muslim immigrants into the society of Thessaloniki, a hundred years after 1912, brings back the fundamental questions raised then by the Greek authorities concerning the building of the Greek state and the relationship between the Greek nation and non-Greeks as members of the same political community of citizens. One hundred years later, although these questions are still timely, especially within the modern context of the rise of the far-right and ethno-racial discourse and action, the issue has changed, under the conditions imposed by the globalisation of migration, into the following: on what terms can a society assure peaceful coexistence between heterogeneous groups through soft assimilation processes between natives and newcomers, processes that are repeated cyclically? The natives of the future are the children of today's newcomers, in a perpetual shift of identities and perceptions. Are the majority of the current inhabitants of Thessaloniki not descendants of refugees and immigrants who settled in the city that was a hostile environment for them? Therefore, what is necessary in contemporary context is the social integration of Muslim immigrants, as of all immigrants who wish to become inhabitants of Thessaloniki, by reducing the issues that bring to the fore Islam's negative image: the ideological disdain with which it is met by the majority of contemporary inhabitants and the legal settlement concerning the founding of a place of worship and a cemetery which is constantly postponed. Only under these circumstances will this New Islam become an element of the city, enrich the city's character and increase its importance, which is *mutatis mutandis* what Venizelos envisioned during his address to the Cretan Parliament in 1906.

Notes

1 For the Muslims of Thessaloniki before the Balkan Wars see Mazower 2004; Dimitriadis 1983, 81, 277, 375; Ginio 2005, 405–416.
2 I refer to the ideas presented by Charles King, without being able to go into more detail on this field (*Thessaloniki: 100 years*, conference presentation 'The making and remaking of cities in comparative perspective').
3 *Gazette of the Cretan State*, 25 November 1906, proceedings of the Second Constitutive Assembly of the Cretans Β΄ Συντακτικής των Κρητών Συνελεύσεως, Hania 1912, D, p. 779.
4 Memorandum: Liste des plaintes adressées au Consulat Gén.Ottoman á Salonique du 15–25 février 1914, AEB, F.9/1914.
5 Venizelos often urged the local authorities and the army to refrain from mistreating Muslims. According to the British Consul in Thessaloniki, 'The petty vexations to which the Moslems are subjected by their Christian neighbors in the country districts and the misery brought on by the war are the most powerful factors in deciding the Moslems to leave Turkey-in-Europe', Elliot to the British Embassy of Athens, No 18, 21 March 1913, British Embassy of Athens, in Destani 2003, 80.
6 According to Ottoman sources, 122,665 Muslim refugees from the New Lands migrated to the Empire, while the Greek authorities estimated that only the Muslims of Macedonia who left their homes amounted to almost 80,000. See Kostopoulos

256 *Konstantinos Tsitselikis*

2007. According to other Greek sources only in 1914, a total of 243,804 Muslims fled Macedonia, *Statistique du mouvement de l'émigration musulmane de la Macédoine durant les 17 premier mois,* AEB, F.10.1914.

7 For example, the Governor General of Macedonia asked for approval to requisition the Mevlevi *tekke* and the community school *Israhane* in Thessaloniki, Th. Sofoulis to the cabinet of Ministers, Thessaloniki 2.6.1914 AEV-ELIA, F.9.3.

8 According to the deputy Governor of Kilkis, the refugees were a real plague for the Muslim population. Telegram of 14.12.1914, GAM, F.14; Glavinas 2005, 162. Ottoman policy exploited the situation to promote emigration from Macedonia. Apparently, this propaganda had more impact on the rural population and less on the urban population of Thessaloniki.

9 More than 100,000 Muslim refugees from Serbia and Bulgaria departed by ship from the ports of Kavala and Thessaloniki respectively, under adverse conditions, with health problems, see Mazower 2004, 337.

10 In his letter of 24 December 1918, the Mufti of Thessaloniki refers to the community buildings destroyed because of the fire of 1917 asking in vain for help from the helpless administration; Dimitradis 1983, 473.

11 According to Themistoklis Sofoulis, Governor General of Thessaloniki, the Greek government should block the passage of foreign Muslim refugees through Greece, because they were spreading propaganda among the Muslims of Asia Minor and thereby endangering the Greeks living there, Sofoulis, AP 28491, MFA, Thessaloniki, 9.6.1914, AEV-ELIA, F.9.3. On several cases of harassment see Glavinas 2013, 56.

12 Hekimoglou 1996, 341. Note that 20,951 Muslims still lived in the Lagkadas region (part of Thessaloniki's wider economic area).

13 For a detailed account of this issue up to 1923, see Glavinas 2013.

14 For the allocation of the workers among the communities including the Muslims, see the exquisite study of Dagkas 2003, 779–795.

15 See, for example, Memorandum of the Muslim deputies of the Greek Parliament to the Greek government (1919), signed by, among others, Hasan Mehmet Ali, AEV-ELIA, F.9.3.

16 Letter of recommendation signed by the last Mufti Souleyman Osman Sirri for Gavriil Filippidis, Thessaloniki, 19 August, 1924, and personal interview with his son Tilemahos Filippidis, whom I thank. Of particular interest is the *Collection of the Greek law regarding the Muslim communities,* edited by Christos Karagiozis and published in the newspaper *Yeni Asır* in Ottoman Turkish in 1921 under the auspices of the Mufti Office of Thessaloniki. I thank the Mufti Office of Komotini for putting it at my disposal.

17 In 1922, the number of schools in the city increased to ten with 1,452 pupils, Inspector of primary education, Doc 10144, Thessaloniki, 26 July 1922, General Archive of Macedonia, F.51.

18 Directorate General of Macedonia, Thessaloniki, 1914.

19 The orphanage operated as a technical school and was of utmost importance for the community, as seen in the relevant archive material in Ankara, AN Adiyeke, *Islamic Community Brotherhood Administrations in Greece: Cemmat-i Islamiye* (1913–1998), Ankara: The National Committee for Strategic Research and Studies, 2002, 63.

20 A conference about the Turkish language in education was organised by the community under the presidency of the Muslim deputy of Thessaloniki (no further details); see Mazower 2004, 341.

21 Kofinas, Governor General of Macedonia ordered in 1913 the attribution of all school *waqf* to the management of the Muslim community of Thessaloniki, 'On the provisional management of the *waqf*', Order of 19 January 1913, Thessaloniki, ap. 1077.

22 According to Nikolaos Eleftheriadis, the most important expert on legal matters concerning the status of Muslims in Greece ('The Mufti Office of Thessaloniki—restitution of schools', (in Greek) *Themis* (LG'1922: 30) three *mearif* (school) estates

The Muslims of Thessaloniki, 1912–2012   257

that were under seizure by the Greek army had to be returned to the Mufti Office of Thessaloniki.

23 It is mentioned that Hassan Mehmet Ali Bey took third place in the region of Thessaloniki with 41,031 votes (elections of 31 May 1915), see Dodos 2005, 107.

24 See A. Papanastasiou's reaction to the demolition of minarets and mosques which he called 'an act of blind chauvinism' and that 'history is not written by destroying innocent buildings that decorated the city'. On the contrary, the harsh line of the nationalists that prevailed was in favour of the demolition of all Muslim buildings, even those for commercial use; (Mazower 2004, 352; Papazoglou 2010).

25 See the undated leaflet (circa 2005) of the Ephorate of Byzantine Antiquities of Thessaloniki 'Monuments of Ottoman period in Thessaloniki'.

26 English report of 1.3.1923, HAMFA/1923/A/5VI/IO, cited by Pelagidis 1994, 244.

27 The case reached the European Court of Human Rights which vindicated the applicant's descendants of the Muslims of Thessaloniki, EctHR, *Yagtzilar et autres v Greece,* 41727/98, 6 December 2001.

28 General Governor of Thessaloniki to the Prefect of Thessaloniki, 11 June 1924, decision, Archive of Alexandros Svolos. I thank Mark Mazower for putting it at my disposal.

29 Kirimis to Ministry of Foreign Affairs, telegram of 14 October 1937, Thessaloniki, MFA, F.1937/58.3.

30 Mufti Office of the Circassians in Thessaloniki AP/59/29.11.1935. Archive of the Mufti Office of Komotini.

31 An informal Mufti Office, not legally recognised was in operation in Veroia (it was of service to 25 families of Circassians, while many Circassians resided at the village Agios Prodromos).

32 Certificate of appointment of the secretary of the Mufti Office signed by the Mufti, 2.7.1932, Minority Schools Archives, General Archives of the State, Kavala, F.93.

33 Report from the Circassians of Thessaloniki, 20.1.1944, MSA, General Archives of the State, Kavala, F.93.

34 Report of the Mufti to the Penal Court of Thessaloniki 19.9.1943, report of Circassians of Thessaloniki, 20.1.1944, letter of Memis Ibrahim Hoca to the Governor General of Macedonia, 2.6.1944, letter of Mahmud Tzellaledin to the Director of Religious Affairs, Directorate General of Macedonia, 28.1.1944. Letter of Bishop of Thessaloniki, Gennadios of 2.6.1944 (all from: MSA, General Archives of the State, Kavala [before 2004], F.93.

35 General Directorate on Aliens, Report on Muslims living in Greece 421/2/20/4, July 1952, MSA, General Archives of State, Kavala, F.93.

36 Tsitselikis 2012, 74. According to Athanasios Papaevgeniou, there were 1,278 Muslims in Western and Central Macedonia at the end of the war; Papaevgeniou 1946.

37 See Act 2833/2000 (FEK A 150) and Act 3512/2006 (FEK A 264).

38 I thank Despoina Syrri for this information (September 2012). See also Tsimpiridou 2011, 48–53.

References

Dagkas, A., *Συμβολή στην έρευνα για την οικονομική και κοινωνική εξέλιξη της Θεσσαλονίκης: Οικονομική δομή και κοινωνικός καταμερισμός της εργασίας 1912–1940* [Contribution to the Research of the Economic and Social Development of Thessaloniki: Economic Structure and Social Distribution of Labour, 1912–1940], Thessaloniki: Professional Chamber of Thessaloniki (1998).

258 Konstantinos Tsitselikis

Dagkas, A., *Recherches sur l'histoire sociale de la Gréce du Nord: Le mouvement des ouvriers du tabac 1918–1928*, Editions de l'Association de Recherchers Interdisciplinaires Pierre Belon, No 6, Paris: De Boccard (2003).

Destani, B., *Ethnic Minorities in the Balkan States 1860–1971*, vol. 3, Slough: Archive Editions (2003).

Dimitriadis, V., *Η Τοπογραφία της Θεσσαλονίκης κατά την Εποχή της Τουρκοκρατίας, 1430–1912* [A Topography of Thessaloniki Under the Turks, 1430–1912], Thessaloniki: Etairia Makedonikon Spoudon (1983).

Dodos, D., *Οι Εβραίοι της Θεσσαλονίκης στις εκλογές του ελληνικού κράτους 1915–1936* [The Jews of Thessaloniki in the Elections of the Greek State 1915–1936], Athens: Exantas (2005).

Ephorate of Byzantine Antiquities of Thessaloniki, *Monuments of Ottoman Period in Thessaloniki*, undated leaflet, Thessaloniki: Ministry of Culture (ca. 2005).

Gavrilidis, G., *Μέγας οδηγός Θεσσαλονίκης και περιχώρων 1932–33* [Great Guide to Thessaloniki and its Suburbs, 1932–33], Thessaloniki: Metochiki Ekdotiki Etaireia (1931).

Gazette of the Cretan State, '25 November 1906, proceedings of the Second Constitutive Assembly of the Cretans, Β' Συντακτικής των Κρητών Συνελεύσεως', Hania 1912, D, 779.

Ginio, E., 'Musulmans et non-musulmans dans la Salonique ottomane (XVIIIe siécle). L'affrontement sur les espaces et les lignes de démarcation', *Revue des mondes musulmanes et de la Méditerrané*, (2005), 405–416.

Glarnetatzis, G., 'Θα χτίσω στους τάφους σας. Αντιπαράθεση για την τύχη των μουσουλμανικών νεκροταφείων (1921)', www.alterthess.gr/content/afieroma-2012-tha-ktiso-stoys-tafous-sas-antiparathesi-gia-tin-tyxi-ton-mousolmanikon-nekron (2012) [broken link].

Glavinas, Y., 'The perceptions of the Muslim minority in Greece in Greek and Bulgarian policy and strategy (1913–1923)', *Etudes Balkaniques*, 4 (2005), 157–172.

Glavinas, Y., *Οι μουσουλμανικοί πληθυσμοί στην Ελλάδα (1912–1923): Από την ενσωμάτωση στην ανταλλαγή* [The Muslim Populations in Greece (1912–23): From Incorporation to Exchange], Thessaloniki: Stamoulis (2013).

Hekimoglou, E., *Θεσσαλονίκη: Τουρκοκρατία και μεσοπόλεμος* [Thessaloniki. Turkish Occupation and Inter War Period], Thessaloniki: University Studio Press (1996).

Kandylakis, M., *Εφημεριδογραφία της Θεσσαλονίκης* [Newspaper-writing of Thessaloniki], Thessaloniki: University Studio Press (1998).

Konortas, P., 'La presse d'expression turque des musulmans de Gréce pendant la periode post-ottomane', *Turcica*, XVII (1985), 245–259.

Kostopoulos, T., *Πόλεμος και εθνοκάθαρση: Η ξεχασμένη πλευρά μιας δεκαετούς εθνικής εξόρμησης (1912–1922)* [War and Ethnic Cleansing], Athens: Vivliorama (2007).

General Archives of Macedonia, F. 51, Doc. 10144, Inspector of elementary schools, 26 July 1922.

Mavrogordatos, G., *1915: Ο εθνικός διχασμός* [1915: The National Schism], Athens: Patakis (2015).

Mazower, *Salonica: City of Ghosts, Christians, Muslims and Jews, 1430–1950*, London: HarperCollins (2004).

Papaevgeniou, A., *Βόρειος Ελλάς: μειονότητες από στατιστικής απόψεως εν σχέσει με τον πληθυσμόν και την εκπαίδευσιν* [Northern Greece: Minorities from a Statistical Viewpoint Relative to Population and Education], Thessaloniki: Syllogos pros diadosin ton ellinikon grammaton (1946).

The Muslims of Thessaloniki, 1912–2012   259

Papazoglou, A., *Οι μιναρέδες της Θεσσαλονίκης* [The Minarets of Thessaloniki], Thessaloniki: Sfakianakis (2010).

Pelagidis, S., *Η αποκατάσταση των προσφύγων στη Δυτική Μακεδονία: 1923–1930* [The Restoration of the Refugees in Western Macedonia (1923–1930)], Thessaloniki: Kyriakidi Brs (1994).

Sakellariou, A., 'Report on Greece', In: Bayrakli, E. and Hafez, F. (eds.), *European Islamophobia Report*, Istanbul: SETA (2015).

Tsibiridou, F., 'Ανάμεσα στο «έθνος και το κράτος»: Η επαναδιαπραγμάτευση της ατελούς σχέσης πολίτη/κράτους στους πλειονοτικούς πληθυσμούς της Θράκης' [Between the 'nation and the state': The renegotiation of the imperfect relation between citizen and state in Thrace], In: Papataxiarhis, E. and Plexousaki, E. (eds.), *Revisions of the Political*, Athens: Alexandreia (2011), 48–53.

Tsitselikis, K., *Old and New Islam in Greece. From Historical Minorities to Immigrant Newcomers*, Leiden: Brill/Nijhoff (2012).

Tsitselikis, K. and Christopoulos, D., 'Από το πολυπολιτισμικό "μέγα όνειρον του Ελληνισμού" των αρχών του 20ού στην "πολυπολιτισμική πραγματικότητα" των αρχών του 21ου' ['From the multicultural "great dream of Hellenism" of the beginning of the 20st century to the "multicultural reality" of the beginning of the 21st century'], In: Christopoulos, D. (ed.), *Το ανομολόγητο ζήτημα των μειονοτήτων στην ελληνική έννομη τάξη* [The Unspoken Issue of Minorities in the Greek Legal Order], Athens: Kritiki (2008).

18 Urban change and the persistence of memory in modern Thessaloniki

Eleni Bastéa[†] and Vilma Hastaoglou-Martinidis

Architects and urban planners often claim that the process of modernizing a city brings about the modernization of its citizens. Is it true, or even possible, that urban change can affect people's beliefs and way of life? What of the ingrained insistence on following the same path while crossing a city, resisting or ignoring change in the built environment.

The sociologist Maurice Halbwachs pointed out:

> The great majority [of a city's inhabitants] may well be more sensitive to a certain street being torn up, or a certain building or home being razed, than to the gravest national, political, or religious events. That is why great upheavals may severely shake society without altering the appearance of the city. Their effects are blunted as they filter down to those people who are closer to the stones than to men—the shoemaker in his shop; the artisan at his bench; the merchant in his store; the people in the market; the walker strolling about the streets, strolling at the wharf, or visiting the garden terraces; the children playing on the corner; the old man enjoying the sunny wall or sitting on a stone bench; the beggar squatting by a city landmark.
>
> (Halbwachs 1980, 131–132)

We will examine these questions by juxtaposing the urban development of post-World War II Thessaloniki with the corresponding literary works that focused on the city. Our aim is to understand if local residents resisted or supported urban modernization and if the memory of the earlier city persisted or faded. Although literary descriptions do not mirror reality directly, they do open a window into the authors' own points of view. A review of Thessaloniki's urban design and literature will shed light onto the city's particular identity, that of a modern regional capital that is also a prominent literary locus.[1]

Thessaloniki: history and urban development

Urban transformation is the rule rather than the exception in the evolution of cities, particularly those like Thessaloniki with a long history. Founded by Cassander, King of Macedonia, around 315 BCE, Thessaloniki was built upon the major

Urban change and the persistence of memory 261

crossroads linking Europe with the maritime routes of the eastern Mediterranean. During the 23 centuries of its continuous existence, Thessaloniki passed successively through the Hellenistic, Roman, Byzantine, and Ottoman periods that restructured its space with their specific architectural and urban models. The city enjoyed prominence and prosperity, as it became an important commercial, administrative, and cultural center. At the end of the 15th century, a large community of Spanish Jews settled in Thessaloniki, further enriching its multiethnic character.

During the last two centuries, the city underwent rapid and dramatic transformations. A pre-modern and multiethnic city of 300 hectares [741.3 acres] and 50,000 inhabitants in 1850, became a modern national center of 6,000 hectares [14,826 acres] and 810,000 inhabitants by 2000. In that period, the city's triple identity, which comprised Jewish, Muslim, and Christian inhabitants in 1850, turned first into a double one, Jewish and Christian, when, in 1923, all Muslim residents were forced to leave Greece and move to Turkey, as part of the 1923 compulsory exchange of minority populations between Greece and Turkey. After the German Occupation of Greece during the Second World War, when over 50,000 Jews were deported to extermination camps, Thessaloniki retained only one, single, that of a Christian Greek city (Mazower 2004; Hastaoglou-Martinidis 1997a, 493–507; Dimitriadis 1983). The profound ethnic and religious population changes parallel the spectacular changes in the city's physical form. Let us take a closer look at these changes.

The pre-modern city of triple identity:
Salonica, Selânik, Σαλονίκη, Solun

In the mid-19th century Thessaloniki still preserved, to a large extent, its 'ancient' scheme, which had been shaped during the five centuries of Ottoman rule (1430–1912). Enclosed within the walls, the population of Jews, Muslims, and Christians lived in separate quarters. Its dense and irregular street network survived, along with its specific socio-economic features. The late 19th-century changes in the geopolitical context affected the city's unique identity of the three ethnic-religious communities but did not alter it drastically. These changes included the integration of the eastern Mediterranean into the international trade, the opening of the Suez Canal (1859), and the Westernizing reforms of Ottoman Empire (Tanzimat, between 1839 and 1876).

From 1869 onwards, Thessaloniki underwent gradual modernization. The Ottoman administration demolished its sea walls, allowing the city to expand toward the sea, where a modern quay was developed. A new rail link with Europe and Istanbul, established after 1872, enhanced the city's Occidental character, as did the newly organized port facilities, a modern central business district, and a growing sector of manufacturing premises at the western side. New residential areas created since the 1890s lay outside the traditional nucleus. The new middle-class districts and fashionable bourgeois suburbs at the southeastern shore were inhabited 'à-la-mixte' by wealthy Jews, Christians, and Muslims. Here, it was

262 Eleni Bastéa and Vilma Hastaoglou-Martinidis

an elevated socio-economic status, rather than religion and ethnicity, that helped bring residents together. These changes sharpened the city's socioeconomic stratification, but did not alter drastically its overall urban character.

By the turn of the 20th century, this cosmopolitan and multicultural city had a population of 150,000 inhabitants and a surface area of 900 hectares [2,224 acres] (Triantaphyllidis 1966). Thessaloniki's commercial prospects attracted many new residents, including Italian Jews, European entrepreneurs, Balkan businessmen, and members of the Greek Diaspora. Similar developments also took place in other cities of the eastern Mediterranean, such as Smyrna (Izmir), Istanbul, and Alexandria.

The turbulent 20th century: transition to single, national identity

At the beginning of the 20th century, Thessaloniki was still part of the Ottoman Empire. A succession of highly significant military and political events during the first decade of the 20th century brought radical changes to the political and cultural profile of the city. These included the Macedonian Struggle, which sought to annex Thessaloniki and the surrounding regions into the Greek state (1904–1908), the Young Turks movement, which sought to align the Ottoman Empire with Western political models (1908), the Balkan Wars, which sought to carve new, independent nation-states out of the Ottoman Empire (1912–1913), and the First World War.

In October 1912, the Greek army succeeded in capturing Thessaloniki and the surrounding regions from the Ottomans, incorporating the new land into the Greek state. During the First World War, some 200,000 Allied troops were stationed in the city. A radical transformation of the urban environment followed the end of the hostilities.

The new national boundaries and the formation of new states in parts of the Ottoman Empire brought to Thessaloniki waves of Greek refugees from the Balkans. Conversely, the exodus of Muslim Thessalonicans towards Turkey and of Jewish Thessalonicans towards Europe and Palestine began to affect the city's demographic composition. In 1916, there were over 31,000 refugees in Thessaloniki, living in precarious conditions. These included Christian Greeks and other minorities who came from Bulgaria, Serbia, and Asia Minor, both because of the changing national borders, and of broader political upheavals, such as the Russian Revolution of 1917. Many of them were to leave a few years later, under the population exchange treaties with Bulgaria and Turkey (Neuilly 1919 and Lausanne 1923). Nevertheless, these resettlements did not radically alter the city's urban profile, whose structure and form remained multiethnic (Penzopoulos 2002).

According to the 1913 census compiled by the new Greek administration, there were 157,889 inhabitants in Thessaloniki, of whom 61,439 (38.9 percent) were Jews, 45,867 (29.0 percent) were Muslims, and 39,956 (23.3 percent) were Orthodox Christians (Dimitriadis 1983, 463–464; Hastaoglou-Martinidis 1997a, 502; Bastéa 2004, 191–210). There were also French, English, and Italian

Urban change and the persistence of memory   263

inhabitants. Thessaloniki's residential and civic/religious sectors reflected the city's multiethnic population. During the Ottoman rule, Thessaloniki enjoyed a central commercial role comparable to that of Izmir or Alexandria. However, after its incorporation into the Greek state, it became a provincial center, under the shadow of Athens. Between 1855 and 1930, Greek literary production in Thessaloniki remained rather slight (Kotopoulos 2006, 43–44). Athens served as the undisputed capital of modern Greek culture and literature (Tsirimokou 1988, 15; Kotopoulos 2006, 15).

The fire of 1917 and the destruction of the historic city

In 1917, a major fire destroyed 128 hectares [316 acres] of the densely populated historical center, where commercial activities and communal institutions were concentrated. The fire destroyed over 9,500 properties, leaving over 73,000 people homeless. This disaster hit the Jewish community hardest: it destroyed three-quarters of the Jewish residential districts, leaving 52,000 persons homeless. Damages reached 1.2 billion francs (Papastathis 1978; Hastaoglou-Martinidis 1997b, 495; Yerolympos 1985, 220). To accommodate the victims of the fire, the Jewish Community, the Municipality, and the Government created seven new quarters on the outskirts of the city, housing 2,500 families in rather poor conditions. In 1924, the city added a new refugee settlement, Campbell, serving the needs of another 200 families from the burned district (Hastaoglou-Martinidis 2000, 6–10).

Joseph Nehama and other Jewish historians regard the fire as the most serious blow to the Jewish community prior to the Holocaust in 1943. Although the issue of Jewish immigration in the interwar period has not been sufficiently studied, it is estimated that more than 10,000 Jews emigrated to Palestine, while a smaller number of mainly well-off people settled in France, the US, and elsewhere (Hastaoglou-Martinidis 1997, 147–174).

The replanning and rebuilding of the city after 1918

Immediately after the fire, the Ministry of Communications (the government department responsible for town planning) set up an International Commission for the New Plan of Thessaloniki, headed by French architect Ernest Hébrard. The government used the reconstruction as a double opportunity: to modernize the urban structure, which was considered 'Oriental' due to its narrow and irregular streets and lack of clear geometry, and to Hellenize a city in which Greeks remained a minority. Following contemporary urban planning methods, the plan proposed the redesign of the intramural city along regular and geometric building blocks and provided a scheme for the whole urban area, including future extensions.

Hébrard's plan, which followed Beaux-Arts principles, radically reshaped the urban space. It proposed the transformation of Thessaloniki into a national urban center of monumental scale. The regular blocks and broad boulevards reflected planning principles of the preceding decades, evident in Georges Haussmann's designs for Paris, the City Beautiful movement in the United States, and contemporary colonial designs around the world. Ancient, Byzantine, and Ottoman historic buildings became focal points of the composition, projected against a neo-Byzantine architectural background. Apartment buildings became the predominant dwelling type, replacing the city's single-family homes. Introverted and irregular roads gave place to new, straight boulevards (Rabinow 1995). The new plan swept away the old city's layout and its characteristic picturesque qualities, now preserved only in the Upper Town. Hébrard's plan echoed the strict grid pattern of Hellenistic Thessaloniki, but articulated it with major diagonal avenues to accommodate modern traffic. This drastic urban undertaking aimed at cementing the Greek presence in the city and signaling a new national beginning.

Under Hébrard's direction, the commission completely redesigned the downtown area, introducing a central north–south civic axis, Aristotelous Avenue, linking the Upper Town with the sea. This major boulevard was to house new public departments and services. It would be lined by new buildings designed in a Neo-Byzantine style in allusion to the city's Byzantine past.

The new plan for the center, coupled with special legislation allowing for the re-distribution of the burned properties, radically altered inherited property patterns and the traditional urban layout. It erased the territorial basis of the ethnic–religious communities. Although new ownership of the historic center included many of its former residents, the numerous poorer inhabitants—mainly Jewish inhabitants—were unable to remain in the center. Social and economic criteria now stratified the new city fabric. The modern urban center, which now included financial, commercial, and civic districts, replaced earlier traditional activities and old business sites (Figure 18.1).

The implementation of Hébrard's design proceeded slowly, frequently adjusted to accommodate property claims, increased speculative activity, and the heightened economic divisions that resulted after the fire. Still, it signaled the radical

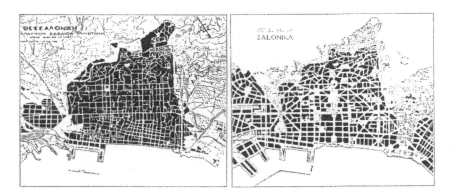

Figure 18.1 Thessaloniki, Greece. The urban fabric before the 1917 fire (left) and after the new plan of 1918 (right). (Yerolympos and Hastaoglou 1992)

Urban change and the persistence of memory 265

modernization of urban structure and form for the intramural city. After the establishment of the Republic of Turkey, planners there followed a similar strategy of *tabula rasa* (a blank slate, i.e. city redesign ignoring every previous trace) when rebuilding Izmir, whose Greek and European neighborhoods were burnt in the catastrophic fire of 1922.

The transition to double identity (1917–1928): refugees and the Population Exchange

Just five years after the fire, and while the rebuilding of the center was in progress, the city faced an unforeseen radical restructuring. Between 1919 and 1922, Greece pressed an eventually disastrous campaign in Asia Minor, aiming to incorporate Izmir and its surrounding areas into the Greek state. After the defeat of the Greek army, Greece and Turkey signed the Treaty of Lausanne (1923), which stipulated the compulsory exchange of minority populations between the two countries. Between 1920 and 1928, more than 1.2 million Orthodox Christians from Asia Minor migrated to Greece, and 355,000 Muslim Turks from Greece migrated to Turkey. At the time, Greece had fewer than five million inhabitants. The Population Exchange was the first large-scale ethnic cleansing in the region, negotiated by the League of Nations. The refugee resettlement in Greece was the biggest organized housing program for refugees of the time.

From the start, Thessaloniki was the main pole of attraction for the urban refugees: 117,000 settled in the city between 1920 and 1928, while approximately 25,000 Muslims left before or during the forced exchange. Along with them a considerable number of *Dönme* or Sabbateans (Jews converted to Islam). The city's multicultural character changed dramatically. In 1926, the population comprised 80% Greek Christians (39.65% refugees) and 15–20% Jews (instead of 40% of 1913) (Census 1926).

These dramatic changes placed extraordinary pressures on the physical resources of the city and strained the finances of the city and the state. To control these changes, the public sector stepped in to approve all levels of planning, from the allocation of refugee settlements to the urban design and building of dwellings. [2]

The Property Law of 1929 established the freehold land system in Thessaloniki's post-fire rebuilding. This 'horizontal land-ownership', as it is described in Greek, allowed the ownership of individual apartments in a multistory building and the corresponding ownership of a percentage of the original building lot. Before the introduction of the freehold system, the owner of a lot was by law also the owner of the building on it. Co-ownership was not permitted within the same building. This freehold land system also made possible the accommodation of the Asia Minor refugees of 1922–1923 and the post-1950s internal migration. It liberated real property from chronic ownership disputes and encouraged the redevelopment of urban centers and the construction of higher density apartment buildings in Thessaloniki.[3]

Housing projects for the refugees bore no resemblance to Hébrard's elaborate design. Given the urgency of these extensive building efforts, planning was reduced to the most rudimentary level, with uniform grid patterns and simple, building codes and construction techniques, without regard to each site's special conditions or the cultural background of each refugee community. As evidenced by the 1923 decree 'On the rural settlement of refugees', every settlement was to be 'planned in a rough manner and divided into building blocks'.[4] New buildings had only the minimum essentials, with little provision for social amenities such as parks or public squares.

In an expedient but haphazard manner, Thessaloniki underwent an unprecedented expansion in all directions, covering a surface area of more than 1,500 hectares (3,706 acres) by 1928 and 2,000 hectares (4,942 acres) by 1940 (Triantaphyllidis 1966). By 1930, the refugees had founded more than 50 settlements on the city's outskirts. These settlements, together with the camps for the Jewish victims of the 1917 fire, formed the 'outcast city', a ring of ghettoized districts around the historic center. In 1932, this 'second' town included 140,750 residents (out of a total of 244,680), of whom 25,750 were Jewish fire victims and 115,000 refugees (Figure 18.2).

Hébrard's redesign of the historic center, along with future extensions, had been intended to accommodate a projected population of 350,000 (twice the existing 170,000) and ultimately cover an area of 2,400 hectares (5,930 acres). Strained economic resources had a negative effect even on the city center. The construction of civic buildings stopped due to lack of funds, while the building blocks of the city bazaars were subdivided to accommodate small shopkeepers. Nevertheless,

Figure 18.2 Thessaloniki. Refugee houses in the Upper Town. An example of vernacular architecture. (Photo by V. Hastaoglou-Martinidis)

Urban change and the persistence of memory 267

the city center emanated an air of vibrant economic activity that did not extend to the refugee developments. Neglect of the cultural particularities of the different refugee groups accelerated Thessaloniki's transformation from a communal to a socially stratified city (Figures 18.3, 18.4).

A series of initiatives sought to counterbalance the loss of Thessaloniki's Ottoman-era hinterland and deal with the repercussions of the refugees' establishment. Projects undertaken between 1916 and 1926 aimed at making Thessaloniki an international transport hub and trade, business, and education center. These included: a rail connection to Athens (1918); creation of the Free Zone in the port (1914 & 1923); establishment of the American Farm School (1918); relocation of Anatolia College, an American missionary school founded in Merzifon, Turkey, in 1886, to Thessaloniki in 1924; establishment of Aristotle University (1926); and founding of the International Trade Fair (1926) (Hekimoglou 2009).

Throughout the city's 20th-century development, the historic center managed to retain some of its earlier character. This historic core overlaps with the Ottoman historic residential and commercial center, stretching north–south from the Upper Town to the Thermaic Gulf, and east–west from the White Tower to Vardari Square and the city's port. Modern architecture was restricted to the city center, with multistory apartment buildings becoming the new form of bourgeois housing. In contrast to the center's modern urban eclecticism, working-class housing on the city's outskirts was modest and semi-rural in appearance. This pattern, urban in the center and semi-rural on the outskirts, persisted for several decades before succumbing to the homogenizing urbanization that followed the post-World War II reconstruction and swept away the physical traces of Jewish and refugee quarters.

Transition to the single-identity city: World War II
and the destruction of the Jewish community

Despite the major political upheavals of the early 20th century and the destructive effects of the 1917 fire on the Jewish population, in 1940 Thessaloniki (278,000 inhabitants, 2,000 hectares) was still home to 52,350 Jews, of whom 47,289 were Greek citizens. The Jewish community, by far the largest in the country, constituted now a minority of 18% (Darques 2002, 78–79).

The German army entered Thessaloniki in April 1941 and soon applied the Nuremberg Laws on Greek Jews. These included the looting of communal treasures, the Yellow Star, forced labor, circulation restrictions, and compulsory relocation into three ghetto districts.

Two events presaged the extermination of the community: in the first one, known as the 'Black Sabbath' of 11 July 1942, the German army summoned 9,000 Jews to Liberty Square for 'registration for labor schemes'. There they were humiliated and beaten. The second involved the destruction of the ancient Jewish necropolis, which included 300,000 burials over 400 years. The 1918 plan had designated the construction of the University campus on the Jewish cemetery, but the removal of the cemetery was at first postponed. Eventually the issue was

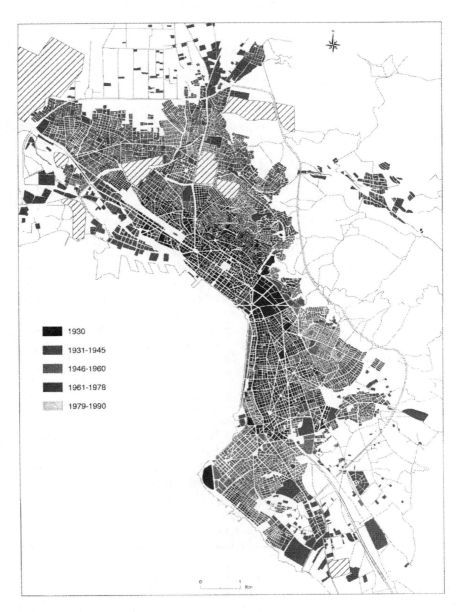

Figure 18.3 Thessaloniki. Urban growth from 1930 to 1990. (Darques 2002; Plan re-elaborated by the authors)

Figure 18.4 Thessaloniki. Street in the Upper town in 1900. (Exhibit of historical documents of Thessaloniki, Center for the History of Thessaloniki, 1985)

'resolved' by the German occupation authorities in cooperation with the municipal authorities in December 1942. Thousands of gravestones became building material, incorporated into new construction (Molho 1948, 407–417).

The Holocaust was the most appalling event in the recent history of Thessaloniki. From March to August 1943, 19 trains left the old railway station carrying some 50,000 Jews to extermination camps. After the liberation in October 1945, only about 2,000 people returned, fewer than 4% of the original community (Molho 2014, 64–73).

Post-war Thessaloniki, 1945–1980: single identity and the turn to modernity

Thessaloniki functioned in the first two post-WWII decades as a frontier town, a conservative provincial center, and a homogeneous city, now re-oriented towards Athens. It endured the consequences of a violent civil war (1946–1949),

270 *Eleni Bastéa and Vilma Hastaoglou-Martinidis*

closed borders to the north, and the Cold War priorities of the NATO alliance (1952). In these harsh conditions, the city received massive waves of internal migrants from the agrarian countryside, which multiplied its population and enlarged its space. The population climbed from 300,000 inhabitants in 1950, to 557,000 in 1971, and 706,000 in 1981. Postwar economic shortages along with the strong demand for housing pushed unregulated urban growth resulting in an over-built urban space, while squatter settlements emerged in the western periphery (Hastaoglou-Martinidis 2008, 169–171). However, this is also the period of re-organization, of the city's effort to find its new identity by squarely embracing modernity.

This new transformation relied heavily on funding from the Marshall Plan. After 1949, large urban projects were put forward by the Ministry of Reconstruction (headed by Constantine Doxiadis), the AMAG (American Mission for Aid to Greece), and the ECA (Economic Cooperation Administration) (Machado 2007, 58–72; Technical Chamber of Greece 2003, 50–61). The 1918 plan envisioned several major public buildings. Lack of funding, however, postponed their construction until after World War II, when the state utilized funds from the Marshall Plan. New buildings included a theater, a stadium, a museum, a hospital, as well as the development of the port and airport (1948).

Unalloyed modernism was first ushered into the city with the design of the Thessaloniki University complex, originally proposed by Hébrard (1919 and 1928) and later developed by Nikolaos Mitsakis (1939). The master plan for the Thessaloniki University campus was completed in 1950 by Vassilios D. Kyriazopoulos. Several prominent architects designed the individual buildings, which are part of a freestanding arrangement in a loosely articulated master plan (Kalogirou n.d., 9–17). Other key architectural elements include the International Fair, which re-opened in 1951 and was soon equipped with new modern buildings; and the Industrial zone on the city's western extension (1962). These new structures endowed Thessaloniki with a decidedly modern character (Figures 18.5, 18.6).

Between 1953 and 1973, a major urban intervention altered drastically the sea front of Thessaloniki: the New Strand, constructed at the southeast seashore, and extending from the White Tower to the Kalamaria boundary line (Figures 18.7, 18.8). Work by the Port Fund had several functions: it served NATO navy vessels, created new traffic arteries, and allowed for the redevelopment of the old coastal zone. It produced a four-kilometer-long quay, with a 150-meter-wide strip of public space. It also included the replacement of the villas once lining the shore with the present row of free-standing massive apartment blocks, specially devised for the well-off landowners of the zone (Figure 18.9). Today, this modernist cityscape dominates the face of the city from the sea. Only a few mansions survive, of more than 120, from the city's cosmopolitan phase (Kalogirou n.d., 9–17).

This was not the only consequence of an unconditioned adherence to modernity: multi-story apartment buildings displaced the modest interwar housing construction in the city center, and at times, additional floors were added to existing low-rise structures.

Figure 18.5 Thessaloniki: the death of the neighborhood: From the original historic fabric, only the monuments survived. All houses have been replaced by multi-story apartment buildings. Visible in this aerial photograph are the Alaca Imaret mosque in the foreground, a multi-dome mosque set in a square; the Yeni Hamam baths, with one dome, mostly visible; and the large basilica church of Hagios Demetrios, near the Yeni Hamam. (Photo by George Tsaousakis, used by permission)

At the same time, however, we notice the first steps towards the protection of the city's past, registering reluctantly but resolutely. The 1918 plan included the development of areas of archaeological significance. Between 1948 and 1962, archaeologists Fotis Petsas and Charalambos Makaronas fought vigorously against the development of two such sites. Thanks to their tireless efforts, the city today can be proud of two major archaeological features, the Roman Forum and the Galerian palace complex (Hastaoglou-Martinidis 2008, 169–171).

From 1980 onwards: the emergence of memory and the transition from the compact to the dispersed city

Before concluding this overview of the city's urban and political history, we would like to underline two themes: new forms of urban growth, and efforts to safeguard the city's heritage.

Starting around 1980, we notice the first efforts to protect and enhance the city's more recent architectural heritage. The first substantive attempt to control urban development involves the Thessaloniki Master Plan (TMP), approved in

Figure 18.6 Thessaloniki. The landscape of Modernism: the International Fair Grounds, the Museums, and the lower part of the historic center. (Aerial photo by George Tsaousakis, used by permission)

Figure 18.7 Thessaloniki. The creation of the modern seafront in the south-eastern shore. Source: plans elaborated by the authors after various sources. (Photo V. Hastaoglou-Martinidis)

1986.[5] The Thessaloniki Master Plan introduced measures for the protection of archaeological and historical monuments and building ensembles and allowed the adoption of special restrictive measures that dealt with circulation and space management. The plan also proposed upgrading and connecting the major historical ensembles and axes of historical importance within a network of historic walks.

Figure 18.8 Thessaloniki. The Aristotelous civic axis in the 1980s. (Aerial photo by George Tsaousakis, used by permission)

Figure 18.9 Thessaloniki. The enhancement of the old harbor with the surviving harbor market. (Aerial photo by George Tsaousakis, used by permission)

274   *Eleni Bastéa and Vilma Hastaoglou-Martinidis*

In it were included the areas from the White Tower to the Byzantine Walls; in the center, from Aristotle Square to the Vlatadon Monastery, and to the west, from the Vardari tower to the Upper Town. Furthermore, the Thessaloniki Master Plan proposed upgrading the traditional parts of Thessaloniki, such as the Upper Town and the commercial center. In 1978, we notice the transformation of the Upper Town through a controversial preservation and redevelopment project that turned the ancient city walls, together with a limited number of the original buildings, into a picturesque backdrop for middle-income housing.

According to the 1991 census, the population of Thessaloniki remained fairly stable, at 750,000 people, even as the city continued to expand towards the suburbs. There has been considerable development during the last 15–20 years towards the east of the city, especially in the suburbs of Panorama and Thermi, where we witness the gradual relocation of middle- and high-income residents, escaping the over-built and congested center. Towards the city's west side, home to a poorer sector of the population, high building coefficients have resulted in densely built blocks, lacking parks and other amenities and any sort of coordinated urban planning, resulting in an area that has been all but forgotten (Christodoulou 2020, 315–322).

Starting in the late 1990s, the compact city, with the dominant historic center and the different urban districts around it, began to split and spread into the peri-urban area. Several recent developments supported this dispersed urban form, including new road construction, the widespread use of private cars, and new development projects by globalized commercial firms. The saturated historic center, with its high land values, appears to be unable to incorporate further development. Thus new patterns of centrality appeared in the periphery of the city, mainly in the southern part, through a dynamic diffusion of the tertiary sector: shopping malls and hotels, movie complexes and casinos, banks and offices, hospitals and schools. Located along expressways, they produce a mosaic of buildings and uses, lacking any sense of coherent urban planning.

From 1992 to 1994, the European Union (sixteenth Directorate) sponsored a pilot plan for the revival of the city's historic commercial center that helped to upgrade and enhance the city's old markets, such as the harbor market (*Ladadika*) and the bazaars. The plan also funded the restoration of the Roman Forum. In 1994, a plan for the renewal and development of Thessaloniki's historic center declared a large part of the intramural city, coinciding more or less with the area destroyed by the fire of 1917, a historical site (European Commission 1992).

With Thessaloniki's designation as 1997 Cultural Capital of Europe, numerous projects and architectural competitions solicited proposals for pedestrian areas, squares, archaeological excavations, and redevelopment, drawing from the planning framework previously described. Most prominent has been the integration of the historic part of the harbor into the city's cultural life. Other important projects included the restoration of the Galerius complex and the Roman Forum, restoration and landscaping of major Byzantine sites, such as the powerful Eptapyrgion Fortress; restoration of Ottoman monuments, such as the Bezesten (Market), the Alaca Imaret (mosque), the Yeni Cami (mosque), and the Bey Hamam and the

Urban change and the persistence of memory 275

Pazar Hamam (Ottoman baths). The city has witnessed the creation of a new generation of museums, enhancing the cultural heritage and life of the city. Other planning projects included the recovery of the fin-de-siècle cosmopolitan physiognomy of the city, with the renovation of more than 30 buildings, such as private mansions, public buildings, manufacturing premises, and religious buildings, renovated to host new uses.[6]

Thus in a belated manner, contemporary urban planning is beginning to recapture and reconstruct the lost image of early 20th-century Thessaloniki, an image preserved and cultivated by the city's writers. Yet the lack of land use regulations and control by the project, and a 'flashy' style usually adopted for the renovation of old buildings has resulted in the conversion of modest retail areas into exclusive recreation spots.

Despite these recent and ambitious planning efforts, Thessaloniki retains its popular identity as the 'refugee capital' and 'mother of the poor', now home to a post-1990 influx of economic migrants from the former Eastern Bloc. The newest arrivals established themselves primarily in the upper part of the historic center, north of Egnatia Street, and in the northwest extensions of the city—that is, in areas that have received migrants to the city since the late 19th century.

The last acquisition of the city is connected to a key, yet incomplete, infrastructure project: the construction of the Metro line in the historic center that since 2006 brought into light an impressive number of finds (more than 100,000 items unearthed). The most important is the 2011 find of an 80-meter-long Byzantine street, dating from the 6th century CE, marble-paved and flanked by commercial and public buildings with colonnades and pilasters. The long debate among the Metro Company, the archaeologists, and the city authorities as to how to maintain this unique discovery in situ remains unresolved.[7] Currently underway is also the conversion of the Hamza Bey Mosque into a museum dedicated to the finds of the Metro excavation works.

Today, in 2020, the city has a population of over one million inhabitants and covers a surface area of 14,000 hectares [34,595 acres]. The increase of the middle-class has created new consumption demands, consumption patterns, and an adopted lifestyle that used to be restricted to a small privileged group. New developments opened the fourth phase of transformations, which started in conditions of prosperity, followed by the on-going overall crisis (Hastaoglou-Martinidis 2008, 169–171).

The literary response: Thessaloniki: 1912–1950s

How did literature respond to the radical urban transformations following the incorporation of Thessaloniki into the Greek state in 1912, the 1917 fire, and the influx of refugees after 1922–1923? As the literary historian Peter Mackridge pointed out, once Thessaloniki became part of the Greek state, the nation-building project included the creation of literature that featured the expanded territories (Mackridge 1997, 175–186). While the architects reshaped Thessaloniki into a modern Greek city, the writers were expected to compose new literary landscapes about Greek Thessaloniki.

276 Eleni Bastéa and Vilma Hastaoglou-Martinidis

The School of Thessaloniki was the first major modern Greek literary movement. It flourished between 1930 and 1940 and represented the work of a close-knit group of writers. They produced the modernist literary journal *Makedonikes Imeres* [Macedonian Days] (1932–1939) and published mainly works of experimental prose. Despite its name, the School of Thessaloniki exemplified rather a *lack* of place specificity and recognizable social and historical settings. Ignoring not only the nationalist propaganda but also the city's historical past, the writers described an introverted and troubled relationship with their environment, reflecting a *private* sense of loss and rootlessness. Most of the members of the School of Thessaloniki focused on the search for self and the cultivation of one's inner world, as articulated in the long interior monologues and their experimental novels. For example, in a poem titled 'Saloniki! Saloniki!' (*Macedonian Days*, September 1932), Petros Spandonidis (1890–1964) describes the city as 'chaos city'. The speaker, as a citizen of 'chaos city', has chaos within himself as well (Mackridge 1997, 180).

We believe that these writers, most of them newcomers to Thessaloniki, avoided specific discussions of the city in part because they did not yet possess a personal and deep familiarity with it. They did not grow up in the city, kicking a ball in the open areas, running by the streams crossing the city. Their focus on the interior world and their experimental prose reflected their engagement with a broader, contemporary European modernist movement.

Thessaloniki between 1950 and today

By the 1950s, we encounter works by writers who grew up in Thessaloniki and who experienced the demolition of old houses and neighborhoods and the destruction of the city of their childhood. Some writers recorded the process of change and the disappearance of the old city with a naturalist's curiosity. Others employed dramatic and apocalyptic visions. Descriptions of destruction may also allude to the greater national losses that resulted from the Asia Minor Catastrophe (Kotopoulos 2006, 55–56). Nikos Gabriil Pentzikis (1908–1993) was the only member of the School of Thessaloniki to describe the city in detail, through the eyes of a narrator who favored long walks. In his collection of essays titled *Mitera Thessaloniki* [Mother Thessaloniki] (1970), he wrote:

> For years now they have been working on widening the road. Workers go up to the old houses and demolish them. At first, the wooden skeleton of the roof is laid bare. The roof tiles are removed. The houses are left without a hat. Then starts the lowering of the walls. Their edges begin to fray. The preserved pieces resemble documents gnawed by mice. On top of the maimed wall, the worker, holding a pickax, balances precariously. A noose brings down the last resisting parts. The interior is revealed in its diverse interior spaces.
>
> (Pentzikis 1980, 13)

Vasilis Vasilikos (born in 1934 and best known for his political novel *Z*) recorded primarily the changes in the historic center and the Upper Town, focusing on the

Urban change and the persistence of memory 277

demolition of old houses, as they entered into an uneven battle with the new apartment buildings. Through vivid and even violent metaphors, he depicted the little houses falling under the ammunition of advancing engineering offices, victims of heavy building artillery (Kotopoulos 2006, 110; Vasilikos 1996).

Most writers criticized the destruction of the city's urban and social fabric. Modernity in Thessaloniki ushered in menacing, tall, anonymous, and unarticulated apartment buildings that destroyed the earlier neighborhoods and turned the streets into dark and narrow passages. Writers often described changes in the city through the eyes of a returning protagonist. For example, the main character in one of Vasilikos's novels returns to Thessaloniki after years abroad and becomes devastated to discover the disappearance of his neighborhood, and with it, 'of many narrow roads, where he had planted his agonies, his heart palpitations, in short, his whole adolescence' (Vasilikos 1999, 159; Kotopoulos 2006, 110).

More often, the narrator reflects on his own childhood memories, as Sakis Papadimitriou (b. 1940) remarked in one of his essays (1960–1973):

> All these years in this quiet neighborhood, I had almost no complaint. Of course, it was not some suburb with trees, green and openness, nevertheless, our house had its own little courtyard and next to us were other single houses or two-story houses. The apartment buildings were approaching in a threatening manner, two or three narrow streets further down. Eventually they would reach us, blocking the air, building up the courtyards, pulpifying the green. Nevertheless, we still had a lot of time ahead of us.
>
> (Papadimitriou 1980; Satrazanis 1996, 230–231)

While demolition crews uncovered the private houses and the lives taking place inside them, something about the mystery of the old city and perhaps the mystery of the narrators' own childhoods suddenly came into sharp focus, and then was lost forever.

Frequently the demolition of traditional buildings became a metaphor for the destruction of traditional neighborhood ties, as expressed in the following prose poem by Dinos Christianopoulos (b. 1931), published in 1986:

> The Death of the Neighborhood
> At night, the son of the neighbor woman, [who lived] across from me,
> was waiting for me at the door. 'Tonight my mother passed away',
> he told me, his eyes filled with tears. For a while we both remained
> silent; at that point, there were no appropriate words. 'I thought of
> letting our neighbors know of the funeral, but aside from Mrs.
> Despoina and you, no one else of the old timers is left. My mother,
> who saw all her neighbors off, will now pass on alone'.
> 'Our neighborhood, too, died with her', I thought, feeling a
> tightness in my heart.
>
> (Christianopoulos 2004a, 38)

278   *Eleni Bastéa and Vilma Hastaoglou-Martinidis*

Despite the city's continuous physical expansion, most authors described a circumscribed area, one that focused on the historic center and on the same major landmarks. These landmarks included not only historic buildings and sites but also commercial establishments, new streets and squares, the seafront, and the sea itself, the Thermaic Gulf. The White Tower continued to be the city's most recognizable symbol, a popular meeting spot and point of orientation. The city's numerous Byzantine churches, especially Hagia Sophia, acted as points of reference, along with the Red Building across from Hagia Sophia, with its ground-floor café, the foreign-language bookstore on Tsimiski Street (now closed), the basement of the (original) Fokas department store (also closed), the Modiano Market, and the Bravo coffee store. Narrators found themselves on Egnatia Street, remarking on its cheap merchandise, and on the shopping street Ermou, aptly named for the god of commerce, Hermes, where one would find most of the shoe stores during the 1960s and 1970s.

'Whether I arrive in Salonica by train, or in my imagination, I head straight up the Via Egnatia, naturally, toward the tall building where I lived for twenty-five years', remarks the narrator in Yorgos Ioannou's book of stories, *Refugee Capital* (1984). Born and raised in Thessaloniki, Ioannou (1927–1985) appeared on the literary scene in the 1960s, by which time he had moved to Athens to work as an educator (Ioannou 1997, 27; 1984, 15).

Modern planning is supposed to produce an open city, legible to newcomers and old-timers alike. Thessaloniki's new plan, ordered according to geometric and transportation axes, transformed it from an inward-focused city, legible only to its own people through a complex system of symbols and references, to a public city that was supposed to be legible to everyone. In the process, writers maintained, the city lost its distinctive interiority and its particular relationship with its inhabitants.

Most writers counterbalanced the effects of new planning by creating their own, private maps of Thessaloniki, organized around daily walks, shopping, and visits to cafés. The image of the city that continued to emerge from these narratives is not the open, modern city of the planners but rather the private city of its long-time inhabitants. In fact, as writers conveyed their own intimacy with Thessaloniki, even when they did not live there permanently, they assumed that their readers experienced the same familiarity with the city.

Consider, for example, the reference to a romantic date, described in one of the short stories by M. Karagatsis (1908–1960): 'At six in the evening. I will be there in my car in the narrow street behind the church of Hagia Sophia' (Karagatsis 1940, 152; Serefas 2006, 25). The author assumes that the reader knows the approximate if not the precise spot of the meeting.

The anti-development criticism regarding the destruction of the neighborhood notwithstanding, literary references to places—be they churches, cafés, or corner dairies—continued to characterize post-World War II literature about Thessaloniki. Moreover, although writers continued to criticize the wholesale destruction of the neighborhood, they made references to specific focal points— churches, cafes, corner stores—proving that many familiar landmarks endured.

Urban change and the persistence of memory 279

Despite the drastic planning changes, the literary city remained legible, and, for the most part, familiar to its residents.

Another example of the writers' continued intimacy with their city is the persistence of Thessaloniki as a *locus eroticus*. In the 1970s, sites of this literary image focused primarily around Vardari Square (near the train station), the still-then undeveloped suburbs of Karabournaki by the sea, in the suburb of Panorama in the hills, and in the unbuilt lots throughout the city. The following poems by Christianopoulos reveal the narrator's search for intimate encounters among the city's familiar landmarks:

Saturday Night

From Vardari to the Fountain
And from the [White] Tower to Dioikitiriou Square,
I look for you in all the sidewalks of love for hire,
I have been by all the construction sites looking for you ....
(Christianopoulos 2004b, 66)

Metaphorically, illicit love took place outside the newly planned city center, or in the undeveloped parts of the city. Nevertheless, as the population continued to expand, these earlier spaces of escape disappeared under the homogenizing effects of growth and development.

Most of the well-known writing on Thessaloniki is the work of male authors. Their views of the city included sites for trysts (homosexual and heterosexual), exploration, and refuge. In their work, the female image is usually a lover or a mother, both objects of desire and memory. Although there were women authors writing in Thessaloniki in the 1950s to 1980s, their sphere of activity remained more limited, focusing on the personal rather than the public urban experience.[8] The novel *Fear* (1998), written in English by the Greek-born Irini Spanidou, who lives and writes in the United States, referred to the exclusion of women in the traditional city:

'You and I should talk', he said.

He took her to a café, a dreary large-scale place with pale green oil-painted walls, a gray-and-black mosaic floor, and bright bare light bulbs hanging on black cords. There was a scattering of customers—two old men playing checkers, four men playing cards, a group of merchant marines drinking ouzo, and a solitary drunk.

There were no women. He always took her places where no women went: the barber, his tailor, men's cafés—places where he should be going alone but needed company.

(Spanidou 1998, 99)

280 *Eleni Bastéa and Vilma Hastaoglou-Martinidis*

From home to apartment: mass construction, evil developers, and provincial newcomers

As the city changed, writers bemoaned not only the loss of its earlier character, but also of its earlier way of life. In one of his novels, Vasilis Vasilikos likened apartment buildings to prisons and apartments to prison cells. In another novel, the protagonist, alienated by the dominant political and social conditions, compared his condition to that of a deserted, traditional, single-family house, surrounded by identical apartment buildings with dirty light wells and no psychological escape (Vasilikos 1996; Bakolas 1990; Kotopoulos 2006, 114). (At the time, the apartment buildings lacked fire escapes as well.)

Although all of these changes were primarily the result of government legislation, most writers did not direct their anger toward the state. Contractors and predatory developers became the villains in many stories, as they exploited *antiparochi* (the exchange of a building plot for apartments in the high-rise built upon it) and destroyed the city forever. Yorgos Ioannou described the situation in one of his short stories (1972–1973):

> The house had already been surrendered to a gang of developers and in its place was erected an apartment building, among the most hideous ones. Now they are getting ready to demolish it, these ridiculous people. Who knows what their cunning brains have conceived for the next business plan?[9]

Perhaps the narrators despised these contractors precisely because they were 'of the people', as they often came from the working class, but profited from the city's loss of character. In a novel by Nikos Bakolas (1927–1999), contractors were compared to the black marketeers who profited from their compatriots during the German occupation (Bakolas 1987, 86; Kotopoulos 2006, 116).

In the 1950s and 1960s, there were only two notable exceptions to the ubiquitous apartment building developments: the flight of many higher income residents to the hills of Panorama, an exclusive Thessaloniki suburb, and the appearance of the 'villa' typology, an expensive, often modernist single-family dwelling surrounded by a large garden. Yet even these villas succumbed to wholesale apartmentization of the 1970s.

The new planning and architecture intensified Thessaloniki's social and economic stratification. Escaping to the city of the past became the defense mechanism for some of the writers, who did not recognize the new city with the newcomers from the villages and the hinterland. In the literature from the 1960s and 1970s, we notice a recurring distinction between the long-time urban residents of the city and the provincial newcomers, who became either excited or alienated by city life. Many of the writers dwelled especially on the inability and unwillingness of these newcomers to integrate themselves into the city's fabric, just as the earlier refugees from Asia Minor had remained apart from the local population for at least one generation.

In a story by Tilemachos Alaveras (1926–2007), published in 1976, the narrator observes that domestic refugees 'from all of Northern Greece, from New

Urban change and the persistence of memory 281

Orestiada, to Tsotyli came and perched in the developers' matchboxes' (Alaveras 1976, 108; Kotopoulos 2006, 116).

Yorgos Ioannou underscored this distinction between old residents and new-comers in the following newspaper chronicle, published in 1978:

> In the wide streets, stroll the people from the provinces on Sundays—in the morning, especially, and in the early afternoon. Of course, the locals stroll, too, but they are a lot fewer.[10]

In his essay collection *Mother Thessaloniki*, Pentzikis reflected on change through the eyes of an older woman:

> Already the street has been widened in parts and buses go by, full of the population that has increased. The little lady in the poor little house across the street does not recognize her neighborhood any more. "Where did all the mansions go" she reflects, looking out of the narrow window of her house [...] The only child of the wealthy home owner, who was planning to get married in that house someday, expired with the demolition of his house. Elsewhere, they destroyed altogether sixty imposing elm trees.
>
> (Pentzikis 1970, 15)

The narrator is not only recording physical change here. He is describing, also, the disappearance of the old, stable social order, as he laces his nostalgia with a conservative and selective reimagining of the past.

Nevertheless, not all literary references were negative. Some of the characters in the work of Vasilikos and Ioannou remark that although the demolitions and higher density new building destroyed old neighborhoods, they did succeed in revealing and highlighting the city's Byzantine physiognomy, as many of the Byzantine landmarks became focal points of the new designs. The authors also acknowledged that from the point of view of the poorer residents, moving into apartment buildings signaled an improvement of their living conditions. Ioannou underscored that, for the first time, many of the refugees were able to move into their own apartments, after suffering through long periods of temporary, make-shift, and crammed housing. Some of the characters in the novels by Vasilikos, return to Thessaloniki after long absences abroad. They acknowledge, then, the overall improvements in the city, even at the cost of the old neighborhoods (Kotopoulos 2006, 116–121).

Contemporary planning and literary sites

On the urban scale, Thessaloniki's historic identity was enriched by three major archeological discoveries: the uncovering of the Forum Romanum, the Palace and parts of the Hippodrome of the complex of Galerius Maximianus (*reg.* 305–311), and a large part of the Hellenistic and Roman city that had been uncovered at the northwest section of the center (Dioikitiriou Square). In addition, for the

282   Eleni Bastéa and Vilma Hastaoglou-Martinidis

first time a concurrent policy of conservation listed all of the city's Ottoman monuments.[11]

Important as these discoveries were from an archeological point of view, they did not feature prominently in the city's literature. Beyond the personal memories that marked the topographies of their novels, writers acknowledged also the presence of the major historical and political landmarks. Several works referred to the political assassination of Grigoris Lambrakis in 1963 near the intersection of Ermou and Venizelou Streets. This assassination became the subject of the book *Z* by Vasilis Vasilikos (1967) and the French-language film of that name (1969).

In a short story by Sakis Serefas (b. 1960), published in 1996, the narrator remarked: 'My girlfriend was standing on the point where Lambrakis was killed right next to the commemorative sculpture' (Kotopoulos 2006, 138–141; Serefas 1996, 63; 2006, 40). Once again, the writer recorded the city's intimate history and topography from a local's point of view, assuming that the reader shares in that knowledge.

In a short story by Dimitris Miggas (b. 1951), published in 2003, the narrator seeks to escape from the present as he routinely climbs up to the Upper Town. Listing a string of streets and bus routes, he aims to fix the city in his memory unchanged:

> It was raining again yesterday. I went up to the Walls by bus and then went down on foot. Akropoleos, Dimitriou Poliorkitou, Tsinari, Athonos, Theophilou, and Akropoleos again.
>
> (Miggas 2003, 61)

We find a similar stringing of place names in the works of Vasilikos and Bakolas. As the literary critic Triantafyllos Kotopoulos remarked, they represent a broken, partial depiction of the city, rather like the tesserae of a large mosaic of a broken image, a multifocal narrative of many heroes (Kotopoulos 2006, 92).

Beginning in the 1970s, the city initiated efforts to protect and enhance the Upper Town's architectural heritage. Until then, one could stroll along narrow streets and gaze at modest, single-family houses from the 19th and early 20th centuries. Since 1978, however, the intramural area of Upper Town underwent changes through a preservation and redevelopment project that allowed the construction of neo-vernacular two- or three-story apartment buildings, akin to the New Urbanism architecture in North America. Before then the Upper Town, with its traditional urban quarters and strong presence of refugee and Jewish residents, played a central role in the city's literary image.

In Vasilikos's novel *Thymata eirinis* [Victims of Peace] (1956) the protagonist brings tour groups to the Upper Town. By always following a strict, predetermined itinerary around the central sites, he is able to describe the city's historical continuity. However, in his story 'To phyllo' [The Page] (1994), the narrator wanders around the narrow and labyrinthine passages of the Upper Town, which reflect his isolation and tangled human relations (Kotopoulos 2006, 105). Thus in some cases, the Upper Town has been depicted as safely retaining the characters'

Urban change and the persistence of memory 283

youthful memories, while at other times it is shown in the throes of change and destruction.

A unified policy of major public works aimed to shape the city's modern character. Both the establishment of the university and the fairgrounds signaled the progressive intellectual and commercial forces that have shaped northern Greece.[12] Despite its central location and its significance as a site of modernist designs, the university campus remains outside of most city inhabitants' daily experience,[13] while the Thessaloniki International Fair has enjoyed the broadest interest among the local population. As an institution, the Fair began in 1926 on the Military Esplanade, moving to its present location in 1939. Its informal layout includes several exhibition pavilions, both permanent and temporary, with the most important structures completed between 1960 and 1975 (Kalogirou n.d., 17). The Fair's populist organization, combining a variety of industrial exhibits with old-style amusement park entertainment, created an open environment for the promotion of modern architecture. For most visitors, the Fair offered one of the few opportunities to experience modern buildings, as most other new structures, primarily apartment buildings, remained modest and utilitarian. The significance of the Fair in people's lives is also evident in the many commemorative family photographs that record annual visits.

The International Fair is the only modern site that features prominently in literary works (Kotopoulos 2006, 263–265). In the following undated poem, Christianopoulos captured the contrast between the urban resident, who yearns to escape the crowds, and his lover from the village, who revels in the Fair's opportunities for popular amusement:

At the Fair

I met you at the Fair, amongst the lights,
amongst the crowd, very tight,
and immediately I suggested we go to some deserted area.

But you had come from the village for entertainment;
we had to get on the bumper cars,
buy ice cream, go into the House of Horrors,
I had to treat you to a sandwich and dark beer,
buy you a lighter as a souvenir.

I didn't realize that you were fed up with deserted areas.

(Christianopoulos 2004b, 88)

The development of the seafront changed the whole face of the city as seen from the sea. In most literature, the seafront represents a central place of escape, entertainment, solitary reflection, and identification with the city (Kotopoulos 2006, 182–190; Karelli 1988). While Pentzikis underscored the picturesque view of the sea from the city, Alaveras focused on the more recent problems regarding the pollution of the Thermaic Gulf (Kotopoulos 2006, 190, 193).

284 *Eleni Bastéa and Vilma Hastaoglou-Martinidis*

The development of Aristotelous Avenue gave the city its most important urban complex, complete with symmetrical neo-Byzantine arcades, and prescribed building façades, terminating in an expansive square with a view of the Thermaic Gulf. This imposing north–south axis, one of the hallmarks of Hébrard's design, appeared in the work of some authors, including Vasilikos and Bakolas (Kotopoulos 2006, 123–124).

In general, writers placed their characters in the city center when the story called for action and in the Upper Town when the story called for reflection, escape, or return to an earlier time. Given the relatively recent experiences of the German occupation and civil war, and considering the city's working-class roots, many stories hinge on political action, with their protagonists crisscrossing the city as they carry out special assignments. According to Kotopoulos, the sites of the city itself became the protagonists in some of the novels by Alaveras and Ioannou, who depicted the city in exhaustive detail (Kotopoulos 2006, 81, 92, 103–104, 106).

Conclusion: literary memory and urban change

Unlike newspaper accounts, which offer an ongoing commentary on contemporary political and urban changes, literature often dwells in the past. Poets and writers may reflect on earlier periods, as the past enjoys a firmer hold on the consciousness of both the writers and their readers. Current research on autobiographical memory concurs that only 'few vivid memories are reported after early adulthood', resulting in 'few new formative experiences occur[ring] after early childhood' (Robinson and Taylor 1998, 125–126). Most individuals, when asked to recount their past, give a very detailed account of their childhood, up to about age 12. After that, their stories tend to trail off, and long periods pass in a cursory manner.

> When I think of Buenos Aires, I think of the Buenos Aires I knew as a child: the low houses, the patios, the porches, the cisterns with turtles in them, the grated windows. That Buenos Aires was all of Buenos Aires,

reflected the Argentine author Jorge Luis Borges (Lopate 1994, 379). Not only are most memories related to childhood, but also memory itself seems to improve, not decay, with time. Encoded childhood memory appears more resistant to forgetting as time passes (Schacter 1996, 72–97 and passim). Notice, for example, how the author Sakis Papadimitriou described the changes in the Thessaloniki of his childhood in an essay collection (1960–1973):

> The imposing new boulevard. All the houses that used to be by the sea retreated by about one hundred meters and in front of them, later, will be planted apartment buildings. And now I think of how we used to plunge into the sea from the courtyards, or go on a boat ride while our family watched us from one of the balconies. Everything was so close, squeezed tightly,

gathered together. As I go by the boulevard by car now, I see the half-demolished single houses, as when we used to go out in the little boat; in a short while, none of the houses will be left. They are counterfeiting our memories, stealing our childhood images.

(Papadimitriou 1980, 76; Satrazanis 1996, 232)

One of Ioannou's narrators acknowledged the disappearance of the picturesque city of his childhood, the 'old', 'moldy', 'burnt-smelling', 'enchanting' city of around 1940. In another story, the narrator recommended better protection and preservation of certain old buildings. Demolishing these buildings betrayed the ignorance of those who control the city's future. Along the same lines, the narrator of another story underscores that the city's plan was drawn by 'people who neither know us nor feel for us'.[14] One of the characters of Alaveras reflects with melancholy that his nephews walk on the same roads, which, however, follow different planning trends. 'The city's color has been altered'. The neighborhood 'is now defined by more multi-story buildings, and from two and three rows of parked cars'.[15] Evocative as these comments are, they do leave open the question of *knowing* a city. How can planners come to know a city? How can newcomers come to know it? Should urban planning acknowledge the sites of specific historical events?

Several prominent themes emerge from the literature on Thessaloniki: nostalgia and sadness, anger, death, loss of recognition and identity, and illicit sex. Writers relied on their own memory to describe the destruction of old neighborhoods and the construction of new buildings. As a whole, literature also waged a direct or indirect critique of various modernization projects. Although some of the writers embraced urban change, most criticized it, longing for the city of their childhood. Nevertheless, we cannot assign the statements or actions of narrators to the writers themselves. In fact, like the majority of the city's inhabitants, most writers lived in the new, poorly constructed, anonymous apartment buildings and only saw the few surviving old buildings in their walks. Nevertheless, they often chose to locate their narratives in the narrow parts of the city that had escaped demolition and rebuilding.

Writers did not criticize urban change only because it disrupted their childhood memories. Surrounded by buildings dating from the 1960s and later, the personal dislocation of the narrators became a metaphor for the dislocation, disorientation, and alienation of the modern inhabitant. Criticism of urban development often reflected criticism of modernization itself. Nevertheless, Greek people continued to oscillate in their position—at times identifying with the writers who held onto a world of the past, while at other times becoming seduced by the siren songs of progress and better life, promised by small-time developers, architects, and the media.

More broadly, urban literature on Thessaloniki mirrored contemporary international literary tropes and themes. Although some writers around the world embraced life in the modern urban environment, others used literature for refuge and escape, making it possible to tolerate the modern city. The writers we

286 *Eleni Bastéa and Vilma Hastaoglou-Martinidis*

reviewed may have criticized the lack of dreaming spaces in the modern city, yet they accepted the inevitability of that city and continued to reside in it.

Notes

1 My dear friend and co-author Eleni Bastéa passed away on January 12, 2020, without seeing the final proofs of a paper that was largely of her inspiration. This theme of memory has been at the heart of Eleni's scientific and literary output, as a place for reflection, modus operandi, and payment of debts to her roots and to present-day experience. She treated her subject with the honesty, generosity and perseverance that distinguished her academic work and presence. Her colleagues will greatly miss her kind disposition, sense of responsibility and creative spirit; and I will miss intensely the summer reunions in our shared home-town, Thessaloniki. (V.H.) An earlier version of this chapter was published as Bastéa and Hastaoglou-Martinidis 2013, 90–117. We would like to thank our colleagues Panayiota Pyla, Carol Krinsky, Yorgo Anagnostou, Christopher Bakken, Tina Godhi, Edmund Keeley, Helen Kolias, Vasili Lambropoulos, Peter Mackridge, and Sakis Serefas for their comments and suggestions regarding the city's urbanism and literary history. Unless otherwise noted, translations from the Greek literary texts are by Eleni Bastéa.
2 This large-scale approach to urban design, unparalleled in Greek planning history, was backed by uniform legislation and made possible only after the reform of the Constitution in 1927 (article 119), permitting the establishment of urban refugee settlements. See Hastaoglou-Martinidis 1996, 499 and 507, note 22.
3 The Property Law of 1929 established the freehold land system on a national scale. Based on the freehold system, all apartment owners in an apartment building today are co-proprietors of the lot and own a percentage of the lot, that is equivalent to the surface area of their apartment. No one knows or can know where exactly this portion is located. The complicated land ownership patterns that have arisen now from this system make it nearly impossible to tear down and rebuild existing apartment buildings to better specifications and building codes. As a result, the city of Thessaloniki has thus become hostage to the system that once allowed it to grow and provide apartment ownership to the majority of its population. On the freehold land system, see Marmaras 1991, 23–32.
4 Refugee settlements, haphazardly built on the city's outskirts, were outside the jurisdiction of the Ministry of Communications. Instead, the settlements fell under the jurisdiction of the Ministry of Social Welfare, a department lacking any city planning competence. See Hastaoglou-Martinidis 2011, 8–48; Kalogirou 1986, 488.
5 Law 1561, *Government Gazette* A–148/6.9.1985, and the General Urban Plan for Thessaloniki, approved early in 1993, *Government Gazette* A-420/27.4.1993.
6 On the strategic plan of Thessaloniki, see Papamichos et al. 1994. On the planning events on the occasion of Thessaloniki, Cultural Capital of Europe, 1997, see Hastaoglou-Martinidis 2002.
7 «Θεσσαλονίκη: Πάνω από 100.000 τα αρχαιολογικά ευρήματα στο Μετρό» [Thessaloniki: over 100,000 archaeological finds in the Metro] www.tovima.gr/cultur e/article/?aid=540497, Athens: *To Vima* 19 November 2013 (consulted July 2019).
8 See, for example, the work of Zoe Karelli, Nina Kokkalidou-Nahmia, and of the authors included in the following anthologies: *Η Θεσσαλονίκη των συγγραφέων: 20 Διηγήματα για τη Θεσσαλονίκη* [Writers' Thessaloniki: 20 Short Stories about Thessaloniki] (Thessaloniki: Ianos, 1996); and Serefas 2006.
9 Yorgos Ioannou, 'Στου Κεμάλ το σπίτι' ['In the house of Kemal'], short story included in Ioannou 1982, 56.
10 Yorgos Ioannou, 'Οι μεγάλοι δρόμοι' ['The large streets'], *Kathimerini* newspaper column, 1978, reprinted in Ioannou 1986, 9, cited in Satrazanis 1996, 107.

Urban change and the persistence of memory 287

11 The Directorate of Byzantine and Post-Byzantine Monuments was established in 1938. The Directorate of Modern Monuments—that is, buildings dating after 1830—was established in 1979.
12 On the cultural and political significance of the university and the International Fair, see also Mackridge 1997, 176.
13 Novels and essays that refer to the university include those whose protagonists are students or faculty there. See Kotopoulos 2006, 265–267.
14 Yorgos Ioannou, 'Σειχ Σου' ['Seich Sou'] and 'Απογραφή ζημιών' ['Inventory of Damages'] in the essay collection *Το δικό μας αίμα* [Our Own Blood] (Athens: Kedros, 1980), pp. 147, 222, and Yorgos Ioannou, 'Τσιρίδες' ['Screams'] in *Η σαρκοφάγος* [The Sarcophagus], 1971, p. 107, all cited in Kotopoulos 2006, 107–110.
15 Tilemachos Alaveras, 'Άρτα κορ' ['in Greek'], short story included in the collection *Απ' αφορμή* [On Occasion], p. 104, cited in Kotopoulos 2006, 108.

References

Adam-Veleni, P., *Θεσσαλονίκη νεράϊδα, βασίλισσα, γοργόνα ; αρχαιολογική περιδιάβαση από την προϊστορία έως την ύστερη αρχαιότητα* [Thessaloniki Fairy, Queen, Mermaid: Archaeological Tour from prehistory to Late Antiquity], Thessaloniki: Zetros (2001).
Alaveras, T., 'Αμιξία', [Separation], short story included in the collection *Απ' αφορμή* [On Occasion], Thessaloniki: Nea Poreia (1976), 108.
Alaveras, T., 'Άρτα κορ' [in Greek], short story included in the collection *Απ' αφορμή* [On Occasion], Athens: Nea Poreia (1976), 104.
Bakolas, N., *Η μεγάλη πλατεία* [The Great Square], Athens: Kedros (1987).
Bakolas, N., *Καταπάτηση* [Violation], Athens: Kedros (1990).
Bastéa, E., 'Storied cities: Literary memories of Thessaloniki and Istanbul', In: Bastéa, E. (ed.), *Memory and Architecture*, Albuquerque: University of New Mexico Press (2004), 191–210.
Bastéa, E. and Hastaoglou-Martinidis, V., 'Modernization and its discontents in post-1950s Thessaloniki: Urban change and urban narratives', In: Pyla, P. (ed.), *Landscapes of Development: The impact of Modernization Discourses on the Physical Environment of the Eastern Mediterranean*, Cambridge, MA: Harvard U. Graduate School of Design (2013), 90–117.
Borges, J. L., 'Blindness', In: Weinberger, E. (tr.), *Jorge Luis Borges: Seven Nights*, New York: New Directions (1980).
Christianopoulos, D., *Πεζά ποιήματα* [Prose Poems], 4th edition, Thessaloniki: Ianos (2004a).
Christianopoulos, D., *Ποιήματα* [Poems], 4th edition, Thessaloniki: Ianos (2004b).
Christodoulou, Ch., 'The post-war transformation of the Thessaloniki periphery: Urbanization and landscape', In: Keridis, D. and J. B. Kiesling (eds.), *Thessaloniki: A City in Transition, 1912–2012* [Thessaloniki: City in Transition, 1912–2012], Oxford: Routledge (2020), 310–322.
Darques, R., *Salonique au XXe siècle: De la cité ottomane à la métropole grecque*, Paris: CNRS (2002).
Dimitriadis, V., *Η Τοπογραφία της Θεσσαλονίκης κατά την εποχή της Τουρκοκρατίας, 1430—1912* [Topography of Thessaloniki under Turkish Rule 1430–1912], Thessaloniki: Society for Macedonian Studies (1983).

288 Eleni Bastéa and Vilma Hastaoglou-Martinidis

European Commission General Directorate 16, *Πρότυπο Σχέδιο για την ανανέωση και ανάπτυξη του ιστορικού κέντρου της Θεσσαλονίκης, 1992–95* [Model Plan for the Renewal and Development of the Historical Center of Thessaloniki], Thessaloniki: Region of Central Macedonia (1992–95). Photocopy.

Halbwachs, M., *The Collective Memory*, Ditter, F. J. Jr. and Ditter, V. Y. (trs.)., New York: Harper Colophon Books (1980).

Hastaoglou-Martinidis, V., 'A Mediterranean City in transition: Thessaloniki between the two wars', *Facta Universitatis, Series: Architecture and Civil Engineering*, 1.4 (1997a), 493–507.

Hastaoglou-Martinidis, V., 'On the state of the Jewish Community of Salonica after the fire of 1917', In: Hassiotis, I. (ed.), *The Jewish Communities of Southeastern Europe from the 15th to the 20th century*, Thessaloniki: Institute for Balkan Studies (1997b), 147–174.

Hastaoglou-Martinidis, V., 'Η κατασκευή των προσφυγικών συνοικισμών Κάμπελ–Βότση, Βυζαντίου' [The construction of refugee settlements Campbell–Votsi, Vizantio], *ΧΡΟΝΙΚΑ, Όργανο του Κεντρικού Ισραηλιτικού Συμβουλίου Ελλάδας*, 23/165 (2000), 6–10.

Hastaoglou-Martinidis, V., 'Looking towards the past, looking towards the future. Urban design projects for Thessaloniki 1997 cultural capital of Europe', *Paper Presented at the Hellenic Studies Conference, Modern Greece and its Monuments*, Whitney Humanities Center, Yale University, April 5–6 (2002).

Hastaoglou-Martinidis, V., 'Νεωτερικότητα και μνήμη στη διαμόρφωση της μεταπολεμικής Θεσσαλονίκης' ['Modernity and memory in the planning of post-war Thessaloniki'], In: Kaukalas, G., Lambrianidis, L. and Papamichos, N. (eds.) *Η Θεσσαλονίκη στο μεταίχμιο. Η πόλη από τη σκοπιά των αλλαγών* [Thessaloniki at the Edge: A City from the Perspective of Changes], Athens: Kritiki (2008), 169–171.

Hastaoglou-Martinidis, V., 'Προσφυγική εγκατάσταση και πολεοδομικοί μετασχηματισμοί της Θεσσαλονίκης, 1922–30' ['Refugee settlement and urban changes in Thessaloniki, 1922–30'], In: *Η μεταμόρφωση της Θεσσαλονίκης. Η εγκατάσταση των προσφύγων στην πόλη (1920–40)* [The Transformation of Thessaloniki. The Settlement of Refugees in the City, 1920–40], Thessaloniki: Historical Archive of Refugee Greeks (2011), 38–48.

Hastaoglou-Martinidis, V., 'Η κατασκευή της Νέας Παραλίας στη Θεσσαλονίκη, 1953–1972' ['The construction of the New Strand in Thessaloniki, 1953–1972'], In: Vitopoulou, A., Karadimou-Gerolympou, A. and Tournikiotis, P. (eds.), *Η ελληνική πόλη και η πολεοδομία του μοντέρνου* [The Greek City and the Urban Design of Modernity], Athens: Futura (2015), 315–329.

Hekimoglou, E., *Θεσσαλονίκη. Τεκμήρια Φωτογραφικού Αρχείου 1900–1980*, [Thessaloniki. Documents of Photographic Archive 1900–1980], Athens: Ministry of the Interior, General Secretariat of Communication (2009).

Ioannou, Y., 'Salonica–Athens: A study in comparative erotics', In: Reed, F. A. (tr.), *Refugee Capital*, Athens: Kedros (1997), Originally in Greek, Yorgos Ioannou, Η πρωτεύουσα των προσφύγων, Athens: Kedros (1984).

Ioannou, Y., 'Τσιρίδες' ['Screams'] in *Η σαρκοφάγος* [The Sarcophagus], Athens: Kedros (1971).

Ioannou, Y., 'Στου Κεμάλ το σπίτι' ['In the house of Kemal'], short story included in the collection Ioannou, Y., *Η μόνη κληρονομιά* [The Only Inheritance], Athens: Kedros (1974, 1982).

Urban change and the persistence of memory 289

Ioannou, Y., 'Σειχ Σου' ['Seich Sou'] and 'Απογραφή ζημιών' ['Inventory of Damages'] in the essay collection *Το δικό μας αίμα* [Our Own Blood], Athens: Kedros (1980).

Ioannou, Y., 'Οι μεγάλοι δρόμοι' ['The large streets'], *Kathimerini* newspaper column, 1978, reprinted in Ioannou, Y., *Εύφλεκτη χώρα* [Flammable Country], Athens: Kedros (1986).

Kalogirou, N. S., *Post-War Architecture and Town Planning in Thessaloniki* (in Greek and English). Athens: Barbounakis (n.d.).

Kalogirou, N., 'La croissance de la banlieue de Thessalonique. Les nouveaux caractères de l'espace urbaine', (in Greek with French summary), In: *Η Θεσσαλονίκη μετά το 1912* [Thessaloniki after 1912] Conference Proceedings, 1–3 Nov. 1985, Thessaloniki: Municipality of Thessaloniki (1986).

Karagatsis, M., *Ο Γιούγκερμαν και τα στερνά του* [Yugerman and his Last Hours], Athens: Estia (1940, 2000).

Karelli, Z., *για τη θάλασσα* [For the Sea], Athens: Roes (1988).

Kotopoulos, T. I., *Η Θεσσαλονίκη στο έργο των Θεσσαλονικέων πεζογράφων* [Thessaloniki in the Work of Thessalonikan Prose Writers], Thessaloniki: Kodikas (2006).

Lopate, P., *The Art of the Personal Essay, An Anthology from the Classical Era to the Present*, New York: Anchor Books, Doubleday (1994).

Machado, B., *In Search of a Usable Past: The Marshall Plan and Postwar Reconstruction Today*, Lexington, VA: George C. Marshall Foundation (2007).

Mackridge, P., 'Cultivating new lands: The consolidation of territorial gains in Greek Macedonia through literature, 1912–40', In: Mackridge, P. and Yannakakis, E. (eds.), *Ourselves and Others: The Development of a Greek Macedonian Cultural Identity since 1912*, Oxford: Berg (1997).

Marmaras, M., *Η αστική πολυκατοικία της μεσοπολεμικής Αθήνας* [The Urban Apartment Building of Inter-War Athens], Athens: Politistiko Technologiko Idryma ETVA (1991).

Mazower, M., *Salonica: City of Ghosts, Christians, Muslims and Jews, 1430–1950*, London: HarperCollins (2004).

Miggas, D., *Της Θεσσαλονίκης μοναχά* [Only for Salonica], Athens: Metaichmio (2003).

Molho, M., *Memoriam: Hommage aux Victimes Juives des Nazis en Grèce*, Thessalonique: Communauté Israélite de Thessalonique (1948).

Molho, R., *Οι Εβραίοι της Θεσσαλονίκης 1856–1919. Μια ιδιαίτερη κοινότητα* [The Jews of Thessaloniki 1856–1919: A distinctive community], Athens: Patakis Editions, [2001] (2014).

National Statistical Service of Greece, Population census, Thessaloniki, Athens: National Statistical Service of Greece, Ministry of the Interior (1926).

Papadimitriou, S., *Πεζά 1960–73* [Prose 1960–73] Thessaloniki: Diagonios (1980).

Papamichos, N., Hastaoglou, V., Hadjimihalis, K., Kafkoula, K., Yerolympos, A., *Thessaloniki in the Twenty-first century: Growth, environment, culture. Contribution towards the development of the Strategic Plan* (in Greek, unpublished research report), Organization for the Master Plan of Thessaloniki, Greek Ministry of Planning (1994–1995).

Papastathis, Ch., 'A memoir on the fire in Thessaloniki in 1917 and the relief victims', *Makedonika*, 18 (1978), 143–170 (in Greek).

Pentzikis, N. G., *Μητέρα Θεσσαλονίκη* [Mother Thessaloniki] Athens: Kedros (1970).

Pentzopoulos, D., *The Balkan Exchange of Minorities and its Impact on Greece*, London: Hurst & Company, [1962] (2002).

290   Eleni Bastéa and Vilma Hastaoglou-Martinidis

Rabinow, P., *French Modern: Norms and Forms of the Social Environment*, Chicago, IL: University of Chicago Press, reprint edition (1995).

Robinson, J. A. and Taylor, L. R., 'Autobiographical memory and self-narratives: A tale of two stories', In: Thompson, C. P., Herrmann, D. J., Bruce, D., Read, J. B., Payne, D. G., Toglia, M. P., (eds.), *Autobiographical Memory: Theoretical and Applied Perspectives*, Mahwah, NJ: Lawrence Erlbaum Associates (1998), 125–126.

Satrazanis, A., *La ville de Thessalonique dans la prose locale, 1935–1985*, Thessaloniki: Centre d'Histoire de Thessalonique (1996).

Schacter, D. L., *Searching for Memory: The Brain, the Mind, and the Past*, New York: Basic Books (1996).

Serefas, S., 'Τελικά μπούτι ήταν' ['At the end, it was a thigh'], short story included in the collection *Το σπίτι υποδέχεται* [The House Receives], Athens: Kedros (1996).

Serefas, S. (ed.), *Θεσσαλονίκη: Μια πόλη στη λογοτεχνία* [Thessaloniki: A City in Literature], Athens: Metaichmio (2006).

Spanidou, I., *Fear*, New York: Alfred A. Knopf (1998).

Technical Chamber of Greece [Τεχνικό Επιμελητήριο Ελλάδος], *80 χρόνια ΤΕΕ, οδοιπορικό στον χρόνο* [80 years, Technical Chamber of Greece, Travelogue in Time], Athens: Technical Chamber of Greece (November 2003), 50–61.

Triantaphyllidis, I., *Χωροταξική Μελέτη Θεσσαλονίκης* [Urban Planning Study of Thessaloniki], Thessaloniki: First Stage (1966) issue 25.

Tsirimokou, L., *Λογοτεχνία της πόλης* [Literature of the City], Athens: Lotos (1988).

Vasilikos, V., *Δεν μετανιώνω για τα δάκρυα που έχυσα για σένα* [I Do Not Regret the Tears I Shed for You], Athens: Nea Synora (1996).

Vasilikos, V., *Ο Ευρωπέος και η ωραία του υπερπέραν* [The European and the Beauty from the World Beyond], Athens: Nea Sinora–A. A. Livani (1999).

Writers' Thessaloniki (collective work), *Η Θεσσαλονίκη των συγγραφέων: 20 Διηγήματα για τη Θεσσαλονίκη* [20 Short Stories about Thessaloniki], Thessaloniki: Ianos (1996).

Yerolympos, A., *The Replanning of Thessaloniki after the Fire of 1917* (in Greek, with summaries in English and French), Thessaloniki: Municipality of Thessaloniki (1985).

Yerolympos, A. and Hastaoglou, V., 'Καταστροφές και μεταπλάσεις. Η γένεση της σύγχρονης πόλης' ['Catastrophes and remolding: The genesis of a contemporary city'], *Themata Chorou kai Technon*, 23 (1992), 17–26.

19 French interests and Salonica's port, 1872–1912

Entrepreneurial and architectural innovation

Vilma Hastaoglou-Martinidis

The period between 1860 and 1900 was a time of intensive harbour construction throughout the eastern Mediterranean, spurred by the opening of the Suez Canal in 1869. The tremendous increase in maritime trade in the Levant went hand in hand with European economic penetration, triggering various processes of modernisation led by transport infrastructure: harbours and railways were developed concurrently, creating a new economic arena in which French, English, and German interests competed. The major cities involved in maritime trade in the Levant—Alexandria, Smyrna, Beirut, Constantinople, and Salonica—acquired modern port facilities, with new quays on extensive embankments, solid moles, spacious wharves, breakwaters, and specialised building equipment. In every case, the harbour works also entailed radical changes to the traditional waterfront (Hastaoglou-Martinidis 2010, 78–99) (Table 19.1).

The port of Salonica, exclusively the work of French contracting companies, would prove the most important and long-lived French enterprise in the city. It lasted from 1896 until 1930, when the Greek State purchased the port operating rights.[1] Its construction implicated prominent French firms, such as the *Société de Construction des Batignolles*, the *Société Anonyme Ottomane du Port de Salonique* of Edmond Bartissol, and the *Bureau Technique de Béton Armé de François Hennebique*. Their work was supported by skilled graduates of the '*grandes écoles*'—mostly the École des Ponts et Chaussées, the École Centrale des Arts et des Manufactures, and the École des Arts et Métiers. The history of this venture includes interesting material regarding entrepreneurial antagonisms, engineering accomplishments, and architectural/urbanist programs, some of which still form part of Salonica's technical inheritance.

This presentation will follow the steps taken in the less well-documented initial phase for the creation of the harbour. It draws on unpublished material held in various archival sources in Greece and abroad, to portray a city under change during a period of fluidity and realignments.

Table 19.1 Harbour works: projects, engineers, contracting companies, and urban transformations

City	Harbour projects engineers	Contracting companies (construction dates)	Commissioned by and coastal landfill
Alexandria West Port:			Khedive of Egypt
	Auguste Stœklin 1863		Non-implemented
	Cordier 1864		Egyptian government
	Joseph Sciama 1865		
	Linant de Bellefords 1869		
	William Janvrin Du Port 1870	William Bruce Greenfield & Co (1870–1880)	15.0 ha landfill
Alexandria East Port—corniche:			Municipality
	Leopold Dietrich & Archondaris	Societa di Eduardo Almagià (1901–1907)	52.6 ha landfill
	Eduard Quellenec 1902–1905		(4 km long)
Smyrna (Izmir):			Vali Sabri Pasha
	English engineer 1867	J. Charnaud, A. Barker et G. Guarracino, Société des Quais de Smyrne (1867)	
	Polycarpe Vitalis 1868	Société des Quais de Smyrne of Dussaud Frères (1868–1875)	40.0 ha landfill (3.5 km long)
Constantinople (Istanbul) Sirkedji & Galata:			Ottoman government
	Louis Barret 1873		
	Hilarion Pascal 1874		
	A. Cingria & A. Guérard 1898–1900	Société des Quais, Docks et Entrepôts de Constantinople of Marius Michel (1890–1900)	3.0 ha landfill
Constantinople (Istanbul) Skutari, Haydar-Pasha:			Ottoman government
	Waldorp 1900	Société du Port de Haydar-pacha, subsidiary of the Baghdad Railway Co (1900–1903)	13.0 ha landfill

Beirut:

		Vali Midhat Pasha
Auguste Stœcklin 1863	Compagnie des Messageries Maritimes	
Austin 1879		
Henri Garetta 1889	Société Impériale Ottomane du Port de Beyrouth (1887–1895)	5–6 ha landfill

Salonica (Thessaloniki) Quay:

		Vali Sabri Pasha
Roch/Rocco Vitalis 1871	Société des Quais de Salonique (1870–1882)	Prefecture

Salonica (Thessaloniki) Harbour:

Louis Barret 1872	Compagnie de Construction des Batignolles (1874–1892)	Non-implemented
Hilarion Pascal 1874		
Aslan 1892		Non-implemented
Adolphe Guérard 1892		
Jules Robert 1897	Société Anonyme Ottomane du Port de Salonique (1896–1904–1930)	Ottoman government
Marcel Pouard 1901		10.0 ha landfill
Alexandre Vallaury, arch. 1907–1911	Bureau Technique de Béton Armé de François Hennebique (1903–1912)	Harbour buildings
André George, engin. 1910–1912	Eli Modiano, contractor 1910–1912	

(from Hastaoglou-Martinidi 2010)

294 Vilma Hastaoglou-Martinidis

The starting point: the construction of the quay, 1869–1882

Until 1870, Salonica (then with fewer than 80,000 inhabitants) was cut off from the sea by its encircling medieval walls. But in 1979 the city's newly appointed Governor-General, Sabri Pasha, took a decisive step in response to the growth of commerce in the region, the considerable maritime traffic it brought, and the resulting pressure from commercial houses and the consuls.[2] On his proposal, the Sublime Porte permitted the demolition of the old sea walls to make room for two vital transit-trade facilities: railway installations and a quay with a length of 1,650 meters along the seafront. Roch (or Rocco) Vitalis, a competent civil engineer who had already worked in Smyrna, was called to finalise a preliminary plan drawn up in 1869[3] and to assume the management of the works.[4] That plan, dated October 29 1871, offered a detailed scheme for the layout of the quay. It provided for a large embankment of 6.2 ha, on which a strip of 16 large building blocks was arranged, six fronting the old harbour market, assigned to port uses, and the remaining ten in front of the housing districts assigned to urban uses. A number of plots were reserved for public facilities—such as the custom house (built in 1873 on Vitalis' design[5]), the headquarters of the Vilayet, a naval hospital, and the municipal market—and the first square of the city was projected at the spot between the two sections of the quay[6] (Figure 19.1).

The work was entrusted to a new state enterprise, the *Société des Quays de Salonique*, established in 1870 with a loan of 15,000 Turkish liras advanced from the Vilayet. The funds necessary for the works, estimated at 80,000 liras, would be raised by auctioning land reclaimed from the sea, circa 62,000 square metres, for an expected return of 100,000 liras.[7]

The ceremonial laying of the cornerstone took place on June 4, 1870, colourfully described by the Press.

> The interesting ceremony of laying the foundation stone of the quay, which is to be constructed here along the whole length of the town fronting the harbour, was inaugurated by his Excellency the Governor-General of the Vilayet, Sabri Pasha, on Saturday the 4th inst. The weather, though hot and sultry, was very fine, and notwithstanding the heat, the Consuls and other dignitaries, the principal merchants, and a large concourse of people were assembled, when his Excellency, the Pasha, made his appearance about midday, and walked slowly and with dignified step along the pier, built for that purpose to the spot in the sea where the foundation stone was to be deposited, and a canopy had been erected of evergreens and decorated with the Turkish flag. The Mufti then offered up a prayer, and the Pasha made a speech, when the marble slab being suspended by a pulley; he overlaid it cement by means of a silver trowel, presented to him for the occasion by the English residents here, as a slight token of regard and esteem for his praiseworthy exertions in ameliorating the condition of our town; he then dealt the slab three blows with a silver hammer, when it was lowered in the clear and placid waters, out of which one day we hope to see a beautiful quay to our astonished senses.
>
> (*The Levant Times and Shipping Gazette*, June 11, 1870)

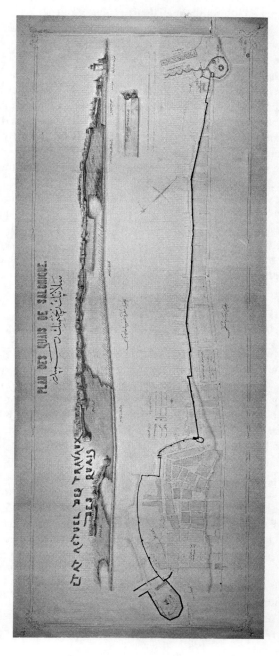

Figure 19.1 Plan of the quay of Salonica, October 29, 1871, by Roch A. Vitalis. (Source: Prime-ministerial Archives of Istanbul)

296   Vilma Hastaoglou-Martinidis

Despite this optimism in the press, and an initial schedule for construction to be completed by the end of 1871, in autumn 1871 construction suddenly stopped, as allegations were advanced concerning the abuse of a considerable sum (12,000 Turkish liras) and an unjustified increase in the scheduled budget. Sabri Pasha and his staff were dismissed after an administrative inquiry.[8] From 1872 onwards the works were pushed forward again by the new Vali, Ismail Pasha. However, in the autumn of 1874, with the quay approaching completion, work stopped again for lack of funds. The next Vali, Omer Fevzi Pasha, traveled to Istanbul to urge the Porte to advance the funds—about 15,000 liras—necessary to resume work.[9] After subsequent delays, the work was undertaken by the *Commission des quais* set up by the Grand Vizier in 1879, and construction was finally completed in 1882, with supplementary public financing. The full length of the quay was paved with basalt. A horse-drawn tram was introduced, and the health of the town greatly improved.[10]

The quay became the busiest and more 'westernised' part of the city. The section in front of the old market was designated for port uses, while the remainder, the 'municipal quay', attracted factories, workshops and warehouses, offices and shops, coffee houses and hotels, recreational spaces, and private residences. Soon, however, the quay became inadequate. First, lighters were still needed for loading and unloading, because the of the shallow depth (2 to 6 m). Second, the railroads were placed since 1874 in the western part of the city, and the railway companies were pressing for tracks to be laid allowing goods trains to reach the dockside for loading and unloading.

The company of Chemins de fer Orientaux of Maurice de Hirsch and the first plans for the harbour

A charter for a railway network in the European provinces of the Ottoman Empire, to link Istanbul with Vienna, was granted in 1869 to a company owned by Belgian banker Baron Maurice de Hirsch, with Austrian, British, French, and Belgian capital. The company *Chemins de fer Orientaux* built in 1871–1874 a first railway line of 355 km, connecting Istanbul to Edirne and the border. In 1872 a 148-km branch line assured Edirne an outlet to the Aegean at Dedeağaç (Alexandroupolis). Between 1871 and 1874, a second line of 362 km linked Thessaloniki to Mitrovitsa and the Balkan hinterland (Hastaoglou-Martinidis 2003, 65).

According to the contract signed with the Hirsh Company, for the efficient operation of the Balkan rail network and the development of agriculture and trade, the Ottoman government bound itself to develop connecting roads, as well as to build harbour facilities in the ports of Salonica, Dedeağaç, and Varna.[11] The preparation of the harbour plans was assigned to the Company, while their financing was to be secured by the government. The Hirsch Company assigned this task to Hilarion Pascal, Director of works in the port of Marseilles.[12] At his order, the engineer of the port, Louis Barret, prepared draft plans for the harbours of Constantinople, Salonica, and Dedeağaç for the Oriental Railways Company.[13]

For Salonica, Barret proposed the development of the harbour along the city front: widening the existing quay from 12 to 80 m on a large landfill, to accommodate rail lines and transit sheds; four moles of 170 m long, arranged at right angles to the quay at intervals of 130 m (their number could be increased in the future to occupy the whole city front); and a breakwater parallel to the quay at a distance of 500 m from the shore (Barret 1875, 85–86) (Figure 19.2).

In 1874, Hilarion Pascal himself was engaged to finalise the project. Pascal proposed a very detailed and realistic plan that limited the harbour to the west end of the quay, in front of the market area, in the immediate vicinity of the railway installations. It included a breakwater of 500 m long parallel to the shore at a distance of 555 m, a docking area 100 m long and 85 m wide on a new embankment, a mole of 150 m long and 130 m wide perpendicular to the quay (to be completed by a second similar one in the future), and the dredging of the basin to a depth of 7 m. His project included a scheme for the future extension of the port along the quay towards the White Tower, plans for the quay-walls and dikes, detailed reports with technical specifications, estimate of costs and quantities, etc. The cost of the works was anticipated at 2,500,000 francs, to be paid by the Ottoman government.[14]

It seems the proposed cost was found to be excessive—not surprisingly, since the heavily indebted Empire declared a suspension of payments in 1875—and the project came to a halt. However, Pascal's project influenced the subsequent laying out of the harbour, both in terms of its positioning next to the railway installations and its modest size.

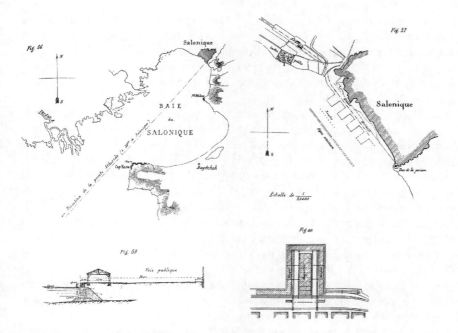

Figure 19.2 Louis Barret's draft project for Salonica's harbour, 1872. (Source: Louis Barret, Note sur l'aménagement des ports de commerce, Paris, Lacroix 1875, 86)

298 *Vilma Hastaoglou-Martinidis*

The entrepreneurial plans of Société de Construction des Batignolles, 1874–1892

By the 1890s, when Salonica had more than 120,000 inhabitants and was a hive of economic activity, the question of a proper harbour was, once again, placed on the agenda. In 1892 another French firm, the *Société de Construction des Batignolles* (SCB) sought the concession for the work. Founded in 1846 by Ernest Goüin (1815–1885), a former pupil of the École Polytechnique, the company (originally *Ernest Goüin et Cie*) initially specialised in locomotive production for the big French railway companies, and later in iron bridges, including the Asnières Bridge in France, the Vistula Bridge in Warsaw, and the famous Trinity Bridge in Saint Petersburg (Park-Barjot 2005).

In 1872, *Ernest Goüin et Cie* turned to a joint stock company, the *Société de Construction des Batignolles* (SCB), which redirected its activities towards the French colonial empire, and obtained important railway and harbour concessions. In 1885, when Jules Goüin succeeded his father, SCB was by far the most important French public works firm.[15]

Its international account includes the Bône-Guelma line (Algeria, 1885–1891), the Beirut-Damascus line in Syria (1892–1895), and the railway from Mudania to Bursa (1891–1892). In partnership with other companies, SCB built railways in Yunnan (south China, 1903–1910), northern Spain, southern Italy (1892), and Greece (1902–1912). Its harbour projects included the ports of Tunis (1888), Burgas (1898–1906), and Pernambuco, Brazil—the biggest in the Atlantic (1905–1915)—together with a large number of non-implemented plans drawn up for various ports in the Eastern Mediterranean.[16] In Greece, SCB obtained in 1900 the concession for the railway line from Piraeus-Athens to the border near Larisa, amounting to 441 km. It cut through the three mountain chains with 56 tunnels and many bridges, the Bralos and Asopos iron viaducts being the most challenging ones (both bombed in WWII).[17]

SCB always carefully studied the local situation and examined schemes previously prepared before deciding what was to be done. In preparation for Salonica's harbour concession, the company sent fact-finding missions headed by Adolphe-Marie-Nicolas Guérard (1841–1921) in 1874 and again in 1892. Guérard, Inspector General of the Ponts et Chaussées and Chief Engineer of the port of Marseilles, had remarkable activity outside France, carrying out missions for foreign governments in Europe and South America, including Costanţa port (1891), Burgas and Varna ports (1895), the Danube ports (1898), and Montevideo port (1895). His activity as consulting harbour engineer for French or foreign private companies is equally impressive: Varna, Dedeağaç, and Salonica harbour projects (1873), Jaffa (1879), Libau, Russia (1880), Tunis (1882), Lisbon (1885), the Suez port and Heraclea (1891), Constantinople (1896–1900), Salonica (1892), and the Moroccan ports (1905). In Latin America: harbour projects in Santa Fé (1903), Buenos Aires (1908), Valparaiso (1906), and Rio de Janeiro-Pernambuco (1910). Between 1870 and the beginning of the 20th century, Guérard accomplished many missions as consulting engineer for the *Société de Construction des Batignolles,*

French interests and Salonica's port 299

and produced thorough documentation, still held in the company's archives. A number of documents presented here are drawn from his files.[18]

The concession for the harbour of Salonica being imminent since 1888, Guérard was sent in 1892 to evaluate on the spot the existing projects and prepare alternative plans.[19] His study was focused on the problem of building quay walls on the unstable seabed along the shore; this was a thorny technical issue he was to resolve successfully in 1896 for the Sirkedji docks in the Golden Horn (Hastaoglou-Martinidis 2011b). His colleague, engineer Aslan of the École des Ponts et Chaussées, produced an alternative project for the layout and the quay-walls of the port, based on a revision of Pascal's designs. None of these materialised, as the concession was granted to the company of Edmond Bartissol[20] (Figure 19.3).

The Concessionaire Company of Edmond Bartissol

Edmond Bartissol (1841–1916) was born in Portel, in Roussillon, southern France, to a family of builders. Self-taught, he managed within two decades to rise from his humble origins and become a prominent public works contractor, industrialist, land and chateau owner and wine-producer, mayor of Fleury-Mérogis, and member of Parliament for the region of Eastern Pyrenees.[21] This spectacular career started in 1866 in the Suez Canal, as a plain foreman under his fellow countryman Ferdinand Lesseps. Upon his return to France in 1870, with the support of his acquaintances (and future partners Alexis Duparchy and Alexandre Lavalley), he was able to obtain contracts for important public works in Portugal (railways and harbours, notably the port of Leixões, 1879–1892). He rapidly extended his business in Brazil where he built the port of Recife/Pernambuco (1908–1913), one of the largest in the Atlantic, but also in Mozambique where for 15 years his company sought concession contracts for mining exploitation, agricultural crops, and undertaking harbour works (Escudier 2000, 47–56, 136–141). Bartissol successfully applied his skills to other industries as well. He founded the first electric power plant of Perpignan (in 1888), the hydroelectric plant in Vinça-Perpignan (1889), and set up the Hydroelectric Company of Roussillon (1901). His manufacturing ventures included cigarette paper with the symbolic name 'Suez' (1893), the aperitif Banyuls-Bartissol (1904), and the fabrication of artificial gemstones (beginning of the 20th century). In 1889, Bartissol made his entrance into politics when elected as MP for the region of Céret, in the Eastern Pyrenees. In Parliament he dealt with issues that matched his expertise, especially legislation for highways, maritime canals, irrigation projects, etc.

Bartissol came to Salonica thanks to his connections with Théodore Berger, member of the Administration Committee of the Ottoman Bank in Paris (1882–1900), who was until his death very influential in the Ottoman Empire (Escudier 2000, 144). The contract for the construction of the port was signed in July 1896 by the Minister of the Civil List, Michel Portugal, and by Edmond Bartissol (Hastaoglou-Martinidis 1999). The next year, under the terms of the contract, Bartissol set up a company, the *Société Anonyme Ottomane de Construction du*

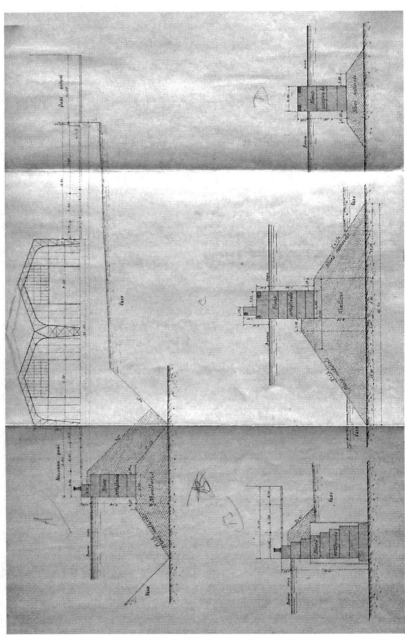

Figure 19.3 'Port de Salonique: Nouveau Project étudié par Monsieur Aslan' (1892). (Centre des Archives du Monde de Travail, Société de Constructions des Batignolles, 89 AQ 2276, used by permission)

French interests and Salonica's port   301

Port de Salonique; its duration was fixed at 24 years, with the permission to operate the harbour for a period of five years. A second contract, signed by Bartissol and Minister Ohannes Sakisian Effendi in December 1904, re-established the company as a *Société d'Exploitation* and extended its rights up to 1944.[22]

The cost of the whole project was estimated at 6,500,000 francs, of which one-fifth would be paid by the Civil List and the remaining 5,200,000 francs by the contractor. The return of the capital advanced would be spread over 20 years, by means of 5% annuities guaranteed by the net proceeds from operating the harbour.[23]

Following his favourite practice, Bartissol set up the company's Board with his family being powerfully represented in it: himself as president, and his three nephews, Jules Robert (engineer), Admiral Louis Cauber (husband of Marie Bartissol), and Admiral Joseph Nabona as members; the remaining three members were local investors H. Salem, Levi Modiano, and Hadjibar Effendi. The company's head office was in Istanbul, but the Board was headquartered in Paris (7 rue La Fayette) (Escudier 2000, 143–146).

Work began in 1897 and was put in the hands of Jules Robert, engineer of the École des Arts et des Manufactures of Paris, who had also worked with his uncle in Spain and Portugal, in Mozambique, as well as in various other projects. Robert had full authority to handle all transactions in the name of Bartissol, and in 1904 became the Company's Executive Director. He is the author of the final plan of the port, which echoed the general lines of the projects drawn up in 1874 by H. Pascal and in 1892 by Aslan. In practice, the construction (1897–1903) was carried out after 1901 by another of Bartissol's relatives, the young Marcel Pouard, engineer of the École Centrale des Arts et Manufactures.

The task included the construction of a docking area 800 m long by 130 m wide by reclaiming land from the sea in front of the old quay built in 1870; the construction of two 200-m-long moles at right angles to the quay (the west mole 50 m wide, the east mole 90 m wide); the construction of a 560-m-long breakwater 530 m from the shore and parallel to the quay, with a protected basin of 13.2 ha; dredging to give the whole basin a uniform depth of 8.5 m; paving the new land with basalt; erecting perimeter walls; provision of water and gas supplies and sewers; laying of 3,000 m of railway lines; the installation of five cranes; the construction of 8,000 square metres of dockside transit sheds, a new custom house, the central railway station (at an estimated cost of 500,000 francs), and a grain silo; and widening the linear quay along the city front from 12 m to 20 m, to serve for the unloading of smaller ships.[24]

The work was scheduled for completion in 1901; but unforeseen problems (soft soil caused underwater foundations to subside) meant that the quays were not finished until 1904. Raw materials for the landfill were conveyed from the Evangelistria quarry (outside the east wall of the city) to the port by a specially installed lorry line (Hastaoglou-Martinidis 1999, 135). As shown in a rare map of the port in 1904, the line ran along the quay and circled the White Tower in order to approach the quarry along modern Angelaki and Ethnikis Aminis streets; of particular interest is the depiction of the eastern part of the city, showing the new

White Tower and Hamidiye neighbourhoods and arrangements for the Jewish, Muslim, and Christian sections of the huge necropolis.

The same year, construction began of the buildings needed for operation of the port, on the quays and open spaces, now equipped with rail lines. First was the construction of the warehouses on the dockside for transit merchandise. These were standardised sheds typical of Levantine ports and railroad depots (Alexandria, Smyrna, Haydar-Pasha/Constantinople) (De Cordemoy 1909; Berthot n.d.). A light, single-storey structure with a visible metal skeleton filled in with bricks, a stone foundation, pitched tile roof, and large metal doors. The open-plan 50 × 20 m interior corresponded to the carrying capacity of cargo ships of the time. The construction, a technical innovation for the city, was adopted for the construction of the railway sheds, the tram depot, and the water company pumping station. A total of nine dockside transit sheds were erected, covering 8,000 square metres, symmetrically lining the dockside in such a way as to facilitate the movement of merchandise.[25] Today four of them survive, converted to cultural uses (Figure 19.4).

In 1909, Serbia, engaged since 1906 in a customs war with Austria, signed an agreement with the port company giving it the right to export bovines, primarily to Egypt, using a separate part of the west mole, for an annual rent of 27,500 francs. The company built new sheds and grain silos, and installed railroad tracks to enable goods trains to run directly onto the quays. This Serbian Free Zone was the first free zone of the port. It lasted for ten years.[26]

Figure 19.4 The dockside transit sheds in 1904, postcard published by David M. Assael, Salonique. (Hastaoglou collection)

The Bureau Technique de Béton Armé de François Hennebique and the construction of port's buildings

The *Bureau Technique de Béton Armé de François Hennebique* was the third French company involved in construction of the harbour. Its creator, François-Benjamin-Joseph Hennebique (1842–1921), builder and self-taught engineer, recorded an impressive course which secured him unchallenged supremacy in the then revolutionary innovation of reinforced concrete. In 1892, he patented his reinforced concrete construction system and successfully resolved the crucial problem of rigidity by integrating columns and beams into a single monolithic structure; in parallel he devised the 'compressol' system of foundation, an innovative technique applicable to heavy structures. His inventions resulted in a rapid expansion of his business, with a worldwide network of associated local companies and licensed contractors acting as agents for the *Hennebique system*. By 1902, his representatives had already undertaken 7,205 structures (civic buildings, industrial facilities, bridges, etc.), and by 1913 his performance had skyrocketed as the number of structures reached 30,000, with a turnover of 600 million francs (Delhumeau 1999).

In the Eastern Mediterranean, the firm launched its activities after 1900. The Hennebique system was rapidly diffused by local agencies of associated concessionaires in Constantinople, Smyrna, Salonica, Athens, Alexandria, and Cairo.[27] In 1903, with the Thessaloniki docks, backfilling, and warehouses almost completed, Bartissol appealed to the *Bureau Hennebique* to undertake projects for harbour buildings imposed by the concession, which required exceptional know-how because of their large size and their setting on the loose, yielding soil of the landfill.

Four of six projects prepared by Hennebique's office were implemented: the widening of the 1871 quay from 12 to 20 m, the Grain Silo, the buildings for the Régie Company, and the custom house. In the same period, the office carried out five more projects in the town, commissioned by other companies and private individuals.[28] The Grain Silo was a challenging project because of the special expertise it required. After a first aborted project in 1903, a second one of a more moderate capacity (3,500 tons) was eventually implemented in 1910. It was destroyed in the 1944 bombing.[29]

Salonica was a cosmopolitan city with a thriving economy, and Bartissol's interest soon turned from the harbour to the city at large. In 1905, on his agreement, Paul Félix founded the *Compagnie immobilière et Régie de terrains de Salonique*, which was to develop the 20,000 square metres of reclaimed land it owned by the terms of the concession.[30] In this case, Bartissol repeated the successful real estate project of the apartment building complex he erected in Perpignan in 1887, the *Cité Bartissol*, which became the administrative centre of his businesses for the next 30 years; it remained his property until his death in 1916, and survives until today next to St Jean Cathedral. Twin five-storey buildings were erected after 1906 on either side of Salaminos Street, flanking the main entrance to Thessaloniki port, to house the Company's local offices. Their eclectic architecture, reminiscent of French urban 'immeubles' with arcades, signalled the presence of the French company until they were bombed in 1944.[31]

304   *Vilma Hastaoglou-Martinidis*

Plans for the General Warehouses of the Ottoman Bank, designed to complete the bank's network of warehouses in the ports of the region, were drawn up in 1906. The plot purchased from the Port was intended for a large two-storey building with loft, of 5,511 square metres, for which the Bank budgeted 4,000 Turkish liras. The plans were not implemented, and in 1909 the Bank—in growing need of storage space—erected on the site a simpler structure of 2,014 square metres; adopting the pattern of the dock-side sheds; it still stands in good condition.[32]

The custom house was by far the biggest project undertaken in the port. Its colossal dimensions and its location on the docks demanded the contribution of three high-ranking professionals: Alexandre Vallaury, the prominent Levantine architect, author of many prestigious buildings in Constantinople, professor in the Imperial School of Fine Arts and architect of the Customs Authority (since 1889); André George, the top engineer of the Hennebique Central Bureau; and engineer Eli Modiano, the authorised Hennebique contractor in Salonica. The building was patterned on the Sirkedji custom house designed by Vallaury few years ago. It was founded using the compressol system and built entirely with reinforced concrete between 1910 and 1912.[33] It is the only one of Hennebique's works that survives today, and is partly used as a passenger terminal (Figure 19.5).

Epilogue

In 1912, the landscape of the harbour was completed. The building of the port constituted a threefold innovation for the city. With regard to the management and financing of urban space, it instituted standard procedures for major public works. From the point of view of town-planning and architecture, it introduced a rational and functional layout, and new types of buildings that contrasted clearly with the oriental appearance of the city (Figure 19.6).

The French company maintained its contract privileges after the incorporation of Salonica into Greece in 1912. Despite its modest size, the port faithfully served the commercial traffic of the city for almost half a century, despite the obvious disproportion between the limited capacity of the harbour (land and sea surface area and technical facilities) and the city's vast hinterland (approximately 130,000 square kilometres and three to four million inhabitants). The port remained unchanged until the eve of WWII, despite successive plans prepared for its extension: the 1914 extension plan by Marcel Pouard, in anticipation of the establishment of a Free Zone (eventually its operation was postponed for 1925); the 1918 extension project by harbour specialist Prof. Angelos Guinis—in the context of the post-fire replanning of the city—redirecting the development of the harbour along the western shore of the city; and the 1932 extension plan by the Consortium Batignolles, Hersent and Schneider, after the Port Trust Fund bought out the French company's operating rights in 1930.

Implementation of the extension plan began only after WWII. Much of the harbour's original stock of buildings and equipment was bombed in 1944, so the present situation is only faintly reminiscent of the pre-war harbour landscape.

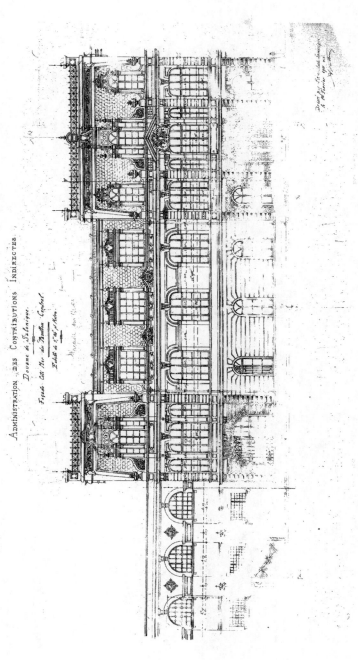

Figure 19.5 Alexandre Vallaury's design for the façade of Salonica's custom house, 1911. (Source: CNAM/SIAF/Cité de l'architecture et du patrimoine/Archives d'architecture du XXe siècle, Fonds BAH, file 'Entrepôts de douane turques, port de Salonique, 1910–1914')

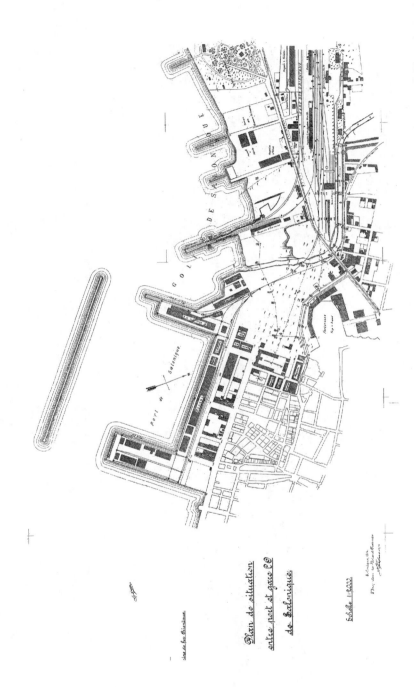

Figure 19.6 Plan of the harbour in 1914, showing the completion of the works. (Gift to the author by the *Institut Français de Thessalonique*)

Notes

1 According to the 1904 report by the French consulate of Salonica giving a catalogue of French interests in the city, notably banks, industrial enterprises, navigation companies, real property, and buildings. Archives du Ministère des Affaires Etrangères, CCC, Salonique 1904.

2 The city's commercial establishment was constantly calling for improved port facilities, and it was a recurrent theme in consular reports during the second half of the nineteenth century. Sabri Pasha introduced a new spirit of governance—it is not a coincidence that the same year the first town council was constituted—and considerable undertakings were pushed forward, the most important being the project for the building of the quay. See Karadimou-Yerolympou 1997, 132–158.

3 This preliminary plan, entitled '*Projet de quai à Salonique*', is held in the Prime-ministerial archives in Istanbul; it is signed by Roch A. Vitalis and dated May 6 1869.

4 The quay of Izmir was constructed between 1869 and 1876 in front of the old shore for a total length of 3.5 km on a large landfill over 40 hectares; it was the work of the French company of Dussaud Frères, known for their harbour building activity in various Mediterranean port-cities. See Hastaoglou-Martinidis 2016.

5 Foreign Office, CR, Salonica 1870.

6 The document, entitled 'Plan des quais de Salonique/État actuel des travaux des quais', is held in the Prime-ministerial Archives of Istanbul; it is signed by Roch Vitalis and dated October 29 1871.

7 Foreign Office, CR, Salonica 1869.

8 Foreign Office, CR, Salonica 1871. Immediately after the event, foreign consuls anxious about the irregularities and delays occurring in the execution of the project, suggested the commissioning of the work to a private company, and the French firm *Piat* proposed a convention for the construction of the quays. Archives du Ministère des Affaires Etrangères, CCC Salonique, vol. 27, doc. 12 and January 26 1872.

9 Foreign Office, CR, Salonica 1874.

10 Foreign Office, CR, Salonica 1882. To cover the budget deficit, the programme for public buildings was abandoned and the plots assigned to that purpose were sold to private individuals. The initial plan changed and the number of building blocks was raised from 16 to 30, to accommodate smaller plots that could more easily be sold to private citizens.

11 Actes de la Concession, 1874.

12 Pascal, born in 1815 in Saint Saturnin-les-Apt, graduated the École des Ponts et Chaussées in 1839; he retired in 1885. He was Chief Engineer in the Port of Marseilles, and responsible for several important projects there. Highly regarded by his superiors, he was offered administrative positions (Secretary General in the Ministry of Public Works in 1876) and membership in various committees (management of railways, lighthouses, etc.). His activity outside France was considerable. Member of the International Commission for the Works of the Universal Company of the Suez Canal, he prepared harbour projects for Constantinople and Salonica for the Oriental Railways Company in 1872 and Varna in 1873. Between 1868 and 1870, he participated in the construction works of the port of Fiume and Trieste, invited by the Austrian-Hungarian government. In 1871, he was invited by the Greek government as consultant engineer for major port projects in Patras, Syros, Kalamata, and elsewhere. (Archives Nationales de France, Ingénieurs des Ponts et Chaussées, dossier individuel F14/2294/1)

13 Louis-Julien Barret (1828–1887) trained at the École des Arts et Métiers in Aix and the École Centrale de Paris. He began his career as an engineer in the Ch. Reynaud shipyard, before moving to the French shipbuilding company Forges et Chantiers de la Méditerranée in La Sevne-sur-Mer, in Provence. In 1859, he entered the service of the *Société des Docks et Entrepôts de Marseille*, where he stayed until his death. He was called to undertake harbours or railway projects in St Petersburg, Odessa,

308 *Vilma Hastaoglou-Martinidis*

Constantinople, Varna, Salonica, Fiume (Rijeka), and Trieste. (*Dictionnaire de Bibliographie Française*, Tome V, 595)

14 Société de Constructions des Batignolles, 89 AQ 2276 Port de Salonique, doc. «Projet présenté par Hilarion Pascal le 17 Févier 1874 pour la construction de ce port et des quais nécessaires au service des Chemins de fer».

15 The company is still active after merging, in 1968, with the *Société Parisienne pour l'Industrie Electrique* to form *Spie-Batignolles*.

16 A detailed account of the projects carried out by SCB is offered in the website www.a rchivesnationales.culture.gouv.fr/camt/index.html

17 Société de Constructions des Batignolles, 89 AQ 2204 à 2216. Years later, in 1920, SCB returned to Thessaloniki and unsuccessfully sought contracts for the extension of the port and irrigation projects of the Vardar plain (1923–1925); and again in 1932, for the extension of the port.

18 Archives Nationales, Ingénieurs des Ponts et Chaussées, Dossier individuel F14/11556, & École Nationale des Ponts et Chaussées, Fichiers des ingénieurs du Corps.

19 See the thorough account by A. Guérard on the projects for the harbour, Société de Constructions des Batignolles, 89 AQ 2276 Port de Salonique, doc. 'Renseignements sur l'exécution des travaux à Salonique'.

20 Société de Constructions des Batignolles, 89 AQ 2276 Port de Salonique, doc. 'Nouveau projet de M. Aslan'.

21 http://histoireduroussillon.free.fr/Thematiques/Biographies/Bartissol.php, and also in www.mairie-fleury-merogis.fr/_recherche/presentation/histoire/celebrites.asp

22 Société Ottomane d'Exploitation du port de Salonique, *Conventions and Other Legal Documents*, Paris: Imprimérie Paix, 1914.

23 The company would deduct 20% to cover operating, administration, and maintenance costs, and the Municipality 3% to cover the work of widening the sea front. The remaining 77% would go towards paying off the total capital, and the surplus, regarded as profit, would be divided equally between the Civil List and the contractor: see Convention 1904, *op. cit.*; Report of the Company 1913, records of the General Administration of Macedonia, f. 35, and Louis Godard, 'Les ports maritimes de la Turquie. Ports existants et ports projetus', *Le Génie Civil*, Tome LV-No 19, 4/1909: 351.

24 Reports of the Port Company.

25 See Convention 1904, *op. cit.*

26 Archives du Ministère des Affaires Etrangères, Turkey file 455, doc. 5 November 1909; Foreign Office, DCR, Salonica, No. 4579, 1909; Dertilis 1928: 7–14.

27 In Istanbul the firm maintained a local office with representative the engineer André George. Among its 37 projects in Istanbul are the Church of Saint-Antoine in Pera, the Custom house in Galata, the Deutsch-Orientbank head office and the First and Fourth Foundation Khans in Eminonü. See Hastaoglou-Martinidis 2011, 144–157.

28 CNAM/SIAF/Cité de l'architecture et du patrimoine/Archives d'architecture du XXe siècle, Fonds BAH (Fonds Béton Armé Hennebique).

29 CNAM/SIAF/Cité de l'architecture et du patrimoine/Archives d'architecture du XXe siècle, Fonds BAH, file 'Silos à grains, Salonique 1910–1911'.

30 A similar arrangement was included in the contracts for the harbours of Smyrna, Constantinople, and Beirut. For *Compagnie immobilière et de Régie de terrains*, see Archives du Ministère des Affaires Etrangères, port de Salonique, v. 455, document dated 6 October 1917.

31 CNAM/SIAF/Cité de l'architecture et du patrimoine/Archives d'architecture du XXe siècle, Fonds BAH, file 'Immeuble d'habitation pour la Cie de Régie immobilière, port de Salonique, 1906–1908'.

32 CNAM/SIAF/Cité de l'architecture et du patrimoine/Archives d'architecture du XXe siècle, Fonds BAH, file 'Magasins généraux de la Banque impériale ottomane, port de Salonique, 1906'. The Ottoman Bank purchased the plot from the port company for

French interests and Salonica's port   309

5,000 Turkish liras in 1908. Public Land Service, Thessaloniki Office, file 'Port', doc. May 13 1981.
33 CNAM/SIAF/Cité de l'architecture et du patrimoine/Archives d'architecture du XXe siècle, Fonds BAH, file 'Entrepôts de douane turques, port de Salonique, 1910–1914'.

References

Barret, L., *Note sur l'aménagement des ports de commerce*, Paris: Lacroix (1875).
Berthot, P., *Traité des ports de mer*, Paris: G. Fanchon (n.d.).
De Cordemoy, C. J., *Exploitation des ports maritimes*, Paris: H. Dunod et E. Pinat (1909).
Delhumeau, G., *L'Invention du Béton Armé - Hennebique 1890–1914*, Paris: Norma (1999).
Dertilis, P., *La zone franche de Salonique et les accords Grèco-Yugoslaves*, Paris, Libr. A. Rousseau (1928).
Escudier, J., *Edmond Bartissol, 1841–1916: du canal de Suez à la bouteille d'apéritif*, Paris: CNRS (2000).
Fonds BAH, (Fonds Béton Armé Hennebique), *CNAM/SIAF/Cité de l'architecture et du patrimoine/Archives d'architecture du XXe siècle*, Paris.
Godard, L., 'Les ports maritimes de la Turquie. Ports existants et ports projetus', *Le Génie Civil*, Tome LV-No 19, 4 (1909), 349–353.
Hastaoglou-Martinidis, V., 'Cartography of harbour-works in the Eastern Mediterranean cities: The paths of modernisation', In: Kolluoglu, B. and Toksoz, M. (eds.), *Mapping out the Eastern Mediterranean*, London: I. B. Tauris (2010), 78–99.
Hastaoglou-Martinidis, V., 'The advent of reinforced concrete technology in Constantinople constructions and the activity of the Greek architects, engineers and contractors, 1902–1913', In: Kuruyazici, H. and Sarlak, E. (eds.), *Greek Architects of Istanbul in the Era of Westernisation*, Athens: Olkos (2011a), 144–157.
Hastaoglou-Martinidis, V., 'The advent of transport and aspects of urban modernisation in the levant during the nineteenth century', In: Roth, R. and Polino, M.-N. (eds.), *The City and the Railway in Europe*, London: Ashgate (2003).
Hastaoglou-Martinidis, V., 'The building of Istanbul docks, 1870–1910. New entrepreneurial and cartographic data', *A/Z, ITU Journal of the Faculty of Architecture*, 8.1 (2011b), 85–99.
Hastaoglou-Martinidis, V., 'The harbour of Thessaloniki, 1896–1920', In: Jarvis, A., (ed.), *Albert Dock 150*, Liverpool: The Centre for Port and Maritime History, Merseyside Maritime Museum, (1999), 133–141.
Hastaoglou-Martinidis, V., 'The transformation of Smyrna's sea front: Projects and facets of a cosmopolitan modernisation, 1860–1910', In: *Proceedings of the International Conference, Smyrna, the Development of an East Mediterranean Metropolis (17th century–1922)*, Athens (2016).
Karadimou-Yerolympou, A., *Μεταξύ Ανατολής και Δύσης: Βορειοελλαδικές πόλεις στην περίοδο των οθωμανικών μεταρρυθμίσεων: Βόλος, Θεσσαλονίκη, Ιωάννινα, Σέρρες, Αλεξανδρούπολη, Καβάλα* [Between East and West. North-Greek cities in the era of Ottoman reforms], Athens: Trochalia (1997).
Park-Barjot, R.-R., *La Société de construction des Batignolles: Des origines à la Première Guerre mondiale (1846–1914)*, Paris: Presses Paris Sorbonne (2005).

20 The post-war transformation of the Thessaloniki periphery

Urbanization and landscape

Charis Christodoulou

Between 1945 and 2010, the city of Thessaloniki sprawled in its surrounding landscape. The primary production areas and informal settlements in the periphery of Thessaloniki gradually transformed into wholly urbanized areas. Inadequate official planning applied since the 1980s shaped this process, along with the mobility and settlement of various social groups. Today one can easily distinguish between officially planned districts and informal peri-urban areas. However, the periphery of Thessaloniki is a hard-to-read patchwork, spatially and socially fragmented, in which past patterns of social division between western and eastern suburbs no longer fully apply. In this context, new settlements have developed as spaces of social exclusion, as refuges, hide-outs, encampments, stigmatized neighbourhoods, ghettos, and microcosms based on concentrations of Roma, Greek Pontians, new migrants, and refugees, but also low-income socio-professional cohorts and the elderly. Based on diverse primary and secondary documentation and extensive empirical research during 2000–2004 and 2013–2014, the chapter places the evolution of the city's socio-spatial constitution within a broader historical and geographical context and beyond dominant narratives.

The urban periphery as a field of research

Urban space is usually approached through the lens of cities' central and compact districts, and their dominant representations. Urban peripheral space is considered secondary and residual to mainstream urban historiography. Despite the fact that Thessaloniki periphery has contributed to a great degree to the city's dynamism and the evolution of its places and people, it mostly remains an 'unknown place' since there is neither a constituted conception nor a single, accepted, or prevalent perception of it today, through time and beyond supposed homogeneous imagery. The making of the Thessaloniki conurbation has been approached so far through the documentation and discussion of the transformation of the city's central or cohesive districts (Hastaoglou-Martinidi 2001; 2008, 12–14; Kalogirou 1986; Karadimou-Yerolympou 1995; 2007, 12–13). Past descriptions presented habitation issues in isolated studies of settlements but did not refer to the overall landscape of the periphery and they were partly influenced by the political atmosphere of the era (Fatouros and Chatzimichalis 1979; Axarli and Kosmaki 1979; Kalogirou 1977, 1980).

Transforming Thessaloniki's periphery 311

This chapter stresses the main attributes of its physiognomy and mutations, the transformation processes, and the official planning framework elements that determined the evolution of its socio-spatial constitution within the broader historical context. Special reference is made to social groups that inhabit the urban periphery (Roma, Greek Pontians, new migrants, and refugees, low rank socio-professional groups, and the elderly), as well as, to social housing complexes as places of distinguished socio-spatial constitution. The reason for this reference is that the attributes of their habitation in the urban periphery represent indications of changes in spatial or social policy forwarded and state practices related to 'otherness' in urban processes.

A method of multiple historical-geographical approaches was adopted while researching into the perimeter of the Urban Complex of Thessaloniki for my doctoral dissertation (Christodoulou 2008, 2015). The research area covered 1,400 hectares, more than 10% of the city's surface area, embracing about 5% of the overall population in the contemporary city (Figure 20.1). The study made use of diverse documentation from primary and secondary sources (maps and aerial pictures, topographic diagrams, archive research in agencies, relevant literature references), and triangulated conclusions out of extensive empirical research (mapping, iconography, inhabitant testimonies, 2000–2004). The space that it refers to comprises most areas where urban planning transformations took place in the last 40 years along with changes in the institutional framework of urban planning and demography shifts (Figure 20.2).

In this paper, the post war era is divided into periods in accordance with commonly accepted historical terminology, that is, before and after the political change brought about after the end of the dictatorship. However, distinct temporal milestones in each period are related to the existence of documents referring to urban space—dated maps, legal texts, etc. The first period, from the end of the wars until the mid-1970s, is marked by rapid urbanization as a result of internal migration from the countryside towards the city, the predominance of the reconstruction model of central urban districts by means of the '*polykatoikia*' (the Greek version of condominium) and their extensions with peripheral illegal/ self-generated settlements. The second, post-dictatorship period, up to the end of the 2000s but before the 2010 'financial crisis', is marked by an attempt to plan for the housing demands in new urban extensions, by urban sprawl and the suburbanization of the population within the wider metropolitan area, and also by new demographic phenomena, such as repatriation, new migration, waves of refugees, and population aging.

The periphery during the first post-war period (1945–1979): physical dispersion, ekistics deterioration, and natural landscape loss

At the end of WWII, the area under study was outside the peripheral refugee settlements and the settlement of the 'locals' of Pylea, both of which in the immediate post-war period were still distinct semi-urban or rather semi-rural neighbourhoods and communities (Figure 20.3). Sparsely populated, nominally homogeneous in

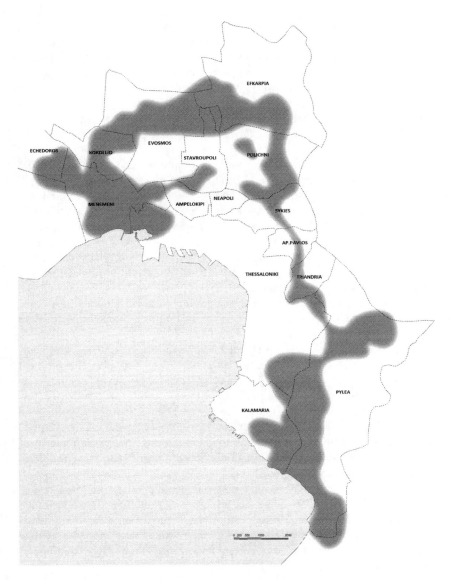

Figure 20.1 Diagram of the area of research in the perimeter of the Thessaloniki Urban Complex. (Christodoulou 2008)

the origin of their inhabitants, these settlements had kept almost their original footprint and were struggling to implement their half-finished settlement plans.

The study area was the threshold of Thessaloniki's productive interior (Figure 20.4). The landscape was dominated by natural features (streams, self-sown pasture, gardens, and field crops). Small lots granted as refugee rural

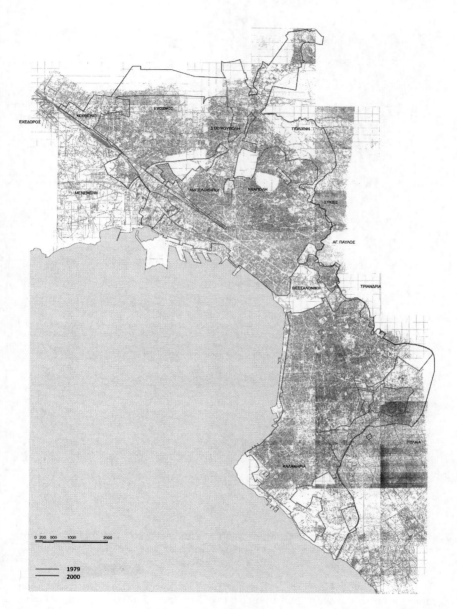

Figure 20.2 Diagram of official urban plan limits for the years 1979 and 2000. (Christodoulou, 2008)

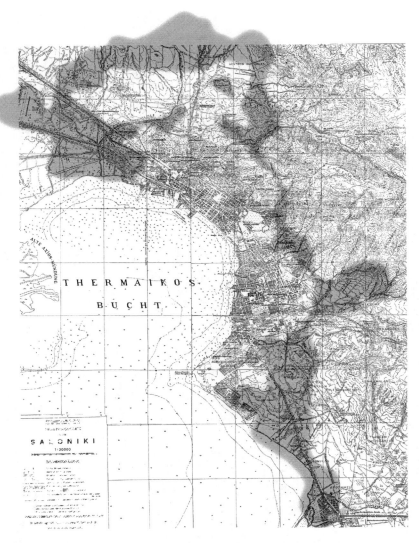

Figure 20.3 The area of research imposed on Thessaloniki urban fabric of the 1930s. (Diagram: Charis Christodoulou, 2008; base map: Aristotle University of Thessaloniki, Central Library Map Collection)

compensation to the west, and bigger parcels of farmland to the east, together with the tiny lots of the exchangeable property, formed a farmland mosaic that extended as far as the yards of the houses that dotted the surrounding countryside. These parcels provided permanent employment to a number of people inhabiting the peripheral settlements. The place names derived from characteristic landscape

Figure 20.4 Aerial view of the eastern periphery of Thessaloniki in the early 1950s; Pylea, Toumpa, Votsi, Nea Krini in the foreground. (Thessaloniki Records of Photography Archive 1900–1980, Athens: Ministry of Internal-General Secretariat of Communication - General Secretariat of Information, 2009, p. 21)

features. The area was traversed by two railways (to Edessa and Pieria) and by the main road network, which developed to serve the city, radiating out from Thessaloniki's compact core. A multitude of country roads served local transportation needs but with no broader structure. The area was difficult to access, and the city appeared to be unaware of it.

The 1950s and 1960s

By the end of the 1960s, Thessaloniki's urban core had virtually merged with the peripheral settlements into one urban complex, thus doubling its population (according to national censuses: 302,635 inhabitants in 1951 versus 557,360 in 1971). The city periphery was transformed from an area of primary sector activity into an area of building plots destined for poorer members of the wave of internal migration. The residential fabric spread beyond the peripheral settlements, overflowing natural or man-made barriers such as roads and railways, streams, and other spaces incompatible with residential use. The whole periphery—including remote corners—became potentially inhabitable by exploiting all the access routes.

The transition was brutally rapid, especially to the west. Public land was occupied, either squatted upon or by irregular sales transactions, while whole neighbourhoods were manipulatively planned depending on local circumstances and

316 *Charis Christodoulou*

land use characteristics (geomorphology, agricultural use, access). Housing tracts sprang out along the main and secondary roads, at the foot of the western and eastern hills, on the flat areas of refugee farmland and on the public land on hills or along streams; these residences gradually filled the spaces between the most cohesive areas of the city and the older peripheral settlements without making any provision for the development of necessary infrastructure. Being still in operation, military camps and cemeteries were the only areas left mostly unbuilt; however, they were soon encircled by this irregular urban continuum. To the south and, the study zone still retained its rural character: cotton, wheat, and okra fields, scattered henhouses and sheep pens belonging mainly to residents of Pylea or (less often) Kalamaria. However, also in the east, in Kifissia, habitation clusters were formed, primarily by internal migrants.

Dwellings here were low and scattered; they covered people's basic accommodation needs but lacked amenities. The majority of people bought the basics not only from peddlers (grocers and greengrocers on carts and later on trucks) but also from shops (bakeries, grocery stores, butcheries, etc.) established in the centre of their peripheral settlement. People could use the buses of the then newly established OASTH (Organization of Urban Transport of Thessaloniki—est. 1957) to get from the locally important centre of their peripheral municipality to the centre of the city of Thessaloniki.[1] The building activity took place without any planning on an unbalanced land market. Without established planning frameworks to determine their location, production sites were 'spontaneously' located just as habitation ones were.

Modern imposing production units and employment firms cropped up to the east and to the west (tobacco shops, manufacturing and transit firms). These buildings were also erected where new dwellings gathered, even next to small fields where crops were still being grown. But it was also next to factories and warehouses where new dwellings sprang up. This apparently controversial mixture of uses, scale, and building styles showed that there was a primary connection between production and the habitation of the necessary workforce. This dramatic unruly image of urban space was the result both of a lack of a rational development policy at a national and regional level which allowed for the politically driven allocation of production and, quoting a researcher of the times, of the ruling 'class politics for the housing of the people' (Kalogirou 1977).

During the same period of time, the first post-war social housing estates were built mainly on the eastern side of the city in an effort to cover part of the population's housing needs. These were erected by the then newly established independent Workers' House Organization (AOEK) (Christodoulou 2015b). At the same time the estates funded by the People & Refugee Housing Programme were built, which aimed both at providing the refugees who had lived in slums with permanent homes and at sanitizing any filthy, unhygienic areas including any Roma encampment, such as the Finikas social housing complex (in cooperation with the Ministries of Social Welfare and Public Works). All these complexes were single-use residential areas which followed the principles of the Modern Movement for industrialized building and free urban layout. They were constructed all at a given point in time all at once and used for residential purposes only. They were all fragments of organized space amidst unformed stretches of land on the edge of the city without any (functional or natural) continuity with the surrounding urban tissue.

During the same period of time, private building associations made their appearance on the east side of town (in the area between Toumba and Pylea: Konstantinoupolitika and Malakopi districts, and in Panorama). To their antipodes, it has been reported that Roma often swarmed 'uncultivated stretches of land' among all these areas, where they settled temporarily.

The new modernization works and the public infrastructure works (some of which were included in the Marshall Plan), such as the widening and improvement of the main roads, the built water reservoir of Kalochori-Dendropotamos, the water supply tanks in Agios Pavlos and Kalamaria, the digging of a flood-control trench which regulated the stream flow on the eastern side of the city (1958), the extension of the electric lighting network by the then newly established Hellenic Public Power Corporation (est. 1950), and other major private investments in infrastructure such as the modern cement quarries in Efkarpia (TITAN) and the petrochemical installations beyond Kordelio with a petrol pipeline reaching out to the sea (Esso-Pappas), marked the beginning of the urbanization of the nature of the periphery. They had an irreversible effect on the natural terrain and the landscape, leaving little room for any future residential development.

The 1970s

During the 1970s, the extension of the city was interrupted by the fall of the migration wave and the reinforcement of planning regulations which permitted an increased building capacity in the central and eastern areas following consecutive increases of the permitted Floor Area Ratio. Thus, the self-generated settlements in the west barely extended, next to the already existing neighbourhoods which were now more densely built and populated. These neighbourhoods failed to develop in the east for reasons of cohesion of the socio-economic tissue of the area that somehow guarded the land.

The major roadworks of the 1970s, that is the ring-road stretching from the north-west to the northern entrance of the city (Langada Avenue) and the new national highway linking Athens to Thessaloniki on the western entrance of the city, which were planned at a prior development phase of the city, had by the end of the decade encircled the western peripheral settlements, crossed their edges and divided previously joined neighbourhoods. In the eastern periphery, the new vast cemetery which had just started to operate played a major role in the development of the area which was not connected to the main road network. As a result, what inevitably gained in importance were the older country roads on the route from Nea Elvetia to Thermi which until then had only been secondary.

In the late 1970s, most residential units in the study zone—with the exception of the social housing complexes—formed a continuous residential fabric even though they lay on a perimeter zone beyond the existing city plan. Such was the plethora of these habitations and so densely and uniformly low-rise were they that they formed distinct cohesive units. However, a number of habitation units in the more remote areas either were sparsely built or included some small scattered cores of dwellings. In most units and mostly in the western areas the problems lingered: the floods caused by blocked streams, the either insufficient or inexistent technical and social infrastructure which turned everyday life into an endless struggle, the unformed urban fabric, the heavy traffic congestion and the environmental problems caused by the irrational mix of wholesale facilities, transit firms and the factories with dwellings. Open streams characterized whole districts, crossed and divided neighbourhoods that resembled an active construction site with open plots and incomplete spaces (Figure 20.5). The multiple stretches

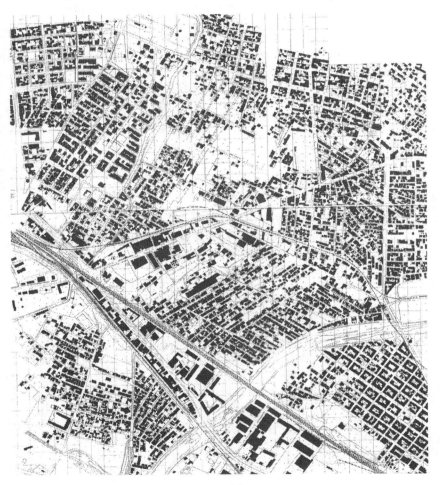

Figure 20.5 Part of the north-western periphery in the late 1970s; densification of unstructured fabric of in-between areas of Kordelio, Evosmos, and Menemeni. (Map: Christodoulou, 2008; base aerotopographic diagrams, 1:1.000, Ministry of Public Works 1978: Prefecture of Thessaloniki, Municipality of Thessaloniki Planning Dept. Archive, used by permission)

Transforming Thessaloniki's periphery 319

of unexploited land in the in-between parts of the expanding urban fabric between compactly built-up areas and peripheral settlements offered nomadic groups such as Roma, lots of options as to where they would settle temporarily within, close to, or far away from inhabited areas.

Newly erected shops specializing in building materials and recreation items along with night clubs lined strips of the northern road axis (entrance/exit to the city) on the extension of Langada Avenue and on Georgikis Scholis Avenue which leads to Chalkidiki (Tsoulouvis et al. 1981). The space around and among these buildings was still being cultivated despite the dispersion of small, large, and medium-sized industries. This mixing of residences with production units went on with the erection of encumbering large new installations adjacent to or within residential areas. Incompatible though they were with the habitations, they were granted planning permission due to the lack of an official city plan.

In the late 1970s, the study zone was considered by the researchers of the time to be covered partly by peripheral illegal/self-generated settlements inhabited by internal migrants and partly by 'vacant stretches of land', located 'outside the city plan' (data from Tsoulouvis et al. 1981). This was a macroscopic picture with many omissions, however, since there were no analytical records or mappings; at the same time, the city was extending following the consecutive approvals of city plans which left inhabited stretches of land outside its boundaries.

The second post-war period (1980–2010): introduction of rational planning principles and intensification of fragmentation

The 1980s

The 1980s were marked by a decrease in residential development and by more intense efforts to introduce the principles of urban planning rationalism into the legislation with the 'Operation for Urban Restructuring' paving the way in 1982. In 1985, the Thessaloniki Master Plan took effect at a time when the local government system became subject to administrative reform. All this coincided with a period of recession, a result of which was that there was less pressure for new large-scale industrial and residential uses and there was also a sharp drop in the rate of the population growth in the Urban Complex of Thessaloniki (Figure 20.6).

In the 1980s, the periphery was no longer an area of only legally built habitations mixed with illegally built ones and of increasing self-generated settlements with characteristics of active neighbourhoods. More public land was now being illegally occupied, old neighbourhoods were being extended in view of the imminent urban restructuring, sparsely built residential areas were sprawling, residential cores were getting squeezed into areas of incompatible uses, temporary encampments were being set up, new social housing estates were making their appearance to the east and west, and the already existing buildings were ageing.

These areas were inhabited not only by the 'typical internal migrants' from the broader area of Macedonia and Thrace but also from co-ethnic immigrants from Central Europe, repatriated political refugees from the countries of the Eastern Bloc (1976–1985), and various groups of Roma. These social groups of distinct

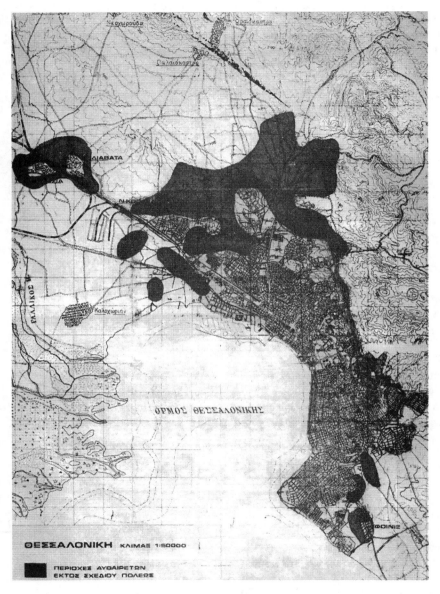

Figure 20.6 Out-of-the-official-plan settlements (in black) in the Thessaloniki periphery of the late 1970s. (*Technika Chronika* – Technical Chamber of Greece, Jan.–Feb. 1977, p. 163)

identity had not been taken into consideration in the promoted city planning which should have been a mechanism for homogenization and relief of social tension; groups which had been struggling to survive and develop in the urban space.

Characteristic are the words of a resident whom I am quoting below:

> Back then things were really weird! People did anything they could or wanted! Our neighbour was a cattle-breeder and a regular contractor of illegally built constructions. My father was a small-scale industry owner and a cattle-breeder. He not only organized the production and the workers in the workshop and supplied products to customers, but he also slaughtered and skinned the animals and then found customers to sell them to. Two businesses on one plot, both illegally built structures, of course. As for me, I was a university student at the Faculty of Engineering back then. On Sunday mornings I grazed the sheep.
>
> (author's interview)

The urban planning process along with the municipalities' General Urban Plans and the parallel urban extension plans, most of which came into effect in 1987–1988, made transitional provisions which allowed urban planning also on land that was not densely built but included limited habitation cores (of illegally or legally built constructions). This provision raised the prospect for an increase in the land value and at the same time it controlled the illegal building activity in all the areas to which the city had extended, with the exception of the Roma settlements.

The only areas which were still being extended with the development of illegally built constructions in the 1980s were those where large stretches of public land were illegally occupied in an organized manner (Figure 20.7).

The serious environmental and residential management problems in the areas of the periphery and the study area persisted, thus aggravating the existing spatial and social inequalities. Although the situation in the western area was more critical due to the greater density of industrial land uses, there were acute environmental problems throughout the periphery, both east and west: uncontrolled waste and rubble disposal into streams and onto unoccupied land, shacks. The streams which divided neighbourhoods were a source of degradation along their length, which revealed a lack of adequate environmental control over the sprawled industries. It was thus typical of the urban planners of the times to cover torrents flow under roads 'for the purposes of sanitation' and to make room for common-use spaces.

In the peri-urban areas, the concentration of industrial and commercial facilities tended to create clearer land use zones; there was a greater density of industrial uses on the north-western side of the city which were close to the main road networks and a linear development of urban services and recreation facilities on the south-eastern side following the establishment of the first two hypermarkets outside the urban fabric. Some areas still engaged in activities of the primary production sector.

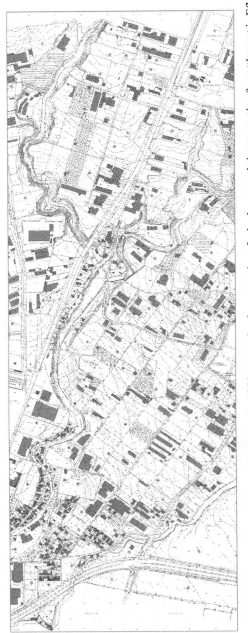

Figure 20.7 Parts of the northern periphery in the 1980s; extensive fragmentation of suburban parcels in preparation for settlement in Efkarpia. (Map: Christodoulou, 2008; base aerotopographic diagrams, 1:1.000, Ministry of Public Works 1982: Prefecture of Thessaloniki, Municipality of Thessaloniki Planning Dept. Archive)

Transforming Thessaloniki's periphery 323

The building of New Diagonios Avenue (known today as K. Karamanli Avenue) and of the National Highway linking Thessaloniki to Moudania in the late 1980s created conditions for better access and improved services in the south-eastern part of the city. Uses involving heavy transport (moving companies, automobile repair shops, etc.) were relocated from compact areas of single or mixed residential use both to the west (to the area of Menemeni) and to the east edge of the city (to the area of Pylea). The official plan for a ring road along the whole perimeter of the Urban Area of Thessaloniki set a natural border which 'hindered the extension of the urban fabric'. It was upon this that the interpretation and implementation of the compact city model was based, which would have to be followed in the development of the urban area as referred to in the Master Plan for the Urban Area of Thessaloniki. This developmental option dimmed the prospects for urban planning in the municipalities located on the edges of the city (Menemeni, Evosmos, Efkarpia, Pylea) and defined them as areas for commercial, manufacturing, or small-scale industry land use in accordance with the provisions covering building on areas located outside the city plan. This was due to an absence of clear rules for development, namely an absence of an effective Land-use Control Zone.

The 1990s

The 1990s were characterized by the improvement of the urban and housing stock, transformation of old and newly dispersed habitations, and new allocations in peri-urban space of several uses in the framework of an intensified spatial fragmentation. Densification and transformation of the peripheral districts followed the spontaneous and cumulative urban extensions of the previous decade by means of a gradual renewal of the urban stock, in specific in the areas where the planning regulation was fulfilled up to the phase of their enactment on property demarcation.

However, the overall scene of improvement of the settlements did not dissolve the already geographically formed, territorial, and socio-spatial inequalities or the serious problems of environmental management and the degradation of natural elements in their surrounding urban and peri-urban areas. Even at present, these areas set up by illegal building and/or land appropriation are differentiated from the initial nuclei of the peripheral planned districts, spatially as well as socially. Their constitutional attributes: problematic neighbouring of incompatible uses or uses disturbing to housing, sites difficult to access, organic development of urban fabric by means of low-quality building stock, restricted surfaces for public/communal infrastructure, fragmentation by technical infrastructure and movement networks passing through, high concentration of low socio-economic profile inhabitants. These drawbacks were not possible to be reversed by the selective interventions of physical planning or infrastructure development of later decades.

In the districts of dense structure, the low Floor Area Ratio, which was applied with planning, did not encourage the radical renewal of the existing stock, in fact it actually conserved the social cohesion of the neighbourhoods and deterred the expulsion of their initial inhabitants. Gradually the areas facing problems in urban living conditions within the urban plan were restricted to small clusters on

324   *Charis Christodoulou*

sites invisible from the main circulation axes. No improvement whatsoever was noted in terms of technical infrastructure in the neighbourhoods that remained suspended as to their perspective of incorporation in the official city plan. In the meantime, absence of Land-use Control Zones in application of the Master Plan for the Urban Area of Thessaloniki intensified the persisting, often contradictory, mixture of land uses and initiatives (collective, private, or belonging to organizations) for provisions for land or housing.

The case of Roma habitation is indicative of the new conditions that were formed. Since the beginning of the 1990s, the districts of sedentarized Roma entered a course of increasing integration and improvement of their socio-economic features, alas not discarding their social and cultural stigmatized identity. Roma living in encampments were submitted to continuous persecutions, displacement, and irrevocable marginalization. They lost their former locations that were to be developed as urban or suburban. Being under persecution, a number of groups accepted to reside in stable organized settlements and to sedentarize in a compulsory manner in locations not suitable for housing development, in a state of a ghetto away from the urban tissue under the pretext of the settlements' 'temporary' character (Figure 20.8).

Indicative for the selective dealing of each case of settlement was also the conservation of the newly built self-generated settlements of Greek Pontians coming from countries of the former Soviet Union. A small number of these people who had migrated in the Urban Complex of Thessaloniki finally selected to settle in the periphery. Kin groups chose to buy land and constructed whole neighbourhoods (Efxinoupolis, Filothei) within the light industry park of Efkarpia-Oreokastro in sites which were previously only sparsely inhabited by locals. The kin network played a decisive role in the selection of settlement sites as well as in the actual constitution of habitation in a collaborative solidarity manner. In the most organized way, since the 1960s well-known process of land parceling or appropriation, construction without planning permission on peri-urban lots, and their consequent political legalization was activated (Figure 20.9).

In the beginning of the 1990s, economic migrants without official papers, workers in the fields, in the construction industry or in light manufacture inhabited the edge of the city in shanties in invisible sites around Kalochori, Menemeni, Evosmos, Efkarpia, and Pylea. Their habitations took place in all possible lodgings (abandoned houses and sheds, etc.) and were rather ephemeral. They appeared and vanished with a weekly rhythm depending on the conditions of official control and supervision. Migrant families resided in the dated social housing complexes, taking advantage of the offer of low rent and sale prices of flats. Their accommodation deterred the social collapse of the complexes which was expected due to the aging of their initial inhabitants.

Since the beginning of the 1990s, the circulation of the ring-road along the whole of the perimeter of the Urban Complex of Thessaloniki, and that of the National Highway linking Thessaloniki to Moudania, as well as the improvement of the features of the western and northern gates of the city, rendered the periphery even more accessible. Soon, the denature of peri-urban landscape was more

Figure 20.8 Views of the western periphery in the 2000s; Roma organized settlement in Menemeni, 2004. (Christodoulou, 2008)

Figure 20.9 Views of the northern periphery in the 2000s; Efxinoupolis, new Pontian neighborhood in Evosmos–Efkarpia, 2001. (Christodoulou 2008)

than obvious, as an effect of a great number of interventions of every scale and type. Dispersed legally and illegally built cells cropped up gradually in formerly agricultural land along the new main highway network and in the interior of the areas it encircled; land filling of streambeds and earthworks modified irreversibly the physical terrain; extensive fencing of lots and high vegetation extinction took place; all these interventions constituted interventions that prepared the intensified use of the peri-urban land that would follow.

New allocation choices of the tertiary sector enterprises taking advantage of the new conditions of accessibility and availability of big land property created the first consumption clusters of large-scale supermarkets, commercial centres, poles of wide public attraction, some of which incorporated entertainment facilities[2] (Figure 20.10). However, the land use and the image of the periphery did not have a homogeneous character in the whole perimeter. In the western suburbs, there were the warehouses and the workshops that prevailed because of the surviving networks of commerce and transportation of the past. The northern districts were marked by specialized commerce and of construction materials and home equipment, offices, retail, and light industry. Finally, the south-eastern ones gathered the most important units of tertiary activities and urban services, as well as a good number of old and new sports, recreation, education, and welfare facilities. There was also abundant violation of planning legislation referring to mainly other than residential uses; that is, preconstructed cells for auxiliary uses, pavilions, all kinds of extensions in shops, sheds, piggeries, fishermen shanties on the coast and others, which documents the change of genre of urbanization of the peri-urban space.

The 2000s

At the beginning of the 2000s, the landscape of the periphery included both compact urbanized clusters and dispersed habitations in the middle of an arising scene of globalized economy. The western and eastern districts followed parallel courses

Figure 20.10 Views of the south-eastern periphery in the 2000s; images of new urbanity and peri-urban consumption, 2001. (Christodoulou 2008)

of improvement without significant population mobility from the one to the other in reference to housing. There were zones of aggravation and zones of amelioration in relation to urban spatial and social specificities which had been consolidated in the 1990s independently of the overall schema of the west-east division. Already a few were the habitations in the periphery that were not compact. The majority of the neighbourhoods that had been incorporated in areas within official General Urban Plans hadn't exhausted their programmed residential capacity. In areas where there had been a recent enactment of the planning regulation on property demarcation—in the east as well as in the west, several sites had a total picture of an open worksite. This reconstruction reinforced their mixing in terms of population.

At the same time in remote habitations which hadn't been integrated in the official plan during the 'Operation for Urban Restructuring' in the 1980s, the inhabitants' identity changed. The ones that survived entrenched in residentially problematic sites were several old landowners who had lost the perspective of their land's integration in the official urban plan, moreover lodgers on low rents. The well-known procedure of degradation and consequent habitation of the housing stock by non-privileged or marginalized groups that had already been observed in central areas of the city appeared in the periphery with the element of exclusion more intense, in constructions either cumulatively renovated or half-ruined, even in trailers: elderly—men and women, people not able to develop an urban mobility, immigrants—mostly single men, but in families as well, obviously poor and unemployed, kin of local Roma groups and groups of Albanian and Bulgarian ones. The outer fringe was marked by contradictions in terms of urban planning as well as socially in unforeseen functionally mixed surroundings (Figure 20.11).

Figure 20.11 Views of the south-eastern periphery in the 2000s; mixture of primary and tertiary sector activities in the peri-urban area of Pylea, 2005. (Photograph by Dimitris Katsapelidis, used with his permission)

Immediately after the completion of the public consultation on the legislation of Land-use Control Zones in the peri-urban area of Thessaloniki in 2002–2003, there was an unprecedented development in the south-eastern periphery out of the simultaneous exploitation of private property. In a very short time span, educational complexes, composite commercial clusters and malls with multi-plex cinemas, cafes and restaurants functioning as entertainment poles, hotels of large-scale, private health and welfare installations, sports facilities, swarmed the area together with industrial and other productive activities of the past (docks, workshops, etc.). The peri-urban out of the official plan area of the municipali-ties of Pylea and Thermi along the coastline was the fastest developing field of installation of all branches of the tertiary sector of economy in the greater area of Thessaloniki. This progress was not anticipated and in fact it was set off by the possibility of enactment of the proposed zones of urban services, ecologi-cal development, and protection. The owners of big land property together with entrepreneurial interests for development were mobilized in order to supersede the imminent enactment of restrictive development conditions on their property. The actual existence of big property land, the coincident quest of globalized enter-prises for new development sites, as well as the new accessibility conditions in the periphery acted simultaneously as catalysts in the formation of the character of the area.

These installations operate today within an in-between zone of the compact urban areas and the suburban residential areas of the countryside which overrules the mono-nuclearity of the Urban Complex of Thessaloniki in the tertiary sector with tricky effects. The case of the south-eastern periphery encapsulates all kinds of facilitation offered by the local and central (national) public administration for the allocation of enterprises of globalized interests. At the same time, relevant but smaller in scale and dispersion was the development of the north-western parts of the periphery between Menemeni-Diavata-Kalochori-Ionia and between Efkarpia-Evosmos-Oreokastro.

The staggering development of central functions in the southeastern periphery lead gradually to the rise of a new dynamic social space and to a dispersed urban landscape on one hand unfamiliar on the other a prominent point of reference in Thessaloniki, in all then Greek cities as well as in the neighbouring Balkan countries. The composition of this space happened in a fragmented and cumula-tive manner taking advantage of and transgressing the legal ordinances for the out-of-the-official-plan construction in absence of an official Land-use Control Zone or overall development plan. Elemental technical infrastructure was missing too. Some of the first indications of the malfunction of the area were the severe traffic problems on the main and secondary road network, the lack of pedestrian security, and the difficulty to provide for infrastructure networks. At the end of the 2000s, the coastline of Mikra as a major natural advantage and public space of the Urban Complex of Thessaloniki had been wasted despite the fact that it had been prescribed as a recreation and environmental protection zone in the city's Master Plan. However, there were still available fields, property of state organizations to which those that came up out of recent deindustrialization were added. These

330 Charis Christodoulou

fields provide a new and unforeseen potential for an active regeneration plan and a new identity of urban life.

Conclusion: the urban periphery of Thessaloniki in transition

The urban periphery of Thessaloniki remains to a great extent an 'unknown land', despite its increasing contribution to the formation of the perception and the actual experience of the city, a meeting point and a transit field of the people of the wider metropolitan area, and possibly the broader area of the Balkans. The description of its urbanization, habitation, and landscape from an historical-geographical approach informs and broadens our understanding and perception of the socio-spatial transition of the city. The pragmatic synthesis of issues regarding both the 'real' space—physical and social—and the widely maintained, perceived or by urban planning programmed space, enhances the processes of gradual transformation of the periphery. During the first post-war period (1940s to 1970s), the primary production space was transformed into urbanized space, and fields into completely inhabited neighbourhoods, and during the post-dictatorship period (1970s to 2010), into compact districts with infrastructural problems and new peri-urban centralities of civic life where unforeseen antagonisms prevailed.

The chapter provides new insights into the changes that the urbanization pattern underwent, from the rapid reconstruction of central urban districts and the peripheral self-generated settlements of the 1960s to the urban tissue consolidation and the staggering urban sprawl in the 2000s. It underlines the change in the degree of tolerance that state and local authorities showed for the arbitrary use of space, not only for housing but also of any use allocation of any powerful interested agency. The sharp contrast between the 'real' city and the 'planned' city has, despite the efforts made in the 1980s to repair it by means of numerous urban plans and institutional tools, persisted and it has also acquired new attributes that are not woven together with the urban evolution as an overall settlement, but derive from its 'spontaneous' uncontrolled metropolitan expansion.

The historical-geographical retrospection documents the conditions that bred a mentality hostile to the natural environment and to the cultural heritage, one of wild environmental exploitation of the urban grounds, which has led to the present degradation of urban and peri-urban landscape.

Since the beginning of the 21st century, new, multi-faceted conditions have been formed, which are more complex and composite than those of the previous decades: planned neighbourhoods exhibit differentiated urban development modes, and either incorporate or exclude different social groups; the habitation of space presents similar features in the urban fringe along the whole perimeter of the Urban Complex of Thessaloniki. Thus, it can be concluded that the widely accepted perception of the dual city of north-west degraded districts and south-east upgraded ones, is valid only as genealogical documentation. The contemporary periphery is a mosaic—fragmented in terms of space and society. It still stands in the shadow of the Thessaloniki central areas and dominant narratives, in a fragile present, evolving at random towards an uncertain future.

Transforming Thessaloniki's periphery   331

Notes

1 See the guide to the bus network of Thessaloniki (from the *Makedonia* newspaper, 1 September 1963) in Ioannidou and Tsironis 2004, 194.
2 The typology and geographical dispersion of the clusters of the tertiary sector that were located in Thessaloniki in the 1990s are described and explained in Kafkalas et al. 1999, 111–119, 123–127, maps 12–13.

References

Axarli, K. and Kosmaki, P., 'Για μια αλλαγη στην παραγωγή και χρήση του χώρου: Ελεγχος δυνατοτήτων στον οικισμό Δενδροπόταμος' [For a change in the production and use of space: Examination of the potential in "Dendropotamos settlement", 1974], In: Fatouros, D. et al. (eds.), *Μελέτες για την κατοικία στην Ελλάδα* [Studies of Housing in Greece], Thessaloniki: Paratiritis (1979), 133–229.

Christodoulou, Ch., *Αστικοποίηση και χώροι κοινωνικού αποκλεισμού: εγκαταστάσεις κατοίκησης στην περιφέρεια της Θεσσαλονίκης, 1980–2000* [Urbanization and Spaces of Social Exclusion: Habitation Patterns in the Periphery of Thessaloniki], Doctoral Dissertation, Dept. of Urban and Regional Planning and Regional Development, School of Architecture, Aristotle University of Thessaloniki (2008). (internet publication https://ikee.lib.auth.gr/record/105525/files/ChristodoulouFinal.pdf) [in Greek with a summary in English].

Christodoulou, Ch., 'Συγκροτήματα κοινωνικής κατοικίας της πρώτης μεταπολεμικής περιόδου στη Θεσσαλονίκη: Μετασχηματισμοί και αστικοί συσχετισμοί στο οικιστικό περιβάλλον της σύγχρονης πόλης' ['Social housing complexes of the first postwar period in Thessaloniki: Transformations and urban interrelations in the residential surroundings of the contemporary city'], In: Vitopoulou, A., Tournikiotis, P. and Yerolympos, A. (eds.), *Η ελληνική πόλη και η πολεοδομία του μοντέρνου* [The Greek City and Modern Planning], DoCoMoMo 05, Athens: Futura (2015b), 297–314.

Christodoulou, Ch., *Τοπία αστικής διάχυσης, αστικοποίηση και πολεοδομικός σχεδιασμός: η περιφέρεια της Θεσσαλονίκης* [Landscapes of Sprawl. Urbanization and Urban Planning. The Periphery of Thessaloniki], Thessaloniki: University Studio Press (2015).

Fatouros, D. A. and Chatzimichalis, K., 'Αυτογενής οικισμός στην περιοχή της Θεσσαλονίκης' ['Spontaneous settlement in the Thessaloniki region'], In: Fatouros, D. et al. (eds.), *Μελέτες για την κατοικία στην Ελλάδα* [Studies of Housing in Greece], Thessaloniki: Paratiritis (1979).

Hastaoglou-Martinidis, V., 'Νεωτερικότητα και μνήμη στη διαμόρφωση της μεταπολεμικής Θεσσαλονίκης' ['Modernity and memory in the planning of post-war Thessaloniki'], In: Kaukalas, G., Lambrianidis, L. and Papamichos, N. (eds.), *Η Θεσσαλονίκη στο μεταίχμιο. Η πόλη από τη σκοπιά των αλλαγών* [Thessaloniki at the Edge: A City from the Perspective of Changes], Athens: Kritiki (2008), 169–171.

Hastaoglou-Martinidi, V. 'O Poleodomikos Metaschimatismos tis Thessalonikis sta Chronia tis Prosfigikis Plimiridas 1922–30' ['Urban planning transformation of Thessaloniki in the years of migrant flood 1922–30'], In: Lavas, G. et al. (eds.), *Η Πόλη στο Καλειδοσκόπιο για την Ιστορία της Πόλης και της Πολεοδομίας* [The City in the Kaleidoscope. Texts on the History of the City and Urban Planning], Athens: Association of the History of the City and Urban Planning, Research Institute of Applied Communication, Athens University (2001), 255–276.

332   Charis Christodoulou

Ioannidou, E. and Tsironis, Th. (eds.), *Η Καλαμάρια γράφει ιστορία 1940–1967*. [Kalamaria Writes History 1950–1967: From Survival to Creation. Historic-Photographic Album], Thessaloniki: Historical Archive of Refugee Hellenism of the Municipality of Kalamaria (2004).

Kafkalas, G. et al. *Μείωση της μονοκεντρικότητας στο πολεοδομικό συγκρότημα Θεσσαλονίκης και ο ρόλος του τριτογενή τομέα* [Thessaloniki: Reduction of Monocentricity in the Urban Complex of Thessaloniki and the Role of the Tertiary Sector], Thessaloniki: Ziti (1999).

Kalogirou, N. S., *Architecture and Urban Planning in Postwar Thessaloniki: A Critical Review*, Thessaloniki: Barbounakis (1986) [in Greek and English].

Kalogirou, N., 'Αστικοποίηση και πολεοδομική πολιτική στην περιοχή Θεσσαλονίκης' ['Urbanization and urban planning policy in the area of Thessaloniki'], *Epitheorisi Koinonikon Erevnon* (Review of Social Research), 30–31 (1977), 355–364 [in Greek].

Kalogirou, N., 'Οργάνωση και παραγωγή του χώρου στους αυθαίρετους οικισμούς Με βάση μια έρευνα πεδίου σε δύο οικισμούς της Θεσσαλονίκης' ['Organization and production of space in illegal settlements based on a field research in two settlements of Thessaloniki'], *Technika Chronika*, 2 (1980), 51–59 [in Greek].

Karadimou-Yerolympou, A., 'Από τον 19ο στον 20ο αιώνα: Η ανάδυση του σύγχρονου αστικού τοπίου της Θεσσαλονίκης' ['From the 19th to the 20th century, the emergence of contemporary urban landscape of Thessaloniki'], *Technografima*, 324 (2007), 12–13 [in Greek].

Karadimou-Yerolympou, A., *Η ανοικοδόμηση της Θεσσαλονίκης μετά την πυρκαγιά του 1917* [The Reconstruction of Salonica after the Fire of 1917], Thessaloniki: University Studio Press (1995).

Tsoulouvis, L. et al. *Μελέτη Οικιστικής Ανάπτυξης Θεσσαλονίκης* [Study of Residential Development of Thessaloniki], Thessaloniki: Technical Chamber of Greece (1981).

21 Land policy in Thessaloniki and the transition to a contemporary metropolitan area, 1922–1967

Athena Yiannakou

Introduction

Understanding a city is a multi-task endeavour 'aiming to reconcile the ways in which urban social processes (comprising of the cultural as well as the political and economic) are constituted at particular historical moments' (Eade and Mele 2002, 3–4). Land is as much the key to understanding the shape, layout, and growth of a city form (Kievel 1993), as it is a determining factor in urban change. The layout and scale of urban development owe much to the nature of landownership (Kievel 1993), while landownership establishes basic interests and outlines a framework of alliances and oppositions that structure society (Elliot and Mc Crone 1982, 97).

The processes and specific patterns of urban growth and spatial structure of the city of Thessaloniki, after its incorporation into the country's national economy, cannot be understood unless we look at the way state, small landownership, residential development, and land-use planning were historically interrelated, in particular after the drastic changes in the city's size and social structure in the post-1922 period (Yiannakou 1993). If the decisive role of the state in land allocation had a determining influence on urban growth and development patterns in Greece generally, Thessaloniki was the place where the implementation of all major inter-war land and housing programmes and policies was in many respects the crucial other side of the abrupt post-war urban transition.

The exchange of Greek and Muslim populations after the Asia Minor Catastrophe marked the beginning of a new stage in the urban history of Thessaloniki (Loukatos 1986; Yerolympos et al. 1988). As the majority of the city's Muslim population left the country and approximately 100,000 Greek refugees arrived in Thessaloniki, the 1920s constituted the beginning of a period of modern urban development in Thessaloniki. This development took place alongside the city's incorporation in the Greek state and its transformation from a cosmopolitan Balkan city into a modern regional metropolis (Hastaoglou-Martinidis 1997). It is difficult to estimate the exact number of refugees who inhabited Thessaloniki (Pentzopoulos 1959; Maravelakis and Vakalopoulos 1955). Hence, it is difficult to estimate the number of families entitled to resettlement. It was estimated that more than 30,000 families (119,000 people) were

334　*Athena Yiannakou*

settled in the Province (eparchy) of Thessaloniki [21,000 in Greater Thessaloniki (GT) and 9,000 in the rest of the region], an area that coincides fairly closely with the Wider Area of Thessaloniki as defined by the 1985 Master Plan (Figure 21.1).

The paper focuses on an analysis of the programmes of land and housing allocation, implemented in the context of refugee rehabilitation after 1922. It analyzes the scope and characteristics of both the Urban and Rural Rehabilitation Progammes to define the significance of these programmes, their influence on the structure of landownership and the nature of land policy incorporated in them. The research is based on unpublished material from the archives of the Ministries of Social Welfare and Agriculture.[1] The first part examines the programme of Urban Rehabilitation and its impact upon urban development of GT. Special attention is paid to the course of its implementation and the form of urban landed property that resulted. The second part provides an account of the Rural Refugee Rehabilitation in eight areas of Thessaloniki's periphery incorporated in the urban area after 1950. One result was the creation of a fragmented system of small rural land holding in these peripheral areas. The third part deals briefly with other sources of state land allocation, so as to provide a comprehensive consideration of state land policy and its impact upon contemporary urban land allocation in GT.

Urban Rehabilitation Programme: consolidating small landholdings as a feature of the modern urban form

In Thessaloniki a total of 19,168 families were resettled through the Urban Rehabilitation Programme (URP), representing 12% of the total number of urban refugee families resettled in various urban areas. URP started in Thessaloniki in 1925 with a major expropriation of land, and opened the way for the city's first stage of suburbanisation. Overall, 445 hectares of land (12% of the total land made available for the needs of the URP nationally) were transferred to public ownership for the implementation of the urban rehabilitation policy in Thessaloniki. The largest part of this land, 395 hectares, came under the jurisdiction of the Refugee Rehabilitation Committee (EAP), and, after its dissolution in 1930, under the administration of the Ministry of Social Welfare (MSW, Table 21.1). In addition, about 50 hectares were transferred to 11 building co-operatives, which were to undertake rehabilitation independently, under the supervision of the MSW.

The largest part of the expropriated land was concentrated in the east and south areas of GT (Table 21.2). It is well known that Thessaloniki had been expanding eastward since 1880 (Dimitriadis 1983; Kolonas 2016). URP drastically transformed the social basis of the city's expansion: new neighbourhoods of low-income refugee communities encircled the middle-class suburbs of the eastern part, thus forming one of the crucial characteristics of a Mediterranean city (Leontidou 1990). This programme was rather limited in the western areas, which were still rural, constituting the basis for the rehabilitation of the peasant refugees, and later, the main location of industrial plants and working-class housing. During 1922–1928, the population of the urban area of Thessaloniki increased by 37.50%,

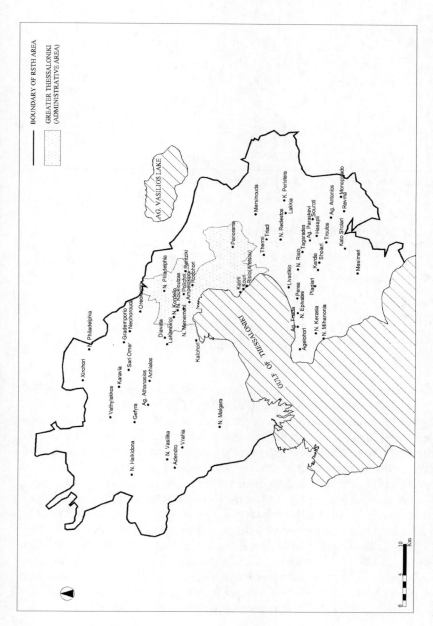

Figure 21.1 Refugee settlements in the province of Thessaloniki. (Map redrawn by the author, based on data from Maravelakis and Vakalopoulos 1955)

336   *Athena Yiannakou*

Table 21.1 Land disposed under the jurisdiction of the EAP, the MSW, and building co-operatives for the URP (in square metres)

Municipality or suburb	EAP/MSW	Co-operatives	TOTAL
Thessaloniki	1,566,103	257,787	1,823,890
Toumpa	−1,370,453	−22,000	−1,392,453
Harilaou	−68,761	−35,095	−103,856
Xerokrene/Kalithea	−126,889	−6,692	−133,581
40 Ekklesies		−194,000	−194,000
Kalamaria	1,975,071	181,600	2,156,671
Agios Pavlos	117,678		117,678
Triandria	44,625		44,625
Neapoli	23,848	65,000	88,848
Ampelokipoi	57,636		57,636
Kordelio	38,078		38,078
Efkarpia	124,857		124,857
TOTAL	3,947,896	504,387	4,452,283

(Yiannakou 1993, elaboration of data from unpublished records of the MSW, Housing Division, Department of Thessaloniki)

Table 21.2 Distribution of the URP and per area of GT

Zone	Area (in square metres)	%
East and South suburbs	3,652,979	82.05
North suburbs	356,303	8
Inner West	280,065	6.29
Outer West	162,935	3.66
TOTAL GT	4,452,282	100

whereas in the period 1917–1927, the urban area of Thessaloniki increased by 600 hectares, 74.17% of which were involved in URP (Figure 21.2).

One of the main characteristics of URP was its gradual implementation over a long period of time, despite the fact that its objectives concerned the specific needs of refugee rehabilitation in the 1920s (Table 21.3). The initial emphasis of the programme was on housing, whereby 9,196 houses were built by the EAP and (later) the MSW, and allocated, together with the titles of ownership of the plots, to an equal number of families. The emphasis on home and landownership is evident in the programme. The latter becomes clearer with the gradual shift towards land allocation and a promotion of self-housing which followed. After the MSW had resumed responsibility for the programme, the programme was split into two parts. Apart from the continuation of the housing programme as set by the EAP, 3,777 families—29% of the total settled in the first period—were provided with urban plots and loans, in order to have their own houses built. One of the most acute social problems during this pre-war period was that 3,096 families were

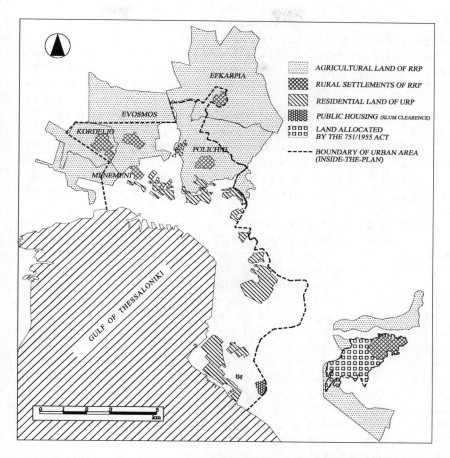

Figure 21.2 Land allocated to refugees by the Refugee Rehabilitation Programmes, including land allocated to building co-operatives. (By the author)

Table 21.3 Number of families settled by the URP in different periods

Year	No. of families	%
1928–1950		
sheltered in houses	12,973	67.68
houses by the EAP	2,138	−11.15
houses by the MSW	7,058	−36.82
'self-housing'	3,777	−19.7
shed-settlers	3,096	16.15
1950–1965	1,771	9.24
1965–1984	1,328	6.93

(Yiannakou 1993)

338   *Athena Yiannakou*

temporarily settled in sheds, a situation that was resolved in the years 1950–1965, partly through the public housing programmes of Phoinikas and Agios Ioannis, and partly through land allocation to shed-dwellers.

In the period 1950–1965, apart from housing shack-dwellers, 1,771 additional families were provided with urban plots for self-housing, whereas after 1965, 1,328 families were provided with 781 plots. Approximately 25–30 hectares of land were allocated during this final period 1965–1984. Despite the fact that house prices and demand for housing were rapidly increasing in the areas where the MSW had been allocating land since the early 1960s, it was only after 1973, at a time when the housing market in the south-eastern areas was flourishing, that the MSW took into consideration the development value of the allocated properties. This was a time which, due to high demand for land in the south-eastern areas in particular, most of these properties immediately entered the speculative housing sector.

Thus URP, as indeed all land allocation programmes, originated in the 1920s, finally constituting a long-standing policy, which encompassed the interdependency between state and small landownership. It is in this context that both the delays in carrying out URP and its legalistic nature should be placed. One could argue that the slow progress of the programme can be attributed to the large scale of the task of rehabilitation and the financial difficulty of accomplishing it. If this is partly true for the pre-war period, the fact that about 32% of URP was carried out throughout the entire post-war period should be considered as indicative, not only of the state bureaucracy and its resultant inefficiency, but also of the specific way the state intervened in residential land allocation. This does not diminish the significance of the public housing programme, particularly if one considers the fact that no other housing programme ever reached even part of URP's proportions, either locally or nationally. However, its significance in the firm establishment of small landownership in the urban area was to become one of the most important factors for housing land allocation and the high share in it held by the owner-occupied sector, as well as it having an enormous impact upon later trends in residential development.

The 'one-family-per-plot' principle, which secured high rates of homeownership for low-income groups in urban areas in the 1920s, was also one of the main factors facilitating the easy transfer of this landed property into the speculative sector (the *antiparohi* market) through which owner-occupation dominated housing allocation in the post-war period. The change of objectives from public housing provision to provision of small landed property, further extended this access to potentially, highly priced land. Altogether 6,876 families, 36% of the total, were settled through the programme of landed property provision.

Taking into consideration land availability, extreme land fragmentation was necessary in order to achieve high rates of small ownership. The average size of the allocated plots varied from 80–200 square metres and was slightly increased to 150–250 square metres in the 1965–1984 co-ownership programme. An examination of the plot size in the area remaining under the ownership of the MSW, for example, shows that 29% of plots do not even fulfil the requirements of the local

Land policy in Thessaloniki, 1922–1967   339

plans and therefore cannot be officially developed. In the case of the allocated plots, this problem has contributed to a large number of digressions from the standards set by local plans, and above all, to strong pressures on behalf of the owners for the revision of these standards. Bearing in mind these problems, one can easily explain how plot ratio has become one of the central issues in planning practice.

By 1984, almost the entire land (99.29%) owned and administered by the MSW throughout 1925–1984 was allocated. That year the government decided to instruct the local department of the MSW to bring an end to the rehabilitation programme.

Rural Rehabilitation Programme: consolidating small land holdings in the post-war urban periphery

If the programme of urban refugee rehabilitation determined the character of urban expansion in the inter-war period, and was to play an important role in the development of the *antiparohi* market in the inner urban areas in the post-war period, it was the Rural Rehabilitation Programme (RRP) that established the patterns of post-war urban expansion and the peculiarities of land market in the outer urban periphery of Thessaloniki.

Since the actual programme of land allocation started in GT in 1930, almost at the time of the dissolution of the EAP, it was undertaken entirely by the Ministry of Agriculture (MA), which was to become the major agent of land allocation in areas subjected to the conversion processes. The RRP in GT was part of the broader land allocation programme implemented in Macedonia, which absorbed 77.07% of the rural refugee population. Seven of the areas in which the RRP was implemented in the county of Thessaloniki, namely Polichni, Menemeni, Evosmos, Kordelio, Efkarpia, Rodohori (Sykies), and Panorama, called *Agroktimata* (farms), were incorporated into the boundaries of GT after 1950 (Figure 21.2). Through the RRP 1,712 families were provided with farming land in these seven areas (Table 21.4). They represent 6.15% and 8.79% of the total families settled in the Province of Thessaloniki and in GT respectively, through the 1920s Rehabilitation Programmes. At the same time, an equal number of rural settlements were established.

In all, 1,163 families or an estimated 4,640 individuals were initially settled in the then periphery of Thessaloniki. To these families, 200 hectares of land were distributed within the 'Settlements', the newly created rural communities, for their housing needs (Figure 21.2). Up to 2,800 hectares of farming land were distributed to 1,712 families throughout the period 1930–1970, representing approximately 34% of the total land and 83% of the cultivated land in these areas. Table 21.5 records the allocated land in six out of the seven areas under investigation. Allocations in Kordelio (estimated at about 200 hectares) are not included due to lack of data.

The implementation of the RRP involved two different stages. First, the stage of initial allocations which involved two procedures. During the first procedure,

340   *Athena Yiannakou*

Table 21.4 Distribution of settled families by the RRP per community

Settlements	Initial allocations	Complementary allocations+	TOTAL
Polichni	183	87	270
Menemeni	149	–	149
Evosmos	341	–	341
Kordelio*	64	–	64
Efkarpia	158	72	230
Rodohori	75	286 **	361
Panorama	193	104	297
TOTAL GT	1,163	549	1,712

(Yiannakou 1993, elaboration of data from Land Allocation Records, MA, Survey Department, County of Thessaloniki)
* Data from Maravelakis and Vakalopoulos (1955).
** Families provided with urban plots.
+ Not including families allocated land after appropriation.

the average size of the 'basic' allotment, the area of allocated land each family was entitled to, was set. Due to the urgency of the refugee problem, land was allocated only temporarily, in which case a family did not always get all the land it was entitled to. These deviations were amended later. In four of the areas under study, Polichni, Evosmos, Efkarpia, and Panorama, final allocations of this first stage took place in the years 1930–1933. In two areas, Menemeni and Rodohori, they took place between 1959 and 1964. Due to the fact that land in these areas was already converted for residential or industrial uses, it was decided to reduce the size of the 'basic' allotments, taking into account their increase in value.

A second stage involved the complementary allocations. New land, 210 hectares overall, was allocated in four areas, Polichni, Efkarpia, Rodohori, and Panorama. Apart from settling new landless peasants, the purpose of these allocations was to resolve the situation of appropriated land, as well as to complete certain land allocations, which old beneficiaries were entitled to from previous stages. In the case of Menemeni and Rodohori where final settlement of the initial allocations took place in the beginning of the 1960s, appropriations were also settled during this stage. As far as old beneficiaries were concerned, this was settled through complementary allocations, due to the fact that during the final stage of the initial allocations certain families had, once again, not been provided with all the land they were entitled to. This was an extremely complicated procedure relating to Greek family law. In brief, given the fact that rural owner-occupation is family based, and that part of the allocated land had already been transferred to inheritors, a new computation of the remaining land had to be carried out. In this case, not only did the land that the new beneficiary had inherited from his/her parents have to be deducted, but also that inherited from his/her in-laws, in case the latter had been distributed by the MA. In the case of Rodohori in particular, due to the delays in finalising the situation of ownership of the allocated land,

Table 21.5 The Rural Rehabilitation Programme and the distribution of land per 'Farm' (area in *stremmata*=0.1 hectare)

FARM	Year of allocation	CULTIVATED LAND		Non-cultivated land	Area of settlement	TOTAL
		Allocated to farmers	Private properties			
POLICHNI						
first allocation	1933	3556.5	1677.6	3644.1	869.7	
second	1961	163.1	–	3481.8	–	
third	1957–1968	358.4	1048.1	2074.5	–	
Total area		4078.0	2725.7	2074.5	869.7	9747.9
%		41.8	28.0	21.3	8.9	100.0
MENEMENI	1959–1962					
total area		2679.6	302.0	1663.5	176.3	4821.4
%		55.6	6.3	34.5	3.7	100.0
EVOSMOS	1930					
total area		8961.1	962.8	844.0	332.1	10830.0
%		80.3	8.9	7.8	3.1	100.0
EFKARPIA						
first allocation	1931	4367.5	883.3	8439.4	155.3	
second	1957	222.3	–	8217.0	–	
third	1967–1968					
total area		4726.7	883.3	8080.1	155.3	13845.3
%		34.1	6.4	58.4	1.1	100.0
RODOHORI						
first allocation	1962–1964	1009.0	44.9	3258.0	–	
second	1969–1970	105.1	–	3152.9	–	
third	1972	25.4	–	3127.5	–	
total area		1139.5	44.9	3127.5	–	4311.9
%		26.4	1.0	72.5	–	100.0

(*Continued*)

Table 21.5 Continued

FARM	Year of allocation	CULTIVATED LAND		Non-cultivated land	Area of settlement	TOTAL
		Allocated to farmers	Private properties			
PANORAMA						
first allocation	1931	3790.3	289.4	28557.2	418.6	
second	1966	121.2	–	28436.0		
third	1967	967.0	–	27469.0		
total area		4878.5	289.4	27469.0	418.6	33055.4
%		14.8	0.9	83.1	1.3	100.0
TOTAL GT		26193.0	5207.0	43258.0	1952.0	76612.0
%		83.4	16.6			
%		34.2	6.8	56.5	2.5	100.0

(Yiannakou 1993)

Land policy in Thessaloniki, 1922–1967 343

43.92 hectares, 43.5% of the total allocated land, was in fact distributed as urban plots. The impact of the above procedures, both on land fragmentation, as well as on the dependence of the rural and the consequent urban land owner-occupation upon the state, was of great importance.

In practice, until the early 1930s, 92% of the RRP's land had been allocated on the periphery of Thessaloniki at a time when the dominant character of these areas was still rural. However, this fact is not enough to diminish its impact on later processes of conversion in these areas, especially if one considers the structure of landed property after the allocation. On the other hand, although the total allocated land distributed in 'complementary' allocations during the years 1957–1972 was only 8%, even this small percentage might have been very significant in an urban land market where ownership of very small plots had predominated. In terms of the final allocation of land in GT, only 77.90% was settled in the inter-war period, while a total of 578.80 hectares—7.55% of the total area under study—was settled after 1957 (Table 21.6).

The average size of a property distributed to landless peasants was 17,931 square metres (Table 21.7). From this figure the part of land in Rodohori had been deducted, since this was distributed in the form of urban plots. This small size of the allotments was one issue that caused a number of claims on behalf of peasant refugees from the beginning of the rural refugee rehabilitation (Pelagidis 1988, 75). A better understanding of the evolution of rural landed property can be also reached from an examination of its average size in different periods. The size of allocated property per family in the inter-war period varied from 19,434 square metres in Polichni to 27,649 square metres in Efkarpia. In the case of post-war allocations there are two figures to be considered. First, as far as Rodohori and Menemeni are concerned the average size of a landed property per family was 10,174 and 17,984 square metres respectively. This was due to a decision taken by the Expropriation Committee of the MA in 1955 to reduce the size of 'basic' allotments in these areas, since the final rehabilitation of the allocated land had taken place at a time when these areas were transformed into urban ones. Secondly, as far as complementary allocations were concerned, the average size of an allocated property varied from 3,509 square metres to 10,744 square metres, because of the time of the allocation but also because part of these properties had already been appropriated by peasant families.

Table 21.6 The implementation of the RRP over time

		Area (in stremmata)	*%*	*% of the total*
Initial allocation				
final stage	1930–1933	20405.4	77.9	
	1957–1964	3688.6	14.1	92.0%
complementary	1957–1961	743.9	2.8	
allocations	1966–1972	1355.5	5.2	8.0%
TOTAL		766111.9	100.0	100.0%

Table 21.7 Average size of farming land in the allocation areas

	No. of allotments	Size of allotments (in stremmas)							Average size (in square metres)
		0–2	*2–4*	*4–6*	*6–10*	*10–15*	*15–20*	*20–*	
POLICHNI	937	172	239	326	190	8	2	–	4,352
first allocation	720	60	193	269	188	8	2	–	4,939
second allocation									1,254
	130	111	13	1				–	
third allocation									4,120
	87	1	28	56	2			–	
MENEMENI	353	155	34	19	59	81	5		7,591
EVOSMOS	1,037	58	154	209	280	240	84	12	8,381
EFKARPIA	680	84	150	162	126	125	31	2	6,951
first allocation	579	58	96	153	115	124	31	2	7,543
second allocation	54	14	23	6	10	1			4,117
third allocation	47	12	31	3	1				2,912
RODOHORI	127	40	40	20	19	8			4,486
PANORAMA	970	72	414	278	188	13	5		5,029
first allocation	762	60	222	274	188	13	5		4,974
second allocation	28	12	13	3					4,327
third allocation	180		179	1					5,372
TOTAL GT	4,104	581	1031	1014	862	475	127	14	6,243

Total allocated area: 25,623.620 *stremmata*

Land policy in Thessaloniki, 1922–1967   345

The problem of land fragmentation and its possible impact on land supply becomes more acute when the average size of a farming land plot is taken into consideration. Overall, the average size of a farming land plot on the periphery of Thessaloniki was a mere 6,245 square metres and the average number of rural sites per family was 2.87. As the continuity of owner-occupation is affected by inheritance patterns which results in further land fragmentation, 20–30 years after the implementation of the bulk of the RRP in GT, a major part of the allocated land was transferred to its inheritors resulting in further land fragmentation.

Apart from the effects of the RRP on the structure of land in the periphery of Thessaloniki, a second important aspect of the programme concerns the way relations between state and small landowners were affected by the structure and implementation of the programme. In other words, a number of characteristics of the RRP, such as its gradual implementation, its bureaucratic nature, or its lack of locational criteria, were related and in turn resulted in a considerable dependence of small landownership upon the state. Although this dependence was initially created in the rural sector, due to the repercussions of the programme upon residential development, it was gradually transferred into the urban sector. Thus, for instance, complementary allocations took on greater significance at a period when land prices were rapidly increasing and, as a consequence, there was a great deal of pressure on the MA to proceed with these allocations.

As a result of the above trends, residential development and land-use planning became, to some extent, dependent upon the extreme bureaucratic nature of the RRP. Despite the fact that most land transactions in these peripheral areas were illegal, both the entry of this land into the *antiparohi* market and land-use planning in these areas became dependent upon the state decision to clarify the situation of ownership in these areas. In addition, with large areas of land, most characteristically in Kordelio, situation of landownership had already become obscure during the course of the RRP's implementation. Practically speaking, according to the records of the MA, all areas studied in this section, which had performed high growth rates since the beginning of the 1950s, were treated as rural until almost the beginning of the 1970s. Even though complementary allocations continued until 1972, they had been officially put on hold by the early 1960s. This action was taken by the Expropriation Committee of the MA in Thessaloniki, and was based on a decision taken by the High Court, according to which, allocation of land was suspended in the area of Thessaloniki. Nevertheless, allocation programmes continued in the Province of Thessaloniki and in certain areas until 1981.

Other forms of land allocation

The Ministries of Social Welfare and Agriculture established themselves as the two major agents of land allocation and, indirectly, land-use planning, through the programmes of urban and rural refugee rehabilitation. However, state involvement in land allocation also operated through other public and non-public agents, as a result of the formation of special categories of land, which also played an

346 *Athena Yiannakou*

important role in land market processes in GT. Two categories of land are mentioned in this section, the remaining exchangeable property, left under state control, and land distributed to building co-operatives. Unfortunately, only very limited information exists about the size, the administration, and the transactions, which took place in these categories of land. This very fact reflects the way land was administered, as well as the established attitude favouring privatisation of large parts of public land.

Exchangeable property

Although a major part of the exchangeable property was transferred into the ownership of the MA, for the needs of the RRP, large stocks of this category of property were administered rather independently by the programme of the National Bank of Greece, and after 1949, by the separate Departments of Public Exchangeable Property of the Ministry of Finance. The basic target of both agents in charge of exchangeable property was its liquidation. Over the years, this liquidation took place in two ways: through sale to the occupants—tenants or through auction. Large sales to tenants of exchangeable property took place during the pre-war period, when the National Bank of Greece was in charge of this property. During the post-war years, however, most exchangeable land was sold to its occupants, as it was gradually appropriated by them (Figure 21.3). Until 1970, no special restrictions were set in respect of these sales, either in terms of the size of the piece of landed property or the economic status of its occupants, or its location. Only in 1970 were there certain restrictions placed on GT—the main urban area in Greece, with a high concentration of exchangeable property. Only landed property, up to 500 square metres could be sold to its occupants, and only if the latter had been using it for over 25 years and had not acquired any other provision through the rehabilitation programmes. Bigger properties could be sold only in cases where they were appropriated by more than one family (Act 547/1970). According to information given by the local Department of Public Exchangeable Property, most estates of exchangeable property in GT belonged to categories that could be sold directly to their occupants. By 1979, DAP estimated that in the county of Thessaloniki exchangeable property amounted to 3,788 estates or 8,710 hectares.

Building co-operatives

Two main types of co-operatives were formed in GT in the period under examination: co-operatives of refugees entitled to rehabilitation as prescribed by the regulations of the URP and co-operatives of special groups entitled to a particular rehabilitation as prescribed by the 751/1955 Act. On the whole, 15 refugee building co-operatives were established in the inter-war period. Table 21.8 indicates the area of land made available to seven of them, while for the rest, no relevant data are available. A number of restrictions were placed, according to which, this land had to be used only for housing members of the co-operative, and not for

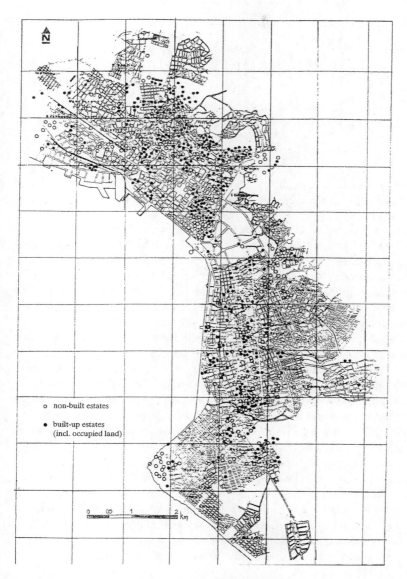

Figure 21.3 The distribution of exchangeable landed property in Greater Thessaloniki in 1966. (from Triantafyllides, 1966)

348   *Athena Yiannakou*

Table 21.8 Land allocation to refugee building co-operatives

Refugee building	Year of allocation	Area of land (in square metres)
Co-operatives		
Kato Toumpa	1928	22,000
Troados	1927–1929	19,122
Sidiridromikon	1926	15,973
40 Ekklesies	1927	194,000
Pamfyliou	1926	6,692
Byzantio	1928	181,600
Neapoli	1928	65,000
TOTAL		504,387

(Yiannakou 1993)

profit making. Taking into account the housing problem of these members, almost all the above building co-operatives were exclusively involved in rehabilitating their own members.

However, the situation was very different with the second type of co-operatives entitled to public housing. These co-operatives were established on the grounds of an ambiguous piece of legislation, the 751/1955 Act, under which, certain special groups (army officers, war victims, victims of natural disasters, and certain refugee groups) were provided with land for self-housing. As this Act was one of the most characteristic by-products of the political situation that prevailed after the Civil War, the criteria for land allocation were purely political.

In GT six such co-operatives were set up by the end of the 1950s. There is no analytical data for the precise area of the allocated land, let alone the actual activities of these co-operatives. Three of them, which were the most important ones, appear to have acquired about 300 hectares of land in Panorama. Taking into consideration the character of the land and housing market in Panorama, an area which has always had the highest concentration of upper-income housing since 1960 (Triantafyllidis 1966), one could easily understand why the bulk of this land entered the speculative sector almost immediately after its allocation. Officially the MSW, in charge of these co-operatives, allowed transfer of the allocated land only five years after its allocation to a member of a building co-operative, provided that, in the meantime, this land would be used for self-housing. Nevertheless, in most cases this prerequisite was actually violated, and land was sold immediately after its allocation to the beneficiaries. According to information given by the local department of the MSW, the Minister of MSW directly intervened in all these sales by enabling the lifting of the legal restrictions acting independently from the local department.

Concluding remarks

Analysis of these programmes shows that their major objective was the establishment of small landownership as the dominant system of land tenure. Though a public housing programme, the URP was extremely influential as far as the structure of landownership in the inner urban periphery was concerned. The latter facilitated the expansion of the *antiparohi* housing market, intrinsically connected with extreme land fragmentation, in these areas. The RRP, on the other hand, established similar patterns in the outer rural zone with its very small farms. A central feature of this policy was the continuous transfer of public land to the small family economy, whether rural or urban. The continuation of these programmes throughout the post-war period, combined with the way exchangeable property was administered, resulted in enormous shortfalls in public land stocks and operated as a major obstacle to effective land-use planning.

It would be wrong to confine the significance of these programmes to the severity of their consequences for the city's land structure at a certain point in time. The fact that their implementation continued throughout most of the period under examination suggests that, above all, they constituted the cornerstone of actual land policy in GT and the main domain, through which, the interdependencies between the state and the residential sector were built-up. Almost 25% of the total area of GT was transferred from big or medium landownership to national, and finally to small, ownership through an extensive programme of land re-allocation. In a situation where the state has historically been the dominant player in allocating land resources, a number of characteristics of the programmes were formed in the course of their implementation, such as appropriation phenomena, obscurities in the situation of ownership, and the bureaucratic nature of implementation, all of which constituted key features in residential land development and allocation.

Land policy was carried out by three major agencies, the Ministry of Social Welfare, the Ministry of Agriculture, and the Departments of Exchangeable Property. The Ministry responsible for use planning did not participate, while the three agencies practically ignored the various urban planning programmes. Our investigation highlights an issue overlooked by previous urban analysts and Greek policy-makers, that the greater part of real property in the second largest urban centre in Greece was formed, shortly before rapid development occurred, by the state's own land policies.

The Programme of Urban Refugee Rehabilitation consolidated a situation of extremely fragmented urban ownership, in turn the basis for the expansion of the *antiparohi* sector in urban (inside-the-plan) areas of Greater Thessaloniki. As this study of the Rural Rehabilitation Programme shows, state protectionism was so powerful a factor in the immediate rural periphery (where migrants were settled after 1950), that all of this zone was treated officially as a rural area during its transformation to an urban area, and even afterwards. The nature of this policy and the process of its implementation were crucial elements affecting the interdependence of the state and new interest groups of land-holders. In this new set of relations, two aspects were of great importance: the subjection of small landholdings to a complex and contradictory institutional framework and its parallel dependence on an equally complex system of allowances, in which political factors played a crucial role; and the interdependence between land policy, the urban development process, and land use planning, with the latter confined to small,

350 *Athena Yiannakou*

isolated extensions of the urban planning zone, based on multiple simple layout plans with numerous amendments (Yiannakou 2008).

Looking in more detail at the structure of landed property in the urban periphery and its changes, one could argue that urban growth and expansion were not purely market-related processes, with the state merely supporting illegal building as a means to cover the housing needs of the immigrants. Rather, the structure of landed property, and the way control over land was subsumed by the former peasant families, played a crucial part in transforming land to an unrestrictedly supplied good. Changes did occur in this pattern, after 1970, but at a very slow rate, and in such a way that wide access to peripheral urban land was a persistent feature of the land market until more recent years.

Note

1 A large part of this paper is based on Yiannakou 1993, chapter 4.

References

Dimitriadis, V., *Τοπογραφία της Θεσσαλονίκης κατά την Εποχή της Τουρκοκρατίας, 1430-1920 [Topography of Thessaloniki under the Turks]*, Thessaloniki: Eteria Makedonikon Spoudon (1983).

Eade J. and Mele C. (eds.), *Understanding the City*, Oxford: Blackwell Publishing (2002).

Elliot B. and McCrone D., *The City: Patterns of Domination and Conflict*, London: Macmillan Press (1982).

Hastaoglou-Martinidis, V., 'A Mediterranean city in transition: Thessaloniki between two world wars', *Facta Univarsitatis: Architecture and Civil Engineering*, 1(4), (1997), 493–507.

Kievel, P., *Land and the City: Patterns and Processes of Urban Change*, London: Routledge (1993).

Kolonas, V., *Η Θεσσαλονίκη εκτός των Τειχών: Εικονογραφία της Συνοικίας των Εξοχών (1885-1912) [Thessaloniki outside the Walls: An Iconography of the Exoches District]*, Thessaloniki: University Studio Press (2016).

Leontidou, L., *The Mediterranean City in Transition: Social Change and Urban Development*, Cambridge: Cambridge University Press (1990).

Loukatos, S. D., 'Πολιτειογραφικά Θεσσαλονίκης, νομού και πόλης, στα μέσα της δεκαετίας του 1910' ['Statistical elements of the city and prefecture of Salonika during the decade of 1910'], In: History Centre of Thessaloniki (ed.), *Thessaloniki After 1912*, Thessaloniki: Municipality of Thessaloniki (1986), 101–129.

Maravelakis, M. and Vakalopoulos, A., *Οι προσφυγικές εγκαταστάσεις στην περιοχή της Θεσσαλονίκης* [Refugee Settlements in the Area of Thessaloniki], Thessaloniki: Eteria Makedonikon Spoudon (1955).

Pelagidis, S., 'Προσφυγικά προβλήματα του βορειοελλαδικού και λοιπού χώρου, στο ελληνικό κοινοβούλιο 1924–28' ['Refugee problems of the northern Greek and elsewhere in the Greek parliament'], *Makedonika*, 26, (1988), 63–97.

Pentzopoulos, D. T., *The 1922–23 Exchange of Minorities and its Impact upon Greece*, Ph.D. Thesis, Princeton University (1959).

Triantaphyllidis, I., *Χωροταξική Μελέτη Θεσσαλονίκης* [Urban Planning Study of Thessaloniki], Thessaloniki: First Stage (1966) issue 25.

Yerolympos, A., Kalogirou, N. and Hatzimichalis, C., *Βορειοελλαδικοί Οικισμοί πριν και μετά την Απελευθέρωση. Μετασχηματισμοί του Αστικού και Περιφερειακού Χώρου* [Northern Greek Settlements before and after the Liberation: Transitions of the Urban and Regional Space] (Research Report), Thessaloniki: Ministry of Industry, Research and Technology (1988).

Yiannakou, A., *Residential Land Development and Urban Policy in Greece: the Case of Greater Thessaloniki*, Ph.D. Thesis, London School of Economics (1993).

Yiannakou, A., 'Πολεοδομικά σχέδια για τη Θεσσαλονίκη: Ιδεολογία και πρακτική κατά τη διάρκεια του 20ου αιώνα' [Urban plans in Thessaloniki: Ideology and practice during the 20th century], In: Kafkalas, G., Lamprianidis, L. and Papamichos, N. (eds.), *Η Θεσσαλονίκη στο Μεταίχμιο: η Πόλη από τη Σκοπιά των Αλλαγών* [Thessaloniki on the Verge: the City from the Viewpoint of Change], Athens: Kritiki (2008), 447–487.

22 The care of monuments in modern Thessaloniki

Perceptions and practices

Kornilia Trakosopoulou-Tzimou

The aim of the present study is to outline the historical evolution of policies and attitudes regarding the protection of the Byzantine, Ottoman, and modern architectural heritage of Thessaloniki over three periods: from the mid-19th century up to 1912; from 1912 until the Second World War; and after the Second World War. Until the mid-19th century, a general lack of interest in preserving the city's architectural heritage is observed. In 1890, following a major fire at Ayasofya mosque (Agia Sophia church), important initiatives in favor of its conservation were taken by European Byzantinists. The initial steps for the protection and preservation of major Christian monuments (that were converted into mosques) were taken by Ottoman Administration, in the years after 1900. The Ernest Hébrard (1875–1933) urbanization plan following the 1917 fire "liberated" byzantine monuments by depriving them of their urban context. The need for larger spaces led to major alteration and demolition of historic buildings. The Greek state was slow to recognize the cultural value of Ottoman monuments, most of which were destroyed or turned to secular uses. Nor was the architecture of the Modernist movement of the Inter-war period exempt from destruction or ill-advised interventions. At the present time, rehabilitation activities are coordinated by the Ministry of Culture and Sports. Efforts are made to preserve what remains of the city's architectural heritage.

The period of Ottoman reforms, 1850s–1912

Thessaloniki was an attractive city that impressed 19th-century travelers with the beauty of its setting, its rich historical past, and significant commercial activity. Viewed from the sea, the city's architecture still reflects the great economic growth of the 19th century (Figure 22.1). From the 1860s on, Thessaloniki experienced a wide range of architectural and urban planning proposals through which it would be transformed into a modern city with a new port and railway stations, theatres, cinemas, commercial buildings, and new residential blocks (Trakosopoulou-Tzimou 2005). The construction of the quay where the sea walls of the city had stood (1869) and the new road axes of the master plan prepared by city engineer Achilles Kampanakis (1889) linked the historic city to the eastern and western suburbs and were completed by the beginning of the 20th century. A new harbor

Figure 22.1 Thessaloniki. The quay in the early 20th century. (Archive of the Thessaloniki History Center)

and an industrial zone, established at the end of the 19th century outside the old city walls, altered the image of the city, as the constantly growing commercial activity of the old historic center was flanked by a new city of transportation links, breweries, tanneries, potteries, and flour mills (Figure 22.2).

During the period of modernization, as well as throughout the period after 1912 (incorporation of Thessaloniki into the Greek state), the care of monuments would be characterized by different approaches, due to the clash of the past and modernization, and also to the overall cultural and political elements of the period.

Traditional approach

Until the mid-19th century, there is no record of any particular concern for the protection and restoration of the city's monuments. Buildings were maintained as long as they were useful, and left standing if there was no specific reason to demolish them. This 'traditional' approach is possibly as old as society itself. But as art historian Alois Riegl notes, certain monuments could occupy a special place in a city as 'memory values' (Jokilehto 1986, 6). In Thessaloniki, such monuments would include the *Incantadas* caryatid porch (Greek *Μαγεμένες*), and the Arch of Galerius, which co-existed harmoniously with other buildings within a complex and irregular traditional layout (Figures 22.3, 22.4).

But such monuments, precisely because of their memory value, could be destroyed or carried off to other countries. This was the case of the *Incantadas*, transported to Paris in 1864 by Emmanuel Miller with the consent of the Sultan

Figure 22.2 Thessaloniki. New-style buildings in the Customs House district. (Archive of the Thessaloniki History Center)

(Vakalopoulos 1991, 50–57), as had happened before with the plunder of the Parthenon sculptures. Although attempts were made to block this pillaging, Miller eventually contrived to accomplish it. So far, unfortunately, no official request has been made by the competent Greek authorities for their return to Thessaloniki.

Quite often, the value of a monument is linked to the purpose it serves. As a consequence, the meaning of restoration can refer either to the maintenance of the monument's original function, or to a new function attached to the monument

Figure 22.3 Thessaloniki 1916. The arch of Galerius. (Archive of the Thessaloniki History Center)

Figure 22.4 Thessaloniki: *Las Incantadas*, by Stuart and Revett 1794. (Source: Wikimedia Commons)

356 Kornilia Trakosopoulou-Tzimou

through a process of renovation that often disregards its original architectural and artistic value. A key example is the conversion of important Christian churches into mosques after the conquest of Thessaloniki by the Ottomans.

With regard to monuments that had lost their usefulness, such as the Byzantine fortification walls made obsolete by the discovery of gunpowder, there was no question of restoration. These could be torn down and their materials reused, as happened in Thessaloniki in the 1870s. The new Governor of the city, Sabri Pasha, was authorized to demolish the sea wall, to construct a promenade, and to link the harbor with the railway station. As the British consul reported, rejecting the idea of repairing the city wall and emphasizing the economic side of the enterprise:

> As a castle, Thessaloniki is without value. All the city walls are in a ruined state and their extent is so great that millions would be required merely for their provisional repair, while as a result of the sale of the land along the city and between the walls and the sea, and as well as the sale of the stone for building purposes and for the construction of a promenade, the Sublime Porte would not only sell millions of piastres-worth of shares, but at the same time would provide a great alleviation to the inhabitants of the city, who would profit by an enjoyable walk along the promenade (09.06.1883).
>
> (Trakosopoulou-Tzimou 2005, 145)

The period in which the city walls would be regarded as a key part of the architectural and historical heritage of the city had not yet arrived. Economic benefits took precedence over the protection of the past. Thus one of the most characteristic elements of Thessaloniki, well documented in old engravings and photographs, was sacrificed.

Similar perceptions and practices led to the demolition and replacement of quite a few public buildings, even imposing landmarks such as the *Konaki* (the Government House) of Thessaloniki. This building, an important example of Ottoman public architecture of the first half of the 19th century, was demolished in 1890. In its place, the new seat of the *vilayet* (province) of Thessaloniki was erected, designed by the Italian architect Vitaliano Poselli along the lines of western architectural models to replace the traditional typology and morphology of Ottoman Government Houses (Trakosopoulou-Tzimou 2005, 185–186)[1] (Figure 22.5).

Archaeological interest and research on the Byzantine monuments

Renaissance humanism and Enlightenment classicism focused on the monuments of classical antiquity and showed little interest in the architecture of later periods. From the mid-19th century, however, Byzantine art became known through the work of European researchers, architects, and archaeologists. In 1847, the French architect Felix Marie Charles Texier (1802–1871) published in the *Bulletin Archéologique* his observations regarding the 'Byzantine Churches of Thessaloniki', including the 'mosaics on a golden background', the wall paintings,

Figure 22.5 Vitaliano Poselli, Government House. (Archive of the Thessaloniki History Center)

and the alterations made in converting these churches into mosques (Texier 1847, 523–540).

The reasons for their interest were multiple and the significance of their research should not be viewed in isolation. Interest in the protection of Byzantine monuments (which, for the Sublime Porte, were considered Muslim religious monuments dating from the conquest) falls within the nationalist and historicist currents of the 19th century, where the study of history and the protection of national monuments were seen as addressing practical national issues. At the same time, Europeans took an interest in the national monuments of other countries, particularly in the Orient, in the context of competitive colonialism as well as scientific curiosity.

Interest in the Byzantine monuments of Thessaloniki heightened significantly after the church of St. Sophia (Aya Sofia Mosque) was seriously damaged by a fire on 27 August, 1890. This event attracted worldwide attention. In response, in October 1890 the English architect, archaeologist, and astronomer Francis Penrose (1817–1903), then director of the British School in Athens, entrusted two BSA architecture students, Robert Weir Schultz (1860–1951) and Sidney Howard Barnsley (1865–1926), with the task of studying the Byzantine monuments devastated by the fire. It was his desire to record at least those monuments for which there would be no possibility of immediate repair, as he regarded such documentation essential for their future restoration. Penrose also published in the London architectural journal *The Builder* (11 and 25 October 1890) his appeal for financial contributions.

358 *Kornilia Trakosopoulou-Tzimou*

Thanks to the notable efforts of Schultz and Barnsley, the Byzantine monuments of Thessaloniki attracted scientific interest. Their work was continued by Walter S. George in 1906–1907 and by William Harvey in 1907–1908. Such research was encouraged by the foundation in 1908 of the *Byzantine Research and Publications Fund*. With its financial assistance, Walter S. George took on the task of recording in colored drawings the ancient mosaics of Saint Demetrios, which had just been discovered. His laborious, brilliant work was completed by September 1909 (Cormak 1985, 13–14).

Restoration of Christian monuments (1907–1912)

In 1907 and 1908, the Ottoman Administration took two noteworthy initiatives, to restore Byzantine monuments that had been converted into mosques, and to uncover mosaics and wall paintings, such as those of the Acheiropoieto and Saint Sophia churches. For the Acheiropoieto church (Eski-Cuma Mosque), the work included a broad programme to remove all Islamic elements but also those additions categorized as part of a 'stylistic revival' of the ancient Christian basilica. According to the French Byzantinist Charles Diehl (1859–1944), the decision to restore the building was taken by the Ottoman government under the guidance of his colleague, architect Marcel Le Tourneau (1874–1912) and 'on the basis of his instructions [...] which resulted in the removal of all those ill-conceived additions' (Diehl 1914, 5–14). The official repair committee comprised the Vali, the municipal engineer G. Menexes, the Belgian engineer Aimé Cuypers, representatives of the Ottoman government, and the archaeological consultant Gogousis. This work, however, showed inadequate respect for all the historical phases of the monument (Theocharidou-Tsaprali and Mavropoulou-Tsiumi 1985, 14).

The work of restoration and beautification of the fire-damaged Hagia Sophia church would become a major project. In 1898, in a publication in the foreign press of Constantinople, it was reported that 'the mosque contains several valuable mosaics and the contractors were specifically trained to take appropriate measures against possible damage during the course of the repair work' (*Levant Herald*, 28 November 1898). Evidently, the work did not begin immediately. In a subsequent article in 1900 in the same newspaper, it is stated that the monument remains in a poor state of preservation and that an order was directed to Demetriades Effendi, engineer and head of the technical service of the *vilayet*, to draw up a plan for its restoration. It was estimated that the repair works would cost 5,700 Ottoman liras (*Levant Herald*, 1 October 1900).

By the spring of 1909 the repairs, undertaken by contractors M. M. Nouridjian and Ethem Bey, had progressed substantially (Diehl 1909, 352). That year, Le Tourneau, in Thessaloniki on assignment for the French Ministry of Education, in his report to the *Académie des Inscriptions et Belles-Lettres*, noted with enthusiasm that:

"The mosaics of St. Sophia now shine in the heaven of the dome and in the depths of the apse in their original state". Moreover, he noted:

The care of monuments in modern Thessaloniki   359

An imperial irade allowed me to work without being afraid of obstacles from the Turkish authorities. In the vali of Thessaloniki and Hilmi pasha I found intelligent and liberal people who helped me, as far as it was possible, in the completion of my mission ... I had the most valuable and most effective advice from our Consul M. Alric, from Mr. M. Steeg the financial advisor, the French architect M. Thirion who directs important projects in Thessaloniki, and from the contractors M. M. Nouridjan and Ethem Bey. Without them I could not proceed correctly in my work [...]. The Academy will allow me to extend my warmest thanks to them. The outcome exceeded all my expectations.

(Diehl and Le Tourneau 1909, 41–42)

The work was completed two years later. For the occasion of Sultan Mehmet V Resat's visit on 21 March 1911, workmen and painters were transferred from Constantinople to Thessaloniki by order of the Minister of Waqf Properties, in order to prepare the monument ('*de mettre celle en état*'), under the supervision of the *vilayet* engineer and the 'distinguished' Belgian director of the Water Supply Company, whose advice on technical matters carried 'great weight' (*Levant Herald*, 11 March 1911).

In addition to the restoration of the damaged part and uncovering the wall paintings, the work on St. Sophia included decorating the interior spaces, the facades and the courtyard area with new ornamentation, restructuring the western entrance, roofing the northwestern tower with an onion dome, constructing a monumental fountain and replacing the Palaeologan propylon of the precinct with a portico of Ottoman style (Theocharidou-Tsaprali and Mavropoulou-Tsiumi 1985, 12–13) (Figure 22.6).

The new decoration was the work of Italian architect Pierro Arrigoni (Kamaraki and Astreinidou 1992, 28–34). Indeed, the entire project of embellishment in a 'neo-Ottoman' style was most probably carried out by the same architect, given that other important buildings designed during that period by Arrigoni were in the same style, including the municipal fish market, the twin kiosks on the quay at the end of Sabri Pasha Street, the entrance gate of the theatre of the White Tower, etc. (Trakosopoulou-Tzimou 2005, 296–299). Unfortunately, none of these buildings have survived.

In my view, the restoration and embellishment of Saint Sophia are impressive, not only because of the consistency and the layering of the interventions (completions, additions), but more importantly, because it achieved the realization of a unified architectural idea, within a neo-Ottoman style derived from Turkish nationalism, that would influence the Young Turks but European architects as well.

According to the sociologist Ziya Golap, the Turks could be contemporary and follow European culture without sacrificing the values related to their identity and religion (Trakosopoulou-Tzimou 2005, 284–285). Architectural pluralism (with the introduction of various European styles) inspired anxiety in Turkish intellectuals and triggered a sense of the need to preserve their heritage. In contrast,

Figure 22.6 The church of Saint Sophia (Aya Sofia Mosque) after restoration. (Archive of the Thessaloniki History Center)

Ottoman architecture, as represented by the work of Sinan, was a matter of pride (Çelik 1986, 148). This ideological context led to the idea of a return to Ottoman architecture and creation of the neo-Ottoman style.

After Thessaloniki was incorporated into the Greek state in November 1912, the projects carried out by the Greek Administration had a 'purifying' aim to remove neo-Ottoman elements from the church of Saint Sophia and replace them in a neo-Byzantine style. An example of this tendency was the replacement of the neo-Ottoman portico with one based on the designs of Ioannis Siagas, in 1919. According to Sfendonis, 'Siagas designed the portico and traced the stones for the arches on the moulds one by one with his own hand, and he used bricks and stones carefully chosen from the ruins of the burnt down houses' (Cholevas 1992, 7).

After the city's incorporation into the Greek state (1912–1940)

If the ideological context of the Ottoman Empire in the early 20th century pointed young Turkish architects towards the study of Ottoman architecture, in the Greek Kingdom the Greek defeat in the 1897 in the Greek-Turkish War followed by its victories in the Balkan Wars led to an escalation of nationalism and a resurgence of the 'Great Idea'. Within this scope, the diplomat and advocate of modern Demotic Greek Ion Dragoumis (1878–1920) wanted to downplay the obsession with classical antiquity and define the components of a new culture with a return to Byzantium and Byzantine architecture, which 'must become the unique

The care of monuments in modern Thessaloniki   361

foundation on which to base the architecture of Greek civilization' (Filippidis 1984, 109–114).

Here we should emphasize that architects interested in Greek popular culture and traditional architecture were a minority in this period, since most of them had followed the Beaux Arts academic tradition (for example the architect Xenophon Paionides) (Trakosopoulou-Tzimou 2005, 292–295). The first architect to react against academic principles and to declare a shift towards anonymous popular tradition was Aristotelis Zachos, who published in 1911 a combative article 'Λαϊκή Αρχιτεκτονική' ('Folk Architecture') in the ground-breaking journal of Gerasimos Vokos, Ο Καλλιτέχνης ('The Artist') (Zachos 1911, 185–186). As the chief exponent of 'Ελληνικότητα' ('Hellenism') in architecture, he was inspired primarily by Byzantine and popular architecture.

Zachos' first concern, as head of the Architectural Office for the Embellishment and Sanitation of Cities and Towns of the Municipality of Thessaloniki in 1912, was the reorganization of the city plan. Until 1914, he would work with enthusiasm on plans for the Macedonian capital, as well as for the restoration of its Byzantine monuments, the repair of which had been interrupted. Zachos used the contemporary city planning practices of Southern Germany as his model, and focused on matters of architectural heritage, among other things (Fessa-Emmanouil and Marmaras 2005, 12). The 1917 fire, however, would burn to ashes not only the historic center of Thessaloniki, but also Zachos' vision for it, since he did not play a significant role in the International Planning Committee, under the guidance of the French architect, city planner and archaeologist Ernest Hébrard, for the preparation of a new urban plan, although he participated (Fessa-Emmanouil and Marmaras 2005, 20).

The restoration of Saint Demetrios

A key event of the decade 1913–1923 was the assignment to Zachos of the work of conserving and consolidating the burnt-out shell of the basilica of Saint Demetrios. In 1927, he was interviewed by a journalist of the *Makedonia* newspaper, who described him as a man 'who understood from the very beginning the importance of the work the city had exclusively entrusted to him'. In this interview the architect spoke of the philosophy of his intervention, arguing that:

> The conclusion of this whole study was that we needed to prop up what was still in existence, to replace what was irreparably damaged, and to create, within the bounds of possibility, the best reconstruction of the church, attributing to it its ancient prestige and something beyond this.
>
> (*Makedonia*, 26 October 1927)

Zachos' final study, which was not implemented, envisaged in addition to the revival of the church, the design of a paved courtyard, which would include an L-shaped arcade 'to lend exceptional charm to the whole, accentuating the whole architectural appearance'; a belfry 'situated on the axis of League of Nations

362 Kornilia Trakosopoulou-Tzimou

Street (today's Aristotelous Street) that would dominate the city'; and a museum (*Makedonia*, 26 October 1927).[2] It is obvious that Zachos was not particularly worried about the historical accuracy of his proposal, which is characterized by arbitrary revivals. Nevertheless, this proposal indicates his interest in redesigning the area of the monument in a neo-Byzantine style and creating an integrated architectural proposal, an approach analogous to that of Arrigoni for the embellishment of Saint Sophia in a neo-Ottoman style.

In conclusion, like Arrigoni, Zachos adopted the stylistic approach for the revival of the church of Saint Demetrios, that was applied in several analogous examples in 19th century Europe. His approach was consistent with the idea of Hellenism expressed in the early 20th century, which looked backward to Byzantine architecture and popular tradition. Two important Christian churches of Thessaloniki, Saint Sophia and Saint Demetrios, enabled architects to arrive at new compositions of neo-Ottoman and neo-Byzantine style respectively, corresponding to the particular cultural requirements of the historic moment.

The role of monuments in the Hébrard-Mawson city plan

The great fire that burnt the central districts of Thessaloniki in 1917, and the implementation of a new city plan to rebuild it, caused the city to lose much of its cosmopolitan architectural character. Ernest Hébrard, a French architect, city planner, and chief of the Committee formed to prepare the redesign of the city, was basically the man who left his imprint on the new urban plan. Zachos' contribution as a member of the Committee seems to have been limited to designing the facades of the buildings in Aristotelous Street in neo-Byzantine style, and the areas surrounding of the Byzantine monuments, since the new urban plan conflicted with the views he held regarding respect for architectural heritage and vernacular tradition.

It should be emphasized that, though Hébrard maintained in a 1927 article that 'during the process of designing the new plan [he] was greatly influenced by the presence of the monuments of the past [...] which were discreetly highlighted' (Hébrard 1927, 99–100), he produced a design that contradicted that approach, due to its radical modifications to the pre-fire plan of the city. Until the early 20th century, the monuments were harmoniously integrated in the traditional urban fabric, forming a particular connection with the surrounding environment in terms of their position and projection (Trakosopoulou-Tzimou, 1988). In the new Hébrard city plan this relationship is completely ignored. The proposed opening of new streets not only 'liberated' the monuments from their environment, but required numerous demolitions around them, even in areas the fire left intact, such as the Frangomahalla and the Rotonda, which would gradually lose their historic character (Figure 22.7).

In my opinion, a lack of appreciation and understanding of the significance of architectural heritage was of crucial importance in the formation of the above plan. Despite the growing attention given to the preservation of monuments and the environment since the beginnings of Romanticism, an approach that found

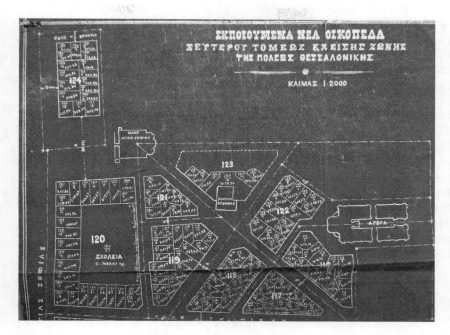

Figure 22.7 The 'liberation' of Agia Sophia from its surroundings, extract from the city plan, 1924. (Archive of the City Planning Department, Thessaloniki)

support among European architects and city planners at the end of the 19th century (Jokilehto 1986, 9), such views were not applied in the case of Thessaloniki. Hébrard's aim, according to François Loyer, was the promotion of French colonial policy, which had no connection to architectural heritage and tradition (Loyer 1966, 333).

The issue of 'highlighting ancient buildings' and their surroundings was commented on by French city planner M. Pierre Lavedan in the journal *Urbanisme* in 1933. His article was inspired by the rebuilding of Thessaloniki on the basis of the plans of Hébrard, whom Lavedan described as 'well-informed and very artistic':

> The liberation of the Byzantine buildings poses a rather delicate issue. [...] the city plan proposes the liberation of the two most important Byzantine buildings, Saint Sophia and Saint Paraskevi. The two are linked by an area of planted trees, which will traverse Egnatia Street. However it does not isolate them on two empty squares. The designs of Hébrard [...] show the buildings surrounded by gardens and cypress-trees and foresee the adaptation of the adjacent buildings.
>
> (Lavedan 1933, 155)

364   Kornilia Trakosopoulou-Tzimou

It is clear that the concept of 'liberating' monuments, on the one hand, and 'adapting' the buildings surrounding the Byzantine monuments with facades in neo-Byzantine style, on the other, bears no relation to the then prevalent architecture of the city. Thus an effort was to be made, through the use of historical neo-Byzantine elements in the facades, to 'recreate' a sense of place that had never existed but would replace an authentic historical environment.

From the above emerges a sense of rejection of the city's architecture and traditional layout where it was preserved. This fact could, to some extent, explain Zachos' dissatisfaction, which he expressed in a sketch (Fessa-Emmanouil and Marmaras 2005, 8).

Preserving the surroundings of monuments had become an issue already since the beginning of the Romantic movement in Europe. It was raised at the First International Congress of Architects and Technicians of Historic Monuments, held in Athens in 1931. The 'Athens Charter for the Restoration of Historic Monuments' noted the importance of preserving authentic historical monuments with respect for their surroundings.[3] However, the seven main resolutions of the Congress would not be widely understood before the Second World War.

'Protection' of Ottoman monuments: demolition, reconstruction/additions

In Thessaloniki during the inter-war period (1918–1939), we find complete indifference and ignorance towards the protection of the Ottoman monuments. The idea that Ottoman monuments were part of Thessaloniki's architectural heritage was very slow to be accepted by state policy and local society.

The fire of 1917 and the 1922/1924 exchange of populations paved the way for the demolition and the sale of mosques and other properties owned by Muslim religion foundations (*waqf*) for the benefit of the community. Once a building ceased to be used as a mosque, the office of the Mufti of Thessaloniki entrusted its management to various administrators (*mütevelli*). With the relevant documents in their hands but with no authorization to sell them, they nevertheless sold several holdings to private individuals and left Greece. This is the case of the *Iskele Mosque* in Aigyptou Street (Ladadika district), about which it was reported in 1926 that 'at the time the real property in Aigyptou Street was being sold, a ring of crafty brokers and administrators and others carried out transactions of a similar nature' (Trakosopoulou-Tzimou 2014, 57–68).[4]

A flagrant example of maladministration of monuments on the exchange lists by Greek authorities of that period is the case of the Hamza Bey Mosque (known as the Alkazar) located at the intersection of Egnatia and Venizelou Streets. The building ceased to function as a mosque after the liberation of Thessaloniki in 1912. In the fire of 1917, it does not appear to have suffered serious damage (Sabanopoulou 2008, 222–223; Theocharidou-Tsaprali and Mavropoulou-Tsioumi 1985, 146). In 1930,

> According to the plan of the city prepared by Messrs. Mawson, Hébrard [...]
> the Hamza Bey Mosque was declared an archaeological relic and remained

The care of monuments in modern Thessaloniki 365

intact. When the estates of the exchanged Moslems and the waqf property devolved to the State for the account of the refugee population as a whole, and responsibility for selling them was assumed by the Refugee Bank, the Director of the City Planning Office Mr. Delladetsimas was questioned by the Refugee Bank whether the sale of the mosque was possible and under which terms. Mr. Delladetsimas promptly replied that the sale of the mosque was possible, under the strict condition that the monument would be by no means altered, especially as regarding to its exterior, due to its great historical significance.

(*Makedonika Nea*, 20 December 1930)

As is clear from what happened afterwards, the above-mentioned condition was ignored. 'As soon as the mosque was purchased, the purchaser repaired it and altered its interior. However, as he was not pleased with the outcome, he demolished the external walls and built shops instead' (*Makedonika Nea*, 20 December 1930). The greatest alteration, however, was the conversion of the atrium, with an open colonnade on four sides, into a cinema (called the Alkazar), initially open-air and later covered with a metal roof (Figure 22.8).

This event provoked the reaction of the local press, not out of sensitivity for the protection of historic buildings, but rather as a reaction to the economic loss to the refugee collectivity (*προσφυγική ολότητα*):

the mosque, with the stores into which it was converted, has become a property worth eight million drachmas, whereas it was purchased for only two million [...] if at the time of the auction, the issue of the restriction requiring for the mosque to remain unchanged was not set [...], the refugee collectivity would not have lost 6 million.

(*Makedonika Nea*, 20 December 1930)

In addition, another 'scandal' (as described by the press) pertained to the sale of the historic complex of the *Karavan Serai*. Delladetsimas was once more held responsible, because 'he damaged the "Real Estate Team" (*Κτηματική Ομάδα*) to the tune of ten million' (*Makedonika Nea*, 20 December 1930). Although the purchasers of this historic complex in 1924 were obligated to keep the part that survived the fire intact, visible and accessible (Figure 22.9), instead they demolished it and erected a new building on the site (in which the City Council of Thessaloniki was housed until recently) (Petridis 1985, 66), in conformity with a study performed by Delladetsimas himself and approved by the Archaeological Service.

In the following period, as well as after the Second World War, numerous Ottoman buildings, e.g. the Iskele Mosque in the Ladadika district, and Saatli Mosque, north-west of the Government House, were left to decay or were demolished all at once or bit by bit in the context of the implementation of the city's urban plan (Figure 22.10). Those that survived underwent transformations incompatible with their historical character. Since the most imposing of these were the

Figure 22.8 Hamza Bey Mosque. View of the atrium, before 1912. (Archive of the Thessaloniki History Center)

Figure 22.9 Karavan Serai. General view of the remains from the fire in 1917. (Author's collection)

Figure 22.10 Saatli Mosque. General view, 1916. Was situated north-west of the Government House of Thessaloniki and was demolished in the context of the implementation of the Hébrard urban plan. (Archive of the Thessaloniki History Center)

religious buildings, they suffered the greatest destruction. In 1925, all the minarets of Thessaloniki were demolished, except that of the Rotonda (Theocharidou-Tsaprali and Mavropoulou-Tsiumi 2005, 146).

A few Greek politicians took up the issue. Alexandros Papanastasiou recognized the historical and architectural value of the minarets. In an interview in 1925, he proved his awareness of the ecumenical character of the cultural heritage of Thessaloniki:

> I am distressed because many of the (Muslim) monuments were mutilated with the demolition of the minarets [...] history cannot be erased by tearing down innocent monuments that once beautified the city [...] they are valuable national property and must be respected.
>
> (*Ephimerida ton Valkanion*, 8 November 1925)

It is a fact that from 1912 onwards, the destruction of quite a few Ottoman mosques, and not only their most prominent elements, meant the loss of valuable information concerning the historical and social development of the city. The exceptions are the New Mosque (a work of the architect Poselli, with neo-Ottoman elements) which was preserved, because the Archaeological Museum was housed in it in 1925, and the Alaca Imaret (or Ishak Pasha Mosque) at the north-east of the basilica of Saint Demetrios.

368 *Kornilia Trakosopoulou-Tzimou*

Protection of modern monuments: demolitions, reconstructions, extensions

We meet with similar indifference and ignorance in matters of protection of more recent monuments (listed buildings or historic sites), that survived the 1917 fire. Many of these were demolished during implementation of the modified Hébrard urban plan, while others underwent alterations and expansions that modified their original form (for instance, the Allatini mansion in the Frangomahalla quarter) (Trakosopoulou-Tzimou 1983, 161–171). Nowadays, it is possible to visit several of them, while in the case of others it is exceptionally difficult, due to their poor state of preservation. For most of them, it is rather uncertain whether their original form is still perceptible, because of the numerous alterations they sustained over time. In addition there are many examples of historic public buildings that were modified by new additions required by changes in their original use, such as the villa of Yako Modiano (Trakosopoulou-Tzimou 2001a, 140–161), the present-day Folk and Ethnological Museum of Macedonia-Thrace, and the villa of Ahmet Kapantzi (Trakosopoulou-Tzimou 2001b, 118–139).

After the Second World War, the '*antiparochi*' system, through which the owner of a building plot was compensated with apartments instead of cash for the land he sold to a builder, and the high built-surface ratio in Thessaloniki, undermined the protection for modern monuments and led to their destruction. Even the historic buildings that had survived were downgraded by badly designed multi-story buildings erected next to them. For certain remarkable buildings that are lost, we have only contemporary photographs and postcards.

Nor was the architecture of the Modernist movement of the Inter-war period exempt from destruction or ill-advised interventions. The state school complexes (designed by the architects Valentis and Mitsakis, Figure 22.11), the military airport cluster SEDES (designed by the architect Valentis), the Archaeological Museum of Thessaloniki (designed by the architect Karantinos), and others, have suffered great damage in comparison with buildings of equivalent importance for the Modernist movement in western Europe (Trakosopoulou-Tzimou 2016, 254–265). The architects who designed the above buildings, apart from providing functional solutions, also produced works of great beauty, by taking advantage of the freedom arising from the lack of historic references.

Important industrial complexes of Thessaloniki, such as the Allatini flour mill, the Allatini brickworks complex, and the FIX brewery were not saved from partial destruction. They remain in a downgraded condition.

During the same period, the range of monuments deemed worthy of protection was further broadened, as it came to be realized that not only monuments of art and archaeological sites had value for the people, but every authentic sample of their cultural heritage, of their traditional or popular architecture.

Figure 22.11 Nikolaos Mitsakis Anotaton Parthenagogeio Thessalonikis: Thessaloniki Secondary Girl's School, Elevation 1933 ANA_14_37_05. (Archive of Nikolaos Mitsakis © 2019 Modern Greek Architecture Archive, Benaki Museum Athens, used by permission)

In 1950, as a result of the above, Law 1469/50 was passed 'concerning the protection of a distinct category of buildings and works of art, later than 1830', expanding the meaning of protection for cultural goods (movable and immovable property) created after 1830 that were monuments or works of art that required special government protection. Nevertheless, the Ephorate of Modern Monuments (Εφορεία Νεωτέρων Μνημείων), to which their protection was assigned, was established only after a delay of three decades.

Although valuable time was lost and the historic image of Thessaloniki was significantly altered, we are obliged to persist in the basic principles and aims of the official documents and instructions, particularly the archaeological law 3028/2002 and the international conventions ratified by the Greek state for protection of architectural heritage, with the goal of limiting the ongoing practice of demolitions, additions, and discordant usages and constructions adjacent to monuments.

In this general context of perceptions and practices of rehabilitation, several attempts by state special regional services for the rehabilitation of modern monuments are encountered, for instance the attempts made by the Ephorate of Modern Monuments of Central Macedonia for the rehabilitation of the Yako Modiano villa (Figure 22.12) and the Ahmet Kapantzi villa, as a result of their incorporation into European financial programmes (Trakosopoulou-Tzimou 2001a; 2001b). Recently, the restoration-rehabilitation work on the Workshop of the Hamidié School of Arts and Crafts (*Islahhane* or *Midhat Pasha Polytechnic*) was also implemented in Thessaloniki[5] (Trakosopoulou-Tzimou 2017) (Figure 22.13).

In conclusion, I would like to underscore that problems in the rehabilitation of modern monuments are due in most cases to economic issues. However, apart from that, today's inadequate recognition of the cultural character of restoration-rehabilitation, and a historical amnesia encouraged by modern lifestyles and shaped by contemporary approaches and practices of private individuals and the state, tend to reproduce the conditions that may lead in future to the deformation or elimination of valuable elements of Thessaloniki's architectural heritage.

Figure 22.12 Yako Modiano's villa, after restoration. Architect Eli Modiano, 1911–1912. (Photograph by the author)

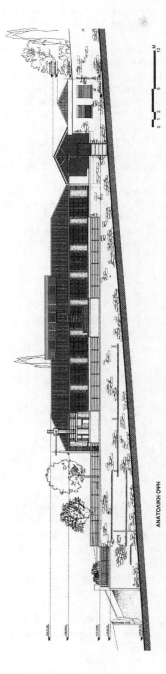

Figure 22.13 The workshop of the School of Arts and Crafts Hamidié (*Islahhane or Midhat Pasha Polytechnic*) in Eleni Zographou Street. (Restoration project for the eastern facade, 2010. Architects: K. Trakosopoulou-Tzimou, A. Syrgianni, K. Parathyra) (Source: K. Trakosopoulou-Tzimou, 2017)

372　Kornilia Trakosopoulou-Tzimou

Notes

1　According to a plan of the building site (1878), the old complex included several public offices (police station, holding cells, prison, archives), built around a wide courtyard. The Government House was in the center of the courtyard and was used as Governor's residence, as well. Next to it, to the east, was the *Haremlik*, separated from the other buildings by a high wall.
2　For the study of the space surrounding the church of Saint Demetrios, see also Fessa-Emmanouil and Marmaras 2005, 20–22 and Chlepa 2011, 196–197.
3　For the Athens Charter for the Restoration of Historic Monuments, see www.icomos .org/en/179-articles-en-francais/ressources/charters-and-standards/167-the-athens-cha rter-for-the-restoration-of-historic-monuments (consulted July 2019).
4　In 1926, the legal proceedings in furtherance of the claims of the 'buyers' were rejected as unacceptable. The building, which was characterized as a historic monument for preservation by the Ministry of Culture in 1995, is among the property of the Greek state (ΔΑΠ). The Iskele Mosque, after 1912, was converted into an ironworks. Later, during the 1960s, a part of it was demolished to open up Fasianou Street.
5　The work of rehabilitation of the Workshop of the School of Arts and Crafts (Islahhane) was incorporated (3261/10.06.2011) into the EU-funded Partnership Agreement for the Development Framework (ESPA) program for Macedonia-Thrace, 2007–2013, upon the proposal of the Ministry of Culture - Ephorate of Modern Monuments (Εφορεία Νεωτέρων Μνημείων Κ-Μ). For the architectural project, see Trakosopoulou-Tzimou 2017.

References

Çelik, Z., *The Remaking of Istanbul: Portrait of an Ottoman City in the Nineteenth Century*, Seattle/London: University of Washington Press (1986).
Chlepa, E. A., *Τα βυζαντινά μνημεία στη νεότερη Ελλάδα. Ιδεολογία και πρακτική των αποκαταστάσεων (1833–1939)*, Athens: Kapon (2011).
Cholevas, N., *Ο αρχιτέκτων Άγγελος Ι. Σιάγας (1899–1987)* [The Architect Angelos I. Siagas], Athens: Papasotiriou (1992).
Cormack, R., *The Church of Saint Demetrios: The Watercolours and Drawings of W.S. George*, Exhibition catalogue, Thessaloniki: Vafopouleio Cultural Center – British Council (October–November 1985).
Diehl, C., 'Les églises Byzantines de Salonique et leurs mosaïques', *Comptes-rendus des séances de l'Académie des Inscriptions et Belles-Lettres*, 5 (1909), 351–353.
Diehl, C., 'La Basilique d'Eski-Djouma à Salonique et sa décoration en mosaïques', *Le Revue de l'art ancien et moderne*, 202 (1914), 5–14.
Diehl, C. and Le Tourneau, M. 'Les Mosaïques de Sainte-Sophie de Salonique', *Monuments et Mémoires de la Fondation Eugène Piot*, 16.2 (1909), 39–60.
Filippidis, D., *Νεοελληνική Αρχιτεκτονική*, Athens: Melissa (1984)
Fessa-Emmanouil, E. and Marmaras, E. V., *Δώδεκα Έλληνες Αρχιτέκτονες του Μεσοπολέμ ου*, Irakleio: Crete University Press (2005).
Hébrard, E., 'La reconstruction de Salonique', *L'Architecture*, 36 (1927), 99–100.
Jokilehto, J., *A History of Architectural Conservation*, D. Phil. Thesis, The University of York, England (1986).
Kamaraki, D. and Astreinidou, P., 'Η Αποκατάσταση της νεότερης ζωγραφικής διακόσμ ησης της Αγίας Σοφίας της Θεσσαλονίκης', *Αρχαιολογία & Τέχνες*, 45 (1992), 28–34.

The care of monuments in modern Thessaloniki 373

Lavedan, M. P., 'L'œuvre d'Ernest Hébrard en Grèce, -I. Salonique', *Urbanisme*, 21 (1933), 148–162.

Loyer, F., *Architecture de la Grèce contemporaine (1834–1966)*, Thèse de Doctorat, Faculté de Lettres et Sciences Humaines, Université de Paris, Paris (1966).

Petridis, E., 'Βενιζέλου και Βαμβακά γωνία', In: *Νεώτερα Μνημεία της Θεσσαλονίκης*, Thessaloniki: Hellenic Ministry of Culture – Ministry of Northern Greece (1985–1986), 66–67.

Sabanopoulou, L., 'Τζαμί Χαμζά Μπέη (ή Αλκαζάρ)', In: Brouskari, E. (ed.), *Η Οθωμανική Αρχιτεκτονική στην Ελλάδα*, Athens: Hellenic Ministry of Culture, Directorate of Byzantine and post-Byzantine Antiquities (2008), 222–223.

Texier, C., 'Églises Byzantines de Salonique', *Bulletin Archéologique* [Comité historique des arts et monuments], 4 (1847–48), 523–540.

Theocharidou-Tsaprali, K. and Mavropoulou-Tsiumi, Ch., *Η αναστήλωση των βυζαντινών και μεταβυζαντινών μνημείων στη Θεσσαλονίκη: Έκθεση Αναστηλωτικών Εργασιών (30.11–31.12.1985)*, Athens: Ministry of Culture –Fund of Archaeological Proceeds (1985).

Trakosopoulou-Tzimou, K., 'Το αρχοντικό του Αλλατίνι στο Φραγκομαχαλά. Η εξέλιξη του αστικού χώρου και ο αρχιτεκτονικός τύπος', In: Karadedos, G. (ed.), *Νεοκλασική Πόλη & Αρχιτεκτονική, Proceedings of the Panhellenic Conference on Neoclassical City and Architecture*, Thessaloniki: Aristotle University of Thessaloniki (1983), 161–171.

Trakosopoulou-Tzimou, K., *Monuments and Urban Fabric. A Study of the Relationship between Monuments and Urban Fabric in Respect to Urban Conservation*, MSc Thesis in Advanced Architectural Studies, University College London, Bartlett School of Architecture and Planning, London (1988).

Trakosopoulou-Tzimou, K., 'Αποκατάσταση και εξυγίανση της Έπαυλης Μοδιάνο στη Θεσσαλονίκη. Προσαρμογή ενός νεότερου μνημείου στη σύγχρονη χρήση του ως μουσείο', In: Nomikos, M. (ed.), *Αποκατάσταση–Επανάχρηση Μνημείων και Ιστορικών κτιρίων στη Βόρεια Ελλάδα*, Thessaloniki: ERGON VI (2001a) t. 2, 140–161.

Trakosopoulou-Tzimou, K., 'Αποκατάσταση της Έπαυλης Α. Καπαντζή στη Θεσσαλον ίκη και επανάχρησή της ως έδρα του Οργανισμού για την Πολιτιστική Πρωτεύουσα της Ευρώπης - Θεσσαλονίκη 97', In: Nomikos, M. (ed.), *Αποκατάσταση–Επανάχρηση Μνημείων και Ιστορικών κτιρίων στη Βόρεια Ελλάδα*, Thessaloniki: ERGON VI (2001b) t. 2, 118–139.

Trakosopoulou-Tzimou, K., *Ο Εκσυγχρονισμός της Βορειοελλαδικής Αρχιτεκτονικής και Πόλης στη διάρκεια του 19ου αιώνα και στις αρχές του 20ού*, Phd Thesis, National Technical University of Athens, Athens (2005).

Trakosopoulou-Tzimou, K., 'Το Εργαστήριο της Σχολής Τεχνών και Επαγγελμάτων (Ισλαχανέ) στη Θεσσαλονίκη. Ιστορική τεκμηρίωση και μελέτη για την αποκατάσταση ενός νεότερου μνημείου', In: P. Adam-Veleni and K. Tzanavari (ed.), *Το Αρχαιολογικό Έργο στη Μακεδονία και στη Θράκη*, 26 (2012) 405–418, Thessaloniki: Ministry of Culture and Sports, Aristotle University of Thessaloniki (2017). Available at: https://www.academia.edu/41241231 (consulted July 2019)

Trakosopoulou-Tzimou, K., 'Η ΞΕΧΑΣΜΕΝΗ ΟΘΩΜΑΝΙΚΉ ΚΛΗΡΟΝΟΜΙΑ: το μικρό τέμενος κοντά στη σκάλα (Ισκελέ Τζαμί) στη Θεσσαλονίκη', In: Hadjitryphon, N. (ed.), *Ιστορικά Ισλαμικά Τεμένη: Τεκμηρίωση–Προστασία–Ανάδειξη, Καινοτόμες προσεγγίσεις*, Proceedings of Scientific Meeting on *Historical Islamic Mosques*

374 *Kornilia Trakosopoulou-Tzimou*

- *Conservation-Enhancement-Innovative Interventions* (19 October 2013), Thessaloniki: Ministry of Culture and Sports (2014), 57–68.

Trakosopoulou-Tzimou, Κ., 'Αρχιτεκτονική του μοντέρνου κινήματος - Ζητήματα προστασίας, διατήρησης και αποκατάστασης', In: Giakoumakatos, A. (ed.), *Ελληνική Αρχιτεκτονική στον 20ό και 21ο αιώνα. Ιστορία – Θεωρία – Κριτική*, Athens: Gutenberg (2016), 254–265.

Trakosopoulou-Tzimou, Κ., 'Το Πολυτεχνείο του Μιδχάτ πασά (Ισλαχανέ) στη Θεσσαλο νίκη: οθωμανική οικοδομική δραστηριότητα και μετασχηματισμοί του αστικού χώρου στα τέλη του 19ου αιώνα', In: *Proceedings of the 2nd Conference on Construction History*, Department of Architecture Engineering DUTH and Ministry of Culture and Sports, Xanthi (5–7 December 2017). Available at: https://www.academia.edu/35383420 (consulted July 2019)

Vakalopoulos, A. E., *Θεσσαλονίκη και άλλα μελετήματα δημοσιευμένα μεταξύ 1981–1990*, Thessaloniki: Vanias (1991).

Zachos, A., 'Λαϊκή Αρχιτεκτονική', *Ο Καλλιτέχνης*, 17 (1911), 185–186.

Newspapers

Εφημερίς των Βαλκανίων: 1925
Μακεδονία: 1927
Μακεδονικά Νέα: 1930
The Levant Herald: 1898–1911

23 A past for every possible future
Concluding remarks

Basil C. Gounaris

The historical bibliography on Thessaloniki is extremely rich, so much so as to make it unlikely that every book and article could ever be captured in a single database. And it is improbable, given the pace at which this bibliography is growing, that a global history of our city, such as that attempted by the late Apostolos Vakalopoulos in 1947, will be ever written again. The benefit of the international conference commemorating the city's centenary in 2012 derives primarily from the questions raised and the debates these questions triggered among the participants.

This commemoration of the 100th anniversary of the entry of the victorious Greek army highlights the importance of the historical 'rupture' it represents. The transition from Ottoman to Greek marks an 'end of history', the closing of a circle. Obviously, the post-war change of administration and redrawn borders were not insignificant historical events for Thessaloniki. The social and economic consequences were dramatic, but they are not the only factors that compel us to examine the transition process. One hundred years after 1912, Thessaloniki has not yet come to terms with its past, has not completed its transformation, has not embraced a final identity; nor, consequently, has it defined with any precision the future it is aspiring to. Suspense regarding the future still haunts a past that is regularly called upon to offer solutions for the present.

We expect that, by deepening our knowledge on the transition process, we will become wiser, for Thessaloniki's benefit. What emerges from this conference, however, is that challenging the past is nothing new. This challenge, impassioned or sedate, has been an integral part of Thessaloniki's history long before it became the concern of Greek authorities. In the era of Ottoman modernization, our city was well-known as a bold and multifaceted experiment in transition from Eastern to Western, a transition that concerned not only geography but also time. For modernizers, the East represented an undesirable past. Moving toward the West was not only about improving the infrastructure or adopting a friendlier attitude towards ancient monuments. It implied a shift of identities. Thessalonians reoriented themselves vis-à-vis tradition, religion, and new nationalisms, sometimes through compromises, other times aggressively. Time, however, was not in their favor. The culture shaped in Thessaloniki over the course of a single transitional generation between 1890 and 1920, an appealing and cosmopolitan one though

376   *Basil C. Gounaris*

wracked with internal conflicts and contradictions, was not solid enough to sustain its own unique modernity. It would be naïve or at least romantic to expect that we could retrospectively impose on that fragile past a future that history denied to it because of the Balkan Wars.

Modernization as an urban process did not end in 1912, of course. The prospect of economic development continued to inspire, although the horizon had changed. The debate with the past, however, assumed new dimensions. Old Greece rediscovered in Thessaloniki its medieval past, almost still living though not unaltered, as a source of inspiration enriched by local Macedonian art and tradition. An artistic marriage was possible and, indeed, rather successful: next to the Byzantine monuments, now refurbished and promoted, the White Tower and other Ottoman monuments survived, even if, as prime minister Alexandros Papanastasiou complained, they had been 'amputated' by the demolition of all but two of the city's minarets.

Human identities, however, followed a different course. The future of Greek national ideology at the time was by no means assured. Under the new administration, Ottoman and Bulgarian cultural options were excluded as incompatible with the Greek, while the Jewish community began a successful 'negotiation' to create a new Greek-Jewish cultural blend. This Greek-Jewish identity was a specific interwar construct, one that, like Ottoman cosmopolitanism some years earlier, was not given time to bear much fruit. On the other hand, the Asia Minor refugee identity proved much stronger and durable. Indeed, in the post-WWII era, refugees transformed the whole city.

Transformation was not just a matter of culture or symbolism but chiefly a social and economic process. After the 1917 fire and the 1922 exchange of population between Greece and Turkey, Thessaloniki had almost nothing in common with Ottoman Selanik apart from sharing the same topography. This new reality—breaking from the past—became the context in which new politics and ideologies were generated and facilitated antagonism between the past and the new modernity, an antagonism sometimes prolific, other times explosive and disruptive. This bipolar scheme which gradually became unipolar, that is strictly hellenocentric, should also be blamed for the eventual extinction of the refugee cultural mosaic as well. The refugee experience soon became a hollow symbol. The sounds of the city had changed. Thessaloniki was still colorful and noisy; but different colors and sounds interested no one, not even the refugees themselves. In fact they were annoying.

This attitude, the negation of syncretism, never abandoned our city. The practices of urban planning left Thessaloniki only with a few disconnected monuments of its urban past. A different city was built all around these scattered places of memory, yet a distant one. It is extremely difficult—if it is desirable at all—to reconnect these places of the past with a single line, into one representative and comprehensible city image, since the original context is long gone. In fact we are scared by such a synthetic approach. Therefore we tend to neglect this approach, although during the last 20 years we have experienced an impressive demographic change, a new wave of refugees, which has produced similar social, economic, and spatial developments. We stand idle as if we suffer from collective amnesia,

A past for every possible future 377

ignorant and fearful, as we face these seemingly 'new' experiences. Yet today's locals are the grandchildren of the then refugees. Much more durable in time and handier for politics proved another narration of the city's past, the story of progressivism, the avant-garde, and social struggles. It starts with the 1908 Ottoman constitution and incorporates conveniently the struggles and the Jewish and Bulgarian laborers and socialists, the interwar supporters of the demotic vernacular, Greek WWII resistance fighters, and strikers of all seasons.

At this point we should explore more systematically the troubled relation of Thessaloniki with its past, through the use of local history books. Around 1914, in his *La ville convoitée*, Joseph Nehama wrote regarding his fellow Thessalonians:

> There is no bond whatsoever between these people. Each one lives in his own dream. There is no unity, no community of views, no co-ordination of efforts. Each one has his own imagined motherland, each one constructs in his own way his future state. They are divided by an ocean of thoughts and feelings. They approach each other; they talk strictly about business. They never converse. What could they say to each other, these people of different races and so dissimilar interests? They are impenetrable to each other. They do not understand each other. The same news rejoices some and bereaves others.
>
> (Nehama 1913, 346)

The 'imagined motherlands' and 'future states' became the Achilles heel for cosmopolitan Thessaloniki in the late Ottoman period. It was not an exclusively local problem; in any case, cosmopolitanism as a by-product of imperial ideology was and remains in opposition to national ideology. It was clear that this detrimental scheme of ideological dichotomy, cosmopolitanism vs. nationalism, was unnatural and should never be allowed to happen again. But the way of bridging effectively the already fragmented past with the precarious present in order to avoid a fragmented national future was not certain for Greek historians who took over.

In 1947, Apostolos Vakalopoulos published his *Istoria tis Thessalonikis*. The purpose of his work, he writes, was to establish 'the uninterrupted course of the city'. This obliged him, though a historian of the modern age, to cover a period stretching from 316 BC to 1912. In this span of 22 centuries, the five centuries of Ottoman rule and Jewish demographic predominance are a brief parenthesis. At a time when the raids and artillery shells of 'Slav-communists' reached even to the outskirts of the city, Thessaloniki needed to be Greek and the capital of a Greek Macedonia. A year later, Nikolas Svoronos, a Marxist historian, completed his doctoral thesis in the École Pratique des Hautes Études. Svoronos studied the 18th-century social and economic history of Thessaloniki to identify the conditions that had given rise to modern Greek society. Despite the multinational approach, his conclusions focused exclusively on the Greek community, and particularly on creating the preconditions for Greek independence, which for him, a political exile then living in Paris, had not yet been achieved.

In 1962, the committee responsible for the commemoration of the 50th anniversary of 1912, headed by the Chair of the Society for Macedonian Studies,

378   *Basil C. Gounaris*

decided not to include even a single chapter referring explicitly to the Jewish community in the massive illustrated book published for the occasion. Numerous pages were dedicated to the struggle against the Bulgarians but none to the Holocaust. In fact, the whole interwar and World War II periods are missing. Apparently, the eminent committee, in choosing 1912 as the end point, intended to avoid the sensitive (especially for the royal family) subject of World War I and the national schism, the leftist-led Resistance, and the Left's brief post-war rule in Thessaloniki; these are extremely vivid chapters of local history, but 'delicate'. Exclusion of the Jews was not intentional, I believe, but instead collateral damage, convenient to some but not the primary purpose of this silence. Kostis Moskof, in his *Tomi tis metapratikis polis* [Profile of a Retail City], written after the restoration of democracy in 1974, probed 19th-century Thessaloniki for something entirely different, a proper paradigm of how Greek history had been derailed with the development of dependency on the West. (Moskof 1978, 9-11)

In 1985, the Municipality of Thessaloniki published a kind of official local history to celebrate 2,300 years from the city's founding by Cassander. In this volume no group goes missing, neither the Jews and the Holocaust nor the left-wing EAM (National Liberation Front). In his preface the then Mayor Theocharis Manavis remarked that it was not an exaggeration to claim that Thessaloniki,

> with its past, present, and mission was a symbol of the Greek nation. Thessaloniki is Greece itself. It is a national duty and objective to familiarize the whole world with its long and impressive contribution to the Greek nation and to all mankind.
>
> (Manavis 1986, 11)

This volume languished uncirculated for many years, allegedly because the next mayor found its content not politically balanced. In 1997, the artistic manager of 'Thessaloniki Cultural Capital of Europe', writer Panos Theodoridis, in his preface to another impressive two-volume publication, *Tois agathois vasileuousa* [Queen city for the virtuous] emphasized the Jewish presence and the coexistence of cultures (Theodoridis 1997, 9). This shift was required not only by the nature of the observance but also by the large-scale change in local demography, in Greece's Balkan policy, and in historiography. In his message to a local economic history conference in 2000, Premier Kostas Simitis expressed his vision of a burgeoning Thessaloniki as the 'metropolis of South-Eastern Europe' (Simitis 2000, 9–10). In his own greeting, Minister for Macedonia and Thrace Yannis Magriotis expressed the expectation—if not certainty—that globalization and open borders would revive the traditional role of Thessaloniki as 'an international metropolitan center', moving beyond the role of 'peripheral center' it played during the 20th century (Magriotis 2000, 11–12). The published minutes of that conference encapsulate a mix of history and economic-political expectations that today seem counterproductive and even pathetic.

A past for every possible future 379

These post-WWII historical publications, and the prior work of Nehama, exemplify how the present and the future have colonized the past of Thessaloniki for various reasons. Obviously, this is a subject still open to research. However it is clear that until the late 1970s, each era's intellectual establishment treated Thessaloniki as a paradigm for the nation's historical progression in whatever direction it preferred, and revised its past accordingly. Thessaloniki was not in fact a very convenient paradigm; still, it possessed great symbolic value, either as co-capital for the historical continuity of Hellenism, or for the rise of a Greek commercial class and the socialist movement, or as a bastion against incursion by Slavs and Communists, or as 'mother of the poor' and capital city for the refugees from Asia Minor. A city with unbroken continuity—like the Greek nation in school textbooks—became, in the hands of the historians, a holy symbol and multi-tool for ambitious local politicians: the once co-capital, overshadowed only by Constantinople itself, was victimized and marginalized by Athens, an ersatz capital city. Thessaloniki has emerged as a prominent symbol of the cleavage between the Byzantine tradition, to which the Asia Minor refugees belong, and Neoclassical modernization—a cleavage that has haunted both Thessaloniki and the country as a whole since its founding. In the witty, poetic words of singer-songwriter Dionysis Savvopoulos, Thessaloniki is the aunt who reminds us of our late lamented mother. In this sense, the cleavage between Thessaloniki and Athens is the revival of the 19th-century split between Constantinople and Athens as rival national centers fighting for the same goal, the Great Idea, but following divergent paths. It is only natural that as the champion of ethnic tradition, Thessaloniki reserves a special place in its history for its brave irregular fighters (*palikaria*); a part of history allotted to successive popular militants from the Left.

If we accept, as I suggest, this deeper and almost dramatic symbolism of Thessaloniki's history as an allegory of the two conflicting natures of Greek national identity, then we should conclude that the historical debate will be endless and hotly contested. The idea of modernization as the dominant force shaping the future of Greece has been seriously undermined by both post-modern and pre-modern critiques, making room for the emergence of different, competing pasts. All these pasts claim authenticity and promise to deliver us safely to the insecure future.

Mayor Yiannis Boutaris, in his address to this conference, stated on behalf of Thessaloniki that he wishes not only to seek out historical memories but to integrate the city's history into a 'tangible social and developmental result, dynamic and visionary, to create a modern model for development'. If history is so indispensable to politicians for discovering and shaping a past worthy of the unpredictable but challenging future for which they are responsible, then historians should seek the assistance of astrologists and fortune-tellers to give them the vision they so desperately seek. Otherwise they will surely fall short and be held responsible for not securing a better future.

380   *Basil C. Gounaris*

References

Magriotis, Y., "Message" in Lois Lamprianidis (ed.), *Proceedings of the Conference Οικονομική Ιστορία της Θεσσαλονίκης, Ο ρόλος της ως περιφερειακό κέντρο της Νοτιοανατολικής Ευρώπης*, Thessaloniki : Ypourgeio Makedonias-Thrakis (2000).

Manavis, Th., "Preface", in *Proceedings of the Conference Η Θεσσαλονίκη μετά το 1912. (1–3 November 1985)*, Thessaloniki: Municipality of Thessaloniki (1986).

Moskof, K., *Θεσσαλονίκη: 1700–1912, τομή της μεταπρατικής πόλης* [Thessaloniki 1700–1912: Profile of a Retail City], Athens: Stochastes (1978).

Nehama, J. [writing as Risal, P.], *La ville convoitée*, Paris: Perrin et Cie (1913).

Simitis, K., "Message" in Lois Lambrianidis (ed.), *Proceedings of the Conference Οικονομική Ιστορία της Θεσσαλονίκης, Ο ρόλος της ως περιφερειακό κέντρο της Νοτιοανατολικής Ευρώπης*, Thessaloniki : Ypourgeio Makedonias-Thrakis (2000).

Theodoridis, P., "Instead of Preface", in Chasiotis, I. (ed.), *Τοις αγαθοίς βασιλεύουσα Θεσσαλονίκη: Ιστορία και Πολιτισμός* [Queen city for the virtuous], Thessaloniki: Paratiritis (1997).

Vakalopoulos, A., *Ιστορία της Θεσσαλονίκης 315 π.Χ.–1912*, Thessaloniki: Εταιρεία των Φίλων της Βυζαντινής Μακεδονίας (1947).

Index

Abatzopoulou, Fragiski 194
Abdul Hamid II, sultan 10, 46, 118, 126,
127, 235; Thessaloniki exile of 3, 22,
132, 134, 249
Abdullah Galib Pasha 109, **115**
Abdul Mejid, sultan 11, 20, 38, 85
Acheiropoieto *see* Eski Cuma mosque
Adil Bey, Osman (mayor) 120, 130
Adrianople *see* Edirne
Aegean Sea 15, 53, 54, 56, 58–9, 75,
147, 296
Aggelakis, Konstantinos 178
Agia Sophia *see* Hagia Sophia
Agios Athanasios *see* Hagios Athanasios
Agios Dimitrios *see* Hagios Demetrios
Agios Pavlos 317, 336
Agrarian Union 246
agriculture 55–6, 67, 144–6, 173, 186–7,
207, 211–12, 339
Akbaytogan, Tuğçe 121
Akif Pasha 65
Aksyón newspaper 198, 204
Alaca Imaret *271*, 274, 367
Alaveras, Tilemachos 280, 283–5
Albania/Albanians 15, 41, 42, 44, 50, 57,
58, 162, 229; in Thessaloniki 24, 39, 46,
251, 252, 328
Alexander the Great 1, 51, 53, 57, 195
Alexandria 5, 8, 12, 35, 38, 40, 47, 263,
291, **292**
Alexandroupolis (Dedeağaç) 296, 298
Alexandrov, Todor 147
Alexiades, Demosthenis 96–9
Alfieri, Vittorio 101
Ali Daniş Bey 119
Ali Sami Bey 249
Alitheia newspaper 102, 120, 140
Allatini, Moses/Moïse 31, 40
Allatini Brothers (Fratelli Allatini) 73,
119, 368

Alliance Israélite Universelle 38, 101, 154,
156, 158, 165
American Farm School 267
American Red Cross 231
Anagnostou, Yorgo 291
Anastassiadou, Meropi 86
Anatolia 2, 41, 106; Greek military
campaign in 202, 250
Anatolia College 267
ancien régime 17, 82
Andreadis, Stavros 2
Andronikos, Manolis 233, 236
Andronopoulos, Vasilis 96, 99
Ankara 62, 243, 256
Anninos, Babis 49
Anthrakitis, Methodios 29
antisemitic violence 10, 23, 163, 193
Antoniades, Antonios 102
Aravantinos, Perikles 96
Archaeological Museum of Thessaloniki
121, 227, 232, 236, 367, 368; *see also*
Yeni Cami
Archaeological Service/Ephorate 233, 236,
239, 365; of Modern Monuments 369,
370, 372
Aristotelous Avenue 264, 273, 274,
284, 362
Aristotle University of Thessaloniki 13,
139, 159, 163, 248, 267, 270; Jewish/
Hebrew studies at 11, 161–2
Arniotakis, Michalis 96
Arrigoni, Pierro 359, 362
Ashkenazi, Saadi Halevi 140
Asia Minor, Greek aspirations in 50,
58–60, 162; refugees from 155, 163,
170, 178, 183, 186–7, 194, 215, 222,
231, 247, 250, 262, 265, 280, 376, 379
Asia Minor Catastrophe 2, 11, 59, 62, 177,
183, 184, 189, 202, 276, 333; *see also*
refugees

382   *Index*

Athens, University of 161, 196
Athens as competitor 6, 187, 191, 252, 263, 379
Athonite Academy 26, 27, 29
Avezou, Charles 120
Axios (Vardar) river 50, 129, 308
Aya Sofya mosque 116, 121, 122, 134, 352, 357, *360*; *see also* Hagia Sophia church
Aya Tanaş *see* Hagios Athanasios

Babanis, Captain Leonidas 195, 204
Bağlamalı Ligor *110*, 122
Bakolas, Nikos 280, 282, 284
Balkan hinterland 1, 40, 46, 57, 58, 64, 128, 186, 267, 296
Balkanlar newspaper 249
Balkan League 171
Balkan Wars 16, 49, 50, 52, 54, 57, 63, 70, 72, 73, 86, 136, 154, 169, 170, 177, 193, 201, 239, 247, 255, 262, 360, 376; *see also* First Balkan War; Second Balkan War
Barnsley, Sidney Howard 357, 358
Barret, Julien 292, 296, *297*, 307
Barret, Louis 296, 307
Bartissol, Edmond 291, 299–303
Bastéa, Eleni 12, 291
Batignolles, Société de Construction des 291, 293, 298, 304
Beaux Arts style 263, 361
Beirut 5, 8, 12, 35, 36, 37, 38, 40, 41, 47, 82, 86, 91, 92, 291, 293, 298, 308
Belgrade 9, 12, 68
Belich, James 20
Bellili, Lazarus 161, 168
Belomoretch newspaper 141, 147, 148
Benaroya, Abraham 1, 70, 133, 145, 150, 188
Benbassa, Esther 197
Bensanchi, Mentesh 164, 165
Berlin, Congress of 3
Beş Çinar 134
Bey Hamam 274
Biazi, Eliyahu 204
Bitola (Manastir) 21, 41, 42, 57, 66–9, 73, 145–7, 220
Black Sea 5, 57, 123, 186
Blagoev, Dimitar 145
Bnai B'rit'h/Bene Berith 158, 159, 160, 165, 168
Boshnak Han 71, 72
Bosnia 5, 15, 35, 131
Bosnian Muslims 43

Boutaris, mayor Ioannis 2, 6, 379
Bozhkov, Stoyan 65
Bozveli, Neofit 64
British consul 36, 126, 136, 255
British Museum 121
Bulgarian-American Agricultural School 73
Bulgarian Army 76, 147
Bulgarian churches 66, 71, 72, 73, 144
Bulgarian Constituent Assembly 76
Bulgarian Constitutional Clubs 131, 142, 143
Bulgarian Consulate 71, *72*, 75
Bulgarian Election Committee 144
Bulgarian Exarchate, Exarchists 4, 8, 10, 62, 65, 67, 73, 140, 142, 143, 146, 148, 218
Bulgarian National Bank 72
Bulgarian press 74, 139–49
Bulgarian Principate 56
Bulgarian schools 70, 71–3, 140, 145, 148
Bulgarian teachers 144
Bulgarin newspaper 141, 147, 148, 153
Bureau Hennebique 303
Byron, Lord 37
Byzantine antiquities 257
Byzantine churches 356
Byzantine civilization 198
Byzantine Empire 82, 198, 199
Byzantine monuments 23, 111, 291, 356, 357, 358, 361, 362, 364, 376
Byzantine Walls 274

Café Cristal 42
Calzoletti, Adelina 100
Campbell neighbourhood 218, 223, 263; *see also* antisemitic violence
Carasso, Emmanuel 38, 131, 135
Cassander 1, 260, 378
Castagna, Eugenio 100
Catholic Church 73, 88
Catholic High School 73
Cavid Bey 135
Central Election Committee 143
Central Financial Service 172
Central Macedonia 257, 370
Chernopeev, Hristo 144, 145
Chief Rabbi 75, 131
Chios Douli, Slave of Chios 96
Christianopoulos, Dinos 277, 279, 283
Christidi, Lambros 115
Christodoulou, Charis 12, 310
Chrysi Avgi 253
Circassians 22, 251, 252, 257

Index   383

citizenship 89, 134, 164, 176, 194, 203, 244, 251–2
City Council 365
City Planning 365
Civil List 299, 301, 308
Civil War (1946–1949) 23, 269, 284, 348
Classical Greece 197, 198–9, 202, 306, 360
class structure 207, 209, 218, 222
Cold War 3, 7, 13, 24, 270
Colocotronis, Major Vladimiros 53, 62
Committee of Union and Progress 10, 42, 43, 46, 127, 129
Communal Council 165
Communist Party of Greece (KKE) 4, 188, 190
Constantine I: crown prince 37; king 46
Constantinople see Istanbul
Constitutional Clubs 144
consuls, European 19, 30, 35–7, 40, 42, 46, 52, 294, 307
Corfu 27, 29, 161
cosmopolitanism 2, 3, 5, 8, 10, 32, 81–4, 88–92, 170, 262, 270, 275, 303, 333, 362, 375–7
Crawfurd Price, W. H. 49
Cretan Issue 143
Cretan Parliament 244, 255
Crete 36, 50, 134, 147, 148, 175
Crimean War 127
Customs Authority 63–4, 172, 304
Customs House (teloneio) 134, 233, 354
Cyril and Methodios 1, 64, 68, 71
Cyril VI, Patriarch 27

Dagkas, Alexandros 216, 219, 220
Dakin, Douglas 221
Danon, Abraham 197
Darzhilovich, Konstantin 65
Dedeağaç see Alexandroupolis
Dendrinos, Ierotheos 29
Dethier, Philipp Anton 108, 109
Diakovich, Ivan 140
Diehl, Charles 358
Dimitriadis, Sotiris 9, 126
Dimov, Dimitar 76
Dioikitiriou Square 279, 281
Diomidis, Alexandros 220
Dönme community 39, 46, 84, 87, 129, 131, 233, 234, 238, 248, 265; and Yeni Cami/Hamidiye 9, 121, 227–308
Dorev, Pancho 146
Doxapatri, Maria 96
Doxiadis, Constantine 183, 270

Dragoumis, Ion 360
Dragoumis, Stefanos 56
Driault, Édouard 50–1

EAP see Refugee Rehabilitation Committee
Eastern Bloc 275, 319
Eastern Europe 2, 5, 378
Eastern Question 50, 53, 56, 57, 147
Eastern Rumelia 5, 56, 214
Eastern Thrace 5, 28, 177, 194
Economic Cooperation Administration 270
Ecumenical Patriarchate see Patriarchate
Edessa/Vodena 65, 66, 111, 135, 136, 315
Edhem Bey, Halil 118, 120
Edirne 57, 67, 73–4, 82, 148, 197, 247, 296
Edson, Charles 122
EEE see National Union Hellas
Egnatias Boulevard/Via Egnatia 21, 230, 275, 278, 363
Eldem, Edhem 9, 105
elections, municipal 135, 170, 176, 177–9
elections, national 176, 188, 189, 190, 249, 253; Muslim representation 250
elections, Ottoman 42, 126, 131, 132, 135, 142, 144
Eleftheriadis, Nikolaos 256
Elliniko Dramatiko Thiaso 96
El Lunar 139
El Makabeo 168
El Mesajero 204
El Progreso 196
El Puevlo 159, 160, 161, 163, 164, 165, 168, 203, 218
Enlightenment 100, 356; Adriatic 27; Epirot 26; Greek/Neohellenic 5, 7, 26, 51; Jewish 31; Septinsular 26; Thessaloniki 26–33, 100
Enver Bey 42
Epirus 28, 56, 58, 75, 143, 147, 169, 180
Eptapyrgion Fortress 274
Erlmann, Veit 237
Ermis newspaper 96, 98, 99, 100, 102, 140
Errera, Yosef 101
Eski Cuma mosque (Acheiropoietos) 116–17, 119, 358
ethnic cleansing 247, 265
Ethnikos Dichasmos see National Schism
ethnological diversity 96, 173, 184, 185
European Court of Human Rights 257
Europeanization 9, 85, 173, 233
European Union 13, 252, 274
Evangelidis, Tryphon 28

384 *Index*

Evangelistria cemetery 72, 301
Evraïkon Vima 158
Evrenos family 44
exchangeable property 184–6, 314, 346, *347*, 349; *see also* population exchange
Expropriation Committee 343, 345

Faik Bey 91
Fardis, Nikolaos 230
Faros tis Makedonias, newspaper 96, 100, 101, 102
Fatzeas, Grigorios 30
Fédération Socialiste Ouvrière 1, 4, 22, 133, 134, 136, 145, 150, 220, 246
Fehmi, Mehmed 42, 119
Fehmi Pasha 42
Fevzi Pasha, Omer 296
Filaretos, George 171, 180
Filekpaideutikos Syllogos Thessalonikis 102
Filippidis, Gavriil 247, 256
fire of 1890 21, 87, 117, 128, 228, 352, 357
fire of 1917 2, 23, 90, 238, 352, 361–6, 368, 376; Jewish community 157; mosques 230; resettlement 184–6, 209–11
First Balkan War 49, 72, 146, 153; Greek entry into Thessaloniki 1, 8, 36, 45, 154, 193, 262
First World War/WWI 2, 4, 5, 22, 23, 57, 63, 73, 89, 90, 178, 179, 183, 202, 230, 250, 262, 378
Fleming, Katherine E. 193, 203, 222
Fotinov, Konstantin 64
Fournier, Narcisse 96
Franses, Eli 204
free port 16
Free Zone 59, 267, 302, 304
French language 36, 37, 38, 40, 45, 46, 73, 95, 101, 122, 140, 145, 148, 155, 156, 159, 183, 193, 198, 199, 200, 228, 249, 282
French Revolution 17, 34
Frick, Otto 107

Galanté, Avraham 197, 198, 204
Galerius, emperor and monuments 45, 116, 117, 274, 281, 353, 355
Galt, John 95
Garbolas, Miltiadis 139
Garbolas, Sophocles 140
Garvanov, Ivan 142
Gedaliah, Don Yehuda 10, 139

Gedeon, Manouil 28, 29
Genç Kalemler 43
General Confederation of Greek Workers (GSEE) 4
Geographia Neoteriki 30, 31, 51
Gerasimov, Konstantin 66
German Occupation *see* World War II
Geshov, Ivan 68, 73
Giannitsa (Yenice) 44, 50, 73, 135
Giassas, Dimitrios 62
Ginio, Eyal 11, 19
Giovannaki Efendi 108
Glavinov, Vasil 70, 144, 145
Godard, Louis 308
Godhi, Tina 291
Golap, Ziya 359
Goüin, Ernest & Jules 298
Gounaris, Basil 13, 221, 375
Government House 126, 356, *357*, 365, 372
Great Depression 216
Greater Bulgaria 52
Greater Greece 49, 53; *see also* Megali Idea
Greater Thessaloniki 334, 347, 349
Great Idea *see Megali Idea*
Greek Americans 54
Greek diaspora 262
Greek Drama Company 96
Greek Parliament 164, 256
Greek Revolution 98, 200
Greek-Jewish League 158
Greek-Turkish war of 1897 360
Gruev, Damyan 68, 142
Gruevski, Tome 139
GSEE *see* General Confederation of Greek Workers
Guinis, Angelos 304
Gypsies *see* Roma

Hadzhidimov, Dimo 70
Hadzhilazarou, Yanis and family 65–6
Hadzhimishev, Pancho 67, 69, 73
Hadzhimishev family 67, 69, 74
Hadzi Theodosij Sinajtski 139
Hafuz Ahmet Efendi 247
Hagia Eirene 107
Hagia Paraskevi 117, 363
Hagia Sophia church 106, 110–12, 115–19, 121, 190, 234, 239, 278, 352, 357–60, 362–3; *see also* Ayasofya mosque
Hagios Athanasios 65, 71, 115, 122
Hagios Demetrios church 39, 116–19, 122, 271, 358, 361–2, 367, 372

Index 385

Hagios Georgios 110, 117, 118, 121
Hagios Panteleimon 117
Hague Convention 171
Haj Agâh Beg 235
Halbwachs, Maurice 260
Halevy, Saadi Bezalel 197
Halil Edhem Bey 118, 120, 135
Halkidiki 52, 56, 75, 247, 251, 319
hamams (baths) 250, *271*, 274–5
Hamdi Bey, Ahmed 87, 118, 129
Hamdi Bey, Osman 118, 123
Hamidiye Boulevard 71, 109, 134
Hamidiye Camii *see* Yeni Cami
Hamidiye district 228–9, 302
Hamilakis, Yannis 233, 234
Hamza Bey Mosque 230, 250, 275,
   364–5, *366*
Hanioğlu, Şükrü M. 4, 14
Harlakov, Nikola 145
Harvey, William 358
Hasan, Galit 36, 37, 119, 256
Hasan Mehmet Ali 256
Hasan Tahsin Pasha 36, 37
Hassan Cavus 43
Hastaoglou, Vilma 12, 260, 291
Hatzi Ahmet, Circassian mufti 251
Hébrard, Ernest 2, 7, 13, 23, 90, 263–6,
   270, 284, 352, 361–8
Hebrew language 11, 109, 155, 157, 159,
   160, 161, 162, 165, 168, 195, 198,
   199, 228
Hekimoglou, Evangelos 11, 207
Hellenization 10, 12, 55, 65, 154, 155, 162,
   164, 170, 172, 173, 176, 203, 222, 237
Hennebique, François 291, *293*, 303–4
Hertog, François 17
Hestia newspaper 175, 180
Hikmet, Nazim 41
Hilmi Pasha, Huseyin 42, 126, 149, 359
Hoidas, Dimitrios 29
Holland, Henry 34
Holocaust 2, 5, 190, 197, 204, 263, 269, 378
Hortacî mosque *see* Rotunda
Houlousi, mufti Mehmet 247
Howes, David 232
Husein Housni Karaoglou 251
Hüseyin Kâzim Paşa 135

Ibrahim Bey 92
İbrahim Pasha 116
Ilinden 8, 50, 52, 142
IMARO/IMRO *see* Internal Macedonian
   Revolutionary Organization
Imdat newspaper 249

Imperial Museum, Istanbul 105, 108, 110,
   111, 117, 118, 119, 120, 122
Incantadas monument 353, *355*
Inspector of Public Instruction 157, 160, 162
Internal Macedonian Revolutionary
   Organization (IMRO, VMRO, IMARO)
   5, 41–2, 67, 69–71, 73, 76, 142, 144,
   146, 147, 149
International Commission for New
   Thessaloniki Plan 263
Ioannidou, Heleni 239, 332
Ioannina 27, 31, 51, 245
Ioannou, Giorgos 5, 189, 191, 278,
   280–1, 284
Ioannou, Stefanos 99
Ionian Islands 10, 27, 96, 169, 171
Iossipos Moisiodax 29
Irredentism *see* Megali Idea
İshakiye Mosque (Hagios
   Panteleimon) 117
Ishak Pasha Mosque 367
Iskele Mosque 364, 365, 372
Iskra newspaper 141, 143, 144, 148
Israel 3, 11, 40, 98, 155, 195
Istanbul 95, 130–2; museums 105–22;
   railroad 40, 296, 302
Italian Philological Circle 102
Ivantsev, Dimitar 139, 143

Jarchev, Yordan 148, 153
Jewish cemetery 109, 161, 163, 267, 269
Jewish Communal Council 158, 165
Jewish Community 11, 31, 32, 75, 83, 87,
   90, 98, 101, 102, 155–64, 168, 193–7,
   200–2, 210, 231, 238, 254, 263, 267,
   376, 378; emigration 11, 90, 193, 196;
   see also Holocaust
Jewish converts *see* dönme
Jewish diaspora 196
Jewish education 155–60, 165, 203;
   see also Superior Commission for
   Jewish Instruction
Jewish Museum 155
Jewish National Fund 200
Jewish press 38, 149, 159, 193, 194,
   196, 198
Jewish Rabbinate 75
Jewish Telegraphic Agency 168
Journal de Salonique newspaper 38, 140,
   229, 230
Judaeo-Spanish (Ladino) 11, 38–9, 95,
   101, 155–6, 194–204, 228; education
   159–62; press 65, 133, 140, 145;
   university chair 161–2

386   Index

Kaiser Wilhelm 118
Kalevras, Achilles 215
Kallimopoulou, Eleni 12, 238
Kalostypis, Ioannis 55, 56, 57
Kampanakis, Achilles 352
Kanchov, Vasil 149
Kandylakis, Manolis 139, 144, 150
Kapantzi, Ahmet 368, 370
Karakanovski, Vasil 66, 76
Karamanlis, Konstantinos 2
Karavan Serai 365, 366
Kasımiye Mosque *see* Hagios Demetrios
   church
Katerinopoulos, Constantinos 11, 183
Kavala, Maria 256, 257
Keeley, Edmund 291
Kemal, Mustafa (Ataturk) 1, 3, 4, 37, 39,
   41, 44, 46, 105
Kemaledin Bey 249
Kemalists 1, 249, 251
Kerem, Yitzchak 101
Keridis, Dimitris 1
Kerim Ağa 134
Kiepert, Heinrich 62
Kilkis 146, 147, 247, 256
King, Charles 35, 255
King Alexander of Greece 195
King Constantine of Greece 37, 46, 202
King George I of Greece 22, 46,
   49, 147
Kitromilides, Paschalis 5, 7, 26
Kızıltan, Zeynep 121
KKE *see* Communist Party of Greece
Knizhiitsi za prachit 141, 148
Kofinas, Georgios 15, 16, 256
Kohn, Jacques 158, 159, 165
Kolias, Helen 291
Kolonas, Vasilis 120
Komotini 251, 256, 257
Konstantinova, Yura 8, 10
Konstitutsionna Zarya 141, 143, 144, 148,
   149, 150
Koretz, Rabbi Tzevi 200, 204
Kornetis, Kostis 12, 227
Korydalleus, Theophilos 29
Kotopouli, Marika 97, 98
Kotopoulos, Triantafyllos 282, 284
Kotzias, Nikolaos 236
Koumas, Constantinos 28
Koutouvalis, Marinos 96
Koutzakiotis, Georgios 34
Krainichanets, Todor 63
Kukush Mahala (neighborhood) 72, 73
Kulturno Edinstvo 146

Kyriaki, Aspa 14
Kyriakos, Nikolaos 96
Kyriazopoulos, Vassilios D. 270

Ladino *see* Judaeo-Spanish
La Epoca newspaper 140, 197, 204
Lafi, Nora 9, 81
Lamb, Harry 126, 135, 136
Lambrakis, Grigoris 282
Lambropoulos, Vassili 291
Lavedan, Pierre 363
Lazarist Order 73
League of Nations 187, 215, 265, 361
Le droit/To Dikaion periodical 249
Lekka, Anastasia 14
Le Tourneau, Marcel 358–9
Levant Herald newspaper 358, 359
Levantine cities 5, 8, 35–47, 51, 302
Liberal Entente 135
Liberal Party 178, 190, 250
Liberty Square 44, 133, 267
lingua franca 37
London 15, 21, 25, 49, 357
Lorandos, Emmanouil 96
Loti, Pierre (Julien Viaud) 21–2, 36
Lower City 2, 7
Loyer, François 363
Lycée Française 159
Lyvanios, Dimitris 13

Macedonian Question 50, 143
Macedonian Slavophones *see* Slav
   Macedonians
Macedonian Struggle 53, 54, 73, 262
Macedonism 51, 53, 57, 60
Mackridge, Peter 275, 291
Magriotis, Yannis 378
Mahmud Pasha 106
Mahmud Şevket Paşa 132
Mahmud Tzellaledin 251, 252, 257
Makaronas, Charalambos 236, 271
Makedonia newspaper 98, 102, 140, 160,
   163, 194, 218, 230, 361
Manastir *see* Bitola
Manavis, Mayor Theocharis 378
Manchov, Dragan 78
Mansel, Philip 5, 8, 35
Marshall Plan 270, 317
Marx, Karl 22, 145
Mavrogordatos, Michael 59
Mawson, Thomas 23, 362, 364
Mazarakis, Alexandros 52, 53, 54
Mazower, Mark 3, 6, 7, 12, 13, 15, 28,
   165, 170, 220, 235, 257

Index   387

Mediterranean city 2, 5, 26, 40, 200, 261, 291, 298, 303, 334
Megali Idea 8, 51, 56, 67, 162, 165, 171, 175, 360, 379
Mehmed Fehmi Efendi 119
Mehmed Hayri Pasha 233
Mehmet Ali 20, 257
Mehmet Cavid Bey 131
Mehmet V Reşad, sultan 132, 359
Memis Ibrahim Hoca 252, 257
Mendel, Gustave 110, 122
Mendelssohn, Moses 31
Merkado Yosef Kovo 197, 199
Merkouris, Spyridon 49
Metaxas regime 11, 154, 161, 188, 200, 204
Middle Ages 40, 64
Middle East 4, 5, 40, 243, 252
Midhat Pasha Polytechnic 370, 371
Miggas, Dimitris 282
Milios, John 221
military occupation 15, 169, 180
Miller, Emmanuel 353, 354
Minardos, press officer 223
Misitzis, Dimosthenes 96
Mithat Pasha 248
Mitsakis, Nikolaos 270, 368, 369
modernization, Ottoman 2, 9, 27, 85–9
Modiano, Yako (villa) 368, *370*
Modiano family 38, 40, 293, 304
Modiano Market 278
Mokrob, Boro 149
Molho, Alberto 204
Molho, Antonis 34
Molho, Michael 160, 166, 197
Molho, Rena 149
Molière 96, 101
Morin, Edgar 38
Moschos, Ioannis 28
Moskof, Kostis 219, 378
mosques 45, 88, 116, 117, 119, 122, 247, 275, 358, 372; destruction/conversion 230, 250, 257, 364–7; minarets 13, 229–31, 250, 367, 376
Mount Athos 26, 29, 249
Mount Lebanon 36, 46
Mount Pelion 27
Muan Zade, Moustafa Namouk 251
Muan Zade, Nedim Almahsit 252
muftis 234, 244–7, 250–2, 256–7, 294, 364
Municipal Hospital 86
municipal institutions 9, 81, 84, 88
municipalities (belediye) 81, 86, 128, 321; reforms 82, 85

Mürzsteg Agreement (1903) 147
Muslim Community 12, 84, 228, 234, 243–52; Community Council 246; schools 248; ulema 131, 133; *see also* Muftis; *Vakif/waqf*
Mustafa Efendi, el-Hac 106

Naar, Devin E. 10, 154
Nahoum, Vidal 38
Napoleonic Wars 20
Narodna Volja 141, 143, 145, 148, 150
Nasi, Don Yosef 204
National Bank of Greece 157, 210, 220, 346
National Liberation Front (EAM) 378
National Schism 10, 177, 179, 202, 250, 254, 378
National Union Hellas (EEE) 23, 163, 218
Natsalo newspaper 141, 143, 145, 148, 150
Naumov, Nikola 144, 147
Navarino Network 14
Nea Alitheia newspaper 102, 135, 136, 147, 175
Nehama, Joseph (pen name Pierre Risal) 31, 154, 197–9, 204, 263, 377, 379
Nehama, Rabbi Judah 139
Nemlizade Hamdi Bey 129
Neo-Byzantine style 264, 284, 360, 362, 364
neoclassicism 13, 23, 379
neo-Ottoman style 359, 360, 362
New Lands (post-1912) 10, 170, 175, 176, 177, 179, 180, 244, 245, 246, 247, 255
New Mosque *see* Yeni Cami
New Zionist Club 158
Nigdelis, Pantelis 121
Nikolaides, Kleanthes 57, 58
North Atlantic Treaty Organization (NATO) 36, 270
Nova Bulgaria 141, 147, 148

Obradović, Dositej 29
Ocoferi, Girolamo 102
Oikonomou, Giorgos 232
Olympos Square *see* Liberty Square
Orfanidis, Theodoros 96
Oriental Railways Company 296, 307
Orient Bank 98, 212
Orthodox Church 6, 131, 234
Osman Adil Bey 130
Osman Bey 71, 72, 245
Osman Hamdi Bey 118, 123
Osman Sait Ibrahim Chaki, mayor 90, 91, 172, 178

388   *Index*

Ottolenghi, Moshe 101
Ottoman administration 352, 358
Ottoman archaeology 9, 105–12
Ottoman architecture 238, 360; *see also* neo-Ottoman style; Ottoman Baroque style
Ottoman army 9, 36, 131, 132, 134, 233
Ottoman Bank 42, 70, 221, 299, 304, 308
Ottoman bankruptcy 10
Ottoman Baroque style 13
Ottoman conquest 356, 357
Ottoman Macedonia 4, 49, 51, 53, 62, 126
Ottoman municipal administration 9, 81–9
Ottoman reforms, reformers 2, 81, 85, 87, 89, 128, 352
Ottoman theatre 100
Ottoman Turkish 65, 100, 133, 193, 228, 256

Paionides, Xenophon 361
Palaiologos, Andronikos 30
Palamas, Gregorios 1
Palestine 4, 108, 160, 199; emigration to 90, 193, 196, 262, 263
Pallikari, Olivia 9, 95
Panfititikis Enosis 163
Papadimitriou, Sakis 277, 284
Papamichos-Chronakis, Paris 237, 238
Papanastasiou, Alexandros 13, 210, 257, 367, 376
Paparrigopoulos, Konstantinos 51, 162
Papazoglou, Dr. 158
Parios, Athanasios 29
Paris Peace Conference 53
Pascal, Hilarion 296, 297, 299, 301, 307, 308
Patriarchal School 27, 29
Patriarchate 4, 27, 60, 65, 66, 73, 142
Patrikios, Minas 177, 178
Paul, apostle 1, 17, 116, 161
Pazar Hamam 275
Pelekidis, Efstratios 232
Penrose, Francis 357
Pentzikis, Nikos Gabriil 276, 281, 283
People's Federative Party 142
Pepelasis, Adamantios 188
Petrov, Gyorche 68
Petsas, Fotis 271
Philippides, Daniel 30, 51
Philosophical School 11
Picard, Charles 120
Ploumidis, Spyridon G. 8, 52, 56, 58, 62
Plovdiv, Philippopolis 95
Polychroniades, Konstantinos 173

Pontic, Pontians 12, 231, 237, 310, 311, 324, *326*
Poppetrov, Sreben 144
Popular Party 190
population exchanges 12, 91, 183, 234, 243, 247–54, 262, 265; Mixed Commission 252
port of Thessaloniki 7, 12, 13, 21, 39, 40, 46, 67, 72, 261, 291–308
Poselli, Vitaliano 88, 238, 356, *357*, 367
Pouard, Marcel 301, 304
Poulos, Panagiotis 12, 121, 227
Prahia, Yehuda Haim Aharon Ha-Cohen 204
Pravo newspaper141, 143, 144, 146, 147, 148, 150, 153
Prilep 65, 67, 146
Progressive Constitutional Party 142
Progressive Party 190
Property Law of 1929 265, 286
Psyroukis, Nikos 221
Public Land Service 309
Public Power Corporation 317
Public Works 239, 307, 316

Qur'an 19, 235

Rabotnik newspaper141, 143, 145, 148
Rabotnitseska Iskra newspaper 141, 143, 145
Rabotnitsesko Vestnik newspaper 141, 143, 145
Radical Party 190
Rahmi Bey 131, 135
railroads 9, 12, 37, 40, 41, 55, 67, 86, 188, 208, 221, 261, 267, 269, 291, 294–302, 307, 315, 352, 356
Raktivan, Konstantinos 15, 172, 173, 174, 175, 180
Ralis, Ioannis 96
Raynov, Bozhil 68
Refugee Housing Programme 316
Refugee Rehabilitation Committee (EAP) 184, 185, 187, 190, 212, 334, 336, 337, 339
refugees 10, 184, 186, 187, 188, 189
Reinach, Salomon 108
Relief Service 231
Reshid Pasha 20
Riegl, Alois 353
Rigas Feraios (Velestinlis) 33, 51
Risal, Pierre *see* Nehama, Joseph
Rizov, Dimitar 73
Robert, Jules 301

Rodina newspaper 141, 143, 148
Rodrigue, Aron 197
Roma minority 84, 95, 253, 310, 316, 317, 319, 321, 324, *325*, 328
Rotunda 13, 45, 116, 117, 233, 362, 367
royalists 201–2
Rozanes, Salomon 197, 198
Rural Refugee Rehabilitation Programme 334, 339, 340, 341, 343, 345, 346, 349
Russia 5, 15, 47, 57, 76, 127, 244, 298
Russian Consulate 67
Russian Revolution 262

Saatli mosque 365, *367*
Sabbatai Zevi 1, 7, 31, 38, 84
Sabri Paşa, governor 7, 9, 20, 65, 85, 86, 108, 128, 293, 294, 296, 307, 356, 359
Saint Demetrios *see* Hagios Demetrios
Saint John Chrysostom church 73
Saint Petersburg 37, 298
Saint Sophia *see* Hagia Sophia
Sakisian Effendi 301
Salgandzhiev, Stefan 66, 76
Samardzhiev, Kone 73, 78, 148, 153
Samartzides, Christoforos 96
Sancak of Salonica 131
Sandanski, Yane 144, 145
San Stefano treaty 52
Schafer, Murray 238
School of Thessaloniki 276
Schultz, Robert Weir 357, 358
Sciacky, Leon 47
Second Balkan War 1, 46, 73, 146, 148, 162, 231, 379
Seferis, George 37
Selanikli Mustafa 39
Selânik Vilâyeti Salnâmesi 65
Sephardic Jews 82, 161, 194, 195, 197, 198, 203
Serapheim II, patriarch 27, 29
Serbia 29, 36, 46, 75, 148, 209, 244, 245, 256, 262, 302
Serbian Free Zone *see* Free Zone
Serefas, Sakis 282, 291
Shapkarev, Kuzman 67, 68
Shevket Pasha 44
Shopov, Atanas 68, 70, 73, 75
Siagas, Ioannis 360
silk industry 56, 207
Simeon, Tsar of Bulgaria 147
Simeonov, Stojan 139
Simitis, Kostas 378
Şiranizade Abdullah Şakir Efendi 106
Sirri, Suleyman Osman 247, 251

Slav Macedonians 5, 10, 53, 155
Smith, Michael Llewellyn 60
Smyrna, Izmir 16, 29, 31, 35–8, 40, 45, 62, 96, 101, 122, 215, 262; loss of 183, 265; port 291, 292; schools 27, 41, 51
Snegarov, Ivan 64–6
Sofia, Bulgaria 64, 69, 75, 95, 144–5, 148
Sofoulis, Themistoklis 256
Sophianos, Nikolaos 51
soundscape 227–37, 238
Soviet Union (USSR) 23, 170, 252, 324
Spandonidis, Petros 276
Spanidou, Irini 279
Spanish Embassy in Athens 161, 162
Spanish Jews *see* Sephardic Jews
Spanish language 161, 168; *see also* Judaeo-Spanish
Sprostranov, Naum 67
Stavroulakis, Nikos 238
Stefanidis, Giannis 13
Strasimirov, Anton 146, 150
Sublime Porte 294, 356, 357
Suez Canal 12, 261, 291, 299, 307
Superior Commission for Jewish Instruction 155, 157–64
Svetlina newspaper 148, 149, 150
Svolopoulos, Konstantinos 13
Svolos, Alexandros 257
Syndikas, mayor Petros 178

Talmud Torah Hagadol 84
Talmud Torah school 101, 157
Tanzimat 9, 20, 91, 127, 155, 248
Terenzio, Tony 108
Texier, Felix Charles 356
theater *43*, 133, 177, 270, 352, 359; Armenian 101; Greek 9, 96, 97, 99, 102; Italian 100; Jewish 101; Ottoman 95–102
Theodor Herzl Club 158
Theodoridis, Panos 378
Thermaic Gulf 26, 30, 34, 267, 278, 283, 284
Thessalonike 1
Thessaloniki as Cultural Capital of Europe 24, 274, 378
Thessaloniki International Fair 187, 253, 267, 270, *272*, 283, 291
Thessaloniki Master Plan 271, 272, 274, 319
Thessaly 27, 56, 57, 58, 75, 147, 169, 244
tobacco industry 4, 56, 59, 67, 130, 187–8, 207, 251
To Fos newspaper 158, 160
Tomov, Angel 145
Touloumi, Olga 237

390   Index

Trakosopoulou, Kornilia 13, 370
Tramway Company 229
Treaty/convention of Athens (1913) 176, 234, 244
Tria Epsilon see National Union Hellas
Tribune Juive newspaper 158
Trieste 46, 307, 308
Tsaldaris, Panagis 202
Tsaousakis, George 271–3
Tsaous Monastery 30
Tsapari, Selo 146, 150
Tsitseklis, Pantelis 170, 180
Tsitselikis, Konstantinos 12, 243

Uchitelski Glas newspaper 141, 143, 145, 148
Uchitelsko Saznanie newspaper 141, 143, 144, 145, 148
United Front 190
United States 3, 264, 279
Upper City (Ano Poli) 2, 7, 21, 264, 266, 267, 274, 276, 282, 284
Urban Refugee Rehabilitation 349
Urban Transport 316
Uziel, Rabbi Jacob 140
Uzilyo, Moïse 196

Vakalopoulos, Apostolos E. 28, 219, 375, 377
vakif/waqf 211, 359; administration 243–9, 256; property 19, 209, 248, 364, 365
Vallaury, Alexandre 293, 304, 305
Vamvakas, Charisios 178, 179
Vardar Gate, district 72, 117, 160
Vardari Square 267, 279
Vardar river *see* Axios
Vasileiades, Spyridon 96, 102
Vasilikos, Vasilis 276, 277, 280, 281, 282, 284
Venetian Republic 29
Venice Charter 368, 372
Venizelos, Eleftherios 46, 171, 175–80, 183, 202; and Jews 76, 90, 154, 157–63; and Muslims 230, 243–5, 249, 250, 255
Venlian theater company 101
Vernardakis, Dimitrios 96
Via Egnatia *see* Egnatias Boulevard
vilayet 65, 67, 128, 147; of Salonica 66, 68, 69, 131, 135, 140, 228, 294, 356–9

Villa Allatini 22, 44, 132, 134, 368
Villa Kapandji 40, 41
Villa Mordoch 88
Vlahov, Dimitar 135, 136, 142, 143, 149
Vlasidis, Vlasis 10
Vlatadon Monastery 274
Vogli, Elpida K. 10, 169
Voulgaris, Evgenios 26, 29

waqf see Vakif
Water Supply Company 359
Western Macedonia 26, 28, 65, 66
Western Thrace 196, 253
White Tower 36, 42, 43, 44, 120, 121, 134, 267, 270, 274, 278, 297, 301, 302, 359, 376
Wiegand, Theodor 118, 123
Workers Socialist Democratic Party 142, 145
working class 89, 188, 267, 280, 334
World War II (WWII) 5, 11, 47, 154, 190, 197, 203, 227, 236, 260, 267, 270, 278, 298, 304, 311, 352, 364, 365, 368, 376, 377, 378, 379; aftermath 2, 261, 284; German occupation 155, 161, 252, 269, 280; *see also* Holocaust

Yadikâr Terakki Mektebi 228, 248
Yeni Asır newspaper 41, 249, 256
Yeni Cami, New Mosque 9, 121, 227–39, 250, 253, 274, 367
Yenice Vardar *see* Giannitsa
Yerolympos, Alexandra 87
Yiannakou, Athena 13, 333
Young Turk Revolution 4, 10, 22, 37, 120, 201, 221, 248
Young Turks in Thessaloniki 1, 3, 9, 43–4, 69, 70, 88, 126–42, 144, 146, 220, 244, 262, 359
Yusuf Sidik Mehmed Pasha 106, 108, **113**

Zachos, Aristotelis 90, 361–4
Zambelios, Ioannis 98, 99
Zerzoulis, Nikolaos 26
Zevi *see* Sabbatai Zevi 1, 7, 38, 84
Zionism 4, 11, 89, 159, 164, 194, 196, 200–3
Ziya, Halid 40
Zographou Monastery 66